Reading the Roots

Reading the Roots

American Nature Writing before *Walden*

EDITED BY MICHAEL P. BRANCH

THE UNIVERSITY OF GEORGIA PRESS ATHENS & LONDON

Athens, Georgia 30602

Designed by Kathi Dailey Morgan
Set in Electra by Graphic Composition, Inc.
Printed and bound by Maple-Vail
The paper in this book meets the guidelines for permanence and durability of the Committee on Production Guidelines for Book Longevity of the Council on Library Resources.

PRINTED IN THE UNITED STATES OF AMERICA

07 06 05 04 03 C 5 4 3 2 1
07 06 05 04 03 P 5 4 3 2 1

LIBRARY OF CONGRESS CATALOGING-IN-PUBLICATION DATA

Reading the roots : American nature writing before Walden / edited by Michael P. Branch.
p. cm.
Includes bibliographical references and index.
ISBN 0-8203-2547-3 (hardcover : alk. paper) — ISBN 0-8203-2548-1 (pbk. : alk. paper)
1. Natural history—United States.
I. Branch, Michael P.
QH104 .R43 2004
508.73—dc22 2003016613

BRITISH LIBRARY CATALOGING-IN-PUBLICATION DATA AVAILABLE

This country, Most Serene Highnesses, is so enchantingly beautiful that it surpasses all others in charm and beauty as much as the light of day surpasses night. Very often I would say to my crew that however hard I tried to give your Highnesses a complete account of these lands my tongue could not convey the whole truth about them nor my hand write it down. I was so astonished at the sight of so much beauty that I can find no words to describe it. For in writing of other regions, their trees and fruit, their harbors and all their other features, I have wrongly used the most exalted language I knew, so that everyone has said that there could not possibly be another region even more beautiful. But now I am silent, only wishing that some other may see this land and write about it. When he sees the extreme beauties of this coast, he will then be able to prove himself more fortunate than I in the use and choice of words with which to describe it.

CHRISTOPHER COLUMBUS

as quoted in *The Life of the Admiral by His Son, Hernando Colón* (1571)

CONTENTS

Acknowledgments / xi

Introduction / xiii

Editorial Criteria and a Note on the Text / xxix

Part I: The Fifteenth, Sixteenth, and Seventeenth Centuries

Christopher Columbus, *Digest of Columbus's Log Book from the First Voyage* (1492–1493) and *Narrative of the Third Voyage* (1498–1500) / 3

Amerigo Vespucci, *Mundus Novus* (1503) / 9

Pietro Martire d'Anghiera, *De Orbe Novo* (1511–1530) / 14

Gonzalo Fernández de Oviedo y Valdés, *Natural History of the West Indies* (1526) / 22

Alvar Núñez Cabeza de Vaca, *The Narrative of Alvar Núñez Cabeza de Vaca* (1542) / 29

Pedro de Castañeda de Nájera, *The Narrative of the Expedition of Coronado* (c. 1562) / 35

Jean Ribaut, *The Whole and True Discovery of Terra Florida* (1563) / 41

Thomas Hariot, *A Brief and True Report of the Newfound Land of Virginia* (1588) / 46

John Smith, *A Description of New England* (1616) and *The General History of Virginia* (1624) / 51

William Wood, *New England's Prospect* (1634) / 57

Thomas Morton, *The New English Canaan* (1637) / 63

Anne Bradstreet, *Meditations Divine and Moral* (1664/1867) / 68

John Josselyn, *Account of the Second Voyage to New England* (1674) / 72

Jasper Danckaerts, *Journal of a Voyage to New York and a Tour in Several of the American Colonies* (1679–1680/1867) / 78

Louis Hennepin, *A New Discovery of a Vast Country in America* (1697) / 84

Part II: The Eighteenth Century

Sarah Kemble Knight, *The Journal of Madam Knight* (1704–1705/1825) / 95

Robert Beverley, *The History and Present State of Virginia* (1705) / 99

John Lawson, *A New Voyage to Carolina* (1709) / 105

Cotton Mather, *The Christian Philosopher* (1721) / 110

Jonathan Edwards, "The Spider Letter" (1723) and "Beauty of the World" (1725) / 117

Paul Dudley, "An Essay upon the Natural History of Whales . . ." (1724) / 125

Mark Catesby, *The Natural History of Carolina, Florida, and the Bahama Islands* (1731) / 131

Eliza Lucas Pinckney, *The Letterbook of Eliza Lucas Pinckney* (1739–1762/1972) / 137

Peter Kalm, *Travels into North America* (1753–1761) / 143

Benjamin Franklin, "The Kite" (1752), "Effect of Oil on Water" (1773), and "Restoration of Life by Sun Rays" (1773) / 149

John Winthrop, *A Lecture on Earthquakes* (1755) / 156

Pedro Font, *Font's Complete Diary* (1775–1776/1933) / 161

J. Hector St. John de Crèvecoeur, *Letters from an American Farmer* (1782) / 166

John Ferdinand Dalziel Smyth, *A Tour in the United States of America* (1784) / 172

Thomas Jefferson, *Notes on the State of Virginia* (1785) / 178

William Bartram, *Travels through North and South Carolina, Georgia, East and West Florida . . .* (1791) / 184

James Smith, *An Account of the Remarkable Occurrences in the Life and Travels of Col. James Smith* (1799) / 191

Charles Willson Peale, "Introduction to a Course of Lectures on Natural History . . ." (1799) / 196

Part III: The Nineteenth Century through Walden

Meriwether Lewis and William Clark,
The Journals of Lewis and Clark (1804–1806) / 205

Alexander Wilson, *American Ornithology; or, The Natural History of the Birds of the United States* (1808–1829) / 212

John Bradbury, *Travels in the Interior of America . . .* (1817) / 217

Henry Rowe Schoolcraft, *Journal of a Tour into the Interior of Missouri and Arkansaw . . .* (1821) / 224

Timothy Dwight, *Travels in New England and New York* (1821–1822) / 230

Edwin James, *Account of an Expedition from Pittsburgh to the Rocky Mountains . . .* (1822–1823) / 236

Solomon Bayley, *A Narrative of Some Remarkable Incidents, in the Life of Solomon Bayley, Formerly a Slave . . .* (1825) / 242

Timothy Flint, *Recollections of the Last Ten Years Passed in Occasional Residences and Journeyings in the Valley of the Mississippi . . .* (1826) / 247

Anne Newport Royall, *Sketches of History, Life, and Manners, in the United States* (1826) / 253

François-René, Vicomte de Chateaubriand, *Travels in America* (1827) / 260

John James Audubon, *Ornithological Biography* (1831–1839) / 266

Ralph Waldo Emerson, "The Uses of Natural History" (1833) / 273

John D. Godman, *Rambles of a Naturalist* (1833) / 280

Washington Irving, *A Tour on the Prairies* (1835) / 286

Thomas Cole, "Essay on American Scenery" (1836) / 292

Harriet Martineau, *Retrospect of Western Travel* (1838) / 298

Jane Johnston Schoolcraft (Bame-wa-was-ge-zhik-a-quay) (Ojibwa) and Henry Rowe Schoolcraft, *Algic Researches, Comprising Inquiries Respecting the Mental Characteristics of the North American Indians* (1839) / 303

John Kirk Townsend, *Narrative of a Journey across the Rocky Mountains, to the Columbia River . . .* (1839) / 308

Nicolas Point, *Recollections of the Rocky Mountains* (1840–1847/1967) / 314

George Catlin, *Letters and Notes on the Manners, Customs, and Conditions of the North American Indians* (1841) / 320

Lucy Hooper, *The Lady's Book of Flowers and Poetry* . . . (1842) / 325

Nathaniel Hawthorne, "Buds and Bird-Voices" (1843) / 330

William Cullen Bryant, "A New Public Park" (1844) and *Letters of a Traveller* . . . (1850) / 336

Margaret Fuller, *Summer on the Lakes, in 1843* (1844) / 342

John C. Frémont and Jessie Benton Frémont, *Report of the Exploring Expedition to the Rocky Mountains in the Year 1842, and to Oregon and North California in 1843–1844* (1845) / 347

George Copway (Kah-ge-ga-gah-bowh) (Ojibwa), *The Life, History and Travels of Kah-ge-ga-gah-bowh, a Young Indian Chief of the Ojebwa Nation* . . . (1847) / 353

Henry David Thoreau, *A Week on the Concord and Merrimack Rivers* (1849) / 358

Susan Fenimore Cooper, *Rural Hours* (1850) / 365

Howard Stansbury, *Exploration and Survey of the Valley of the Great Salt Lake of Utah* . . . (1852) / 371

Fredrika Bremer, *The Homes of the New World: Impressions of America* (1853) / 375

Further Reading / 381

Sources and Credits / 391

About the Editor / 396

Index / 397

ACKNOWLEDGMENTS

It is a pleasure to thank those whose encouragement and support helped make this book possible. All errors of fact and judgment, of course, remain my own.

First, I am honored to thank the students of the Graduate Program in Literature and Environment at the University of Nevada, Reno, many of whom studied with me in various seminars on early American environmental writing; I have learned a tremendous amount from them, and I think of this book as an extension of the shared research ambitions of those seminars. In particular, I want to express my deep gratitude to two people whose excellent work helped bring this project to fruition: Eve Quesnel, whose dedication to *Roots* resulted in crucial assistance with manuscript preparation at all stages; and Madison Furrh, whose resourceful and tenacious research informed many of the headnotes in the book.

For their thorough and helpful reading of the full manuscript of *Roots*, I am deeply grateful to Ian Marshall, John Tallmadge, and Eve Quesnel. Thanks to Madison Furrh and Elaine Egbert for their helpful comments on the book's introduction, and to Elaine Egbert, Frank Tobin, and Bud Soucie for assistance in translating some passages from the Latin and French. And thanks to Monica Bahnsen for help with proofreading and indexing and to Kate Hoagland for helping with additional manuscript preparation in the late stages of the project.

I am obliged to many colleagues in the libraries at the University of Nevada, Reno. For their patience in tracking down numberless interlibrary loan requests, my thanks go to Millie Syring, Carole Keith, and Ann Campbell. For reference support I am grateful to Betty Glass, Richard Grefrath, and Maggie Ressel, as well as Bob Blesse and the staff of the Special Collections Department. In the Circulation Department, special thanks to Vicky Pascucci, Ginny Roecker, and Victor Atkocaitis. Thanks also to Usha Mehta, and to the reference staffs of the UNR Mines and Health Sciences libraries.

For assistance in locating obscure texts by Solomon Bayley, thanks to David Easterbrook of the Northwestern University Library and Sheila Britton of the University of Notre Dame Library.

At the University of Georgia Press, I wish to recognize my friend and colleague Barbara Ras (who has since become Director of Trinity University Press), whose early and unfailing encouragement of this project I deeply appreciate. Jennifer Reichlin did superb work in helping the manuscript through the final stages of editing, and Jane Curran's expert copyediting was invaluable. The efforts of Allison Reid and David Des Jardines were instrumental in helping this book find its audience. And I am very grateful to Nancy Grayson for her excellent work in helping to see *Roots* through to publication.

Thanks to Karla Armbruster and Kathleen Wallace for welcoming my article-length argument on behalf of early American nature writing into their book *Beyond Nature Writing: Expanding the Boundaries of Ecocriticism* (UP of Virginia, 2001), and thanks to the University Press of Virginia for permission to use parts of that article ("Before Nature Writing: Discourses of Colonial American Natural History") in the introduction to this volume. Likewise, thanks to Ken Womack, editor of *Interdisciplinary Literary Studies*, for permission to reprint in my introduction small parts of my article "Saving All the Pieces: The Place of Textual Editing in Ecocriticism" (*ILS* fall, 2001: 4–23). I am also grateful to my friend Jim Warren for inviting me to present parts of this book to the Environmental Studies Colloquium at Washington and Lee University during spring 2002.

In the course of my research I have had the pleasure of discussing early American environmental writing with many gifted scholars, among whom I would especially like to mention a number of colleagues in the Association for the Study of Literature and Environment (ASLE): SueEllen Campbell, Terrell Dixon, Tom Hallock, Christoph Irmscher, Rochelle Johnson, Paul Lindholdt, Tom Lyon, Ian Marshall, David Mazel, Sean O'Grady, Scotti Parrish, Daniel Patterson, Dan Peck, Dan Phillipon, Bill Rossi, Gordon Sayre, Scott Slovic, Bart St. Armand, Tim Sweet, John Tallmadge, and Jim Warren.

For bringing a sense of perspective to my scholar's garret at the Digs, thanks to Raissa and Darcy. For their constant encouragement, thanks to my folks, Stuart and Sharon Branch. And for her infinite patience, insight, and love — the rich soil in which *Roots* grew — my deepest thanks to my wife and best friend, Eryn, to whom this book is appreciatively dedicated.

INTRODUCTION

Far Shores and First Encounters: Approaching Early American Nature Writing

When Christofero Columbo first laid eyes on the shores of the New World in the autumn of 1492, he was overwhelmed by the beauty, richness, and diversity of the natural environment he found there. In trying desperately to describe the unprecedented loveliness of the bays and rivers, the trees and flowers, the fish and birds as he saw them for the first time, the word he used, over and over again, was "marvelous." And though Columbus made landfall in the Bahamas, rather than in the territory eventually called the United States, his reaction to the world of wonders he witnessed is characteristic of the responses of many other explorers, settlers, and travelers who encountered the American land and its flora and fauna during the centuries that followed Columbus's first voyage.

Indeed, to nonnative inhabitants and travelers, vast reaches of the North American land continued to be a "New World"—an expansive, remote, and little-known wilderness—until well into the nineteenth century. A century and a half after Columbus, many experienced explorers believed that the Great Western Ocean (the Pacific) lay just west of the Appalachian Mountains. Three centuries after Columbus, so astute a naturalist as Thomas Jefferson believed the Appalachians to be the highest mountains in North America and even thought it likely that the mastodon still roamed the unexplored interior wilderness. Lewis and Clark did not lead their Corps of Discovery across the vast continent until the early nineteenth century, and even as late as the mid–nineteenth century—when Ralph Waldo Emerson, Henry David Thoreau, and Margaret Fuller were already philosophizing in Concord—American landscapes such as the Rocky Mountains and Sierra Nevada and the Great Basin and Southwestern deserts were largely unknown wildernesses that were still being explored and mapped.

Those who encountered and attempted to describe the "marvelous" landscapes of North America during the first centuries of its nonnative exploration and settlement were, like Columbus, often overwhelmed by the impressive scale, fecundity, and beauty of the wilderness they found here. And early writers were often fascinated by unusual animals such as the opossum and the hummingbird, which had no counterparts among European fauna. But the story of the American land in these early centuries is also a story of the assumptions, projections, hopes, and values of those who recorded what they saw, for while the land exists independently of human perceptions, the literature of the land does not. If the texts included in this book make clear how powerfully New World nature captivated the imagination of early American explorers, writers, and naturalists, they also show that a writer's sensibility is the complex and often distorted lens through which the natural world is invariably experienced and understood.

Of particular interest in considering early descriptions of American environments is the wonderful, fallible lens of language itself. As a tool that humans develop to mediate and express their encounters with the world, language must change and grow to encompass new places, new experiences, and our emotional and intellectual responses to them. But early writers who encountered the remarkably powerful physical geography of North America were equipped with a poorly developed vocabulary by which to express their observations and feelings. How, using language developed to describe European nature, does one depict the marvel of a possum or hummingbird, let alone the wordless magnificence of Niagara Falls or the Grand Canyon? In trying to communicate experiences in terms a European reader of the period might have understood, how does one describe seeing a flock of a billion passenger pigeons roosting in an unbroken forest, or a herd of ten thousand bison roaming the oceanic expanse of a great prairie? In struggling to represent the strange and wonderful landscapes of the New World, early American nature writers try, like Shakespeare's Duke Senior in the forest of Arden, to find "tongues in trees, books in the running brooks, / Sermons in stones and good in every thing" (*As You Like It* 2.2). And yet, like Columbus, they are often paralyzed by what we might call "sublime aphasia"; dumbstruck by overwhelming beauty, they are often left with a poignant sense of the ineffable grandeur of the land. "I was so astonished at the sight of so much beauty that I can find no words to describe it," admits Columbus. "For in writing of other regions, their trees and fruit, their harbors and all their other features, I have wrongly used the most exalted language I knew, so that everyone has said that there could not possibly be another region even more beautiful. But now I am silent, only wishing that some other may see this land and write about it."

Many others did follow Columbus in struggling to express in words their experience of the marvelous American land. In the pages of this book you will discover descriptions of a wide range of American landscapes, plants, and animals by sixty-three writers working during the three and a half centuries between Columbus and the mid–nineteenth century. Although *Reading the Roots* is arranged chronologically and divided by centuries, you will also find larger topical and historical rubrics by which to organize the contents of the book. For example, most of the pieces included in part 1 could be categorized as exploration narratives; many authors in part 2 explore various aspects of colonial settlement; part 3 includes Western exploration narratives, more developed examples of science writing, and a strong ideological movement toward both nationalism and Romanticism. If you approach the book with a special interest — in flowers, birds, or fish, for example, or in travel writing or nationalist prose, or in the literature of a particular region or period — you will find ways to organize your readings by following particular regional, topical, historical, or ideological threads through the text. Each selection is introduced by a brief headnote to help you contextualize the authors and their work within the nature writing tradition, while the Further Reading section identifies many other works — works of literary natural history as well as critical, scholarly, and reference works — that can augment your study of early American environmental writing.

In exploring the often fabulous and relatively uncharted world of early American nature writing, I have sometimes felt as did the early literary naturalists: overwhelmed by a sense of the beauty, diversity, and richness of what I have seen and anxious to share these wonders with friends back home. But the body of work engaged here is also a vast wilderness from which even the most passionate bibliophile might not succeed in returning with stories of the miraculous things discovered there. *Reading the Roots* surveys a wide body of work from an extensive historical period and contains a diversity of authors who employ a variety of rhetorical forms to engage a range of landscapes. Thus, it is necessarily a general book whose selections are both numerous and brief. But my hope is that the book's broad coverage will serve as an invitation and inspiration to further study of early American nature writing, a rich and heterogeneous corpus of fascinating texts that has received too little critical attention. Like many of the early naturalists included here, my goal is to gather, preserve, and ship home enough specimens to allow you a glimpse of the remarkable wilderness from which they come.

It may be best to think of *Reading the Roots* as a sort of intellectual and literary historical trailhead — a place from which you might follow any number of paths (or, if you prefer, bushwhack cross-country) into the little-known wilderness of American nature writing before *Walden*. And as you enter this textual terra incognita, do not be disconcerted by the unfamiliarity of the territory. To our modern ear the language used by these early writers sometimes sounds uncomfortably arcane, while to our twenty-first-century eyes the landscapes they describe may appear impossibly wild. However, recall that what we encounter in these texts cannot seem stranger to us than an opossum or hummingbird seemed to the writers who first attempted to describe these wonders of nature. And if we are entering an unknown country in which we sometimes risk becoming lost, we are also visiting an amazing land where, around the next bend of the river or over the top of the next mesa, we may see Niagara Falls or the Grand Canyon for the first time. Like early literary natural historians, we should enjoy the lovely strangeness of this new world even as we work together to develop a critical language by which to describe and understand it.

Strange Beasts: Why We Hesitate to Study Early American Nature Writing

Because humans have always used art to comprehend, mediate, and express their relationship to the nonhuman world, it might be said that some form of "nature writing" has long been a significant artifact of human culture. In critical practice, however, the term "nature writing" has often been reserved for a type of nature representation that is deemed literary, written in the speculative personal voice, and presented in the form of the nonfiction essay. Such nature writing is often pastoral or Romantic in its philosophical assumptions, tends to be modern or even ecological in its sensibility, and is often in service to an implicit or explicit preservationist agenda. It is to this sort of nature writing that ecocritics — that is, scholars who study representations of the natural environment in literary and cultural texts — have devoted most of their attention thus far.

Given this circumscribed definition of nature writing, it is not surprising that most critical studies of American environmental literature examine works written since the mid–nineteenth century. Indeed, Henry David Thoreau has often been cited as the progenitor of the American nature writing tradition, despite his own explicit and enthusiastic discussions of the many earlier American literary natural historians upon whose work he built. But what if, as a corrective thought experiment, we try to imagine the American nature writing tradition slowly building toward Thoreau, rather than spontaneously issuing from him? In fact, Thoreau's own voluminous journal is replete with references to the early travelers, explorers, and naturalists whose books he sought out and treasured. "What a strong and hearty but reckless, hit-or-miss style had some of the early writers of New England, like [John] Josselyn and William Wood," Thoreau once wrote. "They are not to be caught napping by the wonders of Nature in a new country. . . . The strong new soil speaks through them." "Certainly that generation stood nearer to nature," concludes the author of *Walden*, "nearer to the facts, than this, and hence their books have more life in them" (7: 108–109).

But unlike Thoreau, who deeply appreciated the historical, scientific, and literary importance of early American nature writers, most ecocritics remain unfamiliar with the remarkable body of place-based literature produced during the three and a half centuries separating the earliest documented European explorations of North America in the late fifteenth century from the publication of Thoreau's

Walden in 1854. Indeed, reading the tradition of literary representations of North American landscapes as if that tradition began with *Walden* is akin to studying American history as if it began with the Civil War. Although both *Walden* and the Civil War are clearly monumental, neither springs forth ex nihilo; rather, each must be understood within a long history of antecedent environmental and cultural circumstances.

The lack of attention paid to early American nature writing may seem a logical consequence of the fact that the current blossoming of environmental literature and ecocriticism has been inspired by a particularly modern, ecological sensibility—a sensibility shaped largely in response to the accelerated degradation of American environments during the twentieth and twenty-first centuries. Indeed, the assumption that nature writing should respond to immediate environmental problems has directed ecocritical attention not only toward the twentieth and twenty-first centuries but also toward the handful of well-known contemporary environmental writers whose work appears to most directly address the current crisis. It is not only understandable but absolutely necessary that a major strand of contemporary literature should address itself to issues of environment and culture, and that it should respond deeply and sympathetically to the loss of biodiversity and habitat that constitutes one of the major political and ethical challenges of our age. Nevertheless, considering the demonstrable centrality of the natural landscape throughout American history, literature, and culture—a centrality Perry Miller expressed in calling America "nature's nation"—it is also profitable to examine other reasons why we have been slow to critically examine earlier American writing about nature.

To begin with, our working definition of nature writing (as the contents of numerous "green" anthologies suggest) has often been limited to the modern literary subgenre of the nonfiction personal essay that sympathetically describes nature and the authorial response to it. Unfortunately this restrictive generic definition of nature writing has discouraged us from considering earlier American writing about nature, which usually takes such less familiar rhetorical forms as the report, sermon, tract, letter, providential history, spiritual autobiography, captivity narrative, slave narrative, or personal diary. It is telling that our limited affection for pre-nineteenth-century nature writers—Gilbert White or William Bartram, for example—is usually reserved for authors whose work is essentially essayistic. Undoubtedly this bias is an artifact of our culture's current reading practices. We all read essays in magazines and newspapers, and many of us also write essays—either as students or in some aspect of our professional lives—but how many of us would voluntarily curl up with a good sermon or government report?

In ignoring these seemingly arcane rhetorical forms, however, we risk losing contact with the experiences and sensibilities of American readers and writers of the past, and we miss an opportunity to better understand how our predecessors saw the world around them. The sermon, for example, was the most widely read form of published American writing during the seventeenth century, and if a New England or Virginia family could afford books beyond the Bible (and perhaps *Pilgrim's Progress*, or a pamphlet on animal husbandry), those additional volumes were likely to consist of sermons or other religious tracts. And in these richly metaphorical religious writings, colonists such as Cotton Mather and Jonathan Edwards expressed and explored their relationship not only to God but also to agriculture, animals, wilderness, and the landscape they inhabited. Likewise, one of the most-read rhetorical forms of the early nineteenth century was the government report, which eastern readers used to glimpse the vast landscapes of the American West. Reports by such explorers as John Bradbury, Edwin James, John Kirk Townsend, and, especially, John C. Frémont were so popular that they directly influenced American settlement patterns, Indian policy, resource extraction, and national identity. By reading representations of the American land in various rhetorical forms — however unfamiliar these strange beasts may at first seem — we thus encourage a deeper understanding of the American environmental and literary history encoded within them.

I also believe we are uncomfortable engaging writers whose approach to the natural world threatens or offends our own literary, environmental, or ethical sensibilities. Exploration narratives, promotional tracts, and religious writings may be so imperialist in their ideology, so anthropocentric in their natural philosophy, or so orthodox in their Christianity that we are disconcerted by their approach to nature. How comfortable are we as readers of Columbus's lyrical descriptions of the New World, when we are also painfully aware that, like many early explorers, the admiral sought gold and converts to Catholicism and was willing to enslave and kill Native Americans to achieve his aims? How should we respond to John Smith, who deeply appreciated the fecundity and biodiversity of the New World yet often wrote as if every plant and animal was adorned with a price tag — created only to satisfy the inordinate craving of the colonist for easy wealth or the aristocratic entertainments of hunting and falconry? And what of Cotton Mather, who studied astronomy and Newtonian physics and yet shared in the speculation that God created blazing comets in order to have a handy place to put lowly sinners for an eternity of suffering? Similar problems arise in other early depictions of the American land. In the fugitive slave narrative written by Solomon Bayley, for example, we may appreciate Bayley's deep faith in the divine power of sheltering wilderness, while also being appalled that he is driven to the woods by slave owners who would separate him from his family and subject him to extreme racial injustice for their own gain.

Also unsettling is the surprising frequency with which early American nature writers engage in the immoderate slaughter of the very animals they profess to admire. This is a matter not simply of subsistence hunting, so common in these early accounts, but of wanton destruction, as when John Bradbury blasts 271 (now extinct) passenger pigeons in a few hours, or Washington Irving kills a buffalo merely for sport and takes only the tongue as a "trophy," or John Kirk Townsend shoots a helpless doe antelope only because his "evil genius and love of sport" triumph over his better angel of self-restraint. A good example of how radically our environmental sensibility differs from that of these early writers may be found in our likely reaction to so unexceptional a passage as the following by John C. Frémont: "I gave Godey leave to kill our little dog (Klamath), which he prepared in Indian fashion—scorching off the hair, and washing the skin with soap and snow, and then cutting it up into pieces, which were laid on the snow. Shortly afterward the sleigh arrived with a supply of horse meat; and we had tonight an extraordinary dinner—pea soup, mule, and dog." These few examples suggest that when we say "nature writing," we often mean to indicate (however unintentionally) the work of writers who share with us certain philosophical or ideological assumptions about nature and our relationship to it—assumptions that can rarely be assumed to guide the environmental values of the writers (especially pre-nineteenth-century writers) included in this book.

In addition, we may be uncertain about how to discuss American nature writing from the period before it became identifiably "American." Not only is much early American natural history literature written before America gained political sovereignty and, subsequently, national identity, but it is also frequently written by native European settlers, explorers, or travelers who are only emigrants to or temporary residents in the New World. Of the fifteen authors included in part 1 of this book, for example, none was born in North America; instead, they are Italian, Spanish, French, Dutch, Belgian, and English. In what sense, then, can we classify them as "American" nature writers? In part 2 of the book we still find that many of these important "American" writers, such as Englishman Mark Catesby and Swede Peter Kalm, are European travelers. Even the most "American" of writers—founding fathers including Benjamin Franklin and Thomas Jefferson—are, of course, colonials who must assist in the creation of the sovereign nation with which they are now associated. And J. Hector St. John de Crèvecoeur, famous for his *Letters from an American Farmer*, was a French nobleman and, when the Revolution came, a pro-Tory loyalist! So, if we insist that important literary representations of the American land may be created only by those born in America—or that such representations must express the sensibility we associate with such American cultural nationalists as Ralph Waldo Emerson or Thomas Cole—we not only miss the valuable perspective on American landscape that comes from international travelers, but we also isolate ourselves from nearly three centuries of our own environmental literary history. If ecocriticism is to establish legitimacy as the scholarly study of the literature of *place*—rather than *nation*, which has long been the more conventional approach to taxonomizing literary history—then it must broaden its scope to include the work of any writer who substantially engages the natural world and our human relationship with it.

It may also embarrass some scholars to take seriously representations of nature that are badly flawed in matters of scientific accuracy. Yet even the giants of early natural history believed that snakes paralyzed their prey with a gaze, or that swallows hibernated underwater, or that insects spontaneously generated in the carcasses of animals (even if they did not believe, as did early eighteenth-century Turkish writer Ibrahim Effendi, that the American "Wakwak" tree blossomed with beautiful women as fruit). Because positivist science is arguably the dominant worldview of our own age, the surprising credulity of these early writers—their quick willingness to embrace what seems idle speculation or, worse, egregious superstition—may strike us as awkward, if not intellectually weak. After all, shouldn't nature writing accurately represent the natural world it describes? However, to dismiss the earliest naturalists on the grounds that they are mere purveyors of bad science is to hold them to an anachronistic standard that has little relevance to the pre-rationalist worldview within which they actually wrote. Not only does it fail to appreciate the obvious limitations of pre-industrial technologies of "scientific" communication and investigation, but it also ignores the unprecedented newness of the New World, the degree to which North America was to early explorers and settlers what outer space is to us today: a little-known and poorly understood realm that captures the imagination while eluding comprehensive intellectual understanding. Three centuries from now our own impressive scientific knowledge is likely to appear as rudimentary, politicized, and superficial as the work of sixteenth- and seventeenth-century natural philosophers now seems to us. More importantly, though, in rejecting the fabulous in early nature writing we turn our backs on some of the most interesting writing we could hope to discover—engaged, imaginative, fantastic writing in which the mystery and beauty of nature is celebrated by writers whose wildest dreams are being tested by the wonders of an unknown world.

There is also a troubling dearth of scholarly editions of works of early American natural history. Although textual editing has long been understood as central to the project of literary studies (especially in such areas as medieval and Renaissance literature, where the rarity of many texts renders their proper preservation and presentation essential), scholars of environmental literature have been slow to recognize the need for and importance of textual editing. Furthermore, few ecocritics are trained in methodologies of textual editing; most literary scholars receive years of instruction in the myriad ways of taking a text apart analytically, but very few are trained in the painstaking techniques necessary to put a text together literally — or put it back together when it has been corrupted by a complicated textual history. Advanced instruction in the principles of documentary editing is rare, and many scholars remain understandably intimidated by an enterprise Arthur Plotnik accurately describes as "an excruciating act of self-discipline, mind-reading, and stable cleaning" (34). As a result, many texts that are important to the tradition of early American natural history writing remain inaccessible — either because they have never been edited from manuscript sources, or because they have never been re-edited from inaccurate or corrupted editions.

In concluding this substantial list of disincentives to the study of early American nature writing we might also mention the following: the earliest reports from the New World are often available only in eighteenth- or nineteenth-century translations (and in many cases, because original manuscripts have been lost, are available only in unverifiable transcriptions); many early works are steeped in a tradition of natural philosophy or *materia medica* that is not only archaic but also alien to the modern sensibility; among the most interesting early works are examples of a sort of theoretical science writing that may appear to fall outside the purview of the humanities; ecocritics have so far demonstrated a special interest in literary celebrations of Western American landscapes, which of course were largely unknown to writers before the nineteenth century; and, finally, the texts we might classify as early nature writing have often been categorized under a competing array of critical and generic rubrics including exploration literature, settlement or promotional tracts, historical writing, philosophical literature, memoir, theology, and science writing, among others. In short, early American nature writing is a strange beast, not easily captured and, once captured, not easily taxonomized; therein lies its beauty, as well as its potential to enrich ecocritical studies.

Widening the Field: The Value of Studying Early American Nature Writing

In spite of these temporary limitations on the bailiwick of ecocriticism, it is clearly time for scholars to closely examine environmental writing in many literary genres and rhetorical forms, from various periods, and organized according to a range of ideological assumptions. Just as ecocritics have in recent years expanded their work in many important new directions (among which I would especially note international environmental literature, urban nature writing, and green cultural and film studies), we are now poised to extend our work to the predecessors of Henry Thoreau. Indeed, one of the richest areas of study in this second generation of ecocritical scholarship is likely to be representations of nature in the diverse and challenging writing of the American exploration, colonial, revolutionary, and early Romantic periods — a body of work that rewards ecocritical attention in a number of ways.

To begin with, early American natural history writing gives us a remarkable window onto the American land in its earliest stages of European occupation. As Henry Savage Jr. notes, "[t]he vanished world of the unravaged American wilderness can be seen by us most clearly now through the eyes of pioneer naturalists" (23). One of the great tragedies of American environmental history is the amount of habitat and number of species that have been irrevocably lost. In this sense, early American nature writing is sometimes our only imaginative means to see places, flora, and fauna that simply no longer exist. In this book, for example, you will read Lewis and Clark's observations of wild rivers that are now dammed, Washington Irving's account of vast grassland prairies now displaced by industrial agriculture, and John Bradbury's description of herds of bison that were, before their near extermination, many thousands strong. Here, too, is Alexander Wilson's wonderful description of the ivory-billed woodpecker and, even earlier, William Wood's account of the passenger pigeon, in which he writes, "I have seen them fly as if the airy regiment had been pigeons, seeing neither beginning nor ending, length or breadth of these millions of millions." Both birds are now extinct. Through early American nature writing, we glimpse a lost world that we need to understand, remember, and mourn.

Henry Thoreau certainly appreciated the environmental historical value of early natural history literature when, on January 3, 1855, he devoted a lengthy journal entry to comparing then-current New England plant and animal populations to the prevalence of the same flora and fauna as described in William Wood's *New England's Prospect* (1634), which he was then reading. "The wild meadow-grasses appear to have grown more rankly in those days," writes Thoreau, noting that Wood "describes them as 'thick and long, as high as a man's middle; some as high as the shoulders'" (7: 132). "Strawberries too were more abundant and large before they were so cornered up by cultivation," he adds (132–33). And we sense Thoreau's excitement as he reads Wood's report of the commonness of various birds that had already become rare or extinct in Massachusetts by the mid–nineteenth century: "Think of that! They had not only brant and common gray wild geese, but 'a white goose,' probably the snow goose" (136). The following year Thoreau's journal contained a lengthy quotation from Cotton Mather's 1717 letter describing a record snowfall. Here Thoreau notes appreciatively that Mather's "simple testimony" of the storm is "worth all the philosophy he might dream of" (8: 165). The work of early American literary natural historians thus allows readers — whether Thoreau or ourselves — an extremely valuable glimpse of the lost wildernesses of North America.

In their effort to identify the roots of a sustainable land ethic, ecocritics must also search for a marginalized tradition of earlier American literature in which love of nature finds expression. In recovering what Pamela Regis rightly calls the "lost paradigm" of natural history (xi), we find that many early writers not studied by ecocritics anticipate modern environmental sensitivity by showing genuine concern for the aesthetic, spiritual, and intellectual value of the natural world. Writing in 1679, for example, Jasper Danckaerts describes a beautiful evening in which he "not only saw all the colors of the rainbow, but all hues and colors, all shining according to their natures, with a brilliancy of their own, displaying them in that perfect splendor, which is so agreeable, and capable of enrapturing man." And Cotton Mather's *The Christian Philosopher* (1721) includes many wonderful moments, such as Mather's pledge to attend closely to the sermons of God's silent ministers, the fishes: "As *mute* as they are, they are *plain* and *loud* Preachers," he writes, "I want nothing but an *Ear* to make me a profitable Hearer of them." Or think of Quaker botanist William Bartram, who encouraged readers to expand their appreciation of the divine intelligence of our fellow creatures: "If we bestow but very little attention to the economy of the animal creation, we shall find manifest examples of premeditation, perseverance, resolution, and consummate artifice," he wrote in *Travels* (1791).

By attending more closely to early American representations of nature, we can discover texts that—precisely because of their iconoclastic or unpopular celebration of nature—have been suppressed, corrupted, or lost. The aphorism that "the winners write the histories" suggests the predicament of the American environmental historian or ecocritic, for the dominant American environmental ethic has long been one of instrumental valuation, capitalist utility, and short-term profit. This dominant, utilitarian ethic has ensured that, until fairly recently, the attention and resources of publishers, funding sources, and paying audiences have been directed primarily toward writing that maintains the status quo while refusing to challenge the wisdom of this dominant environmental ethic. Studying the early roots of modern nature writing is particularly valuable in helping us rediscover otherwise obscure texts whose environmental sympathy or advocacy may have caused them to meet with resistance at all levels of cultural production and dissemination. In finding early texts that demonstrate a deep appreciation for the natural world, we can thus identify important historical moments when individual writers made nascent attempts to cultivate a more carefully considered relationship with the land.

Equally important, we need to study earlier American conceptions of nature in order to better understand how certain misguided and destructive ideas gained prominence in our culture. After all, environmental degradation during the past half century has often been the logical consequence of such earlier American environmental attitudes as fear of wilderness, narrow adherence to theological imperatives of predestination and conversion, ignorance of functional interrelationships in ecological systems, and the sanctioned exploitation of women, indentured servants, Native Americans, and African Americans. By looking more closely at early works that express a strongly anthropocentric, dangerously instrumentalist, or ecologically illiterate approach toward nature, ecocriticism can help reveal the origins of ideas that have often resulted in the destruction of ecosystems and the species that depend upon them.

Indeed, we should study forms of environmental representation that we find ideologically offensive precisely because their thorough theologizing of landscape may be alien to our modern secular sensibility, or because their scientific understanding of nature is by our own standards so fatally flawed, or because their mercantilist interpretation of the landscape appears so reductive in its ignorance of the aesthetic and spiritual value of the natural world. We need to understand, for example, that in the eyes of many early explorers the wilderness of the New World was little more than a well-stocked larder, ripe for the taking by whichever European monarchy could secure its treasures. We must realize that animals such as the passenger pigeon were driven to extinction not because they were rare, but because most nineteenth-century Americans subscribed to the myth of inexhaustible natural resources—the view that species of North American plants and animals were so fantastically numerous as to be impervious to the effects of hunting and agriculture. We should acknowledge that concepts of American national identity are closely entwined with the physical geography of our land, and that in our country environmental destruction has often proceeded under the imprimatur of nationalist ideology. Likewise, the beliefs that rationalized gratuitous trophy hunting, vicious environmental racism, carelessly applied technologies, and widespread destruction of habitat are all visible in the pages of this book. Only by exploring these earlier American environmental ideas and assumptions might we begin to transcend the inevitable limitations of our own vision in order to see this land through the eyes of those who came before us—and only in this informed engagement of other perspectives might we fully understand the roots of our own environmental assumptions and values, however different from those of our predecessors.

Ecocriticism will also be enriched by new attention to works in genres other than the nonfiction essay. Because the nonfiction personal essay, like all literary genres, has developed a set of conventions that privilege certain assumptions about the author and the world—in this case, assumptions such as the availability of leisure time, the primacy of personal experience, the inherent value of philosophical reflection, and the beneficence of nature—it tends to offer a deep but rather narrow view of how writers have perceived and represented American environments. Unfortunately, ecocritics often find early American works unfamiliar in their language, rhetorical conventions, and ideological approach to nature. However, if we are to construct a more accurate view of how this land has been understood and depicted in American culture, it is essential that we broaden our thinking to imagine "nature writing" as a category that describes literary and nonliterary rhetorical forms including the scientific report, religious tract, captivity narrative, slave narrative, letter, and diary.

As I've suggested, then, I believe the circumscription of ecocritical attention to post-Thoreauvian nature writing deprives us of a full understanding of American attitudes toward and descriptions of the land. Such a limitation in vision keeps us from seeing the American wilderness before its rivers were dammed, its forests cut, its prairies broken and harrowed. It prevents us from realizing how many interesting environmental perceptions are contained in the pages of texts we dismissively label bad science. It discourages us from recognizing how powerfully the early ideas of economy, religion, and nation have shaped the environmental problems and values that condition our culture's relationship to nature in the twenty-first century. By reading the roots of contemporary American nature writing, however, we can gain a much deeper and more enriching sense of this environmental literary history. Regarding early American natural history writing, then, I propose adherence to Aldo Leopold's ecological maxim that it is always wisest to "save all the pieces" (146–47). I believe we should preserve, circulate, and study these early American texts as "pieces" that may ultimately be necessary for the reconstruction of a more complete history of the American land and the ways it has been encountered, understood, and represented in the literature of the last five centuries.

Tracing Back Tracks: An Exercise in Imaginative Time Travel

Henry Thoreau once alluded to the reading of early American natural history writing as an intellectually orienting activity by which a person might "trace back his own tracks in the snow" (7: 108–9). It would seem, somewhat ironically, that Thoreau knew something that ecocritics have so far failed to adequately recognize: American nature writing did not begin with Thoreau, but rather, with those "hearty but reckless, hit-or-miss" early American natural history writers whose work Thoreau valued so highly (108). If the environmental crises of the twentieth and twenty-first centuries suggest that our culture has often been "lost" in its attempt to find workable approaches to environmental protection and ecological sustainability, we might do well to "trace back" our own tracks — back to the origins of the attitudes and values that shape our environmental ethics today. One way to do so is to follow the flowering branches of contemporary environmental literature to their nineteenth-century trunk and, from there, trace the tradition to its earlier, deeper roots.

In order to appreciate the circumstances under which early American literary naturalists wrote, however, we must attempt the difficult task of imagining the world from their perspective — a perspective we may be able to glimpse if we imaginatively strip away the accreted strata of assumptions and information that so thoroughly inform our twenty-first-century view of the natural world. In preparing to encounter the earliest texts in this book, try to make an imaginative journey back — before the current heyday of nature writing as it is suggested by the cultural status of Barry Lopez, Wendell Berry, Gary Snyder, Terry Tempest Williams, or Rick Bass; before Earth Day, the Endangered Species Act, or the popular environmentalism that enabled the writing of Edward Abbey; before the advent of the scientific ecology that informed the work of Rachel Carson; before the literary environmental ethics articulated by Aldo Leopold. Go back still further, before the wilderness preservation movement as personified by John Muir; before the establishment of the national parks and forests associated with Theodore Roosevelt, or the urban parks inspired by William Cullen Bryant and Andrew Jackson Downing; before the popular vogue for natural history that was so expertly tapped by John Burroughs.

Now imagine attempting a comprehensive description of nature absent the benefit of Darwin's insights into the origin of species and without the pioneering literary ecology of Henry Thoreau to suggest a rhetorical and epistemological model for your work. Go back still further, before the Romanticism and Transcendentalism of Rousseau, Goethe, Coleridge, Wordsworth, Carlyle, and Emerson had placed a blessing upon the literary celebration of nature; before Herman Melville had described the wilderness of the sea and James Fenimore Cooper had described the wilderness of the forest; before the writing of John Wesley Powell and, even earlier, Lewis and Clark, revealed something of the other side of the continent.

Go back still further, before the flowering of the literary natural history essay in the work of William Bartram; before the pastoral agrarian philosophy of Thomas Jefferson and Hector St. John de Crèvecoeur; before Enlightenment and Deist ideas of natural philosophy and their elaboration in the scientific accomplishments of David Rittenhouse and Benjamin Franklin. Return to a time when natural history was not taught in American colleges or schools; when there were no American museums of natural history; when paper, books, and scientific instruments sufficient for the study of natural history were beyond the means of most colonists; when, in fact, few in the New World even imagined the idea of professional natural history. Go back before the formation of the American Philosophical Society provided naturalists a sense of community, even before the British colonies of North America declared their independence from England. Now take a very large step back before the more than fifty editions and three hundred abridgments of Buffon's monumental, fifteen-volume *Histoire naturelle* (1749–67) and, finally, one giant leap back to a time before Linnaeus's revolutionary *Species Plantarum* (1753) and *Systema Naturae* (10th ed., 1758) provided naturalists a systematic means by which to observe, classify, and describe every living thing on Earth.

Pausing here, note that our imaginative return has so far brought us only to the mid–eighteenth century, an age of impressive literary and philosophical productivity, and a time of tremendous advances in the practice and technologies of all branches of the natural sciences! Were we to go even further back, we would enter a period in which the natural world was much less studied, understood, or appreciated: the seventeenth century, during which many colonists believed that storms, earthquakes, and comets were agents of divine retribution; the sixteenth century, during which explorers scanned the sea for mermaids and searched the land for golden cities; and the fifteenth century, during which the wilderness of the New World was the purest terra incognita—a land so entirely unfathomed and unfathomable that Columbus himself died believing he had actually discovered the marvelous, prelapsarian Eden described in the biblical Genesis.

Finally, try your best to imagine that without the benefit of any of the ideas, insights, information, achievements, methodologies, technologies, institutions, or assumptions that we have shed during this imaginative voyage back in time, *you* were to sit down, dip your quill pen, and attempt to write literary natural history. It is in that imagination that our story begins.

WORKS CITED
(exclusive of works contained within this book)

Leopold, Aldo. *Round River: From the Journals of Aldo Leopold.* Ed. Luna B. Leopold. London: Oxford UP, 1972.

Miller, Perry, ed. *Nature's Nation.* Cambridge, Mass.: Harvard UP, 1967.

Plotnik, Arthur. *The Elements of Editing: A Modern Guide for Editors and Journalists.* New York: Macmillan, 1982.

Regis, Pamela. *Describing Early America: Bartram, Jefferson, Crèvecoeur, and the Rhetoric of Natural History.* DeKalb: Northern Illinois UP, 1992.

Savage, Henry, Jr. *Lost Heritage: Wilderness America through the Eyes of Seven Pre-Audubon Naturalists.* New York: William Morrow, 1970.

Shakespeare, William. *As You Like It.* Ed. Alan Brissenden. London: Oxford UP, 1998.

Thoreau, Henry David. *The Journal of Henry D. Thoreau.* 14 vols. Ed. Bradford Torrey and Francis H. Allen. Boston: Houghton Mifflin, 1906.

EDITORIAL CRITERIA AND A NOTE ON THE TEXT

Editorial Criteria

In selecting the contents of this book I have tried to offer a wide range of examples of nonfiction early American nature writing. For the purposes of this project, my operational definitions are as follows: "nonfiction" is prose writing in any rhetorical form and in any written language (translations are thus included, while narratives based in oral literatures are not); "early" is that which falls before the publication of Henry Thoreau's *Walden* in 1854 (important because *Walden* has often been credited with initiating the American nature writing tradition); "American" is writing that deals with the geographical space later called the United States (even if written before American political sovereignty, and whether written by native-born Americans, émigrés, or travelers—the exceptions are Columbus, Vespucci, and Oviedo, who are vitally important for their representation of the *idea* of America although their writing does not properly concern the landscapes of what is now the United States); and, "nature writing" is literary or nonliterary prose that substantially engages landscape, plants, animals, weather, or other natural phenomena (including human ideas about, responses to, and experiences within nature).

In selecting authors for inclusion I have attempted to represent a diversity of voices and approaches while being guided by several criteria, including the writer's importance to one or more of the following: American literary history, American environmental history, the history of American natural science, and the developing idea of nature in America. I have also considered the literary and scientific interest of the prose itself, and I have made a special effort to include important canonical authors while also introducing many accomplished writers who are less well known. The inclusion of increasingly more authors per century as the book moves forward toward the mid–nineteenth century is intended to mirror the proliferation of literary and scientific responses to American nature that occurred during the periods being represented. I have also sought to represent a diversity of regions (North, South, East, West), landscapes (ocean, coastal, mountain, forest, river, lake, swamp, prairie, desert, cave), subjects (plants, animals, birds, fish, marine mammals, weather, earthquakes, Native American environmental practices), rhetorical forms (exploration account, settlement narrative, promotional tract, spiritual autobiography, captivity narrative, fugitive slave narrative, diary, letter, scientific report), "disciplinary" approaches (exploration, agriculture, hunting and fishing, theology, botany, zoology, ornithology, geology, astronomy, anthropology, aesthetics, natural philosophy, mountaineering), nationalities or cultural affiliations (Italian, Spanish, French, Dutch, Belgian, English, Swedish, Scottish, Anglo-American, African American, Native American), and religious or ideological perspectives (Catholic, Huguenot, Calvinist, Labadist, Quaker, Deist, pantheist, utilitarian, rationalist, nationalist, conservationist, preservationist, Romantic, Transcendentalist).

Even with diversity as a goal, several important constraints deserve special mention. The limitation of the book to written literatures has necessitated the omission of Native American oral narrative, a richly imaginative, nonliterary form of cultural expression that has important environmental implications; however, several Native American writers are included in the book, and engagement with Indian cultures (and their environmental narratives, practices, and beliefs) is central to many of the pieces included here. The case is similar with African American nature writing; although the early folk tradition is prolific, a written literary tradition that is particularly concerned with the natural world truly blossoms during the decades following the Civil War. The initial remoteness of the New World and the subsequent severe restrictions on women's cultural production before the nineteenth century has also made representation of women writers quite challenging; although eleven women writers are included here, an extension of the scope of the project into the late nineteenth century (a veritable heyday for American women nature writers) would have resulted in the inclusion of many more. Finally, the need to restrict this book to a length that allows publication as a single volume has made it necessary to omit scores of interesting and important early American writers whose work engages the natural landscape; however, the Further Reading section lists works by more than one hundred writers who would very likely have been included in *Reading the Roots* had space permitted.

A Note on the Text

The names of authors included in this collection are spelled in accordance with their main entry in the Library of Congress documentary system. The texts in this book are presented as originally published, with the following exceptions. Although original paragraphing, capitalization, and italicization have generally been retained, archaic spelling and British spelling (but not diction) have been modernized and regularized. Where called for, words in titles and subtitles have been capitalized, as have the first words of sentences. Likewise, end-line punctuation has been added where missing. For words that were unclear in the manuscript source, the likely reading has been silently adopted. In a very few cases, obvious typographical errors have been silently corrected. Ellipses have been added to indicate the omission of text from an excerpt, while ornaments separate selections from two different texts by the same author. Throughout this book, the dates of journal and diary entries have been standardized to month, day, and year for the first entry of a given year; and month and day for subsequent entries within the same year. All texts are arranged chronologically by the year of first publication, except in cases of manuscripts that remained unpublished until long after they were written; in these cases the piece is arranged chronologically by year of composition, with first the composition and then the publication year indicated in parentheses, thus: (1739/1972). The specific editions used in rendering the selections contained in this book are listed in the credits, where permissions credits may also be found.

PART ONE

The Fifteenth, Sixteenth, and Seventeenth Centuries

As long as Plum Island shall faithfully keep the commanded post, notwithstanding all the hectoring words and hard blows of the proud and boisterous ocean; as long as any salmon or sturgeon shall swim in the streams of Merrimack; or any perch or pickerel in Crane Pond; as long as the seafowl shall know the time of their coming, and not neglect seasonably to visit the places of their acquaintance; as long as any cattle shall be fed with the grass growing in the meadows, which do humbly bow down themselves before Turkey Hill; as long as any sheep shall walk upon Old Town Hills, and shall from thence pleasantly look down upon the River Parker, and the fruitful marshes lying beneath; as long as any free and harmless doves shall find a white oak or other tree within the township, to perch, or feed, or build a careless nest upon, and shall voluntarily present themselves to perform the office of gleaners after barley harvest; as long as nature shall not grow old and dote, but shall constantly remember to give the rows of Indian corn their education, by pairs: So long shall Christians be born there; and being first made meet, shall from thence be translated, to be made partakers of the inheritance of the saints in light.

SAMUEL SEWALL

from *Phaenomena quaedam Apocalyptica . . .* (1697)

Christopher Columbus
(1451–1506)

Although the glory of his discoveries went to Spain, which had supported his expeditions, Christofero Columbo was a Genoese Italian who had distinguished himself as a captain in the merchant service. After years of petitioning first Portugal and then Spain to finance an attempt to find passage to the riches of the East by sailing west from Europe, Columbus secured Spanish patronage and embarked, in August, 1492, on the first of his four voyages (1492–93, 1493–96, 1498–1500, 1502–4). A month of sailing brought him to his first landfall in the New World, on the Caribbean island he named San Salvador. Believing the Caribbean archipelago to be islands off mainland Cipangu (Japan) and Cathay (China), Columbus claimed to have succeeded in discovering Marco Polo's fabled Indies, even going so far as to incorrectly label the Natives he found there "Indians." Although Columbus's complex motives for exploration included a desire for glory and gold, slaves and spices, he was certainly not without an aesthetic sensibility. If Columbus's descriptions of New World landscapes are mercantilistic and self-promotional, they also demonstrate a genuine enthusiasm for the overwhelming beauty of the new land. Indeed, the following excerpts from the *Digest of Columbus's Log Book from the First Voyage,* which was redacted by Bartolomé de las Casas, suggest a startling encounter with a *terra incognita* of ineffable loveliness: "I was so astonished at the sight of so much beauty," he writes, "that I can find no words to describe it." Although the Spanish monarchy rewarded Columbus's achievement with various appointments and titles, including "Admiral of the Ocean Sea," Columbus himself never fathomed that he had discovered a New World, instead persisting in his claim to have found the Indies. As his subsequent voyages failed to yield the desired proof, however, he became increasingly convinced that he had actually discovered the "earthly Paradise" described in the Bible. In the following selection from the *Narrative of the Third Voyage,* Columbus explains his own theory of world geography: that the earth is pear-shaped, and that Eden exists at the apex of its watery "stem."

From *Digest of Columbus's Log Book from the First Voyage* (1492–1493)

October 19, 1492. I raised anchor at dawn and sent the caravel *Pinta* to the east-southeast and the *Niña* to the south-southeast and myself went south-southeast. I ordered them to follow these courses till midday and that both should then change their courses and rejoin me, and soon, before we had sailed three hours, we saw an island to the east, towards which we steered, and all three vessels reached its northern point before midday. Here there is an islet and a reef of rocks, on the seaward side to the north and another between this and the island itself, which the Indians whom I had with me called "Samoet." I named it Isabela.

The wind was northerly and this islet lay on the course from Fernandina, from which I had sailed due west. I then followed the coast of this island westwards for twelve leagues as far as a cape which I named Cape Hermoso (Beautiful) which is on its western coast. It is indeed lovely, rounded and in deep water, with no shoals lying off it. At first the shore is low and stony, but further on there is a sandy beach which continues along most of this coast. Here I anchored on this night of Friday until morning. The whole of this coast and all of the island that I saw is more or less beach, and, beautiful though the others are, this island is the most beautiful I have seen. There are many trees, very green and tall, and the land is higher than on the other islands. On it there is a hill which cannot however be called a mountain, but which makes the whole island more beautiful. There seems to be a lot of water in the middle of the island. On this northeastern side the coast turns sharply and is thickly covered with very large trees.

I wished to go in, anchor and land in order to see all this beauty, but the water was shallow and I could only anchor some way off shore. The wind was very favorable for sailing to this point where I am now anchored, which I named Cape Hermoso, and beautiful it is. And so I did not anchor in that bay, seeing as I did this green and lovely cape in the distance. Everything on all these coasts is so green and lovely that I do not know where to go first, and my eyes never weary of looking on this fine vegetation, which is so different from that of our own lands. I think that many trees and plants grow there which will be highly valued in Spain for dyes and medicinal spices. But I am sorry to say that I do not recognize them. When I reached this cape, the scent of flowers and trees blew offshore and this was the most delightful thing in the world.

In the morning before I sail away I will land to see what is growing on this cape. There is no village, for this lies further inland, and it is there, according to the men I have with me, that the king lives who wears so much gold. Tomorrow I intend to go so far inland as to find this village and see and speak with this king, who, according to their signs, rules all the islands in this neighborhood and wears much gold on his clothes and person. I do not attach much belief to their statements, however, because I do not understand them very well, and know that they are so poor in gold that any small amount this king may wear will seem much to them.

I have called this cape here Cape Hermoso and I believe that it is an island separate from Samoet and that there is another small island also lying between them.

I did not examine this matter minutely because I could not do all this even in fifty years, being anxious to see and discover as much as I could in order to return to your Highnesses, God willing, in April. It is true that if I find any place where there is gold or spices in quantity I shall wait until I've collected as much as I can. Therefore I continue to sail on in search of such a place. . . .

October 21. At ten o'clock I reached this Cabo del Isleo and anchored, as did the caravels. After eating a meal I went ashore, but there was no village—only one house in which I found nobody. I think they had all run away from fright, for all their things were there.

I wouldn't allow anything to be touched but went with the captains and men to examine the island. Though all the others we had seen were beautiful, green and fertile, this was even more so. It has large and very green trees, and great lagoons, around which these trees stand in marvelous groves. Here and throughout the island the trees and plants are as green as in Andalusia in April. The singing of small birds is so sweet that no one could ever wish to leave this place. Flocks of parrots darken the sun and there is a marvelous variety of large and small birds very different from our own; the trees are of many kinds, each with its own fruit, and all have a marvelous scent. It grieves me extremely that I cannot identify them, for I am quite certain that they are all valuable and I am bringing samples of them and of the plants also.

As I was walking beside one of the lagoons I saw a snake, which we killed. I am bringing the skin to your Highnesses. As soon as we saw it, it swam into the lagoon and we followed it, for the water was not very deep, and we killed it with spears. It is almost five foot long and I believe there are many of them in this lagoon. Here I recognized aloe, and tomorrow I intend to have half a ton brought aboard, for they tell me it's very valuable. . . .

October 23. I should like to depart today for the island of Colba, which I believe according to the indications of its site and riches given us by these people must be Chipangu. I shall not stay here any longer, to round this island or go to the village as I had intended, to have speech with the king or lord. I do not wish to delay long, since I see that there is no goldfield here and to round these islands one needs many changes of wind and the wind doesn't blow as one wishes. It is best to go where there is much to be done and so it is right not to stay here but to continue on our course, discovering many lands until we find one that is truly profitable. I think, however, that this place is very rich in spices. I am extremely sorry that I cannot recognize them, for I see a very great number of trees each bearing its own kind of fruit, and they are as green now as trees in Spain in the months of May and June. There are a thousand kinds of plants also, all in flower. But the only one I recognize is this aloe, which I ordered to be taken aboard yesterday and brought for your Highnesses.

From *Narrative of the Third Voyage* (1498–1500)

I have always read that the world of land and sea is spherical. All authorities and the recorded experiments of Ptolemy and the rest, based on the eclipses of the moon and other observations made from east to West, and on the height of the Pole Star made from north to south, have constantly drawn and confirmed this picture, which they held to be true. Now, as I said, I have found such great irregularities that I have come to the following conclusions concerning the world: that it is not round as they describe it, but the shape of a pear, which is round everywhere except at the stalk, where it juts out a long way; or that is like a round ball, on part of which is something like a woman's nipple. This point on which the protuberance stands is the highest and nearest to the sky. It lies below the Equator, and in this ocean, at the farthest point of the east, I mean by the farthest point of the east the place where all land and islands end.

In support of this belief, I urge all the arguments which I have stated concerning the line from north to south a hundred leagues west of the Azores. As we passed it in a westerly direction, the ships mounted gently nearer to the sky, and we enjoyed the mildest weather. On account of this mildness the needle shifted by a quarter northwestwards, and continued to shift farther to the northwest as we sailed on. It is this increase of height that causes the changes in the circle described by the Pole Star and the Guards. The closer I came to the Equator the higher they rose, and the greater the alteration in these stars and their orbits.

Ptolemy and the other geographers believed that the world was spherical and that the other hemisphere was as round as the one in which they lived, its center lying on the island of Arin, which is below the Equator between the Arabian and Persian gulfs; and that the boundary passes over Cape St. Vincent in Portugal to the west, and eastward to China and the *Seres*. I do not in the least question the roundness of that hemisphere, but I affirm that the other hemisphere resembles the half of a round pear with a raised stalk, as I have said, like a woman's nipple on a round ball. Neither Ptolemy nor any of the other geographers had knowledge of this other hemisphere, which was completely unknown, but based their reasoning on the hemisphere in which they lived, which is a round sphere, as I have said.

Now that your Highnesses have commanded navigation, exploration and discovery, the nature of this other hemisphere is clearly revealed. For on this voyage I was twenty degrees north of the Equator in the latitude of Arguin and the African mainland, where the people are black and the land very parched. I then went to the Cape Verde Islands, whose inhabitants are blacker still, and the farther south

I went the greater the extremes. In the latitude in which I was, which is that of Sierra Leone, where the Pole Star stood at five degrees at nightfall, the people are completely black, and when I sailed westwards from there the heats remained excessive. On passing the line of which I have spoken, I found the temperatures growing milder, so that when I came to the island of Trinidad, where the Pole Star also stands at five degrees at nightfall, both there and on the mainland opposite the temperatures were extremely mild. The land and the trees were very green and as lovely as the orchards of Valencia in April, and the inhabitants were lightly built and fairer than most of the other people we had seen in the Indies. Their hair was long and straight and they were quicker, more intelligent and less cowardly. The sun was in Virgo above their heads and ours. All this is attributable to the very mild climate in those regions, and this in its turn to the fact that this land stands highest on the world's surface, being nearest to the sky, as I have said. This confirms my belief that the world has this variation of shape which I have described, and which lies in this hemisphere that contains the Indies and the Ocean Sea, and stretches below the Equator. This argument is greatly supported by the fact that the sun, when Our Lord made it, was at the first point of the east; in other words the first light was here in the east, where the world stands at its highest. Although Aristotle believed that the Antarctic Pole, or the land beneath it, is the highest part of the world and nearest to the sky, other philosophers contest it, saying that the land beneath the Arctic Pole is the highest. This argument shows that they knew one part of the world to be higher and nearer to the sky than the rest. It did not strike them however that, for the reasons of shape that I have set down, this part might lie below the Equator. And no wonder, since they had no certain information about this other hemisphere, only vague knowledge based on deduction. No one had ever entered it or gone in search of it until now when your Highnesses commanded me to explore and discover these seas and lands.

It was discovered that the distance between these two straits which lie, as I have said, opposite one another on a line from north to south, is twenty-six leagues. There can be no mistake in this because I took the readings on a quadrant. From these two straits westward to the gulf which I have mentioned and I called the Golfo de las Perlas is another sixty-eight leagues of four miles (as is generally reckoned at sea). The water runs continuously and very fiercely out of these two straits towards the east, which accounts for its battle with the salt water outside. In that southern strait which I named the Boca de la Sierpe, I found that at nightfall the Pole Star stood at about five degrees above the horizon, and in the northern strait, which I called the Boca del Drago, it was at about seven. I found that the Golfo de las Perlas itself is almost 3,900 miles westwards of the first meridian of Ptolemy, which is nearly seventy degrees along the Equator, reckoning each degree as fifty-six and two-thirds miles.

Holy Scripture testifies that Our Lord made the earthly Paradise in which he placed the Tree of Life. From it there flowed four main rivers: the Ganges in India, the Tigris and the Euphrates in Asia, which cut through a mountain range and form Mesopotamia and flow into Persia, and the Nile, which rises in Ethiopia and flows into the sea at Alexandria.

I do not find and have never found any Greek or Latin writings which definitely state the worldly situation of the earthly Paradise, nor have I seen any world map which establishes its position except by deduction. Some place it at the source of the Nile in Ethiopia. But many people have traveled in these lands and found nothing in the climate or altitude to confirm this theory, or to prove that the waters of the Flood which covered, etc., etc. reached there. Some heathens tried to show by argument that it was in the Fortunate Islands (which are the Canaries); and St. Isidore, Bede, Strabo, the Master of Scholastic History, St. Ambrose and Scotus and all learned theologians agree that the earthly Paradise is in the East, etc.

I have already told what I have learnt about this hemisphere and its shape, and I believe that, if I pass below the Equator, on reaching these higher regions I shall find a much cooler climate and a greater difference in the stars and waters. Not that I believe it possible to sail to the extreme summit or that it is covered by water, or that it is even possible to go there. For I believe that the earthly Paradise lies here, which no one can enter except by God's leave. I believe that this land which your Highnesses have commanded me to discover is very great, and that there are many other lands in the south of which there have never been reports. I do not hold that the earthly Paradise has the form of a rugged mountain, as it is shown in pictures, but that it lies at the summit of what I have described as the stalk of a pear, and that by gradually approaching it one begins, while still at a great distance, to climb towards it. As I have said, I do not believe that anyone can ascend to the top. I do believe, however, that, distant though it is, these waters may flow from there to this place which I have reached, and form this lake. All this provides great evidence of the earthly Paradise, because the situation agrees with the beliefs of those holy and wise theologians and all the signs strongly accord with this idea.

Amerigo Vespucci
(c. 1452–1512)

Like Christopher Columbus, Amerigo Vespucci was an Italian whose explorations were made under the standard of Spain. And like Columbus, Vespucci claimed to have made four voyages to the New World (1497–98, 1499–1500, 1501–2, 1503–4), though there is evidence that he may actually have made only two. A Florentine born into a banking and business family, Vespucci spent a number of years in Paris before entering the service of Lorenzo di Pierfrancesco de' Medici as a city and state administrator. In the early 1490s Vespucci traveled to Seville, where, in addition to serving Lorenzo's financial interests, he was briefly engaged in a business partnership with Christopher Columbus himself. Although a 1505 letter from Columbus referred to Vespucci as a "worthy person," the Florentine's letters, which were being published at about this time, offered an implicit challenge to Columbus's understanding of western geography and were thus seen by many as an attack upon Columbus. Perhaps the most important of Vespucci's letters is the famous *Mundus Novus* ("New World"), a Latin translation of a letter, written in Italian but now lost, from Vespucci to his old patron, Lorenzo di Pierfrancesco de' Medici. In the letter (probably published in 1503), which was soon translated into a number of languages and widely circulated throughout Europe, Vespucci declares that the "new regions" from which he had recently returned "can be called a new world." Although Columbus had "discovered" the New World, it was Vespucci who recognized it as such. And while Vespucci's voyages were to the regions that are now Venezuela and Brazil, his influential concept of the New World changed the way the mysterious western lands were regarded ever after. In recognition of his achievements as a navigator and explorer—achievements Vespucci takes pains to emphasize in the following excerpt—the Spanish Crown appointed him to the new post of "piloto mayor" ("pilot major"). The suggestion that the recently discovered *Mundus Novus* be named after Vespucci rather than Columbus was promoted by a 1507 map of the known world, where the name "America" first appears.

From *Mundus Novus* (1503)

Amerigo Vespucci to Lorenzo di Pierfrancesco de' Medici, with many salutations

In the past I have written to you in rather ample detail about my return from those new regions which we searched for and discovered with the fleet, at the expense and orders of His Most Serene Highness the King of Portugal, and which can be called a new world, since our ancestors had no knowledge of them and they are entirely new matter to those who hear about them. Indeed, it surpasses the opinion of our ancient authorities, since most of them assert that there is no continent south of the equator, but merely that sea which they called the Atlantic; furthermore, if any of them did affirm that a continent was there, they gave many arguments to deny that it was habitable land. But this last voyage of mine has demonstrated that this opinion of theirs is false and contradicts all truth, since I have discovered a continent in those southern regions that is inhabited by more numerous peoples and animals than in our Europe, or Asia or Africa, and in addition I found a more temperate and pleasant climate than in any other region known to us, as you will learn from what follows, where we shall briefly write only of the main points of the matter, and of those things more worthy of note and record, which I either saw or heard in this new world, as will be evident below.

We set out from Lisbon under favorable conditions on 14 May 1501 by order of the aforesaid king, with three ships, to go in quest of new regions to the south, and we sailed steadily for twenty months, and the route was as follows. We sailed to what were formerly called the Fortunate Islands and are now the Grand Canary Islands, which are in the third climate and at the bounds of the inhabited West. From there, we traveled on the Ocean Sea along the entire African coast and part of the Ethiopian, as far as the Ethiopian promontory, as Ptolemy called it, which is now called Cape Verde by our people, and Bezeguiche by the Ethiopians. The region is Mandanga, fourteen degrees north of the equator within the Torrid Zone, and it is inhabited by black tribes and peoples. There, once we had recovered our strength and procured all the necessities for our voyage, we weighed anchor and spread our sails to the winds; and set our course across the very vast Ocean toward the Antarctic, steering somewhat to the west with the wind known as Vulturnus: and from the day we left the aforesaid promontory, we sailed for two months and three days before sighting any land. What we suffered in that vast expanse of sea, what dangers of shipwreck, what physical discomforts we endured, what anxieties beset our spirits, I leave to the understanding of those who have learned well and from much experience what it means to quest after uncertain things, things they have dared to investigate without prior knowledge of them. And that I might condense the whole story into one sentence, know that out of the sixty-seven days we sailed, we had forty-four continuous days of rain, thunder, and lightning, so dark that we never saw sunlight in the day, nor clear sky at night. Fear so overwhelmed us that we had almost abandoned all hope of survival. However, in those frequent, terrible tempests of sea and sky, it pleased the Most High to show us a nearby continent, and new regions and an unknown world. Sighting them, we were filled with joy, which, as one can well imagine, seizes those who have found safety after calamities and misfortunes. Thus, on 7 August 1501, we dropped anchor off the shores of those regions, thanking our God with solemn prayer and the singing of a Mass. There we learned that the land was not an island but a continent, both because it extends over very long, straight shorelines, and because it is filled with countless inhabitants. For in it we encountered innumerable peoples and tribes, and all kinds of sylvan animals not found in our regions, and many other things we had never seen before, which would take too long to describe individually. God's mercy shone about greatly when we entered those regions; for our firewood and water supplies were dwindling, and in a few days we might have perished at sea. Honor be to Him, and glory, and thanks.

We decided to sail along the shore of that continent to the east, and never to lose sight of it. Soon we came to a bend where the shore curved to the south: the distance from where we first touched land to this bend was about three hundred leagues. In this phase of the voyage we landed on several occasions and conversed in friendly fashion with the people, as you will hear below. I had forgot to write to you that from the promontory of Cape Verde to the start of that continent is a distance of about seven hundred leagues, although I estimate that we sailed more than eighteen hundred, owing in part to our ignorance of the place and the ignorance of the pilot, and in part because of the storms and winds which blocked our direct course and forced us to make frequent turns. For if my companions had not relied upon me and my knowledge of cosmography, there would have been no pilot or captain on the voyage to know within five hundred leagues where we were. Indeed, we were wandering with uncertainty, with only the instruments to show us accurate altitudes of the heavenly bodies: those instruments being the quadrant and astrolabe, as everyone knows. After this, everyone held me in great honor. For I truly showed them that, without any knowledge of sea charts, I was still more expert in the science of navigation than all the pilots in the world: for they know nothing of any places beyond those where they have often sailed before. In any case, where the aforementioned bend in the land curved southward on the coast, we agreed to sail beyond it and explore what was in those regions. Therefore we sailed along the shore, approximately six hundred leagues, and we often landed and conversed with the inhabitants of those regions, and were warmly received by them, and sometimes stayed with them fifteen or twenty days at a time, always in a very friendly and hospitable way, as you will hear in the following. . . .

The air there is very temperate and good, and, as I was able to learn by conversing with the people, there is no pestilence or illness there deriving from contaminated air, and unless they die a violent death, they live a long life: I think this is due to the southern winds blowing constantly there, especially the one we call Eurus, which is to them as Aquilo is to us. They are very zealous fishermen, and the sea there is full of fish of all sorts. They are not hunters: I think this is because there are many kinds of forest animals there, especially lions, bears, countless snakes, and other dreadful and ill-formed beasts, and forests on all sides with trees of enormous size, that they do not dare to expose themselves, naked and without any protection or weapons, to such dangers.

The land of those regions is very fertile and pleasant, abundant in hills and mountains, countless valleys and huge rivers, watered by healthful springs, and filled with broad, dense, barely penetrable forests and all sorts of wild beasts. Great trees grow there without cultivation, and many of them produce fruits delicious to taste and beneficial to the human body, though several indeed are the opposite, and none of the fruits there are like our own. Numberless kinds of herbs and roots grow there as well, from which the people make bread and excellent foods. They also have many seeds, totally different from ours. There are no kinds of metal there except gold, in which those regions abound, although we did not bring any back with us on this our first voyage. The inhabitants apprised us of it, and told us that in the interior there is great abundance of gold, which they do not at all value or consider precious. They are rich in pearls, as I wrote to you elsewhere. If I wanted to mention separately all the things which are there, and to write about the numerous kinds of animals and their great numbers, I would grow too prolix with a matter so vast; and I certainly believe that our Pliny did not come within a thousandth part of the types of parrots and other birds and animals which are in those regions, with such great diversity of forms and colors that even Polycletus, master of painting in all its perfection, would have failed to depict them adequately. All the trees there are fragrant, and all produce gum or oil or some liquor, and I do not doubt that their properties, if they were known to us, would be salubrious for the human body; and certainly, if anywhere in the world there exists an Earthly Paradise, I think it is not far from those regions, which lie, as I said, to the south, and in such a temperate climate that they never have either icy winters or scorching summers.

Sky and air are clear for most of the year and free from dense vapors. The rains there fall delicately and last three or four hours, then vanish like mist. The sky is adorned with very beautiful signs and figures, in which I noticed twenty stars as bright as we sometimes see Venus or Jupiter. I considered their movements and orbits and measured their circumferences and diameters with geometric methods, and determined that they are of great magnitude. . . .

In that hemisphere I saw things which do not agree with the arguments of philosophers: a white rainbow was seen twice around midnight, not only by me, but also by all the sailors. Likewise, several times we saw a new moon on the day when it was in conjunction with the sun. Every night in that part of the sky, innumerable vapors and bright flares streak across. A bit earlier I spoke of the hemisphere, although, properly speaking, it is not fully a hemisphere with respect to ours; but since it approaches the shape of one, it is permissible to call it so.

Therefore, as I said, from Lisbon, our point of departure, 39½ degrees from the equator, we sailed fifty degrees beyond the equator, which together make about ninety degrees, and since this sum makes a quarter of the great circle, according to the true reasoning of measurement passed on to us by the ancients, it is clear that we sailed around a quarter of the world. And by this logic, we who live in Lisbon, 39½ degrees this side of the equator in the northern latitude, are at an angle of five degrees in the transverse line to those who live at the fiftieth degree beyond the same line in the southern latitude, or, so that you may understand more clearly: a perpendicular line, which hangs over our heads from a point directly above us while we stand upright, hangs pointing toward their sides or ribs: thus we are in an upright line, and they in a transverse line, and a kind of orthogonal triangle is formed thereby, of which we form the perpendicular line, they the base, and the hypotenuse extends from our vertex to theirs. . . . And let these words suffice for cosmography.

These were the more noteworthy things I saw on this last navigation of mine, which I call the "third journey." The other two "journeys" were my two other navigations, which I made toward the west on a mandate from the Most Serene King of the Spains; on those voyages I noted the marvels accomplished by the sublime creator of all, our God: I kept a diary of the noteworthy things, so that, if ever I am granted the leisure, I may gather together all these marvels one by one and write a book, either of geography or of cosmography, so that my memory will live on for posterity, and so that the immense creation of almighty God, unknown in part to the ancients yet known to us, may be recognized. I pray, therefore, to the most merciful God that He may prolong the days of my life, that by His good grace, and for the salvation of my soul, I may attain the fullest realization of my goals. The other two "journeys" I keep among my private papers, and when the Most Serene Highness returns the "third journey" to me, I shall try to return to tranquility and my homeland, where I will be able to confer with experts and, with the help and encouragement of my friends, to complete that work.

I ask your forgiveness for not sending you this last navigation, or rather this last "journey," as I had promised to do in my last letter: you know the reason, since I could not yet have the original back from His Most Serene Highness. I still plan to make a fourth voyage, and have already received the promise of two ships together with their equipment, so that I may prepare to search for new regions to the south, traveling from the east with the wind called Africus; on this voyage I think I will accomplish many things to the praise of God, the benefit of this kingdom, and the honor of my old age; and I await nothing but the consent of His Most Serene Highness. May God permit whatever is for the best. You will learn of whatever happens.

The interpreter Giocondo has translated this letter from Italian to Latin, so that all the Latins may understand how many marvelous things are being discovered every day, and to curb the audacity of those people who wish to study the heavens and their majesty and to know more than they are permitted to know, for, ever since the world began, the earth's vastness and all things contained in it have been unknown.

Praise to God.

Pietro Martire d'Anghiera
(1457–1526)

Italian-born Pietro Martire d'Anghiera was an influential humanist and historian who helped bring the light of the Italian Renaissance to Spain and the news of the New World to Europe. Born at Arona, near Milan, Martire went to Rome when he was twenty years old. After many years as an Italian courtier, in 1487 he went to Spain, where he soon became an important member of the Spanish intelligentsia. Martire lectured at the university in Salamanca, instructed members of the court of King Ferdinand and Queen Isabella, and in 1511 was appointed by Emperor Charles V to serve as Spanish Royal Chronicler—a challenging position that required him to study, synthesize, and present the many findings of Spanish explorers in the New World. Martire's epic work of history, geography, anthropology, and natural history is his *De Orbe Novo* (known in English as *The Decades of the New World*), published in phases from 1511 to 1530. These chronicles describe the New World as it was then being reported by Columbus, Balboa, Cortes, Magellan, and many others who sailed under the standard of Spain. It was through *De Orbe Novo* that many early-sixteenth-century Europeans learned of the landscape of the New World, the conquest of Mexico, the discovery of the Pacific Ocean, and the nature of Native American cultures throughout the Americas. Italian, French, and German translations of the work appeared throughout the century; when Richard Eden's translation of parts of the *De Orbe Novo* was published in London in 1555 as *The Decades of the Newe Worlde* . . . , it was only the second book in English to contain information about New World explorations. Although Martire was, by the standards of his day, a well-educated and well-informed geographer and naturalist, the wild stories included in the excerpt below—so credulous and so outrageous by later standards—suggest how little was actually known of the peoples and creatures of the new lands. The fantastic descriptions of the *De Orbe Novo* reveal Martire's wonderful literary imagination but also demonstrate that a willing belief in the wonders of the New World was common among even the best-educated sixteenth-century European readers.

From *De Orbe Novo* (1511–1530)

A certain cacique of the region, Caramatexius by name, was very fond of fishing. Upon one occasion a young fish of the gigantic species called by the natives *manatí* was caught in his nets. I think this species of monster in unknown in our seas. It is shaped like a turtle and has four feet, but is covered with scales instead of shell. Its skin is so tough that it fears nothing from arrows, for it is protected by a thousand points. This amphibious creature has a smooth back, a head resembling that of a bull, and is tame rather than fierce. Like the elephant or the dolphin, it likes the companionship of men and is very intelligent. The cacique fed this young fish for several days with yucca bread, millet, and the roots the natives eat. While it was still young, he put it in a lake near to his house, as in a fishpond. This lake, which had been called Guaurabo, was henceforth called Manatí. For twenty-five years this fish lived at liberty in the waters of the lake, and grew to an extraordinary size. All that has been told about the lake of Baiae or the dolphins of Arion is not to be compared with the stories of this fish. They gave it the name of Matu, meaning generous or noble, and whenever one of the king's attendants, specially known by him, called from the bank Matu, Matu, the fish, remembering favors received, raised its head and came towards the shore to eat from the man's hand. Anyone who wished to cross the lake merely made a sign and the fish advanced to receive him on its back. One day it carried ten men altogether on its back, transporting them safely, while they sang and played musical instruments. If it perceived a Christian when it raised its head it dived under water and refused to obey. This was because it had once been beaten by a peevish young Christian, who threw a sharp dart at this amiable and domesticated fish. The dart did it no harm because of the thickness of its skin, which is all rough and covered with points, but the fish never forgot the attack, and from that day forth every time it heard its name called, it first looked carefully about to see if it beheld anybody dressed like the Christians. It loved to play upon the bank with the servants of the cacique, and especially with the young son who was in the habit of feeding it. It was more amusing than a monkey. This manatí was for long a joy to the whole island, and many natives and Christians daily visited this animal.

It is said that the flesh of manatís is of good flavor, and they are found in great numbers in the waters of the island. The manatí Matu finally disappeared. It was carried out to sea by the Attibunico, one of the four rivers which divide the island into equal parts, during an inundation accompanied by horrible typhoons which the islanders call hurricanes. The Attibunico overflowed its banks and inundated the entire valley, mingling its waters with those of all the lakes. The good, clever, sociable Matu, following the tide of the torrent, rejoined its former mother and the waters of its birth; it has never since been seen. . . .

There is another system of bird hunting which is quite original and diverting to relate. We have already stated that there exist in the islands, and especially at Hispaniola, stagnant lakes and ponds upon whose waters flutters a whole world of aquatic birds, because those waters are covered with grasses, and little fish and a thousand varieties of frogs, worms, and insects live in that liquid mud. The work of corruption and generation ordained by the secret decree of providence is promoted in these depths by the heat of the sun. Different species of birds swarm in these waters: ducks, geese, swans, divers, gulls, sea mews, and countless similar.

We have elsewhere related that the natives cultivate a tree in their gardens, whose fruit resembles a large gourd. The natives throw a large quantity of these gourds into the ponds, after having carefully stopped up the holes by which water is introduced into them, to prevent their sinking. These gourds, floating about on the water, inspire the birds with confidence; the hunter then covers his head with a sort of cask made of a gourd, one in which there are little holes for his eyes, like in a mask. He wades into the water up to his chin, for from their infancy they are all accustomed to swim, and do not fear to remain a long time in the water. As the birds find the gourd which conceals the hunter similar to all the others floating about, the man is able to approach the flock. Imitating with his head the movements of the floating gourd, he follows the little waves produced by the wind, and gradually approaches the birds. Stretching out his right hand he seizes a bird by the foot, and without being seen, quickly jerks it under the water and thrusts it into a bag he carries. The other birds imagining their companion has dived in search of food, as they all do, fearlessly continue their movements, and in their turns become victims of the hunter. . . .

In my first Decades I spoke of a vast maritime cavern in the province of Guaccaiarima in Hispaniola, which extends a distance of several stadia into the heart of the lofty mountains along the west coast. The interior of this cavern is navigable. In its gloomy depths, where the sun's rays hardly penetrate save for a moment at sunset, is heard such a roaring from a waterfall that those who enter shiver with horror. The following is the ancient tradition believed by the islanders concerning this cavern, and the story is a pleasing one. They ascribe life to the island, believing that it breathes, eats, and digests. They compare it to a monstrous female beast. This cavern corresponds to the sex organs of the woman, and at the same time to the anal canal, through which she discharges her excrement and impurities. This is proven by the name the region takes from this cavern; *guacca* means region or neighborhood, and *tarima* means behind, or a place where filth accumulates. Upon hearing this I recollected the story of the fabulous Demogorgon, breathing in the bowels of the earth and, according to the ancient belief, producing the ebb and flow of the sea. It is just as well, however, to mix a little truth with these legends. . . .

Let us now consider the hunting fish. This fish formerly vexed me somewhat.

In my first Decades, addressed to Cardinal Ascanio, I stated amongst other marvels, if I remember properly, that the natives had a fish which was trained to hunt other fish just as we use quadrupeds for hunting other quadrupeds, or birds for hunting other birds. So are the natives accustomed to catch fish by means of other fish. Many people, given to detraction, ridiculed me at Rome in the time of Pope Leo for citing this and other facts. It was only when Giovanni Rufo di Forli, Archbishop of Cosenza, who was informed of all I wrote, returned to Rome after fourteen years' absence as legate of Popes Julius and Leo in Spain, stopped the mouths of many mockers, and restored me my reputation for veracity. In the beginning I also could hardly believe the story, but I received my information from trustworthy men whom I have elsewhere cited, and later from many others.

Everybody has assured me that they have seen fishermen use this fish just as commonly as we chase hares with French dogs, or pursue the wild deer with Molossians. They say that this fish makes good eating. It is shaped like an eel, and is no larger. It attacks fish larger than itself, or turtles larger than a shield; it resembles a weasel seizing a pigeon or still larger animal by its throat, and never leaving go until it is dead. Fishermen tie this fish to the side of their bark, holding it with a slender cord. The fish lies at the bottom of the bark, for it must not be exposed to the bright sun, from which it shrinks.

The most extraordinary thing is that it has at the back of its head a sort of very tough pocket. As soon as the fisherman sees any fish swimming near the bark, he gives the signal for attack and lets go the little cord. Like a dog freed from its leash, the fish descends on its prey and, turning its head, throws the skin pouch over the neck of the victim, if it is a large fish. On the contrary, if it is a turtle, the fish attaches itself to the place where the turtle protrudes from its shell, and never lets go till the fisherman pulls it with the little cord to the side of the bark. If a large fish has been caught (and the fishermen do not trouble about the small ones), the fishermen fasten stout cords to it and pull it into the air, and at that moment the hunting fish lets go of its prey. If, on the contrary, a turtle has been caught, the fishermen spring into the sea and raise the animal on their shoulders to within reach of their companions. When the prey is in the bark, the hunting fish returns to its place and never moves, save when they give it a piece of the animal, just as one gives a bit of a quail to a falcon; or until they turn it loose after another fish. I have elsewhere spoken at length concerning the method of training it. The Spaniards call this fish *reverso,* meaning one who turns round, because it is when turning that it attacks and seizes the prey with its pocket-shaped skin. . . .

Let me quote some amusing details concerning certain seabirds larger than eagles or vultures. According to the descriptions given me, they appear to me to be pelicans. These birds have such enormous mouths that a soldier, who used his military cloak to protect himself against one that attacked him, saw the entire cloak disappear into the creature's throat, and when the bird was afterwards killed, he got it back intact; his companions witnessed this incident. This bird can swallow a five-pound fish or even a larger one at one gulp. It swims about seeking fish which it catches in the following manner. In the first place it does not dive as other seabirds, such as geese, ducks, and divers do, but rises high into the air like birds of prey circling about and waiting until a fish, attracted by the noise, rises to the surface. Great flocks of these birds may be seen hovering about, and from time to time they drop with such force on their prey that they dive half an arm's length under the water. The fish, astonished by the noise of the wings, do not move, and so let themselves be caught.

It sometimes happens that two birds seize upon a fish. Nothing is more entertaining than to watch, either from on board ship or from the shore, the battle that follows between them, for neither bird relinquishes the prey which is finally torn in pieces, each one carrying off his share. Their beaks are half a palm long, and are more curved than those of any other birds of prey. They are, indeed, longer, and their wings more spreading than those of eagles or vultures. On the other hand, their bodies are so lean that they are scarcely larger than pigeons. Provident nature has given them strong wings to sustain the weight of their enormous beak, for they do not require them for such a meager body. The Spaniards call these birds alcatraz.

Many other birds, unknown to us, are found in this country. Most remarkable for the variety of their plumage and their forms are the parrots; some are as large or even larger than our cocks, while others are scarcely the size of a sparrow. Flocks of parrots are as numerous as are flocks of ravens, crows, or jays in Europe. The natives use them for food, just as we do pigeons and blackbirds, rearing them about their houses for their entertainment, for they take the place of our linnets and magpies. . . .

Let us now consider another of nature's marvels. In Hispaniola and the other islands of the ocean, there are swampy districts well adapted for cattle raising. The colonies in the neighborhood of these swampy places are infested by all kinds of gnats, produced by the damp heat; and these insects do not attack people only at night, as in other countries. This is the reason why the natives do not build lofty houses, and make their entrance doors only wide enough to barely admit a man and without any windows at all. For the same reason they do without torches, for the gnats instinctively follow the light; nevertheless the insects get into the houses. While Nature has bestowed this pest on the islanders, she has at the same time supplied a remedy, just as we have the cat to rid us of the filthy nuisance of rats. The gnat chasers, which likewise serve other purposes, are called *cucurios* and are winged worms, inoffensive, a little smaller than butterflies, and resembling rather a scarabaeus, since their wings are protected by a tough outer covering, into which they are drawn when the insect stops flying. These insects, like the fireflies we see shining at night or certain luminous worms found in hedgerows, have been supplied by provident nature with four luminous points, two of which occupy the place of the eyes, and the other two are hidden inside the body under the shell, and are only visible when they put out their little wings like the scarabs, and begin to fly. Each cucurio thus carries four lanterns, and it is pleasing to learn how people protect themselves against the pestiferous gnats, which sting every one and in some places are a trifle smaller than bees.

As soon as one knows that these dangerous gnats have invaded his house, or wishes to prevent them doing so, cucurios are immediately procured by the following artifice; necessity, the mother of invention, has taught this method. To catch cucurios one must go out at nightfall, carrying a burning coal, mount upon a neighboring hut in sight of the cucurios, and then call in a loud voice, "cucurios, cucurios!"

Simple people imagine that the cucurios are charmed by this noise and answer the call. As a matter of fact they quickly appear in masses. We believe they are attracted by the light, as clouds of gnats also rush towards it, just as the martins and swallows do, only to be devoured by the cucurios. When a sufficient number of cucurios have assembled, the hunter throws down the coal, and the cucurios, following the direction of the fire, fall to the earth, where it is as easy to catch them as for the traveler to catch a scarabaeus creeping along with its wings under its shell. It is also alleged that cucurios are not caught at all in this manner, but rather by knocking them to the ground with branches or broad strips of linen, when they are flying; they lie there stupefied and are caught. It is also said they are caught as birds are, by throwing the linen cloth or the branches of leaves over them. However this may be, as soon as the hunter has got his supply of these cucurios, he takes them home, and closely shutting his house, he lets them loose. The cucurio immediately flies about the room seeking the gnats. He acts as though he mounted guard over the hammocks and the faces of the sleepers, which the gnats attack, assuming the duty of ensuring them a night's rest.

This is not the only service the cucurio renders. Another sufficiently curious one is the following: each eye of this insect is a lamp for the benefit of its owner; and by the light emitted by these cucurios one can sew, spin, and even dance. May it not be imagined that the cucurios, charmed by the songs of the singers and their movements in the dance, also follow in their flight the rhythmical movements? In chasing the gnats, the cucurios are obliged to execute turnings and returnings in their flight.

By the light shed by this insect, as long as his hunger is not satisfied, it is possible to read or write. When the cucurio's hunger is appeased by the gnats he has caught and swallowed, his light grows dim; and when the natives perceive this, they open the door and let the insect regain his liberty and search for food elsewhere. As a joke, and to scare people who are afraid of specters, the facetious sometimes rub their faces with a dead cucurio, and show themselves, with flaming countenances, to their neighbors at night, asking them where they are going. Our own young people in like manner, when they wish to joke, put on a mask with gaping mouth well furnished with teeth, and seek to scare children or womanish-hearted people who are easily frightened. The face smeared with the cucurios looks like a bright flame; but this luminous property quickly grows dim and goes out.

There is another extraordinary advantage derived from the cucurio; the natives, whom the Spaniards send on errands, prefer to go at night; attaching two cucurios to their toes, they walk as easily as though they carried as many lanterns as the cucurios have lights. They also carry others in their hands, which help them to catch utias. These utias are a sort of rabbit, a little larger than a rat, and before the arrival of the Spaniards, the natives knew of no other and ate no other quadruped. They also fish by means of cucurios, this being a sport of which they are passionately fond and which they follow from their cradles. . . .

Near the source of the Dabaiba River lies a country called Camara, the last syllable pronounced long. The recollection is still preserved amongst its inhabitants of a frightful tempest mingled with whirlwinds, which suddenly broke from the east upon that country, tearing up all the trees by the roots and carrying off many houses, especially those built of wood. While the tempest raged two birds, almost similar to the harpies of the Strophades celebrated by the poets, were blown into the country. They had the face, chin, mouth, nose, teeth, eyes, eyebrows, and physiognomy of a virgin; one of these birds was so heavy that no tree was strong enough to support it. It is even alleged that when it rested on a rock to pass the night, the mark of its talons was distinguishable. It seized people in its claws, and carried them off to devour them on the summit of the mountains, as easily as hawks rob chickens. The other bird was not so large, and was doubtless the offspring of the first.

The Spaniards who went up that river a distance of four hundred leagues into the interior in their boat, talked with many natives who witnessed the death of the larger of those birds. They are trustworthy men, to whose testimony I have often had recourse: the jurisconsult, Coral, Osorio, and Espinosa. It will be interesting to learn how the people of Camara on the Dabaiba got rid of this terrible pest. As necessity is the mother of invention, so the people of Camara found the means of killing that bird, of which history should preserve the recollection. Cutting a huge piece of wood, they carved on one of its extremities the image of a man; after which they carried it to a place where this monstrous bird often passed when descending from the mountain in search of prey. Profiting by a clear night and the full moon, they dug a hole and set up the beam in such wise that only the human figure should be visible. Just near the ditch was a thick forest, in which they placed themselves, in ambuscade, armed with bows and javelins. At dawn the frightful monster appeared, descending upon its prey. It swooped upon the statue, seizing it and plunging its claws so deeply into the wood that it could no longer fly away; upon which the barbarians ran from their hiding place and dealt it so many blows that it was more full of holes than a sieve. It finally fell dead. They bound it with cords and suspended it upon long lances, transporting it throughout the whole neighborhood in order to allay the general terror and to make known the fact that the roads, which no one had ventured to use because of that bird, were now free. . . .

There is an amusing story Your Holiness may read, growing out of a bat's bite. A servant of the monks who suffered from a pleurisy was at death's door, and needed to be quickly bled. Two or three times the surgeon tried to open a vein with his razor, but could not draw a drop of blood. He was therefore abandoned as one who had but a few hours to live; and the monks, after bidding him a last farewell, made preparations for his burial. Meanwhile a bat dropped on the abandoned unfortunate, opened a vein in one of his feet which was uncovered, and only after gorging himself with blood did he quit, leaving the vein open. When the monks returned at daybreak, instead of dead, as they expected, they found the man fresh and lively and almost out of danger; he convalesced rapidly and resumed his former occupation. The bat had acted as doctor, and merited thanks. The bite of these creatures kills dogs, cats, and chickens. The natives call them *rere*; I give things the names they use, which are not many.

There are crows, not black, with hooked aquiline beaks, rapacious and slow of flight, as we commonly see in the case of the *avitade* in Spain, which is larger than a goose. At sunset they exhale fragrant perfumes, but at midday, or when the air is heavy, they have no odor. Large quantities of partridges, chickens, and doves are found in this country, as are likewise sparrows smaller than our wrens. Marvelous things are told of their industry in building their nests to protect themselves against birds of prey and other animals.

The neighboring district to Chiribichi is called Atata, and is remarkable for its salt ponds, as we have already said. While the Spaniards were exploring their banks, those who were looking towards the sea while their companions were playing games or resting, beheld an unrecognizable object floating on the waves. It seemed to be a human head covered with hair and a thick beard, and with arms moving. As long as they watched it without speaking, the monster moved quietly as though admiring the ship, but when the sailors shouted to draw their comrades' attention, the noise frightened the creature, which dived, but not without exposing that part of its body concealed under water. It ended in a fish's tail, and its lashings stirred up the hitherto tranquil waters. I believe it was a Triton, one of those named by the fables of old, the trumpeters of Neptune.

Gonzalo Fernández de Oviedo y Valdés (1478–1557)

A Spaniard from Madrid, Gonzalo Fernández de Oviedo y Valdés spent most of his life as a courtier in the service of Spanish royalty including King Ferdinand and Queen Isabella and, for nearly forty years, the Spanish emperor Charles V (Ferdinand's grandson). Oviedo met Columbus as early as 1490—several years before the older man's first voyage into the unknown—and was friends with Columbus's sons. Already a man in his mid-thirties when he first sailed to the New World in 1514, Oviedo directed the Crown's operations in mining and smelting gold in Tierra Firme; in the years that followed he would cross the Atlantic a remarkable total of twelve times. Although Oviedo may have begun his *Natural History* as early as in 1515—and although his work was encouraged by Charles V, who in 1519 gave him a commission to write the official history of the New World—the bulk of the book was probably not written until 1524. The *Natural History*, composed in Spanish rather than Latin, was published in Toledo in 1526 and was translated into nearly all the European languages. It was so popular in its day that many Europeans (including, according to some scholars, Sir Walter Raleigh) received their first glimpses of the marvelous new land and its strange creatures through Oviedo's eyes. Perhaps because a full, uncorrupted English translation did not appear until 1959, the vital importance of the *Natural History* to New World nature writing has gone largely unrecognized. In addition to being a widely read and extremely influential book, the *Natural History* is also the first book to describe the wonders of New World nature methodically, carefully, and on the basis of firsthand observations. Although Oviedo's models were Pliny and Aristotle, his results are strikingly modern in both sensibility and style. His lucid, engaged, richly descriptive prose suggests a deliberately literary approach—an observation supported by the fact that he also wrote a Chivalric romance, *Don Claribalte* (1519). In his later years Oviedo continued to enlarge his most important work, publishing the first part of his *General and Natural History of the Indies* in 1535; part two was published just after his death in 1557.

From *Natural History of the West Indies* (1526)

Armadillo

The armadillo is a very strange animal to the Christians, and quite different from any animal in Spain or anywhere else. This animal is a quadruped. Its whole body and tail are covered with skin. Its hide is like the skin of a lizard, between white and gray, but somewhat more white. In appearance it is exactly like an armored horse, with its caparison and armor completely covering its body. From under the armor the tail comes out, and in their proper place the legs, and the neck and the ears in their place. In short, it is exactly like a warhorse with armor. This animal is about the size of a small dog, or common cur dog, and is not vicious, but rather timid. They make their homes in mounds of earth, and by digging with their paws they hollow out their caves and burrows, somewhat like those made by rabbits. They are excellent food and are captured in nets, and some are killed by crossbowmen. Most often these animals are taken when the fields are burned over in preparation for planting or to renew the grass for cows and cattle.

I have eaten of them several times, and the flavor is better than that of kid. It is healthful food. I cannot help suspecting that this animal was known by those who first put horses in full trappings, for from the appearance of these animals they could have learned the form of the trappings for the armored horse. . . .

Nighthawk

In Tierra Firme there are some birds which the Christians call "night birds." They come out at sunset at the same time as the bats, with whom they have constant war, pursuing them and beating them. That is always a source of pleasure to those who observe it. There are many of these birds in Darién, and they are somewhat larger than swifts, and have the same kind of wings and are as fast or faster in flight. Across the middle of each wing there is a band of white feathers. All the rest of its plumage is brown, almost black. These birds fly all night long, and at daybreak hide themselves and are not seen again until sunset, when they come out again to continue their customary feud with the bats.

Bats

Since in the chapter above I spoke of the struggle between the nighthawks and bats, I must now say something about bats. There are many bats in Tierra Firme. They were very dangerous to Christians when first Vasco Núñez de Balboa and the bachelor Encisco went there at the time of the conquest of Darién. Although it was not known then, there is a simple and efficacious cure for the bite of the bat. At that time some Christians died of it and others were critically ill, but later the Indians taught them how to treat the bite.

Those bats are exactly like these in Spain but usually they bite at night, and most commonly they bite the tip of the nose or the tip of the fingers or toes, and suck such a great amount of blood from the wound that it is difficult to believe unless one has observed it. They have another peculiarity, and this is that if among one hundred men they bite one man, they will return to the same man on successive nights even though he be among a great number.

The remedy for this bite is to take a small amount of hot embers from the fire, as hot as can be tolerated, and place them on the wound. There is also another remedy: take water as hot as can be tolerated and wash the wound; then the bleeding stops and a cure is effected very shortly. The wound itself is small, for the bat takes out only a small circle of flesh. They have bitten me, and I have cured myself with hot water as I have described.

There are other bats in the island of St. John that are eaten. They can be skinned very easily in scalding water. Then they appear like reed birds, very white, and fat and of good flavor, according to the Indians. Also some Christians have eaten them, especially those who are inclined to eat what they see others eat.

Pelican

There are birds in the Indies called pelicans which are larger than large geese. Most of their plumage is brown, and in some parts yellow. They have a beak about two spans long, very wide near the head, gradually growing smaller toward the tip. They have a very large gular pouch. They are very much like a bird I saw in your Majesty's place in Brussels in Flanders. They call this bird "hayna."

I remember one day when your Majesty was dining in the large salon, they brought to your royal presence a large kettle of water containing live fish, and this bird ate them whole. I am of the opinion that that must have been a seabird, for it had feet like those of a water bird or a goose. The pelican has that sort also, for they too are seabirds. In Panama, in 1521, I saw a man's coat placed in the pouch of a pelican. On the coast of Panama there are so many flocks of pelicans that they merit description. There are also many men in this capital of your Majesty's who have seen many times what I am about to describe.

Your Majesty knows, as I have already pointed out, that in Panama the tide of the South Sea rises and falls every six hours over a stretch of two leagues and more of land. At high tide the sea comes as close to the houses of Panama as the Mediterranean comes to the houses of Barcelona or Naples. The high tide brings many sardines—a marvelous thing—and one could not believe there would be such an abundance of sardines without seeing them. The chief of that land, when I was there, every day was obligated and ordered by your Majesty's governor to bring usually three dugouts or boats filled with these sardines, and to empty them out in the public square. This he did day after day, and one of the councilmen of the city without charge divided these fish among the Christians. There would have been enough of those fish to sustain many more people, a population even larger than the city of Toledo, and even if they had nothing more to eat, the large numbers of sardines would have been more than enough to sustain them.

The pelicans appeared always at high tide with the sardines, so many of them flying over the water that they filled the air. They would always dive into the water, catch as many sardines as they could, then rise from the water again. After gobbling down the fish, they would dive into the sea again, then rise again without ever resting. When the tide goes out, the pelicans go with it, continuing their fishing as I have described. Along with the pelicans come the frigate birds, described above. As soon as a pelican rises with the fish it has caught, the frigate bird beats it and pursues it so closely that it casts up the fish it has swallowed. As soon as a fish is thrown out, the frigate bird catches it before it falls into the water. It is a pleasure to watch this game that goes on every day.

There are so many of these pelicans that the Christians send dugouts and boats to islands and reefs near Panama to get young pelicans that are not old enough to fly. They kill as many as they want with sticks and fill their dugouts with them. They are fat and good to eat. The adults are not good to eat but they are taken for their fat, which is made into very good oil for burning in lamps. This oil gives a gentle light which burns very beautifully. In this manner and for this reason many pelicans are slaughtered, and yet it always seems that the number that can be seen fishing for sardines is on the increase. . . .

Crabs

Crabs are land animals that come from holes they make in the earth. The head and body are entirely round and in some measure resemble a falcon's hood. Four feet come from each side, and two mouths, like pincers, one larger than the other, with which they bite. The bite is very painful but is not poisonous. Its shell or body is smooth and thin like the shell of an egg except that it is harder. The color is gray or white or bluish purple. They walk sideways and are good to eat. The Indians are very fond of them, and in Tierra Firme there are many crabs, and there are many Christians who like them. Crabs are inexpensive and tasty. When Christians go inland this is food readily available, and very good when roasted over coals. Finally, the form of the crab is about the same as we depict the sign of Cancer.

In Andalusia, on the seacoast and on the banks of the Guadalquivir where it enters the Atlantic ocean at San Lúcar, and in many other places, there are many crabs, but they are water crabs. Those I speak of here are land crabs. Sometimes those of the Indies are harmful, and those who eat them die, especially if the crabs have eaten poisonous things or manchineel apples, which will be described later, from which the Carib Indians make poison for their arrows. Christians protect themselves by not eating the crabs which are found near manchineel trees. Even if one eats many of these good crabs, they will not hurt one and it is not food that causes indigestion.

Toads

There is an offensively large number of nonpoisonous toads in Tierra Firme. The greatest number that I have seen was in the city of Darién. They were so large that when they died during the dry season such large bones remained, especially the ribs, that they looked like the bones of a cat or some other animal about that size. As the waters go down, the toads gradually disappear until the following year, when they reappear with the rains. There are not so many now as there used to be. The reason is that the land is being drained and cultivated by Spaniards, and many trees and forests are being cleared, and with the breeding of cows, mares, and cattle the land is being dried up and each day it is becoming more healthful and beautiful.

These toads sing in three or four ways, and not one is pleasing. Some sing like those here in Spain, others whistle, and others make still different sounds. Some of these toads are green, some are gray, and others are almost black. But they are all ugly, large, and annoying—since there are so many. As I have said, they are not poisonous. Wherever precautions are taken against water damming up, and when the water flows freely or is used up, there are no toads. Then they go in search of swamps. . . .

Fishes and Fishing

In Tierra Firme I have seen a great abundance and many different species of fishes. Since it will be impossible to describe all of them here, I shall speak of a few. First I will say that there are broad sardines which have red tails; they are excellent food and among the best fish found there. There are also mojarras, "biajacas," jurels, "dajaos," rays and trout. These, and many others whose names I do not remember, are caught in great abundance in the rivers. Also very good shrimp are to be had there. Likewise some of the above-named fish are caught in the sea, as well as pompanos, acedias, porgies, mullet, octopi, dolphins, very large shad, lobsters, crabs, oysters, and very large turtles. Very large sharks, manatees and morays are also caught there. There are many other fish and so many species and such a large quantity of them that it would require great space and time to describe them.

However, here I want to speak in detail only about three of these fish named above: the turtle, the shark, and the manatee. Beginning with the first, I say that in the island of Cuba large turtles are found, sometimes so large that ten or fifteen men are necessary to pull one of them from the water. I have heard this from so many reliable people on that island that I consider it to be true. I can testify as an eyewitness about those killed in Tierra Firme. In the village of Acla I saw one so large that six men were hard put to it to carry it, and ordinarily the smaller ones are quite a burden for two men. The large one that I saw there carried by six men had a shell seven spans long, measured down the middle of its back, and more than five spans wide. The turtles are captured in the following manner: Often turtles are caught in drag nets, but the way in which they are caught in quantity is when they leave the sea to come out on the beach to lay their eggs or to feed. When the Spaniards or Indians find their tracks in the sand, they follow them. The turtles, being surprised, run toward the water, but since they are heavy and slow they are easily overtaken. Then a stick is placed under its front legs and as it runs along, the turtle is turned over on its back. Since the turtle cannot turn over from its back to an upright attitude, it must stay there. Leaving the turtle upside down, the hunters can follow tracks of any others that may be there, and handle that turtle in the same fashion. In this way many are caught. This is a very good fish of good flavor and healthful.

The second of the three fishes mentioned above is called *tiburón*. This fish is very large, swift in the water, and very bloodthirsty. Many are caught, especially the small ones, by the ships sailing the Atlantic or while at anchor and in other ways. The large ones are caught while the ships are under way and in the following manner: when the shark sees a ship, it swims after the ship, eating the refuse and garbage thrown overboard. The shark can keep up with the ship regardless of its speed and even swim around it, and often follows the ship one hundred and fifty leagues or more. When the sailors want to catch one, they throw over the stern a hook about as thick as a thumb and about three palms long, bent in the fashion of other fishhooks and with its barb in proportion to its size; attached to the end of the shank of the hook are four or five heavy links of a chain, and in the last link is tied a line two or three times as big as the hook. On the hook they place a piece of fish or bacon or any kind of meat, or part of the entrails of another shark if they have killed one. In one day I have seen nine caught, and more could have been taken if they had been desired.

The shark follows the ship regardless of its speed, as I have said, and swallows the whole fishhook. As soon as the shark swallows the bait it tries to get away, but from the very force of the strike and from the tug of the ship the fishhook pierces the fish, and the point comes through its jaw, and the fish is caught. Some of these fish are so large that twelve to fifteen men or more are necessary to hoist and pull them on board. When they are in the boat a sailor kills the shark with several blows on the head from the flat side of an axe. Some of these fish are ten or twelve feet long or longer, and the widest are five, six, or seven spans wide. They have very big mouths in proportion to the body and have two separate rows of large fierce teeth, each row being quite distinct from the other. These fish are cut into strips and the strips hung in the open air on the rigging for two or three days. Then they can be eaten. The fish has a fine flavor, and because of its size furnishes food for the crew for several days. The young ones naturally are best and more tender and more easily digested. These fish are covered with skin, like the dogfish and spotted dogfish. For these fish as well as sharks are all viviparous. I mention this because Pliny in his *Natural History* does not include any of the three among animals producing living young.

These sharks leave the sea, go up the rivers, and there they are no less dangerous than the large alligators, which have already been described in detail, because they too eat men, cows, and horses, and they are very dangerous in the fords and other places where they have feasted.

There are many other species of fish large and small, that are caught by boats under full sail, and I shall describe the manatee, which is the third of the three fish I said I would describe.

The manatee is a sea fish, much larger than the shark. It is very ugly and resembles those large ox skins used to carry must in Medina del Campo and Arévalo. The head of this fish is as big as a cow's head, and it has eyes like a cow's. It has large stumps instead of arms, with which it swims. It is a very tame animal and comes up to the shore and if there is any grass there that it can reach, it eats it. Since these fish, and many others too, often swim on the surface of the water, they are killed by bowmen in dugouts and boats. When such a fish is sighted, the Indians shoot it with a heavy arrow to which is tied a thin strong cord which has been tarred. Then the fish swims away rapidly and the bowman plays out many yards of the cord, to the end of which is tied a cork or stick. As the fish grows weaker, the sea is covered with blood, and the fish turns toward the shore. The bowman begins to pull in his cord, and when he has pulled in all but a few yards, he draws the cord toward the shore and the manatee finally touches bottom. Then the waves help the fisherman to land the manatee. And the bowman and those who help him drag the manatee up on the shore. A pair of oxen, sometimes two, is required to pull the cart that carries the manatee to the city. Sometimes the fish is loaded into the dugout instead of being towed to shore, because as soon as it dies it floats on the surface. I think that it is one of the tastiest of all fish, and one that tastes most like meat.

It looks so much like a cow that a person seeing only a part that has been cut off could not tell whether it was beef or veal. In fact, it tastes so much like beef that it would fool anyone in the world. It also tastes like the best veal, and it is especially good when dried. None of our fish in Spain, not even the sturgeon, is so good.

The manatee has a certain stone or bone in its head, in the brain or medulla oblongata, which is very useful in curing pain in the side. First the stone is burned, then pulverized. When the pain appears, the patient takes this powder in the morning on an empty stomach. He takes as much as can be picked up on a small coin and follows it with a swallow of good white wine. After continuing this treatment for three or four mornings the pain disappears. Some who have tried the remedy have told me about it. Also I have seen many persons search diligently for this stone for the purpose I have described.

There are other fish almost as large as the manatee that are called red sawfish, which have a sword on the snout. This sword, which is about four or five spans long, is very strong and on both sides it has very sharp teeth. There are other fish that range in size from those smaller than sardines to those so large that two pairs of oxen are necessary to draw them in a cart.

Alvar Núñez Cabeza de Vaca
(c. 1490–1557)

Published in 1542, Cabeza de Vaca's *La Relación* is among the most fascinating and valuable sixteenth-century accounts of New World exploration. In it, the author describes his epic eight-year journey (1528–36) across the then unknown wilderness of what is now the American Gulf Coast and Southwest. As one of only four survivors of the disastrous three-hundred-man Narváez expedition of 1527, Cabeza de Vaca managed — by courage, resourcefulness, perseverance, and luck — to survive shipwreck, storms, hunger, thirst, exposure, illness, injury, enslavement, and Indian attacks, and live to tell the story of his six-thousand-mile walk across what is now Florida, Texas, New Mexico, Arizona, and northern Mexico. By turns adventure story, autobiography, travel narrative, anthropological tract, and nature writing, *La Relación* describes the land and its Native inhabitants and narrates Cabeza de Vaca's remarkable personal transformation from conquistador to castaway to merchant to slave to faith healer. Because it contains the earliest known extant descriptions of the geography, flora, and fauna of the American Southwest, *La Relación* is of special value to students of nature writing. Unlike Columbus and Oviedo, whose descriptions were of the West Indies, Cabeza de Vaca is among the first Europeans to record his impressions of the North American wilderness, which he calls "a difficult and marvelous country of vast forests, the trees astonishingly high." Cabeza de Vaca is the first European explorer to describe that "vast river," the Mississippi. He is also the first to witness and record the impressive movements of that great beast, the buffalo, and is likewise the first to describe other wild American animals, "including one which carries its young in a pouch on its belly until they are big enough to find food by themselves"—the opossum. Indeed, his observations are sufficiently astute to allow him to distinguish among three kinds of mosquitoes he encounters during his travels. Of the Southwestern American landscapes described in the following excerpts from *La Relación*, Cabeza de Vaca concluded, appreciatively, "[t]his land, in short, lacks nothing to be regarded as blest."

From *The Narrative of Alvar Núñez Cabeza de Vaca* (1542)

The Character of the Country

The terrain we had suffered through since first landing in Florida is mostly level, the soil sandy and stiff. Throughout are immense trees and open woods, containing nut varieties, laurels, a species called liquidambar, cedars, junipers, live oaks, pines, red oaks, and low palmettos like those of Castile.

Everywhere are lakes, large and small, some hard to cross because of their depth and/or profusion of fallen trees. They have sand bottoms. The lakes in the Apalachen country are far larger than any we had seen earlier.

This province has many cornfields, and houses are scattered over the countryside as at Gelves.

We saw three kinds of deer; rabbits and jackrabbits; bears and lions; and other wild animals, including one which carries its young in a pouch on its belly until they are big enough to find food by themselves; but, even then, if someone approaches while they are foraging, the mother will not run before the little ones get into her pouch.

The country is very cold. It has fine pastures for cattle. The wide variety of birds in abundance includes geese, ducks, royal drakes, ibises, egrets, herons, partridges, falcons, marsh hawks, sparrow hawks, goshawks, and numerous other fowl. . . .

The Life of the Mariames and Yguaces

. . . Many times while we were among this people and there was nothing to eat for three or four days, they would try to revive our spirits by telling us not to be sad; soon there would be prickly pears in plenty; we would drink the juice, our bellies would get big, and we would be content. From the first talk like this we heard to the first ripening of the prickly pears was an interval of five or six months. This period having lapsed and the season come, we went to eat the fruit.

We found mosquitoes of three sorts, all abundant in every part of the region. They poison and inflame and, through most of the summer, exasperated us. For protection, we encircled ourselves with smudge fires of rotten and wet wood. We did little else all night than shed tears from the smoke of this remedy, besides roasting from the intense heat of the many fires. If at any time we took refuge to the seaside and fell asleep, we were reminded with blows to feed the fires. The Indians of the interior have another intolerable method, even worse than the one I have just mentioned, which is to fire the plains and forests within reach with brands, both to drive the mosquitoes away and at the same time drive lizards and like things from the earth to eat.

They also kill antelope by encircling fires; deprived of pasturage, the animals are forced to seek it where the Indians may trap them. The Indians encamp only where they can find wood and water. Sometimes everybody carries loads of these to hunt deer, which usually are found where wood and water are not. The Indians kill all the deer and other animals they can the day of their arrival, then consume the whole of their water and wood in cooking and smudge fires. They tarry the next day to get something to sustain their homeward hike. By the time they go, the ravages of those insects make them look as if they had the affliction of holy Lazarus.

In this way they appease their hunger two or three times a year, at the cost I have stated. I can declare from sad experience that there is no torment in the world to equal it.

Inland are many deer, fowl, and beasts other than those I have spoken of. Buffalo come as far as here. Three times I have seen and eaten them. I think they are about the size of those in Spain. They have small horns like the cows of Morocco; their hair is very long and flocky like merinos'. Some are tawny, others black. In my opinion the meat is finer and fatter than the beef of this country. The Indians make blankets out of the skins of cows not full grown; and shoes and shields from the full-grown. These cattle come from as far away as the seacoast of Florida, from a northerly direction, and range over a tract of more than 400 leagues. Throughout this whole range, the people who dwell nearby descend and live upon them and distribute an incredible number of hides into the interior.

The Tribal Split and News of the Remaining Barge

When the six months I had been biding my time were up, the Indians proceeded to the prickly pears thirty leagues away, and the moment to execute our escape plan drew nigh. When we drew near the point of flight, our Indian masters quarreled over a woman. After a scuffle in which heads were bruised with fists and sticks, each took his lodge and went his own way. So we Christians found ourselves separated with no means of reuniting for another year.

During this year my lot was hard, as much from hunger as harsh treatment. Three times I had to run from my masters, who came after me with intent to kill;

but each time, God our Lord preserved me. When the prickly pear season at last arrived again, we Christians came together with the aggregation of all the tribe in the cactus thickets.

We set a time for our escape, but that same day the Indians dispersed to different locales of the cactus country. I told my comrades I would wait for them at a certain spot among the prickly pear plants until the full moon. This day I was speaking to them was the new moon, September 1, 1534. I said that if they did not appear by the time the moon was full, I would go on alone. So we parted, each going with his Indian group.

On the thirteenth day of the moon, Andrés Dorantes came with Estevánico and told me they had left Castillo with other Indians nearby, called Anagados; that they had encountered great obstacles and got lost; that tomorrow the Mariames were going to move to the place where Castillo was and unite in friendship with this tribe which held him, having heretofore been at war with them. In this way we would recover Castillo.

The thirst we had all the while we ate the pears, we quenched with their juice. We caught it in a hole we hollowed out in the ground. When the hole was full, we drank until slaked. The juice is sweet and must-colored. The Indians collect it like this for lack of vessels. There are many kinds of prickly pear, some very good; they all seemed so to me, hunger never leaving me the leisure to discriminate.

Aside from prickly pear juice, nearly all these people drink rainwater, which lies about in puddles. There are rivers; but since the Indians know no fixed abode, they have no familiar places for getting water.

Over all the region we saw vast and beautiful plains that would make good pasture. I think the land would prove very productive if developed by civilized men. We saw no mountains. . . .

Our Success with Some of the Afflicted and My Narrow Escape

The very evening of our arrival, some Indians came to Castillo begging him to cure them of terrible headaches. When he had made the sign of the cross over them and commended them to God, they instantly said that all pain had vanished and went to their houses to get us prickly pears and chunks of venison, something we had tasted of precious little.

We returned many thanks to God, Whose compassion and gifts day by day increased. After the sick had been tended, the Indians danced and sang in festivity till sunrise. The celebration of our coming extended to three days.

When it ended, we inquired of the region farther on, of its people and subsistence. Prickly pears were plentiful throughout, they answered, but this season's had all been gathered by now and the tribes returned home. We would find the country very cold and skins scarce. Reflecting on this, and winter being already upon us, we concluded to stay with these Indians till spring.

Five days after our arrival, the tribe took us with them to gather more prickly pears, at a place where other peoples of different tongues converged. There being no fruit of any kind along the way, we walked five days in gnawing hunger, to a river, where we put up our houses and then went to look for the pods which grow on certain trees.

The awkwardness of picking one's way in this vicinity of no paths slowed my own rounds and when, after dark, I went to join the others, who had returned to camp, I got lost. Thank God I found a burning tree, by the warmth of which I passed that cold night.

In the morning I loaded up with sticks and continued my search, carrying two burning brands. For five days I wandered in this way with my fire and my load; otherwise, had my wood failed me where none could be found, I would have lost my kindling fire by the time I located sticks elsewhere. This was all the protection I had against cold, as I wended my way naked as the day I was born.

I would go into the low woods by the river before sunset to prepare myself for the night. First I hollowed out a hole in the ground and threw in fuel, of which there was plenty from the fallen, dry trees in the woods. Then I built four fires around the hole in the form of a cross, and slept in this hole with my fuel supply, covering myself with bundles of the coarse grass which grows thick in those parts. Thus I managed shelter from the cold of night.

One night, the fire fell on the straw as I slept, and blazed so suddenly that it singed my hair in spite of my haste to get out. All this while, I tasted not a mouthful nor found anything to eat. My bare feet bled. By the mercy of God, the wind did not blow from the north in the whole time or I would have died.

At the end of the fifth day I reached the riverbank where the Indians were then camped. They and the Christians had given me up for dead, supposing I had been bitten by a snake. Everybody rejoiced to see me; my companions said it had been their great struggle with hunger that kept them from looking for me. All shared prickly pears with me that night, and the next morning we set out for a place where they still abounded. When we got there, we satisfied our great craving, and the Christians gave thanks to the Lord. . . .

Rabbit Hunts and Processions of Thousands

We traveled in that region through so many different villages of such diverse tongues that my memory gets confused. They ever plundered each other, and those who lost were as content as those who gained. We attracted more followers than we could employ or manage.

As we went through these valleys, every Indian carried a club three palms long and kept alert. When a rabbit jumped (the country teems with these animals), they quickly surrounded him and threw their clubs with amazing accuracy, driving him from one man to another. I cannot imagine a sport that is more fun, as often the rabbit runs right into your hand. By the time we stopped for the night, the Indians had provided us with eight or ten backloads of rabbits apiece.

The archers, instead of staying with us, deployed in the mountains after deer and came back at dark with five or six for each of us, besides quail and other game. Whatever the Indians killed or found, they brought before us, not daring to eat anything until we had blessed it, even if they were desperately hungry. They themselves had established this rule when they took up their march with us.

The women brought many mats, of which the men made us houses—a separate one for each of us together with his personal attendants. When these were put up, we ordered the deer and hares roasted, and the rest of what had been taken. They did this efficiently in ovens they constructed for the purpose. We took a little from each ovenload and gave the rest to the principal personage of our procession to divide among his people. Every Indian brought his portion to us to be breathed on and blessed before he would dare touch it. When you consider that we were frequently accompanied by three or four thousand Indians and were obliged to sanctify the food and drink of each one, as well as grant permission for the many things they asked to do, you can appreciate our inconvenience. The women would bring us prickly pears, spiders, worms—whatever they might gather—strictly forgoing even these until we had made the sign of the cross over them, though the women might have been starving at the time.

Our enormous escort still with us, we crossed a large river which flowed from the north; we then traversed thirty leagues of plains, to be met by a throng who had come a long way to give us a reception on the trail comparable to the ones we had been receiving in the villages and *rancherías* lately. . . .

The Town of Hearts

In the town where the emeralds were presented us, the people gave Dorantes over 600 opened deer hearts, which they always kept in great supply for food. So we called this place the Town of Hearts. It is the gateway to many provinces on the South Sea, and whoever seeks them without entering here will surely be lost.

The timid, surly Indians of the coast grow no corn; they eat powdered rushes, straw, and fish, which they catch from rafts, having no canoes. The women cover themselves somewhat, with grass and straw.

We think that near the coast, along the line of those permanent towns we came through, must be more than a thousand leagues of settled, productive land, where three crops a year of corn and beans are sown.

Pedro de Castañeda de Nájera
(n.d.)

Although he was the most important chronicler of the adventures and discoveries of the Coronado expedition (1540–42), very little is known about Pedro de Castañeda, a Spaniard from the Biscayan town of Nájera. Castañeda was a common soldier stationed at the Spanish colonial detachment at Culiacán, in northwestern Mexico, before joining the Coronado expedition that left from Compostela, Mexico, on February 23, 1540. Having heard rumors of the fabulous wealth of the legendary Seven Cities of Cibola (rumors derived from the journeys of Cabeza de Vaca, Fray Marcos de Niza, and Hernando de Soto), Coronado marched north to seek his golden dream, followed by a force of more than 1,600 horsemen, soldiers, archers, guides, and servants. It was to be an ill-fated journey in which the mythic geography of the West, with its cities of gold, ultimately gave way to the hardships of survival within the physical geography of a vast, unknown country. But if on his long journey with Coronado through northern Mexico and the Southwest (and as far north and east as present-day Kansas) Castañeda found no gold, he did witness amazing lands and creatures, as his narrative shows. The opening section of the following excerpt records the first European encounter with the Grand Canyon of the Colorado ("Firebrand") River—an encounter so unprecedented in scale that the Spaniards assumed the river to be no more than six feet wide, though Indian guides assured them it was immense. Castañeda is also among the first writers to describe the continent's oceanic prairies and the great herds of bison that roamed there. Indeed, he predicted that his account, "describing only the truth, will be so remarkable that it will seem incredible." Castañeda's narrative, written long after the Coronado expedition (probably in the mid-1560s), is also special because it was written not by a military leader or priest, but rather by a common man who, though he regrets his lack of literary polish, promises to offer an accurate account of "that which happened—that which I heard, experienced, saw, and did" in the wilderness of the New World. Although Castañeda's original account, *Relación de la jornada de Cíbola. . .*, has been lost, this important work survives in a 1596 copy that is still extant.

From *The Narrative of the Expedition of Coronado* (c. 1562)

How Don Pedro de Tovar Discovered Tusayan or Tutahoaco and Don Garcia Lopez de Cardenas Saw the Firebrand River . . .

This country was elevated and full of low twisted pines, very cold, and lying open toward the north, so that, this being the warm season, no one could live there on account of the cold. They spent three days on this bank looking for a passage down to the river, which looked from above as if the water was 6 feet across, although the Indians said it was half a league wide. It was impossible to descend, for after these three days Captain Melgosa and one Juan Galeras and another companion, who were the three lightest and most agile men, made an attempt to go down at the least difficult place, and went down until those who were above were unable to keep sight of them. They returned about 4 o'clock in the afternoon, not having succeeded in reaching the bottom on account of the great difficulties which they found, because what seemed to be easy from above was not so, but instead very hard and difficult. They said that they had been down about a third of the way and that the river seemed very large from the place which they reached, and that from what they saw they thought the Indians had given the width correctly. Those who stayed above had estimated that some huge rocks on the sides of the cliffs seemed to be about as tall as a man, but those who went down swore that when they reached these rocks they were bigger than the great tower of Seville. They did not go farther up the river, because they could not get water.

Before this they had had to go a league or two inland every day late in the evening in order to find water, and the guides said that if they should go four days farther it would not be possible to go on, because there was no water within three or four days, for when they travel across this region themselves they take with them women loaded with water in gourds, and bury the gourds of water along the way, to use when they return, and besides this, they travel in one day over what it takes us two days to accomplish.

This was the Tison (Firebrand) river, much nearer its source than where Melchior Diaz and his company crossed it. These were the same kind of Indians, judging from what was afterward learned. They came back from this point and the expedition did not have any other result. On the way they saw some water falling over a rock and learned from the guides that some bunches of crystals which were hanging there were salt. They went and gathered a quantity of this and brought it back to Cibola, dividing it among those who were there. They gave the general a written account of what they had seen, because one Pedro de Sotomayor had gone with Don Garcia Lopez as chronicler for the army. The villages of that province remained peaceful, since they were never visited again, nor was any attempt made to find other peoples in that direction. . . .

Of How the Army Went from Cibola to Tiguex and What Happened to Them on the Way, on Account of the Snow

. . . The army continued its march from here after it stopped snowing, and as the season had already advanced into December, during the ten days that the army was delayed, it did not fail to snow during the evenings and nearly every night, so that they had to clear away a large amount of snow when they came to where they wanted to make a camp. The road could not be seen, but the guides managed to find it, as they knew the country. There are junipers and pines all over the country, which they used in making large brushwood fires, the smoke and heat of which melted the snow from 2 to 4 yards all around the fire. It was a dry snow, so that although it fell on the baggage and covered it for half a man's height it did not hurt it. It fell all night long, covering the baggage and the soldiers and their beds, piling up in the air, so that if any one had suddenly come upon the army nothing would have been seen but mountains of snow. The horses stood half buried in it. It kept those who were underneath warm instead of cold. The army passed by the great rock of Acuco, and the natives, who were peaceful, entertained our men well, giving them provisions and birds, although there are not many people here, as I have said. Many of the gentlemen went up to the top to see it, and they had great difficulty in going up the steps in the rock, because they were not used to them, for the natives go up and down so easily that they carry loads and the women carry water, and they do not seem even to touch their hands, although our men had to pass their weapons up from one to another. . . .

Of How the Army Returned to Tiguex and the General Reached Quivira

. . . The army waited for its messengers and spent a fortnight here, preparing jerked beef to take with them. It was estimated that during this fortnight they killed 500 bulls. The number of these that were there without any cows was something incredible. Many fellows were lost at this time who went out hunting and did not get back to the army for two or three days, wandering about the country as if they were crazy, in one direction or another, not knowing how to get back where they started from, although this ravine extended in either direction so that they could find it. Every night they took account of who was missing, fired guns and blew trumpets and beat drums and built great fires, but yet some of them went off so far and wandered about so much that all this did not give them any help, although it helped others. The only way was to go back where they had killed an animal and start from there in one direction and another until they struck the ravine or fell in with somebody who could put them on the right road. It is worth noting that the country there is so level that at midday, after one has wandered about in one direction and another in pursuit of game, the only thing to do is to stay near the game quietly until sunset, so as to see where it goes down, and even then they have to be men who are practiced to do it. Those who are not, had to trust themselves to others.

Which Treats of the Plains That Were Crossed, of the Cows, and of the People Who Inhabit Them

. . . Now we will speak of the plains. The country is spacious and level, and is more than 400 leagues wide in the part between the two mountain ranges — one, that which Francisco Vazquez Coronado crossed, and the other that which the force under Don Fernando de Soto crossed, near the North sea, entering the country from Florida. No settlements were seen anywhere on these plains.

In traversing 250 leagues, the other mountain range was not seen, nor a hill nor a hillock which was three times as high as a man. Several lakes were found at intervals; they were round as plates, a stone's throw or more across, some fresh and some salt. The grass grows tall near these lakes; away from them it is very short, a span or less. The country is like a bowl, so that when a man sits down, the horizon surrounds him all around at the distance of a musket shot. There are no groves of trees except at the rivers, which flow at the bottom of some ravines where the trees grow so thick that they were not noticed until one was right on the edge of them. They are of dead earth. There are paths down into these, made by the cows when they go to the water, which is essential throughout these plains.

As I have related in the first part, people follow the cows, hunting them and tanning the skins to take to the settlements in the winter to sell, since they go there to pass the winter, each company going to those which are nearest, some to the settlements at Cicuye, others toward Quivira, and others to the settlements which are situated in the direction of Florida. These people are called Querechos and Teyas. They described some large settlements, and judging from what was seen of these people and from the accounts they gave of other places, there are a good many more of these people than there are of those at the settlements. They have better figures, are better warriors, and are more feared. They travel like the Arabs, with their tents and troops of dogs loaded with poles and having Moorish pack saddles with girths. When the load gets disarranged, the dogs howl, calling some one to fix them right. These people eat raw flesh and drink blood. They do not eat human flesh. They are a kind people and not cruel. They are faithful friends. They are able to make themselves very well understood by means of signs. They dry the flesh in the sun, cutting it thin like a leaf, and when dry they grind it like meal to keep it and make a sort of sea soup of it to eat. A handful thrown into a pot swells up so as to increase very much. They season it with fat, which they always try to secure when they kill a cow. They empty a large gut and fill it with blood, and carry this around the neck to drink when they are thirsty. When they open the belly of a cow, they squeeze out the chewed grass and drink the juice that remains behind, because they say that this contains the essence of the stomach. They cut the hide open at the back and pull it off at the joints, using a flint as large as a finger, tied in a little stick, with as much ease as if working with a good iron tool. They give it an edge with their own teeth. The quickness with which they do this is something worth seeing and noting.

There are very great numbers of wolves on these plains, which go around with the cows. They have white skins. The deer are pied with white. Their skin is loose, so that when they are killed it can be pulled off with the hand while warm, coming off like pigskin. The rabbits, which are very numerous, are so foolish that those on horseback killed them with their lances. This is when they are mounted among the cows. They fly from a person on foot.

Which Describes Some Remarkable Things That Were Seen on the Plains, with a Description of the Bulls

My silence was not without mystery and dissimulation when, in chapter 7 of the second part of this book, I spoke of the plains and of the things of which I will give a detailed account in this chapter, where all these things may be found together; for these things were remarkable and something not seen in other parts. I dare to write of them because I am writing at a time when many men are still living who saw them and who will vouch for my account. Who could believe that 1,000 horses and 500 of our cows and more than 5,000 rams and ewes and more than 1,500 friendly Indians and servants, in traveling over those plains, would leave no more trace where they had passed than if nothing had been there — nothing — so that it was necessary to make piles of bones and cow dung now and then, so that the rear guard could follow the army. The grass never failed to become erect after it had been trodden down, and, although it was short, it was as fresh and straight as before.

Another thing was a heap of cow bones, a crossbow shot long, or a very little less, almost twice a man's height in places, and some 18 feet or more wide, which was found on the edge of a salt lake in the southern part, and this in a region where there are no people who could have made it. The only explanation of this which could be suggested was that the waves which the north winds must make in the lake had piled up the bones of the cattle which had died in the lake, when the old and weak ones who went into the water were unable to get out. The noticeable thing is the number of cattle that would be necessary to make such a pile of bones.

Now that I wish to describe the appearance of the bulls, it is to be noticed first that there was not one of the horses that did not take flight when he saw them first, for they have a narrow, short face, the brow two palms across from eye to eye, the eyes sticking out at the side, so that, when they are running, they can see who is following them. They have very long beards, like goats, and when they are running they throw their heads back with the beard dragging on the ground. There is a sort of girdle round the middle of the body. The hair is very woolly, like a sheep's, very fine, and in front of the girdle the hair is very long and rough like a lion's. They have a great hump, larger than a camel's. The horns are short and thick, so that they are not seen much above the hair. In May they change the hair in the middle of the body for a down, which makes perfect lions of them. They rub against the small trees in the little ravines to shed their hair, and they continue this until only the down is left, as a snake changes his skin. They have a short tail, with a bunch of hair at the end. When they run, they carry it erect like a scorpion. It is worth noticing that the little calves are red and just like ours, but they change their color and appearance with time and age.

Another strange thing was that all the bulls that were killed had their left ears slit, although these were whole when young. The reason for this was a puzzle that could not be guessed. The wool ought to make good cloth on account of its fineness, although the color is not good, because it is the color of buriel.

Another thing worth noticing is that the bulls traveled without cows in such large numbers that nobody could have counted them, and so far away from the cows that it was more than 40 leagues from where we began to see the bulls to the place where we began to see the cows. The country they traveled over was so level and smooth that if one looked at them the sky could be seen between their legs, so that if some of them were at a distance they looked like smooth-trunked pines whose tops joined, and if there was only one bull it looked as if there were four pines. When one was near them, it was impossible to see the ground on the other side of them. The reason for all this was that the country seemed as round as if a man should imagine himself in a three-pint measure, and could see the sky at the edge of it, about a crossbow shot from him, and even if a man only lay down on his back he lost sight of the ground.

Jean Ribaut
(c. 1520–1565)

A Frenchman from the village of Dieppe, on the English Channel, Jean Ribaut was perhaps the most accomplished French seaman of his day. He was also a member of the new Protestant sect and was, like other Huguenots, persecuted for his faith. In 1562 Ribaut commanded an expedition to Florida, where he was to help establish Protestant colonies despite the opposition of Spanish Catholic interests in the region. On this first voyage Ribaut "discovered" and named many of Atlantic Florida's capes, bays, and rivers—including the lovely River of May (St. Johns)—and established Charlesfort, the first Protestant outpost in North America, at what is now Parris Island, South Carolina. Ribaut returned to France in June 1562, where he and his fellow Huguenots fought against Catholic France before escaping across the Channel to England. While in exile Ribaut completed his firsthand account of the wonders of the New World, *The Whole and True Discovery of Terra Florida,* which was published in London in May 1563. The following month Ribaut was captured while attempting to help French war hostages escape England and was imprisoned in the Tower of London. Upon his release in 1565, he was again entrusted with a French fleet bound for Florida; meanwhile, however, the Spanish had also dispatched a small armada, under Pedro Menéndez de Avilés, to challenge French settlement efforts in Florida. During a series of violent clashes with the Spanish near St. Augustine—which was established by Menéndez himself—Ribaut's fleet was swept south by a hurricane and shipwrecked near current-day Daytona Beach. The Spanish captured the French survivors and, under Menéndez's order, massacred all who were Protestant. On October 12, 1565, the captive Ribaut refused to renounce his Protestantism—instead asserting the biblical injunction that "From earth we come, and unto earth must we return"—and was subsequently impaled with a pike and decapitated. Ribaut's literary legacy, *The Whole and True Discovery of Terra Florida,* is among the richest sixteenth-century descriptions of the bounty and beauty of the New World, an "incomparable land" that he calls "the pleasantest and most commodious dwelling of all the world."

From *The Whole and True Discovery of Terra Florida* (1563)

Thursday the last of April at the break of the day we discovered and clearly perceived a fair coast, stretching of a great length, covered with an infinite number of high and fair trees, we being not past 7 or 8 leagues from the shore, the country seeming unto us plain, without any show of hills, and approaching nearer within 4 or 5 leagues of the land, we cast anchor at ten fathom water, the bottom of the sea being plain with much ooze and of fast hold. On the south side as far as a certain point or cape, situated under the latitude of 29 degrees and a half, which we have named the cape Francoys, we could espy neither river nor bay, wherefore we sent our boats, furnished with men of experience, to sound and know the coast near the shore, who returning again unto us about one of the clock at afternoon, declared that they had found, among other things, 8 fathom water at the hard bank of the sea. Whereupon, having diligently weighed up our anchors and hoist up sail, with wind at will we sailed and viewed the coast all along with an unspeakable pleasure of the odoriferous smell and beauty of the same. And because there appeared unto us no sign of any port, about the setting of the sun, we cast anchor again, which done, we did behold to and fro the goodly order of the woods wherewith God hath decked everywhere the said land. Then perceiving towards the north a leaping and breaking of the water, as a stream falling out of the land unto the sea, forthwith we set again up sail to double the same while it was yet day. And as we had so done, and passed beyond it, there appeared unto us a fair entry of a great river, which caused us to cast anchor again and tarry there near the land, to the end that the next morning we might see what it was. And though that the wind blew for a time vehemently to the shoreward, yet the hold and anchorage is so good there, that one cable and one anchor held us fast without driving or sliding.

The next day in the morning, being the first of May, we assayed to enter this port with two row barges and a boat well trimmed, finding little water at the entry and many surges and breakings of the water which might have astuned and caused us to return back to shipboard, if God had not speedily brought us in, where finding forthwith 5 or 6 fathom water, entered in to a goodly and great river, which as we went we found to increase still in depth and largeness, boiling and roaring through the multitude of all sorts of fishes. . . .

We entered and viewed the country thereabout, which is the fairest, fruitfullest and pleasantest of all the world, abounding in honey, venison, wildfowl, forests, woods of all sorts, palm trees, cypress, cedars, bays, the highest, greatest and fairest vines in all the world with grapes accordingly, which naturally and without man's help and trimming grow to the top of oaks and other trees that be of a wonderful greatness and height. And the sight of the fair meadows is a pleasure not able to be expressed with tongue, full of herons, curlews, bitterns, mallards, egrets, woodcocks, and of all other kind of small birds, with harts, hinds, bucks, wild swine, and sundry other wild beasts as we perceived well both then by their footing there and also afterwards in other places by their cry and braying which we heard in the night time. Also there be coneys, hares, guinea cocks in marvelous number, a great deal fairer and better than be ours, silk worms, and to be short it is a thing unspeakable, the commodities that be seen there and shall be found more and more in this incomparable land, never as yet broken with plow irons, bringing forth all things according to his first nature, whereof the eternal God endowed it. . . .

It is a place wonderfully fertile, and of strong situation, the ground fat so that it is likely that it would bring forth wheat and all other corn twice a year, and the commodities there for livelihood and the hope of more riches be like unto those we found and considered upon the river of May, and men may travel thither through a great arm of the sea in hoys and barks as great as ye may do in the river of May without coming into the sea. This arm doth divide and make the Isle of May, as many other rivers and arms of the sea which we have discovered divide and make many other great islands, by the which we may travel from one island to another between land and land. And it seemeth that men may go and sail without danger through all the country, and never enter in to the great seas, which were a wonderful advantage. This is the land of Chicore whereof some have written, and which many have gone about to find, for the great riches they perceived by some Indians to be found there. It is set under so good a climate, that none of all our men, though we were there in the hottest time of the year, the sun entering into Cancer, were troubled with any sickness. The people there live long and in great health and strength, so that aged men go without staves, and are able to do and run like the youngest of them, who only are known to be old by the wrinkles in their face and decay of sight.

We departed from them very friendly and with their contentation, but the flood and the night overtaking us, we were constrained to lie in our boats all that night, till it was day, floating upon this river which we have called Seyne, because at the entry it is as broad as from Havre de Grace unto Honefleu. At the break of the day we espied on the south side one of the fairest, pleasantest and greatest meadow ground that might be seen, into the which we went, finding at the very entry a long a fair and great lake and an innumerable number of footsteps of harts and hinds of a wonderful greatness, the steps being all fresh and new. And it seemeth that the people do nourish them like tame cattle, in great herds; for we saw the footsteps of an Indian that followed them. The channel and depth of this river of Seyne is on the side of the meadow that is on the isle of May.

Being returned to our ships, we sailed to know more and more of the coast, going as near the shore as we could. And as we had sailed so all along about six or seven leagues, there appeared unto us another bay where we cast anchor athwart of it, tarrying so all the night. In the morrow we went thither, and finding by our sounding at the entry many banks and beatings, we durst not venture to enter there with our great ships, we having named this river Some, which within is a league over and of 8, 9, 10, and 11 fathom depth, dividing itself into many great rivers, that sever the country into many fair and great islands and small goodly meadow ground and pastures, and everywhere such abundance of fish as is incredible. And on the west northwest side there is a great river that cometh from the high country, of a great league over, and on the other on the northeast side which return into the sea. So that (my lord) it is a country full of havens, rivers and islands of such fruitfulness as cannot with tongue be expressed, and where in short time great and precious commodities might be found. And besides this, we discovered and found also seven rivers more, as great and as good, cutting and dividing the land into fair and great islands, the Indian inhabitants thereof like in manners, and the country in fertility apt and commodious throughout to make sugar and to bear and bring forth plentifully all that men would plant or sow upon it. There be everywhere the highest, fairest and greatest fir trees that can be seen, very well smelling and whereout might be gotten with cutting only the bark, as much rosin, turpentine and frankincense as men would have; and to be short, there lacketh nothing. Wherefore being not able to enter and lie with our great vessels there, where we would make no long abode, nor enter so far into the rivers and countries as we would fain have done: for it is well enough known how many inconveniences have happened unto men, not only in attempting of new discoveries, but also in all places by leaving their great vessels in the sea, far from the land, unfurnished of their heads and best men. As for the other rivers, we have given them such names as follow, and unto the Indians joining to them, the same name that the next river unto it hath, as ye shall see by the protracture or carte I have made thereof, as to the fourth the name of Loire, to the fifth Charent, to the sixth Garone, to the seventh Riviere Belle, to the eighth Riviere Grande, to the ninth Porte Royall, to the tenth Belle a Veoir.

Upon Whitsuntide, Sunday the 17 of May, after we had well perceived and considered that there was no remedy but to assay to find the means to harbor our ships, as well for to amend and trim them as to get us fresh water, wood and other necessaries whereof we had need, being of opinion that there was no fairer or fitter place for the purpose than Porte Royall. And when we had sounded the entry and the channel, (thanked be God) we entered safely therein with our ships against the opinion of many, finding the same one of the greatest and fairest havens of the world. Howbeit, it must be remembered, lest that men approaching near it within 7 leagues of the land, be abashed and afraid, finding on the east side, drawing towards the southeast, the ground to be flat, for nevertheless at a full sea there is everywhere four fathom water keeping the right channel.

In this port are many arms of the sea deep and large, and here and there of all sides many rivers of a mean bigness, where without danger all the ships in the world might be harbored. We found no Indians inhabiting thereabout the port and river side nearer than 10 or 12 leagues upward into the countries, although it be one of the goodliest, best and fruitfullest countries that ever was seen, and where nothing lacketh, and also where as good and likely commodities be found as in the other places thereby; for we found there a great number of pepper trees, the pepper upon them yet green and not ready to be gathered; also the best water of the world, and so many sorts of fishes that ye may take them without net or angle, as many as you will; also guinea fowl and innumerable wildfowl of all sorts, and in a little island at the entry of this haven, on the east-northeast side, there is so great number of egrets that the bushes be all white and covered with them, so that one may take of the young ones with his hand as many as he will carry away. There be also a number of other fowl, as herons, bitterns, curlews, and to be short, so many small birds that it is a strange thing to be seen. We found the Indians there more doubtful and fearful than the others before; yet after we had been at their houses, and congratulated with them, and showed courtesy to those that we found to have abandoned their trough-boats, meal, victuals, and small household stuff, as both in not taking away or touching any part thereof, and in leaving in the place where they dressed their meat, knives, looking glasses and little beads of glass, which they love and esteem above gold and pearls for to hang them at their ears and neck, and to give them to their wives and children, they were somewhat emboldened; for some of them came to our boat, of the which we carried two goodly and strong aboard our ships, clothing and using them as gently and lovingly as it was possible; but they never ceased day nor night to lament and at length they escaped away. Wherefore, albeit I was willing, according to your commandment and memorial, to bring away with us some of that people, yet by the advice of those that were sent with us on the Prince's behalf and yours, I forbear to do so for many considerations and reasons that they told me, and for that also we were in doubt that, leaving some of our men to inhabit there, all the country, man, woman, and child would not have ceased to have pursued them for to have theirs again, seeing they be not able to consider nor weigh to what intent we should have carried them away. And this may be better done to their contentation when they have better acquaintance of us, and know that there is no such cruelty in us as in other people and nations, of whom they have been beguiled under color of good faith, which usage in the end turned to the doers to no good.

This is the river of Jordan in mine opinion, whereof so much hath been spoken, which is very fair, and the country good and of great consequence, both for their easy habitation and also for many other things which should be too long to write. The 22 of May we planted another column graven with the King's arms, on the south side, in a commodious pleasant and high place, at the entry of a fair great river, which we have called Lybourne where there is a fair lake of fresh water very good, and on the same side a little lower towards the entry of the haven, is one of the fairest and best fountains that a man may drink of, which falleth with violence down to the river from a high place out of a red and sandy ground, and yet for all that fruitful and of good air, where it should seem that the Indians have had some fair habitation.

There we saw the fairest and the greatest vines with grapes according, and young trees, and small woods very well smelling, that ever were seen, whereby it appeareth to be the pleasantest and most commodious dwelling of all the world.

Thomas Hariot
(1560–1621)

An English mathematician, astronomer, and naturalist who graduated from Oxford, Thomas Hariot was an important ally of the earliest English colonizer of the New World, Sir Walter Raleigh. It is likely that Hariot instructed Raleigh and his men in navigational techniques during the early 1580s, and Hariot served as a scientific adviser to Arthur Barlowe's expedition to the New World in 1584. Hariot himself accompanied the 1585 expedition, led by Sir Richard Grenville, to Raleigh's fledgling colony at Roanoke Island, off the Carolina coast. Arriving in April of that year, Hariot remained until July 1586, during which time he traveled widely—exploring as far as the northern Chesapeake—collecting, sketching, and describing flora and fauna and studying Native American cultures and languages. During this relatively brief but extremely productive sojourn in the New World, he was accompanied by the illustrator John White, whose paintings of the people, plants, and animals there gave many Europeans their first "view" of the new lands. After returning to England, Hariot published his observations in 1588 as *A Brief and True Report of the Newfound Land of Virginia*, an important book that described many plants and trees, eighty-six kinds of birds, and twenty-eight mammals, including such New World "curiosities" as the opossum. Although Hariot's *Report*, like the work of John Smith and others who followed, is a promotional tract designed to encourage settlers to emigrate to the struggling colonies, it is also a book in which mild salesmanship is ultimately eclipsed by richly detailed description. If Hariot's is among the first English accounts of the New World landscape, it is also among the most precise. In the following selection, which focuses upon New World agricultural products and Native American farming techniques, Hariot takes special care in describing such unfamiliar plants as a "kind of grain" called "Maize" (corn), a "great herb, in form of a Marigold, about six foot in height" (sunflower), and Uppowoc (tobacco)—an herb so healthful that a relation of its many virtues, Hariot asserts, would "require a volume by itself."

From A *Brief and True Report of the Newfound Land of Virginia* (1588)

Pagatowr, a kind of grain so called by the inhabitants: the same in the West Indies is called Maize: English men call it Guinea wheat, or Turkey wheat, according to the names of the countries from whence the like hath been brought. The grain is about the bigness of our ordinary English peas, and not much different in form and shape: but of divers colors: some white, some red, some yellow, and some blue. All of them yield a very white and sweet flower: being used according to his kind, it maketh a very good bread. We made of the same in the country some malt, whereof was brewed as good ale as was to be desired. So likewise by the help of hops, thereof may be made as good beer. It is a grain of marvelous great increase: of a thousand, fifteen hundred, and some two thousand fold. There are three sorts, of which two are ripe in eleven and twelve weeks at the most, sometimes in ten, after the time they are set, and are then of height in stalk about six or seven foot. The other sort is ripe in fourteen, and is about ten foot high, of the stalks, some bear four heads, some three, some one, and two: every head containing five, six, or seven hundred grains, within a few more or less. Of these grains, besides bread, the inhabitants make victual, either by parching them, or seething them whole until they be broken: or boiling the flower with water into a pap.

Okingier, called by us Beans, because in greatness and partly in shape they are like to the beans in England, saving that they are flatter, of more divers colors, and some pied. The leaf also of the stem is much different. In taste they are altogether as good as our English peas.

Wickonzowr, called by us Peas, in respect of the beans for distinction sake because they are much less, although in form they little differ: but in goodness of taste much like, and are far better than our English peas. Both the beans and peas are ripe in ten weeks after they are set. They make them victual either by boiling them all to pieces into a broth, or boiling them whole until they be soft, and begin to break, as is used in England, either by themselves, or mixed together: sometime they mingle of the wheat with them: sometime also, being whole sodden, they bruise or pun them in a mortar, and thereof make loaves or lumps of doughish bread, which they use to eat for variety.

Macocquer, according to their several forms, called by us Pumpkins, Melons, and Gourds, because they are of the like forms as those kinds in England. In Virginia such of several forms are of one taste, and very good, and do also spring from one seed. There are of two sorts: one is ripe in the space of a month, and the other in two months.

There is an herb which in Dutch is called Melden. Some of those that I describe it unto, take it to be a kind of Orage: it groweth about four or five foot high; of the seed thereof they make a thick broth, and pottage of a very good taste: of the stalk by burning into ashes they make a kind of salt earth, wherewithal many use sometimes to season their broths: other salt they know not. We ourselves used the leaves also for potherbs.

There is also another great herb, in form of a Marigold, about six foot in height, the head with the flower is a span in breadth. Some take it to be Planta Solis: of the seeds hereof they make both a kind of bread and broth. . . .

I thought also good to note this unto you, that you which shall inhabit, and plant there, may know how specially that country corn is there to be preferred before ours: Besides, the manifold ways in applying it to victual, the increase is so much, that small labor and pains is needful in respect that must be used for ours. For this I can assure you, that according to the rate we have made proof of, one man may prepare and husband so much ground (having once borne corn before) with less then four and twenty hours labor, as shall yield him victual in a large proportion for a twelve month, if he have nothing else but that which the same ground will yield, and of that kind only which I have before spoken of: the said ground being also but of five and twenty yards square. And if need require, but that there is ground enough, there might be raised out of one and the selfsame ground two harvests or offcomes: for they sow or set, and may at any time when they think good, from the midst of March until the end of June: so that they also set when they have eaten of their first crop. In some places of the country notwithstanding they have two harvests, as we have heard, out of one and the same ground.

For English corn nevertheless, whether to use or not to use it, you that inhabit may do as you shall have farther cause to think best. Of the growth you need not to doubt: for barley, oats, and peas, we have seen proof of, not being purposely sown but fallen casually in the worst sort of ground, and yet to be as fair as any we have ever seen here in England. But of wheat, because it was musty, and had taken salt water, we could make no trial: and of rye we had none. Thus much have I digressed, and I hope not unnecessarily: now will I return again to my course, and entreat of that which yet remaineth appertaining to this chapter.

There is an herb which is sowed apart by itself, and is called by the inhabitants Uppowoc: In the West Indies it hath divers names, according to the several places and countries where it groweth, and is used: the Spaniards generally call it Tobacco. The leaves thereof being dried and brought into powder: they use to take the fume or smoke thereof, by sucking it through pipes made of clay, into their stomach and head: from whence it purgeth superfluous flame and other gross humors, and openeth all the pores and passages of the body: by which means the use thereof not only preserveth the body from obstructions, but also (if any be, so that they have not been of too long continuance) in short time breaketh them: whereby their bodies are notably preserved in health, and know not many grievous diseases, wherewithal we in England are oftentimes afflicted.

This Uppowoc is of so precious estimation amongst them, that they think their gods are marvelously delighted therewith: whereupon sometime they make hallowed fires, and cast some of the powder therein for a sacrifice: being in a storm upon the waters, to pacify their gods, they cast some up into the air and into the water: so a weir for fish being newly set up, they cast some therein and into the air: also after an escape of danger, they cast some into the air likewise: but all done with strange gestures, stamping, sometime dancing, clapping of hands, holding up of hands and staring up into the heavens, uttering therewithal, and chattering strange words and noises.

We ourselves during the time we were there, used to suck it after their manner, as also since our return, and have found many rare and wonderful experiments of the virtues thereof: of which the relation would require a volume by itself: the use of it by so many of late, men and women of great calling as else, and some learned Physicians also, is sufficient witness. . . .

The Conclusion

Now I have (as I hope) made relation not of so few and small things, but that the Country (of men that are indifferent and well disposed) may be sufficiently liked: If there were no more known than I have mentioned, which doubtless and in great reason is nothing to that which remaineth to be discovered, neither the soil nor commodities. As we have reason so to gather by the difference we found in our travails, for although all which I have before spoken of, have been discovered and experimented not far from the Sea coast, where was our abode and most of our travailing: yet sometimes as we made our journeys further into the main and Country; we found the soil to be fatter, the trees greater and to grow thinner, the ground more firm and deeper mold, more and larger champions, finer grass, and as good as ever we saw any in England; in some places rocky and far more high and hilly ground, more plenty of their fruits, more abundance of beasts, the more inhabited with people, and of greater policy and larger dominions, with greater towns and houses.

Why may we not then look for in good hope from the inner parts of more and greater plenty, as well of other things, as of those which we have already discovered: Unto the Spaniards happened the like in discovering the main of the West Indies. The main also of this Country of Virginia, extending some ways so many hundredth of leagues, as otherwise than by the relation of the inhabitants we have most certain knowledge of, where yet no Christian prince hath any possession or dealing, cannot but yield many kinds of excellent commodities, which we in our discovery have not yet seen.

What hope there is else to be gathered of the nature of the climate, being answerable to the Island of Japan, the land of China, Persia, Jury, the Islands of Cyprus & Candy, the South parts of Greece, Italy, and Spain, and of many other notable and famous Countries, because I mean not to be tedious, I leave to your own consideration.

Whereby also the excellent temperature of the air there at all seasons, much warmer than in England, and never so vehemently hot, as sometimes is under and between the Tropics, or near them, cannot be known unto you without further relation.

For the wholesomeness thereof I need to say but thus much: that for all the want of provision, as first of English victual, excepting for twenty days, we lived only by drinking water, and by the victual of the Country, of which some sorts were very strange unto us, and might have been thought to have altered our temperatures in such sort, as to have brought us into some grievous and dangerous diseases: Secondly the want of English means, for the taking of beasts, fish, and fowl, which by the help only of the inhabitants and their means, could not be so suddenly and easily provided for us, nor in so great number and quantities, nor of that choice as otherwise might have been to our better satisfaction and contentment. Some want also we had of clothes. Furthermore, in all our travails which were most special and often in the time of winter, our lodging was in the open air upon the ground. And yet I say for all this, there were but four of our whole company (being one hundred and eight) that died all the year and that but at the latter end thereof and upon none of the aforesaid causes. For all four, especially three were feeble, weak, and sickly persons before ever they came thither, and those that knew them, much marveled that they lived so long being in that case, or had adventured to travail.

Seeing therefore the air there is so temperate and wholesome, the soil so fertile, and yielding such commodities, as I have before mentioned, the voyage also thither to and fro being sufficiently experimented, to be performed twice a year with ease, and at any season thereof: And the dealing of Sir Walter Raleigh so liberal in large giving and granting land there, as is already known, with many helps and furtherances else: (The least that he hath granted hath been five hundred acres to a man only for the adventure of his person) I hope there remains no cause whereby the action should be misliked.

If that those which shall thither travail to inhabit and plant, be but reasonably provided for the first year, as those are which were transported the last, and being there, do use but that diligence and care, as is requisite, and as they may with ease: There is no doubt, but for the time following, they may have victuals that are excellent good and plenty enough, some more English sorts of cattle also hereafter, as some have been before, and are there yet remaining, may, and shall be (God willing) thither transported. So likewise, our kind of fruits, roots, and herbs, may be there planted and sowed, as some have been already, and prove well: And in short time also they may raise of those sorts of commodities which I have spoken of, as shall both enrich themselves, as also others that shall deal with them.

John Smith
(1580–1631)

A skilled geographer, cartographer, explorer, and soldier, John Smith was among the most energetic and entrepreneurial of the early colonial promoters of what he insisted was a remarkable land of opportunity in the New World. Smith was one of the 144 English settlers who, under the banner of King James I, arrived in North America in 1606, where they established Jamestown colony on the Virginia shores. Although more than half of the colonists died of starvation, sickness, and Indian attack during their first winter, Smith soon assumed direction of the infant colony and helped to ensure its survival, thus making Jamestown the first permanent English colony in the New World. From Jamestown Smith sent back to England his descriptions of the land; published in 1608, *A True Relation of Occurrences and Accidents in Virginia* was the first English book written in America. Smith went to England the following year but returned to North America in 1614—this time exploring and mapping the New England coast and eventually publishing his findings in *A Description of New England* (1616). His most substantial literary accomplishment was *The Generall Historie of Virginia, New-England, and the Summer Isles. . .*, published almost a decade later (1624). In all his writing Smith insists that America is a second paradise, a land of unimaginable natural plenitude and fertility in which a man may work three days each week and yet grow rich. Although Smith's dizzying lists of the plants and animals he observes resemble those common to natural historical tracts of the period, Smith's catalogs are more suggestive of a ledger book, in which the economic value of the land and its creatures is constantly being reckoned. While the promotional tract was a fairly common rhetorical form during the early seventeenth century, few have handled the form with greater panache than did Smith. As the following descriptions of New England and Virginia demonstrate, he created an indelible image of America as the land of plenty; in so doing, however, he also helped initiate a tradition within which the natural world is considered primarily in terms of its mercantile value.

From *A Description of New England* (1616)

In March, April, May, and half June, here is Cod in abundance; in May, June, July, and August Mullet and Sturgeon; whose roes do make Caviar and Puttargo. Herring, if any desire them, I have taken many out of the bellies of Cods, some in nets; but the Savages compare their store in the Sea, to the hairs of their heads: and surely there are an incredible abundance upon this Coast. In the end of August, September, October, and November, you have Cod again, to make Cor fish, or Poor John: and each hundred is as good as two or three hundred in the Newfound Land. So that half the labor in hooking, splitting, and turning, is saved: and you may have your fish at what Market you will, before they can have any in Newfound Land; where their fishing is chiefly but in June and July: whereas it is here in March, April, May, September, October, and November, as is said. So that by reason of this plantation, the Merchants may have freight both out and home: which yields an advantage worth consideration.

Your Cor-fish you may in like manner transport as you see cause, to serve the Ports in Portugal (as Lisbon, Avera, Porta port, and divers others, or what market you please) before your Islanders return: They being tied to the season in the open Sea; you having a double season, and fishing before your doors, may every night sleep quietly ashore with good cheer and what fires you will, or when you please with your wives and family: they only, their ships in the main Ocean.

The Mullets here are in that abundance, you may take them with nets, sometimes by hundreds, where at Cape blank they hook them; yet those but one foot and a half in length; these two, three, or four, as oft I have measured: much Salmon some have found up the Rivers, as they have passed: and here the air is so temperate, as all these at any time may well be preserved. . . .

Of Beavers, Otters, Martins, Black Foxes, and Furs of price, may yearly be had 6 or 7000: and if the trade of the French were prevented, many more: 25000 this year were brought from those Northern parts into France; of which trade we may have as good part as the French, if we take good courses.

Of Mines of Gold and Silver, Copper, and probabilities of Lead, Crystal, and Alum, I could say much if relations were good assurances. It is true indeed, I made many trials according to those instructions I had, which do persuade me I need not despair, but there are metals in the Country: but I am no Alchemist, nor will promise more then I know: which is, Who will undertake the rectifying of an Iron forge, if those that buy meat, drink, coals, ore, and all necessaries at a dear rate gain; where all these things are to be had for the taking up, in my opinion cannot lose.

Of woods seeing there is such plenty of all sorts, if those that build ships and boats, buy wood at so great a price, as it is in England, Spain, France, Italy, and Holland, and all other provisions for the nourishing of man's life; live well by their trade: when labor is all required to take those necessaries without any other tax; what hazard will be here, but do much better? And what commodity in Europe doth more decay than wood? For the goodness of the ground, let us take it fertile, or barren, or as it is: seeing it is certain it bears fruits, to nourish and feed man and beast, as well as England, and the Sea those several sorts of fish I have related. Thus seeing all good provisions for man's sustenance, may with this facility be had, by a little extraordinary labor, till that transported be increased; and all necessaries for shipping, only for labor: to which may be added the assistance of the Savages, which may easily be had, if they be discreetly handled in their kinds; towards fishing, planting, and destroying woods. . . .

The chief headlands are only Cape Tragabigzanda and Cape Cod.

The chief mountains, them of Pennobscot; the twinkling mountain of Aucocisco; the great mountain of Sasanou; and the high mountain of Massachusit: each of which you shall find in the Map; their places, forms, and altitude. The waters are most pure, proceeding from the entrails of rocky mountains; the herbs and fruits are of many sorts and kinds: as alkermes, currants, or a fruit like currants, mulberries, vines, respices, gooseberries, plums, walnuts, chestnuts, small nuts, etc. pumpkins, gourds, strawberries, beans, peas, and maize; a kind or two of flax, wherewith they make nets, lines and ropes both small and great, very strong for their quantities.

Oak, is the chief wood; of which there is great difference in regard of the soil where it groweth. Fir, pine, walnut, chestnut, birch, ash, elm, cypress, cedar, mulberry, plumtree, hazel, saxefrage, and many other sorts.

Eagles, Gripes, diverse sorts of Hawks, Cranes, Geese, Brants, Cormorants, Ducks, Sheldrakes, Teal, Mews, Gulls, Turkeys, Dive-doppers, and many other sorts, whose names I know not.

Whales, Grampus, Porpoises, Turbot, Sturgeon, Cod, Hake, Haddock, Coal, Cusk, or small Ling, Shark, Mackerel, Herring, Mullet, Bass, Pinacks, Cunners, Perch, Eels, Crabs, Lobsters, Mussels, Whelks, Oysters, and diverse others etc.

Moose, a beast bigger then a Stag; deer, red, and Fallow; Beavers, Wolves, Foxes, both black and other; Aroughconds, Wildcats, Bears, Otters, Martins, Fitches, Musquashes, and diverse sorts of vermin, whose names I know not. All these and diverse other good things do here, for want of use, still increase, and decrease with little diminution, whereby they grow to that abundance. You shall scarce find any Bay, shallow shore, or Cove of sand, where you may not take many Clams, or Lobsters, or both at your pleasure, and in many places load your boat if you please; Nor Isles where you find not fruits, birds, crabs, and mussels, or all of them, for taking, at a low water. And in the harbors we frequented, a little boy might take of Cunners, and Pinacks, and such delicate fish, at the ship's stern, more than six or ten can eat in a day; but with a casting net, thousands when we pleased: and scarce any place, but Cod, Cusk, Halibut, Mackerel, Skate, or such like, a man may take with a hook or line what he will. And, in diverse sandy Bays, a man may draw with a net great store of Mullets, Basses, and diverse other sorts of such excellent fish, as many as his Net can draw on shore: no River where there is not plenty of Sturgeon, or Salmon, or both; all which are to be had in abundance observing but their seasons. But if a man will go at Christmas to gather Cherries in Kent, he may be deceived; though there be plenty in Summer: so, here these plenties have each their seasons, as I have expressed. We for the most part had little but bread and vinegar: and though the most part of July when the fishing decayed they wrought all day, lay abroad in the Isles all night, and lived on what they found, yet were not sick: But I would wish none put himself long to such plunges; except necessity constrain it: yet worthy is that person to starve that here cannot live; if he have sense, strength and health: for, there is no such penury of these blessings in any place, but that a hundred men may, in one hour or two, make their provisions for a day: and he that hath experience to manage well these affairs, with forty or thirty honest industrious men, might well undertake (if they dwell in these parts) to subject the Savages, and feed daily two or three hundred men, with as good corn, fish, and flesh, as the earth hath of those kinds, and yet make that labor but their pleasure: provided that they have engines, that be proper for their purposes.

Who can desire more content, that hath small means; or but only his merit to advance his fortune, then to tread, and plant that ground he hath purchased by the hazard of his life? If he have but the taste of virtue, and magnanimity, what to such a mind can be more pleasant, than planting and building a foundation for his Posterity, got from the rude earth, by God's blessing and his own industry without prejudice to any? If he have any grain of faith or zeal in Religion, what can he do less hurtful to any; or more agreeable to God, than to seek to convert those poor Savages to know Christ, and humanity, whose labors with discretion will triple requite thy charge and pains? What so truly suits with honor and honesty, as the discovering things unknown? erecting Towns, peopling Countries, informing the ignorant, reforming things unjust, teaching virtue; and gain to our Native mother country a kingdom to attend her; find employment for those that are idle, because they know not what to do: so far from wronging any, as to cause Posterity to remember thee; and remembering thee, ever honor that remembrance with praise? . . .

But if an Angel should tell you, that any place yet unknown can afford such fortunes; you would not believe him, no more than Columbus was believed there was any such Land as is now the well known abounding America; much less such large Regions as are yet unknown, as well in America, as in Africa, and Asia, and Terra incognita; where were courses for gentlemen (and them that would be so reputed) more suiting their qualities, than begging from their Prince's generous disposition, the labors of his subjects, and the very marrow of his maintenance. . . .

Here nature and liberty affords us that freely, which in England we want, or it costeth us dearly. What pleasure can be more, than (being tired with any occasion ashore) in planting Vines, Fruits, or Herbs, in contriving their own Grounds, to the pleasure of their own minds, their Fields, Gardens, Orchards, Buildings, Ships, and other works, etc. to recreate themselves before their own doors, in their own boats upon the Sea, where man woman and child, with a small hook and line, by angling, may take diverse sorts of excellent fish, at their pleasures? And is it not pretty sport, to pull up two pence, six pence, and twelve pence, as fast as you can haul and veer a line? He is a very bad fisher, cannot kill in one day with his hook and line, one, two, or three hundred Cods: which dressed and dried, if they be sold there for ten shillings the hundred, though in England they will give more than twenty; may not both the servant, the master, and merchant, be well content with this gain? If a man work but three days in seven, he may get more than he can spend, unless he will be excessive. Now that Carpenter, Mason, Gardener, Tailor, Smith, Sailor, Forgers, or what other, may they not make this a pretty recreation though they fish but an hour in a day, to take more than they eat in a week: or if they will not eat it, because there is so much better choice; yet sell it, or change it, with the fishermen, or merchants, for any thing they want. And what sport doth yield a more pleasing content, and less hurt or charge than angling with a hook, and crossing the sweet air from Isle to Isle, over the silent streams of a calm Sea? wherein the most curious may find pleasure, profit, and content. Thus, though all men be not fishers: yet all men, whatsoever, may in other matters do as well. For necessity doth in these cases so rule a Commonwealth, and each in their several functions, as their labors in their qualities may be as profitable, because there is a necessary mutual use of all.

For Gentlemen, what exercise should more delight them, than ranging daily those unknown parts, using fowling and fishing, for hunting and hawking? and yet you shall see the wild hawks give you some pleasure, in seeing them stoop (six or seven after one another) an hour or two together, at the skulls of fish in the fair harbors, as those ashore at a fowl; and never trouble nor torment yourselves, with watching, mewing, feeding, and attending them: nor kill horse and man with running and crying, See you not a hawk?

For hunting also: the woods, lakes, and rivers, afford not only chase sufficient, for any that delights in that kind of toil, or pleasure; but such beasts to hunt, that besides the delicacy of their bodies for food, their skins are so rich, as may well recompense thy daily labor, with a Captain's pay.

For laborers, if those that sow hemp, rape, turnips, parsnips, carrots, cabbage, and such like; give 20, 30, 40, 50 shillings yearly for an acre of ground, and meat drink and wages to use it, and yet grow rich: when better, or at least as good ground, may be had and cost nothing but labor; it seems strange to me, any such should there grow poor.

From *The General History of Virginia* (1624)

The Commodities in Virginia, or That May Be Had by Industry

The mildness of the air, the fertility of the soil, and situation of the rivers are so propitious to the nature and use of man, as no place is more convenient for pleasure, profit, and man's sustenance, under that latitude or climate. Here will live any beasts, as horses, goats, sheep, asses, hens, etc. as appeared by them that were carried thither. The waters, Isles, and shoals, are full of safe harbors for ships of war or merchandise, for boats of all sorts, for transportation or fishing, etc. The Bay and rivers have much merchantable fish, and places fit for Salt coats, building of ships, making of Iron, etc.

Muscovia and Polonia do yearly receive many thousands, for pitch, tar, soapashes, Rosen, Flax, Cordage, Sturgeon, Masts, Yards, Wainscot, Firs, Glass, and such like; also Swethland for Iron and Copper. France in like manner, for Wine, Canvas, and Salt. Spain as much for Iron, Steel, Figs, Raisins, and Sacks. Italy with Silks and Velvets consumes our chief Commodities. Holland maintains itself by fishing and trading at our own doors. All these temporize with other for necessities, but all as uncertain as peace or wars. Besides the charge, travel, and danger in transporting them, by seas, lands, storms, and Pirates. Then how much hath Virginia the prerogative of all those flourishing Kingdoms, for the benefit of our Land, when as within one hundred miles all those are to be had, either ready provided by nature, or else to be prepared, were there but industrious men to labor. Only of Copper we may doubt is wanting, but there is good probability that both Copper and better Minerals are there to be had for their labor. Other Countries have it. So then here is a place, a nurse for soldiers, a practice for mariners, a trade for merchants, a reward for the good, and that which is most of all, a business (most acceptable to God) to bring such poor Infidels to the knowledge of God and his holy Gospel.

William Wood
(n.d.)

Little is known about Englishman William Wood, who spent four years in New England between 1629 and 1634. It is probable that Wood was a member of John Endecott's scouting party, sent to Salem to open the way for the settlement of the Massachusetts Bay Colony, established in 1630. It is certain, however, that William Wood has left students of nature writing one of the most unusual and valuable literary artifacts of the seventeenth century. In *New England's Prospect* (1634), Wood was devoted (as many writers of his day were not) to accurate, detailed descriptions that were "experimental"—that is, derived from the author's personal experiences and observations. At a time when English readers were hungry for reports from the New World, Wood's book was the earliest comprehensive, firsthand description of New England geography, climate, flora, and fauna; indeed, it was not until John Josselyn published *New England's Rarities Discovered* in 1672 that any book could challenge Wood's for the honor of being the most complete natural history of colonial New England. In a series of well-organized and clearly written chapters, Wood describes New England's geography, climate, soil, plants and minerals, terrestrial mammals, marine mammals, birds, and fish. In these chapters, roughly structured according to the pre-Linnaean taxonomy common to seventeenth-century natural histories, Wood demonstrates an appreciation for the ingenuity and beauty of the natural world that is quite unusual in writers of his day. *New England's Prospect* is also rare as a record of the New England landscape written from a secular point of view; unlike better known literary colonists John Winthrop and William Bradford, Wood does not view nature through the providential filter of Puritan theology. Wood's genuine appreciation for the intellectual and aesthetic value of nature is especially clear in his admiration for the beaver, hummingbird, and other animals described in the following excerpt. This sympathy makes Wood an important forerunner of Henry Thoreau, who read and reread *New England's Prospect,* and whose journals repeatedly note admiration for the comprehensiveness of Wood's descriptions and the vigor of his literary style.

From *New England's Prospect* (1634)

Beasts Living in the Water

For all creatures that lived both by land and water, they be first otters, which be most of them black, whose fur is much used for muffs and are held almost as dear as beaver. The flesh of them is none of the best meat, but their oil is of rare use for many things. Secondly, martins, a good fur for their bigness. Thirdly, musquashes, which be much like a beaver for shape, but nothing near so big. The male hath two stones which smell as sweet as musk, and being killed in winter and the spring, never lose their sweet smell. These skins are no bigger than a coney skin, yet are sold for five shillings apiece, being sent for tokens into England. One good skin will perfume a whole house full of clothes if it be right and good. Fourthly, the beaver, concerning whom, if I should at large discourse according to knowledge or information, I might make a volume.

The wisdom and understanding of this beast will almost conclude him a reasonable creature. His shape is thick and short, having likewise short legs, feet like a mole before and behind like a goose, a broad tail in form like a shoe sole, very tough and strong. His head is something like an otter's head, saving that his teeth before be placed like the teeth of a rabbit, two above and two beneath, sharp and broad, with which he cuts down trees as thick as a man's thigh, sometimes as big as a man's body, afterwards dividing them into lengths according to the use they are appointed for. If one beaver be too weak to carry the log, then another helps him; if they two be too weak, then *multorum manibus grande levatur onus*, four more adding their help, being placed three to three, which set their teeth in one another's tough tails, and laying the load on the two hindermost, they draw the log to the desired place, also tow it in the water, the strongest getting under, bearing it up that it may swim the lighter. That this may not seem altogether incredible, remember that the like almost may be seen in our ants, which will join sometimes seven or eight together in the carrying of a burthen.

These creatures build themselves houses of wood and clay close by the pond's side, and knowing the seasons build them answerable houses, having them three stories high so that as land-floods are raised by great rains, as the water arise they mount higher in their houses; as they assuage they descend lower again. These houses are so strong that no creature saving an industrious man with his penetrating tools can prejudice them, their ingress and egress being under water. These make likewise very good ponds, knowing whence a stream runs from between two rising hills they will there pitch down piles of wood, placing smaller rubbish before it with clay and sods, not leaving till by their art and industry they have made a firm and curious damhead which may draw admiration from wise, understanding men.

These creatures keep themselves to their own families, never parting so long as they are able to keep house together. And it is commonly said, if any beaver accidentally light into a strange place, he is made a drudge so long as he lives there, to carry at the greater end of the log, unless he creep away by stealth. Their wisdom secures them from the English who seldom or never kills any of them, being not patient to lay a long siege or to be so often deceived by their cunning evasions, so that all the beaver which the English have comes first from the Indians whose time and experience fits them for that employment.

Of the Birds and Fowls Both of Land and Water

Having showed you the most desirable, useful, and beneficial creatures, with the most offensive carrions that belong to our wilderness, it remains in the next place to show you such kinds of fowl as the country affords. They are many, and we have much variety both at sea and on land, and such as yield us much profit and honest pleasure, and are these that follow; as

The princely eagle, and the soaring hawk,
Whom in their unknown ways there's none can chalk:
The humbird for some queen's rich cage more fit,
Than in the vacant widerness to sit.
The swift-winged swallow sweeping to and fro,
As swift as arrow from Tartarian bow.
When as Aurora's infant day new springs,
There the morning mounting lark her sweet lays sings.
The harmonious thrush, swift pigeon, turtledove,
Who to her mate doth ever constant prove.
The turkey-pheasant, heath cock, partridge rare,
The carrion-tearing crow, and hurtful stare,
The long-lived raven, the ominous screech owl,
Who tells, as old wives say, disasters foul.
The drowsy madge that leaves her day-loved nest,
And loves to rove when day-birds be at rest;
The eel-murthering hearn, and greedy cormorant,
That near the creeks in moorish marshes haunt.
The bellowing bittern, with the long-legged crane,
Presaging winters hard, and dearth of grain.

The silver swan that tunes her mournful breath,
To sing the dirge of her approaching death.
The tattling oldwives, and the cackling geese,
The fearful gull that shuns the murthering piece.
The strong winged mallard, with the nimble teal,
And ill-shaped loon who his harsh notes doth squeal.
There widgins, sheldrakes, and humilites,
Snites, doppers, sea-larks, in whole millions flee.

The eagles of the country be of two sorts, one like the eagles that be in England, the other is something bigger with a great white head and white tail. These be commonly called gripes; they prey upon ducks and geese and such fish as are cast upon the seashore. And although an eagle be counted king of that feathered regiment, yet is there a certain black hawk that beats him so that he is constrained to soar so high till heat expel his adversary. This hawk is much prized of the Indians, being accounted a sagamore's ransom.

To speak much of hawks were to trespass upon my own judgment and bring upon myself a deserved censure for abusing the falconer's terms. But by relation from those that have more insight into them than myself, there be diverse kinds of hawks. Their aeries are easy to come by, being in the holes of rocks near the shore, so that any who are addicted to that sport — if he will be but at the charge of finding poultry for them — may have his desires. We could wish them well mewed in England, for they make havoc of hens, partridges, heath cocks, and ducks, often hindering the fowler of his long looked-for shoot.

The humbird is one of the wonders of the country, being no bigger than a hornet, yet hath all the dimensions of a bird, as bill and wings, with quills, spider-like legs, small claws. For color, she is as glorious as the rainbow. As she flies, she makes a little humming noise like a humblebee: wherefore she is called the humbird.

The pigeon of that country is something different from our dovehouse pigeons in England, being more like turtles, of the same color. They have long tails like a magpie. And they seem not so big, because they carry not so many feathers on their backs as our English doves, yet are they as big in body. These birds come into the country to go to the north parts in the beginning of our spring, at which time (if I may be counted worthy to be believed in a thing that is not so strange as true) I have seen them fly as if the airy regiment had been pigeons, seeing neither beginning nor ending, length or breadth of these millions of millions. The shouting of people, the rattling of guns, and pelting of small shot could not drive them out of their course, but so they continued for four or five hours together. Yet it must not be concluded that it is thus often, for it is but at the beginning of the spring, and at Michaelmas when they return back to the southward; yet are there some all the year long, which are easily attained by such as look after them. Many of them build amongst the pine trees, thirty miles to the northeast of our plantations, joining nest to nest and tree to tree by their nests, so that the sun never sees the ground in that place, from whence the Indians fetch whole loads of them.

The turkey is a very large bird, of a black color yet white in flesh, much bigger than our English turkey. He hath the use of his long legs so ready that he can run as fast as a dog and fly as well as a goose. Of these sometimes there will be forty, threescore, and an hundred of a flock, sometimes more and sometimes less. Their feeding is acorns, haws and berries; some of them get a haunt to frequent our English corn. In winter when the snow covers the ground, they resort to the seashore to look for shrimps and such small fishes at low tides. Such as love turkey hunting must follow it in winter after a new fallen snow, when he may follow them by their tracks. Some have killed ten or a dozen in half a day. If they can be found towards an evening and watched where they perch, if one come about ten or eleven of the clock, he may shoot as often as he will; they will sit unless they be slenderly wounded. These turkey remain all the year long. The price of a good turkey cock is four shillings, and he is well worth it, for he may be in weight forty pound, a hen two shillings.

Pheasants be very rare, but heath cocks and partridges be common. He that is a husband, and will be stirring betime, may kill half a dozen in a morning. The partridges be bigger than they be in England. The flesh of the heath cocks is red and the flesh of a partridge white; their price is four pence apiece.

The ravens and the crows be much like them of other countries. There are no magpies, jackdaws, cuckoos, jays, sparrows, etc. The stares be bigger than those in England, as black as crows, being the most troublesome and injurious bird of all others, pulling up the corns by the roots when it is young so that those who plant by reedy and sedgy places, where they frequent, are much annoyed with them, they being so audacious that they fear not guns or their fellows hung upon poles. But the corn having a week or nine days growth is post their spoiling. The owls be of two sorts: the one being small, speckled like a partridge, with ears; the other being a great owl, almost as big as an eagle, his body being as good meat as a partridge.

Cormorants be as common as other fowls, which destroy abundance of small fish. These be not worth the shooting because they are the worst of fowls for meat, tasting rank and fishy. Again, one may shoot twenty times and miss, for seeing the fire in the pan, they dive under the water before the shot comes to the place where they were. They used to roost upon the tops of trees and rocks, being a very heavy drowsy creature, so that the Indians will go in their canoes in the night and take them from the rocks as easily as women take a hen from roost. No ducking ponds can afford more delight than a lame cormorant and two or three lusty dogs.

The crane, although he be almost as tall as a man by reason of his long legs and neck, yet is his body rounder than other fowls, not much unlike the body of a turkey. I have seen many of these fowls, yet did I never see one that was fat—though very sleeky. I suppose it is contrary to their nature to grow fat. Of these there be many in summer but none in winter. Their price is two shillings. There be likewise many swans which frequent the fresh ponds and rivers, seldom consorting themselves with ducks and geese. These be very good meat; the price of one is six shillings.

The geese of the country be of three sorts: first a brant goose, which is a goose almost like the wild goose in England; the price of one of these is six pence. The second kind is a white goose, almost as big as an English tame goose. These come in great flocks about Michaelmas. Sometimes there will be two or three thousand in a flock; those continue six weeks and so fly to the southward, returning in March and staying six weeks more, returning again to the northward. The price of one of these is eight pence. The third kind of geese is a great gray goose with a black neck and a black and white head, strong of flight, and these be a great deal bigger than the ordinary geese of England, some very fat, and in the spring so full of feathers that the shot can scarce pierce them. Most of these geese remain with us from Michaelmas to April. They feed on the sea, upon grass in the bays at low water and gravel, and in the woods of acorns, having as other fowl have their pass and repass to the northward and southward. The accurate marksmen kill of these both flying and sitting; the price of a good gray goose is eighteen pence.

The ducks of the country be very large ones and in great abundance, so is there of teal likewise. The price of a duck is six pence, of a teal three pence. If I should tell you how some have killed a hundred geese in a week, fifty ducks at a shot, forty teals at another, it may be counted impossible though nothing more certain.

The oldwives be a fowl that never leave tattling day or night, something bigger than a duck. The loon is an ill-shaped thing like a cormorant, but that he can neither go nor fly. He maketh a noise sometimes like a sowgelder's horn. The humilities or simplicities (as I may rather call them) be of two sorts, the biggest being as big as a green plover, the other as big as birds that we call knots in England. Such is the simplicity of the smaller sorts of these birds that one may drive them on a heap like so many sheep, and seeing a fit time shoot them. The living seeing the dead, settle themselves on the same place again, amongst which the fowler discharges again. I myself have killed twelve score at two shoots. These bird are to be had upon sandy brakes at the latter end of summer before the geese come in.

Thus much have I showed you as I know to be true concerning the fowl of the country. But methinks I hear some say that this is very good if it could be caught, or likely to continue, and that much shooting will fright away the fowls. True it is that everyone's employment will not permit him to fowl: what then? Yet their employments furnish them with silver guns with which they may have it more easy.

For the frighting of the fowl, true it is that many go blurting away their powder and shot that have no more skill to kill or win a goose than many in England that have rusty muskets in their houses knows what belongs to a soldier, yet are they not much afrighted. I have seen more living and dead the last year than I have done in former years.

Thomas Morton
(c. 1579–1647)

The Royalist and speculator Thomas Morton first came to Massachusetts in 1622, where he set up a fur trading post on the hilltop of Mount Wollaston, above Quincy Bay, just south of present-day Boston. From this outpost, which he happily called "Ma-re" (Merry) Mount, Morton gamboled and gambled, drank and danced, consorted freely with Native "maidens," and set up a lucrative Indian trade (including the sale of guns and liquor) that threatened the security and business interests—as well as the moral values—of his more serious neighbors, the Separatist "Pilgrims" of Plymouth, just thirty miles away. His most famous clash with the Pilgrims came in the spring of 1627, when Morton and his men erected an eighty-foot maypole, around which they engaged in various forms of "frisking" and licentiousness that led William Bradford to condemn his rowdy neighbor as the "Lord of Misrule." Morton was arrested and sent back to England, where charges were quickly dropped. He soon returned to Massachusetts, this time angering the Salem Puritans, who also arrested and deported him. After this second enforced voyage to England, Morton composed *The New English Canaan,* published in 1637. Although Bradford later called it an "infamous and scurrilous book," it was a brilliantly satirical work, unusual in its willingness to criticize the Pilgrims and Puritans for what Morton viewed as their sanctimonious, hypocritical persecution of "strangers"—nonseparatist settlers who were usually Anglicans and often business competitors. It has been less often recognized, however, that *The New English Canaan* is also an important work of early American environmental writing, for the second of its three parts is devoted to "A Description of the Beauty of the Country with her Natural Endowments." In this part, excerpted below, Morton offers a rich description of an untrammeled natural world that the Puritan fathers often regarded solely as a "howling wilderness" in need of literal and symbolic transformation. A much more sympathetic observer of nature, Morton characterizes the wilderness as fecund and nurturing—an Edenic land he finds worthy "to be entitled by the name of the second Canaan."

From *The New English Canaan* (1637)

The General Survey of the Country

In the Month of June, Anno Salutis 1622, it was my chance to arrive in the parts of New England with 30 Servants, and provision of all sorts fit for a plantation: and while our houses were building, I did endeavor to take a survey of the Country: The more I looked, the more I liked it. And when I had more seriously considered of the beauty of the place, with all her fair endowments, I did not think that in all the known world it could be paralleled, for so many goodly groves of trees, dainty fine round rising hillocks, delicate fair large plains, sweet crystal fountains, and clear running streams that twine in fine meanders through the meads, making so sweet a murmuring noise to hear as would even lull the senses with delight asleep, so pleasantly do they glide upon the pebble stones, jetting most jocundly where they do meet and hand in hand run down to Neptune's Court, to pay the yearly tribute which they owe to him as sovereign Lord of all the springs. Contained within the volume of the Land, are Fowls in abundance, Fish in multitude; and I discovered, besides, Millions of Turtledoves on the green boughs, which sat pecking of the full ripe pleasant grapes that were supported by the lusty trees, whose fruitful load did cause the arms to bend: among which here and there dispersed, you might see Lilies and of the Daphnean-tree: which made the Land to me seem paradise: for in mine eye 'twas Nature's Masterpiece; Her chiefest Magazine of all where lives her store: if this Land be not rich, then is the whole world poor.

What I had resolved on, I have really performed; and I have endeavored to use this abstract as an instrument, to be the means to communicate the knowledge which I have gathered, by my many years residence in those parts, unto my Countrymen: to the end that they may the better perceive their error, who cannot imagine that there is any Country in the universal world which may be compared unto our native soil. I will now discover unto them a Country whose endowments are by learned men allowed to stand in a parallel with the Israelites' Canaan, which none will deny to be a land far more excellent than Old England, in her proper nature.

This I consider I am bound in duty (as becometh a Christian man) to perform for the glory of God, in the first place; next, (according to Cicero,) to acknowledge that, *Non nobis solum nati sumus, sed partim patria, partim parentes, partim amici vindicant* [We have been born not for ourselves alone, but partly our native land, partly parents, partly friends lay claim to us].

For which cause I must approve of the endeavors of my Countrymen, that have been studious to enlarge the territories of his Majesty's empire by planting Colonies in America.

And of all other, I must applaud the judgment of those that have made choice of this part, (whereof I now treat,) being of all other most absolute, as I will make it appear hereafter by way of parallel. Among those that have settled themselves in new England, some have gone for their conscience sake, (as they profess,) and I wish that they may plant the Gospel of Jesus Christ, as becometh them, sincerely and without satisme or faction, whatsoever their former or present practices are, which I intend not to justify: however, they have deserved (in mine opinion) some commendations, in that they have furnished the Country so commodiously in so short a time; although it hath been but for their own profit, yet posterity will taste the sweetness of it, and that very suddenly.

And since my task, in this part of mine abstract, is to entreat of the natural endowments of the Country, I will make a brief demonstration of them in order, severally, according to their several qualities: and show you what they are, and what profitable use may be made of them by industry.

What Trees Are There and How Commodious

Oaks are there of two sorts, white and red; excellent timber for the building both of houses and shipping: and they are found to be a timber that is more tough than the oak of England. They are excellent for pipe-staves, and such like vessels; and pipe-staves at the Canary Islands are a prime commodity. I have known them there at 35 p. the 1000, and will purchase a freight of wines there before any commodity in England, their only wood being pine, of which they are enforced also to build shipping; of oaks there is great abundance in the parts of New England, and they may have a prime place in the Catalogue of commodities.

Ash there is store, and very good for staves, oars or pikes; and may have a place in the same Catalogue.

Elm: of this sort of trees there are some; but there hath not yet been found any quantity to speak of.

Beech there is of two sorts, red and white; very excellent for trenchers or chairs, and also for oars; and may be accounted for a commodity.

Walnut: of this sort of wood there is infinite store, and there are 4 sorts: it is an excellent wood, for many uses approved; the younger trees are employed for hoops, and are the best for that employment of all other stuff whatsoever. The Nuts serve when they fall to feed our swine, which make them the delicatest bacon of all other food: and is therein a chief commodity.

Chestnut: of this sort there is very great plenty, the timber whereof is excellent for building; and is a very good commodity, especially in respect of the fruit, both for man and beast.

Pine: of this sort there is infinite store in some parts of the Country. I have traveled 10 miles together where is little or no other wood growing. And of these may be made rosin, pitch and tar, which are such useful commodities that if we had them not from other Countries in Amity with England, our Navigation would decline. Then how great the commodity of it will be to our Nation, to have it of our own, let any man judge.

Cedar: of this sort there is abundance; and this wood was such as Solomon used for the building of that glorious Temple at Jerusalem; and there are of these Cedars, fir trees and other materials necessary for the building of many fair Temples, if there were any Solomons to be at the Cost of them: and if any man be desirous to find out in what part of the Country the best Cedars are, he must get into the bottom grounds, and in valleys that are wet at the spring of the year, where the moisture preserves them from the fire in spring time, and not in a wooden prospect. This wood cuts red, and is good for bedsteads, tables and chests; and may be placed in the Catalogue of Commodities.

Cypress: of this there is great plenty; and vulgarly this tree hath been taken for another sort of Cedar; but workmen put a difference between this Cypress, and the Cedar, especially in the color; for this is white and that red white: and likewise in the fineness of the leaf and the smoothness of the bark. This wood is also sweeter than Cedar, and, (as it is in Garret's herbal,) a more beautiful tree; it is of all other, to my mind, most beautiful, and cannot be denied to pass for a commodity.

Spruce: of these there are infinite store, especially in the Northern parts of the Country; and they have been approved by workmen in England to be more tough than those that they have out of the east country: from whence we have them for masts and yards of ships.

The Spruce of this country are found to be 3 and 4 fathom about: and are reputed able, single, to make masts for the biggest ship that sails on the main Ocean, without peesing; which is more than the East country can afford. And seeing that Navigation is the very sinews of a flourishing Commonwealth, it is fitting to allow the Spruce tree a principal place in the Catalogue of commodities.

Alder: of this sort there is plenty by riversides, good for turners.

Birch: of this there is plenty in divers parts of the Country. Of the bark of these the Savages of the Northern parts make them delicate Canoes, so light that two men will transport one of them over Land whither they lift; and yet one of them will transport ten or twelve Savages by water at a time.

Maple: of those trees there is great abundance; and these are very excellent for bowls. The Indians use of it to that purpose; and is to be accounted a good commodity.

Elder: there is plenty in that Country; of this the Savages make their Arrows, and it hath no strong unsavory scent like our Elder in England.

Hawthorne: of this there is two sorts, one of which bears a well tasting berry as big as one's thumb, and looks like little Queen apples.

Vines: of this kind of trees there are that bear grapes of three colors: that is to say, white, black and red.

The Country is so apt for vines, that, but for the fire at the spring of the years, the vines would so overspread the land that one should not be able to pass for them; the fruit is as big, of some, as a musket bullet, and is excellent in taste.

Plum trees: of this kind there are many; some that bear fruit as big as our ordinary bullace: others there be that do bear fruit much bigger than pear plums; their color red, and their stones flat; very delicious in taste.

Cherry trees there are abundance; but the fruit is as small as our sloes; but if any of them were replanted and grafted, in an orchard, they would soon be raised by means of such; and the like fruits.

There is great abundance of Musk Roses in divers places: the water distilled excelleth our Rosewater of England.

There is abundance of Sassafras and Sarsaparilla, growing in divers places of the land; whose buds at the spring do perfume the air.

Other trees there are not greatly material to be recited in this abstract, as gooseberries, raspberries, and other berries.

There is Hemp that naturally groweth, finer than our Hemp of England.

A Perspective to View the Country By

As for the Soil, I may be bold to commend the fertility thereof, and prefer it before the Soil of England, (our Native Country); and I need not to produce more than one argument for proof thereof, because it is so infallible.

Hemp is a thing by Husbandmen in general agreed upon to prosper best in the most fertile Soil: and experience hath taught this rule, that Hemp seed prospers so well in New England that it shooteth up to be ten foot high and ten foot and a half, which is twice so high as the ground in old England produceth it; which argues New England the more fertile of the two.

As for the air, I will produce but one proof for the maintenance of the excellency thereof; which is so general, as I assure myself it will suffice.

No man living there was ever known to be troubled with a cold, a cough, or a murr; but many men, coming sick out of Virginia to New Canaan have instantly recovered with the help of the purity of that air; no man ever surfeited himself either by eating or drinking.

As for the plenty of that Land, it is well known that no part of Asia, Africa or Europe affordeth deer that do bring forth any more than one single fawn; and in New Canaan the Deer are accustomed to bring forth 2 and 3 fawns at a time.

Besides, there are such infinite flocks of Fowl and Multitudes of fish, both in the fresh waters and also on the Coast, that the like hath not elsewhere been discovered by any traveler.

The winds there are not so violent as in England; which is proved by the trees that grow in the face of the wind by the Sea Coast; for there they do not lean from the wind as they do in England: as we have heard before.

The Rain is there more moderate than in England; which thing I have noted in all the time of my residence to be so.

The Coast is low Land, and not high Land: and he is of a weak capacity that conceiveth otherwise of it, because it cannot be denied but that boats may come aground in all places along the Coast, and especially within the Compass of the Massachusetts patent, where the prospect is fixed.

The Harbors are not to be bettered for safety and goodness of ground, for anchorage, and, (which is worthy observation,) shipping will not there be furred; neither are they subject to worms, as in Virginia and other places.

Let the Situation also of the Country be considered, (together with the rest which is discovered in the front of this abstract,) and then I hope no man will hold this land unworthy to be entitled by the name of the second Canaan.

Anne Bradstreet
(c. 1612–1672)

Widely celebrated as the first American woman poet, Anne Bradstreet came to the colonies in 1630, sailing to the Massachusetts Bay Colony aboard the *Arabella* as a member of John Winthrop's congregation. Like most Puritan women, Bradstreet was denied any important public role within the patriarchal theocracy of the Bay Colony. But as both the daughter and the wife of prominent Puritan leaders, Bradstreet was better educated and more widely read than most women of her day. She also managed to write poetry regularly, even as her family moved from Salem, to Charlestown, to Newtowne (Cambridge), to Ipswich, and, finally, to Andover, on the same Merrimack River that would, two centuries later, be celebrated by Henry Thoreau. In 1647 Bradstreet's brother-in-law, John Woodbridge, sailed to England with copies of her poems, which were published—without her knowledge—under the title *The Tenth Muse Lately Sprung Up in America . . . By a Gentlewoman in Those Parts* (1650). It was the first book of poetry published by an American writer and was so successful in England that even King George III was said to have owned and read it. Though often immersed in the domestic responsibilities occasioned by her eight children and the hardships of a frontier life, Bradstreet continued to write, revising earlier poems, composing new ones, and also writing prose. Much of her finest work was published posthumously. Bradstreet's "Meditations Divine and Moral," excerpted below, were written during the early 1660s but remained in manuscript until the Ellis edition of Bradstreet's work appeared in 1867. In the "Meditations" we see a woman, mother, wife, daughter, and literary artist whose understanding of the natural world was deeply conditioned by her Puritan faith. However, we also see a writer who understood nature to have value as a world full of lessons, a moral text in which the wisdom of the Creator could be read by the attentive observer. In linking the natural world to spiritual insights, Bradstreet not only anticipated the late Puritan naturalists Cotton Mather and Jonathan Edwards but also helped initiate a spiritually concerned tradition of nature writing that would eventually run through Emerson and Thoreau and into the environmental writing of the twentieth century.

From *Meditations Divine and Moral* (1664/1867)

It is reported of the peacock that priding himself in his gay feathers he ruffles them up, but spying his black feet, he soon lets fall his plumes, so he that glories in his gifts and adorings, should look upon his Corruptions, and yet will damp his high thoughts.

The finest bread hath the least bran the purest honey the least wax and the sincerest Christian the least self-love.

Diverse children, have their different natures, some are like flesh which nothing but salt will keep from putrefaction, some again like tender fruits that are best preserved with sugar, those parents are wise that can fit their nurture according to their Nature.

If we had no winter the spring would not be so pleasant, if we did not some times taste of adversity, prosperity would not be so welcome.

He that will undertake to climb up a steep mountain with a great burden on his back, will find it a wearisome if not an impossible task so he that thinks to mount to heaven clogged with the Cares and riches of this Life, 'tis no wonder if he faint by the way.

He that walks among briars and thorns will be very careful, where he sets his foot. And he that passes through the wilderness of this world, had need ponder all his steps.

The skillful fisher hath his several baits, for several fish, but there is a hook under all, Satan that great Angler hath his sundry baits for sundry tempers of men, which they all catch greedily at but few perceives the hook till it be too late.

Lightning doth usually precede thunder, and storms rain, and strokes do not often fall till after threatening.

Yellow leaves argue want of sap and gray hairs want of moisture so dry and sapless performances are symptoms of little spiritual vigor.

Iron till it be thoroughly heat is incapable to be wrought, so god sees good to cast some men into the furnace of affliction and then beats them on his anvil into what frame he pleases.

Ambitious men are like hops that never rest climbing so long as they have anything to stay upon, but take away their props and they are of all, the most dejected.

Some children are hardly weaned although the teat be rubbed with wormwood or mustard, they will either wipe it off, or else suck down sweet and bitter together so is it with some Christians, let god embitter all the sweets of this life, that so they might feed upon more substantial food, yet they are so childishly sottish that they are still hugging and sucking these empty breasts, that god is forced to hedge up their way with thorns or lay affliction on their loins that so they might shake hands with the world before it bid them farewell.

The spring is a lively emblem of the resurrection, after a long winter we see the leafless trees and dry stocks (at the approach of the Sun) to resume their former vigor and beauty in a more ample manner then what they lost in the Autumn so shall it be at that great day after a long vacation, when the Sun of righteousness shall appear those dry bones shall arise in far more glory, than that which they lost at their creation, and in this transcends the spring, that their leaf shall never fail nor their sap decline.

Fire hath its force abated by water not by wind, and anger must be allayed, by cold words and not by blustering threats.

We often see stones hang with drops not from any innate moisture, but from a thick air about them so may we sometime see, marble hearted sinners, seem full of contrition, but it is not from any dew of grace within, but from some black Clouds that impends them, which produces these sweating effects.

A shadow in the parching sun, and a shelter in a blustering storm are of all seasons the most welcome so a faithful friend in time of adversity, is (of all other) most Comfortable.

The treasures of this world may well be compared to husks, for they have no kernel in them, and they that feed upon them, may soon Stuff their throats, but cannot fill their bellies, they may be choked by them, but cannot be satisfied with them.

Sometimes the sun is only shadowed by a cloud, that we cannot see his luster, although we may walk by his light, but when he is set, we are in darkness till he arise again, so god doth sometime veil his face but for a moment that we cannot behold the light of his Countenance, as at some other time, yet he affords so much light as may direct our way, that we may go forwards to the City of habitation, but when he seems to set and be quite gone out of sight then must we needs walk in darkness and see no light, yet then must we trust in the lord and stay upon our god, and when the morning (which is the appointed time) is come the Sun of righteousness will arise with healing in his wings.

Corn is produced with much labor (as the husbandman well knows) and some land asks much more pains, then some other doth to be brought into tilth yet all must be ploughed and harrowed. Some children (like sour land) are of so tough and morose a disposition that the plough of correction must make long furrows on their back and the Harrow of discipline go often over them, before they be fit soil, to sow the seed of morality, much less of grace in them. But when by prudent nurture they are brought into a fit capacity, let the seed of good instruction and exhortation be sown, in the spring of their youth, and a plentiful crop may be expected in the harvest of their years.

We see in orchards, some trees so fruitful, that the weight of their Burden, is the breaking of their limbs, some again, are but meanly loaden, and some have nothing to show but leaves only, and some among them are dry stocks. So is it in the church which is god's orchard, there are some eminent Christians, that are so frequent in good duties, that many times, the weight thereof impairs both their bodies and estates, and there are some (and they sincere ones too) who have not attained to that fruitfulness, although they aim at perfection. And again there are others that have nothing to commend them, but only a gay profession, and these are but leafy Christians, which are in as much danger of being cut down, as the dry stock, for both cumber the ground.

We see in the firmament there is but one Sun, among a multitude of stars and those stars also, to differ much one from the other, in regard of bigness and brightness, yet all receive their light from that one Sun, so is it in the Church both militant and triumphant, there is but one Christ, who is the Sun of righteousness, in the midst of an innumerable Company of Saints, and Angels those Saints have their degrees, even in this life, some are Stars of the first magnitude, and some of a less degree, & others (and they indeed the most in number) but small and obscure, yet all receive their luster (be it more or less) from that glorious sun that enlightens all in all, and if some of them shine so bright while they move on earth, how transcendently splendid shall they be, when they are fixed in their heavenly spheres.

All the Comforts of this Life, may be compared to the gourd of Jonah, that notwithstanding we take great delight, for a season in them, and find their shadow very comfortable, yet there is some worm or other, of discontent or fear, or grief that lies at the root which in great part withers the pleasure which else we should take in them, and well it is that we perceive a decay, in their greenness for were earthly comforts permanent who would look for heavenly?

All weak and diseased bodies, have hourly mementos of their mortality. But the soundest of men, have likewise their nightly monitor, by the emblem of death, which is their sleep (for so is death often called) and not only their death, but their grave, is lively represented before their eyes, by beholding their bed, the morning may mind them of the resurrection, and the sun approaching, of the appearing of the Sun of righteousness, at whose coming they shall all rise out of their beds. The long night shall fly away, and the day of eternity shall never end, seeing these things must be what manner of persons ought we to be, in all good conversation.

As the brands of a fire, if once severed, will of themselves go out although you use no other means to extinguish them so distance of place together with length of time (if there be no intercourse) will cool the affections of intimate friends, though there should be no displeasence between them.

God hath by his providence so ordered, that no one Country hath all Commodities within itself, but what it wants, another shall supply, that so there may be a mutual commerce through the world. As it is with Countries so it is with men, there was never yet any one man that had all excellences, let his parts natural and acquired spiritual and moral, be never so large, yet he stands in need of something which another man hath (perhaps meaner than himself) which shows us perfection is not below, as also that god will have us beholden one to another.

John Josselyn
(c. 1608–c. 1675)

Among the most interesting and colorful of the colonial literary naturalists, Englishman John Josselyn is sometimes remembered for his credulous acceptance of mythic legends describing a New World inhabited by tritons, mermen, and sea monsters. Josselyn's North American connection came through his brother Henry, an early settler of Maine who in 1645 was made deputy governor of that province. John Josselyn visited his brother at Black Point (Scarborough), Maine, briefly in 1638–39 and, after the Restoration, returned to live in New England from 1663 to 1671. During this second, longer visit Josselyn studied Native American culture, collected plants, and kept notebooks describing the flora and fauna of the New World. And while Josselyn's special interest was the study of plants, he was not a scientific botanist but rather an herbalist whose sensibility and methodology was rooted in the ancient tradition of *materia medica:* the use of natural materials as medicinal curatives. As a practitioner of botany in the service of "physick," Josselyn was somewhere between the popular folk superstitions common in his day and the new science of the systematic taxonomists then in ascendancy within the Royal Society. In 1671 Josselyn returned to England permanently and wrote his two books: *New England's Rarities Discovered* . . . was published in 1672; his expanded work, *An Account of Two Voyages to New-England,* came out several years later, in 1674. Like John Smith, whom he read, Josselyn was a promoter of a New World whose wonders he celebrated; yet Josselyn was a closer observer of nature than was Smith. Like William Wood, whose *New England's Prospect* he knew, Josselyn aspired to write a comprehensive natural history of New England; despite its scientific weaknesses, Josselyn's work did eclipse Wood's as the most expansive natural historical treatment of the region. And like Thomas Morton, whom he also read, Josselyn was a Royalist and raconteur who ran afoul of the Puritans; he complained, for example, that he had been repeatedly fined for failing to attend church services. Josselyn is refreshingly original in his unique combination of natural history and folklore. And though his books are plagued by "vulgar error," as the following selections demonstrate, his appealing accounts of a fabulous New World wilderness also caused his writing to have wide appeal among the popular readership of his day.

From *Account of the Second Voyage to New England* (1674)

Of Beasts of the earth there be scarce 120 several kinds, and not much more of the Fowls of the Air, is the opinion of some Naturalists; there are not many kinds of Beasts in *New England,* they may be divided into Beasts of the Chase of the stinking foot, as *Roes, Foxes, Jackals, Wolves, Wild cats, Raccoons, Porcupines, Skunks, Musquashes, Squirrels, Sables,* and *Mattrises;* and Beasts of the Chase of the sweet foot, *Buck, Red Deer, Reindeer, Elk, Marouse, Maccarib, Bear, Beaver, Otter, Marten, Hare.*

The *Roe* a kind of Deer, and the fleetest Beast upon earth is here to be found, and is good venison, but not overfat.

The *Fox,* the male is called a dog fox, the female a bitch-fox, they go a clicketing the beginning of the spring, and bring forth their cubs in *May* and *June.* There are two or three kinds of them; one a great yellow *Fox,* another gray, who will climb up into Trees; the black *Fox* is of much esteem. *Foxes* and *Wolves are* usually hunted in *England* from *Holy Rood* day, till the *Annunciation.* In *New England* they make best sport in the depth of winter: they lay a sledge-load of Cods-heads on the other side of a paled fence when the moon shines, and about nine or ten of the clock the *Foxes* come to it, sometime two or three, or half a dozen, and more; these they shoot, and by that time they have cased them, there will be as many; So they continue shooting and killing of *Foxes* as long as the moon shineth: I have known half a score killed in one night. Their pisles are bony like a dog's, their fat liquefied and put into the ears easeth the pain, their tails or bushes are very fair ones and of good use, but their skins are so thin (yet thick set with deep fur) that they will hardly hold the dressing.

Jackals there be abundance, which is a Creature much like a *Fox*, but smaller, they are very frequent in *Palestine*, or the *Holy Land*.

The *Wolf* seeketh his mate and goes a clicketing at the same season with *Foxes*, and bring forth their whelps as they do, but their kennels are under thick bushes by great Trees in remote places by the swamps, he is to be hunted as the *Fox* from *Holy Rood* day till the *Annunciation*. But there they have a quicker way to destroy them. See *New England's* rarities. They commonly go in routs, a rout of *Wolves* is 12 or more, sometimes by couples. In 1664 we found a *Wolf* asleep in a small dry swamp under an Oak, a great mastiff which we had with us seized upon him, and held him till we had a rope about his neck, by which we brought him home, and tying of him to a stake we baited him with smaller Dogs, and had excellent sport; but his hinder leg being broken, they knocked out his brains. Sometime before this we had an excellent course after a single *Wolf* upon the hard sands by the Sea-side at low water for a mile or two, at last we lost our dogs, it being (as the *Lancashire* people phrase it) twilight, that is almost dark, and went beyond them, for the mastiff-bitch had seized upon the *Wolf* being gotten into the Sea, and there held him till one went in and led him out, the bitch keeping her hold till they had tied his legs, and so carried him home like a Calf upon a staff between two men; being brought into the house they unbound him and set him upon his legs, he not offering in the least to bite, or so much as to show his teeth, but clapping his stern betwixt his legs, and leering towards the door would willingly have had his liberty, but they served him as they did the other, knocked his brains out, for our dogs were not then in a condition to bait him; their eyes shine by night as a Lanthorn: the Fangs of a *Wolf* hung about children's necks keep them from frighting, and are very good to rub their gums with when they are breeding of Teeth, the gall of a *Wolf* is sovereign for swelling of the sinews; the fiants or dung of a *Wolf* drunk with white wine helpeth the *Colic*.

The Wildcat, Lusern or *luceret*, or Ounce as some call it, is not inferior to Lamb, their grease is very sovereign for lameness upon taking cold.

The *Raccoon* or *Rattoon* is of two sorts, gray *Rattoons*, and black *Rattoons*, their grease is sovereign for wounds with bruises, aches, strains, bruises; and to anoint after broken bones and dislocations.

The *Skunk* is almost as big as a *Raccoon*, perfect black and white or piebald, with a bush-tail like a *Fox*, an offensive Carrion. The Urine of this Creature is of so strong a scent, that if it light upon any thing, there is no abiding of it, it will make a man smell, though he were of *Alexander's* complexion; and so sharp that if he do but whisk his bush which he pisseth upon in the face of a dog hunting of him, and that any of it light in his eyes it will make him almost mad with the smart thereof.

The *Musquashes* is a small Beast that lives in shallow ponds, where they build them houses of earth and sticks in shape like molehills, and feed upon *Calamus Aromaticus:* in *May* they scent very strong of Musk; their fur is of no great esteem; their stones wrapped in Cotton wool will continue a long time, and are good to lay amongst clothes to give them a grateful smell.

The *Squirrel,* of which there are three sorts, the mouse-squirrel, the gray squirrel, the flying squirrel, called by the *Indian Assapanick.* The mouse-squirrel is hardly so big as a Rat, streaked on both sides with black and red streaks, they are mischievous vermin destroying abundance of Corn both in the fields and in the house, where they will gnaw holes into Chests, and tear clothes both linen and woolen, and are notable nut-gatherers in *August;* when hazel and filbert nuts are ripe you may see upon every Nut-tree as many mouse-squirrels as leaves; So that the nuts are gone in a trice, which they convey to their Drays or Nests. The gray squirrel is pretty large, almost as big as a Coney, and are very good meat: in some parts of the Country there are many of them. The flying squirrel is so called, because (his skin being loose and large) he spreads it on both sides like wings when he passeth from one Tree to another at great distance. I cannot call it flying nor leaping, for it is both.

The *Mattrise* is a Creature whose head and foreparts is shaped somewhat like a Lion's, not altogether so big as a housecat, they are innumerable up in the Country, and are esteemed good fur.

The *Sable* is much of the size of a *Mattrise* perfect black, but what store there is of them I cannot tell, I never saw but two of them in Eight years space.

The *Martin* is as ours are in *England,* but blacker, they breed in holes which they make in the earth like Conies, and are innumerable, their skins or fur are in much request.

The *Buck, Stag,* and Reindeer are Creatures that will live in the coldest climates, here they are innumerable, bringing forth three *Fawns* or *Calves* at a time, which they hide a mile asunder to prevent their destruction by the *Wolves,* wild-*Cats, Bears,* and *Mequans:* when they are in season they will be very fat; there are but few slain by the *English.* The *Indians* who shoot them, and take of them with toils, bring them in with their suet, and the bones that grow upon *Stags-Hearts.*

The *Moose* or *Elk* is a Creature, or rather if you will a Monster of superfluity; a full grown *Moose* is many times bigger than an *English* Ox, their horns as I have said elsewhere, very big (and branched out into palms) the tips whereof are sometimes found to be two fathom asunder, (a fathom is six feet from the tip of one finger to the tip of the other, that is four cubits) and in height from the toe of the forefoot, to the pitch of the shoulder twelve foot, both of which hath been taken by some of my skeptic Readers to be monstrous lies. If you consider the breadth that the beast carrieth, and the magnitude of the horns, you will be easily induced to contribute your belief. . . .

There are certain transcendentia in every Creature, which are the indelible Characters of God, and which discover God. There's a prudential for you, as *John Rhodes* the Fisherman used to say to his mate, *Kitt Lux.* But to go on with the *Moose;* they are accounted a kind of Deer, and have three *Calves* at a time, which they hide a mile asunder too, as other Deer do, their skins make excellent Coats for Martial men, their sinews which are as big as a man's finger are of perdurable toughness and much used by the *Indians,* the bone that grows upon their heart is an excellent Cordial, their blood is as thick as an *Ass's* or *Bull's* who have the thickest blood of all others, a man the thinnest. To what age they live I know not, certainly a long time in their proper climate. *Some particular living Creatures cannot live in every particular place or region, especially with the same joy and felicity as it did where it was first bred, for the certain agreement of nature that is between the place and the thing bred in that place: As appeareth by* Elephants, *which being translated or brought out of the Second or Third Climate, though they may live, yet will they never engender or bring forth young.* So for plants, Birds, &c. Of both these Creatures, some few there are have been brought into *England,* but did not long continue. Sir *R. Baker* in his Chronicle tells us of an *Elephant* in *Henry* the Third's Reign, which he saith was the first that was ever seen there, which as it seems is an error, unless he restrain it to the *Normans'* time. For Mr. *Speed* writeth that *Claudius Drusus* Emperor of *Rome* brought in the first in his Army; the bones of which digged up since are taken for Giant's bones. As for the *Moose* the first that was seen in *England,* was in King *Charles* the First's Reign; thus much for these magnals amongst the Creatures of God to be wondered at, the next beast to be mentioned is

The *Marouse,* which is somewhat like a *Moose,* but his horns are but small, and himself about the size of a *Stag,* these are the Deer that the flat-footed *Wolves* hunt after.

The *Maccarib* is a Creature not found that ever I heard yet, but upon *Cape-Sable* near to the *French* plantations.

The *Bear* when he goes to mate is a terrible Creature, they bring forth their Cubs in *March,* hunted with dogs they take a Tree where they shoot them, when he is fat he is excellent Venison, which is in *Acorn* time, and in winter, but then there is none dares to attempt to kill him but the *Indian.* He makes his Den amongst thick Bushes, thrusting in here and there store of *Moss,* which being covered with snow and melting in the daytime with heat of the Sun, in the night is frozen into a thick coat of Ice; the mouth of his Den is very narrow, here they lie single, never two in a Den all winter. The *Indian* as soon as he finds them, creeps in upon all four, seizes with his left hand upon the neck of the sleeping *Bear*, drags him to the mouth of the Den, where with a club or small hatchet in his right hand he knocks out his brains before he can open his eyes to see his enemy. But sometimes they are too quick for the *Indians*, as one amongst them called black *Robin* lighting upon a male-*Bear* had a piece of his buttock torn off before he could fetch his blow: their grease is very sovereign. One Mr. *Purchase* cured himself of the *Sciatica* with *Bears-grease*, keeping some of it continually in his groin. It is good too for swelled Cheeks upon cold, for Rupture of the hands in winter, for limbs taken suddenly with *Sciatica, Gout*, or other diseases that cannot stand upright nor go, bedrid; it must be well chaft in, and the same cloth laid on still; it prevents the shedding of the hair occasioned by the coldness of winter's weather; and the yard of a *Bear* which as a Dog's or Fox's is bony, is good for to expel Gravel out of the kidneys and bladder, as I was there told by one Mr. *Abraham Philater* a *Jerseyman*.

The *Beaver* or Pound-dog is an Amphibious Creature, lives upon the land as well as in the water. I suppose they feed upon fish, but am sure that the Bark of Trees is also their food; there is an old proverbial saying, *sic me jubes quotidie, ut fiber salicem:* you love me as the *Beaver* doth the willow; who eateth the Bark and killeth the Tree. They will be tame, witness the *Beaver* that not long since was kept at *Boston* in the *Massachusetts Bay*, and would run up and down the streets, returning home without a call. Their skins are highly valued, and their stones are good for the palsy, trembling, and numbness of the hands, boiling of them in Oil of *Spike*, and anointing the sinews in the neck. If you take of *Castorium* two drams, of woman's hair one dram, and with a little Rosin of the *Pine Tree*, make it up into pills as big as Filberts and perfume a woman in a fit of the mother with one at a time laid upon coals under her nostrils, it will recover her out of her fit. The grease of a *Beaver* is good for the Nerves, Convulsions, Epilepsies, Apoplexies &c. The tail as I have said in another Treatise, is very fat and of a masculine virtue, as good as *Eringo's* or *Satyrion*-Roots.

The *Otter* or River-Dog is Amphibious too, he hunteth for his kind in the spring, and bringeth forth his whelps as the *Beaver* doth, they are generally black, and very numerous, they are hunted in *England* from *Shrovetide* until *Midsummer*, but in *New England* they take them when they can. The skin of an *Otter* is worth Ten Shillings, and the gloves made thereof are the best fortification for the hands against wet weather that can be thought of, the fur is excellent for muffs, and is almost as dear as *Beaver*, the grease of an *Otter* will make fish turn up their bellies, and is of rare use for many things.

The *Hare*, I have no more to write of them than that they kindle in hollow Trees. What else concerns him, or any of the fore-mentioned Creatures you may have in my *New England's* rarities, to which I refer you.

The *Porcupine* likewise I have treated of, only this I forgot to acquaint you with, that they lay Eggs, and are good meat.

The last kind of Beasts are they that are begot by equivocal generation, as *Mules* and several others, that when the Beasts were brought by the Almighty Creator to *Adam*, who gave them names, were not then in *rerum natura*. Of these there are not many known in *New England*. I know of but one, and that is the *Indian* dog begotten betwixt a *Wolf* and a *Fox*, or between a *Fox* and a *Wolf*, which they made use of, taming of them, and bringing of them up to hunt with, but since the *English* came amongst them they have gotten store of our dogs, which they bring up and keep in as much subjection as they do their webbs.

Jasper Danckaerts
(1639–c. 1703)

Born in Zeeland, Netherlands, Jasper Danckaerts was a cooper, an employee of the Dutch West India Company, and a member of the Labadist sect that flourished during the second half of the seventeenth century. The Labadists were a relatively small group of radical Protestants who, following the preaching of Jean de Labadie (1610–74), pursued a mystical, reformist, rather narrow interpretation of Calvinism. The religious persecution of the Labadists forced them to move from place to place within Europe and eventually to seek asylum abroad. Jasper Danckaerts and fellow church member Petrus (Peter) Sluyter (1645–1722) traveled to America in 1679 in search of a safe place to establish a Labadist settlement. Danckaerts and Sluyter—who, fearing persecution, used the aliases Schilders and Vorstman, respectively—traveled through New York, New Jersey, Delaware, Maryland, and Massachusetts before deciding to establish a colony on part of the 24,000-acre estate of Bohemian adventurer Augustine Herrman (whose son, Ephraim, was a Labadist) in Maryland, within the domain of Lord Baltimore. In 1680 the men went home to Europe, returning in 1683 with others to establish their Labadist commune on a 3,750-acre tract of land near the Bohemia River. The colony never had more than a hundred members, and by about 1730 both the colony and the sect it represented had disappeared. Despite the strong religious biases evident in Danckaerts's journal, the document is a literary treasure from the Dutch colonies of North America. Rediscovered nearly a century after its composition, the work was first translated from the Dutch and published in 1867 as *Journal of a Voyage to New York and a Tour in Several of the American Colonies. . . .* Danckaerts's *Journal* is also a treasure of colonial American nature writing, for although it has remained virtually unknown among students of environmental literature, it contains some of the most lyrical and eloquent literary celebrations of American seascapes and landscapes written prior to the eighteenth century. Danckaerts's description of the sunset and moonrise in the passage that opens the following excerpt from the *Journal*, for example, demonstrates a subtle, delicate, painterly prose that was highly unusual for writers of his day.

From *Journal of a Voyage to New York and a Tour in Several of the American Colonies* (1679–1680/1867)

August 21, 1679. . . . The sea, which was exceedingly smooth, and a very clear and soft sky, made the evening hour extremely fine. The sky, with thin transparent snow-white clouds upon its glittering blue, was adorned by a bright, clear setting sun, which, in proportion as it declined and departed to another world, there to display the splendor which the creator has bestowed upon him, changed these clouds from white to shining brightness, and imparted to them for a while the golden luster of his fire. The sky around was not a pure sky-blue, but was of a mixed blue and green, sparkling like the flame when copper is brought to a glowing heat; that which was nearer the sun being more like the sun, and that further removed from him, gradually fading into bright blue mingled with silver; so that we not only saw all the colors of the rainbow, but all hues and colors, all shining according to their natures, with a brilliancy of their own, displaying them in that perfect splendor, which is so agreeable, and capable of enrapturing man. But one of the greatest beauties to be observed was their wonderful unity or harmony, or blending together; for although these colors and shining splendors were as manifold as the degrees and minutes, yea points of removal from their center, the sun, which shone the brightest and most, yet one could not discover where they separated or where they united, or even a point where one could be distinguished from the next, so united were they all, and so manifold and distinct was their unity without being divided. And although all this had a great and starry brightness, it was nevertheless so moderated and tempered through all the diversity of colors that we could not only look at each one in particular, but also the whole together, yea even at the sun itself, the center of this lordly perspective, and distinct from these surrounding splendors, as the extreme point of their concentration. No part lost anything by viewing the whole, and the whole lost nothing by viewing a part, nor did any one part lose by viewing any other part, nor the most excellent by viewing the least, nor the least, by viewing the most excellent, so exact was their unity in their multiplicity, and their multiplicity in their unity. No sooner had their glorious beauty left us, than turning around we saw not indeed the same, but its expression and projection, in a full moon, coming up in the east, as the sun was setting in the west. And as the one had shown himself like burning gold, the other showed herself as well polished, or burnished silver, upon the same field as the sun had done, but according to her nature and power and color; for as the sky and the clouds which were next the sun participated most in the color of the sun, so those nearest the moon had the greatest resemblance to the moon. These indeed were as white as snow and transparent, so that the light of the moon shining through the white thinness gave them a luster like silver and that upon a heaven's blue field. The outermost clouds were black or dark, while the outermost of the other (the sun) were a pure white, so that the one began with a color and glory with which the other terminated.

The peculiar feelings which the Lord excited in us over these and the like occurrences are not the material for the relation of a voyage. They can be expressed in some other place or perhaps never. . . .

August 22. . . . A great fleet of porpoises came from the south, extending as far off as we could see, leaping and tumbling with such swiftness and speed towards our ship, that it seemed as if they would certainly have taken it by storm. It is incredible how far they sprang up into the air; but as they came near to us they checked themselves, and went swimming, leaping and tumbling around us. One of the largest of them sprung full the length of a man high out of the water, and cutting capers in the air, made every one laugh; then fell backwards between two waves and disappeared beneath them, and we saw him no more. This was the final exhibition in the scene, which lasted half an hour, and then they all left. There were flying fish also flying out of the water while the others were swimming in it. Some are of opinion that these do not fly, but only spring out of the water; but I am certain such persons have never well looked at this fish, or observed how it flies. It is about the size of a herring, though we saw none as large as that during the voyage; it is more like the smelt. Close behind the head where other fish usually have two small fins, the flying fish has two long ones, which when stretched out, reach nearly to the tail. The fins have five or six little bones in them, which beginning at the end of the fin run finer and finer to nothing, and constitute the strength of the fin. You never see this fish spring out of the water like other fish, and fall in it again; but it comes from the water not upward, but like an arrow shot from a bow, spreading its two fins like wings which it does not flap as the feathered tribe does, for it is not of that nature; but moves them quickly and gently, the same as a certain insect which I have seen in Europe, and which in Friesland they call *coolwachter* and in the land of Cleves *rontbout*. It is true it does not fly high, although sometimes it flies as high as a ship; nor far, yet as far as a musket shot; but whether it be true that it cannot fly any further, because its wings are dry, or because it has no power to sustain its body longer in the air, which is more probably the truth, or for both reasons, I cannot say, nor do I believe anybody can. It flies seldom alone, but in schools sometimes of hundreds together. Fish in the sea swim together much in schools or fleets, and it seldom happens when you see a fish of a certain kind alone that there are not more of the same sort to be seen about. When a school of other fish, whether dorados or others, come among a school of flying fish, which serve as food for them, and the large fish hunt the flying fish for this purpose, the flying fish strive to save themselves by flying. . . .

September 5. It still continued calm. We caught a dolphin early in the morning. It is a very pretty fish, a species of round fish, but flat on the sides. Its color is a sky-blue ground with a golden hue over it, and I observed the older it is the more golden it is. On account of this golden appearance, I believe it is called *dorado* by the Portuguese, who doubtless were the first to eat it, when they began to make their long voyages. On the blue skin there are spots of a darker blue, which look pretty, and are set off by the gold color. It has no scales, or very small ones; its fins and tail are very bright, and exhibit great brilliancy when it is swimming. Its flesh is good but rather dry, as is the case generally with all sea fish. The captain had this one prepared and dressed with sauce; it was good and refreshed and strengthened us very much; but when we went to breakfast, we found there had happened a great misfortune to our mess. All our butter had been lost during the storm, through the negligence of the person having it in charge. The latitude at noon to-day was 36° 45′, the distance sailed forty miles; the course W. by N., the longitude 312° 20′. Shortly after midday we caught a shark which had been swimming for an hour alongside of the ship. He was so heavy that it was as much as three of us could do, to haul him on deck. When we got him in the ship, every body had to keep out of his way. He tried hard to bite, for which purpose there were three rows of teeth in his mouth close to each other. They endeavored to thrust a stick of wood down his throat, into his belly, in order to prevent his biting; but he struck around lustily whenever they came near him for that purpose. They cut off his tail with an ax, thus depriving him of his greatest power, and he soon bled to death. They then opened his head and took the brains out, which were as white as snow; these are esteemed a valuable medicine for women in childbirth; for which purpose the English use it a great deal. They also skinned him. The skin when dried is used to smooth and polish woodwork. If the sailors wish to eat the flesh they cook it by the fire as ours did; but this desire generally passes off with their first voyage, for the flesh is not good for much. It is like that of the thorndike or skate, but hard, and of a strong flavor. There is only one bone in the body, the backbone, which the sailors cut out and preserve as a rarity, and make buttons out of it for their frocks and trousers. We also caught several small fish of different kinds, like the carp, sole, seableak and others. . . .

October 6. We remained in the house during the forenoon, but after having dined we went out about two o'clock to explore the island of *Manathans*. This island runs east and west, or somewhat more northerly. On the north side of it is the North river, by which it is separated from the main land on the north; on the east end it is separated from the main land by a creek, or rather a branch of the North river, emptying itself into the East river. They can go over this creek at dead low water, upon rocks and reefs, at the place called *Spyt den duyvel.* This creek coming into the East river forms with it the two *Barents islands.* At the west end of these two running waters, that is, where they come together to the east of these islands, they make, with the rocks and reefs, such a frightful eddy and whirlpool that it is exceedingly dangerous to pass through them, especially with small boats, of which there are some lost every now and then, and the persons in them drowned; but experience has taught men the way of passing through them with less danger. Large vessels have always less danger because they are not capable of being carried along so quickly. There are two places where such whirling of the stream occurs, which are on account of the danger and frightfulness called the Great and Little Hell-gate. After these two streams are united, the island of *Manathans* is separated on the south from Long Island by the East river, which, beginning at the bay before New York, runs eastwardly, after forming several islands, again into the sea. This island is about seven hours' distance in length, but it is not a full hour broad. The sides are indented with bays, coves and creeks. It is almost entirely taken up, that is, the land is held by private owners, but not half of it is cultivated. Much of it is good woodland. The west end on which the city lies, is entirely cleared for more than an hour's distance, though that is the poorest ground; the best being on the east and north side. There are many brooks of fresh water running through it, pleasant and proper for man and beast to drink, as well as agreeable to behold, affording cool and pleasant resting places, but especially suitable places for the construction of mills, for although there is no overflow of water, yet it can be shut off and so used. A little eastward of *Nieu Haerlem* there are two ridges of very high rocks with a considerable space between them, displaying themselves very majestically, and inviting all men to acknowledge in them the majesty, grandeur, power and glory of their creator, who has impressed such marks upon them. Between them runs the road to *Spyt den duyvel.* The one to the north is most apparent; the south ridge is covered with earth on its north side, but it can be seen from the water or from the main land beyond to the south. The soil between these ridges is very good, though a little hilly and stony, and would be very suitable in my opinion for planting vineyards, in consequence of its being shut off on both sides from the winds which would most injure them, and is very warm. We found blue grapes along the road which were very good and sweet, and as good as any I have tasted in the Fatherland.

We went from the city, following the Broadway, over the *valey,* or the fresh water. Upon both sides of this way were many habitations of negroes, mulattoes and whites. These negroes were formerly the proper slaves of the (West India) company, but, in consequence of the frequent changes and conquests of the country, they have obtained their freedom and settled themselves down where they have thought proper, and thus on this road, where they have ground enough to live on with their families. We left the village, called the *Bouwerij*, lying on the right hand, and went through the woods to New Harlem, a tolerably large village situated on the south side of the island, directly opposite the place where the northeast creek and the East river come together, situated about three hours journey from New Amsterdam, like as old Harlem, in Europe, is about three hours distance from old Amsterdam. . . .

April 23, 1680. Mr. Sanders having provided us with horses, we rode out about nine o'clock, to visit the *Cahoos* which is the falls of the great *Maquas kil* (Mohawk river), which are the greatest falls, not only in New Netherland, but in North America, and perhaps, as far as is known, in the whole New World. We rode for two hours over beautiful, level, tillable land along the river, when we obtained a guide who was better acquainted with the road through the woods. He rode before us on horseback. In approaching the Cahoos from this direction, the roads are hilly and in the course of half an hour you have steep hills, deep valleys and narrow paths, which run round the precipices, where you must ride with care, in order to avoid the danger of falling over them, as sometimes happens. As you come near the falls, you can hear the roaring which makes everything tremble, but on reaching them and looking at them you see something wonderful, a great manifestation of God's power and sovereignty, of his wisdom and glory. We arrived there about noon. They are on one of the two branches into which the North river is divided up above, of almost equal size. This one turns to the west out of the highland, and coming here finds a blue rock which has a steep side, as long as the river is broad, which, according to my calculation is two hundred paces or more, and rather more than less, and about one hundred feet high. The river has more water at one time than another; and was now about six or eight feet deep. All this volume of water coming on this side, fell headlong upon a stony bottom this distance of an hundred feet. Anyone may judge whether that was not a spectacle, and whether it would not make a noise. There is a continual spray thrown up by the dashing of the water, and when the sun shines the figure of a rainbow may be seen through it. Sometimes there are two or three of them to be seen one above the other, according to the brightness of the sun and its parallax. There was now more water than usual in consequence of its having rained hard for several days, and the snow water having begun to run down from the high land. . . .

August 1. The beginning of this month brought to mind that we were in this region a year ago. We made good progress last night, east northeast. It was misty and rainy for which reason we could not take an observation. We reckoned we were in 45° 20′ and had sailed 96 miles, being about 100 miles northeast by north from Cape Race. The water was very clear which induced us to believe we were on a bank, not the great bank of Newfoundland, but the bank they call *Banc au vert.* After dinner the deep lead was thrown, as we had done for two or three days previously without sounding bottom. We now found thirty-eight fathoms of water and a bottom of white sand and small pebbles. Every thing was prepared in order to fish, most of the sails taken in, and the rest muzzled. We had at first three hooks and towards the last another, and in about three hours caught one hundred and fifty large codfish, which the captain salted down for the ship's provision. We had fresh fish for a day or two, but the English do not understand how to cook or dress fish. Catching such a large quantity of fish in such a short time was very exciting; it seemed as if the entire bottom of the sea were covered with them, but you did not see them. Two hooks were constantly being pulled up while the others were being let down. Our hearts could not otherwise than ascend to God, admiring him as the source of such abundance, in the bosom of the wide ocean as well as upon the land, of creatures which he subjects as it were by force, to unworthy and sinful men, who instead of being drawn thereby to him to glorify him and sanctify themselves and these creatures, by their use, to God, are not only not affected at his plenitude and goodness, but misuse such good creatures to the scorn and dishonor of their Creator. . . .

Louis Hennepin
(c. 1640–c. 1702)

Born at Ath, Belgium (then in Spanish possession), Father Louis Hennepin was a Franciscan priest of the austere Récollect branch of the Order. After time spent in Belgium, France, Germany, and Holland, he was sent as a willing missionary to New France (Canada) in 1675. The New World expedition he joined had been ordered by King Louis XIV and was led by the celebrated René Robert, Sieur de la Salle. Once in Quebec, Hennepin made many wilderness journeys in the region—often by canoe or snowshoes—in order to learn the Native American customs and languages that would facilitate his missionary work. In 1678 Hennepin accompanied La Salle on his famous exploration of the Great Lakes and much of what is now Michigan, Wisconsin, and Minnesota. Many of his greatest adventures occurred in 1680, when La Salle ordered Hennepin, along with several other men, to travel down the Illinois River and then up the Mississippi as far as possible. The men were taken captive by a band of Issati Sioux Indians, under whose control they traveled the upper Mississippi region; while captive, Hennepin came to the site of present-day Minneapolis, where he named the Falls of St. Anthony in honor of his patron saint, St. Anthony of Padua. After various wilderness adventures, Hennepin's freedom was negotiated by the French explorer Daniel Greysolon Du Lhut, with whom he subsequently traveled down the Mississippi, then up the Wisconsin River, and eventually back to St. Ignace, where he wintered before proceeding to Montreal, then Quebec and, in the autumn of 1681, back to Europe. There Hennepin crafted his journals into several important books. *Description de la Louisiane* (*A Description of Louisiana*; 1683) was considered not only lively but also reasonably accurate; *Nouvelle Découverte d'un très grand Pays, situé dans l'Amerique* (*A New Discovery of a Vast Country in America*; 1697), however, was popular but also deliberately inaccurate (for example, Hennepin here makes the false claim that he explored the lower Mississippi as far south as the Gulf). Exaggerations notwithstanding, the Franciscan explorer did offer richly detailed descriptions of the upper Mississippi and Great Lakes landscape. The excerpt that opens the following selection is the first published eyewitness account of the great Niagara Falls—although Hennepin wildly exaggerates the actual height of the "wonderful Downfall."

From *A New Discovery of a Vast Country in America* (1697)

A Description of the Fall of the River Niagara . . .

Betwixt the Lake *Ontario* and *Erié*, there is a vast and prodigious Cadence of Water which falls down after a surprising and astonishing manner, insomuch that the universe does not afford its Parallel. 'Tis true, *Italy* and *Suedeland* boast of some such Things; but we may well say they are but sorry Patterns, when compared to this of which we now speak. At the foot of this horrible Precipice, we meet with the River *Niagara*, which is not above half a quarter of a League broad, but is wonderfully deep in some places. It is so rapid above this Descent, that it violently hurries down the wild Beasts while endeavoring to pass it to feed on the other side, they not being able to withstand the force of its Current, which inevitably casts them down headlong above Six hundred foot.

This wonderful Downfall is compounded of two great Cross-streams of Water, and two Falls, with an Isle sloping along the middle of it. The Waters which fall from this vast height, do foam and boil after the most hideous manner imaginable, making an outrageous Noise, more terrible than that of Thunder; for when the Wind blows from off the South, their dismal roaring may be heard above fifteen Leagues off.

The River *Niagara* having thrown itself down this incredible Precipice, continues its impetuous course for two Leagues together, to the great Rock above-mentioned, with an inexpressible Rapidity: But having passed that, its Impetuosity relents, gliding along more gently for two Leagues, till it arrives at the Lake *Ontario* or *Frontenac.*

Any Bark or greater Vessel may pass from the Fort to the foot of this huge Rock above-mentioned. This Rock lies to the Westward, and is cut off from the Land by the River *Niagara,* about two Leagues farther down than the great Fall; for which two Leagues the People are obliged to carry their Goods overland; but the way is very good, and the Trees are but few, and they chiefly Firs and Oaks.

From the great Fall unto this Rock, which is to the West of the River, the two Brinks of it are so prodigious high, that it would make one tremble to look steadily upon the Water, rolling along with a Rapidity not to be imagined. Were it not for this vast Cataract, which interrupts Navigation, they might sail with Barks or greater Vessels, above Four hundred and fifty Leagues further, cross the Lake of Hurons, and up to the farther end of the Lake *Illinois;* which two Lakes we may well say are little Seas of fresh Water. . . .

A Particular Account of the River Mississippi; of the Country through Which It Flows . . .

From thirty Leagues below *Maroa,* down to the Sea, the Banks of the *Mississippi* are full of Reeds or Canes; but we observed about forty places, where one may land with great facility. The River overflows its Banks now and then; but the Inundation is not very considerable, because of the little Hills which stop its Waters. The Country beyond those Hills is the finest that ever I saw, it being a Plain, whose Bounds I don't know, adorned now and then with some Hills and Eminences covered with fine Trees, making the rarest Prospect in the World. The Banks of the small Rivers flowing through the Plain, are planted with Trees, which look as if they had been disposed into that curious Order by the Art of Men; and they are plentifully stocked with Fish, as well as the *Mississippi.* The Crocodiles are very dangerous upon this great River, as I have already observed; and they devour a Man if they can surprise him; but 'tis easy to avoid them, for they don't swim after Men, nor follow them ashore.

The Country affords all sorts of Game, as Turkey Cocks, Partridges, Quails, Parrots, Woodcocks, Turtledoves, and Wood Pigeons; and abundance of wild Bulls, wild Goats, Stags, Beavers, Otters, Martins, and wild Cats: But as we approached nearer the Sea, we saw no Beavers. I design to give a particular Account of these Creatures in another place; in the meantime we shall take notice of two others, who are unknown in *Europe.*

I have already mentioned a little Animal, like a Muskrat, that M. *la Salle* killed as we came from Fort *Miamis* to the *Illinois,* which deserves a particular Description. It looks like a Rat as to the Shape of its Body, but it is as big as a Cat: His Skin looks Silver-like, with some fair black Hair, which makes the Color the more admirable. His Tail is without any Hair, as big as a Man's Finger, and about a Foot long, wherewith he hangs himself to the Boughs of Trees. That Creature has under the Belly a kind of a Bag, wherein they put their young ones when they are pursued; which is one of the most wonderful things of the World, and a clear Demonstration of the Providence and Goodness of the Almighty, who takes so particular a Care of the meanest of his Creatures.

There is no fierce Beast in all that Country that dares attack Men; for the *Mechibichi,* the most terrible of all, and who devours all other Beasts whatsoever, runs away upon the approach of a Savage. The Head of that Creature is very like that of the spotted Lynx, but somewhat bigger: his Body is long, and as large as a wild Goat, but his Legs are shorter; his Paws are like a Cat's Foot; but the Claws are so long and strong, that no other Beast can resist them. When they have killed any Beast, they eat part of it, and carry the rest upon their Back, to hide it in the Woods; and I have been told that no other Beast dare meddle with it. Their Skin is much like that of a Lion, as well as their Tail; but their Head is much bigger.

The Savages gave us to understand that to the Westward of their Habitation, there are some Beasts who carry Men upon their Backs, and showed us the Hoof and part of the Leg of one, which was certainly the Hoof of a Horse; and surely Horses must not be utterly unknown in the Northern *America:* for then how could the Savages have drawn upon the Rock I have mentioned, the Figure of that Animal? . . .

The Great Straits Which the Author and His Companion Are Reduced to in Their Voyage

Picard, who had been very ill used by the Savages, had rather venture all than go up the River with *Aquipaguetin.* Six Charges of Powder was all that we had left, which obliged us to husband it as well as we could; wherefore we divided it into twenty, to shoot only for the future at Turtles or Wild Pigeons. When these also were spent, we had recourse to three Hooks, which we baited with some stinking Barbel that an Eagle happened to drop. We took nothing the two first Days, and were destitute of all means of subsistence. This made us, you must think, betake ourselves to Prayers with greater fervency than ever. And yet *Picard,* 'midst all our Misfortunes, could not forbear telling me, that he should pray to God with a much better Heart if his Belly were full.

I comforted both him and myself as well as I could, and desired him to row with all the force he had left, to see if we could catch a Tortoise. The next Morning, having rowed the best part of the Night, we found a Tortoise, which was no bigger than an ordinary Plate. We went to boiling him the same Minute on the Fire that we had kindled. We devoured it so hastily, that I did not observe that I cut the Gall, which made my Mouth as bitter as itself; but I ran immediately and gargled my Throat, and so fell to again, with the same eagerness as before.

Notwithstanding our famished Condition, we got at last to the *River of Bulls:* Here we cast our Hooks, which we baited with a white Fish that an Eagle had let fall. God, who never abandons those that trust in him, succored us very visibly on this occasion; for we had scarce finished our Prayers towards ten at Night, when *Picard,* who heard the Noise, quitted his Devotion, and ran to the Hooks, where he found two Barbels hung, which were so large, that I was forced to help him to get them out of the Water. We did not stand to study what Sauce we should make for these monstrous Fish, which weighed above twenty-five pound both; but having cut them to pieces, broiled 'em on the Coals. . . .

The Author's Reflections upon the Voyage to China; the Opinion of Most of the Savages of North America Concerning the Creation of the World, and the Immortality of the Soul

Our Discoveries have acquainted us with most part of *North America,* so that I don't question if the King of *Great Britain,* and the States of *Holland* should think fit to send us back thither to finish what we have so happily begun, but we should demonstrate what we could never yet give a clear account of, though many attempts have been made to it. It has been found impossible hitherto to go to *Japan* by the Frozen Sea; that Voyage has often been frustrated; and I am morally assured, that we can never succeed in it, till we have first discovered the Continent betwixt the Frozen Sea and *New Mexico.* I am persuaded that God preserved me in all the great dangers of my long voyages, that I might perfect that happy Discovery; and I here offer myself to undertake it, not doubting the success of the Enterprise (God willing) provided I am furnished with convenient means.

I don't wonder, that the learned are at a loss how *America* was peopled, and that infinite numbers of Nations settled upon that vast Continent. *America* is half the terrestrial Globe. The most expert Geographers are not thoroughly acquainted with it, and the inhabitants themselves, whom we discovered, and who in all likelihood should know best, don't know how their Ancestors came thither; and certainly if in *Europe* we wanted the Art of Writing (as those People do) which in a manner makes the dead live again, recalls what's past, and preserves the memory of things, I am afraid we should not be less ignorant than those Savages.

The greatest part of the Barbarians in *North America* have generally a Notion of some sort of Creation of the World; they say, Heaven, Earth and Mankind were made by a Woman, and that she and her Son govern the World, and for this reason, perhaps it is, that they reckon their Genealogies by Women. They say farther, that the Son is the Author of all good things, and the Woman of all Evil. That both of them enjoy perfect Felicity. The Woman, they say, fell out of Heaven big with Child, and lighted upon the back of a Tortoise, who saved her from drowning. When we object against the Ridiculousness of their Belief, they usually answer, that such an Objection is of force with them that make it, but is of no weight against them, because they look upon themselves to be created after another manner than the *Europeans* are.

Other Savages upon the same Continent, are of opinion, that a certain Spirit called *Otkon* by the *Iroquois,* and *Atahauta* by the other Barbarians at the Mouth of the River of St. *Laurence,* is the Creator of the World, and that one *Messou* repaired it after the Deluge. In this manner do they alter and confound by their Traditions that Knowledge of the universal Deluge, which their Ancestors probably had: they say, that this *Messou* or *Otkon* being a hunting one day, his Dogs lost themselves in a great Lake, which thereupon overflowing, covered the whole Earth in a short time, and swallowed up the World. They add, that this *Messou* or *Otkon* gathered a little Earth together by the help of some Animals, and made use of this Earth to repair the World again. They think the *Europeans* inhabit another World different from theirs; and when we go about to undeceive them, and teach them truly how the universe was created, they say all that may be true enough of the World we live upon, but 'tis quite another thing with theirs; Nay, they often ask us, whether we have a Sun and Moon in *Europe* as well as they.

There are another sort of Savages who dwell at the Mouth of the River of St. *Laurence* and *Mississippi,* that tell us a very odd Story; they say much like the former that a Woman came down from Heaven, and hovered a while in the Air, because she could find no place to set her Foot upon. The Fish of the Sea compassionating her, held a Council to determine who should receive her. The Tortoise offered himself, and presented his Back above Water, the Woman placed herself upon it, and stayed there. In time the Filth of the Sea gathering and settling about the Tortoise by little and little, formed a great extent of Land, which at present is that we call *America.* . . .

Though they believe that the Soul is Corporeal (for they understand nothing else by their *Otkon, Atahauta,* or *Manitou,* but some material principal Being, that gives life and motion to all things) nevertheless they profess their Belief of the Immortality of the Soul, and a Life to come, in which they shall enjoy all sorts of pleasure; as Hunting, and Fish in abundance, Corn for those that sow it, for some never sow Corn; Tobacco, and a thousand other Curiosities and Conveniences. They say the Soul does not leave the Body as soon as it dies, and therefore they take care to lay by the Body a Bow, Arrows, Corn, and fat Meat, for the Dead to subsist upon till they reach the Country of Souls.

And because they think all sensible things have Souls, therefore they reckon that after Death, men hunt the Souls of Beavers, Elks, Foxes, Otters, and other Animals. They believe that the Souls of those Rackets which they wear under their Feet in Wintertime to keep 'em from sinking into the Snow, serve 'em for the same use in the next Life, as well as the Souls of Bows and Arrows to kill Beasts with. And so they fancy of the Fish likewise, and therefore the Souls will have occasion say they for the Arms interred with the Dead; the dead Bodies have no need of the Arms and Victuals that are set by 'em, no longer than till they get to the Country of Souls. . . .

Of Their Manner of Fishing

The Savages that dwell in the North fish in a different manner from those of the South: The first catch all sorts of Fish with Nets, Hooks, and Harping-irons, as they do in *Europe*. I have seen them fish in a very pleasant manner: They take a Fork of Wood with two Grains or Points, and fit a Gin to it, almost the same way that in *France* they catch Partridges: After they put it in the Water, and when the Fish, which are in greater plenty by far than with us, go to pass through, and find they are entered into the Gin, they snap together this sort of Nippers or Pinchers, and catch the Fish by the Gills.

The *Iroquois* in the fishing season sometimes make use of a Net of forty or fifty fathom long, which they put in a great *Canoe*; after they cast it in an oval Form in convenient places in the Rivers. I have often admired their dexterity in this Affair. They take sometimes four hundred white Fish, besides many Sturgeons, which they draw to the Bank of the River with Nets made of Nettles. To fish in this manner, there must be two Men at each end of the Net to draw it dexterously to the shore. They take likewise a prodigious quantity of Fish in the River of *Niagara*, which are extremely well tasted.

The Fishery is so great in this place, that it's capable to furnish with Fish of several sorts the greatest City in *Europe*. It's not to be wondered at. The Fish continually swim up the River from the Sea towards the Spring, to find convenient places to spawn in. The River of St. *Laurence* receives in this part of *Niagara* an infinite quantity of Water from the four great Lakes of which we have spoke, and which may properly be called little freshwater Seas. This great deluge of Water tumbling furiously over the greatest and most dreadful Leap in the World, an infinite number of Fish take great delight to spawn here, and as it were stagnate here, because they cannot get over this huge Cataract: So that the quantity taken here is incredible.

Whilst I was in the Mission of the Fort *Frontenac*, I went to see this Leap, which comes from a River in the North, and falls into a great *Basin* of the Lake *Ontario*, big enough to hold a hundred Men of War. Being there, I taught the Savages to catch Fish with their Hands: I caused Trees to be cut down in the Spring, and to be rolled down to the Bank of the River, that I might lie upon them without wetting me; and after I thrust my Arm into the Water up to the Elbow, where I found a prodigious quantity of Fish of different Species; I laid hold on them by the Gills, gently stroking them; and when I had at several times taken fifty or sixty large Fish, I went to warm and refresh me, that I might return fresher to the Sport: I cast them into a Sack which a Savage held in his hand. With these I fed above fifty *Iroquois* Families of *Ganneousse*, and by the assistance of *Monsieur de la Salle*, taught them to plant the Indian Corn, and to instruct their Children in the Christian Religion at the Fort *Frontenac*.

PART TWO

The Eighteenth Century

One day I undertook a tour through the country, and the diversity and beauties of nature I met with in this charming season, expelled every gloomy and vexatious thought. Just at the close of day the gentle gales retired, and left the place to the disposal of a profound calm. Not a breeze shook the most tremulous leaf. I had gained the summit of a commanding ridge, and, looking round with astonishing delight, beheld the ample plains, the beauteous tracts below. On the other hand, I surveyed the famous river Ohio, that rolled in silent dignity, marking the western boundary of Kentucky with inconceivable grandeur. At a vast distance I beheld the mountains lift their venerable brows, and penetrate the clouds. All things were still. I kindled a fire near a fountain of sweet water, and feasted on the loin of a buck, which a few hours before I had killed. The fallen shades of night soon overspread the whole hemisphere, and the earth seemed to gasp after the hovering moisture. My roving excursion this day had fatigued my body, and diverted my imagination. I laid me down to sleep, and I awoke not until the sun had chased away the night.

DANIEL BOONE

The Adventures of Colonel Daniel Boon . . . (1784)

Sarah Kemble Knight
(1666–1727)

Bostonian Sarah Kemble was married to a much older man, Richard Knight, while in her early twenties. Well before her husband's death (probably in 1706), Knight had become skilled in various matters of practical business and law, particularly those having to do with the settlement of estates. When, in 1704, her cousin Caleb Trowbridge died, leaving a young widow, Knight decided to travel from Boston to New Haven, Connecticut (a journey of approximately 150 miles), to help settle her cousin's estate. Perhaps appreciating how unusual it was for a woman to travel alone so far through the wilderness, "Madam Knight" decided to keep a journal of her adventures traveling to Connecticut and back. Written in 1704–5, but not published until 1825, Knight's *Journal* is a rare and valuable document for a number of reasons. In addition to being one of the relatively few surviving early-eighteenth-century documents written by a woman, the *Journal* also offers a surprisingly secular account of a wilderness that, even in its darkest aspects, is not represented as the realm of demons and devils. And Knight's keen eye for detail, incisive observations on nature and culture, use of humor, and focus on movement make her one of America's earliest woman travel writers. In addition, the *Journal* offers a lively narrative within which the trials of the protagonist are framed in terms of challenge, adventure, and accomplishment. With the help of hired guides Knight traveled rough forest roads on horseback — often at night, on exhausted mounts, and in inclement weather — fording swollen streams or stemming them in a small canoe. The following brief selection from the *Journal* demonstrates the legitimate fear that wilderness could inspire in a woman traveler of this period, but it also suggests that Knight appreciated the challenge of the adventure, the beauty of the wilderness, and the warmth of the homecoming she received at the conclusion of what was then a very long and arduous journey.

From *The Journal of Madam Knight* (1704–1705/1825)

Having here discharged the Ordinary for self and Guide, (as I understood was the custom,) About Three, afternoon, went on with my Third Guide, who Rode very hard; and having crossed Providence Ferry, we come to a River which they Generally Ride through. But I dare not venture; so the Post got a Lad and Canoe to carry me to t'other side, and he rid through and Led my horse. The Canoe was very small and shallow, so that when we were in she seemed ready to take in water, which greatly terrified me, and caused me to be very circumspect, sitting with my hands fast on each side, my eyes steady, not daring so much as to lodge my tongue a hair's breadth more on one side of my mouth than t'other, nor so much as think on Lott's wife, for a wry thought would have overset our wherry: But was soon put out of this pain, by feeling the Canoe on shore, which I as soon almost saluted with my feet; and Rewarding my sculler, again mounted and made the best of our way forwards. The Road here was very even and the day pleasant, it being now near Sunset. But the Post told me we had near 14 miles to Ride to the next Stage, (where we were to Lodge) I asked him of the rest of the Road, foreseeing we must travail in the night. He told me there was a bad River we were to Ride through, which was so very fierce a horse could sometimes hardly stem it: But it was but narrow, and we should soon be over. I cannot express the concern of mind this relation set me in: no thoughts but those of the dangerous River could entertain my Imagination, and they were as formidable as various, still Tormenting me with blackest Ideas of my Approaching fate — Sometimes seeing myself drowning, otherwhiles drowned, and at the best like a holy Sister Just come out of a Spiritual Bath in dripping Garments.

Now was the Glorious Luminary, with his swift Coursers arrived at his Stage, leaving poor me with the rest of this part of the lower world in darkness, with which we were soon Surrounded. The only Glimmering we now had was from the spangled Skies, Whose Imperfect Reflections rendered every Object formidable. Each lifeless Trunk, with its shattered Limbs, appeared an Armed Enemy; and every little stump like a Ravenous devourer. Nor could I so much as discern my Guide, when at any distance, which added to the terror.

Thus, absolutely lost in Thought, and dying with the very thoughts of drowning, I come up with the Post, who I did not see till even with his Horse: he told me he stopped for me; and we Rode on Very deliberately a few paces, when we entered a Thicket of Trees and Shrubs, and I perceived by the Horse's going, we were on the descent of a Hill, which, as we come nearer the bottom, 'twas totally dark with the Trees that surrounded it. But I knew by the Going of the Horse we had entered the water, which my Guide told me was the hazardous River he had told me of; and he, Riding up close to my Side, Bid me not fear — we should be over Immediately. I now rallied all the Courage I was mistress of, Knowing that I must either Venture my fate of drowning, or be left like the Children in the wood. So, as the Post bid me, I gave Reins to my Nag; and sitting as Steady as Just before in the Canoe, in a few minutes got safe to the other side, which he told me was the Narragansett country.

Here We found great difficulty in Travailing, the way being very narrow, and on each side the Trees and bushes gave us very unpleasant welcomes with their

Branches and boughs, which we could not avoid, it being so exceeding dark. My Guide, as before so now, put on harder than I, with my weary bones, could follow; so left me and the way behind him. Now Returned my distressed apprehensions of the place where I was: the dolesome woods, my Company next to none, Going I knew not whither, and encompassed with Terrifying darkness; The least of which was enough to startle a more Masculine courage. Added to which the Reflections, as in the afternoon of the day that my Call was very Questionable, which till then I had not so Prudently as I ought considered. Now, coming to the foot of a hill, I found great difficulty in ascending; But being got to the Top, was there amply recompensed with the friendly Appearance of the Kind Conductress of the night, just then Advancing above the Horizontal Line. The Raptures which the Sight of that fair Planet produced in me, caused me, for the Moment, to forget my present weariness and past toils; and Inspired me for most of the remaining way with very divining thoughts, some of which, with the other Occurrences of the day, I reserved to note down when I should come to my Stage. My thoughts on the sight of the moon were to this purpose:

Fair Cynthia, all the Homage that I may
Unto a Creature, unto thee I pay;
In Lonesome woods to meet so kind a guide,
To Me's more worth than all the world beside.
Some Joy I felt just now, when safe got o're
Yon Surly River to this Rugged shore,
Trees Deeming Rough welcomes from these clownish
Better than Lodgings with Nereides.
Yet swelling fears surprise; all dark appears —
Nothing but Light can dissipate those fears.
My fainting vitals can't lend strength to say,
But softly whisper, O I wish 'twere day.
The murmur hardly warmed the Ambient air,
E're thy Bright Aspect rescues from despair:
Makes the old Hag her sable mantle loose,
And a Bright Joy does through my Soul diffuse.
The Boistero's Trees now Lend a Passage Free,
And pleasant prospects thou givest light to see.

From hence we kept on, with more ease than before: the way being smooth and even, the night warm and serene, and the Tall and thick Trees at a distance, especially when the moon glared light through the branches, filled my Imagination with the pleasant delusion of a Sumptuous city, filled with famous Buildings and churches, with their spiring steeples, Balconies, Galleries and I know not what:

Grandeurs which I had heard of, and which the stories of foreign countries had given me the Idea of.

> Here stood a Lofty church—there is a steeple,
> And there the Grand Parade—O see the people!
> That Famous Castle there, were I but nigh,
> To see the mote and Bridge and walls so high—
> They're very fine! says my deluded eye.

Being thus agreeably entertained without a thought of any thing but thoughts themselves, I on a sudden was Roused from these pleasing Imaginations, by the Post's sounding his horn, which assured me he was arrived at the Stage, where we were to Lodge: and that music was then most musical and agreeable to me. . . .

The next night at Haven's and had Roast fowl, and the next day we come to a river which by Reason of the Freshets coming down was swelled so high we feared it impassable and the rapid stream was very terrifying—However we must over and that in a small Canoe. Mr. Rogers assuring me of his good Conduct, I after a stay of near an hour on the shore for consultation went into the Canoe, and Mr. Rogers paddled about 100 yards up the Creek by the shore side, turned into the swift stream and dexterously steering her in a moment we come to the other side as swiftly passing as an arrow shot out of the Bow by a strong arm. I stayed on the shore till He returned to fetch our horses, which he caused to swim over himself bringing the furniture in the Canoe. But it is past my skill to express the Exceeding fright all their transactions formed in me. We were now in the colony of the Massachusetts and taking Lodgings at the first Inn we come to had a pretty difficult passage the next day which was the second of March by reason of the sloughy ways then thawed by the Sun. Here I met Capt. John Richards of Boston who was going home, So being very glad of his Company we Rode something harder than hitherto, and missing my way in going up a very steep Hill, my horse dropped down under me as Dead; this new surprise no little hurt me meeting it Just at the Entrance into Dedham from whence we intended to reach home that night. But was now obliged to get another Horse there and leave my own, resolving for Boston that night if possible. But in going over the Causeway at Dedham the Bridge being overflowed by the high waters coming down I very narrowly escaped falling over into the river Horse and all which 'twas almost a miracle I did not—now it grew late in the afternoon and the people having very much discouraged us about the sloughy way which they said we should find very difficult and hazardous it so wrought on me being tired and dispirited and disappointed of my desires of going home that I agreed to Lodge there that night which we did at the house of one Draper, and the next day being March 3d we got safe home to Boston, where I found my aged and tender mother and my Dear and only Child in good health with open arms ready to receive me, and my Kind relations and friends flocking in to welcome me and hear the story of my transactions and travails I having this day been five months from home and now I cannot fully express my Joy and Satisfaction. But desire sincerely to adore my Great Benefactor for thus graciously carrying forth and returning in safety his unworthy handmaid.

Robert Beverley
(c. 1673–1722)

A Virginia gentleman, politician, and agriculturist, Robert Beverley held various offices in the Virginia legislature and was married to Ursula Byrd, sister of the influential colonial writer and intellectual William Byrd II. Many of Beverley's natural historical observations were made on and around Beverley Park, the six-thousand-acre estate where, among other agricultural experiments, he attempted to introduce successful viniculture to the colonies. Born and bred in Virginia, though educated in England (as was then common for the sons of landed gentry), Beverley is notable for writing from the position of a Virginian; he differed from many colonials in thinking of himself as an American, rather than as a displaced Englishman abroad in the colonies simply to make his fortune. In his major work, *The History and Present State of Virginia*, Beverley deliberately employed a simple, direct American idiom that he hoped would accurately convey the life and landscape of the colonial South. His sympathetic portrayals of Native Americans often displeased fellow Virginia planters, for whom Indian attacks along the frontier represented a serious hazard. Indeed, Beverley went so far as to assert that Indians had legitimate reasons to "lament the arrival of the Europeans," who had deprived them of their ancestral lands while introducing "drunkenness and luxury" among them. And although Beverley was interested in agricultural improvements, he also had an unusual appreciation for wilderness, a "simple state of nature" he felt offered the naturalist-observer an "endless Succession of Native Pleasures." Despite its occasional borrowings from Thomas Hariot and John Smith, part 2 of *The History and Present State of Virginia*, "The Natural Productions and Conveniences of the Country. . . ," is the most detailed natural historical account written by a colonial southerner. The following selections demonstrate Beverley's remarkably thorough knowledge of regional natural history, while also suggesting his genuine interest in local Native American fishing and hunting practices.

From *The History and Present State of Virginia* (1705)

Of the Fish

As for Fish, both of Fresh and Saltwater, of Shellfish, and others, no Country can boast of more Variety, greater Plenty, or of better in their several Kinds.

In the Spring of the Year, Herrings come up in such abundance into their Brooks and Fords, to spawn, that it is almost impossible to ride through, without treading on them. Thus do those poor Creatures expose their own Lives to some Hazard, out of their Care to find a more convenient Reception for their Young, which are not yet alive. Thence it is, that at this Time of the Year, the Freshes of the Rivers, like that of the *Broadruck*, stink of Fish.

Besides these Herrings, there come up likewise into the Freshes from the Sea, Multitudes of Shads, Rocks, Sturgeon, and some few Lampreys, which fasten themselves to the Shad, as the *Remora* of *Imperatus* is said to do to the Shark of *Tiburone*. They continue their stay there about Three Months. The Shads at their first coming up, are fat and fleshy; but they waste so extremely in Milting and Spawning, that at their going down they are poor, and seem fuller of Bones, only because they have less Flesh. It is upon this Account, (I suppose) that those in the *Severn*, which in *Gloucester* they call *Twaits*, are said at first to want those intermusculary Bones, which afterwards they abound with. As these are in the Freshes, so the Salts afford at certain Times of the Year, many other Kinds of Fish in infinite Shoals, such as the Oldwife, a Fish not much unlike an Herring, and the Sheepshead, a Sort of Fish, which they esteem in the Number of their best.

There is likewise great Plenty of other Fish all the Summer long; and almost in every Part of the Rivers and Brooks, there are found of different Kinds: Wherefore I shall not pretend to give a Detail of them, but venture to mention the Names only of such as I have eaten and seen myself, and so leave the rest to those that are better skilled in Natural History. However, I may add, that besides all those that I have met with myself I have heard of a great many very good sorts, both in the Salts and Freshes; and such People too, as have not always spent their Time in that Country have commended them to me, beyond any they had ever ate before.

Those which I know of myself, I remember by the Names. Of Herrings, Rocks, Sturgeons, Shads, Oldwives, Sheepsheads, Black and red Drums, Trouts, Taylors, Green-Fish, Sunfish, Bass, Chub, Place, Flounders, Whitings, Fatbacks, Maids, Wives, Small-Turtle, Crabs, Oysters, Mussels, Cockles, Shrimps, Needlefish, Bream, Carp, Pike, Jack, Mullets, Eels, Conger Eels, Perch, and Cats, *&c.*

Those which I remember to have seen there, of the Kinds that are not eaten, are the Whale, Porpoise, Shark, Dogfish, Gar, Stingray, Thornback, Sawfish, Toadfish, Frogfish-Fish, Land Crabs, Fiddlers, and Periwinkles. One Day as I was hauling a Seine upon the Salts, I caught a small Fish, about Two Inches and an Half long, in Shape something resembling a Scorpion, but of a Dirty dark Color; I was a little shy of handling it, though, I believe, there was no Hurt in it. This I judged to be that Fish, which Mr. *Purchase* in his *Pilgrims*, and Capt. *Smith* in his General History, Pag. 28. affirm to be extremely like St. *George's* Dragon, except only that it wants Feet and Wings.

Before the Arrival of the *English* there, the *Indians* had Fish in such vast Plenty, that the Boys and Girls would take a pointed Stick, and strike the lesser sort, as they Swam upon the Flats. The larger Fish, that kept in deeper Water, they were put to a little more Difficulty to take; But for these they made Weirs; that is, a Hedge of small rived Sticks, or Reeds, of the Thickness of a Man's Finger, these they wove together in a Row, with Straps of Green Oak, or other tough Wood, so close that the small Fish could not pass through. Upon High-Water Mark, they pitched one End of this Hedge, and the other they extended into the River, to the Depth of Eight or Ten Foot, fastening it with Stakes, making Cods out from the Hedge on one side, almost at the End, and leaving a Gap for the Fish to go into them, which were contrived so, that the Fish could easily find their Passage into those Cods, when they were at the Gap but not see their Way out again, when they were in: Thus if they offered to pass through, they were taken.

Sometimes they made such a Hedge as this, quite across a Creek at High Water, and at Low would go into the Run, so contracted into a narrow Compass, and take out what Fish they pleased.

At the Falls of the Rivers, where the Water is shallow, and the Current strong, the *Indians* use another kind of Weir, thus made: They make a Dam of loose Stone, whereof there is plenty at hand, quite across the River, leaving One, Two, or more Spaces or Trunnels, for the Water to pass through; at the Mouth of which they set a Pot of Reeds, wove in Form of a Cone, whose Base is about Three Foot, and perpendicular Ten, into which the Swiftness of the Current carries the Fish, and wedges them so fast, that they cannot possibly return.

The *Indian* Way of Catching Sturgeon, when they came into the narrow part of the Rivers, was by a Man's clapping a Noose over their Tail, and by keeping fast his hold. Thus a Fish finding itself entangled, would flounce, and often pull him under Water, and then that Man was counted a *Cockarouse*, or brave Fellow, that would not let go; till with Swimming, Wading, and Diving, he had tired the Sturgeon, and brought it ashore. These Sturgeons would also often leap into their Canoes, in crossing the River, as many of them do still every Year, into the Boats of the *English*.

They have also another Way of Fishing like those on the *Euxine* Sea, by the Help of a blazing Fire by Night. They make a Hearth in the Middle of their Canoe, raising it within Two Inches of the Edge; upon this they lay their burning

Lightwood, split into small Shivers, each Splinter whereof will blaze and burn End for End, like a Candle: 'Tis one Man's Work to tend this Fire and keep it flaming. At each End of the Canoe stands an *Indian*, with a Gig, or pointed Spear, setting the Canoe forward with the Butt-end of the Spear, as gently as he can, by that Means stealing upon the Fish, without any Noise, or disturbing of the Water. Then they with great Dexterity, dart these Spears into the Fish, and so take them. Now there is a double Convenience in the Blaze of this Fire; for it not only dazzles the Eyes of the Fish, which will lie still, glaring upon it, but likewise discovers the Bottom of the River clearly to the Fisherman, which the Daylight does not. . . .

'Tis a good Diversion to observe the Manner of the Fishing-Hawks preying upon Fish, which may be seen every fair Day all the Summer long, and especially in a Morning. At the first coming of the Fish in the Spring, these Birds of Prey are surprisingly eager. I believe, in the Dead of Winter, they Fish farther off at Sea, or remain among the craggy uninhabited Islands, upon the Sea Coast. I have often been pleasantly entertained, by seeing these Hawks take the Fish out of the Water, and as they were flying away with their Quarry, the bald Eagles take it from them again. I have often observed the first of these hover over the Water, and rest upon the Wing, some Minutes together, without the least change of Place, and then from a vast Height, dart directly into the Water, and there plunge down for the Space of Half a Minute, or more, and at last bring up with him a Fish, which he could hardly rise with; then, having got upon the Wing again, he would shake himself so powerfully, that he threw the Water like a Mist about him; afterwards away he'd fly to the Woods with his Game, if he were not overlooked by the Bald Eagle, and robbed by the Way, which very frequently happens. For the Bald Eagle no sooner perceives a Hawk that has taken his Prey, but he immediately pursues, and strives to get above him in the Air, which if he can once attain, the Hawk for fear of being torn by him, lets the Fish drop, and so by the Loss of his Dinner, compounds for his own Safety. The poor Fish is no sooner loosed from the Hawk's Talons, but the Eagle shoots himself, with wonderful Swiftness, after it, and catches it in the Air, leaving all further Pursuit of the Hawk, which has no other Remedy, but to go and fish for another.

Walking once with a Gentleman in an Orchard by the Riverside, early in the Spring, before the Fish were by us perceived to appear in Shoal-Water, or near the Shores, and before any had been caught by the People, we heard a great Noise in the Air just over our Heads, and looking up, we see an Eagle in close pursuit of a Hawk, that had a great Fish in his Pounces. The Hawk was as low as the Apple-Trees, before he would let go his Fish, thinking to recover the Wood, which was just by, where the Eagles dare never follow, for fear of bruising themselves. But, notwithstanding the Fish was dropped so low, and though it did not fall above Thirty Yards from us, yet we with our Hallooing, Running and casting up our Hats, could hardly save the Fish from the Eagle, and if it had been dropped Two Yards higher, he would have got it: But we at last took Possession of it alive, carried it Home, and had it dressed forthwith. It served Five of us very plentifully, without any other Addition, and some to the Servants. This Fish was a Rock near Two Foot long, very fat, and a great Rarity for the Time of Year, as well as for the Manner of its being taken.

These Fishing-Hawks, in more plentiful Seasons, will catch a Fish, and loiter about with it in the Air, on purpose to have a Chase with an Eagle; and when he does not appear soon enough, the Hawk will make a saucy Noise, and insolently defy him. This has been frequently seen, by Persons who have observed their Fishings. . . .

Of Wild Fowl, and Hunted Game

As in Summer, the Rivers and Creeks are filled with Fish, so in Winter they are in many Places covered with Fowl. There are such a Multitude of Swans, Geese, Brants, Sheldrakes, Ducks of several Sorts, Mallard, Teal, Bluewings, and many other Kinds of Waterfowl, that the Plenty of them is incredible. I am but a small Sportsman, yet with a Fowling Piece, have killed above Twenty of them at a Shot. In like manner are the Millponds, and great Runs in the Woods stored with these Wildfowl, at certain Seasons of the Year.

The Shores, Marshy Grounds, Swamps, and Savannahs, are also stored with the like plenty of other Game of all Sorts, as Cranes, Curlews, Herons, Snipes, Woodcocks, Saurers, Ox-eyes, Plover, Larks, and many other good Birds for the Table that they have not yet found a Name for. Not to mention Beavers, Otters, Muskrats, Minxes, and an infinite Number of other wild Creatures.

Although the Inner Lands want these Benefits (which, however, no Pond or Slash is without,) yet even they, have the Advantage of Wild Turkeys, of an incredible Bigness, Pheasants, Partridges, Pigeons, and an Infinity of small Birds, as well as Deer, Hares, Foxes, Raccoons, Squirrels, Possums. And upon the Frontier Plantations they meet with Bears, Panthers, Wildcats, Elks, Buffaloes and Wild Hogs, which yield Pleasure, as well as Profit to the Sportsman. And though some of these Names may seem frightful to the *English*, who hear not of them in their own Country; yet they are not so there; for all these Creatures ever fly from the Face of Man, doing no Damage but to the Cattle and Hogs, which the *Indians*, never troubled themselves about.

Here I can't omit a strange Rarity in the Female *Possum*, which I myself have seen. They have a false Belly, or loose Skin quite over the Belly; this never sticks to the Flesh of the Belly, but may be looked into at all Times, after they have been concerned in Procreation. In the Hinder-part of this, is an Overture big enough for a small Hand to pass into: Hither the young Ones, after they are full haired, and strong enough to run about, do fly whenever any Danger appears, or when they go to rest, or suck. This they continue till they have learned to live without the Dam: But, what is yet stranger, the young Ones are bred in this false Belly without ever being within the true One. They are formed at the Teat, and there they grow for several Weeks together into perfect Shape, becoming visibly larger, till at last they get Strength, Sight, and Hair; and then they drop off, and rest in this false Belly, going in and out at Pleasure. I have observed them thus fastened at the Teat, from the Bigness of a Fly, until they became as large as a Mouse. Neither is it any Hurt to the old One to open this Budget, and look in upon her Young.

The *Indians* had no other Way of taking their Water or Land-Fowl, but by the Help of Bows, and Arrows: Yet, so great was their Plenty that with this Weapon only, they killed what Numbers they pleased. And when the Waterfowl kept far from Shore, (as in warmer Weather they sometimes did,) they took their Canoes, and paddled after them.

But they had a better Way of killing the Elks, Buffaloes, Deer, and greater Game, by a Method which we call Fire-Hunting: That is, a Company of them would go together back into the Woods, any time in the Winter, when the Leaves were fallen, and so dry, that they would burn; and being come to the Place designed, they would Fire the Woods, in a Circle of Five or Six Miles Compass; and when they had completed the first Round, they retreated inward, each at his due Distance, and put Fire to the Leaves and Grass afresh, to accelerate the Work, which ought to be finished with the Day. This they repeat, till the Circle be so contracted, that they can see their Game herded all together in the Middle, panting and almost stifled with Heat and Smoke; for the poor Creatures being frightened at the Flame, keep running continually round, thinking to run from it, and dare not pass through the Fire; by which Means they are brought at last into a very narrow Compass. Then the *Indians* let fly their Arrows at them, and (which is very strange) though they stand all round quite clouded in Smoke, yet they rarely shoot each other. By this means they destroy all the Beasts, collected within that Circle. They make all this Slaughter only for the sake of the Skins, leaving the Carcasses to perish in the Woods.

John Lawson
(d. 1711)

Although nothing is known of the birth or early life of John Lawson, he was, during the final decade of his life, among the most important scientific observers and travel writers in the southern colonies, and his major work, *A New Voyage to Carolina*, was the only book to come out of North Carolina during its administration by the Lords Proprietors. Lawson came to the colonies in the summer of 1700, probably as a collector for and correspondent to James Petiver, a London-based naturalist who was a great scientific patron. That winter Lawson surveyed interior Carolina, then a trackless wilderness virtually unknown to white settlers. Traveling with the aid of Indian guides, Lawson completed a 59-day, 550-mile journey through the wilds of what is now South and North Carolina—observing, recording, and collecting as he went. In 1701 he built a cabin near what is now New Bern, North Carolina, and by turns traveled, collected, and surveyed. In 1708, or early 1709, Lawson returned to England to arrange publication of *A New Voyage* and, while there, was appointed a commissioner to settle the disputed boundary between Virginia and North Carolina. Returning to North Carolina in 1710, he co-founded Bath and New Bern, the two oldest towns in the state. Although fully occupied with settlements and surveys, Lawson aspired to follow *A New Voyage* with a more comprehensive natural history of the plants, beasts, birds, fishes, insects, fossils, and soils of the region—"a compleat history of these parts which I heartily wish I may live to see publisht." Lawson's wish was in vain. His role as an agent of incursion into Native American lands had earned him the enmity of various tribes, and in September 1711 he was captured and tortured to death by a band of Coree Indians. *A New Voyage* was widely plagiarized by John Brickell and even William Byrd, but Lawson received little credit for his important work, which was subsequently eclipsed by the more comprehensive natural history published by Mark Catesby. Although it contains several of the "vulgar errours" characteristic of natural historians of the period, the following selection also suggests the breadth of Lawson's observations and the liveliness of his prose.

From *A New Voyage to Carolina* (1709)

The *Panther* is of the Cat's kind; about the height of a very large Greyhound of a reddish Color, the same as a Lion. He climbs Trees with the greatest Agility imaginable, is very strong-limbed, catching a piece of Meat from any Creature he strikes at. His Tail is exceeding long; his Eyes look very fierce and lively, are large, and of a grayish Color; his Prey is, Swine's-flesh, Deer, or any thing he can take; no Creature is so nice and clean, as this, in his Food. When he has got his Prey, he fills his Belly with the Slaughter, and carefully lays up the Remainder covering it very neatly with Leaves, which if anything touches, he never eats any more of it. He purrs as Cats do; if taken when Young, is never to be reclaimed from his wild Nature. He hollows like a Man in the Woods, when killed, which is by making him take a Tree, as the least Cur will presently do; then the Huntsmen shoot him; if they do not kill him outright, he is a dangerous Enemy, when wounded, especially to the Dogs that approach him. This Beast is the greatest Enemy to the Planter, of any Vermin in *Carolina.* His Flesh looks as well as any Shambles-Meat whatsoever; a great many People eat him, as choice Food; but I never tasted of a Panther, so cannot commend the Meat, by my own Experience. His Skin is a warm Covering for the *Indians* in Winter, though not esteemed amongst the choice Furs. This Skin dressed, makes fine Women's Shoes, or Men's Gloves.

The Mountain-Cat, so called, because he lives in the Mountainous Parts of *America.* He is a Beast of Prey, as the Panther is, and nearest to him in Bigness and Nature.

This Cat is quite different from those in *Europe;* being more nimble and fierce, and larger; his Tail does not exceed four Inches. He makes a very odd sort of Cry in the Woods, in the Night. He is spotted as the Leopard is, though some of them are not (which may happen, when their Furs are out of Season) he climbs a Tree very dexterously, and preys as the Panther does. He is a great Destroyer of young Swine. I knew an Island, which was possessed by these Vermin, unknown to the Planter who put thereon a considerable Stock of Swine; but never took one back; for the wild Cats destroyed them all. He takes most of his Prey by Surprise, getting up the Trees, which they pass by or under, and thence leaping directly upon them. Thus he takes Deer (which he cannot catch by running) and fastens his Teeth into their Shoulders and sucks them. They run with him, till they fall down for want of strength, and become a Prey to the Enemy. Hares, Birds, and all he meets, that he can conquer, he destroys. The Fur is approved to wear as a Stomacher, for weak and cold Stomachs. They are likewise used to line Muffs, and Coats withal, in cold Climates.

The Wolf of *Carolina,* is the Dog of the Woods. The *Indians* had no other Curs, before the Christians came amongst them. They are made domestic. When wild, they are neither so large, nor fierce, as the *European* Wolf. They are not Manslayers; neither is any Creature in *Carolina,* unless wounded. They go in great Droves in the Night, to hunt Deer, which they do as well as the best Pack of Hounds. Nay, one of these will hunt down a Deer. They are often so poor, that they can hardly run. When they catch no Prey, they go to a Swamp, and fill their Belly full of Mud; if afterwards they chance to get any thing of Flesh, they will disgorge the Mud, and eat the other. When they hunt in the Night, that there is a great many together, they make the most hideous and frightful Noise, that ever was heard. The Fur makes good Muffs. The Skin dressed to a Parchment makes the best Drum-heads, and if tanned makes the best sort of Shoes for the Summer-Countries.

Tigers are never met withal in the Settlement; but are more to the Westward, and are not numerous on this Side the Chain of Mountains. I once saw one, that was larger than a Panther, and seemed to be a very bold Creature. The *Indians* that hunt in those Quarters, say, they are seldom met withal. It seems to differ from the Tiger of *Asia* and *Africa*.

Polecats or Skunks in *America*, are different from those in *Europe*. They are thicker, and of a great many Colors; not all alike, but each differing from another in the particular Color. They smell like a Fox, but ten times stronger. When a Dog encounters them, they piss upon him, and he will not be sweet again in a Fortnight or more. The *Indians* love to eat their Flesh, which has no manner of ill Smell, when the Bladder is out. I know no use their Furs are put to. They are easily brought up tame. . . .

The Alligator is the same, as the Crocodile, and differs only in Name. They frequent the sides of Rivers, in the Banks of which they make their Dwellings a great way under Ground; the Hole or Mouth of their Dens lying commonly two Foot under Water, after which it rises till it be considerably above the Surface thereof. Here it is, that this amphibious Monster dwells all the Winter, sleeping away his time till the Spring appears, when he comes from his Cave, and daily swims up and down the Streams. He always breeds in some fresh Stream, or clear Fountain of Water, yet seeks his Prey in the broad Salt Waters, that are brackish, not on the Seaside, where I never met with any. He never devours Men in *Carolina*, but uses all ways to avoid them, yet he kills Swine and Dogs, the former as they come to feed in the Marshes, the others as they swim over the Creeks and Waters. They are very mischievous to the Weirs made for taking Fish, into which they come to prey on the Fish that are caught in the Weir, from whence they cannot readily extricate themselves, and so break the Weir in Pieces, being a very strong Creature. This Animal, in these Parts, sometimes exceeds seventeen Foot long. It is impossible to kill them with a Gun, unless you chance to hit them about the Eyes, which is a much softer Place, than the rest of their impenetrable Armor. They roar, and make a hideous Noise against bad Weather, and before they come out of their Dens in the Spring. I was pretty much frightened with one of these once; which happened thus: I had built a House about half a Mile from an *Indian* Town, on the Fork of *Neus*-River, where I dwelt by myself, excepting a young *Indian* Fellow, and a Bull-dog, that I had along with me. I had not then been so long a Sojourner in *America*, as to be thoroughly acquainted with this Creature. One of them had got his Nest directly under my House, which stood on pretty high Land, and by a Creekside, in whose Banks his Entering-place was, his Den reaching the Ground directly on which my House stood. I was sitting alone by the Fireside (about nine o'Clock at Night, some time in *March*) the *Indian* Fellow being gone to the Town, to see his Relations; so that there was nobody in the House but myself and my Dog; when, all of a sudden, this ill-favored Neighbor of mine, set up such a Roaring, that he made the House shake about my Ears, and so continued, like a Bittern, (but a hundred times louder, if possible) for four or five times. The Dog stared, as if he was frightened out of his Senses; nor indeed, could I imagine what it was, having never heard one of them before. Immediately again I had another Lesson; and so a third. Being at that time amongst none but Savages, I began to suspect, they were working some Piece of Conjuration under my House, to get away my Goods; not but that, at another time, I have as little Faith in their, or any others working Miracles, by diabolical Means, as any Person living. At last, my Man came in, to whom when I had told the Story, he laughed at me, and presently undeceived me, by telling me what it was that made that Noise. These Alligators lay Eggs, as the Ducks do; only they are longer shaped, larger, and a thicker Shell, than they have. How long they are in hatching, I cannot tell; but, as the *Indians* say, it is most part of the Summer, they always lay by a Spring-Side, the young living in and about the same, as soon as hatched. Their Eggs are laid in Nests made in the Marshes, and contain twenty or thirty Eggs. Some of these Creatures afford a great deal of Musk. Their Tail, when cut of, looks very fair and white, seemingly like the best of Veal. Some People have eaten thereof, and say, it is delicate Meat, when they happen not to be musky. Their Flesh is accounted proper for such as are troubled with the lame Distemper, (a sort of Rheumatism) so is the Fat very prevailing to remove Aches and Pains, by Unction. The Teeth of this Creature, when dead, are taken out, to make Chargers for Guns, being of several Sizes, fit for all Loads. They are white, and would make pretty Snuff Boxes, if wrought by an Artist. After the Tail of the Alligator is separated from the Body, it will move very freely for four days. . . .

Our wild Pigeons, are like the Wood Geese or Stock-Doves, only have a longer Tail. They leave us in the Summer. This sort of Pigeon (as I said before) is the most like our Stock-Doves, or Wood Pigeons that we have in *England*; only these differ in their Tails, which are very long, much like a Parakeet's. You must understand, that these Birds do not breed amongst us, (who are settled at, and near the Mouths of the Rivers, as I have intimated to you before) but come down (especially in hard Winters) amongst the Inhabitants, in great Flocks, as they were seen to do in the Year 1707, which was the hardest Winter that ever was known, since *Carolina* has been seated by the Christians. And if that Country had such hard Weather, what must be expected of the severe Winters in *Pennsylvania*, *New York*, and *New England*, where Winters are ten times (if possible) colder than with us. Although the Flocks are, in such Extremities, very numerous; yet they are not to be mentioned in Comparison with the great and infinite Numbers of these Fowl, that are met withal about a hundred, or a hundred and fifty, Miles to the Westward of the Places where we at present live; and where these Pigeons come down, in quest of a small sort of Acorns, which in those Parts are plentifully found. They are the same we call Turkey-Acorns, because the wild Turkeys feed very much thereon; And for the same Reason, those Trees that bear them, are called Turkey Oaks. I saw such prodigious Flocks of these Pigeons, in *January* or *February*, 1701–2, (which were in the hilly Country, between the great Nation of the *Esaw Indians*, and the pleasant Stream of *Sapona*, which is the West Branch of *Clarendon*, or *Cape-Fair* River) that they had broke down the Limbs of a great many large Trees all over those Woods, whereon they chanced to sit and roost; especially the great Pines, which are a more brittle Wood, than our sorts of Oak are. These Pigeons, about Sunrise, when we were preparing to march on our Journey, would fly by us in such vast Flocks, that they would be near a Quarter of an Hour, before they were all passed by; and as soon as that Flock was gone, another would come; and so successively one after another, for great part of the Morning. It is observable, that wherever these Fowl come in such Numbers, as I saw them then, they clear all before them, scarce leaving one Acorn upon the Ground, which would, doubtless, be a great Prejudice to the Planters that should seat there, because their Swine would be thereby deprived of their Mast. When I saw such Flocks of the Pigeons I now speak of, none of our Company had any other sort of Shot, than that which is cast in Molds, and was so very large, that we could not put above ten or a dozen of them into our largest Pieces; Wherefore, we made but an indifferent Hand of shooting them; although we commonly killed a Pigeon for every Shot. They were very fat, and as good Pigeons, as ever I ate. I inquired of the *Indians* that dwelled in those Parts, where it was that those Pigeons bred, and they pointed towards the vast Ridge of Mountains, and said, they bred there. Now, whether they make their Nests in the Holes in the Rocks of those Mountains, or build in Trees, I could not learn; but they seem to me to be a Wood Pigeon, that build in Trees, because of their frequent sitting thereon, and their Roosting on Trees always at Night, under which their Dung commonly lies half a Foot thick, and kills every thing that grows where it falls. . . .

[O]ur Distance from the Sea rids us of two Curses, which attend most other Parts of *America*, *viz*. Mosquitoes, and the Worm-biting, which eats Ships' Bottoms out; whereas at *Bath-Town*, there is no such thing known; and as for Mosquitoes, they hinder us of as little Rest, as they do you in *England*. Add to this, the unaccountable Quantities of Fish this great Water, or Sound, supplies us withal, whenever we take the Pains to fish for them; Advantages I have nowhere met withal in *America*, except here. As for the Climate, we enjoy a very wholesome and serene Sky, and a pure and thin Air, the Sun seldom missing to give us his daily

Blessing, unless now and then on a Winter's Day, which is not often; and when cloudy, the first Appearance of a Northwest Wind clears the Horizon, and restores the Light of the Sun. The Weather, in Summer, is very pleasant; the hotter Months being refreshed with continual Breezes of cool reviving Air; and the Spring being as pleasant, and beautiful, as in any Place I ever was in. The Winter, most commonly, is so mild, that it looks like an Autumn, being now and then attended with clear and thin Northwest Winds, that are sharp enough to regulate *English* Constitutions, and free them from a great many dangerous Distempers, that a continual Summer afflicts them withal, nothing being wanting, as to the natural Ornaments and Blessings of a Country, that conduce to make reasonable Men happy. And, for those that are otherwise, they are so much their own Enemies, where they are, that they will scarce ever be anyone's Friends, or their own, when they are transplanted; so, it's much better for all sides, that they remain as they are. Not but that there are several good People, that, upon just Grounds, may be uneasy under their present Burdens; and such I would advise to remove to the Place I have been treating of, where they may enjoy their Liberty and Religion, and peaceably eat the Fruits of their Labor, and drink the Wine of their own Vineyards, without the Alarms of a troublesome worldly Life. If a Man be a *Botanist*, here is a plentiful Field of *Plants* to divert him in; If he be a *Gardener*, and delight in that pleasant and happy Life, he will meet with a Climate and Soil, that will further and promote his Designs, in as great a Measure, as any Man can wish for; and as for the Constitution of this Government, it is so mild and easy, in respect to the Properties and Liberties of a Subject, that without rehearsing the Particulars, I say once for all, it is the mildest and best established Government in the World, and the Place where any Man may peaceably enjoy his own, without being invaded by another; Rank and Superiority ever giving Place to Justice and Equity, which is the Golden Rule that every Government ought to be built upon, and regulated by.

Cotton Mather
(1663–1728)

Cotton Mather was a prolific Puritan theologian and author, prominent among the leading intellectuals of early-eighteenth-century America. He was also responsible for helping to introduce Enlightenment thinking to colonial America. Although early Puritans often held a virulent antipathy toward wilderness, Cotton Mather was a late Puritan who demonstrated genuine enthusiasm for the study of nature, albeit as a means to the end of achieving orthodox religious piety. In his later years Mather studied various fields of natural philosophy including agriculture and animal husbandry, biology and medicine, astronomy and physics, zoology and botany, and geography and climatology. Among his most important contributions to colonial American natural science is the "Curiosa Americana," a series of letters describing American natural "curiosities," which he sent to the Royal Society in London between 1712 and 1724, and which earned him the coveted title of F.R.S., Fellow of the Royal Society. Mather's monumental contribution to the literature of American natural history, however, is *The Christian Philosopher: A Collection of the Best Discoveries in Nature, with Religious Improvements,* a rather derivative and allusive treatise that is nevertheless among the most important works of its kind published during the eighteenth century. Mather's book clearly demonstrates a transition from the Puritans' providential worldview toward the scientific paradigm that would ultimately displace it. *The Christian Philosopher* is also the first American book to systematically promote the "argument from design"—the assertion that the natural world should be studied as evidence of the Creator. Throughout his book Mather argues strongly that the study of natural objects, from gnats to comets, can produce spiritual insights. Mather ultimately embraces the idea of "a *Twofold Book* of God: the Book of the *Creatures* and the Book of the *Scriptures,*" and concludes that "the *Former* of these *Books,* 'twill help us in reading the *Latter.*"

From *The Christian Philosopher* (1721)

The Introduction

The Essays now before us will demonstrate, that *Philosophy* is no *Enemy,* but a mighty and wondrous *Incentive* to *Religion;* and they will exhibit that PHILOSOPHICAL RELIGION, which will carry with it a most sensible *Character,* and victorious *Evidence* of a *reasonable Service. GLORY TO GOD IN THE HIGHEST,* and *GOODWILL TOWARDS MEN,* animated and exercised; and a Spirit of *Devotion* and of *Charity* inflamed, in such Methods as are offered in these *Essays,* cannot but be attended with more Benefits, than any *Pen* of ours can declare, or any *Mind* conceive.

In the *Dispositions* and *Resolutions* of PIETY thus enkindled, a *Man* most effectually *shows himself* a MAN, and with unutterable Satisfaction answers the grand END of his Being, which is, *To glorify God.* He discharges also the Office of a *Priest* for the *Creation,* under the Influences of an admirable Savior, and therein asserts and assures his Title unto that *Priesthood,* which the Blessedness of the *future State* will very much consist in being advanced to. The whole *World* is indeed a *Temple* of GOD, *built* and *filled* by that Almighty *Architect;* and in this *Temple,* every such one, affecting himself with the Occasions for it, will *speak of His Glory.* He will also rise into that *Superior Way* of *Thinking* and of *Living,* which the *Wisest* of Men will choose to take; which the more *Polite Part* of Mankind, and the *Honorable of the Earth,* will esteem it no Dishonor for them to be acquainted with. Upon that Passage occurring in the best of Books, *Ye Sons of the Mighty, ascribe unto the Lord Glory and Strength;* it is a Gloss and an Hint of *Munster,* which carries with it a Cogency: *Nihil est tam sublime, tamque magnificum, quod non teneatur laudare & magnificare Deum Creatorem suum* [Nothing is so elevated, so august, that it is not compelled to praise and glorify God its creator]. Behold, a *Religion,* which will be found *without Controversy;* a *Religion,* which will challenge all possible Regards from the *High,* as well as the *Low,* among the People; I will resume the Term, a PHILOSOPHICAL RELIGION: And yet how *Evangelical!* . . .

The Works of the Glorious GOD in the *Creation* of the World, are what I now propose to exhibit; in brief *Essays* to enumerate *some of them,* that He may be glorified in them: And indeed my *Essays* may pretend unto no more than *some of them;* for, *Theophilus* writing, *of the Creation,* to his Friend *Autolycus,* might very justly say, That if he should have a *Thousand Tongues,* and live a *Thousand Years,* yet he were not able to describe the admirable Order of the Creation, διὰ τὸ ὑπερβάλλον μέγεθος καὶ τὸυ πλοῦτον σοφίας τοῦ Θεοῦ [Such a Transcendent Greatness of God, and the Riches of his Wisdom appearing in it]!

Chrysostom, I remember, mentions a *Twofold Book* of GOD; the Book of the *Creatures,* and the Book of the *Scriptures:* GOD having taught first of all us δια πραγμάτων, by his *Works,* did it afterwards δια γράμματων, by his *Words.* We will now for a while read the *Former* of these *Books,* 'twill help us in reading the *Latter:* They will admirably assist one another. The Philosopher being asked, What his *Books* were; answered, *Totius Entis Naturalis Universitas* [The whole universe of natural things]. All Men are accommodated with that *Public Library. Reader,* walk with me into it, and see what we shall find so legible there, *that he that runs may read it.* Behold, a Book, whereof we may agreeably enough use the words of honest *Aegardus; Lectu hic omnibus facilis, et si nunquam legere didicerint, & communis est omnibus, omniumque oculis expositus* [This is easy for all to read, even if they have not learned to read, and it is common to all and it is open to the eyes of all]. . . .

Of Comets

'Tis an admirable Work of our GOD, that the many *Globes* in the Universe are placed at such Distances, as to avoid all violent Shocks upon one another, and everything wherein they might prove a prejudice to one another.

Even *Comets* too, move so as to serve the Holy Ends of their Creator! COMETS, which are commonly called *Blazing Stars,* appear unto later Observations to be a sort of *Eccentrical Planets,* that move periodically about the *Sun.*

Sir *Isaac Newton,* from whom 'tis a difficult thing to dissent in any thing that belongs to *Philosophy,* concludes, That the Bodies of *Comets* are solid, compact, fixed, and durable, even like those of the other *Planets.*

He has a very critical Thought upon the *Heat,* which these *Bodies* may suffer in their Transits near the *Sun.* A famous one, in the Year 1680, passed so near the *Sun,* that the *Heat* of the *Sun* in it must be twenty-eight thousand times as intense as it is in *England* at Midsummer; whereas the Heat of boiling Water, as he tried, is but little more than the dry Earth of that Island, exposed unto the Midsummer-Sun: and the *Heat of red-hot Iron* he takes to be three or four times as great as that of *boiling Water.* Wherefore the *Heat* of that *Comet* in its *Perihelion* was near two thousand times as great as that of *red-hot Iron.* If it had been an Aggregate of nothing but Exhalations, the *Sun* would have rendered it invisible. A Globe of *red-hot* Iron, of the Dimensions of our Earth, would scarce be cool, by his Computation, in 50,000 Years. If then this *Comet* cooled an hundred times as fast as *red-hot Iron,* yet, since his Heat was 2,000 times greater than that of *red-hot Iron,* if you suppose his Body no greater than that of this Earth, he will not be cool in a Million of Years.

The *Tails* of *Comets,* which are longest and largest just after their *Perihelions,* he takes to be a long and very thin Smoke, or a mighty Train of Vapors, which the ignited *Nucleus,* or the Head of the *Comet,* emits from it. And he easily and thoroughly confounds the silly Notion of their being only the *Beams of the Sun,* shining through the Head of the *Star.* . . .

The Sentiments of so acute a Philosopher as Dr. *Cheyne* upon *Comets,* deserve to be transcribed. "I think it most probable, that these frightful Bodies are the Ministers of *Divine Justice,* and in their Visits lend us *benign* or *noxious* Vapors, according to the Designs of Providence; That they may have brought, and may still bring about the great Catastrophe of our System; and, That they may be the Habitation of *Animals* in a State of *Punishment,* which if it did not look too notional, there are many Arguments to render not improbable."

And elsewhere: " 'Tis most likely, they are the Ministers of Divine justice, sending baneful Steams, from their long Trains, upon the *Planets* they come nigh. However, from them we may learn, that the Divine Vengeance may find a *Seat* for the *Punishment* of his disobedient Creatures, without being put to the expense of a New Creation."

When I see a vast Comet, blazing and rolling about the unmeasurable *Aether,* I will think; "Who can tell, but I now see a wicked World *made a fiery Oven in the Time of the Anger of GOD! The Lord swallowing them* up in *his Wrath, and the Fire devouring them!*

"What prodigious Mischief and Ruin might such a *Ball of Confusion* bring upon our sinful *Globe,* if the Great GOD order its Approach to us!

"How happy they, that are in the Favor and Friendship of that Glorious Lord, who *knows how to deliver the Pious* out of Distresses, and *reserve the Unjust for a Punishment of a Day of Judgment!"* . . .

Of Insects

. . . The *spontaneous Generation of Insects* has at last been so confuted by *Redi,* and *Malpighi,* and *Swammerdam,* and our excellent *Ray,* and others, that no Man of Sense can any longer believe it. Indeed such a *spontaneous Generation* would be nothing less than a *Creation.* That all Animals are generated of *Parent Animals,* is a thing so cleared up from Observation and Experiment, that we must speak of it in the Language of those who have lately writ of it, *Nous croyons absolument* [We believe it absolutely]. And of their *Generation* any other way, we cannot but use the Language of Dr. *Lyster, Non inducor ut credam* [I cannot be persuaded to believe]. If an *Insect* may be *equivocally generated,* then, as Dr. *Robinson* justly enquires, *why not sometimes a Bird, yea, a Man? Or why no new Species of Animals now and then? For there is as much Art shown in the Formation of those, as of these.* Dr. *Cheyne* assures us, nobody nowadays, that understands anything of Nature, can so much as imagine, that any Animal, how abject soever, can be produced by an *equivocal Generation,* or without the Conjunction of Male and Female *Parents,* in the same or in two different Individuals. And there are very few who have considered the Matter, but what own that every *Animal* proceeds from a preexistent *Animalcule,* and that the *Parents* conduce nothing but a convenient *Habitation* to it, and suitable *Nourishments,* till it be fit to be trusted with Light, and capable of enjoying the Benefits of the Air. There is nothing in the *Animal Machine,* but an inconceivable number of branching and winding *Canals,* filled with Liquors of different natures, going a perpetual round, and no more capable of producing the wonderful Fabric of another Animal, than a thing is of making itself. There is besides in the *Generation* of an Animal, a necessity that the *Head, Heart, Nerves, Veins* and *Arteries,* be formed at the same time, which never can be done by the motion of any Fluid, which way soever moved.

Great GOD, Thou art the Father of all things; even the Father of Insects, as well as the Father of Spirits: And Thy Greatness appears with a singular Brightness in the least of Thy Creatures!

Concerning *Frogs* generated in the *Clouds,* there has been a mighty Noise; the *Thunder* scarce makes a greater! But Mr. *Ray* says well, it seems no more likely than *Spanish* Jennets begotten by the *Wind,* for that has good Authors too. He adds, *He that can swallow the raining of Frogs, hath made a fair Step towards be-*

lieving that it may rain Calves also; for we read that one fell out of the Clouds in Avicen's *Time. Fromondus*'s Opinion, that the *Frogs* which appear in great multitudes after a Shower, are not indeed generated in the Clouds, but are coagulated of *Dust,* commixed and fermented with *Rainwater,* is all over as impertinent. It is very certain that *Frogs* are of two different Sexes, and have their spermatic Vessels; and their Copulation is notorious (*per integrum aliquando Mensem continuata* [Continuing for a whole month sometimes]) and after the Spawn must be cast into the Water, where the Eggs lie in the midst of a copious Jelly; then must appear a Feetless *Tadpole,* in which Form it must continue a long while, till the Limbs be grown out, and it arrives to the perfect Form of a *Frog.* To what purpose all this, if your way, Gentlemen, [*Fromondus,* and the rest] may suffice? . . .

Even the more noxious *Insects* and *Vermin* are such, that we may consider in them *the Finger of God!* The *Sufferings* they inflict upon us, may be considered as the *Scourges* of God upon us for our Miscarriages, and be improved as Excitations to *Repentance.* I have read somewhere a Passage to this purpose: "I would carry on the Matter to so much of *Watchfulness,* in my apprehending Opportunities for *Thoughts of Repentance,* that the Provocations that may happen to be given to my *Bodily Senses* at any time, shall provoke such *Thoughts* in my Soul. If I happen to lodge where any *Insect* or *Vermin* assaults me, it shall *humble* me. I will think *I have been one among the Enemies of God in the World. These uneasy Creatures are part of the Armies which the Lord of Hosts employs, and with some Contempt, against his Enemies!* . . .

"For what ENDS are all these little Creatures made? Most certainly for great ENDS, and for such as are worthy of a GOD!

"The exquisite Artifice which is conspicuous in the *Make* of these Creatures, does proclaim a marvelous and matchless *Wisdom* in the *Maker* of them; and Wisdom will *make nothing in vain.*

"Though the more *special Uses* of these Creatures be as yet unknown to us, the *only wise God* sends to us this Advice concerning them: *What I do thou knowest not now, but thou shalt know hereafter.*

"However, this we *know* NOW; for these and all Creatures this END is great enough, *that the Great God therein beholds with pleasure the various and curious Works of His Hands.* Behold a sufficient END, as well for a *World* as for a *Worm,* that the infinite God may with delight *behold His own Glories* in the Works which His Hands have wrought. *My Readers,* let us come to a Comfort in the Doxology, *O Lord, thou hast created all things and for thy Pleasure they are and were created!* The Great God has contrived a mighty *Engine,* of an Extent that cannot be measured, and there is in it a Contrivance of wondrous *Motions* that cannot be *numbered.* He is infinitely gratified with the View of this *Engine* in all its *Motions,* infinitely grateful to Him so glorious a Spectacle! when it becomes grateful to *us,* then *we* come into some Communion with Him. I will esteem it a sufficient END for the whole Creation of God, *that the Great Creator may have the Gratification of beholding His own admirable Workmanship.* And I will esteem it a part of the Homage I owe to His Eternal Majesty, to be satisfied in such an END as this. . . .

Of the Fishes

. . . As the *smallest* Animals are bred in the Waters, witness those in *Pepper-water,* so are the *largest;* those of the *cetaceous* Kind are there.

Pliny mentions the *Balaenae* of the *Indian Sea,* which were nine hundred and sixty Foot long; and he mentions *Whales* that were six hundred Foot long, and three hundred and sixty broad, which came into a River of *Arabia.* In the second Chapter of his ninth Book he offers a Reason why the *largest Animals* are bred in the Sea.

But I love to pass from him to a more trusty and modern *Pliny,* our industrious *Ray;* and we will now see something of his Remarks upon these *Belluae Marinae:* The *Tail* in these has a different position from what it has in all other *Fishes;* it lies parallel to the Horizon in these, and it is perpendicular in the rest; hereby it supplies the use of the hinder pair of *Fins;* which these Creatures lack; and it serves both to raise and sink their Body at their pleasure. It is necessary that these Creatures frequently ascend to the top of the Water to *breathe,* and therefore they should be furnished with an Organ, by which their ascent and descent might be facilitated. The turning of their Bodies in the Water they perform like the *Birds,* by the motion of one of their *Fins,* while the other is quiescent. It is very remarkable that their whole Body is compassed round with a copious *Fat,* which we call *the Blubber,* whereby their Bodies are poised, and rendered equiponderant to the Water, and the Water also is kept off at some distance from the *Blood,* the immediate Contact whereof might else have had some chilling force upon it; it serves likewise, as our Clothes do for us, to keep the *Fish warm,* in reflecting the hot Steams of their Body; and so redoubling the Heat thereof: hence they can abide the greatest Cold of the *Northern Seas,* to which they chiefly resort, not only for the Quiet which they enjoy there, but because the *Northern Air,* which is more fully charged with the Particles which we suppose to be *nitrous,* and that are the Aliment of Fire, is fittest of all to maintain their vital Heat in that Activity, which may be sufficient for to move such an unwieldy Bulk as theirs. The *stupendous Magnitude* of these Animals! . . .

Even in the *cold Sea* too, what a *Warmth* of Parental Affection do the *old ones* express for their *young ones,* and how distinguishing! When the *Seals* are hundreds of thousands of them lying in a Bay coming out of the Sea, they bleat like Sheep for their Young; and though they pass through hundreds, yea, thousands of other young ones before they come to *their own*, yet they will suffer none but *their own* to suck them. *Even the Sea-Monsters draw out the Breast, they give suck to their young ones. Monstrous Parents*, that are *without natural Affection!* These Inhabitants of the *Sea* with open Mouth cry out against you.

"I remember a *Crassus*, of whom 'tis reported, that he so tamed a *Fish* in his Pond, as to make him come to him at his calling him; verily, I shall have a Soul deserving *his Name*, and be more stupid than the *Fish*, if I do not hear the Calls which the *Fish* give to me to glorify the God that made them; and who has in their *Variety*, in their *Multitude*, in their *Structures*, their *Dispositions* and *Sagacities*, displayed his Glories. The *Papists* have a silly and foolish Legend of their St. *Anthony* preaching to the *Fishes*; it will be a Discretion in me to make the reverse of the *Fable*, and hear the *Fishes* preaching to me, which they do many Truths of no small importance. As *mute* as they are, they are *plain* and *loud* Preachers; I want nothing but an *Ear* to make me a profitable Hearer of them.

"It is a good Wish to be *in virtute Delphinus* [To have the qualities of a dolphin], to use the Dispatch of the quick *Dolphin* in all good Purposes.

Jonathan Edwards
(1703–1758)

Often remembered as the author of *Sinners in the Hands of an Angry God* (1741), a stinging jeremiad that has become the best-known sermon in American history, Jonathan Edwards was a leading late Puritan theologian whose intellectual interests ranged far beyond the pulpit. Beneath the Great Awakening's sulfurous rhetoric of damnation and salvation, influential new studies in natural science were changing fundamental assumptions about the nature of the physical world. Edwards was deeply engaged in the new rationalism of Newtonian science and was particularly fascinated with physics and optics. Throughout the 1720s he worked on a series of papers organized under the rubric of "Natural Philosophy," including preliminary treatises on atomic structure, the colors of the rainbow, and the speed of light. Although the rationalism of Edwards's scientific work demonstrates his important role in the period's shift from Scholasticism toward modern scientific inquiry, he also shared Cotton Mather's faith that the invisible laws of nature would, as they were better understood, provide insights into the perfection of God's Creation. But Edwards also extended Mather's work—and anticipated the metaphysics of Transcendentalists including Emerson and Thoreau—by searching for a grand synthesis within which God's plan could be read in the patterns of the physical world. Beginning in 1728

Edwards kept a notebook called "Images of Divine Things," in which he worked to decipher and express the spiritual significance of natural objects. In his most famous scientific essays — those of the "Of Insects" series, which includes the "Spider Letter" excerpted here — Edwards sought "corollaries" linking his field observations with the elusive laws of the soul. As his "Beauty of the World" shows, Edwards's aesthetic philosophy held that the loveliness of nature is an enticement to the study of it, and thus a proof that science could be a means to the higher goal of spiritual awakening.

"The Spider Letter" (1723)

Sir:

In the postscript of your letter to my father you manifest a willingness to receive anything else that he has observed in nature worthy of remark; that which is the subject of the following lines by him was thought to be such: he has laid it upon me to write the account, I having had advantage to make more full observations. If you think, Sir, that they are not worthy the taking notice of, with greatness and goodness overlook and conceal. They are some things that I have happily seen of the wondrous and curious works of the spider. Although everything pertaining to this insect is admirable, yet there are some phenomena relating to them more particularly wonderful.

Everybody that is used to the country knows of their marching in the air from one tree to another, sometimes at the distance of five or six rods, though they are wholly destitute of wings: nor can one go out in a dewy morning at the latter end of August and beginning of September but he shall see multitudes of webs reaching from one tree and shrub to another; which webs are commonly thought to be made in the night because they appear only in the morning by reason of the dew that hangs on them, whereas they never work in the night, they love to lie still when the air is dark and moist; but these webs may be seen well enough in the daytime by an observing eye, by their reflection of the sunbeams; especially late in the afternoon may those webs that are between the eye, and that part of the horizon that is under the sun, be seen very plainly, being advantageously posited to reflect the rays, and the spiders themselves may be very often seen traveling in the air from one stage to another amongst the trees in a very unaccountable manner. But, Sir, I have often seen that which is yet more astonishing. In a very calm serene day in the forementioned time of year, standing at some distance between the end of an house or some other opaque body, so as just to hide the disk of the sun and keep off his dazzling rays, and looking along close by the side of it, I have seen vast multitudes of little shining webs and glistening strings, brightly reflecting the sunbeams, and some of them of a great length, and at such a height that one would think that they were tacked to the vault of the heavens and would be burnt like tow in the sun, making a very pleasing as well as surprising appearance. It is wonderful at what a distance these webs may plainly be seen in such a position to the sunbeams, which are so fine that they cannot be seen in another position, though held near to the eye; some that are at a great distance appear (it cannot be otherwise) several thousands of times as big as they ought: They doubtless appear under as great an angle as a body of a foot diameter ought to do at such a distance; so greatly doth coruscation increase the apparent bigness of bodies at a distance, as is observed in the fixed stars. But that which is most astonishing is that very often there appears at the end of these webs, spiders sailing in the air with them, doubtless with abundance of pleasure, though not with so much as I have beheld them and showed them to others. And since I have seen these things I have been very conversant with spiders. Resolving if possible to find out the mysteries of these their amazing works, and pursuing my observations, I discovered one wonder after another till I have been so happy as very frequently to see their whole manner of working; which is thus:

When a spider would go from one tree or branch to another, or would recreate himself by sailing or floating in the air, he first lets himself down a little way from the twig he stands on by a web, as in Fig. 1; and then taking hold of it by his forefeet as in Fig. 2, and then separates or loosens the part of the web *cd* from the part *bc* by which he hangs; which part of the web *cd*, being thus loosened, will by the motion of the air be carried out towards *e*, which will by the sufferance of the spider be drawn out of his tail with infinite ease by the moving air, to what length the spider pleases, as in Fig. 3: And if the further end of the web *de*, as it is running out and moving to and fro, happens to catch by a shrub or the branch of a tree, the spider immediately feels it and fixes the hither end of it, *d*, to the web *bc*, and goes over as by a bridge by the web *de*. Every particular of this, Sir, my eyes have innumerable times made me sure of, saving that I never could distinctly see how they separated the part of the web *cd* (Fig. 2) from the part *bc*, whether it be done by biting of it off or how, because so small a piece of so fine a web is altogether imperceptible amongst the spider's legs, and because the spider is so very quick and dexterous in doing of it all. But I have seen that it is done, though I have not seen how they do it. For this, Sir, I can see: that the web *bc* (Fig. 3) is separated, and not joined to the spider's tail, while the web *de* is drawing out.

Now, Sir, it is certain that these webs, when they first come from the spider, are so rare a substance that they are lighter than the air, because they will immediately ascend in a calm air, and never descend except driven by a wind: and 'tis as certain that what swims and ascends in the air is lighter than the air, as that what ascends and swims in water is lighter than that: So that if we should suppose any such time wherein the air is perfectly calm, this web is so easily drawn out of the

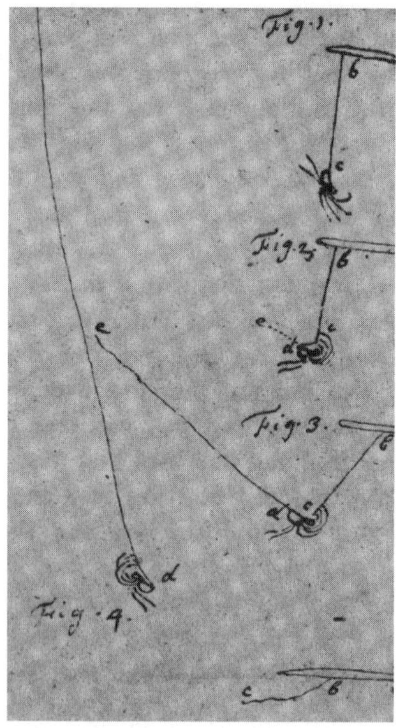

spider's tail, that barely the levity of it is sufficient to carry it out to any length. But at least its levity, or ascending inclination, together with so much motion as the air is never without, will well suffice for this. Wherefore, if it be so that the end of the web *de* (Fig. 3) catches by no tree nor other body till it be drawn out so long that its levity shall be so great as to be more than equal to the gravity of the spider, or so that the web and the spider taken together shall be lighter than such a quantity of air as takes up equal space, then according to the universally acknowledged laws of nature the web and the spider together will ascend and not descend in the air. As when a man is at the bottom of the water, if he has hold of a piece of timber so great that the wood's tendency upwards is greater than the man's tendency downwards, he together with the wood will ascend to the surface of the water. Therefore, when the spider perceives that the web *de* is long enough to bear him up by its ascending force (which force the spider feels by its drawing of him towards *e*), he lets go his hold of the web *bc* (Fig. 4) and, holding by the web *de*, ascends and floats in the air with it. If there be not web more than enough just to equal with its levity the gravity of the spider, the spider together with the web will hang *in equilibrio*, neither ascending nor descending, otherwise than as the air moves; but if there be so much web that its ascending tendency, or rather the buoying force of the air upon it, shall be greater than the descending tendency of the spider, they will ascend till the air is so thin, till they together are just of an equal weight with so much air. But if the web be so short as not to counterpoise the weight of the spider, the web and spider will fall till they come to the ground.

And this very way, Sir, I have multitudes of times seen spiders mount away into the air with a vast train of this silver web before them from a stick in mine hand; for if the spider be disturbed upon the stick by shaking of it he will presently in this manner leave it. Their way of working may very distinctly be seen if they are held up in the sun, in a calm day, against a dark door or anything that is black.

And this, Sir, is the way of spiders' working. This is the way of their going from one thing to another at a distance, and this is the way of their flying in the air. And although I can say I am certain of it, I don't desire that the truth of it should be received upon my word, though I could bring others to testify to it to whom I have shown it, and who have looked on with admiration: But everyone's eyes who will take the pains to observe will make them equally sure of it; only those who would make experiment must take notice that it is not every sort of spider that is a flying spider, for those spiders that keep in houses are a quite different sort, as also those that keep in the ground, and those that keep in swamps upon the ground amongst the bogs, and those that keep in hollow trees and rotten logs; but those spiders that keep on branches of trees and shrubs are the flying spiders. They delight most in walnut trees, and are that sort of spiders that make those curious, network, polygonal webs that are so frequently to be seen in the latter end of the year. There are more of this sort of spider by far than of any other.

Corol. 1. Hence the wisdom of the Creator in providing of the spider with that wonderful liquor with which their bottle tail is filled, that may so easily be drawn out so exceeding fine, and being in this way exposed to the air will so immediately convert to a dry substance that shall be so very rare as to be lighter than the air, and will so excellently serve to all their purposes.

Corol. 2. Hence the exuberant goodness of the Creator, who hath not only provided for all the necessities, but also for the pleasure and recreation of all sorts of creatures, even the insects.

But yet, Sir, I am assured that the chief end of this faculty that is given them is not their recreation but their destruction, because their destruction is unavoidably the constant effect of it; and we find nothing that is the continual effect of nature but what is the end of the means by which it is brought to pass: but it is impossible but that the greatest part of the spiders upon the land should every year be swept into the ocean. For these spiders never fly except the weather be fair and the atmosphere dry, but the atmosphere is never clear and dry, neither in this nor any other continent, only when the wind blows from the midland parts, and consequently towards the sea; as here in New England, the fair weather is only when the wind is westerly, the land being on that side and the ocean on the easterly. I scarcely ever have seen any of these spiders flying but when they have been hastening directly towards the sea. And the time of their flying being so long, even from about the middle of August, every sunshiny day till about the end of October (though their chief time, as was observed before, is the latter end of August and beginning of September). And they, never flying from the sea but always towards it, must get there at last. And it seems unreasonable to think that they have sense to stop themselves when they come near the sea, for then we should see hundreds of times more spiders on the seashore than anywhere else. When they are once carried over the water their webs grow damp and moist and lose their levity and their wings fail them, and let them down into the water.

The same also holds true of other sorts of flying insects, for at those times that I have viewed the spiders with their webs in the air there has also appeared vast multitudes of flies at a great height, and all flying the same way with the spiders and webs, direct to the ocean. And even such as butterflies, millers, and moths, which keep in the grass at this time of year, I have seen vastly higher than the tops of the highest trees, all going the same way. These I have seen towards evening, right overhead, and without a screen to defend my eye from the sunbeams, which I used to think were seeking a warmer climate. The reason of their flying at that time of year I take to be because the ground and trees and grass, the places of their residence in summer, begin to be chill and uncomfortable. Therefore when the sun shines pretty warm they leave them, and mount up into the air and expand their wings to the sun, and flying for nothing but their own ease and comfort, they suffer themselves to go that way that they can go with the greatest ease, and so where the wind pleases: and it being warmth they fly for, they never fly against the wind nor sidewise to it, they find it cold and laborious; they therefore seem to use their wings but just so much as to bear them up, and suffer themselves to go with the wind. So that it must necessarily be that almost all aerial insects, and spiders which live upon them and are made up of them, are at the end of the year swept away into the sea and buried in the ocean, and leave nothing behind them but their eggs for a new stock the next year.

Corol. 1. Hence there is reason to admire at the wisdom of the Creator, and to be convinced that it is exercised about such little things in this wonderful contrivance of annually carrying off and burying the corruption and nauseousness of the air, of which flying insects are little collections, in the bottom of the ocean where it will do no harm; and especially the strange way of bringing this about in spiders, which are collections of these collections, their food being flying insects, flies being the poison of the air, and spiders are the poison of flies collected together. And what great inconveniences should we labor under if it were not so, for spiders and flies are such exceedingly multiplying creatures, that if they only slept or lay benumbed in winter, and were raised again in the spring, which is commonly thought, it would not be many years before we should be plagued with as vast numbers as Egypt was. And if they died ultimately in winter, they by the renewed heat of the sun would presently again be dissipated into the nauseous vapors of which they are made up, and so would be of no use or benefit in that in which now they are so very serviceable and which is the chief end of their creation.

Corol. 2. The wisdom of the Creator is also admirable in so nicely and mathematically adjusting their plastic nature, that notwithstanding their destruction by this means and the multitudes that are eaten by birds, that they do not decrease and so by little and little come to nothing; and in so adjusting their destruction to their multiplication they do neither increase, but taking one year with another, there is always an equal number of them.

These, Sir, are the observations I have had opportunity to make on the wonders that are to be seen in the most despicable of animals. Although these things appear for the main very certain to me, yet, Sir, I submit it all to your better judgment, and deeper insight. I humbly beg to be pardoned for running the venture, though an utter stranger, of troubling you with so prolix an account of that which I am altogether uncertain whether you will esteem worthy of the time and pains of reading. Pardon me if I thought it might at least give you occasion to make better observations on these wondrous animals, that should be worthy of communicating to the learned world, from whose glistening webs so much of the wisdom of the Creator shines.

Pardon, Sir, your most obedient humble servant,
Jonathan Edwards

"Beauty of the World" (1725)

The beauty of the world consists wholly of sweet mutual consents, either within itself, or with the Supreme Being. As to the corporeal world, though there are many other sorts of consents, yet the sweetest and most charming beauty of it is its resemblance of spiritual beauties. The reason is that spiritual beauties are infinitely the greatest, and bodies being but the shadows of beings, they must be so much the more charming as they shadow forth spiritual beauties. This beauty is peculiar to natural things, it surpassing the art of man.

Thus there is the resemblance of a decent trust, dependence and acknowledgment in the planets continually moving round the sun, receiving his influences by which they are made happy, bright and beautiful, a decent attendance in the secondary planets, an image of majesty, power, glory and beneficence in the sun in the midst of all; and so in terrestrial things, as I have shown in another place.

'Tis very probable that that wonderful suitableness of green for the grass and plants, the blue of the sky, the white of the clouds, the colors of flowers, consists in a complicated proportion that these colors make one with another, either in the magnitude of the rays, the number of vibrations that are caused in the optic nerve, or some other way. So there is a great suitableness between the objects of different senses, as between sounds, colors, and smells — as between the colors of the woods and flowers, and the smell, and the singing of birds — which 'tis probable consist in a certain proportion of the vibrations that are made in the different organs. So there are innumerable other agreeablenesses of motions, figures, etc.: the gentle motions of trees, of lily, etc., as it is agreeable to other things that represent calmness, gentleness and benevolence, etc. The fields and woods seem to rejoice, and how joyful do the birds seem to be in it. How much a resemblance is there of every grace in the fields covered with plants and flowers, when the sun shines serenely and undisturbedly upon them. How a resemblance, I say, of every grace and beautiful disposition of mind; of an inferior towards a superior cause, preserver, benevolent benefactor, and a fountain of happiness.

How great a resemblance of a holy and virtuous soul in a calm serene day. What an infinite number of such-like beauties is there in that one thing, the light; and how complicated an harmony and proportion is it probable belongs to it.

There are beauties that are more palpable and explicable, and there are hidden and secret beauties. The former pleases and we can tell why: we can explain and particularly point forth agreements that render the thing pleasing. Such are all artificial regularities: we can tell wherein the regularity lies that affects us. The latter sort are those beauties that delight us and we can't tell why. Thus we find ourselves pleased in beholding the color of the violets, but we know not what secret regularity or harmony it is that creates that pleasure in our minds. These hidden beauties are commonly by far the greatest, because the more complex a beauty is, the more hidden is it. In this latter sort consists principally the beauty of the world; and very much in light and colors. Thus, mere light is pleasing to the mind. If it be to the degree of effulgence, 'tis very sensible, and mankind have agreed in it: they all represent glory and extraordinary beauty by brightness. The reason of it is either that light, or our organ of seeing, is so contrived that an harmonious motion is excited in the animal spirits and propagated to the brain. That mixture of all sorts of rays, which we call white, is a proportionate mixture that is harmonious (as Sir Isaac Newton has shown) to each particular simple color and contains in it some harmony or other that is delightful. And each sort of rays play a distinct tune to the soul, besides those lovely mixtures that are found in nature — those beauties, how lovely, in the green of the face of the earth, in all manner of colors in flowers, the color of the skies, and lovely tinctures of the morning and evening.

Corol. Hence the reason why almost all men, and those that seem to be very miserable, love life: because they cannot bear to lose the sight of such a beautiful and lovely world — the ideas, that every moment whilst we live have a beauty that we take not distinct notice of, but bring a pleasure that, when we come to the trial, we had rather live in much pain and misery than lose.

Paul Dudley
(1675–1751)

A contemporary of Cotton Mather and Jonathan Edwards, Paul Dudley was the son of Massachusetts governor Joseph Dudley and was descended from a prominent Bay Colony family that was also related to the Sewalls and Winthrops. Paul Dudley received his bachelor's and master's degrees at Harvard (1690, 1693) before going on to study law, eventually serving as attorney general of Massachusetts, judge in the Massachusetts Superior Court, and chief justice of the Court. Throughout his distinguished career in politics and law, however, Dudley maintained a keen interest in the study of American natural history. For seventeen years, from 1719 until 1736, he sent to the Royal Society a remarkable series of letters covering a wide range of topics: from maple sugar production, locating bee trees, and identifying moose to Niagara Falls (in which he corrected Hennepin's exaggeration of the height of the cataract), smallpox inoculation, and sweat lodge cures; from types of rattlesnakes, local horticulture and orchardry, and the life cycles of cicadas (which, however, he mistook for locusts) to various other phenomena including lightning, earthquakes, and the aurora borealis. In recognition of his contributions to American natural science, the members of the Royal Society elected him a Fellow in 1721. Because Dudley's natural history essays were never arranged in book form and have never been reprinted since their initial publication in early-eighteenth-century volumes of the Royal Society's *Transactions,* they have remained "lost classics" of colonial American nature writing. Although Dudley, like many intellectuals of his day, was deeply interested in the study of theology, he was much less inclined than his contemporaries Mather and Edwards to cast his field observations in religious terms. As a result his work is quite secular, more closely reflecting the positivist approach to natural science that by the early eighteenth century was beginning to displace the previously dominant providential worldview. The following essay on the natural history of whales, sent to the Royal Society in 1725 and subsequently published in the *Transactions*, is the work of a sharp observer and clear writer whose approach to cetacean taxonomy, physiology, breeding, and feeding is quite modern.

"An Essay upon the Natural History of Whales . . ." (1724)

Sir,

I am very sensible that the World has long since, and often been entertained with various Relations of this wonderful Creature: But as I shall endeavor to avoid any vain Repetition, so I flatter myself with the Hopes of presenting the Royal Society with some Particulars not yet published, both of the Whale in general, and more especially of that Species or Kind of Whale, which our People call the *Spermaceti*, but, in my Opinion, much rather deserves the Name of the Ambergris Whale. But here I would have it noted, that the following Account respects only such Whales, as are found on the Coast of *New England.*

And of these there are divers Sorts or Kinds.

As first, The Right, or Whalebone Whale is a large Fish, measuring sixty or seventy Feet in Length, and very bulky, having no Scales, but a soft fine smooth Skin, no Fins, but only one on each Side, from five to eight Feet long, which they are not observed to use, but only in turning themselves, unless while young, and carried by the Dam on the Flukes of their Tails, when with those Fins they clasp about her Small, and so hold themselves on. This Fish, when first brought forth, is about twenty Feet long, and of little Worth, but then the Dam is very fat. At a Year old, when they are called Short-heads, they are very fat, and yield to fifty Barrels of Oil, but by that Time the Dam is very poor, and termed a Dry-skin, and won't yield more than thirty Barrels of Oil, though of large Bulk. At two Years old, they are called Stunts, being stunted after weaning, and will then yield generally from twenty-four to twenty-eight Barrels. After this, they are termed Scull-fish, their Age not being known, but only guessed at by the Length of the Bone in their Mouths. The Whalebone, so called, grows in the upper Jaw on each Side, and is sometimes six or seven Feet in Length. A good large Whale has yielded a thousand Weight of Bone. 'Tis thought by some, that the hairy Part of the Whalebone, and which is next to the Tongue, serves in the Nature of a Strainer of their Food.

The Eye of a Whale is about the Bigness of an Ox's Eye, and they are situated in the After-part of the Head on each Side, and where the Whale is broadest; for his Head tapers away forward from his Eyes, and his Body tapers backward; his Eyes are more than half way his Depth, or nearest his Under-part; just under his Eyes are his two Fins before-mentioned; he carries his Tail horizontally, and with that he sculls himself along.

The Entrails of this Whale are made and situated much like those of an Ox, and their Scalps are sometimes found covered with Thousands of Sea-lice. One of these Whales has yielded one hundred and thirty Barrels of Oil, and near twenty out of the Tongue. The Whalebone Whale is the most valuable, except the *Spermaceti* Whale.

The Scrag Whale is near akin to the Finback, but, instead of a Fin upon his Back, the Ridge of the Afterpart of his back is scragged with half a Dozen Knobs or Knuckles; he is nearest the right Whale in Figure and for Quantity of Oil; his Bone is white, but won't split.

The Finback Whale is distinguished from the right Whale, by having a great Fin on his Back from two Feet and a Half, to four Feet long, which gives him the Name; he has also two side Fins, as the Whalebone Whale, but much longer, measuring six or seven Feet. This Fish is somewhat longer than the other, but not so bulky, much swifter, and very furious when struck, and very difficultly held; their Oil is not near so much, as that of the right Whale, and the Bone of little Profit, being short and knobby. The Belly of this Whale is white.

The Bunch or humpback Whale, is distinguished from the right Whale, by having a Bunch standing in the Place where the Fin does in the Finback. This Bunch is as big as a Man's Head, and a Foot high, shaped like a Plug pointing backwards. The Bone of this Whale is not worth much, though somewhat better than the Finback's. His Fins are sometimes eighteen Feet long, and very white; his Oil much as that of the Finback. Both the Finbacks and Humpbacks are shaped in Reeves longitudinal from Head to Tail on their Bellies and their Sides, as far as their Fins, which are about halfway up their Sides.

The *Spermaceti* Whale. This Fish is much of the same Dimension with the other, but of a grayish color, whereas the others are black; he has a Bunch on his Back like the Humpback, but then he is distinguished by not having any Whalebone in the Mouth; but instead of that, there are Rows of fine ivory Teeth in each Jaw, about five or six Inches long. One of these Teeth I have done myself the Honor to send the Society. The Man, who gave it me, says, the Whale was forty-nine Foot long, and his Head made twelve Barrels of *Spermaceti* Oil. They are a more gentle Fish than the other Whales, and seldom fight with their Tails; but when struck, usually turn upon their Backs, and fight with their Mouths. The Oil, which is made of the Body of this Fish, is much clearer and sweeter than that of the other Whales.

The *Spermaceti* Oil, so called, lies in a great Trunk about four or five Feet deep, and ten or twelve Feet long, near the whole Depth, Breadth, and Length of the Head, in the Place of the Brains, and seems to be the same, and disposed in several membranous Cells, and covered not with a Bone, but a thick grisly Substance below the Skin, through which they dig a Hole, and lade our the clear Oil. Not but that the Head, and other Glandulous Parts of this Fish, will make the *Spermaceti*

Oil; but the best, and that which is prepared by Nature, is in the Trunk aforesaid: And an ingenious Man, who has himself killed many of these Whales, assures me, that only the Trunk will afford from ten to twenty Barrels. Besides the *Spermaceti* Oil, this Fish will yield from twenty to fifty Barrels of common Oil.

One of our Country Doctors tells me, that the Tooth of this Fish, shaved or powdered, and so infused in Liquor, equals the Hartshorn, and has been used in the Smallpox, and given to Lying-in-Women, in Case of Sickness, with Success. The Quantity is as much as will lie upon an *English* Shilling. . . .

I go on therefore, in the second Place, to give an Account of the Manner of the Propagation of Whales. They generate much like to our neat Cattle, and therefore they are termed Bull, Cow, and Calf. The *Latins* called the Whale *Bellua Marina*. They bring forth but one at a Time, and but every other Year. When the Cow takes Bull, she throws herself upon her Back, sinking her Tail, and so the Bull slides up, and, when the Bull is slid up, she clasps him with her Fins. A Whale's Pissel is six Feet long, and at the Root is seven or eight Inches Diameter, and tapers away till it comes to about an Inch Diameter: his Stones would fill half a Barrel, but his Genitals are not open or visible, like those of the true Bull. The Calf, or young Whale, has been found perfectly formed in the Cow, when not above seventeen Inches long, and white; yet, when brought forth, is usually twenty Feet, but of a black Color; it is supposed they go with their Young about nine or ten Months, and are very fat in that Time, especially when they bring forth. When the Female suckles her Young, she turns herself almost upon her Back, upon the Run of the Water, she has two Teats of six or eight Inches long, and ten or twelve Inches round. The Milk is white, like that of a Cow; and upon opening a young sucking Whale, the Milk was found curdled in his Bag, just like that of a Calf.

The Care of their Young is very remarkable, they not only carrying them on their Tails, and suckling them, but often rising with them for the Benefit of the Air; and however they are chased or wounded, yet as long as they have Sense, and perceive Life in their Young, they will never leave them, nor will they then strike with their Tail, and if, in their running, the young one loses his Hold and drops off, the Dam comes about, and passing underneath, takes it on again. And therefore Care is taken by those who kill these Mate Fish (as they are called) only to fasten the Calf, but not to kill her, till they have first secured the Cow. For so soon as ever the Calf is dead, the Cow perceives it, and grows so violent, that there is no managing her.

The Whales are very gregarious, being sometimes found a Hundred in a Scull, and are great Travelers. In the Fall of the Year, the right or Whalebone Whales go Westward, and in the Spring they are headed Eastward. But here it must be noted, that the several Kinds of Whales don't mix with one another, but keep by themselves.

Respiration. Their Way of Breathing is by two Spout-Holes in the Top of the Head. The *Spermaceti* has but one, and that on the left Side of the Head. Once in a Quarter of an Hour, when not disturbed, they are observed to rise and blow, spouting out Water and Wind, and to draw in fresh Air: but, when pursued, they will sometimes keep under Water half an Hour or more; though 'tis observed when any Cow has her Calf on her Tail, she rises much oftener (through a natural Instinct) for the young one to breath, without breathing herself. Out of their breathing Holes they spout great Quantities of Blood, when they have received their Death Wound.

Food or Sustentation. For the first Year, as has been already observed, they all suck the Dam. After they are weaned, the right Whales, as is generally supposed, live upon some oozy Matter, which they suck up from the Bottom of the Sea. The Triers, that open them when dead, acquaint me, that they never observed any Grass, Fish, or any other Sort of Food in the right or Whalebone Whale, but only a grayish soft Clay, which the People call *Bole Armoniac;* and yet an experienced Whale-man tells me, that he has seen this Whale in still Weather, skimming on the Surface of the Water, to take in a Sort of reddish Spawn or Brett, as some call it, that at some Times will lie upon the Top of the Water, for a Mile together. Here also it may be observed, that though the Body of this Whale is so very bulky, and so exceeding fat; yet when cut open, they are seldom found to have much more Draught than that of an Ox, and they dung much as neat Cattle do. Their Swallow is not much bigger than an Ox's; but the Finback Whale has a larger Swallow: for he lives upon the smaller Fish, as Mackerel, Herring, *&c.* great Sculls of which they run through, and, with a short Turn, cause an Eddy or Whirlpool, by the Force of which, the small Fish are brought into a Cluster; so that this Fish, with open Mouth, will take in some Hundreds of them at a Time. The *Spermaceti* Whale, besides other Fish, feeds much upon a small Fish that has a Bill; our Fishermen call them Squid Fish. The small Pieces of these Squid Bills are plainly to be discerned in the Ambergris, and may be picked out of it; they appear glazy, and like little Pieces of broken Shells.

The Way and Manner of killing Whales. Mr. *Harris* in his *Bibliotheca Navigantium, &c.* has given a very particular Account of the Method of taking Whales at *Greenland,* and though our Way in *New England* differs very much from that, yet I shall wave it, as not so strictly appertaining to Philosophy. Only I would take notice of the Boats our Whale-men use in going from the Shore after the Whale: They are made of Cedar Clapboards, and so very light, that two Men can conveniently carry them, and yet they are twenty Feet long, and carry six Men, *viz.* The Harpooner in the Forepart of the Boat, four Oarsmen, and the Steersman. These Boats run very swift, and by reason of their Lightness can be brought on and off, and so kept out of Danger. The Whale is sometimes killed with a single Stroke, and yet at other Times she will hold the Whale-men in Play, near half a Day together, with their Lances, and sometimes they will get away after they have been lanced and spouted blood, with Irons in them, and Drugs fastened to them, which are thick Boards about fourteen inches square. Our People formerly used to kill the Whale near the Shore; but now they go off to Sea in Sloops and Whaleboats, in the Months of *May, June,* and *July,* between *Cape Cod* and *Bermudas;* where they lie by in the Night, and sail to and again in the Day, and seldom miss of them; they bring home the Blubber in their Sloops. The true Season, for taking the right or Whalebone Whale, is from the Beginning of *June,* to the End of *May;* for the *Spermaceti* Whale, from the Beginning of *June,* to the End of *August.* And it has been observed by our Fishermen, that when a *Spermaceti* Whale is struck, he usually, if not always, throws the Excrements out of the *Anus.*

The wonderful, and even prodigious Strength of this Creature, which lies principally in their Tails, that being both their offensive and defensive Weapon. Many Instances of this Kind I have had from credible Persons, who were Eyewitnesses; I will mention but a few. A Boat has been cut down from Top to Bottom with the Tail of a Whale, as if cut with a Saw, the Clapboards scarce splintered, though the Gunnel upon the Top is of tough Wood. Another has had the Stern, or Sternpost of about three Inches through, and of the toughest Wood that can be found, into which the Ends of the Cedar Clapboards are nailed, cut off smooth above the Cuddy, without so much as shattering the Boat, or drawing the Nails of the Clapboards. An Oar has been cut off with a Stroke upwards, and yet not so much as lifted up out of the Tholepin. One Person had an Oar cut off, while in his Hand, and yet never felt any Jarring.

A few Years since, one of the Finback Whales came into an Harbor near *Cape Cod,* and towed away a Sloop of near forty Ton, out of the Harbor into the Sea. This Accident happened thus: It is thought the Whale was rubbing herself upon the Fluke of the Anchor, or going near the Bottom, got the Fluke into her Nisket, or the Orifice of the *Uterus,* and, finding herself caught, tore away with such Violence, and towed the Sloop out of the Harbor, as fast as if she had been under Sail with a good Gale of Wind, to the Astonishment of the People on Shore, for there was nobody on board. When the Whale came into deep Water, she went under, and had like to have carried the Sloop with her, but the Cable gave Way, and so the Boats that were out after her, recovered it. This Whale was found dead some Days after on that Shore, with the Anchor sticking in her Belly.

After a Whale is dead, it has been observed, that the same way the Head lies, so the Head will lie if not forcibly turned, and let the Wind blow which Way it will, that Way they will scull a Head, though right in the Eye of the Wind, and they are much easier towed to the Shore, if they die that Way with their Head, than any other.

The Enemies of the Whale, or the Fish that prey upon the Whales, and often kill the young ones, for they won't venture upon an old one, unless much wounded, Our Whale-men have given this Fish the Name of Killers. These Killers are from twenty to thirty Feet long, and have Teeth in both Jaws that lock one within another. He has a Fin, near the Middle of his Back, four or five Foot long. They go in Company by Dozens, and set upon a young Whale, and will bait him like so many Bulldogs; some will lay hold of his Tail to keep him from thrashing, while others lay hold of his Head, and bite and thrash him, till the poor Creature, being thus heated, lolls out his Tongue, and then some of the Killers catch hold of his Lips, and if possible of his Tongue; and after they have killed him, they chiefly feed upon the Tongue and Head, but when he begins to putrefy, they leave him. This Killer is without doubt the *Orca*, that Dr. *Frangius* describes in his Treatise of Animals. His Words are these, *Quando Orca insequitur Balaenam, ipsa Balaena horibilem edit Mugitum, non aliter quam cum Taurus mordetur a Cane* [When a killer whale attacks a whale, the whale itself gives forth a horrible roar, not otherwise than when a bull is bitten by a dog]. These Killers are of such invincible Strength, that when several Boats together have been towing a dead Whale, one of them has come and fastened his Teeth in her, and carried her away down to the Bottom in an Instant. And sometimes again, they have bit out a Piece of Blubber of about two Foot square, which is of that Toughness, that an Iron, with little Beards being struck into it, will hold it till it draws the Boat under Water. The Killers are sometimes taken, and make good Oil, but have no Whalebone. The Carcasses, or Bodies of dead Whales in the Sea, serve for food for Gulls, and other Seafowl, as well as Sharks, for they are not very nice.

Mark Catesby
(1683–1749)

Although we identify the eighteenth-century naturalists Linnaeus and Buffon with monumental projects of collecting and describing flora and fauna, it was Englishman Mark Catesby who published the first relatively comprehensive account of the plants and animals of the British colonies of North America. In natural history expeditions to the wilderness of Virginia (1712–19) and Carolina (1722–26), Catesby attempted to collect, sketch, and describe as many species as possible. His great work, *The Natural History of Carolina, Florida, and the Bahama Islands,* published in two volumes (1731–1743, with an appendix in 1747), became the main study upon which naturalists (including Franklin and Jefferson) depended throughout the eighteenth century. So accomplished was this work (although it occasionally borrowed directly from John Lawson) that in 1733 Catesby was made a Fellow of the Royal Society on the basis of the first volume alone—and so proud was he of the distinction that he had it engraved upon his tombstone. That first volume, consisting primarily of plates and descriptions of birds, also established Catesby as the first great American ornithologist; indeed, his depictions of birds were the best available until the work of Alexander Wilson and John James Audubon, nearly a century later. Though he was self-taught as an engraver, Catesby's 220 plates of the *Natural History* captured the imagination of readers. Equally significant, however, was Catesby's approach to both prose and visual description: he was among the first naturalists to deliberately sketch flora and fauna *in situ* and *ad vivum* to ensure accuracy in the depiction of morphology, color, and posture. Catesby also demonstrated a proto-ecological sensibility when he arranged his plates to depict plants and animals in natural association. In the following selection, his division of land into zones by types of vegetation (rice, oak-hickory, pine, shrub oak) is also an early example of the ecological technique of defining local environments according to the presence of key species. Catesby's accomplishments were honored in the naming of several species, including *Rana catesbeiana*, the bullfrog.

From *The Natural History of Carolina, Florida, and the Bahama Islands* (1731)

The Preface

The inhabited parts of Carolina extend west from the sea about sixty miles, and almost the whole length of the coast, being a level, low country. In these parts I continued the first year searching after, collecting and describing the animals and plants. I then went to the upper uninhabited parts of the country, and continued at and about Fort Moore, a small fortress on the banks of the River Savanna, which runs from thence a course of 300 miles down to the sea, and is about the same distance from its source, in the mountains.

I was much delighted to see nature differ in these upper parts, and to find here abundance of things not to be seen in the lower parts of the country. This encouraged me to take several journeys with the Indians higher up the rivers, towards the mountains, which afforded not only a succession of new vegetable appearances, but the most delightful prospects imaginable, besides the diversion of hunting buffalo, bears, panthers, and other wild beasts. In these excursions I employed an Indian to carry my box, in which, besides paper and materials for painting, I put dried specimens of plants, seeds, etc.—as I gathered them. To the hospitality and assistance of these friendly Indians, I am much indebted, for I not only subsisted on what they shot, but their first care was to erect a bark hut, at the approach of rain to keep me and my cargo from wet. . . .

Of the Soil of Carolina

The whole coast of Florida, particularly Carolina, is low; defended from the sea by sandbanks, which are generally two or three hundred yards from low-water mark, the sand rising gradually from the sea to the foot of the bank, ascending to the height of fourteen or sixteen feet. These banks are cast up by the sea, and serve as a boundary to keep it within its limits. But in hurricanes, and when strong winds set on the shore, they are then overflowed, raising innumerable hills of loose sand further within land, in the hollows of which, when the water subsides, are frequently left infinite variety of shells, fish, bones, and other refuse of the ocean. The sea on these coasts seldom makes any sudden or remarkable revolution, but gets and loses alternately and gradually.

A grampus cast on the shore of North Edisto River, sixteen feet long, I observed was in less than a month covered with sand. Great winds often blow away the sand two or three feet deep, and expose to view numbers of shells and other things, that has lain buried many months, and sometimes years.

At Sullivans Island, which is on the north side of the entrance of Charleston harbor, the sea on the west side has so encroached (though most defended, it being on the contrary side to the ocean) that it has gained in three years time, a quarter of a mile laying prostrate, and swallowing up vast pine and palmetto trees. By such a progress, with the assistance of a few hurricanes, it probably, in some few years, may wash away the whole island, which is about six miles in circumference.

At about half a mile back from the sandbanks before mentioned, the soil begins to mend gradually, producing bays, and other shrubs; yet, till at the distance of some miles, it is very sandy and unfit for tillage, lying in small hills, which appear as if they had been formerly some of those sandhills formed by the sea, though now some miles from it.

Most of the coast of Florida and Carolina, for many miles within land, consists of low islands and extensive marshes, divided also by innumerable creeks, and narrow muddy channels, through which only boats, canoes, and periaguas can pass.

These creeks, or rather gutters, run very intricately through the marshes, by which in many places a communication is necessitated to be cut from one creek to another, to shorten the passage, and avoid those tedious meanders.

These inland passages are of great use to the inhabitants, who without being exposed to the open sea, travel with safety in boats and periaguas; yet are necessitated sometimes to cross some rivers and sounds, eight or ten miles wide, or go far about. The further parts of these marshes from the sea, are confined by higher lands, covered with woods, through which, by intervals, the marsh extends in narrow tracts higher up the country, and contracts gradually as the ground rises; these upper tracts of marshland, by their advantageous situation, might with small expense be drained, and made excellent meadowlands the soil being exceeding good. But so long as such spacious tracts of higher lands lie uncultivated, and continue of no other use than for their cattle to range in, such improvements are like to lie neglected, and the marshes, which is a considerable part of the country, remain of little or no use.

The soil of Carolina is various; but that which is generally cultivated consists principally of three kinds, which are distinguished by the names of rice land, oak and hickory land, and pine barren land. Rice land is most valuable, though only productive of that grain, it being too wet for anything else. The situation of this land is various, but always low, and usually at the head of creeks and rivers, and before they are cleared of wood are called swamps; which being impregnated by the washings from the higher lands, in a series of years are become vastly rich, and deep of soil, consisting of a sandy loam of a dark brown color. These swamps, before they are prepared for rice, are thick, overgrown with underwood and lofty trees of mighty bulk, which by excluding the sun's beams, and preventing the exhalation of these stagnating waters, occasions the land to be always wet, but by cutting down the wood is partly evaporated, and the earth better adapted to the culture of rice; yet great rains, which usually fall at the latter part of the summer, raises the water two or three feet, and frequently cover the rice wholly, which nevertheless, though it usually remains in that state for some weeks, receives no detriment.

The next land in esteem is that called oak and hickory land; those trees, particularly the latter, being observed to grow mostly on good land. This land is of most use, in general producing the best grain, pulse, roots, and herbage, and is not liable to inundations; on it are also found the best kinds of oak for timber, and hickory, an excellent wood for burning. This land is generally light and sandy, with a mixture of loam.

The third and worst kind of land is the pine barren land, the name implying its character. The soil is a light sterile sand, productive of little else but pine trees, from which notwithstanding are drawn beneficial commodities, of absolute use in shipping, and other uses, such as masts, timber, etc. pitch, tar, rosin and turpentine. One third part of the country is, I believe, of this soil.

Though what is already said may suffice for a general description of the inhabited lands of Carolina, and of which the greatest part of the soil consists, yet there are some tracts interspersed of a different nature and quality; particularly pine lands are often intermixed with narrow tracts of low lands, called bay swamps, which are not confined by steep banks, but by their gradual sinking seem little lower than the pine land through which they run. In the middle of these swamps, the water stands two or three feet deep, shallowing gradually on each side. Their breadth is unequal, from a quarter to half a mile, more or less, extending in length several miles. On this wet land grows a variety of evergreen trees and shrubs, most of them aquatics, as the *Akea floridana,* red bay, water tupelo, alaternus, whorts, smilax, *Cistus virg.* or the upright honeysuckle, *Magnotia lauri, folio,* etc.

The swamps so filled with a profusion of flagrant and beautiful plants, give a most pleasing entertainment to the senses; therein excelling other parts of the country; and by their closeness and warmth in winter are a recess to many of the wading and waterfowls. This soil is composed of a blackish sandy loam, and proves good rice land; but the trouble of grubbing up, and clearing it of the trees and underwood has been hitherto a discouragement to the culture of it.

Another kind of land may be observed more sterile than that of pine barren land. This land is rejected, and not capable of cultivation, and produces nothing but shrubby oaks, bearing acorns at the height of two feet. I think it is called shrubby oak land.

All the lower (which are the inhabited) parts of Carolina, are a flat sandy country; the land rising imperceptibly to the distance of about an hundred miles from the sea, where loose stones begin to appear, and at length rocks, which at the nearer approach to the mountains, increase in quantity and magnitude, forming gradual hills, which also increase in height, exhibiting extensive and most delightful prospects. Many spacious tracts of meadowland are confined by these rugged hills, burdened with grass six feet high. Other of these valleys are replenished with brooks and rivulets of clear water, whose banks are covered with spacious tracts of canes, which retaining their leaves the year round, are an excellent food for horses and cattle, and are of great benefit particularly to Indian traders, whose caravans travel these uninhabited countries; to these shady thickets of canes (in sultry weather) resort numerous herds of buffalo where solacing in these limpid streams they enjoy a cool and secret retreat. Pine barren, oak, and hickory land, as has been before observed to abound in the lower parts of the country, engross also a considerable share of these upper parts.

The richest soil in the country lies on the banks of those larger rivers, that have their sources in the mountains, from whence in a series of time has been accumulated by inundations such a depth of prolific matter, that the vast burden of mighty trees it bears, and all other productions, demonstrates it to be the deepest and most fertile of any in the country. Yet pity it is that this excellent soil should be liable to annual damage from the same cause that enriched it, for being subject to be overflowed lessens the value of it. In other places on the banks of these rivers extend vast thickets of cane, of a much larger stature than those before mentioned, they being between twenty and thirty feet high, growing so close, that they are hardly penetrable but by bears, panthers, wild cats, and the like. . . .

Of the Water

The larger rivers in Carolina and Virginia have their sources in the Appalachian mountains, generally springing from rocks, and forming cascades and waterfalls in various manners, which being collected in their course, and uniting into single streams, cause abundance of narrow rapid torrents, which falling into the lower grounds, fill innumerable brooks and rivulets, all which contribute to form and supply the large rivers.

All those rivers which have their sources in the mountains, have cataracts about one-third of the distance from the mountains to the sea. These cataracts consist of infinite numbers of various sized rocks, scattered promiscuously in all parts of the river, so close to one another, and in many places so high, that violent torrents and lofty cascades are continually flowing from between and over them. The extent of these cataracts (or falls, as they are commonly called) is usually four or five miles; nor are the rivers destitute of rocks all the way between them and the mountains; but between these falls and the sea, the rivers are open, and void of rocks, and consequently are navigable so far, and no further, which necessitates the Indians in their passage from the mountains, to drag their canoes some miles by land, till they get below the cataracts, from which they have an open passage down to the sea, except that the rivers in some places are encumbered by trees carried down and lodged by violent torrents from the mountains.

The coasts of Florida, including Carolina and Virginia, with the sounds, inlets, and lower parts of the rivers, have a muddy and soft bottom.

At low water there appears in the rivers and creeks immense beds of oysters, covering the muddy banks many miles together; in some great rivers extending thirty or forty miles from the sea, they do not lie separate, but are closely joined to one another, and appear as a solid rock a foot and a half or two feet in depth, with their edges upwards.

The rivers springing from the mountains are liable to great inundations, occasioned not only from the numerous channels feeding them from the mountains, but the height and steepness of their banks, and obstructions of the rocks.

When great rains fall on the mountains, these rapid torrents are very sudden and violent; an instance of which may give a general idea of them, and their ill consequences.

In September 1722, at Fort Moore, a little fortress on the Savannah river, about midway between the sea and mountains, the waters rose twenty-nine feet in less than forty hours. This proceeded only from what rain fell on the mountains, they at the fort having had none in that space of time.

It came rushing down the river so suddenly, and with that impetuosity that it not only destroyed all their grain, but swept away and drowned the cattle belonging to the garrison. Islands were formed, and others joined to the land. And in some places the course of the river was turned. A large and fertile tract of low land, lying on the south side of the river, opposite to the fort, which was a former settlement of the Savannah Indians, was covered with sand three feet in depth, and made unfit for cultivation. This sterile land was not carried from the higher grounds, but was washed from the steep banks of the river. Panthers, bears and deer were drowned, and found lodged on the limbs of trees. The smaller animals suffered also in this calamity; even reptiles and insects were dislodged from their holes, and violently hurried away, and mixing with harder substances were beat in pieces, and their fragments (after the waters fell) were seen in many places to cover the ground.

There is no part of the globe where the signs of a deluge more evidently appears than in many parts of the northern continent of America; which, though I could illustrate in many instances, let this one suffice. Mr. Woodward, at his plantation in Virginia, above an hundred miles from the sea, towards the sources of Rappahannock river, in digging a well about seventy feet deep, to find a spring, discovered at that depth a bed of the Glossopetrae, one of which was sent me.

All parts of Virginia, at the distance of sixty miles, or more, abound in fossil shells of various kinds, which in stratums lie imbedded a great depth in the earth, in the banks of rivers and other places, among which are frequently found the vertebras, and other bones of sea animals.

Eliza Lucas Pinckney
(1722–1793)

Elizabeth Lucas was the daughter of George Lucas, a British Army officer who ran a sugar plantation on Antigua, in the West Indies, where "Eliza" was born. Fearing for his wife's health — and for his family's safety, should tensions between Britain and Spain escalate into war — Lucas moved his family to the mainland province of South Carolina in 1738, when Eliza was fifteen. The family established at "Wappoo," an estate on Wappoo Creek, seventeen (land) miles from Charleston, but also administered several other plantations in the area. In 1739 duty called Lucas back to Antigua, leaving responsibility for management of the Carolina estates to sixteen-year-old Eliza, whose mother was too ill to be of much help. Showing tremendous courage, energy, and business acumen, young Eliza managed not only to keep the plantations solvent, but also developed remunerative new agricultural techniques and products.

Most importantly, she is credited with successfully introducing indigo—a crop that proved vital to the regional economy—to America from the Caribbean during the early 1740s. She also experimented with domestic silk manufacture, and she was a devoted orchardist and arborist who followed Virgil in planting cedar groves, and who had the foresight to plant oak groves in anticipation of increasing demand for timber by shipbuilders. In 1744 she married Charles Pinckney, a prominent colonial lawyer and jurist, and had four children—of which two, Charles and Thomas, became prominent Federalist leaders. Eliza Pinckney's *Letterbook*, which remained in manuscript until 1972, provides a rare glimpse into the life of a remarkable eighteenth-century woman horticulturalist, arborist, and agriculturalist. The first four letters excerpted below were written when Pinckney was a teenager and had just received responsibility for her father's plantations; the last three were written in the 1760s, when she was again thrust into the role of estate administrator by her husband's death in 1758. Although the Pinckney estates and fortunes were ravaged during the Revolutionary War, the family survived the trial to become one of the most prominent families of the early national period. When Eliza Pinckney died of cancer in 1793, President Washington himself insisted upon serving as her pallbearer.

From *The Letterbook of Eliza Lucas Pinckney* (1739–1762/1972)

[circa 1742]
To Miss Bartlett
Dr. Miss B

. . . O! I had like to forgot the last thing I have done a great while. I have planted a large fig orchard with design to dry and export them. I have reckoned my expense and the profits to arise from these figs, but was I to tell you how great an Estate I am to make this way, and how 'tis to be laid out you would think me far gone in romance. Your good Uncle I know has long thought I have a fertile brain at scheming. I only confirm him in his opinion; but I own I love the vegetable world extremely. I think it an innocent and useful amusement. Pray tell him, if he laughs much at my project, I never intend to have my hand in a silver mine and he will understand as well as you what I mean.

Our best respects wait on him and Mrs. Pinckney. If my Eyes don't deceive me you in your last letter talk of coming very soon by water to see how my oaks grow. Is it really so, or only one of your unripe schemes? While 'tis in your head put it speedily into execution and you will give great pleasure to

Y m o s
E. Lucas

[circa 1742]
[To Miss Bartlett]
Dr. Miss B

I have got no further than the first volume of Virgil but was most agreeably disappointed to find myself instructed in agriculture as well as entertained by his charming pen; for I am persuaded though he wrote in and for Italy, it will in many instances suit Carolina. I had never perused those books before and imagined I should immediately enter upon battles, storms and tempest that puts one in a maze and makes one shudder while one reads. But the calm and pleasing diction of pastoral and gardening agreeably presented themselves, not unsuitably to this charming season of the year, with which I am so much delighted that had I but the fine soft language of our poet to paint it properly, I should give you but little respite till you came into the country and attended to the beauties of pure nature unassisted by art. The majestic pine imperceptibly puts on a fresher green; the young myrtle joining its fragrance to that of the Jessamin of golden hue perfumes all the woods and regales the rural wanderer with its sweets; the daisies, the honeysuckles and a thousand nameless beauties of the woods invite you to partake the pleasures the country affords.

You may wonder how I could in this gay season think of planting a Cedar grove, which rather reflects an Autumnal gloom and solemnity than the freshness and gaiety of spring. But so it is. I have begun it last week and intend to make it an Emblem not of a lady, but of a compliment which your good Aunt was pleased to make to the person her partiality has made happy by giving her a place in her esteem and friendship. I intend then to connect in my grove the solemnity (not the solidity) of summer or autumn with the cheerfulness and pleasures of spring, for it shall be filled with all kind of flowers, as well wild as Garden flowers, with seats of Camomile and here and there a fruit tree — oranges, nectrons, Plums, &c. . . .

Yr. m. o. St.
E. Lucas

[circa 1742]
[To Miss Bartlett]
Dr. Miss B

Won't you laugh at me if I tell you I am so busy in providing for Posterity I hardly allow myself time to Eat or sleep and can but just snatch a minute to write to you and a friend or two now. I am making a large plantation of Oaks which I look upon as my own property, whether my father gives me the land or not; and therefore I design many years hence when oaks are more valuable than they are now — which you know they will be when we come to build fleets. I intend, I say, 2 thirds of the produce of my oaks for a charity (I'll let you know my scheme another time) and the other 3rd for those that shall have the trouble of putting my design in Execution. I suppose according to custom you will show this to your Uncle and Aunt. "She is a good girl," says Mrs. Pinckney. "She is never Idle and always means well." "Tell the little Visionary," says your Uncle, "come to town and partake of some of the amusements suitable to her time of life." Pray tell him I think these so, and what he may now think whims and projects may turn out well by and by. Out of many surely one may hit.

I promised to tell you when the mockingbird began to sing. The little warbler has done wonders; the first time he opened his soft pipe this spring, he inspired me with the spirit of Rhyming, and I produced the 3 following lines while I was lacing my stays:

> Sing on thou charming mimic of the feathered kind
> and let the rational a lesson learn from thee,
> to Mimic (not defects) but harmony.

If you let any mortal besides yourself see this exquisite piece of poetry, you shall never have a line more than this specimen; and how great will be your loss you who have seen the above may judge as well as

Yr. m. obedt. Servt.

Eliza. Lucas

May 22nd, 1742

[To Thomas Lucas]

I am now set down, my Dear Brother, to obey your commands and give you a short description of the part of the world I now inhabit. South Carolina then is a large and Extensive Country Near the Sea. Most of the settled parts of it is upon a flat—the soil near Charleston sandy, but further distant clay and swamplands. It abounds with fine navigable rivers, and great quantities of fine timber. The Country at a great distance, that is to say about a hundred or a hundred and fifty mile from Charleston, is very hilly.

The Soil in general is very fertile, and there is very few European or American fruits or grain but what grow here. The Country abounds with wild fowl, Venison and fish. Beef, veal and mutton are here in much greater perfection than in the Islands though not equal to that in England; but their pork exceeds any I ever tasted anywhere. The Turkeys are extremely fine, especially the wild, and indeed all their poultry is exceeding good; and peaches, Nectrons and melons of all sorts extremely fine and in profusion, and their Oranges exceed any I ever tasted in the West Indies or from Spain or Portugal.

The people in general are hospitable and honest, and the better sort add to these a polite gentile behavior. The poorer sort are the most indolent people in the world or they could never be wretched in so plentiful a country as this. The winters here are very fine and pleasant, but 4 months in the year is extremely disagreeable, excessive hot, much thunder and lightning, and mosquitoes and sand flies in abundance.

Charleston, the Metropolis, is a neat pretty place. The inhabitants are polite and live in a very gentile manner; the streets and houses regularly built; the ladies and gentlemen gay in their dress. Upon the whole you will find as many agreeable people of both sexes for the size of the place as almost anywhere. St. Phillips church in Charleston is a very Elegant one, and much frequented. There are several more places of public worship in this town and the generality of people are of a religious turn of mind.

I began in haste and have observed no method or I should have told you before I came to Summer that we have a most charming spring in this country, especially for those who travel through the Country for the scent of the young myrtle and Yellow Jessamin with which the woods abound is delightful. . . .

My dr. brother
Your most affectionately
E. Lucas

[circa 1761]
[To Mrs. King]
Dear Madam,

'Tis with great regret I send Mr. King so small a collection of seeds, especially as I have an opportunity to send them by a private hand; but I was taken in Sept. with a most severe fever which held me many days without intermission and seized my spirits in such a manner as brought me to the Verge of the grave 3 times in 2 months, and several relapses afterwards has confined me to my chamber 4 months.

As soon as I was able I inquired how my directions were observed concerning the Seeds, and though I had sent positive orders to 3 places for different sorts of seeds, they were observed but at one. Poor Mr. Drayton had also promised me a large quantity of Magnolia and Bay seed, but he was taken ill about the same time I was, and died. I am a good deal mortified at the disappointment as there will be a year lost by it, but please God I live this year, I will endeavor to make amends and not only send the Seeds but plant a nursery here to be sent you in plants at 2 year old. And I think I know a method that will preserve the trees very well, by which means I imagine you will save 2 if not 3 years growth in your trees, for I believe a tree will grow as much in 2 years here as in 4 or 5 in England. . . .

[Eliza Lucas]

Febr. 1762
[To Mr. Keate]
. . . What great doings you have had in England since I left it. You people that live in the great world in the midst of Scenes of entertainment and pleasure abroad, of improving studies and polite amusement at home, must be very good to think of your friends in this remote Corner of the Globe. I really think it a great virtue in you; and if I could conceal the selfish principle by which I am actuated I could with a better grace attempt to persuade you that there is so much merit in setting down at home and writing now and then to an old woman in the Wilds of America that I believe I should take you off an hour sometimes from attending Matinee and the other gay scenes you frequent.

How different is the life we live here; visiting is the great and almost only amusement of late years. However, as to my own particular, I live agreeable enough to my own taste, as much so as I can separated from my dear boys.

I love a Garden and a book; and they are all my amusement except I include one of the greatest Businesses of my life (my attention to my dear little girl) under that article. For a pleasure it certainly is to cultivate the tender mind, to teach the young Idea how to shoot, &c., especially to a mind so tractable and a temper so sweet as hers. For, I thank God, I have an excellent soil to work upon, and by the Divine Grace hope the fruit will be answerable to my endeavors in the cultivation. . . .

Your most obliged friend and most obedt. servant,
E. Pinckney

Febr. 27th, 1762
To Mrs. Onslow
. . . I am glad Col. Onslow takes pleasure in his Garden. 'Tis natural to be pleased at others taking pleasure in the same things we do. I think it an Innocent and delightful amusement. I have a little hovel about 5 mile from town, quite in a forest where I find much amusement 4 or 5 months in the year, and where I have room enough to exercise my Genius that way, If I had any. However, I please myself and a few that are partial to me. I am myself head gardener, and I believe work much harder than most principal ones do. We found it in such ruins when we arrived from England that I have had a wood to clear, and indeed it was laid out in the old taste so that I have been modernizing it, which has afforded me much employment.

Being a sort of enthusiast in my Veneration for fine trees, I look upon the destroyers of Pyrford Avenue as sacrilegious Enemies to posterity, and upon an old oak with the reverential Esteem of a Druid. It staggered my philosophy to bear with patience the Cutting down one remarkable tree which was directed by an old man by mistake, and I could not help being very angry with the old fellow though he had never offended me before in his life. Indeed it was planted by my dear Mr. Pinckney's own hand, which made it doubly mortifying to me. What must Col. Onslow's vexation or Philosophy be if he loves trees but half as well as I do to see so many fallen — and probably planted by some of his ancestors.

I will now conclude. Surely 'tis time when I can find nothing more animated to entertain you with than stocks and stones, or you will think me as senseless as they which I must be to be any other than what I am

My dr madam
Your most affectionate
Most obliged and obedient Servt.
E. Pinckney

Peter Kalm
(1716–1779)

Born in Sweden to a family from Swedish Finland, Pehr Kalm had intended to study theology when he entered the University of Åbo (Turku), Finland, in 1735, the same year fellow Swede Linnaeus published his monumental *Systema Naturae*. But Kalm soon devoted himself to studying the new Linnaean botanical taxonomy and by 1741 had crossed the Baltic to study with Linnaeus at Uppsala University, in southeastern Sweden. Linnaeus's tutelage made Kalm an accomplished botanist and an able disciple of the new taxonomic system, and his influence allowed Kalm to make a great collecting expedition to North America from 1748 to 1751. The young botanist traveled to the colonies via England, where he consulted with Mark Catesby before sailing for Philadelphia. Once in Philadelphia he was befriended by Benjamin Franklin, John Bartram, and other prominent naturalists, among whom he helped to spread his mentor's system of classification. Kalm traveled widely in the British colonies and in Canada, studying new species and recording detailed observations in his journal; when Franklin published Kalm's account of Niagara Falls in the *Pennsylvania Gazette* on September 20, 1750, it was the first description of the falls to be published in English. Kalm's impressive North American botanical collection added at least fifty new species to the American plants included in the 1753 edition of Linnaeus's *Species Plantarum*, and in appreciation Linnaeus named the mountain laurel, *Kalmia latifolia*, in Kalm's honor. In 1751 Kalm returned to Swedish Finland to assume the position of professor of "Oeconomy" at the University of Åbo. There he worked on his American journals and specimens, eventually publishing his great work, the three-volume *En Resa Til Norra Amerika* (*Travels into North America*), between 1753 and 1761 (the first English translation appeared in 1770–71). And while Kalm is best known as a botanist, the following excerpts from *Travels* show that he was also a careful observer of animals who was keenly aware of the adverse effects of colonial expansion upon native species.

From *Travels into North America* (1753–1761)

October 24, 1748. Of all the rare birds of *North America, the Hummingbird* is the most admirable, or at least most worthy of peculiar attention. Several reasons induce me to believe, that few parts of the world can produce its equal. Dr. *Linnaeus* calls it *Trochilus Colubris.* The *Swedes,* and some *Englishmen,* call it the *King's bird;* but the name of Hummingbird is more common. *Catesby,* in his *Natural History of Carolina,* Vol. 1. page 65. tab. 65. has drawn it, in its natural size, with its proper colors, and added a description of it. In size it is not much bigger than a large *humble-bee,* and is therefore the least of all birds, or it is much if there is a lesser species in the world. Its plumage is most beautifully colored, most of its feathers being green, some gray, and others forming a shining red ring round its neck; the tail glows with fine feathers, changing from green into a brass color. These birds come here in spring, about the time when it begins to grow very warm, and make their nests in summer; but, towards autumn, they retreat again into the more southern countries of *America.* They subsist barely upon the nectar, or sweet juice of flowers, contained in that part which botanists call the *nectarium,* and which they suck up with their long bills. Of all the flowers, they like those most, which have a long tube; and I have observed that they have fluttered chiefly about the *Impatiens Noli-tangere,* and the *Monarda* with crimson flowers. An inhabitant of the country is sure to have a number of these beautiful and agreeable little birds before his windows all the summer long, if he takes care to plant a bed with all sorts of fine flowers under them. It is indeed a diverting spectacle to see these little active creatures flying about the flowers like bees, and sucking their juices with their long and narrow bills. The flowers of the above-mentioned *Monarda* grow *verticillated,* that is, at different distances they surround the stalk, as the flowers of our mint (*Mentha*), bastard hemp (*Galeopsis*), motherwort (*Leonurus*), and dead nettle (*Lamium*). It is therefore diverting to see them putting their bills into every flower in the circle. As soon as they have sucked the juice of one flower, they flutter to the next. One that has not seen them would hardly believe in how short a space of time they have had their tongues in all the flowers of a plant, which when large, and with a long tube, the little bird, by putting its head into them, looks as if it crept with half its body into them.

During their sucking the juice out of the flowers, they never settle on it, but flutter continually like bees, bend their feet backwards, and move their wings so quick, that they are hardly visible. During this fluttering, they make a humming like bees, or like that which is occasioned by the turning of a little wheel. After they have thus, without resting, fluttered for a while, they fly to a neighboring tree or post, and resume their vigor again. They then return to their humming and sucking. They are not very shy; and I, in company with several other people, have not been full two yards from the place where they fluttered about and sucked the flowers; and though we spoke and moved, yet they were no ways disturbed; but, on going towards them, they would fly off with the swiftness of an arrow. When several of them were on the same bed, there was always a violent combat between them, in meeting each other at the same flower (for envy was likewise predominant amongst these little creatures) and they attacked with such impetuosity, that it would seem as if the strongest would pierce its antagonist through and through with its long bill. During the fight, they seem to stand in the air, keeping themselves up by the incredibly swift motion of their wings. When the windows towards the garden are open, they pursue each other into the rooms, fight a little, and flutter away again. Sometimes they come to a flower which is withering, and has no more juice in it; they then, in a fit of anger, pluck it off, and throw it on the ground, that it may not mislead them for the future. If a garden contains a great number of these little birds, they are seen to pluck off the flowers in such quantities, that the ground is quite covered with them, and it seems as if this proceeded from a motion of envy.

Commonly you hear no other sound than their humming; but when they fly against each other in the air, they make a chirping noise like a sparrow or chicken. I have sometimes walked with several other people in small gardens, and these birds have on all sides fluttered about us, without appearing very shy. They are so small that one would easily mistake them for great humming-bees or butterflies, and their flight resembles that of the former, and is incredibly swift. They have never been observed to feed on insects or fruit; the nectar of flowers seems therefore to be their only food. Several people have caught some hummingbirds, on account of their singular beauty, and have put them into cages, where they died for want of a proper food. However, Mr. *Bartram* has kept a couple of them for several weeks together, by feeding them with water in which sugar had been dissolved; and I am of opinion, that it would not be difficult to keep them all winter in a hothouse.

The hummingbird always builds its nest in the middle of a branch of a tree, and it is so small, that it cannot be seen from the ground, but he who intends to see it must get up to the branch. For this reason it is looked upon as a great rarity if a nest is accidentally found, especially as the trees in summer have so thick a foliage. The nest is likewise the least of all; that which is in my possession is quite round, and consists in the inside of a brownish and quite soft down, which seems to have been collected from the leaves of the great mullein or *Verbascum Thapsus,* which are often found covered with a soft wool of this color, and the plant is plentiful here. The outside of the nest has a coating of green moss, such as is common on old pales, or enclosures, and on trees; the inner diameter of the nest is hardly a geometrical inch at the top, and its depth half an inch. It is however known, that the hummingbirds make their nests likewise of flax, hemp, moss, hair, and other such soft materials; they are said to lay two eggs, each of the size of a pea. . . .

November 9. All the old *Swedes* and *Englishmen,* born in *America,* whom I ever questioned, asserted that there were not near so many birds fit for eating at present, as there used to be when they were children, and that their decrease was visible. They even said, that they had heard their fathers complain of this, in whose childhood the bays, rivers, and brooks were quite covered with all sorts of waterfowl, such as wild geese, ducks, and the like. But at present there is sometimes not a single bird upon them; about sixty or seventy years ago, a single person could kill eighty ducks in a morning; but at present you frequently wait in vain for a single one. A *Swede* above ninety years old assured me, that he had in his youth killed twenty-three ducks at a shot.

This good luck nobody is likely to have at present, as you are forced to ramble about for a whole day, without getting a sight of more than three or four. *Cranes* at that time came hither by hundreds in the spring: at present there are but very few. The *wild Turkeys,* and the birds, which the *Swedes* in this country call *Partridges* and *Hazel hens,* were in whole flocks in the woods. But at this time a person is tired with walking before he can start a single bird.

The cause of this diminution is not difficult to find. Before the arrival of the *Europeans,* the country was uncultivated, and full of great forests. The few *Indians* that lived here seldom disturbed the birds. They carried on no trade among themselves, iron and gunpowder were unknown to them. One hundredth part of the fowl, which at that time were so plentiful here, would have sufficed to feed the few inhabitants; and considering that they cultivated their small maize fields, caught fish, hunted stags, beavers, bears, wild cattle, and other animals whose flesh was delicious to them, it will soon appear how little they disturbed the birds. But since the arrival of great crowds of *Europeans,* things are greatly changed: the country is well peopled, and the woods are cut down: the people increasing in this country, they have by hunting and shooting in part extirpated the birds, in part scared them away: in spring the people still take both eggs, mothers, and young indifferently, because no regulations are made to the contrary. And if any had been made, the spirit of freedom which prevails in the country would not suffer them to be obeyed. But though the eatable birds have been diminished greatly, yet there are others, which have rather increased than decreased in number, since the arrival of the *Eu-*

ropeans: this can most properly be said of a species of daws, which the *English* call *Blackbirds,* and the *Swedes, Maize thieves;* Dr. *Linnaeus* calls them *Gracula Quiscula.* And together with them, the several sorts of *Squirrels* among the quadrupeds have spread; for these and the former live chiefly upon maize, or at least they are most greedy of it. But as population increases, the cultivation of maize increases, and of course the food of the above-mentioned animals is more plentiful: to this it is to be added, that these latter are rarely eaten, and therefore they are more at liberty to multiply their kind. There are likewise other birds which are not eaten, of which at present there are nearly as many as there were before the arrival of the *Europeans.* On the other hand I heard great complaints of the great decrease of eatable fowl, not only in this province, but in all the parts of *North America,* where I have been.

Aged people had experienced that with the fish, which I have just mentioned of the birds: in their youth, the bays, rivers, and brooks, had such quantities of fish, that at one draught in the morning, they caught as many as a horse was able to carry home. But at present things are greatly altered; and they often work in vain all the night long, with all their fishing tackle. The causes of this decrease of fish, are partly the same with those of the diminution of the number of birds; being of late caught by a greater variety of contrivances, and in different manners than before. The numerous mills on the rivers and brooks likewise contribute to it in part: for it has been observed here, that the fish go up the river in order to spawn in a shallow water; but when they meet with works that prevent their proceeding, they turn back, and never come again. Of this I was assured by a man of fortune at *Boston:* his father was used to catch a number of herrings throughout the winter, and almost always in summer, in a river, upon his country seat: but he having built a mill with a dike in this water, they were lost. In this manner they complained here and everywhere of the decrease of fish. Old people asserted the same in regard to oysters at *New York;* for though they are still taken in considerable quantity, and are as big, and as delicious as can be wished, yet all the oyster-catchers own, that the number diminishes greatly every year: the most natural cause of it, is probably the immoderate catching of them at all times of the year.

Mr. *Franklin* told me, that in that part of *New England* where his father lived, two rivers fell into the sea, in one of which they caught great numbers of herrings, and in the other not one. Yet the places where these rivers discharged themselves into the sea, were not far asunder. They had observed that when the herrings came in spring to deposit their spawn, they always swam up the river, where they used to catch them, but never came into the other. This circumstance led Mr. *Franklin's* father, who was settled between the two rivers, to try whether it was not possible to make the herrings likewise live in the other river. For that purpose he put out his nets, as they were coming up for spawning, and he caught some. He took the spawn out of them, and carefully carried it across the land into the other river. It was hatched, and the consequence was, that every year afterwards they caught more herrings in that river; and this is still the case. This leads one to believe that the fish always like to spawn in the same place where they were hatched, and from whence they first put out to sea; being as it were accustomed to it. . . .

May 5, 1749. . . . *Bullfrogs* are a large species of frogs, which I had an opportunity of hearing and seeing today. As I was riding out, I heard a roaring before me; and I thought it was a bull in the bushes, on the other side of the dike, though the sound was rather more hoarse than that of a bull. I was however afraid, that a bad goring bull might be near me, though I did not see him; and I continued to think so till some hours after, when I talked with some *Swedes* about the *Bullfrogs*, and, by their account, I immediately found that I had heard their voice; for the *Swedes* told me, that there were numbers of them in the dike. I afterwards hunted for them. Of all the frogs in this country, this is doubtless the greatest. I am told, that towards autumn, as soon as the air begins to grow a little cool, they hide themselves under the mud, which lies at the bottom of ponds and stagnant waters, and lie there torpid during winter. As soon as the weather grows mild, towards summer, they begin to get out of their holes, and croak. If the spring, that is, if the mild weather, begins early, they appear about the end of *March*, old style; but if it happens late, they tarry underwater till late in *April*. Their places of abode are ponds, and bogs with stagnant water; they are never in any flowing water. When many of them croak together, they make an enormous noise. Their croak exactly resembles the roaring of an ox or bull, which is somewhat hoarse. They croak so loud, that two people talking by the side of a pond cannot understand each other. They croak all together; then stop a little, and begin again. It seems as if they had a captain among them: for when he begins to croak, all the others follow; and when he stops, the others are all silent. When this captain gives the signal for stopping, you hear a note like *poop* coming from him. In daytime they seldom make any great noise, unless the sky is covered. But the night is their croaking time; and, when all is calm, you may hear them, though you are near a mile and a half off. When they croak, they commonly are near the surface of the water, under the bushes, and have their heads out of the water. Therefore, by going slowly, one may get close up to them before they go away. As soon as they are quite underwater, they think themselves safe, though the water be very shallow.

Sometimes they sit at a good distance from the pond; but as soon as they suspect any danger, they hasten with great leaps into the water. They are very expert at hopping. A full-grown *Bullfrog* takes near three yards at one hop. I have often been told the following story by the old *Swedes*, which happened here, at the time when the *Indians* lived with the *Swedes*. It is well known, that the *Indians* are excellent runners; I have seen them, at Governor *Johnson's*, equal the best horse in its swiftest course, and almost pass by it. Therefore, in order to try how well the bullfrogs could leap, some of the *Swedes* laid a wager with a young *Indian,* that he could not overtake the frog, provided it had two leaps beforehand. They carried a bullfrog, which they had caught in a pond, upon a field, and burnt his backside; the fire, and the *Indian,* who endeavored to be closely up with the frog, had such an effect upon the animal, that it made its long hops across the field, as fast as it could. The *Indian* began to pursue the frog with all his might at the proper time: the noise he made in running frightened the poor frog; probably it was afraid of being tortured with fire again, and therefore it redoubled its leaps, and by that means it reached the pond before the *Indian* could overtake it.

In some years they are more numerous than in others: nobody could tell, whether the snakes had ever ventured to eat them, though they eat all the lesser kinds of frogs. The women are no friends to these frogs, because they kill and eat young ducklings and goslings: sometimes they carry off chickens that come too near the ponds. I have not observed that they bite when they are held in the hands, though they have little teeth; when they are beaten, they cry out almost like children. I was told that some eat the thighs of the hind legs, and that they are very palatable.

Benjamin Franklin
(1706–1790)

Although he began life as the fifteenth child of a poor chandler, Benjamin Franklin lived to become the most famous American in the world in the eighteenth century. A gifted statesman, philosopher, writer, humorist, businessman, pragmatist, and inventor whose character is deeply intertwined with American secular individualism and self-reliance, Franklin was also well known as an accomplished natural scientist. Perhaps most striking is Franklin's sensibility: during the eighteenth century those who explored the mysteries of nature were often referred to as "the curious," a title that describes Franklin perfectly. Although he is probably best known for his statesmanship, his *Autobiography* (1784, 1788), and his *Poor Richard's Almanac* (1732–58), Franklin wrote many scientific papers and letters documenting the results of his various inquiries and experiments. As a virtuoso, he studied all the major scientific fields of his day, including chemistry, medicine, botany, geology, physics, and meteorology; as a Deist, he defended the work of Newton, Locke, and Boyle against objections that the scientific theories proposed by such men were anathema to the orthodox biblical understanding of the physical world; as an Enlightenment rationalist, he interrogated natural phenomena including the Gulf Stream, the aurora borealis, fossils, earthquakes, combustion, magnetism, acoustics, and optics. Franklin's *Experiments and Observations on Electricity,* published beginning in 1751, established him as a leader in the new science of electricity. The following letters — just a few among his voluminous scientific correspondence — give a sense of Franklin's approach to what we would now call the "scientific method": a disciplined and deliberate movement from curiosity to questioning to experimentation to theorizing and, finally, to considerations of the pragmatic applications of his results. Literary botanist William Bartram honored Ben Franklin when he asked that one of his own greatest discoveries, the genus of rare flowering tree, be named *Franklina* in Franklin's honor.

"The Kite" (1752)

Letter to Peter Collinson

Sir,

As frequent mention is made in public papers from *Europe* of the success of the *Philadelphia* experiment for drawing the electric fire from clouds by means of pointed rods of iron erected on high buildings, &, it may be agreeable to the curious to be informed, that the same experiment has succeeded in *Philadelphia,* though made in a different and more easy manner, which is as follows:

Make a small cross of two light strips of cedar, the arms so long as to reach to the four corners of a large thin silk handkerchief when extended; tie the corners of the handkerchief to the extremities of the cross, so you have the body of a kite; which being properly accommodated with a tail, loop, and string, will rise in the air, like those made of paper; but this being of silk, is fitter to bear the wet and wind of a thunder-gust without tearing. To the top of the upright stick of the cross is to be fixed a very sharp-pointed wire, rising a foot or more above the wood. To the end of the twine, next the hand, is to be tied a silk ribbon, and where the silk and twine join, a key may be fastened. This kite is to be raised when a thunder-gust appears to be coming on, and the person who holds the string must stand within a door or window or under some cover, so that the silk ribbon may not be wet; and care must be taken that the twine does not touch the frame of the door or window. As soon as any of the thunder-clouds come over the kite, the pointed wire will draw the electric fire from them, and the kite, with all the twine, will be electrified, and the loose filaments of the twine will stand out every way, and be attracted by an approaching finger. And when the rain has wet the kite and twine, so that it can conduct the electric fire freely, you will find it stream out plentifully from the key on the approach of your knuckle. At this key the vial may charged; and from electric fire thus obtained, spirits may be kindled, and all the other electric experiments be performed, which are usually done by the help of a rubbed glass globe or tube, and thereby the sameness of the electric matter with that of lightning completely demonstrated.

B. Franklin

From "Effect of Oil on Water" (1773)

Letter to William Brownrigg

Dear Sir,

I thank you for the remarks of your learned friend at Carlisle. I had, when a youth, read and smiled at Pliny's account of a practice among the seamen of his time, to still the waves in a storm by pouring oil into the sea; which he mentions, as well as the use made of oil by the diver; but the stilling a tempest by throwing vinegar into the air had escaped me. I think with your friend, that it has been of late too much the mode to slight the learning of the ancients. The learned, too, are apt to slight too much the knowledge of the vulgar. The cooling by evaporation was long an instance of the latter. This art of smoothing the waves by oil is an instance of both.

Perhaps you may not dislike to have an account of all I have heard, and learned, and done in this way. Take it if you please as follows.

In 1757, being at sea in a fleet of ninety-six sail bound against Louisbourg, I observed the wakes of two of the ships to be remarkably smooth, while all the others were ruffled by the wind, which blew fresh. Being puzzled with the differing appearance, I at last pointed it out to our captain, and asked him the meaning of it. "The cooks," says he, "have, I suppose, been just emptying their greasy water through the scuppers, which has greased the sides of those ships a little"; and this answer he gave me with an air of some little contempt, as to a person ignorant of what everybody else knew. In my own mind I at first slighted his solution, though I was not able to think of another; but recollecting what I had formerly read in Pliny, I resolved to make some experiment of the effect of oil on water, when I should have opportunity.

Afterwards being again at sea in 1762, I first observed the wonderful quietness of oil on agitated water, in the swinging glass lamp I made to hang up in the cabin, as described in my printed papers. This I was continually looking at and considering, as an appearance to me inexplicable. An old sea captain, then a passenger with me, thought little of it, supposing it an effect of the same kind with that of oil put on water to smooth it, which he said was a practice of the Bermudians when they would strike fish, which they could not see, if the surface of the water was ruffled by the wind. This practice I had never before heard of, and was obliged to him for the information; though I thought him mistaken as to the sameness of the experiment, the operations being different as well as the effects. In one case, the water is smooth till the oil is put on, and then becomes agitated. In the other it is agitated before the oil is applied, and then becomes smooth. The same gentleman told me, he had heard it was a practice with the fishermen of Lisbon when about to return into the river (if they saw before them too great a surf upon the bar, which they apprehended might fill their boats in passing) to empty a bottle or two of oil into the sea, which would suppress the breakers and allow them to pass safely. A confirmation of this I have not since had an opportunity of obtaining; but discoursing of it with another person, who had often been in the Mediterranean, I was informed, that the divers there, who, when under water in their business, need light, which the curling of the surface interrupts by the refractions of so many little waves, let a small quantity of oil now and then out of their mouths, which rising to the surface smoothes it, and permits the light to come down to them. All these informations I at times revolved in my mind, and wondered to find no mention of them in our books of experimental philosophy.

At length being at Clapham, where there is, on the common, a large pond, which I observed one day to be very rough with the wind, I fetched out a cruet of oil, and dropped a little of it on the water. I saw it spread itself with surprising swiftness upon the surface; but the effect of smoothing the waves was not produced; for I had applied it first on the leeward side of the pond, where the waves were largest, and the wind drove my oil back upon the shore. I then went to the windward side where they began to form; and there the oil, though not more than a teaspoonful, produced an instant calm over a space several yards square, which spread amazingly, and extended itself gradually till it reached the lee side, making all that quarter of the pond, perhaps half an acre, as smooth as a looking glass.

After this I contrived to take with me, whenever I went into the country, a little oil in the upper hollow joint of my bamboo cane, with which I might repeat the experiment as opportunity should offer, and I found it constantly to succeed.

In these experiments, one circumstance struck me with particular surprise. This was the sudden, wide, and forcible spreading of a drop of oil on the face of the water, which I do not know that anybody has hitherto considered. If a drop of oil is put on a highly polished marble table, or on a looking glass that lies horizontally, the drop remains in its place, spreading very little. But, when put on water, it spreads instantly, many feet round, becoming so thin as to produce the prismatic colors, for a considerable space, and beyond them so much thinner as to be invisible, except in its effect of smoothing the waves at a much greater distance. It seems as if a mutual repulsion between its particles took place as soon as it touched the water, and a repulsion so strong as to act on other bodies swimming on the surface, as straw, leaves, chips, &c. forcing them to recede every way from the drop, as from a center, leaving a large, clear space. The quantity of this force, and the distance to which it will operate, I have not yet ascertained; but I think it a curious inquiry, and I wish to understand whence it arises.

In our journey to the North, when we had the pleasure of seeing you at Ormathwaite, we visited the celebrated Mr. Smeaton, near Leeds. Being about to show him the smoothing experiment on a little pond near his house, an ingenious pupil of his, Mr. Jessop, then present, told us of an odd appearance on that pond, which had lately occurred to him. He was about to clean a little cup in which he kept oil, and he threw upon the water some flies that had been drowned in the oil. These flies presently began to move, and turned round on the water very rapidly, as if they were vigorously alive, though on examination he found they were not so. I immediately concluded that the motion was occasioned by the power of the repulsion above mentioned, and that the oil issuing gradually from the spongy body of the fly continued the motion. He found some more flies drowned in oil, with which the experiment was repeated before us. To show that it was not any effect of life recovered by the flies, I imitated it by little bits of oiled chips and paper, cut in the form of a comma, of the size of a common fly; when the stream of repelling particles issuing from the point made the comma turn round the contrary way. This is not a chamber experiment; for it cannot be well repeated in a bowl or dish of water on a table. A considerable surface of water is necessary to give room for the expansion of a small quantity of oil. In a dish of water, if the smallest drop of oil be let fall in the middle, the whole surface is presently covered with a thin greasy film proceeding from the drop; but as soon as that film has reached the sides of the dish, no more will issue from the drop, but it remains in the form of oil, the sides of the dish putting a stop to its dissipation by prohibiting the farther expansion of the film.

Our friend Sir John Pringle, being soon after in Scotland, learned there, that those employed in the herring fishery could at a distance see where the shoals of herrings were, by the smoothness of the water over them, which might possibly be occasioned, he thought, by some oiliness proceeding from their bodies.

A gentleman from Rhode Island told me, it had been remarked, that the harbor of Newport was ever smooth while any whaling vessels were in it; which probably arose from hence, that the blubber which they sometimes bring loose in the hold, or the leakage of their barrels, might afford some oil, to mix with that water, which from time to time they pump out, to keep their vessel free, and that some oil might spread over the surface of the water in the harbor, and prevent the forming of any waves.

This prevention I would thus endeavor to explain. . . .

Now I imagine that the wind, blowing over water thus covered with a film of oil, cannot easily *catch* upon it, so as to raise the first wrinkles, but slides over it, and leaves it smooth as it finds it. It moves a little the oil indeed, which being between it and the water, serves it to slide with, and prevents friction, as oil does between those parts of a machine, that would otherwise rub hard together. Hence the oil dropped on the windward side of a pond proceeds gradually to leeward, as may be seen by the smoothness it carries with it, quite to the opposite side. For the wind being thus prevented from raising the first wrinkles, that I call the elements of waves, cannot produce waves, which are to be made by continually acting upon, and enlarging those elements, and thus the whole pond is calmed.

Totally therefore we might suppress the waves in any required place, if we could come at the windward place where they take their rise. This in the ocean can seldom if ever be done. But perhaps, something may be done on particular occasions, to moderate the violence of the waves when we are in the midst of them, and prevent their breaking where that would be inconvenient. . . .

Your most obedient humble servant,
B. Franklin

"Restoration of Life by Sun Rays" (1773)

Letter to Barbeu Dubourg

Your observations on the causes of death, and the experiments which you propose for recalling to life those who appear to be killed by lightning, demonstrate equally your sagacity and your humanity. It appears that the doctrines of life and death in general are yet but little understood.

A toad buried in sand will live, it is said, till the sand becomes petrified; and then, being enclosed in the stone, it may still live for we know not how many ages. The facts which are cited in support of this opinion are too numerous, and too circumstantial, not to deserve a certain degree of credit. As we are accustomed to see all the animals with which we are acquainted eat and drink, it appears to us difficult to conceive how a toad can be supported in such a dungeon; but if we reflect that the necessity of nourishment which animals experience in their ordinary state proceeds from the continual waste of their substance by perspiration, it will appear less incredible that some animals in a torpid state, perspiring less because they use no exercise, should have less need of aliment; and that others, which are covered with scales or shells, which stop perspiration, such as land and sea turtles, serpents, and some species of fish, should be able to subsist a considerable time without any nourishment whatever. A plant, with its flowers, fades and dies immediately, if exposed to the air without having its root immersed in a humid soil, from which it may draw a sufficient quantity of moisture to supply that which exhales from its substance and is carried off continually by the air. Perhaps, however, if it were buried in quicksilver, it might preserve for a considerable space of time its vegetable life, its smell, and color. If this be the case, it might prove a commodious method of transporting from distant countries those delicate plants, which are unable to sustain the inclemency of the weather at sea, and which require particular care and attention. I have seen an instance of common flies preserved in a manner somewhat similar. They had been drowned in Madeira wine, apparently about the time when it was bottled in Virginia, to be sent hither (to London). At the opening of one of the bottles, at the house of a friend where I then was, three drowned flies fell into the first glass that was filled. Having heard it remarked that drowned flies were capable of being revived by the rays of the sun, I proposed making the experiment upon these; they were therefore exposed to the sun upon a sieve, which had been employed to strain them out of the wine. In less than three hours, two of them began by degrees to recover life. They commenced by some convulsive motions of the thighs, and at length they raised themselves upon their legs, wiped their eyes with their forefeet, beat and brushed their wings with their hind feet, and soon after began to fly, finding themselves in Old England, without knowing how they came thither. The third continued lifeless till sunset, when, losing all hopes of him, he was thrown away.

I wish it were possible, from this instance, to invent a method of embalming drowned persons, in such a manner that they may be recalled to life at any period, however distant; for having a very ardent desire to see and observe the state of America a hundred years hence, I should prefer to any ordinary death the being immersed in a cask of Madeira wine, with a few friends, till that time, to be then recalled to life by the solar warmth of my dear country! But since in all probability we live in an age too early and too near the infancy of science, to hope to see such an art brought in our time to its perfection, I must for the present content myself with the treat, which you are so kind as to promise me, of the resurrection of a fowl or a turkey cock.

I am, &c.

B. Franklin

John Winthrop
(1714–1779)

A descendant of Governor John Winthrop, the first governor of the Massachusetts Bay Colony, Professor John Winthrop earned bachelor's and master's degrees at Harvard (1732, 1735) before becoming Harvard's Hollis Professor of Mathematics and Natural Philosophy (1738)—a chair he held for four decades. Although well trained in literature and philosophy, Winthrop's love of science was apparently inspired by his early reading of *The Christian Philosopher* (1721), a book written by the man who baptized him: Cotton Mather. Often considered the leading American scientist of his day, Winthrop was largely responsible for introducing Newtonian science to Harvard, where he taught in such innovative areas as mechanics, electricity, optics, motion, magnetism, astronomy, and "fluxions" (calculus). With the help of Benjamin Franklin, he also established the first true experimental chemistry and physics laboratory in the colonies. And though he twice declined the Harvard presidency, he was elected to fellowship in the Royal Society (1766) and the American Philosophical Society (1769). Winthrop was well known for his important astronomical observations of the aurora borealis, sunspots, comets, meteors, eclipses, and the transits of both Mercury and Venus. But his greatest scientific insights came in response to earthquakes—terrifying natural phenomena that he helped demystify by denying the popular belief that such disturbances were a form of divine retribution. Treating earthquakes as physical events that required rational explanation, he made careful measurements and fashioned plausible theories that helped initiate the science of seismology; for example, Winthrop was the first to observe that during tremors the earth moves with an "undulatory motion"—in shock waves. But if Winthrop's rational explanation of the 1755 quake that hit Boston comforted some, it angered others, sparking a public debate in which Winthrop argued the controversial position that earthquakes were not evidence of God's wrath. The following selection from his lecture on the subject demonstrates his ability to combine powerful, visual descriptions of natural phenomena with rational theories to explain them. Winthrop concludes by speculating that, even if divinely sent, quakes abide by natural laws — laws that, he speculates, "tend to promote the good of the whole."

From A *Lecture on Earthquakes* (1755)

You may justly expect, that the great EARTHQUAKE, which so lately spread terror, and threatened desolation throughout *New England*, should take me off from my stated course of lectures, to inquire into the probable causes of so formidable a phenomenon. The subject is curious, and at present engages the attention of many persons; and the discussion of it may help to extend your views.

An Earthquake, you all know, is an agitation or shaking of some *considerable* part of the earth, and that by *natural* causes; in contradistinction to the shaking of a *small* part of it by *artificial* methods. The degrees of this shaking are very various;— from the small jarrings, which are but just perceptible, to those violent succussions, which have altered the face of whole countries. These shakings are for the most part (I believe, always) preceded or attended by an hollow rumbling noise, something like what is called *heavy thunder*; which is usually greater or less, according to the degree of the shake. Naturalists have distinguished earthquakes into two kinds; one, when the motion is horizontal, or from side to side; the other, when it is perpendicular, or right up and down. This distinction may, for what I know, be just; and yet perhaps earthquakes more commonly consist in a kind of *undulatory* motion, which may include both the others. For as a wave of water, when raised to its greatest height, subsides, and in subsiding spreads itself horizontally; so in like manner, a *wave of earth*, if I may be allowed the expression, must in its descent partake both of an horizontal and perpendicular motion at the same time. And for the same reason, it must have had both these motions in its ascent; but those particles, which had been carried forward in one direction in the ascent, will return in a contrary direction in the descent. This has been evidently found to be the case in the more violent earthquakes; and probably the reason why it has not been universally found so, was, the difficulty of distinguishing these two motions from one another, when each of them has been but small. Though the ancient Egyptians and *Chaldeans* are said to have been able to foretell earthquakes, yet it is very certain, from all the accounts we have, that these agitations of the earth do nowhere observe any order or regular period in their returns; but at some times, recur more frequently; at others, after longer intermissions. If therefore they pretended to foretell them at all, they must have done it, not from any knowledge they had of their nature and causes; but only by the vain arts of judicial astrology;—a kind of learning, it seems, which, futile as it is, was held in high repute among them. No countries, of which we have any knowledge, are exempt from these agitations: but some are more subject to them than others; and it is observable, that those which abound most with combustible minerals, as fossil coals, sulfur, niter, &c. are the most exposed to them. Many of these countries, too, have certain mountains called *volcanoes*, which are almost perpetually burning, and throwing out fire, and smoke, and ashes; their entrails probably consisting chiefly of such sort of minerals. It is observed, however, that about the time of an earthquake in those places, these volcanoes rage more furiously, projecting stones and cinders to a great height in the air; and pouring out whole rivers of liquid fire, which carry such a devastation, wherever they run, as no human art can either prevent or repair. Several such there are in the *Molucca* islands in the *East Indies*, almost under the equinoctial; and *Iceland*, under the polar circle, has four or five besides the noted *Hecla*. *Vesuvio* near *Naples* is very remarkable; but there is none more famous than that in *Sicily*, now known there by the name of *Monte Gibello*, as it was formerly by that of Etna. . . .

That the earth has been, in all ages, and in most parts of it, subject to these agitations, history affords us but too many proofs. It is not, however, my design to enter into a detail of the dismal events of this sort, left upon record. I shall only extract from authentic accounts a few of the most striking particulars, in order to give you some idea of the dire effects, which such convulsions of the earth are capable of producing.

Imagine then the earth trembling with a huge thundering noise, or heaving and swelling like a rolling sea:—now gaping in chasms of various sizes, and then immediately closing again; either swallowing up the unhappy persons who chanced to be over them, or crushing them to death by the middle:—from some, spouting up prodigious quantities of water to a vast height, or belching out hot, offensive and suffocating exhalations; while others are streaming with torrents of melted minerals:—some houses moving out of their places; others cracking and tumbling into heaps of rubbish; and others again, not barely by whole streets, but by whole cities at a time, sinking downright to a great depth in the earth, or under water:—on the shore, the sea roaring and rising in billows; or else retiring to a great distance from the land, and then violently returning like a flood to overwhelm it; vessels driven from their anchors; some overset and lost, others thrown up on the land:—in one place, vast rocks flung down from mountains, and choking up rivers, which, being then forced to find themselves new channels, sweep away such trees, houses, &c. as had escaped the fury of the shock; in another, mountains themselves sinking in a moment, and their places possessed by pools of water:—some people running about pale, with fear, trembling for the event, and ignorant whither to fly for shelter; others thrown with violence down on the ground, not being able to keep on their feet; and others shrieking or groaning in the agonies of death:—even the brute creation manifesting all the signs of consternation and astonishment:—Imagine these things to yourselves, and you will then have a view, though but an imperfect one, of some of those images of horror and desolation, which accompany the more violent earthquakes.

But I will dwell no longer on these tragical scenes. Those of you, who are desirous of farther information, may meet with it in the Philosophical Transactions; particularly in the accounts of those horrible earthquakes, which almost desolated the islands of *Jamaica* and *Sicily*, 63 years ago; in the latter of which it was computed, that about 60,000 persons perished; which was very near one quarter of the whole number of inhabitants. To relieve you and myself under such melancholy prospects, I will turn my thoughts to the theory of these most formidable phenomena, as soon as I have made two or three observations on the earthquakes we lately felt.

GOD be thanked, all earthquakes are not formidable in so high a degree. Those of *New England*, in particular, which have indeed greatly and justly alarmed the inhabitants, have never destroyed them. For though this country, we know, has been visited with earthquakes from its first settlement by the *English*; yet, so far as my information reaches, not a single life has been lost by any of them; and perhaps never so much damage done to our buildings as by the last great shock. . . .

That the agents, which are able to produce effects so extraordinary as those before recited, which can heave up such enormous masses of matter, and put into the most vehement commotion vast tracts of land and sea, of many hundred miles in extent;—that the agents, I say, which can do all this, and more, must be very powerful, will not admit of a doubt. Now we know of nothing in nature more powerful than the particles of certain bodies converted into vapor by the action of fire. Fire then, and proper materials for it to act upon, it is probable, are the principal agents in this affair. And what greatly strengthens the probability is, an observation before-mentioned, that those countries, which have burning mountains, are more subject to earthquakes; and that these mountains rage with uncommon fury, about the time when the circumadjacent countries are torn with convulsions;—an argument this, that the eruptions of such mountains, and earthquakes, are owing to one and the same cause. . . .

It is a known property of heat to expand bodies, to rarefy them, and enlarge their dimensions; and, when raised to an higher degree, to separate their parts, and make them fly from each other; as in some measure appears already from the instances mentioned under the foregoing article. This effect heat has upon solid as well as fluid bodies;—upon the hardest, as well as the softest. It is observable here, that such particles as cohere by the strongest attraction, do most forcibly repel one another, when they are once separated by heat. And when the heat is intense, and the particles of the heated body are prevented from flying away, till they become thoroughly hot; it will require very strong vessels to hinder their hurling forth with a violent explosion. Thus, a single drop of common water, enclosed in a glass bubble, and laid upon the fire; as soon as it becomes hot, will burst the bubble, with a report scarce inferior to that of a pistol. And water in larger quantities has been heated to that degree, as to rend in sunder very strong vessels of iron, in which it has been endeavored to be confined. What the consequence then would be, of a great body of water's suddenly making its way into a flaming cavern, whose sulfurous or bituminous fires are not extinguished but enraged by water; and of its being there, almost instantaneously, converted into vapor; your own imaginations may easily represent to you. This, it is very likely, has sometimes been the case with respect to those famous volcanoes, *Etna* and *Vesuvio;* both which border the sea. You see here what water may do; but there are many other bodies, which cohere more strongly, as sulfur and niter, for example, whose vapor is still more powerful than that of water. . . .

By this time, enough has been said, I should think, to convince you, that the earth contains within itself the seeds of earthquakes in great abundance. And all these things being considered, it may seem rather a wonder that we have no more earthquakes, than that we have so many. The causes of earthquakes are incessantly at work and although it may require a course of years to ripen the proper materials to that pitch, as that they can force for themselves a passage through the earth; yet it is reasonable to expect, that they will from time to time be collected in such quantities, and ferment to such degrees, as to make these explosions unavoidable. As therefore our globe has been subject to such concussions from the earliest accounts of antiquity, we have no room to doubt but that it will continue to be so, as long as the present frame of nature subsists. For this we may be assured of, that though that imprisoned vapor be discharged into the open air, which, by its struggles to escape, has caused an earthquake; yet the fermenting minerals, from which it was generated, will be continually supplying new quantities of the same; and even those very minerals may from time to time be reproduced, as they are consumed; as was before observed. Thus we see, that in the very structure and constitution of this globe, provision has been made to continue these agitations of it, at proper intervals of time, during the whole period of its existence in its present form; and that in every climate, from the equator to the pole. This suggests a reflection, with which I shall close the present discourse. It is this: That though these explosions, and consequent concussions of the earth, have indeed occasioned most terrible desolations, and in this light may justly be regarded as the tokens of an incensed DEITY; yet it can by no means be concluded from hence, that they are not of real and standing advantage to the globe *in general.* Multitudes, it is true, have at different times suffered by them; multitudes have been destroyed by them; but much greater multitudes may have been every day benefited by them. The all-wise CREATOR could not but foresee all the effects of all the powers he implanted in matter; and, as we find in innumerable instances (and the more we know of his works, the more such instances we discover) that he has established such laws for the government of the world, as tend to promote the good of *the whole*, we may reasonably presume, that he has done it in this case as well as others. To me, at least, the argument on this side the question, drawn from the general analogy of nature, appears to have more force, than any that I have seen offered on the other. For there is nothing, however useful, however necessary, but what is capable of producing, and in fact has produced, damage, in single instances.

Pedro Font
(d. 1781)

Originally from Catalonia, Franciscan missionary Fray Pedro Font was a Spanish chaplain, cartographer, and diarist who during the early 1770s was charged with the Indian mission at San José de los Pimas, in Sonora, Mexico. Because he was a well-educated man as well as a capable missionary, Font was asked to accompany the explorer Juan Bautista de Anza on the second of his famous explorations of California (1775–76). This expedition, which had been ordered by Antonio Maria Bucareli, Viceroy of New Spain, was designed to extend the Spanish colonial network farther north in California, from Monterey Bay to a recently discovered and little-known bay called San Francisco. Spain was mildly concerned about competition from the English and extremely concerned about the Russians, who, from their stronghold in the Aleutian Islands, threatened to spread their colonial empire as far south as Alta California. In its comprehensiveness, its level of detail, and its demonstration of a keen geographical and aesthetic sensibility, *Font's Complete Diary*, copied out in 1777 but not published until 1933, is a masterpiece of eighteenth-century Western American literature. Throughout his journey with Anza, Font drew maps, kept meticulous notes of his observations and activities, and used his watch, compass, and quadrant to measure directions and latitudes. Indeed, Font even used his graphometer (a surveying tool used for calculating angles) to measure the height of a remarkably tall redwood tree: the *palo alto*, after which Palo Alto, California, is named. In the following selections from *Font's Complete Diary*, we see a man who is a devoted Franciscan chaplain but also a talented cartographer, an imperialist explorer but also a graceful writer whose rich prose admirably captures the beauty of the coastal Northern California landscape. Upon his first "delightful view" of San Francisco Bay, Font enthusiastically declares it a "marvel of nature," a "harbor of harbors." In 1776, as the American colonists on the other side of the continent were declaring their independence from Britain, Fray Font was choosing for Spain the site of the modest but beautiful mission of San Francisco.

From *Font's Complete Diary* (1775–1776/1933)

March 27, 1776. We again ascended the sand hills, descended to the arroyo, and crossed high hills until we reached the edge of the white cliff which forms the end of the mouth of the port, and where begins the great estuary containing islands. The cliff is very high and perpendicular, so that from it one can spit into the sea. From here we saw the pushing and resistance which the outgoing water of the estuary makes against that of the sea, forming there a sort of a ridge like a wave in the middle, and it seems as if a current is visible. We saw the spouting of whales, a shoal of dolphins or tunny fish, sea otter, and sea lions. On this elevation the commander decided to erect a cross, ordering it made at once so that he might set it up the next day. We now returned to the camp, which was not far away, and where we arrived at five o'clock, having traveled in all this journey some three leagues.

This place and its vicinity has abundant pasturage, plenty of firewood, and fine water, all good advantages for establishing here the presidio or fort which is planned. It lacks only timber, for there is not a tree on all those hills, though the oaks and other trees along the road are not very far away. The soldiers chased some deer, of which we saw many today, but got none of them. We also found antlers of the large elk which are so very plentiful on the other side of the estuary. The sea is so quiet in the harbor that the waves scarcely break, and from the campsite one scarcely heard them, although it was so near. Here and near the lake there are *yerba buena* and so many lilies that I had them almost inside my tent. Today the only Indians we saw were one who was far away on the beach of the estuary, and two who came to the camp as soon as we arrived. They were of good body and well bearded. They were attentive and obsequious, and brought us firewood. They remained at camp a while, but when the commander gave them glass beads they departed. While we were on the cliff at the mouth, some Indians on the other side of the port yelled at us several times, according to what the soldiers said; but I did not see them or hear them.

The port of San Francisco . . . is a marvel of nature, and might well be called the harbor of harbors, because of its great capacity, and of several small bays which it enfolds in its margins or beach and in its islands. The mouth of the port, which appears to have a very easy and safe entrance, must be about a league long and somewhat less than a league wide on the outside, facing the sea, and about a quarter of a league on the inside, facing the harbor. The inner end of the passage is formed by two very high and perpendicular cliffs almost due north and south of each other, on this side a white one and on the other side a red one. The outer end of the passage is formed on the other side by some large rocks, and on this side by a high and sandy hill which ends almost in a round point, and has on its skirts within the water some white rocks, like small farallones. It was this point which

Commander Ribera reached and on which he placed a cross when he went to reconnoiter this port. . . .

From the inner terminus of the passage extends the remarkable port of San Francisco. This harbor consists of a great gulf or estuary, as they call it, which must be some twenty-five leagues long. Viewed from the mouth it runs about southeast and northwest, the entry or mouth being in the middle. Most of the beach of the harbor, according to what I saw when we went around it, is not clean, but muddy, miry and full of sloughs, and for this reason bad. The width of the port is not uniform, for at the southern end it must be a league wide and in the middle some four leagues. At the extreme northwest it ends in a great bay more than eight leagues in extent, as it seemed to me, whose beach appeared to me clean and not miry like the other, and which is nearly round in shape, although several inlets are seen in it, so that at so long a distance I was not able accurately to distinguish its form.

About the middle of the bay on this side is the outlet or mouth of what hitherto has been taken for a very large river and has been called the Rio de San Francisco, but from here forward I shall call it the Boca del Puerto Dulce, from the experiments which were made when we went to explore it, as I shall set forth hereinafter.

Within the harbor I counted eight islands, and I am not able to say whether there are more or not. . . .

March 28. I said Mass. In the morning the weather was fair, although there were some clouds which scarcely permitted me to observe; but at length by dint of care and patience I succeeded in making the observation. The commander decided to erect the holy cross, which I blessed after Mass, on the extreme point of the white cliff at the inner terminus of the mouth of the port. At eight o'clock in the morning he and I went there with the lieutenant and four soldiers, and the cross was erected on a place high enough so that it could be seen from all the entry of the port and from a long distance away, and at the foot of it the commander left written on a paper under some stones a notice of his coming and of his exploration of this port.

On leaving we ascended a small hill and then entered upon a mesa that was very green and flower-covered, with an abundance of wild violets. The mesa is very open, of considerable extent, and level, sloping a little toward the harbor. It must be about half a league wide and somewhat longer, getting narrower until it ends right at the white cliff. This mesa affords a most delightful view, for from it one sees a large part of the port and its islands, as far as the other side, the mouth of the harbor, and of the sea all that the sight can take in as far as beyond the farallones. Indeed, although in my travels I saw very good sites and beautiful country, I saw none which pleased me so much as this. And I think that if it could be well settled like Europe there would not be anything more beautiful in all the world, for it has the best advantages for founding in it a most beautiful city, with all the conveniences desired, by land as well as by sea, with that harbor so remarkable and so spacious, in which may be established shipyards, docks, and anything that might be wished. . . .

March 29. . . . Passing through wooded hills and over flats with good lands, in which we encountered two lagoons and some springs of good water, with plentiful grass, fennel, and other useful herbs, we arrived at a beautiful arroyo which, because it was Friday of Sorrows, we called the Arroyo de los Dolores. On its banks we found much and very fragrant manzanita and other plants, and many wild violets. Near it the lieutenant planted a little maize and chickpeas to test the soil, which to us appeared very good, and I concluded that this place was very pretty and the best for the establishment of one of the two missions. It appeared to me that the other might be founded at the arroyo of San Matheo, so that in this way they would have the two missions near the port, as it was desired, and to this opinion of mine the fathers were inclined.

We went a little further, and from a small elevation there I observed the trend of the port in this direction. I saw that its extremity was toward the east-southeast, and that a very high redwood, which stands on the bank of the arroyo of San Francisco, visible from a long distance, rising like a great tower in the Llano de los Robles, and whose height I afterward measured, lay to the southeast. Near this elevation, at the end of the hill on the side toward the port, there is a good piece of level land dominated by the Arroyo de los Dolores. This arroyo enters the plain by a fall which it makes on emerging from the hills, and with it everything can be irrigated, and at the same fall a mill can be erected, for it is very suitable for this purpose.

We traveled about three leagues more to the south and southwest and west, and finally, making a turn around the hills, we came out to the plain. In this stretch we found the land good like the rest, and a small spring of water like a well very near the water of the estuary. Some bearded and gentle Indians who live around there came out to see us, and followed us for a short distance. Afterward, now apart from the hills, we came to a small arroyo with very little water, which was called by Father Palou the arroyo of San Bruno, and near which there were signs of a good-sized abandoned village. Having eaten a bite here, we continued on our way till we struck the road taken on going, along which we traveled a short distance to the southeast.

Here the commander decided to go to explore a nearby valley called San Andrés, which is in the range of the spruce trees, also called redwoods, which ends at the Punta de Almejas, as I have said, to see if it had good timber for the settlement at the port. Therefore, leaving the road, we traveled about a short league to the southwest and somewhat to the south, passing an abandoned village. Afterward we came to the Laguna de la Merced, where Senor Ribera, with Father Palóu, stopped a few days when he came to explore the port and it rained on him, as I said above.

Then we entered the valley named. In it we saw, as we went through, extensive groves with many and various trees of good timber, such as live oaks, madroños, spruce, and also cottonwoods and other trees, with much brush on the banks of the arroyo or long and narrow lake, which runs through this valley and forms the arroyo of San Matheo, which runs out upon the plain by a narrow pass through some hills, and consists of two arroyos that join before emerging. . . .

April 3. . . . We climbed to the top of this hill, which commands all the plain, to view the country, and from it we saw a confusion of water, tulares, some trees near the sierra to the south, and a level plain of immeasurable extent. In fact, in all my life I have never seen and I never expect again to see another horizon with so extended a view. If we looked to the east we saw on the other side of the plain at a distance of some thirty leagues a great Sierra Nevada, white from the summit to the skirts, and running diagonally almost from south-southeast to north-northwest. And, according to the part of its course which I was able to sketch, I concluded that perhaps toward the south that range might have some connection with the Sierra Nevada which branches off from the Sierra Madre de California above the Puerto de San Carlos; or better, that it is the same Sierra Madre, which runs about northwest as far as the mission of San Gabriel and beyond; and, moreover, I am convinced that this Sierra Nevada is connected with the large range which Father Garcés saw and in his diary calls the Sierra de San Marcos. But we were not able to see either extremity of it.

We turned to the west and saw the hills which we had been passing on the road, through which ran or extended the assembled waters; and we saw that on the other side of the water there opened a low range of hills whose terminus, seen at a distance of some fifteen leagues, lay about to the northwest, and that from there forward nothing was to be seen but the plain.

We looked to the south and saw a high sierra, bald on the outside, and running about southeast and northwest. This is the range of which I spoke on the 8th of March, and which we had on our right during all our outward journey from the neighborhood of the mission of San Luís until we reached the mouth of the Puerto Dulce, where it ends, and on whose skirts are the valley of Santa Delfina, through which runs the Rio de Monterey, the valley of San Bernardino, and others, including the Llano de los Robles, which runs toward the mouth of the port of San Francisco. A soldier said and was certain that he recognized a peak which was visible at the end of what we could see of this sierra toward the southeast. He said that it was not very far from a place called Buenavista, which the soldiers explored when they went to the tulares which lie near the mission of San Luís in pursuit of some deserters, and that if we should direct our way toward it we would come out in the vicinity of the mission of San Luís or of San Antonio.

We again looked toward the north, and between the low range to the northwest and the Sierra Nevada we saw an immense plain which on that side apparently ran in the same direction as the Sierra Nevada; but on the other side it opened about to the west, with such a sweep that it embraced almost the entire semicircle of the horizon. This is the plain through which the sea of fresh water extends, not continuously but in places leaving great areas uncovered or with little water, forming those great green tulares that begin near the mission of San Luís.

J. Hector St. John de Crèvecoeur
(1735–1813)

Michel-Guillaume-Jean de Crèvecoeur was born in France, the son of a nobleman. In 1755 he came to North America, where he served in the French and Indian War (1756–63) and traveled the English colonies as an Indian trader and surveyor before becoming an American citizen in 1765 under the name J. Hector St. John de Crèvecoeur. Having purchased farmland (which he named "Pine Hill") about sixty miles from New York City, Crèvecoeur at last settled down to a simple life of farming and husbandry. In *Letters from an American Farmer* (1782), his series of essays on American life and character, Crèvecoeur uses the literary persona Farmer James to detail and celebrate the rural life of the independent American yeoman agriculturalist. Although *Letters* is best known for examining the question of American national identity in such essays as "What Is an American?" the book is also an exploration of American pastoralism that frequently invokes natural history, as in the essays on the daily life of the planter (letter 2), on the whale fishery (letter 6), and on snakes and hummingbirds (letter 10); one of the letters even describes a visit to John and William Bartram's botanical gardens outside Philadelphia (letter 11). Because *Letters* was an idealized portrait of the ennobling virtues of rural American life, it found enthusiastic readers — especially among Europeans then enamored with Rousseau's idyllic valorization of a life lived close to the "state of nature." The degree to which Crèvecoeur's American farmer is a self-conscious literary creation is suggested by the fact that Crèvecoeur remained pro-Tory during the American Revolution — a British loyalist whose fear of living among patriot neighbors compelled him to leave Pine Hill and return to Europe during the war. As the following selections from *Letters* show, Crèvecoeur's idealization of the American farmer's pastoral relationship to nature often depends upon romanticized descriptions of the nonhuman beings who share in the domestic tranquility of the American woods and fields.

From *Letters from an American Farmer* (1782)

"On the Situation, Feelings, and Pleasures of an American Farmer"

. . . It is my bees, however, which afford me the most pleasing and extensive themes; let me look at them when I will, their government, their industry, their quarrels, their passions, always present me with something new; for which reason, when weary with labor, my common place of rest is under my locust-tree, close by my bee-house. By their movements I can predict the weather, and can tell the day of their swarming; but the most difficult point is, when on the wing, to know whether they want to go to the woods or not. If they have previously pitched in some hollow trees, it is not the allurements of salt and water, of fennel, hickory leaves, etc., nor the finest box, that can induce them to stay; they will prefer those rude, rough habitations to the best polished mahogany hive. When that is the case with mine, I seldom thwart their inclinations; it is in freedom that they work; were I to confine them, they would dwindle away and quit their labor. In such excursions we only part for a while; I am generally sure to find them again the following fall. This elopement of theirs only adds to my recreations; I know how to deceive even their superlative instinct; nor do I fear losing them, though eighteen miles from my house, and lodged in the most lofty trees, in the most impervious of our forests. I once took you along with me in one of these rambles, and yet you insist on my repeating the detail of our operations; it brings back into my mind many of the useful and entertaining reflections with which you so happily beguiled our tedious hours.

After I have done sowing, by way of recreation, I prepare for a week's jaunt in the woods, not to hunt either the deer or the bears, as my neighbors do, but to catch the more harmless bees. I cannot boast that this chase is so noble, or so famous among men, but I find it less fatiguing, and full as profitable; and the last consideration is the only one that moves me. I take with me my dog, as a companion, for he is useless as to this game; my gun, for no man you know ought to enter the woods without one; my blanket, some provisions, some wax, vermilion, honey, and a small pocket compass. With these implements I proceed to such woods as are at a considerable distance from any settlements. I carefully examine whether they abound with large trees, if so, I make a small fire on some flat stones, in a convenient place; on the fire I put some wax; close by this fire, on another stone, I drop honey in distinct drops, which I surround with small quantities of vermilion, laid on the stone; and then I retire carefully to watch whether any bees appear. If there are any in that neighborhood, I rest assured that the smell of the burnt wax will unavoidably attract them; they will soon find out the honey, for they are fond of preying on that which is not their own; and in their approach they will necessarily tinge themselves with some particles of vermilion, which will adhere long to their bodies. I next fix my compass, to find out their course, which they keep invariably straight, when they are returning home loaded. By the assistance of my watch, I observe how long those are returning which are marked with vermilion. Thus possessed of the course, and, in some measure, of the distance, which I can easily guess at, I follow the first, and seldom fail of coming to the tree where those republics are lodged. I then mark it; and thus, with patience, I have found out sometimes eleven swarms in a season; and it is inconceivable what a quantity of honey these trees will sometimes afford. It entirely depends on the size of the hollow, as the bees never rest nor swarm till it is all replenished; for like men, it is only the want of room that induces them to quit the maternal hive. Next I proceed to some of the nearest settlements, where I procure proper assistance to cut down the trees, get all my prey secured, and then return home with my prize. The first bees I ever procured were thus found in the woods, by mere accident; for at that time I had no kind of skill in this method of tracing them. The body of the tree being perfectly sound, they had lodged themselves in the hollow of one of its principal limbs, which I carefully sawed off and with a good deal of labor and industry brought it home, where I fixed it up again in the same position in which I found it growing. This was in April; I had five swarms that year, and they have been ever since very prosperous. This business generally takes up a week of my time every fall, and to me it is a week of solitary ease and relaxation.

The seed is by that time committed to the ground; there is nothing very material to do at home, and this additional quantity of honey enables me to be more generous to my home bees, and my wife to make a due quantity of mead. The reason, Sir, that you found mine better than that of others is that she puts two gallons of brandy in each barrel, which ripens it, and takes off that sweet, luscious taste, which it is apt to retain a long time. If we find anywhere in the woods (no matter on whose land) what is called a bee-tree, we must mark it; in the fall of the year when we propose to cut it down, our duty is to inform the proprietor of the land, who is entitled to half the contents; if this is not complied with we are exposed to an action of trespass, as well as he who should go and cut down a bee-tree which he had neither found out nor marked.

We have twice a year the pleasure of catching pigeons, whose numbers are sometimes so astonishing as to obscure the sun in their flight. Where is it that they hatch? For such multitudes must require an immense quantity of food. I fancy they breed toward the plains of Ohio, and those about Lake Michigan, which abound in wild oats; though I have never killed any that had that grain in their craws. In one of them, last year, I found some undigested rice. Now the nearest rice fields from where I live must be at least 560 miles; and either their digestion must be suspended while they are flying, or else they must fly with the celerity of the wind. We catch them with a net extended on the ground, to which they are allured by what we call tame wild pigeons, made blind, and fastened to a long string; his short flights, and his repeated calls, never fail to bring them down. The greatest number I ever catched was fourteen dozen, though much larger quantities have often been trapped. I have frequently seen them at the market so cheap, that for a penny you might have as many as you could carry away; and yet from the extreme cheapness you must not conclude, that they are but an ordinary food; on the contrary, I think they are excellent. Every farmer has a tame wild pigeon in a cage at his door all the year round, in order to be ready whenever the season comes for catching them.

The pleasure I receive from the warblings of the birds in the spring, is superior to my poor description, as the continual succession of their tuneful notes is forever new to me. I generally rise from bed about that indistinct interval, which, properly speaking, is neither night nor day; for this is the moment of the most universal vocal choir. Who can listen unmoved to the sweet love tales of our robins, told from tree to tree? Or to the shrill catbirds? The sublime accents of the thrush from on high always retard my steps that I may listen to the delicious music. The variegated appearances of the dewdrops, as they hang to the different objects, must present even to a clownish imagination the most voluptuous ideas. The astonishing art which all birds display in the construction of their nests, ill provided as we may suppose them with proper tools, their neatness, their convenience, always make me ashamed of the slovenliness of our houses; their love to their dame, their incessant careful attention, and the peculiar songs they address to her while she tediously incubates their eggs, remind me of my duty could I ever forget it. Their affection to their helpless little ones, is a lively precept; and in short, the whole economy of what we proudly call the brute creation, is admirable in every circumstance; and vain man, though adorned with the additional gift of reason, might learn from the perfection of instinct, how to regulate the follies, and how to temper the errors which this second gift often makes him commit. This is a subject, on which I have often bestowed the most serious thoughts; I have often blushed within myself, and been greatly astonished, when I have compared the unerring path they all follow, all just, all proper, all wise, up to the necessary degree of perfection, with the coarse, the imperfect systems of men, not merely as governors and kings, but as masters, as husbands, as fathers, as citizens. But this is a sanctuary in which an ignorant farmer must not presume to enter.

If ever man was permitted to receive and enjoy some blessings that might alleviate the many sorrows to which he is exposed, it is certainly in the country, when he attentively considers those ravishing scenes with which he is everywhere surrounded. This is the only time of the year in which I am avaricious of every moment; I therefore lose none that can add to this simple and inoffensive happiness.

I roam early throughout all my fields; not the least operation do I perform, which is not accompanied with the most pleasing observations; were I to extend them as far as I have carried them, I should become tedious; you would think me guilty of affectation, and I should perhaps represent many things as pleasurable from which you might not perhaps receive the least agreeable emotions. But, believe me, what I write is all true and real.

Some time ago, as I sat smoking a contemplative pipe in my piazza, I saw with amazement a remarkable instance of selfishness displayed in a very small bird, which I had hitherto respected for its inoffensiveness. Three nests were placed almost contiguous to each other in my piazza: that of a swallow was affixed in the corner next to the house, that of a phoebe in the other, a wren possessed a little box which I had made on purpose, and hung between. Be not surprised at their tameness; all my family had long been taught to respect them as well as myself. The wren had shown before signs of dislike to the box which I had given it, but I knew not on what account; at last it resolved, small as it was, to drive the swallow from its own habitation, and to my very great surprise it succeeded. Impudence often gets the better of modesty, and this exploit was no sooner performed, than it removed every material to its own box with the most admirable dexterity; the signs of triumph appeared very visible, it fluttered its wings with uncommon velocity, an universal joy was perceivable in all its movements. Where did this little bird learn that spirit of injustice? It was not endowed with what we term reason! Here then is a proof that both those gifts border very near on one another; for we see the perfection of the one mixing with the errors of the other! The peaceable swallow, like the passive Quaker, meekly sat at a small distance and never offered the least resistance; but no sooner was the plunder carried away, than the injured bird went to work with unabated ardor, and in a few days the depredations were repaired. To prevent however a repetition of the same violence, I removed the wren's box to another part of the house.

In the middle of my new parlor I have, you may remember, a curious republic of industrious hornets; their nest hangs to the ceiling by the same twig on which it was so admirably built and contrived in the woods. Its removal did not displease them, for they find in my house plenty of food; and I have left a hole open in one of the panes of the window, which answers all their purposes. By this kind usage they are become quite harmless; they live on the flies, which are very troublesome to us throughout the summer; they are constantly busy in catching them, even on the eyelids of my children. It is surprising how quickly they smear them with a sort of glue, lest they might escape, and when thus prepared, they carry them to their nests, as food for their young ones. These globular nests are most ingeniously divided into many stories, all provided with cells, and proper communications. The materials with which this fabric is built, they procure from the cottony furze, with which our oak rails are covered; this substance tempered with glue, produces a sort of pasteboard, which is very strong, and resists all the inclemencies of the weather. By their assistance, I am but little troubled with flies. All my family are so accustomed to their strong buzzing, that no one takes any notice of them; and though they are fierce and vindictive, yet kindness and hospitality has made them useful and harmless.

We have a great variety of wasps; most of them build their nests in mud, which they fix against the shingles of our roofs, as nigh the pitch as they can. These aggregates represent nothing, at first view, but coarse and irregular lumps, but if you break them, you will observe, that the inside of them contains a great number of oblong cells, in which they deposit their eggs, and in which they bury themselves in the fall of the year. Thus immured they securely pass through the severity of that season, and on the return of the sun are enabled to perforate their cells, and to open themselves a passage from these recesses into the sunshine. The yellow wasps, which build under ground, in our meadows, are much more to be dreaded, for when the mower unwittingly passes his scythe over their holes they immediately sally forth with a fury and velocity superior even to the strength of man. They make the boldest fly, and the only remedy is to lie down and cover our heads with hay, for it is only at the head they aim their blows; nor is there any possibility of finishing that part of the work until, by means of fire and brimstone, they are all silenced. But though I have been obliged to execute this dreadful sentence in my own defense, I have often thought it a great pity, for the sake of a little hay, to lay waste so ingenious a subterranean town, furnished with every conveniency, and built with a most surprising mechanism.

I never should have done were I to recount the many objects which involuntarily strike my imagination in the midst of my work, and spontaneously afford me the most pleasing relief. These appear insignificant trifles to a person who has traveled through Europe and America, and is acquainted with books and with many sciences; but such simple objects of contemplation suffice me, who have no time to bestow on more extensive observations. Happily these require no study; they are obvious, they gild the moments I dedicate to them, and enliven the severe labors which I perform. At home my happiness springs from very different objects; the gradual unfolding of my children's reason, the study of their dawning tempers, attract all my paternal attention. I have to contrive little punishments for their little faults, small encouragements for their good actions, and a variety of other expedients dictated by various occasions. But these are themes unworthy your perusal, and which ought not to be carried beyond the walls of my house, being domestic mysteries adapted only to the locality of the small sanctuary wherein my family resides. Sometimes I delight in inventing and executing machines, which simplify my wife's labor. I have been tolerably successful that way; and these, sir, are the narrow circles within which I constantly revolve, and what can I wish for beyond them? I bless God for all the good he has given me; I envy no man's prosperity, and with no other portion of happiness than that I may live to teach the same philosophy to my children; and give each of them a farm, show them how to cultivate it, and be like their father, good substantial independent American farmers — an appellation which will be the most fortunate one a man of my class can possess, so long as our civil government continues to shed blessings on our husbandry. Adieu.

John Ferdinand Dalziel Smyth

(1745–1814)

John F. D. Smyth (or Smith) was a British soldier who traveled widely in the mid-Atlantic colonies during the mid–eighteenth century, recording the many local customs, manners, and landscapes he observed. For a time Smyth settled down to farming in Maryland — much like Crèvecoeur, whose *Letters from an American Farmer* he read — but soon found his interests threatened by the outbreak of the American Revolution. When war came, Smyth, a devout loyalist, was repeatedly hounded by patriot forces, from which he made a number of narrow escapes before being captured and imprisoned in Philadelphia. Eventually escaping from prison in Baltimore, where he and other loyalist prisoners had been transferred, Smyth secured safe passage to England. In 1784 he published *A Tour in the United States of America* . . . (a French translation followed in 1791), a detailed account that provides an excellent window onto mid-eighteenth-century America. In his introduction to the book Smyth reports that, after reading many accounts of American life and lands, he unfortunately found no author "descending to the minutiae, which compose as well the true perspective, as the real grand intercourse and commerce of life." Unlike many other literary travelers of the period, Smyth devoted himself, to use his own analogy, to describing the individual "bricks" from which the American "edifice" was constructed. And if his book teaches us a great deal about horse races and ordinaries, inns and agriculture, regulators and soldiers, it is also a volume that is rich in close observations of specific places, plants, and animals — the natural parts of which the "singular, wonderful, and astonishing" whole of the American landscape was formed. Although Smyth pledged "implicit obedience" to the "venerable dictates" of "nature and truth," Virginian John Randolph was at least partially right when he declared Smyth's book "replete with falsehood." The following selections, for example, include a highly imaginative description of a snake "charming" a bird into its mouth — a description suggesting Smyth's willingness to stretch his supposed "first-hand" observations into engaging but inaccurate stories based on popular folk beliefs regarding nature.

From A *Tour in the United States of America* (1784)

Indeed the whole appearance of the country, and face of nature, is strikingly novel and charming to an European, especially to a Briton.

The air, the sky, the water, the land, and the inhabitants, being two-thirds blacks, are objects entirely different from all that he had been accustomed to see before. The sky clear and serene, very seldom overcast, or any haze to be observed in the atmosphere, the rains falling in torrents, and the clouds immediately dispersing. Frequent dreadful thunder in loud contending peals; thunder gusts happening often daily, and always within every two or three days, at this season of the year. Eruscations and flashes of lightning, constantly succeeding each other, in quick and rapid transitions. The air dry, and intensely hot in the summer, cold and piercing in the winter, and always keen and penetrating. During the night, thousands of lights, like bright burning candles, being large winged insects, called fireflies, gliding through the air in every direction; frequently vanishing, and perpetually succeeded by new ones. The rivers, large expanses of water, of enormous extent, and spreading under the eye as far as it can comprise; nature here being on such a scale, that what are called great rivers in Europe, are here considered only as inconsiderable creeks or rivulets. The land, an immense forest, extended on a flat plain, almost without bounds; or arising into abrupt ascents, and at length swelling into stupendous mountains, interspersed with rocks and precipices, yet covered with venerable trees, hoary with age, and torn with tempests. The mountains suddenly broken through, and severed by mighty rivers, raging in torrents at the bottom of the tremendous chasm, or gliding in awful majestic silence along the deep valleys between them. The agriculture on the plantations is different from everything in Europe; being either tobacco, three feet high, with the plants a yard apart; or Indian corn, at the distance of six feet between each stalk, in regular straight rows, or avenues, frequently twelve or fifteen feet in height.

While the mind is filled with astonishment, and novel objects, all the senses are gratified.

The flowery shrubs which overspread the land, regale the smell with odoriferous perfumes: and fruits of exquisite relish and flavor, delight the taste, and afford a most grateful refreshment.

The prodigious multitude of green frogs, reptiles, and large insects, on the trees, as well as the bullfrogs in the swamps, ponds, and places of water, during the spring, summer, and fall, make an incessant noise and clamor; the bullfrogs, in particular, emitting a most tremendous roar, louder than the bellowing of a bull, from the similarity of whose voice they obtained their name, but their note is harsh, sonorous, and abrupt, frequently appearing to pronounce articulate sounds, in striking resemblance to the following words, *Hogshead tobacco, Knee deep. Ankle deep. Deeper and deeper. Piankitank,* and many others; but all equally grating and dissonant. They surprise a man exceedingly, as he will hear their hoarse, loud, bellowing clamor just by him, and sometimes all around him, yet he cannot discover from whence it proceeds; they being all covered in water, and just raising their mouth only a little above the surface when they roar out, then instantly draw it under again. They are of the size of a man's foot.

Nor can you perceive the animals from whence the sounds in the trees proceed, they being most effectually hid among the leaves and branches. So that at first this absolutely appears to be a country of enchantments. . . .

My principal amusement was walking: I took great delight in wandering alone among the rocks and solitary romantic situations, around the falls. In these excursions I always carried a book in my pocket, and when I came to any place that commanded my attention, either from the wildness and grandeur of the perspective, or from the observation of the raging torrent below, after admiring the beauties of the scene, I would frequently lie down in the shade, and amuse myself with reading, until I insensibly dropped asleep. This was my daily recreation, which I never neglected.

But I was once extremely surprised at beholding, as soon as I opened my eyes, a prodigious large snake, within a few feet of me, basking himself in the sun. He was jet black, with a copper-colored belly, very fine sparkling eyes, and at least seven feet long. However he did me no injury; for I did not disturb him nor did he molest me; but as soon as he heard the rustling of the leaves, on my moving, he went off with great precipitation and speed.

Another time, whilst I was reading in a very solitary retired place among the rocks and trees, on hearing some little noise near me, I looked around, and just had the glimpse of a very strange and singular animal, such as I had never seen even any resemblance of before. It appeared to me more like a fiddle with feet, than any thing else that I know; the sight I had of it was just as it was running behind a rock. I sought there, and everywhere for it immediately, to no purpose, for I could not discover even a trace thereof remaining.

When I returned, I mentioned what I had seen, but no one, from my description, could inform me what animal it was.

However, nothing is more common here than the black snake. He is very bold and daring; yet, to the human race, entirely harmless and inoffensive; nor is his bite poisonous, and is as readily cured as the scratch of a briar: notwithstanding which, it is said, and I believe with truth, that he is master of all other snakes; even the rattle-snake submits to him. This superiority arises from the strength and power of his muscles, for he insinuates himself in spiral wreaths around his antagonist, and then contracting, by that means conquers or kills him. His prey, for food, he swallows whole.

It is confidently reported, and universally credited, that they devour squirrels, and that they have been found with squirrels whole in their bellies. I myself have seen them swallow frogs of a very large size. After the frog is almost wholly in, if you strike the snake, he will instantly disgorge it, and the frog will leap away.

The black snakes are particularly serviceable in destroying rats and mice, which they seek after very eagerly, and devour for food; for this purpose, they are even more useful than cats, because, by their slender form and peculiar make, they are enabled to pursue these vermin into their lurking holes and hiding places, which they generally do, and thereby at once destroy the whole progeny.

But the Americans, one and all, have such an aversion and antipathy to the very appearance of the whole species, that notwithstanding this kind of serpents are absolutely harmless, and indeed extremely serviceable for the purposes just mentioned, yet they are as eager to kill and destroy them, as the most noxious, virulent, and deleterious of the species, the rattle, moccasin, and horn-snakes.

I have heard many strange relations of the power of snakes, in charming birds, and drawing them down out of the air, to devour them, by a certain fascination in their eyes. To these tales I formerly gave no credit; but I have now had conviction of their truth, by frequent ocular demonstration.

I have observed a little bird, fluttering in the air, within a small compass, gradually descending until it came down on a bush, then hopping from spray to spray, every time lower, constantly sending forth a tremulous, doleful note, expressive of dread and surprise, until at length it would drop into the jaws of a snake on the ground, that was gaping open ready to devour it.

On such occasions, I always struck the snake, and the instant he moved, the bird became liberated from his fascination, flying away with the greatest alertness, and would chirp, and soar over my head in the air, for some little distance, as if grateful for its deliverance from so formidable an enemy. This very extraordinary circumstance I have taken particular notice of several different times. . . .

Having heard much of the Wart Mountain, one of the first, but most considerably of the Alleghenies, or rather the Blue Mountains, for height, as well as for its amazing extent of perspective, I determined to visit it, and ascend the summit thereof on my way; for which reason we bent our course towards it, and crossed Smith's River about nine miles above the fort, at a very bad ford, which was deep and dangerous.

After traveling through an exceedingly rough country, and in extreme bad paths indeed, frequently without any, as also crossing several deep creeks, or water-courses, we found ourselves at night beginning to ascend the Wart Mountain, which is upon the southwest side of Smith's River; and we alighted on an agreeable and convenient spot, near the side of a brook of water, to put up for the night, turning our horses out with their bells and hobbles on, to prevent our losing them.

We struck up and kindled a large fire, gathered leaves for us to lie upon, eat heartily of our jerked (or dried) venison, drank some brandy and water, (for we had brought a pretty large stock along us), wrapped ourselves up in our blankets, and lay down under a large tree, with our feet towards the fire; having traveled about forty-six miles that day.

I cannot undertake to pronounce whether it is owing to the salubrity and elasticity of the air, thus in free circulation, and totally unconfined, but certain it is, that I never found myself dejected, indisposed, or low-spirited in the morning, after pausing the night in this manner.

I arose in the morning as gay and cheerful as a lark, and set out at the dawn of day to ascend the mountain, with my mind filled with the most agreeable expectations of the vast pleasure I should enjoy from the amazingly great extent of the perspective from the summit, which is reckoned equal, if not superior to any, even the highest and most commanding inland situation in the world, at a distance from the sea.

As we approached the summit we found the journey exceedingly troublesome, the ascent becoming more and more perpendicular, until at length we were obliged to alight from our horses, and lead them after us.

Even this we found the greatest difficulty in performing, and we should not have attempted it had there been any place where we could have left our horses with the least certain prospect, or indeed probability of being able to find them again when we returned.

The height of the Wart Mountain may be about six or eight miles; but the extreme steepness thereof towards the summit retards the progress of a traveler so very much, that it is absolutely a severe day's journey to visit the highest part and return, making but a very short stay to enjoy the beauties of the almost unbounded and wonderful perspective.

After many halts we reached the summit of the mountain about eleven o'clock, and were then amply rewarded for the great perils and fatigue we had undergone to attain it.

Language fails in attempting to describe this most astonishing and almost unbounded perspective.

The mind was filled with a reverential awe, but at the same time the ideas, and I had almost said the very soul was sensibly enlarged.

The reflection on our own littleness did not diminish our intellectual faculties nor consequence; and the mind would boldly soar over the vast extent of the earth and water around, and even above the globe itself, to contemplate on, and admire the amazing works of the great Creator of all.

In short, the strong, mighty, pointed, and extended sensations of the mind, at this astonishing period are far beyond the power of human language to describe, or convey any idea of.

On the east you could perceive the deep and broken chasms where the rivers Dan, Mayho, Smith's, Bannister's, and Stanton direct their courses; some raging in vast torrents, and some gliding in silent gentle meanders.

On the north you see the Black Water, a branch of the Stanton; and the break in the mountains where the Fluvannah, a vast branch of the James, pass through in a northeast direction.

On the northwest you will observe with great astonishment and pleasure, the tremendous and abrupt break in the Allegheny Mountains, through which the mighty waters of the New River, and the Great Kanawha pass, the latter directing its course northward, a distance no less than two hundred miles from its source, where the New River meets the Green Briar river which comes from the northeast, a distance also of an hundred and fifty miles.

After the confluence, being then named the Great Kanawha, it proceeds westward inclining to the north, until it falls into the mighty river Ohio, after a course of more than two hundred miles from the junction.

On the west you can very plainly discover the three forks or branches of the Holston, where they break through the Great Allegheny Mountains, forming striking and awful chasms.

And still beyond them you may observe Clinch's River, or Pellissippi, that is almost equal to all the three branches of the Holston, with which it unites, after a course of three hundred and fifty or four hundred miles: the length of the course of the Holston being also above four hundred miles before they unite and form the mighty river Hogohegee or Cherokee, which afterwards flows a course of two hundred and fifty miles in extent before it falls into the Ohio, to which it is at least equal, in the vast quantity of water it contains, as well as the fertility of the soil on its banks, and far superior to it in the excellence of the climate it passes through.

On the south you can see the Dan, the Catawba, the Yadkin, and the Haw, breaking through the mighty mountains that appear in confused heaps, and piled on each other in almost every direction.

Throughout the whole of this amazing and most extensive perspective, there is not the least feature or trace of art or improvement to be discovered.

All are the genuine effects of nature alone, and laid down on her most extended and grandest scale.

Contemplating thereon fills the eye, engrosses the mind, and enlarges the soul.

It totally absorbs the senses, overwhelms all the faculties, expands even the grandest ideas beyond all conception, and occasions you almost to forget that you are a human creature.

Thomas Jefferson
(1743–1826)

Author of the Declaration of Independence and third president of the United States (1801–9), polymath Thomas Jefferson was also one of the premier literary naturalists of the Revolutionary period. Indeed, fellow naturalist Benjamin Smith Barton honored Jefferson the scientist in naming the Twin-leaf flower *Jeffersonia*. As president, Jefferson doubled the size of the United States with the Louisiana Purchase (1803) and subsequently sent the Lewis and Clark expedition (1804–6) to survey an interior wilderness then so little known to Anglo-Americans that Jefferson himself believed the mastodon might still roam there. Jefferson's *Notes on the State of Virginia* (1785), written in response to a 1780 questionnaire sent him by French diplomat François Marbois, was widely read in its day and was one of the most important scientific books by an eighteenth-century American. In *Notes*, the only book he published in his lifetime, Jefferson demonstrates the braiding of close observation, scientific acumen, and lyrical prose that was to become characteristic of nature writing in the centuries that followed. Jefferson's literary sensibility and style also suggest an important transition from the Enlightenment rationalism championed by John Locke to the more romantic appreciation of nature inspired by Edmund Burke's celebration of an aesthetic of the sublime. In the selections that follow, Jefferson's account of the confluence of the Potomac and Shenandoah Rivers at Harpers Ferry demonstrates a dual passion for geology and painterly prose, while his description of Virginia's Natural Bridge blends accurate scientific measurement with an emotional account of the personal experience of the viewer. In his section on "Animals" Jefferson devotes himself to repudiating the infamous "theory of degeneration" advanced by the French naturalist Buffon, who argued that the flora and fauna of the New World were but degenerated (and degenerating) versions of their European counterparts. In a clear example of how politicized science can often be, Jefferson offers a forceful, nationalistic counterargument to redeem American animals — both human and nonhuman — from the "wretched philosophy" that would rank them "among the degeneracies of nature."

From *Notes on the State of Virginia* (1785)

Mountains

For the particular geography of our mountains I must refer to Fry and Jefferson's map of Virginia; and to Evans's analysis of his map of America for a more philosophical view of them than is to be found in any other work. It is worthy notice, that our mountains are not solitary and scattered confusedly over the face of the country; but that they commence at about 150 miles from the seacoast, are disposed in ridges one behind another, running nearly parallel with the seacoast, though rather approaching it as they advance northeastwardly. To the southwest, as the tract of country between the seacoast and the Mississippi becomes narrower, the mountains converge into a single ridge, which, as it approaches the Gulf of Mexico, subsides into plain country, and gives rise to some of the waters of that Gulf, and particularly to a river called the Apalachicola, probably from the Appalachies, an Indian nation formerly residing on it. Hence the mountains giving rise to that river, and seen from its various parts, were called the Appalachian mountains, being in fact the end or termination only of the great ridges passing through the continent. European geographers however extended the name northwardly as far as the mountains extended; some giving it, after their separation into different ridges, to the Blue ridge, others to the North mountain, others to the Allegheny, others to the Laurel ridge, as may be seen in their different maps. But the fact I believe is, that none of these ridges were ever known by that name to the inhabitants, either native or emigrant, but as they saw them so called in European maps. In the same direction generally are the veins of limestone, coal and other minerals hitherto discovered: and so range the falls of our great rivers. But the courses of the great rivers are at right angles with these. James and Potomac penetrate through all the ridges of mountains eastward of the Allegheny; that is broken by no watercourse. It is in fact the spine of the country between the Atlantic on one side, and the Mississippi and St. Lawrence on the other. The passage of the Potomac through the Blue ridge is perhaps one of the most stupendous scenes in nature. You stand on a very high point of land. On your right comes up the Shenandoah, having ranged along the foot of the mountain an hundred miles to seek a vent. On your left approaches the Potomac, in quest of a passage also. In the moment of their junction they rush together against the mountain, rend it asunder, and pass off to the sea. The first glance of this scene hurries our senses into the opinion, that this earth has been created in time, that the mountains were formed first, that the rivers began to flow afterwards, that in this place particularly they have been dammed up by the Blue ridge of mountains, and have formed an ocean which filled the whole valley; that continuing to rise they have at length broken over at this spot, and have torn the mountain down from its summit to its base. The piles of rock on each hand, but particularly on the Shenandoah, the evident marks of their disrupture and avulsion from their beds by the most powerful agents of nature, corroborate the impression. But the distant finishing which nature has given to the picture is of a very different character. It is a true contrast to the foreground. It is as placid and delightful, as that is wild and tremendous. For the mountain being cloven asunder, she presents to your eye, through the cleft, a small catch of smooth blue horizon, at an infinite distance in the plain country, inviting you, as it were, from the riot and tumult roaring around, to pass through the breach and participate of the calm below. Here the eye ultimately composes itself; and that way too the road happens actually to lead. You cross the Potomac above the junction, pass along its side through the base of the mountain for three miles, its terrible precipices hanging in fragments over you, and within about 20 miles reach Frederic town and the fine country around that. This scene is worth a voyage across the Atlantic. Yet here, as in the neighborhood of the natural bridge, are people who have passed their lives within half a dozen miles, and have never been to survey these monuments of a war between rivers and mountains, which must have shaken the earth itself to its center. The height of our mountains has not yet been estimated with any degree of exactness. The Allegheny being the great ridge which divides the waters of the Atlantic from those of the Mississippi, its summit is doubtless more elevated above the ocean than that of any other mountain. But its relative height, compared with the base on which it stands, is not so great as that of some others, the country rising behind the successive ridges like the steps of stairs. The mountains of the Blue ridge, and of these the Peaks of Otter, are thought to be of a greater height, measured from their base, than any others in our country, and perhaps in North America. From data, which may found a tolerable conjecture, we suppose the highest peak to be about 4000 feet perpendicular, which is not a fifth part of the height of the mountains of South America, nor one third of the height which would be necessary in our latitude to preserve ice in the open air unmelted through the year. The ridge of mountains next beyond the Blue ridge, called by us the North mountain, is of the greatest extent; for which reason they were named by the Indians the Endless mountains. . . .

Natural Bridge

The *Natural bridge*, the most sublime of Nature's works, though not comprehended under the present head, must not be pretermitted. It is on the ascent of a hill, which seems to have been cloven through its length by some great convulsion. The fissure, just at the bridge, is, by some admeasurements, 270 feet deep, by others only 205. It is about 45 feet wide at the bottom, and 90 feet at the top; this of course determines the length of the bridge, and its height from the water. Its breadth in the middle, is about 60 feet, but more at the ends, and the thickness of the mass at the summit of the arch, about 40 feet. A part of this thickness is constituted by a coat of earth, which gives growth to many large trees. The residue, with the hill on both sides, is one solid rock of limestone. The arch approaches the Semi-elliptical form; but the larger axis of the ellipsis, which would be the cord of the arch, is many times longer than the (semi-axis which gives its height). Though the sides of this bridge are provided in some parts with a parapet of fixed rocks, yet few men have resolution to walk to them and look over into the abyss. You involuntarily fall on your hands and feet, creep to the parapet and peep over it. Looking down from this height about a minute, gave me a violent headache. (This painful sensation is relieved by a short, but pleasing view of the Blue ridge along the fissure downwards, and upwards by that of the Short hills, which, with the Purgatory mountain is a divergence from the North ridge; and, descending then to the valley below, the sensation becomes delightful in the extreme. It is impossible for the emotions, arising from the sublime, to be felt beyond what they are here: so beautiful an arch, so elevated, so light, and springing, as it were, up to heaven, the rapture of the Spectator is really indescribable! The fissure continues deep and narrow and, following the margin of the stream upwards about three eights of a mile you arrive at a limestone cavern, less remarkable, however, for height and extent than those before described. Its entrance into the hill is but a few feet above the bed of the stream.) This bridge is in the county of Rockbridge, to which it has given name, and affords a public and commodious passage over a valley, which cannot be crossed elsewhere for a considerable distance. The stream passing under it is called Cedar creek. It is a water of James river, and sufficient in the driest seasons to turn a gristmill, though its fountain is not more than two miles above. . . .

Animals

Our quadrupeds have been mostly described by Linnaeus and Mons. de Buffon. Of these the Mammoth, or big buffalo, as called by the Indians, must certainly have been the largest. Their tradition is, that he was carnivorous, and still exists in the northern parts of America. A delegation of warriors from the Delaware tribe having visited the governor of Virginia, during the present revolution, on matters of business, after these had been discussed and settled in council, the governor asked them some questions relative to their country, and, among others, what they knew or had heard of the animal whose bones were found at the Saltlicks, on the Ohio. Their chief speaker immediately put himself into an attitude of oratory, and with a pomp suited to what he conceived the elevation of his subject, informed him that it was a tradition handed down from their fathers, "That in ancient times a herd of these tremendous animals came to the Bigbone licks, and began an universal destruction of the bear, deer, elks, buffaloes, and other animals, which had been created for the use of the Indians: that the Great Man above, looking down and seeing this, was so enraged that he seized his lightning, descended on the earth, seated himself on a neighboring mountain, on a rock, of which his seat and the print of his feet are still to be seen, and hurled his bolts among them till the whole were slaughtered, except the big bull, who presenting his forehead to the shafts, shook them off as they fell; but missing one at length, it wounded him in the side; whereon, springing round, he bounded over the Ohio, over the Wabash, the Illinois, and finally over the great lakes, where he is living at this day." It is well known that on the Ohio, and in many parts of America further north, tusks, grinders, and skeletons of unparalleled magnitude, are found in great numbers, some lying on the surface of the earth, and some a little below it. A Mr. Stanley, taken prisoner by the Indians near the mouth of the Tennessee, relates, that, after being transferred through several tribes, from one to another, he was at length carried over the mountains west of the Missouri to a river which runs westwardly; that these bones abounded there; and that the natives described to him the animal to which they belonged as still existing in the northern parts of their country; from which description he judged it to be an elephant. . . .

But to whatever animal we ascribe these remains, it is certain such a one has existed in America, and that it has been the largest of all terrestrial beings. It should have sufficed to have rescued the earth it inhabited, and the atmosphere it breathed, from the imputation of impotence in the conception and nourishment of animal life on a large scale: to have stifled, in its birth, the opinion of a writer, the most learned too of all others in the science of animal history, that in the new world, "La nature vivante est beaucoup moins agissante, beaucoup moins forte": that nature is less active, less energetic on one side of the globe than she is on the other. As if both sides were not warmed by the same genial sun; as if a soil of the same chemical composition, was less capable of elaboration into animal nutriment; as if the fruits and grains from that soil and sun, yielded a less rich chyle, gave less extension to the solids and fluids of the body, or produced sooner in the cartilages, membranes, and fibers, that rigidity which restrains all further extension, and terminates animal growth. The truth is, that a Pigmy and a Patagonian, a Mouse and a Mammoth, derive their dimensions from the same nutritive juices. The difference of increment depends on circumstances unsearchable to beings with our capacities. Every race of animals seems to have received from their Maker certain laws of extension at the time of their formation. Their elaborative organs were formed to produce this, while proper obstacles were opposed to its further progress. Below these limits they cannot fall, nor rise above them. What intermediate station they shall take may depend on soil, on climate, on food, on a careful choice of breeders. But all the manna of heaven would never raise the Mouse to the bulk of the Mammoth.

The opinion advanced by the Count de Buffon, is 1. That the animals common both to the old and new world, are smaller in the latter. 2. That those peculiar to the new, are on a smaller scale. 3. That those which have been domesticated in both, have degenerated in America: and 4. That on the whole it exhibits fewer species. And the reason he thinks is, that the heats of America are less; that more waters are spread over its surface by nature, and fewer of these drained off by the hand of man. . . .

So far the Count de Buffon has carried this new theory of the tendency of nature to belittle her productions on this side of the Atlantic. Its application to the race of whites, transplanted from Europe, remained for the Abbé Raynal. "One must be astonished (he says) that America has not yet produced one good poet, one able mathematician, one man of genius in a single art or a single science." "America has not yet produced one good poet." When we shall have existed as a people as long as the Greeks did before they produced a Homer, the Romans a Virgil, the French a Racine and Voltaire, the English a Shakespeare and Milton, should this reproach be still true, we will enquire from what unfriendly causes it has proceeded, that the other countries of Europe and quarters of the earth shall not have inscribed any name in the roll of poets. But neither has America produced "one able mathematician, one man of genius in a single art or a single science." In war we have produced a Washington, whose memory will be adored while liberty shall have votaries, whose name will triumph over time, and will in future ages assume its just station among the most celebrated worthies of the world, when that wretched philosophy shall be forgotten which would have arranged him among the degeneracies of nature. In physics we have produced a Franklin, than whom no one of the present age has made more important discoveries, nor has enriched philosophy with more, or more ingenious solutions of the phenomena of nature. We have supposed Mr. Rittenhouse second to no astronomer living: that in genius he must be the first, because he is self-taught. As an artist he has exhibited as great a proof of mechanical genius as the world has ever produced. He has not indeed made a world; but he has by imitation approached nearer its Maker than any man who has lived from the creation to this day. As in philosophy and war, so in government, in oratory, in painting, in the plastic art, we might show that America, though but a child of yesterday, has already given hopeful proofs of genius, as well of the nobler kinds, which arouse the best feelings of man, which call him into action, which substantiate his freedom, and conduct him to happiness, as of the subordinate, which serve to amuse him only. We therefore suppose, that this reproach is as unjust as it is unkind; and that, of the geniuses which adorn the present age, America contributes its full share.

William Bartram
(1739–1823)

Son of colonial naturalist John Bartram, whom Linnaeus declared "the greatest natural botanist in the world," William Bartram grew up working, studying, and sketching under his father's direction in the famous Bartram botanical gardens at Kingsessing, outside Philadelphia. Having traveled extensively with his father to collect plants and seeds, William set off alone in 1773 on the four years of wilderness rambles documented in *Travels through North and South Carolina, Georgia, East and West Florida* . . . , a book eventually published in 1791 with the help of a subscription encouraged by prominent American natural scientists including Benjamin Franklin and Thomas Jefferson. In *Travels*, a work as important to eighteenth-century nature writing as Henry Thoreau's *Walden* (1854) was to environmental writing of the nineteenth century, we see what is possible when a talented writer and expert naturalist combines close observation with dynamic narrative. If Bartram's famous account of the alligators (which he also calls "crocodiles") of "Battle Lagoon" is among the most informed descriptions of those reptiles penned in this period, it is also a literary set piece that suggests the author's deliberate narrative strategies. Indeed, in an age in which literary capital generally flowed westward across the Atlantic, Bartram was widely read by Europeans — including, notably, William Wordsworth, Samuel Taylor Coleridge, Thomas Carlyle, and François-René, Vicomte de Chateaubriand — whose imaginative conceptions of nature were informed by Bartram's romantic descriptions of American wilderness. But there is in William Bartram an additional quality that offers a bridge between the Calvinist typology of a Cotton Mather or Jonathan Edwards and the reverential awe of an Annie Dillard or Barry Lopez. As a Quaker who believed deeply in the "doctrine of inner light" — which posits that nonhuman as well as human nature is graced by God with spiritual value — Bartram is among the most eloquent American voices for the spiritual richness of the natural world. So gentle and peaceful was William Bartram that he earned from the Seminoles of Florida the affectionate nickname *Puc-Puggy*, the "Flower Hunter." Given William Bartram's close study of even the most minute members of the plant community, it is fitting that bryologists have memorialized him in the name of the *Bartramia* moss.

From
Travels through North and South Carolina, Georgia, East and West Florida . . . (1791)

The most apparent difference between animals and vegetables is, that animals have the powers of sound, and are locomotive, whereas vegetables are not able to shift themselves from the places where nature has planted them: yet vegetables have the power of moving and exercising their members, and have the means of transplanting and colonizing their tribes almost over the surface of the whole earth; some seeds, for instance, grapes, nuts, smilax, peas, and others, whose pulp or kernel is food for animals, will remain several days without being injured in stomachs of pigeons and other birds of passage; by this means such sorts are distributed from place to place, even across seas; indeed some seeds require this preparation by the digestive heat of the stomach of animals, to dissolve and detach the oily, viscid pulp, or to soften the hard shells. Small seeds are sometimes furnished with rays of hair or down; and others with thin light membranes attached to them, which serve the purpose of wings, on which they mount upward, leaving the earth, float in the air, and are carried away by the swift winds to very remote regions before they settle on the earth; some are furnished with hooks, which catch hold of the wool and hair of animals passing by them, and are by that means spread abroad; other seeds ripen in pericarps, which open with elastic force, and shoot their seed to a very great distance round about; some other seeds, as of the Mosses and Fungi, are so very minute as to be invisible, light as atoms, and these mixing with the air, are wafted all over the world.

The animal creation also excites our admiration, and equally manifests the almighty power, wisdom, and beneficence of the Supreme Creator and Sovereign Lord of the universe; some in their vast size and strength, as the mammoth, the elephant, the whale, the lion, and alligator; others in agility; others in their beauty and elegance of color, plumage, and rapidity of flight, having the faculty of moving and living in the air; others for their immediate and indispensable use and convenience to man, in furnishing means for our clothing and sustenance, and administering to our help in the toils and labors of life: how wonderful is the mechanism of these finely formed self-moving beings, how complicated their system, yet what unerring uniformity prevails through every tribe and particular species! the effect we see and contemplate, the cause is invisible, incomprehensible; how can it be otherwise? when we cannot see the end or origin of a nerve or vein, while the divisibility of matter or fluid, is infinite. We admire the mechanism of a watch, and the fabric of a piece of brocade, as being the production of art; these merit our admiration, and must excite our esteem for the ingenious artist or modifier; but nature is the work of God omnipotent; and an elephant, nay even this world, is comparatively but a very minute part of his works. If then the visible, the mechanical part of the animal creation, the mere material part, is so admirably beautiful, harmonious, and incomprehensible, what must be the intellectual system? that inexpressibly more essential principle, which secretly operates within? that which animates the inimitable machines, which gives them motion, empowers them to act, speak, and perform, this must be divine and immortal?

I am sensible that the general opinion of philosophers has distinguished the moral system of the brute creature from that of mankind, by an epithet which implies a mere mechanical impulse, which leads and impels them to necessary actions, without any premeditated design or contrivance; this we term instinct, which faculty we suppose to be inferior to man.

The parental and filial affections seem to be as ardent, their sensibility and attachment as active and faithful, as those observed in human nature.

When traveling on the east coast of the isthmus of Florida, ascending the south Musquito river, in a canoe, we observed numbers of deer and bears, near the banks, and on the islands of the river: the bears were feeding on the fruit of the dwarf creeping Chamaerops; (this fruit is of the form and size of dates, and is delicious and nourishing food:) we saw eleven bears in the course of the day, they seemed no way surprised or affrighted at the sight of us. In the evening, my hunter, who was an excellent marksman, said that he would shoot one of them for the sake of the skin and oil, for we had plenty and variety of provisions in our bark. We accordingly, on sight of two of them, planned our approaches as artfully as possible, by crossing over to the opposite shore, in order to get under cover of a small island; this we cautiously coasted round, to a point, which we apprehended would take us within shot of the bears; but here finding ourselves at too great a distance from them, and discovering that we must openly show ourselves, we had no other alternative to effect our purpose, but making oblique approaches. We gained gradually on our prey by this artifice, without their noticing us: finding ourselves near enough, the hunter fired, and laid the target dead on the spot where she stood; when presently the other, not seeming the least moved at the report of our piece, approached the dead body, smelled, and pawed it, and appearing in agony, fell to weeping and looking upwards, then towards us, and cried out like a child. Whilst our boat approached very near, the hunter was loading his rifle in order to shoot the survivor, which was a young cub, and the slain supposed to be the dam. The continual cries of this afflicted child, bereft of its parent, affected me very sensibly; I was moved with compassion, and charging myself as if accessary to what now appeared to be a cruel murder, endeavored to prevail on the hunter to save its life, but to no effect! for by habit he had become insensible to compassion towards the brute creation: being now within a few yards of the harmless devoted victim, he fired, and laid it dead upon the body of the dam.

If we bestow but very little attention to the economy of the animal creation, we shall find manifest examples of premeditation, perseverance, resolution, and consummate artifice. . . .

The evening was temperately cool and calm. The crocodiles began to roar and appear in uncommon numbers along the shores and in the river. I fixed my camp in an open plain, near the utmost projection of the promontory, under the shelter of a large live oak, which stood on the highest part of the ground, and but a few yards from my boat. From this open, high situation, I had a free prospect of the river, which was a matter of no trivial consideration to me, having good reason to dread the subtle attacks of the alligators, who were crowding about my harbor. Having collected a good quantity of wood for the purpose of keeping up a light and smoke during the night, I began to think of preparing my supper, when, upon examining my stores, I found but a scanty provision. I thereupon determined, as the most expeditious way of supplying my necessities, to take my bob and try for some trout. About one hundred yards above my harbor began a cove or bay of the river, out of which opened a large lagoon. The mouth or entrance from the river to it was narrow, but the waters soon after spread and formed a little lake, extending into the marshes: its entrance and shores within I observed to be verged with floating lawns of the pistia and nymphea and other aquatic plants; these I knew were excellent haunts for trout.

The verges and islets of the lagoon were elegantly embellished with flowering plants and shrubs; the laughing coots with wings half spread were tripping over the little coves, and hiding themselves in the tufts of grass; young broods of the painted summer teal, skimming the still surface of the waters, and following the watchful parent unconscious of danger, were frequently surprised by the voracious trout; and he, in turn, as often by the subtle greedy alligator. Behold him rushing forth from the flags and reeds. His enormous body swells. His plaited tail brandished high, floats upon the lake. The waters like a cataract descend from his opening jaws. Clouds of smoke issue from his dilated nostrils. The earth trembles with his thunder. When immediately from the opposite coast of the lagoon, emerges from the deep his rival champion. They suddenly dart upon each other. The boiling surface of the lake marks their rapid course, and a terrific conflict commences. They now sink to the bottom folded together in horrid wreaths. The water becomes thick and discolored. Again they rise, their jaws clap together, re-echoing through the deep surrounding forests. Again they sink, when the contest ends at the muddy bottom of the lake, and the vanquished makes a hazardous escape, hiding himself in the muddy turbulent waters and sedge on a distant shore. The proud victor exulting returns to the place of action. The shores and forests resound his dreadful roar, together with the triumphing shouts of the plaited tribes around, witnesses of the horrid combat.

My apprehensions were highly alarmed after being a spectator of so dreadful a battle. It was obvious that every delay would but tend to increase my dangers and difficulties, as the sun was near setting, and the alligators gathered around my harbor from all quarters. From these considerations I concluded to be expeditious in my trip to the lagoon, in order to take some fish. Not thinking it prudent to take my fusee with me, lest I might lose it overboard in case of a battle, which I had every reason to dread before my return, I therefore furnished myself with a club for my defense, went on board, and penetrating the first line of those which surrounded my harbor, they gave way; but being pursued by several very large ones, I kept strictly on the watch, and paddled with all my might towards the entrance of the lagoon, hoping to be sheltered there from the multitude of my assailants; but ere I had half-way reached the place, I was attacked on all sides, several endeavoring to overset the canoe. My situation now became precarious to the last degree: two very large ones attacked me closely, at the same instant, rushing up with their heads and part of their bodies above the water, roaring terribly and belching floods of water over me. They struck their jaws together so close to my ears, as almost to stun me, and I expected every moment to be dragged out of the boat and instantly devoured. But I applied my weapons so effectually about me, though at random, that I was so successful as to beat them off a little; when, finding that they designed to renew the battle, I made for the shore, as the only means left me for my preservation; for, by keeping close to it, I should have my enemies on one side of me only, whereas I was before surrounded by them; and there was a probability, if pushed to the last extremity, of saving myself, by jumping out of the canoe on shore, as it is easy to outwalk them on land although comparatively as swift as lightning in the water. I found this last expedient alone could fully answer my expectations, for as soon as I gained the shore, they drew off and kept aloof. This was a happy relief, as my confidence was, in some degree, recovered by it. . . .

It was by this time dusk, and the alligators had nearly ceased their roar, when I was again alarmed by a tumultuous noise that seemed to be in my harbor, and therefore engaged my immediate attention. Returning to my camp, I found it undisturbed, and then continued on to the extreme point of the promontory, where I saw a scene, new and surprising, which at first threw my senses into such a tumult, that it was some time before I could comprehend what was the matter; however, I soon accounted for the prodigious assemblage of crocodiles at this place, which exceeded everything of the kind I had ever heard of.

How shall I express myself so as to convey an adequate idea of it to the reader, and at the same time avoid raising suspicions of my veracity? Should I say, that the river (in this place) from shore to shore, and perhaps near half a mile above and below me, appeared to be one solid bank of fish, of various kinds, pushing through this narrow pass of St. Juan's into the little lake, on their return down the river, and that the alligators were in such incredible numbers, and so close together from shore to shore, that it would have been easy to have walked across on their heads, had the animals been harmless? What expressions can sufficiently declare the shocking scene that for some minutes continued, whilst this mighty army of fish were forcing the pass? During this attempt, thousands, I may say hundreds of thousands, of them were caught and swallowed by the devouring alligators. I have seen an alligator take up out of the water several great fish at a time, and just squeeze them betwixt his jaws, while the tails of the great trout flapped about his eyes and lips, ere he had swallowed them. The horrid noise of their closing jaws, their plunging amidst the broken banks of fish, and rising with their prey some feet upright above the water, the floods of water and blood rushing out of their mouths, and the clouds of vapor issuing from their wide nostrils, were truly frightful. This scene continued at intervals during the night, as the fish came to the pass. After this sight, shocking and tremendous as it was, I found myself somewhat easier and more reconciled to my situation; being convinced that their extraordinary assemblage here was owing to the annual feast of fish; and that they were so well employed in their own element, that I had little occasion to fear their paying me a visit. . . .

The noise of the crocodiles kept me awake the greater part of the night; but when I arose in the morning, contrary to my expectations, there was perfect peace; very few of them to be seen, and those were asleep on the shore. Yet I was not able to suppress my fears and apprehensions of being attacked by them in future; and indeed yesterday's combat with them, notwithstanding I came off in a manner victorious, or at least made a safe retreat, had left sufficient impression on my mind to damp my courage; and it seemed too much for one of my strength, being alone in a very small boat, to encounter such collected danger. To pursue my voyage up the river, and be obliged every evening to pass such dangerous defiles, appeared to me as perilous as running the gauntlet betwixt two rows of Indians armed with knives and firebrands. I however resolved to continue my voyage one day longer, if I possibly could with safety, and then return down the river, should I find the like difficulties to oppose. Accordingly I got every thing on board, charged my gun, and set sail, cautiously, along shore. As I passed by Battle lagoon, I began to tremble and keep a good lookout; when suddenly a huge alligator rushed out of the reeds, and with a tremendous roar came up, and darted as swift as an arrow under my boat, emerging upright on my lee quarter, with open jaws, and belching water and smoke that fell upon me like rain in a hurricane. I laid soundly about his head with my club, and beat him off; and after plunging and darting about my boat, he went off on a straight line through the water, seemingly with the rapidity of lightning, and entered the cape of the lagoon. I now employed my time to the very best advantage in paddling close along shore, but could not forbear looking now and then behind me, and presently perceived one of them coming up again. The water of the river hereabouts was shoal and very clear; the monster came up with the usual roar and menaces, and passed close by the side of my boat, when I could distinctly see a young brood of alligators, to the number of one hundred or more, following after her in a long train. They kept close together in a column, without straggling off to the one side or the other; the young appeared to be of an equal size, about fifteen inches in length, almost black, with pale yellow transverse waved clouds or blotches, much like rattlesnakes in color. I now lost sight of my enemy again.

Still keeping close along shore, on turning a point or projection of the river-bank, at once I beheld a great number of hillocks or small pyramids, resembling haycocks, ranged like an encampment along the banks. They stood fifteen or twenty yards distant from the water, on a high marsh, about four feet perpendicular above the water. I knew them to be the nests of the crocodile, having had a description of them before; and now expected a furious and general attack, as I saw several large crocodiles swimming abreast of these buildings. These nests being so great a curiosity to me, I was determined at all events immediately to land and examine them. Accordingly, I ran my bark on shore at one of their landing-places, which was a sort of nick or little dock, from which ascended a sloping path or road up to the edge of the meadow, where their nests were; most of them were deserted, and the great thick whitish eggshells lay broken and scattered upon the ground round about them.

The nests or hillocks are of the form of an obtuse cone, four feet high and four or five feet in diameter at their bases; they are constructed with mud, grass and herbage. At first they lay a floor of this kind of tempered mortar on the ground, upon which they deposit a layer of eggs, and upon this a stratum of mortar, seven or eight inches in thickness, and then another layer of eggs; and in this manner one stratum upon another, nearly to the top. I believe they commonly lay from one to two hundred eggs in a nest: these are hatched, I suppose, by the heat of the sun; and perhaps the vegetable substances mixed with the earth, being acted upon by the sun, may cause a small degree of fermentation, and so increase the heat in those hillocks. The ground for several acres about these nests showed evident marks of a continual resort of alligators; the grass was every where beaten down, hardly a blade or straw was left standing; whereas, all about, at a distance, it was five or six feet high, and as thick as it could grow together. The female, as I imagine, carefully watches her own nest of eggs until they are all hatched; or perhaps while she is attending her own brood, she takes under her care and protection as many as she can get at one time, either from her own particular nest or others; but certain it is, that the young are not left to shift for themselves; for I have had frequent opportunities of seeing the female alligator leading about the shores her train of young ones, just as a hen does her brood of chickens; and she is equally assiduous and courageous in defending the young, which are under her care, and providing for their subsistence; and when she is basking upon the warm banks, with her brood around her, you may hear the young ones continually whining and barking like young puppies. I believe but few of a brood live to the years of full growth and magnitude, as the old feed on the young as long as they can make prey of them. . . .

Having gratified my curiosity at this general breeding-place and nursery of crocodiles, I continued my voyage up the river without being greatly disturbed by them. In my way I observed islets or floating fields of the bright green Pistia, decorated with other amphibious plants, as Senecio Jacobea, Persicaria amphibia, Coreopsis bidens, Hydrocotyle fluitans, and many others of less note.

James Smith
(1737–1814)

During the seventeenth and eighteenth centuries, the Indian captivity narrative enjoyed "best seller" status, as readers hungry for vicarious adventure and depictions of "savage" life devoured the many firsthand accounts penned by whites who had lived as prisoners among the Indians. Although James Smith's book, *An Account of the Remarkable Occurrences in the Life and Travels of Col. James Smith*, was not published until 1799, his captivity among the Iroquois had taken place four decades earlier, during the Seven Years' War (1756–63). Fearing increasing French control of Canada and the Mississippi crescent, the British sent Gen. Edward Braddock to attack the French at Fort Duquesne (now Pittsburgh); the British force of 1,400, weakened by rough terrain and repeated ambushes, would eventually lose this battle for mastery of the Ohio River corridor. James Smith, a member of Braddock's force, was taken captive by a band of Caughnawaga Mohawk Indians in a raid that occurred in July 1755. After his adoption (a common practice among many Indian peoples) he remained a prisoner of the Native Americans for four years, until he was ransomed in the fall of 1759. Like many captivity narratives, Smith's is interesting for its delicate negotiation of the issue of liminal cultural identity: Smith the captive must assimilate into Indian culture in order to survive, yet Smith the author must also reassure himself and his audience of his essentially white identity. However, Smith's book is also fascinating as nature writing, for in addition to being replete with detailed observations made in the deep wilderness, it shows how his captivity is also a form of apprenticeship through which Indian masters such as Tecaughretanego provide him with what we might call an environmental education — a complete course of study in plants, animals, and the medicinal and cultural contexts of their use. Indeed, the dramatic scene depicted at the conclusion of the following excerpt from *An Account* suggests how crucial Smith's acquired knowledge and fortitude was to his survival in the wilderness.

From *An Account of the Remarkable Occurrences in the Life and Travels of Col. James Smith* (1799)

After the departure of these warriors we had hard times; and though we were not altogether out of provisions, we were brought to short allowance. At length Tontileaugo had considerable success, and we had meat brought into camp sufficient to last ten days. Tontileaugo then took me with him in order to encamp some distance from this winter cabin, to try his luck there. We carried no provision with us; he said he would leave what was there for the squaws and children, and that we could shift for ourselves. We steered about a south course up the waters of this creek, and encamped about ten or twelve miles from the winter cabin. As it was still cold weather and a crust upon the snow, which made a noise as we walked and alarmed the deer, we could kill nothing, and consequently went to sleep without supper. The only chance we had, under these circumstances, was to hunt bear holes; as the bears about Christmas search out a winter lodging place, where they lie about three or four months without eating or drinking. This may appear to some incredible; but it is now well known to be the case, by those who live in the remote western parts of North America.

The next morning early we proceeded on, and when we found a tree scratched by the bears climbing up, and the hole in the tree sufficiently large for the reception of the bear, we then fell a sapling or small tree, against or near the hole; and it was my business to climb up and drive out the bear, while Tontileaugo stood ready with his gun and bow. We went on in this manner until evening, without success; at length we found a large elm scratched, and a hole in it about forty feet up; but no tree nigh, suitable to lodge against the hole. Tontileaugo got a long pole and some dry rotten wood, which he tied in bunches with bark; and as there was a tree that grew near the elm, and extended up near the hole, but leaned the wrong way, so that we could not lodge it to advantage; to remedy this inconvenience, he climbed up this tree and carried with him his rotten wood, fire and pole. The rotten wood he tied to his belt, and to one end of the pole he tied a hook, and a piece of rotten wood which he set fire to, as it would retain fire almost like spunk, and reached this hook from limb to limb as he went up; when he got up, with this pole he put dry wood on fire into the hole; after he put in the fire he heard the bear snuff, and he came speedily down, took his gun in his hand, and waited until the bear would come out; but it was some time before it appeared, and when it did appear, he attempted taking sight with his rifle; but it being then too dark to see the sights, he set it down by a tree, and instantly bent his bow, took hold of an arrow, and shot the bear a little behind the shoulder; I was preparing also to shoot an arrow, but he called to me to stop, there was no occasion; and with that the bear fell to the ground.

Being very hungry we kindled a fire, opened the bear, took out the liver, and wrapped some of the caul fat round, and put it on a wooden spit, which we stuck in the ground by the fire to roast; we then skinned the bear, got on our kettle, and had both roast and boiled, and also sauce to our meat, which appeared to me to be delicate fare. . . .

Some time in February the four warriors returned, who had taken two scalps, and six horses from the frontiers of Pennsylvania. The hunters could then scatter out a considerable distance from the winter cabin, and encamp, kill meat and bring it in upon horses; so that we commonly after this had plenty of provision.

In this month we began to make sugar. As some of the elm bark will strip at this season, the squaws, after finding a tree that would do, cut it down, and with a crooked stick, broad and sharp at the end, took the bark off the tree, and of this bark made vessels in a curious manner, that would hold about two gallons each: they made above one hundred of these kinds of vessels. In the sugar-tree they cut a notch, sloping down, and at the end of the notch, stuck in a tomahawk; in the place where they stuck the tomahawk, they drove a long chip, in order to carry the water out from the tree, and under this they set their vessel, to receive it. As sugar-trees were plenty and large here, they seldom or never notched a tree that was not two or three feet over. They also made bark vessels for carrying the water, that would hold about four gallons each. They had two brass kettles, that held about fifteen gallons each, and other smaller kettles in which they boiled the water. But as they could not at all times boil away the water as fast as it was collected, they made vessels of bark, that would hold about one hundred gallons each, for retaining the water; and though the sugar-trees did not run every day, they had always a sufficient quantity of water to keep them boiling during the whole sugar season.

The way that we commonly used our sugar while encamped, was by putting it in bears' fat until the fat was almost as sweet as the sugar itself, and in this we dipped our roasted venison. . . .

In conversation with Tecaughretanego, I happened to be talking of the beavers' catching fish. He asked me why I thought that the beaver caught fish? I told him that I had read of the beaver making dams for the conveniency of fishing. He laughed, and made game of me and my book. He said the man that wrote that book knew nothing about the beaver. The beaver never did eat flesh of any kind; but lived on the bark of trees, roots, and other vegetables.

In order to know certainly how this was, when we killed a beaver I carefully examined the intestines, but found no appearance of fish; I afterward made an experiment on a pet beaver which we had, and found that it would neither eat fish nor flesh; therefore I acknowledged that the book that I had read was wrong.

I asked him if the beaver was an amphibious animal, or if it could live under water? He said that the beaver was a kind of subterraneous water animal, that lives in or near the water, but they were no more amphibious than the ducks and geese were—which was constantly proven to be the case, as all the beavers that are caught in steel traps are drowned, provided the trap be heavy enough to keep them under water. As the beaver does not eat fish, I inquired of Tecaughretanego why the beaver made such large dams? He said they were of use to them in various respects—both for their safety and food. For their safety, as by raising the water over the mouths of their holes, or subterraneous lodging places, they could not be easily found; and as the beaver feeds chiefly on the bark of trees, by raising the water over the banks, they can cut down saplings for bark to feed upon without going out much upon the land: and when they are obliged to go out on land for this food, they frequently are caught by the wolves. As the beaver can run upon land but little faster than a water tortoise, and is no fighting animal, if they are any distance from the water, they become an easy prey to their enemies.

I asked Tecaughretanego, what was the use of the beaver's stones, or glands, to them; as the she beaver has two pair, which is commonly called the oil stones, and the bark stones? He said that as the beavers are the dumbest of all animals, and scarcely ever make any noise; and as they were working creatures, they made use of this smell in order to work in concert. If an old beaver was to come on the bank and rub his breech upon the ground, and raise a perfume, the others will collect from different places and go to work; this is also of use to them in traveling, that they may thereby search out and find their company. Cunning hunters finding this out, have made use of it against the beaver, in order to catch them. What is the bait which you see them make use of, but a compound of the oil and bark stones? By this perfume, which is only a false signal, they decoy them to the trap.

Near this pond, beaver was the principal game. Before the water froze up, we caught a great many with wooden and steel traps: but after that, we hunted the beaver on the ice. Some places here the beavers build large houses to live in; and in other places they have subterraneous lodgings in the banks. Where they lodge in the ground, we have no chance of hunting them on the ice; but where they have houses, we go with malls and handspikes, and break all the hollow ice, to prevent them from getting their heads above the water under it. Then we break a hole in the house, and they make their escape into the water; but as they cannot live long under water, they are obliged to go to some of those broken places to breathe, and the Indians commonly put in their hands, catch them by the hind leg, haul them on the ice, and tomahawk them. Sometimes they shoot them in the head, when they raise it above the water. I asked the Indians if they were not afraid to catch the beavers with their hands? they said no: they were not much of a biting creature; yet if they would catch them by the forefoot they would bite.

I went out with Tecaughretanego, and some others a beaver hunting: but we did not succeed, and on our return we saw where several raccoons had passed, while the snow was soft; though there was now a crust upon it, we all made a halt looking at the raccoon tracks. As they saw a tree with a hole in it, they told me to go and see if they had gone in thereat; and if they had, to halloo, and they would come and take them out. When I went to that tree, I found they had gone past; but I saw another the way they had went, and proceeded to examine that, and found they had gone up it. I then began to halloo, but could have no answer.

As it began to snow and blow most violently, I returned and proceeded after my company, and for some time could see their tracks; but the old snow being about three inches deep, and a crust upon it, the present driving snow soon filled up the tracks. As I had only a bow, arrows, and tomahawk with me, and no way to strike fire, I appeared to be in a dismal situation—and as the air was dark with snow, I had little more prospect of steering my course, than I would in the night. At length I came to a hollow tree, with a hole at one side that I could go in at. I went in, and found that it was a dry place, and the hollow about three feet diameter, and high enough for me to stand in. I found that there was also a considerable quantity of soft, dry rotten wood, around this hollow: I therefore concluded that I would lodge here, and that I would go to work, and stop up the door of my house. I stripped off my blanket, (which was all the clothes that I had, excepting a breechclout, leggings, and moccasins,) and with my tomahawk, fell to chopping at the top of a fallen tree that lay near, and carried wood and set it up on end against the door, until I had it three or four feet thick, all round, excepting a hole I had left to creep in at. I had a block prepared that I could haul after me, to stop this hole: and before I went in I put in a number of small sticks, that I might more effectually stop it on the inside. When I went in, I took my tomahawk and cut down all the dry, rotten wood I could get, and beat it small. With it I made a bed like a goosenest or hog-bed, and with the small sticks stopped every hole, until my house was almost dark. I stripped off my moccasins, and danced in the center of my bed for about half an hour, in order to warm myself. In this time my feet and whole body were agreeably warmed. The snow, in the meanwhile, had stopped all the holes, so that my house was as dark as a dungeon; though I knew that it could not yet be dark out-of-doors. I then coiled myself up in my blanket, lay down in my little round bed, and had a tolerable night's lodging. When I awoke, all was dark—not the least glimmering of light to be seen. Immediately I recollected that I was not to expect light in this new habitation, as there was neither door nor window in it. As I could hear the storm raging, and did not suffer much cold, as I was then situated, I concluded I would stay in my nest until I was certain it was day. When I had reason to conclude that it surely was day, I arose and put on my moccasins, which I had laid under my head to keep from freezing. I then endeavored to find the door, and had to do all by the sense of feeling, which took me some time. At length I found the block, but it being heavy, and a large quantity of snow having fallen on it, at the first attempt I did not move it. I then felt terrified—among all the hardships I had sustained, I never knew before, what it was to be thus deprived of light. This, with the other circumstances attending it, appeared grievous. I went straightway to bed again, wrapped my blanket round me, and lay and mused awhile, and then prayed to Almighty God to direct and protect me, as he had done heretofore. I once again attempted to move away the block, which proved successful; it moved about nine inches. With this a considerable quantity of snow fell in from above, and I immediately received light; so that I found a very great snow had fallen, above what I had ever seen in one night. I then knew why I could not easily move the block, and I was so rejoiced at obtaining the light, that all my other difficulties seemed to vanish. I then turned into my cell, and returned God thanks for having once more received the light of Heaven. At length I belted my blanket about me, got my tomahawk, bow and arrows, and went out of my den.

I was now in tolerable high spirits, though the snow had fallen above three feet deep, in addition to what was on the ground before; and the only imperfect guide I had, in order to steer my course to camp, was the trees; as the moss generally grows on the northwest side of them, if they are straight. I proceeded on, wading through the snow, and about twelve o'clock (as it appeared afterward, from that time to night, for it was yet cloudy,) I came upon the creek that our camp was on, about half a mile below the camp; and when I came in sight of the camp, I found that there was great joy, by the shouts and yelling of the boys, etc.

Charles Willson Peale
(1741–1827)

Born in Maryland, the son of a forger who had been exiled from England, Charles Willson Peale moved to Philadelphia in 1776 and fought as a commander under George Washington during the American Revolution. Peale's gift, however, was not combat but portraiture: he was a talented painter (most of Peale's sixteen children, including the naturalist Titian Ramsay Peale, were named for painters) who executed likenesses of many of the founding fathers. A personal friend of Franklin and

Jefferson, Peale was also a zealous amateur naturalist, though of a more entrepreneurial and less disciplined sensibility than many other scientists of the age. Peale's great dream was to open a public museum of natural history — an idea that was quite radical at a time when collections of natural history were quite modest and were generally restricted to the "cabinets of curiosities" kept by wealthy gentlemen. Peale's was the first natural history museum in America; a century later, there would be 250. As the lecture excerpted below demonstrates, Peale believed that a museum could be a vital agent of public education, and he further held — in a sentiment that anticipates the nationalist tone of nineteenth-century American scientific discourse — that natural history "ought to become a NATIONAL CONCERN, since it is a NATIONAL GOOD." Peale persevered, at first setting up displays in his home (1786) and later moving his ever-expanding collections to the American Philosophical Society (1794) and eventually to the Pennsylvania State House (1802). Peale's "American Museum" was a major public attraction, and many of its thousands of visitors (including Anne Newport Royall, whose account of the museum appears later in this volume) enthusiastically described the wonders they saw there. Peale did his own specimen taxidermy and painted the backdrops against which animals were carefully posed (in later years the collections were reorganized according to the Linnaean system), but he was perhaps most famous for being the first to excavate, reconstruct, and display a full mastodon skeleton — an event that captured the public imagination, encouraged public science education, and inspired a generation of Americans to use the new tools of natural science to further investigate the wonders of the Creation.

From "Introduction to a Course of Lectures on Natural History . . ." (1799)

What more pleasing prospect can be opened to our view than the boundless field of nature? not only comprehending the inhabitants of earth, sea, and air; but earth, sea and air themselves — presenting an inexhaustible fund for amusing and useful enquiry.

The comfort, happiness and support of all ranks, depend upon their knowledge of nature. In the early periods of society, man was compelled more by necessity than mere amusement to investigate the qualities of those objects which a munificent author had opened to his view — That necessity taught him how to feed, clothe and shelter himself from the inclemencies of the weather; and though her calls of necessity are now much weakened, who will deny that the condition of man may not, by a still closer and more extensive investigation, be considerably improved.

No one therefore need blush at having ranked among his earnest pursuits, the study of a science, whose truths so immediately interest him and contain the strongest evidence of an existing all-perfect and omnipotent author, even from the smallest survey; but when minutely examined, when extensively surveyed, how wonderful—how sublime are our ideas of the Deity!

The injunction given to Adam to name the works of creation, implied a necessity to become acquainted with those works, in order to name and characterize them, without confusion.—Let this early ordinance extend to us, and teach us, not only their names and uses but their cause; for I am bold to say that every one who really delights in the contemplation of nature *must* be virtuous.—Those

"Whom nature's works can charm, with God himself
Hold converse; grow familiar, day by day,
With his conceptions, act upon his plan;
And form to his the relish of their souls."

Revealed religion commands our attention to the practice of moral duties; and her injunction gains tenfold influence, when all nature enforces our attention to them, if we would not be surpassed by those animals which we often think beneath us—How weak, how poor, how contemptible, must that human creature be, who, destitute of virtue, will neither learn from man, nor the animals around him, the proper exercise of his faculties.

Pope only limited the voice of nature, when he advised man to

"Learn from the birds what food the thickets yield;
Learn from the beasts the physic of the field;
The art of building from the bee receive;
Learn from the mule to plow, the worm to weave;
Learn from the little nautilus to sail,
Spread the thin oar and catch the driving gale."

Example is the most powerful instructor, and it is to be wished that our divines would more generally enforce their observations on the duties of man, by instances of propriety, I may say virtue, from among the brute creation.

Whenever they *are* introduced universal satisfaction is observed and if more attended to, a novel and beneficial field is opened for the advancement of happiness and the display of talents. Hence would this important truth be more generally received; that the world is destined to manifest the glory of the Creator, and that man is just in a situation to be the interpreter and publisher of the divine wisdom; for, indeed he who knows it not from observation on nature, can scarcely learn it from another source.

A taste for natural enquiries is not only useful in the highest degree, but a never failing source of the most exalted enjoyment; a more rational pleasure cannot possibly occupy the attention or captivate the affections of mankind, than that which arises from a due consideration of the works of nature.

The pains, evils and uneasiness which unavoidably occur in life, must be tempered with a large portion of pleasure to render them tolerable — and it is in the power of the naturalist to point out the most exalted of pleasures as well as the most innocent and advantageous: For what use would the sun display its beams? for what use would this spacious world be furnished by the great and bountiful Author of Nature, were there no rational beings capable of admiring and turning them to their advantage — for this enjoyment, our senses, the inlets to knowledge, are bestowed upon us.

Frequent contemplations of the magnificence, beauty, regularity, proportion and utility in the works of creation, cannot but impress the minds of men, not only with ideas of wonder, admiration, and gratitude; but induce the most cheerful acquiescence in the dispensations of a wise providence. To him who considers not this as the end of knowledge, the voice of nature speaks in vain, and all his wisdom is but madness.

When we are convinced that the laws of the omniscient, are unchangeable and admit of no improvement, we may admire,—adore,—and be happy. . . .

Natural history is not only interesting to the individual, it ought to become a NATIONAL CONCERN, since it is a NATIONAL GOOD,—of this, agriculture, as it is the most important occupation, affords the most striking proof.

The farmer ought to know the characteristic properties of those tame animals in his use, to derive proper advantage from them, and to know whether other animals might not be brought into subjection to supply their place with advantage — and how to procure and support them: He ought to know the qualities of the soil which he cultivates and the means of managing and improving it. The nature of the grain which he raises; and whether there are not others which he might introduce with greater profit; whether his land contains substances suitable to manure and meliorate the soil; and whether it contains fossils, such as turf or coal, &c. fit for fuel, in order to save his timber; or minerals useful in the mechanic arts.

He ought to know what reptiles best aid and protect the fruit of his labor, and not through ignorance destroy such as feed on animals *more* destructive of his grain and fruits; nor ridiculously possess antipathies to those which he ought to *cherish*—but, as it is to be lamented that man receives these as part of his early education; so it is to be hoped that when the knowledge of our favorite science shall be more extended, man shall not merit this stigma on his reason.

Why is it so? Whence these antipathies?—Is there any being ugly or hateful in the eyes of the Creator?—This is a serious question and important to our happiness in many respects.

Never shall I forget my disagreeable sensations, when a naturalist, my friend, demanded of me, why I called a toad, ugly?—My conscience instantly smote me for presuming to depreciate the works of *Divine Wisdom;* and from that moment became convinced, that everything is beautiful in its kind; and I have now a continued pleasure in the contemplation of many things which once appeared disgusting and terrible to me.

The farmer ought to know that snakes feed on field mice and moles, which would otherwise destroy whole fields of corn; and that those birds which pick and appear to injure the trees, there find innumerable worms and beetles, which, left to commit their ravages, would sap and destroy whole orchards of the best fruit. Nature is perfect in all her works, nor is there anything made in vain; and it is our duty to study her ways, in order that we may know what is meant for our particular benefit. . . .

How delightfully may the leisure of a country life be enjoyed, instead of finding it a burden, by directing our inquisitive spirit to the works of nature. How much more harmless and agreeable this enjoyment of a vacant hour, than in the too common practices of idleness, vain curiosity and slander—the greatest evils of society.

Men of a studious and sedentary life in searching for an agreeable relaxation to their minds, pay a necessary condescension to the weakness of human nature—These, amid the inhabitants of the grove, may innocently beguile the dream of life, and find an useful relaxation from the severity of wisdom—But to the musician, poet, painter and sculptor, whose delightful arts give a kind of second existence to nature, is it peculiarly important to be acquainted with the beauties of their model.

The field of natural history is almost boundless; is a science so copious, affording such a variety of studies, that whatever may be the particular talents of the individual, he will here find abundant matter to exercise his genius—But to persons, whose situation in life, leave them without the necessity of employment for a considerable part of their waking hours; who suffer that *ennui*—that dejection of spirits, from which, to relieve themselves, they too often have recourse to habits, the forerunners of vice and misery, it is of inexpressible benefit!

Oh! could they be induced to taste the sweets resulting from reflections on the rise, progress and qualities of natural objects, whether animate or inanimate, which they occasionally meet with in the earth, air, or water—so far would they be from desiring to *kill* their time, that they would have full enjoyment for every moment of life.

The world is a museum in which all men are destined to be employed and amused, and they cannot be too much interested in the objects around them. Goldsmith the elegant imitator of Buffon, says "The mere uninformed spectator passes on in gloomy solitude; while the naturalist in every plant, in every insect, and in every pebble, finds something to entertain his curiosity and excite his speculation."

But it is only by order and system that a general view may be had of so extensive a subject, and that the great book of nature may be opened and studied, leaf by leaf, and a knowledge gained of the character which the great Creator has stamped on each being—without this, our desire would very soon be arrested by confusion and perplexity.

The credit of having first given natural history the form of system, is justly given to the celebrated Linnaeus of Sweden; to whom I am infinitely indebted for the present arrangement of my Museum.

I have long wished to be in a situation to point out to others, the various beauties which have delighted me while in the pursuit of my unremitted labors for years; with the view of establishing a PUBLIC MUSEUM.

The longest life is too short to accomplish the work I had undertaken; and foreseeing the risk, that my labors might be lost, I have hastened to put all I have been able to collect into such good preservation, as to ensure their duration. . . .

Since many of my audience may not know under what difficulties I have formed a *Museum*—permit me here to give a concise account of its rise and progress.—In speaking for a moment of myself, I hope I shall not be accused of the vanity of egotism.

For a number of years I followed the profession of a portrait painter; and by the labors of my pencil alone, supported a large family and might have acquired a fortune; but, like many others of my countrymen, was more active for the public good, than solicitous of acquiring wealth.

At length I found it absolutely necessary to determine, whether to continue my political career, or leave it for the more peaceful studies of the fine arts: When the merit of each was put in the balance, the peaceful muse outweighed political warfare—and since that period I have been scarcely so much as a common observer of the political world.

Leaving the walks of public life, I soon found leisure; and began to paint a collection of the portraits of characters distinguished in the American revolution—which may now justly be considered a valuable one.

I often view it with a pleasing pain, as it brings to my memory the agreeable converse of a Randolph, a Laurens, a Washington, a Green; the philosophic Franklin and Rittenhouse; and of the hair-breadth escapes of Decalb, Paul Jones, and Wayne, and the meritorious exertions and services of many others recognized in those monumental tablets.

From this digression I return to the subject—Having made some progress in the portraits of those worthies—my friend Col. Ramsey suggested the idea of amusing the public curiosity by putting into one corner of my picture-gallery some bones of the mammoth, the enormous non-descript of America. Mr. Patterson

(Professor of Mathematics in our University) encouraged the plan, and presented me with the first article, a curious fish of western waters, with which to begin my Museum.

From so *small* a beginning, arose a fabric, which in some future day may be an honor to America.

Little did I then know of the labor I was bringing on these shoulders.—Though I was called *mad* and cautioned to beware of the gulf into which many others of greater merit had fallen,—*neglect and poverty,*—yet, so irresistibly bewitching is the thirst of knowledge in the science of nature that neither the want of funds, nor leisure from other occupations, could damp my ardor, though a thousand difficulties rose in succession.

Foreigners are surprised to hear this is the work of an individual, unsupported by public bodies! yet it is a fact, which in future will scarcely be credited, *that neither to the government of the United States,* the *state of Pennsylvania,* nor any *other state am I under the least obligation for the present appearance of the Museum.* To individuals only, can I say I am indebted—for whose numerous donations I shall ever be thankful.

Curiosities which are accidentally acquired cannot be better disposed of than by putting them into *a repository for the public inspection,* where they may become immensely *useful* to thousands; otherwise, however valued at first, they are commonly shown only to a few friends—the novelty subsides, and they are *lost* or sent, as many have regretted, to Europe's overflowing stores. The attention paid in the old world to collections of this nature, is a sufficient proof of their importance; where they are often the nurseries of the greatest scientific characters. It is to the Museum of a country, that travelers, after their more local and characteristic enquiries, should sedulously attend, in order to gain correct information on some of its most important peculiarities. Knowledge thus collected might often be the source of infinite benefit to their countrymen.—But in order that the benefit may be *certain,* every traveler should be acquainted with the product of his *own,* to enable him to enquire after and distinguish the peculiarities of *other* countries; and should particularly be acquainted *with some kind of system,* by which to direct those enquiries; for it is only by method in collecting and storing our ideas, when a multiplicity is presented to us, that the knowledge of them is retained and rendered of service.

How often have I been surprised, in my Museum, to observe multitudes of my fellow citizens not even acquainted with the most common and valuable productions of our country!

If the labors attending my Museum will have the effect of making general this necessary acquaintance, in remarking the benefit which must follow to the public, I shall feel no inconsiderable reward.

PART THREE

The Nineteenth Century through *Walden*

A more picturesque scene could hardly be imagined. The night was very dark, but as far as the eye could reach, all across the horizon, about four miles in front of us, was a broad, bright, lurid glare of fire, with a thick canopy of smoke hanging over it, whose fantastic wreaths, as they curled in the breeze, were tinged with the red reflection of the flames. Even at that distance we could hear the crackling and rushing of the fire, which, as it advanced, caused a strong wind, and every now and then a brighter flame would shoot high up into the black cloud of smoke over the top of the hill, illuminating for an instant our tents and wagons in the dark hollow. . . . I ran up for an instant to the top, and shall never forget the scene. Although still half a mile off, the fire seemed close to me, and the heat and smoke were almost intolerable, while the dazzling brightness of the flames made it painful to look at them. . . . Every now and then a prairie hen would flirr past, flying in a wild uncertain manner, as if fear had almost deprived it of the use of its wings; while all the songsters of the grove were wheeling about among the trees, uttering the most expressive cries of alarm, and the melancholy hooting of several owls, and wailing yells of the wolves, together with the shouts and cries of the men almost drowned occasionally by the roaring of the flames, added to the savage grandeur of the scene, and one could have fancied the end of all things was at hand.

JOHN PALLISER

Solitary Rambles and Adventures of a Hunter in the Prairies (1853)

Meriwether Lewis (1774–1809) and William Clark (1770–1838)

When Thomas Jefferson became president in 1801, the little-known territory between the Mississippi and the Rockies was owned by Spain (shortly thereafter it was ceded to France), and the terra incognita west to the Pacific was a pastiche of lands variously controlled by Native American peoples and by Spain, France, Britain, and Russia. When, in 1803, Jefferson negotiated the Louisiana Purchase — by which the United States bought the vast Louisiana territory from France for three cents an acre — he doubled the size of his country. Jefferson had already made secret plans to send explorers west, but the Louisiana Purchase allowed him to make public the Corps of Discovery, the first and most important of many nineteenth-century explorations of the American continent. To lead the expedition he chose young Meriwether Lewis, a man he felt had "a talent for observation which had led him to an accurate knowledge of the plants and animals of his own country," and William Clark, an experienced military man seasoned by frontier Indian campaigns. From 1804 to 1806 these co-captains led their Corps of Discovery, which consisted of about fifty members, from the mouth of the Missouri all the way to the Pacific at the outlet of the Columbia. Along the way they observed and reported on the virtually unknown prairie, mountain, and desert wilderness of the American West, and they cataloged hundreds of species new to science, including the bighorn sheep, coyote, jackrabbit, prairie dog, and grizzly bear; many of the specimens they collected ended up in Peale's natural history museum in Philadelphia. During their voyage both Lewis and Clark kept the sort of thorough, daily, and descriptive diary that Jefferson had specifically requested of them. The result, *The Journals of Lewis and Clark* (the first complete version of which appeared in 1904–5), is an epic narrative of environmental history that has introduced generations of Americans to the vast, presettlement country west of the Mississippi. Their journals are by turns personal diary, field report, adventure story, and natural history journal, and the dual authorship also gives the document an interesting dialogic or contrapuntal structure: the full experience of the expedition emerges only through the intertwining, mutually referential voices of both Lewis and Clark. In the following descriptions of the Great Falls of the Missouri, for example, we notice the tension between Lewis's effusive style, which celebrates the sublime spectacle before him, and Clark's terse prose, which concerns itself more directly with the logistical challenges of the journey. In addition to the birds Clark's Nutcracker (*Nucifraga columbiana*) and Lewis's woodpecker (*Melanerpes lewis*), several plants are named in the explorers' honor: *Clarkia*, a genus of wildflower related to the evening primrose, and *Lewisia*, the bitterroot.

From *The Journals of Lewis and Clark* (1804–1806)

[Lewis]

June 13, 1805. I had proceeded about two miles with Goodrich at some distance behind me when my ears were saluted with the agreeable sound of a fall of water and advancing a little further I saw the spray arise above the plain like a column of smoke which would frequently disappear again in an instant caused I presume by the wind which blew pretty hard from the S.W. I did not however lose my direction to this point which soon began to make a roaring too tremendous to be mistaken for any cause short of the great falls of the Missouri.

I hurried down the hill which was about 200 feet high and difficult of access, to gaze on this sublimely grand spectacle.

Immediately at the cascade the river is about 300 yards wide; about ninety or a hundred yards of this next the Lard. bluff is a smooth even sheet of water falling over a precipice of at least eighty feet, the remaining part of about 200 yards on my right forms the grandest sight I ever beheld. The height of the fall is the same as the other but the irregular and somewhat projecting rocks below receives the water in its passage down and breaks it into a perfect white foam which assumes a thousand forms in a moment sometimes flying up in jets of sparkling foam to the height of fifteen or twenty feet and are scarcely formed before large rolling bodies of the same beaten and foaming water is thrown over and conceals them. In short the rocks seem to be most happily fixed to present a sheet of the whitest beaten froth for 200 yards in length and about 80 feet perpendicular. The water after descending strikes against the abutment before mentioned or that on which I stand and seems to reverberate and being met by the more impetuous current they roll and swell into half formed billows of great height which rise and again disappear in an instant.

The buffalo have a large beaten road to the water, for it is but in very few places that these animals can obtain water near this place owing to the steep and inaccessible banks. I see several skeletons of the buffalo lying in the edge of the water near the Stard. bluff which I presume have been swept down by the current and precipitated over this tremendous fall.

From the reflection of the sun on the spray or mist which arises from these falls there is a beautiful rainbow produced which adds not a little to the beauty of this majestically grand scenery. After writing this imperfect description I again viewed the falls and was so much disgusted with the imperfect idea which it conveyed of the scene that I determined to draw my pen across it and begin again, but then reflected that I could not perhaps succeed better than penning the first impressions of the mind; I wished for the pencil of Salvator Rosa or the pen of Thompson, that I might be enabled to give to the enlightened world some just idea of this truly magnificent and sublimely grand object, which has from the commencement of time been concealed from the view of civilized man; but this was fruitless and vain. I most sincerely regretted that I had not brought a camera obscura with me by the assistance of which even I could have hoped to have done better but alas this was also out of my reach; I therefore with the assistance of my pen only endeavored to trace some of the stronger features of this scene by the assistance of which and my recollection aided by some able pencil I hope still to give to the world some faint idea of an object which at this moment fills me with such pleasure and astonishment; and which of its kind I will venture to assert is second to but one in the known world. I retired to the shade of a tree where I determined to fix my camp for the present and dispatch a man in the morning to inform Capt. C. and the party of my success in finding the falls and settle in their minds all further doubts as to the Missouri.

Goodrich had caught half a dozen very fine trout and a number of both species of the white fish. These trout are from sixteen to twenty-three inches in length, precisely resemble our mountain or speckled trout in form and the position of their fins, but the specks on these are of a deep black instead of the red or gold color of those common to the U. States. These are furnished long sharp teeth on the pallet and tongue and have generally a small dash of red on each side behind the front ventral fins; the flesh is of a pale yellowish red, or when in good order, of a rose red.

I am induced to believe that the Brown, the white and the Grizzly bear of this country are the same species only differing in color from age or more probably from the same natural cause that many other animals of the same family differ in color. One of those which we killed yesterday was of a cream-colored white while the other in company with it was of the common bay or reddish brown, which seems to be the most usual color of them.

My fare is really sumptuous this evening; buffalo's humps, tongues and marrowbones, fine trout parched meal pepper and salt, and a good appetite; the last is not considered the least of the luxuries.

[Clark]

June 13. A fair morning, some dew this morning. The Indian woman very sick I gave her a dose of salts. We set out early, at a mile & ½ passed a small rapid stream on the Lard. side which heads in a mountain to the S.E. 12 or 15 miles, which at this time is covered with Snow. We call this stream Snow river, as it is the conveyance of the melted snow from that mountain at present. Numbers of Geese & Goslings, the geese cannot fly at this season. Gooseberries are ripe and in great abundance, the yellow currant is also common, not yet ripe. Killed a buffalo & camped on the Lard. side near an old Indian fortified camp. One man sick & 3 with swellings, the Indian woman very sick. Killed a goat & Fraser 2 Buffalo.

The river very rapid many shoals great numbers of large stones, passed some bluffs or low cliffs of slate today.

[Lewis]

June 14. This morning at sunrise I dispatched Joseph Fields with a letter to Capt. Clark and ordered him to keep sufficiently near the river to observe its situation in order that he might be enabled to give Capt. Clark an idea of the point at which it would be best to halt to make our portage. About ten o'clock this morning while the men were engaged with the meat I took my Gun and espontoon and thought I would walk a few miles and see where the rapids terminated above, and return to dinner. After passing one continued rapid and three small cascades of about four or five feet each at the distance of about five miles I arrived at a fall of about 19 feet; the river is here about 400 yards wide. This pitch which I called the crooked falls occupies about three-fourths of the width of the river.

I should have returned from hence but hearing a tremendous roaring above me I continued my route across the point of a hill a few hundred yards further and was again presented by one of the most beautiful objects in nature, a cascade of about fifty feet perpendicular stretching at right angles across the river from side to side to the distance of at least a quarter of a mile. Here the river pitches over a shelving rock, with an edge as regular and as straight as if formed by art, without a niche or break in it; the water descends in one even and uninterrupted sheet to the bottom where dashing against the rocky bottom it rises into foaming billows of great height and rapidly glides away, hissing flashing and sparkling as it departs. The spray rises from one extremity to the other to 50 feet. I now thought that if a skillful painter had been asked to make a beautiful cascade that he would most probably have presented the precise image of this one; nor could I for some time determine on which of those two great cataracts to bestow the palm, on this or that which I had discovered yesterday; at length I determined between these two great rivals for glory that this was *pleasingly beautiful*, while the other was *sublimely grand*.

A beautiful little Island well timbered is situated about the middle of the river. In this Island on a Cottonwood tree an Eagle has placed her nest; a more inaccessible spot I believe she could not have found; for neither man nor beast dare pass those gulfs which separate her little domain from the shores. The water is also broken in such manner as it descends over this pitch that the mist or spray rises to a considerable height. This fall is certainly much the greatest I ever beheld except those two which I have mentioned below, it is incomparably a greater cataract and a more noble interesting object than the celebrated falls of Potomac or Schuylkill &c.

Just above this is another cascade of about 5 feet, above which the water as far as I could see began to abate of its velocity, and I therefore determined to ascend the hill behind me which promised a fine prospect of the adjacent country, nor was I disappointed on my arrival at its summit, from hence I overlooked a most beautiful and extensive plain reaching from the river to the base of the Snow-clad mountains to the S. and S. West; I also observed the Missouri stretching its meandering course to the South through this plain to a great distance filled to its even and grassy brim; in these plains and more particularly in the valley just below me immense herds of buffalo are feeding. The Missouri just above this hill makes a bend to the South where it lies a smooth even and unruffled sheet of water of nearly a mile in width bearing on its watery bosom vast flocks of geese which feed at pleasure in the delightful pasture on either border, the young geese are now completely feathered except the wings which both in the young and old are yet deficient. After feasting my eyes on this ravishing prospect and resting myself a few minutes I determined to proceed as far as the river which I saw discharge itself on the West side of the Missouri convinced that it was the river which the Indians call *medecine river* and which they informed us fell into the Missouri just above the falls.

I descended the hill and directed my course to the bend of the Missouri near which there was a herd of at least a thousand buffalo; here I thought it would be well to kill a buffalo and leave him until my return from the river and if I then found that I had not time to get back to camp this evening to remain all night here there being a few sticks of driftwood lying along shore which would answer for my fire, and a few scattering cottonwood trees a few hundred yards below which would afford me at least the semblance of a shelter. Under this impression I selected a fat buffalo and shot him very well, through the lungs; while I was gazing attentively on the poor animal discharging blood in streams from his mouth and nostrils, expecting him to fall every instant, and having entirely forgotten to reload my rifle, a large white, or rather brown bear, had perceived and crept on me within 20 steps before I discovered him; in the first moment I drew up my gun to shoot, but at the same instant recollected that she was not loaded and that he was too near for me to hope to perform this operation before he reached me, as he was then briskly advancing on me; it was an open level plain, not a bush within miles nor a tree within less than three hundred yards of me; the river bank was sloping and not more than three feet above the level of the water; in short there was no place by means of which I could conceal myself from this monster until I could charge my rifle; in this situation I thought of retreating in a brisk walk as fast as he was advancing until I could reach a tree about 300 yards below me, but I had no sooner turned myself about but he pitched at me, open mouthed and full speed, I ran about 80 yards and found he gained on me fast, I then ran into the water. The idea struck me to get into the water to such depth that I could stand and he would be obliged to swim, and that I could in that situation defend myself with my espontoon; accordingly I ran hastily into the water about waist deep, and faced about and presented the point of my espontoon, at this instant he arrived at the edge of the water within about 20 feet of me; the moment I put myself in this attitude of defense he suddenly wheeled about as if frightened, declined the combat on such unequal grounds, and retreated with quite as great precipitation as he had just before pursued me. As soon as I saw him run off in that manner I returned to the shore and charged my gun, which I had still retained in my hand throughout this curious adventure. I saw him run through the level open plain about three miles, till he disappeared in the woods on medecine river; during the whole of this distance he ran at full speed, sometimes appearing to look behind him as if he expected pursuit.

I now began to reflect on this novel occurrence and endeavored to account for this sudden retreat of the bear. I at first thought that perhaps he had not smelt me before he arrived at the water's edge so near me, but I then reflected that he had pursued me for about 80 or 90 yards before I took to the water and on examination saw the ground torn with his talons immediately on the impression of my steps; and the cause of his alarm still remains with me mysterious and unaccountable, so it was and I felt myself not a little gratified that he had declined the combat. My gun reloaded I felt confidence once more in my strength; and determined not to be thwarted in my design of visiting medecine river, but determined never again to suffer my piece to be longer empty than the time she necessarily required to charge her.

Having examined Medecine river I now determined to return, having by my estimate about 12 miles to walk. I looked at my watch and found it was half after six P.M. In returning through the level bottom of Medecine river and about 200 yards distant from the Missouri, my direction led me directly to an animal that I at first supposed was a wolf; but on nearer approach or about sixty paces distant I discovered that it was not, its color was a brownish yellow; it was standing near its burrow, and when I approached it thus nearly, it couched itself down like a cat looking immediately at me as if it designed to spring on me. I took aim at it and fired, it instantly disappeared in its burrow; I loaded my gun and examined the place which was dusty and saw the track from which I am still further convinced that it was of the tiger kind. Whether I struck it or not I could not determine, but I am almost confident that I did; my gun is true and I had a steady rest by means of my espontoon, which I have found very serviceable to me in this way in the open plains.

It now seemed to me that all the beasts of the neighborhood had made a league to destroy me, or that some fortune was disposed to amuse herself at my expense, for I had not proceeded more than three hundred yards from the burrow of this tiger cat, before three bull buffalo, which were feeding with a large herd about half a mile from me on my left, separated from the herd and ran full speed towards me, I thought at least to give them some amusement and altered my direction to meet them; when they arrived within a hundred yards they made a halt, took a good view of me and retreated with precipitation. I then continued my route homewards past the buffalo which I had killed, but did not think it prudent to remain all night at this place which really from the succession of curious adventures wore the impression on my mind of enchantment; at sometimes for a moment I thought it might be a dream, but the prickly pears which pierced my feet very severely once in a while, particularly after it grew dark, convinced me that I was really awake, and that it was necessary to make the best of my way to camp.

It was sometime after dark before I returned to the party; I found them extremely uneasy for my safety; they had formed a thousand conjectures, all of which equally foreboding my death, which they had so far settled among them, that they had already agreed on the route which each should take in the morning to search for me. I felt myself much fatigued, but ate a hearty supper and took a good night's rest.

[Clark]

June 14. A fine morning. The Indian woman complaining all night & excessively bad this morning, her case is somewhat dangerous. Two men with the Toothache 2 with Tumors, & one man with a Tumor & a slight fever. Passed the camp Capt. Lewis made the 1st night at which place he had left part of two bear their skins &c. Three men with Tumors went on shore and stayed out all night. One of them killed 2 buffalo, a part of which we made use of for breakfast, the current excessively rapid more so as we ascend we find great difficulty in getting the Perogue & canoes up in safety, canoes take in water frequently. At 4 o'Clock this evening Jo: Fields returned from Capt. Lewis with a letter for me. Capt. Lewis dates his letter from the Great falls of the Missouri, which Fields informs me is about 20 miles in advance & about 10 miles above the place I left the river the time I was up last week. Capt L. informs me that those falls in part answer the description given of them by the Indians, much higher the Eagle's nest which they describe is there, from those signs he is convinced of this being the river the Indians call the Missouri.

[Lewis]

June 15. This morning the men again were sent to bring in some more meat which Drewyer had killed yesterday, and continued the operation of drying it. I amused myself in fishing, and sleeping away the fatigues of yesterday. I caught a number of very fine trout which I made Goodrich dry; Goodrich also caught about two dozen and several small cat of a yellow color which would weigh about 4 lbs. The tail was separated with a deep angular notch like that of the white cat of the Missouri from which indeed they differed only in color. When I awoke from my sleep today I found a large rattlesnake coiled on the leaning trunk of a tree under the shade of which I had been lying at the distance of about ten feet from him. I killed the snake and found that he had 176 scuta on the abdomen and 17 half formed scuta on the tail; it was of the same kind which I had frequently seen before; they do not differ in their colors from the rattlesnake common to the middle Atlantic states, but considerably in the form and figures of those colors. This evening after dark Joseph Fields returned and informed me that Capt. Clark had arrived with the party at the foot of a rapid about 5 miles below which he did not think proper to ascend and would wait my arrival there. I had discovered from my journey yesterday that a portage on this side of the river will be attended by much difficulty in consequence of several deep ravines which intersect the plains.

Alexander Wilson
(1766–1813)

Born in Paisley, Scotland, Alexander Wilson was a smuggler's son who, from his youth, was a peddler, weaver, wanderer, and poet. Emboldened by the American and French revolutions to make claims on behalf of the working poor of his own country, Wilson wrote satirical poems lambasting wealthy mill owners for exploiting laborers — a form of literary activism for which he was fined, imprisoned, and forced to publicly burn his poems. Wishing to escape oppressive millwork and repressive government, he came to America in 1794, arriving in Delaware shortly after his twenty-eighth birthday. After living and working at a number of places in Pennsylvania and New Jersey, in 1802 Wilson accepted a teaching job at the Union School of Kingsessing, just outside Philadelphia — and, more importantly, just down the road from the Bartrams' famous botanical garden. By about 1804 Wilson, with neighbor William Bartram's help and encouragement (and, subsequently, with the help of Bartram's friends, including Thomas Jefferson and Charles Willson Peale), had resolved to collect, describe, and depict all the birds of America. He ultimately identified many more than the 215 species Bartram had cataloged, including many that were new to science. In the years that followed, Alexander Wilson became one of the most intrepid itinerant naturalists America has ever known. In his epic search for all the birds of America he traveled the fields, forests, and swamps from Maine to the Gulf of Mexico, often capturing live birds so as to accurately draw them from life. Wilson obsessively devoted himself to his life's work, the nine-volume *American Ornithology* (1808–29), a project so ambitious that he did not live to see the publication of its final volumes. The following description of the ivory-billed woodpecker, which is now believed to be extinct, demonstrates the primary elements of Wilson's engaging approach to literary natural history: he combines careful description of the species' appearance, habits, and habitat with personal, anecdotal, sometimes humorous accounts of his own experiences studying it. And while he often uses scientific evidence (including evidence gained from his own dissections of birds) to correct common errors regarding his subjects, his sensibility is that of an enthusiastic admirer of the beauty and behavior of birds. The genus of warblers *Wilsonia* is named in his honor, as are the species Wilson's storm-petrel, Wilson's phalarope, and Wilson's plover.

From *American Ornithology; or, The Natural History of the Birds of the United States* (1808–1829)

*Ivory-Billed Woodpecker (*Picus principalis*)*

This majestic and formidable species, in strength and magnitude, stands at the head of the whole class of woodpeckers, hitherto discovered. He may be called the king or chief of his tribe; and Nature seems to have designed him a distinguished characteristic in the superb carmine crest and bill of polished ivory with which she has ornamented him. His eye is brilliant and daring; and his whole frame so admirably adapted for his mode of life, and method of procuring subsistence, as to impress on the mind of the examiner the most reverential ideas of the Creator. His manners have also a dignity in them superior to the common herd of woodpeckers. Trees, shrubbery, orchards, rails, fence posts, and old prostrate logs, are alike interesting to those, in their humble and indefatigable search for prey; but the royal hunter now before us, scorns the humility of such situations, and seeks the most towering trees of the forest; seeming particularly attached to those prodigious cypress swamps, whose crowded giant sons stretch their bare and blasted or moss-hung arms midway to the skies. In these almost inaccessible recesses, amid ruinous piles of impending timber, his trumpet-like note and loud strokes resound through the solitary, savage wilds, of which he seems the sole lord and inhabitant. Wherever he frequents, he leaves numerous monuments of his industry behind him. We there see enormous pine trees with cartloads of bark lying around their roots, and chips of the trunk itself, in such quantities as to suggest the idea that half a dozen of axmen had been at work there for the whole morning. The body of the tree is also disfigured with such numerous and so large excavations, that one can hardly conceive it possible for the whole to be the work of a woodpecker. With such strength, and an apparatus so powerful, what havoc might he not commit, if numerous, on the most useful of our forest trees! and yet with all these appearances, and much of vulgar prejudice against him, it may fairly be questioned whether he is at all injurious; or, at least, whether his exertions do not contribute most powerfully to the protection of our timber. Examine closely the tree where he has been at work, and you will soon perceive, that it is neither from motives of mischief nor amusement that he slices off the bark, or digs his way into the trunk.—For the sound and healthy tree is the least object of his attention. The diseased, infested with insects, and hastening to putrefaction, are *his* favorites; there the deadly crawling enemy have formed a lodgment between the bark and tender wood, to drink up the very vital part of the tree. It is the ravages of these vermin, which the intelligent proprietor of the forest deplores as the sole perpetrators of the destruction of his timber. Would it be believed that the larvae of an insect, or fly, no larger than a grain of rice, should silently, and in one season, destroy some thousand acres of pine trees, many of them from two to three feet in diameter, and a hundred and fifty feet high? Yet whoever passes along the high road from Georgetown to Charlestown, in South Carolina, about twenty miles from the former place, can have striking and melancholy proofs of this fact. In some places the whole woods, as far as you can see around you, are dead, stripped of the bark, their wintry-looking arms and bare trunks bleaching in the sun, and tumbling in ruins before every blast, presenting a frightful picture of desolation. And yet ignorance and prejudice stubbornly persist in directing their indignation against the bird now before us, the constant and mortal enemy of these very vermin; as if the hand that probed the wound to extract its cause, should be equally detested with that which inflicted it; or as if the thief-catcher should be confounded with the thief. Until some effectual preventive or more complete mode of destruction can be devised against these insects, and their larvae, I would humbly suggest the propriety of protecting, and receiving with proper feelings of gratitude, the services of this and the whole tribe of woodpeckers, letting the odium of guilt fall upon its proper owners.

In looking over the accounts given of the ivory-billed woodpecker by the naturalists of Europe, I find it asserted, that it inhabits from New Jersey to Mexico. I believe, however, that few of them are ever seen to the north of Virginia, and very few of them even in that state. The first place I observed this bird at, when on my way to the south, was about twelve miles north of Wilmington in North Carolina. There I found the bird from which the drawing of the figure in the plate was taken. This bird was only wounded slightly in the wing, and, on being caught, uttered a loudly reiterated, and most piteous note, exactly resembling the violent crying of a young child; which terrified my horse so, as nearly to have cost me my life. It was distressing to hear it. I carried it with me in the chair, under cover, to Wilmington. In passing through the streets, its affecting cries surprised every one within hearing, particularly the females, who hurried to the doors and windows with looks of alarm and anxiety. I drove on, and on arriving at the piazza of the hotel, where I intended to put up, the landlord came forward, and a number of other persons who happened to be there, all equally alarmed at what they heard; this was greatly increased by my asking, whether he could furnish me with accommodations for myself and my baby. The man looked blank and foolish, while the others stared with still greater astonishment. After diverting myself for a minute or two at their expense, I drew my woodpecker from under the cover, and a general laugh took place. I took him upstairs and locked him up in my room, while I went to see my horse taken care of. In less than an hour I returned, and, on opening the door, he set up the same distressing shout, which now appeared to proceed from grief that he had been discovered in his attempts at escape. He had mounted along the side of the window, nearly as high as the ceiling, a little below which he had begun to break through. The bed was covered with large pieces of plaster; the lath was exposed for at least fifteen inches square, and a hole, large enough to admit the fist, opened to the weather-boards; so that, in less than another hour he would certainly have succeeded in making his way through. I now tied a string round his leg, and, fastening it to the table, again left him. I wished to preserve his life, and had gone off in search of suitable food for him. As I reascended the stairs, I heard him again hard at work, and on entering had the mortification to perceive that he had almost entirely ruined the mahogany table to which he was fastened, and on which he had wreaked his whole vengeance. While engaged in taking the drawing, he cut me severely in several places, and, on the whole, displayed such a noble and unconquerable spirit, that I was frequently tempted to restore him to his native woods. He lived with me nearly three days, but refused all sustenance, and I witnessed his death with regret.

The head and bill of this bird is in great esteem among the southern Indians, who wear them by way of amulet or charm, us well as ornament; and, it is said, dispose of them to the northern tribes at considcrable prices. An Indian believes that the head, skin, or even feathers of certain birds, confer on the wearer all the virtues or excellencies of those birds. Thus I have seen a coat made of the skins, heads, and claws of the raven; caps stuck round with heads of butcher birds, hawks, and eagles; and as the disposition and courage of the ivory-billed woodpecker are well known to the savages, no wonder they should attach great value to it, having both beauty, and, in their estimation, distinguished merit to recommend it.

This bird is not migratory, but resident in the countries where it inhabits. In the low countries of the Carolinas it usually prefers the large timbered cypress swamps for breeding in. In the trunk of one of these trees, at a considerable height, the male and female alternately, and in conjunction, dig out a large and capacious cavity for their eggs and young. Trees thus dug out have frequently been cut down, with sometimes the eggs and young in them. This hole, according to information,—for I have never seen one myself,—is generally a little winding, the better to keep out the weather, and from two to five feet deep. The eggs are said to be generally four, sometimes five, as large as a pullet's, pure white, and equally thick at both ends—a description that, except in size, very nearly agrees with all the rest of our woodpeckers. The young begin to be seen abroad about the middle of June. Whether they breed more than once in the same season is uncertain.

So little attention do the people of the countries where these birds inhabit pay to the minutiae of natural history, that, generally speaking, they make no distinction between the ivory-billed and pileated woodpecker, represented in the same plate; and it was not till I showed them the two birds together, that they knew of any difference. The more intelligent and observing part of the natives, however, distinguish them by the name of the large and lesser *logcocks*. They seldom examine them but at a distance, gunpowder being considered too precious to be thrown away on woodpeckers; nothing less than a turkey being thought worth the value of a load.

The food of this bird consists, I believe, entirely of insects and their larvae. The pileated woodpecker is suspected of sometimes tasting the Indian corn: the ivory-billed never. His common note, repeated every three or four seconds, very much resembles the tone of a trumpet, or the high note of a clarionet, and can plainly be distinguished at the distance of more than half a mile; seeming to be immediately at hand, though perhaps more than one hundred yards off. This it utters while mounting along the trunk or digging into it. At these times it has a stately and novel appearance; and the note instantly attracts the notice of a stranger. Along the borders of the Savannah river, between Savannah and Augusta, I found them very frequently; but my horse no sooner heard their trumpet-like note, than, remembering his former alarm, he became almost ungovernable.

The ivory-billed woodpecker is twenty inches long, and thirty inches in extent; the general color is black, with a considerable gloss of green when exposed to a good light; iris of the eye, vivid yellow; nostrils, covered with recumbent white hairs; fore part of the head black; rest of the crest, of a most splendid red, spotted at the bottom with white, which is only seen when the crest is erected, as represented in the plate; this long red plumage being ash-colored at its base, above that white, and ending in brilliant red; a stripe of white proceeds from a point, about half an inch below each eye, passes down each side of the neck, and along the back, where they are about an inch apart, nearly to the rump; the first five primaries are wholly black; on the next five the white spreads from the tip, higher and higher, to the secondaries, which are wholly white from their coverts downward. These markings, when the wings are shut, make the bird appear as if his back were white: hence he has been called by some of our naturalists the large white-backed woodpecker. The neck is long; the beak an inch broad at the base, of the color and consistence of ivory, prodigiously strong and elegantly fluted. The tail is black, tapering from the two exterior feathers, which are three inches shorter than the middle ones, and each feather has the singularity of being greatly concave below; the wing is lined with yellowish white; the legs are about an inch and a quarter long; the exterior toe about the same length, the claws exactly semicircular and remarkably powerful,—the whole of a light blue or lead color. The female is about half an inch shorter, the bill rather less, and the whole plumage of the head black, glossed with green; in the other parts of the plumage, she exactly resembles the male. In the stomachs of three which I opened, I found large quantities of a species of worm called borers, two or three inches long, of a dirty cream color, with a black head; the stomach was an oblong pouch, not muscular like the gizzards of some others. The tongue was worm-shaped, and for half an inch at the tip as hard as horn, flat, pointed, of the same white color as the bill and thickly barbed on each side.

John Bradbury
(1768–1823)

Although Lewis and Clark had explored the Western wilderness in 1804–6 and had collected species that were new to science, neither man was a trained scientist. Among the first professional naturalists to visit the Missouri and Ohio River valleys was John Bradbury, a British botanist who came to America in 1809 under the patronage of the Liverpool Botanic Garden. After arriving in America, Bradbury hastened to Monticello to consult with Thomas Jefferson, who persuaded him to base his explorations of the recently acquired Louisiana territory in the north, at St. Louis. From St. Louis Bradbury made a number of short collecting trips before joining Wilson Hunt's 1811 "Astoria" expedition, made on behalf of businessman John Jacob Astor in an attempt to open routes for the lucrative interior fur trade all the way to the Pacific. On this remarkable expedition—which at times included other superb naturalists such as Henry Marie Brackenridge and Thomas Nuttall — Bradbury traveled 1,800 miles up the Missouri River as far as the Arikara Indian villages, where he separated from Hunt's group and went another 200 miles upriver. On his 2,000-mile voyage Bradbury collected approximately a hundred previously unknown plants. From St. Louis Bradbury later traveled the Mississippi all the way to New Orleans, and from there sailed to New York, where he was prevented from returning to England by the outbreak of the War of 1812. He did not reach England until 1816, by which time the specimens he had sent ahead had been described for science by others, several of whom gave Bradbury no credit for his discoveries. Bradbury did, however, secure the publication of his *Travels in the Interior of America, in the Years 1809, 1810, and 1811 . . .* (1817) before returning to America with his family. A lively adventure story as well as a rich natural history tract, *Travels* was so popular in both Britain and America that Washington Irving used it as the source for much of *Astoria* (1836). The following passages from *Travels* show that Bradbury observed much more than plants, while his objections to the slaughter of bison suggests his ethical concern for nature. The tremendous earthquake Bradbury describes here occurred in December 1811 as he sailed down the Mississippi.

From *Travels in the Interior of America . . .* (1817)

April 6, 1811. Walked all day, and in the afternoon met the hunters, who had found a bee tree, and were returning to the boat for a bucket, and a hatchet to cut it down. I accompanied them to the tree. It contained a great number of combs, and about three gallons of honey. The honeybees have been introduced into this continent from Europe, but at what time I have not been able to ascertain. Even if it be admitted that they were brought over soon after the first settlement took place, their increase since appears astonishing, as bees are found in all parts of the United States, and since they have entered upon the fine countries of the Illinois and Upper Louisiana, their progress westward has been surprisingly rapid. It is generally known in Upper Louisiana, that bees had not been found westward of the Mississippi prior to the year 1797. They are now found as high up the Missouri as the Maha nation, having moved westward to the distance of 600 miles in 14 years. Their extraordinary progress in these parts is probably owing to a portion of the country being prairie, and yielding therefore a succession of flowers during the whole summer, which is not the case in forests. Bees have spread over this continent in a degree and with a celerity so nearly corresponding with that of the Anglo-Americans, that it has given rise to a belief, both amongst the Indians and the whites, that bees are their precursors, and that to whatever part they go the white people will follow. I am of opinion that they are right, as I think it as impossible to stop the progress of the one as of the other. We encamped this night at the bottom of an island.

April 7. This morning I went upon the island, accompanied by one of the Frenchmen named Guardepee, to look for game. We were wholly unsuccessful in our pursuit, although the island is of considerable extent. On arriving at the upper end of it, we perceived a small island, of about two acres, covered with grass only, and separated from the large one by a narrow channel, the mouth of which was covered with drift timber. We passed over, and walked through the grass, and having given up all hopes of game, we were proceeding to the river to wait for the boat, when suddenly my companion, who was before me, stopped, fired, and jumped aside, crying out, "*Voila O diable, tirez,*" ["There, oh hell, shoot!"] at the same time pointing towards the grass a few steps before him. I looked, and saw a bear not five yards from us. I immediately fired, and we retired to a short distance to reload, but on our return found the animal expiring. It was a female, with three small cubs in her bed, about two yards from where she was killed. She had heard us approach, and was advancing to defend them. I took one of the cubs in my arms. It seemed sensible of its misfortune, and cried at intervals. It was evident that whenever it uttered a cry the convulsions of the dying mother increased, and I really felt regret that we had so suddenly cut the ties of so powerful an affection. Whilst we breakfasted the bear was cut up, and, with the young ones, taken on board. We encamped this night about twelve miles below Fort Osage. . . .

April 16. We began to notice more particularly the great number of the bodies of drowned buffaloes floating on the river; vast numbers of them were also thrown ashore, and upon the rafts, on the points of the Islands. These carcasses had attracted an immense number of turkey buzzards, (*Vultur aura*) and as the preceding night had been rainy, multitudes of them were sitting on the trees, with their backs towards the sun, and their wings spread out to dry, a common practice with these birds, after rain. . . .

April 18. I proceeded to examine the neighboring country, and soon discovered that pigeons were in the woods. I returned, and exchanged my rifle for a fowling piece, and in a few hours shot 271, when I desisted. I had an opportunity this day of observing the manner in which they feed, it affords a most singular spectacle, and is also an example of the rigid discipline maintained by gregarious animals. This species of pigeon associates in prodigious flocks: one of these flocks, when on the ground, will cover an area of several acres in extent, and are so close to each other that the ground can scarcely be seen. This phalanx moves through the woods with considerable celerity, picking up as it passes along, everything that will serve for food. It is evident that the foremost ranks must be the most successful, and that nothing will remain for the hindermost. That all may have an equal chance, the instant that any rank becomes the last, they rise, and flying over the whole flock, alight exactly ahead of the foremost. They succeed each other with so much rapidity, that there is a continued stream of them in the air, and a side view of them exhibits the appearance of the segment of a large circle, moving through the woods. I observed that they cease to look for food a considerable time before they become the last rank, but strictly adhere to their regulations, and never rise until there are none behind them. . . .

June 20. We were on horseback on the first appearance of day, and immediately abandoned the river, passed over the bluffs, and struck into the interior of the country. Besides my rifle and other equipments, similar to those of the rest of the party, I had a portfolio for securing the specimens of plants. I had contrived already to collect some interesting specimens by frequently alighting to pluck them, and put them into my hat. For these opportunities, and to ease my horse, I ran many miles alongside of him. Notwithstanding this, about noon he seemed inclined to give up, and I proposed to Mr. Crooks that I should turn back: this he would by no means agree to, but prevailed on the lightest man in company to exchange horses with me for the rest of the day. Soon after noon, some deer were observed grazing at a distance, and we halted in a small valley, suffered the horses to graze, and one of the men was dispatched to look after them, who soon returned, having killed one. As we had not eaten any thing from the morning of the preceding day, this news was very acceptable, and some were dispatched to fetch the meat, whilst others gathered dry buffalo dung to boil our kettle. This opportunity afforded me the pleasure of adding to my little collection, besides securing in my portfolio what I had before gathered. . . .

June 21. We arose before day. Each man cooked his own breakfast, cutting what suited him from the venison, and fixing it on a stick set in the ground, which inclined over the fire. At break of day we were on horseback, and soon after ascended the bluffs, and proceeded on our route. I noticed a sensible change in the face of the country, after we had left the river. We now found some of the more elevated places covered with small stones, and divested of herbage, and throughout, the soil was of less depth, and the grass shorter and more scanty. About ten o'clock we again found the country to assume the same fertile appearance as on the preceding day; and saw herds of buffalo in every direction: before midday two were killed, but very little was taken, except the marrowbones; each man, who chose to take one, hung it to his saddle. In the course of this forenoon we observed three rattlesnakes, of an entirely new and undescribed species; one of them I killed and carried in my shot-pouch, and during the time we stopped to feed our horses, I secured the skin. We passed very close to several herds of buffalo during the afternoon, near which we always observed a number of wolves lurking. I perceived that those herds that had wolves in their vicinity, were almost wholly females with their calves; but noticed also, that there were a few bulls with them, and that these were always stationed at the outside of the herd enclosing the cows with their calves within. We came suddenly on one of these herds, containing, as we judged, from six to eight hundred; they immediately galloped off; one of our party rode after them, and overtook a calf which could not keep pace with the rest: he instantly dismounted, caught it by the hind-leg, and plunged his knife into its body. We took what we wanted, and rode on. This afternoon I noticed a singularly formed hill on our right, in the direction of the Missouri, apparently about 10 miles from us. It is of an oblong shape, nearly perpendicular at the ends, and level at the top, so as to resemble a regular building: near the center there rises a peak, very steep, which seems to be elevated at least 100 feet above the hill on which it stands. We rode this day almost without intermission, and late in the evening arrived at *Rivière de Coeur,* or Heart River, and encamped on its banks, or, more properly, lay down in our blankets. I found that my horse did not get worse, although he showed a great disposition to lag behind, a certain proof of his being very much tired, as the Indian horses, when on a journey, have an aversion to be separated from their companions.

June 22. Although the distance from this place to the Missouri Fur Company's fort was estimated at about sixty miles, we determined if possible to reach it this day, and were, as usual, on horseback at daybreak, having previously breakfasted on veal. I observed the preceding days a sufficient number of buffaloes to induce me to credit the hunters in their reports of the vast numbers they had seen, but this day afforded me ample confirmation. Scarcely had we ascended the bluffs of Heart River, when we began to discern herds in every direction; and had we been disposed to devote the day to hunting, we might have killed a great number, as the country north of Heart River is not so uniform in its surface as that we had passed. It consists of ridges, of small elevation, separated by narrow valleys. This renders it much more favorable for hunting, and although we did not materially deviate from our course, five were killed before noon. Mr. Crooks joined me in remonstrating against this waste; but it is impossible to restrain the hunters, as they scarcely ever lose an opportunity, if it offers, even although not in want of food. About two o'clock we arrived on the summit of a ridge more elevated than any we had yet passed. From thence we saw before us a beautiful plain, as we judged, about four miles across, in the direction of our course, and of similar dimension from east to west. It was bounded on all sides by long ridges, similar to that which we had ascended. The scene exhibited in this valley was sufficiently interesting to excite even in our Canadians a wish to stop a few minutes and contemplate it. The whole of the plain was, perfectly level, and, like the rest of the country, without a single shrub. It was covered with the finest verdure, and in every part herds of buffalo were feeding. I counted seventeen herds, but the aggregate number of the animals it was difficult even to guess at: some thought upwards of 10,000. . . .

December 14. . . . As it required every effort of skill and exertion to pass through this channel in safety, and as the sun had set, I resolved to wait until the morning, and caused the boat to be moored to a small island, about 500 yards above the entrance into the channel. After supper, we went to sleep as usual: about ten o'clock, and in the night I was awakened by a most tremendous noise, accompanied by an agitation of the boat so violent, that it appeared in danger of upsetting. Before I could quit the bed, or rather the skin, upon which I lay, the four men who slept in the other cabin rushed in and cried out in the greatest terror, "*O mon Dieu! Monsieur Bradbury, qu'est ce? qu'il y a?*" ["Oh my God! Mr. Bradbury, what is it? what's going on?"]. I passed them with some difficulty, and ran to the door of the cabin, where I could distinctly see the river as if agitated by a storm; and although the noise was inconceivably loud and terrific, I could distinctly hear the crash of falling trees, and the screaming of the wildfowl on the river, but found that the boat was still safe at her moorings. I was followed out by the men and the patron, still in accents of terror, inquiring what it was: I tried to calm them by saying, "*Restez vous tranquil, c'est un tremblement de terre,*" ["Don't worry, it's an earthquake"] which they did not seem to understand.

By the time we could get to our fire, which was on a large flag, in the stern of the boat, the shock had ceased; but immediately the perpendicular banks, both above and below us, began to fall into the river in such vast masses, as nearly to sink our boat by the swell they occasioned; and our *patron*, who seemed more terrified even than the men, began to cry out, "*O mon Dieu! nous perirons!*" ["Oh my God! We shall die!"]. I wished to consult with him as to what we could do to preserve ourselves and the boat, but could get no answer except "*O, mon Dieu! nous perirons!*" and "*Allons à terre! Allons à terre!*" ["Let's get to shore!"]. As I found Mr. Bridge the only one who seemed to have retained any presence of mind, we consulted, and agreed to send two of the men with a candle up the bank, in order to examine if it had separated from the island, a circumstance that we suspected, from hearing the snapping of the limbs of some drift trees, which were deposited betwixt the margin of the river, and the summit of the bank. The men, on arriving at the edge of the river, cried out "*Venez à terre! Venez à terre!*" ["Come to shore!"] and told us there was a chasm formed already, so wide that it would be difficult to pass it, to attain the firm ground. I ordered them to go upon the island and make a fire, and desired Mr. Bridge and the *patron* to follow them, and as it now occurred to me that the preservation of the boat in a great measure depended on the depth of the river, I tried with a sounding pole, and to my great joy, found it did not exceed eight or ten feet.

Immediately after the shock we noticed the time, and found it was near two o'clock. It was now nearly half past, and I determined to go ashore myself, after securing some papers and money, and was employed in taking them out of my trunks, when another shock came on, terrible indeed, but not equal to the first. Morin, our *patron*, called out from the island, "*Monsieur Bradbury! Sauvez vous, sauvez vous!*" ["Mr. Bradbury! Save yourself!"]. I went ashore, and found the chasm really frightful, as it was not less than four feet in width, and besides the bank had sunk at least two feet. I took the candle, and examined to determine its length, and concluded that it could not be less than eighty yards; and where it terminated at each end, the banks had fallen into the river. I now saw clearly that our lives had been saved by having moored to a sloping bank. Before we had completed our fire, we had two more shocks, and they occurred during the whole night, at intervals of from six to ten minutes, but slight in comparison with the first and second. At four o'clock I took a candle, and again examined the bank, and found to my great satisfaction that no material alteration had taken place; I also found the boat safe, and secured my pocket compass. I had already noticed that the sound which was heard at the time of every shock, always preceded it at least a second, and that it always proceeded from the same point, and went off in the opposite direction. I now found that the shock came from a little northward of east, and proceeded to the westward. At daylight we had counted twenty-seven shocks, during our stay on the island, but still found the chasm so that it might be passed. The river was covered with foam and drift timber, and had risen considerably, but our boat was safe. Whilst we were waiting till the light became sufficient for us to embark, two canoes floated down the river, in one of which we could perceive some Indian corn and some clothes. We considered this as a melancholy proof that some of the boats we passed the preceding day had perished. Our conjectures were afterwards confirmed, as three had been overwhelmed, and all on board perished. When the daylight appeared to be sufficient for us I gave orders to embark, and we all went on board. Two men were in the act of loosening the fastenings, when a shock occurred nearly equal to the first in violence. The men ran up the bank, in order to save themselves on the island, but before they could get over the chasm, a tree fell close by them, and stopped their progress. The bank appeared to me to be moving rapidly into the river, and I called out to the men in the boat "*Coupez les cordes!*" ["Cut the lines!"]. On hearing this, the two men ran down the bank, loosed the cords, and jumped into the boat. We now found ourselves again on the river: the *Chenal du Diable* was in sight, and appeared absolutely impassable, from the quantity of trees and driftwood, that had lodged during the night against the planters fixed in the bottom of the river; and in addition to our difficulties, I noticed that the *patron* and the men appeared to be so terrified and confused, as to be almost incapable of action. I determined to stop, previous to passing the channel, in order that the men might have time to become more composed. I had the good fortune to discover a bank, rising with a gentle slope, where we again moored, and prepared to breakfast on the island. Whilst that was preparing, I walked down the island, in company with Morin, our *patron*, to view the channel, in order to ascertain the safest part, which we soon agreed upon. Whilst we were thus employed, we experienced a very severe shock, and found some difficulty in preserving ourselves from being thrown down; another occurred during the time we were at breakfast, and a third as we were preparing to reembark. In the last, Mr. Bridge, who was standing within the declivity of the bank, narrowly escaped being thrown into the river, as the sand continued to give way under his feet. As I observed that the men were still very much under the influence of terror, I desired Morin to give to each a glass of spirits, and reminded them that their safety depended on their exertions, and we pushed out into the river. The danger we had now to encounter was of a nature which they understood: the nearer we approached it, the more confidence they appeared to gain; and indeed, all their strength, and all the skill of Morin, was necessary, as there was no direct channel through the trees, and we were several times under the necessity of changing our course in the space of a few seconds, and that instantaneously, not a moment being left for deliberation. Immediately after we had cleared all danger, the men dropped their oars, crossed themselves, and gave a shout, congratulating each other on our safety.

Henry Rowe Schoolcraft
(1793–1864)

Born on the banks of the Hudson River, Henry Rowe Schoolcraft was a mineralogist, traveler, writer, and ethnographer of great skill and ambition. After graduating from Middlebury College in Vermont, where he was a devoted student of geology, he worked in his family's wood-fired glass factory before deciding to light out for the wilderness at age twenty-five. Traveling with his friend Levi Pettibone, Schoolcraft left western New York in 1819 on a three-month journey through the little-known wilderness of the Ozark Mountains. His *Journal of a Tour into the Interior of Missouri and Arkansaw* . . . (1821) was the earliest firsthand account of the interior Ozarks. Although Henry Marie Brackenridge's *Views of Louisiana* (1814) and John Bradbury's *Travels* (1817) had described the Mississippi River and Missouri River valley, respectively, there existed no detailed description of the forests, prairies, and glades, savannahs, rivers, and caves, barrens, balds, and bottoms of the Ozark wilderness. Schoolcraft spoke honestly when, in the opening line of his *Journal*, he wrote: "I begin my tour where other travelers have ended theirs." Although his adventure was motivated largely by a desire to investigate mining prospects in the region, Schoolcraft is a sharp observer of plants, animals, and landscapes who takes a deliberately literary and aesthetic approach to his subjects. Although his lack of wilderness experience and proper equipment caused him to be lost, wet, and hungry during much of his trip, his appreciation for the beauty of the wild country he sees is seldom eclipsed by his uncomfortable circumstances. In his later years, H. R. Schoolcraft became an Indian agent, married Jane Johnston, the daughter of an Ojibwa chief, and eventually gathered and published extensive anthropological studies of Native American languages and lifeways. The Schoolcraft of the Ozark journals, however, is an energetic young geologist and adventurer who, even while trapped in a cave by a storm, philosophizes happily that his misadventure affords him "ample leisure to reflect upon the solitude of [his] condition."

From *Journal of a Tour into the Interior of Missouri and Arkansaw* . . . (1821)

November 12, 1818. We find ourselves in a highly interesting section of country, and which affords some of the most picturesque and sublime views of rural scenery which I have ever beheld. The little brush camp we hastily erected last night, and in which I now write, is situated in a beautiful valley, on the banks of a small clear stream, with a rocky and gravelly bottom. The width of this valley is about 800 yards, and is bounded on the west by a perpendicular wall of limestone rock 200 feet in height, and rising in some places in cubical masses, resembling the moldering towers of some antique ruin. On the east the bluffs are neither so high nor precipitous, and are intersected by hollows worn out of the rock by the action of rain operating, for many centuries, on calcareous rock. Down one of these hollows we descended into the valley, not, however, without leading our horse in the most cautious and circuitous manner. The top of these bluffs supports a substratum of a very sterile, gravelly alluvion, and is covered by tall pines, which add much to the beauty of the prospect from the valley below. In the stupendous wall of rocks before me are situated several caves, whose dark and capacious mouths indicate their extent. Many of these, however, cannot be visited without ladders, as they are situated forty or fifty feet above the level of the creek. With considerable difficulty and labor we entered one of them, by means of a large oak which had fallen partly against the mouth of the cave. We found it a spacious chamber, connected with others of less size, and affording both *stalactites*, and *stalagmites*. The former hang like icicles from the roof in various fanciful forms, and some specimens which we succeeded in detaching were translucent, and exhibited much beauty and regularity in the arrangement of their colors, consisting of concentric lines of yellow and brown passing by imperceptible shades into each other. We also obtained in this cave native saltpeter, very white and beautiful. It was found filling small crevices in the rock. The number of caves which we have this day visited, large and small, is seven, and all afford saltpeter. In the largest of these, great quantities of this article are annually collected and manufactured by Col. Ashley, of Mine à Burton, and transported to his powder-manufactory, in Washington county. The cavernous nature of the country bordering this stream is one of its most distinguishing characteristics, and I have seized upon this fact in calling it Cave Creek. This little stream is one of the most interesting objects in the natural physiognomy of the country, which we have thus far met with, and affords a striking instance of that wonderful arrangement in the physical construction of the surface of the earth, which gives valleys to the smallest streams, and tears asunder rocks to allow them passages into rivers, and through them into their common basin, the ocean. Its banks rise in majestic walls of limestone, which would form the most ample barrier to the waves of the sea, and they occasionally rise into peaks, which if located on the coast of the ocean, would be hailed as landmarks by the mariner. The opposite banks correspond with general exactness in their curves, height, composition, and thickness of strata, and other characters evincing their connection at a former period. Yet the only object apparently affected by the separation of such immense strata of rocks, a change which I cannot now contemplate without awe and astonishment, is to allow a stream of twenty yards across a level and undisturbed passage into the adjacent river, the Currents, which it joins, after winding in the most circuitous manner about four miles below. In the course of this distance, the views which are presented are commanding and delightful, and to the painter who wishes to depict the face of nature in its wildest aspect of rocky grandeur, I could recommend this valley, and the adjacent county, as one of unrivaled attractions. A scene so full of interest could not fail to receive the homage of our admiration, and we rambled about the country, until night almost imperceptibly approached, when we returned to our camp, repacked our horse, and moved up the valley of Cave Creek, one mile to Ashley Cave, in which we encamped safe from the weather, turning our horse loose to feed about its mouth. . . .

November 14. A rainstorm which commenced during the night, has continued with little intermission, all day, so that we have been confined to the cave. Thus situated, beyond the boundaries of the civilized world, shut up in a dreary cavern, without books to amuse the mind, or labor to occupy the body, we have had ample leisure to reflect upon the solitude of our condition, and in reverting to the scenes of polished life, to contrast its comforts, attractions, and enjoyments, with the privations and danger by which we are surrounded. There springs, however, a pleasure from our very regrets; we are pleased in reflecting on scenes of former gratification; of lands that are distant, and of times that are past; and the mind is insensibly led to hope for their repetition. We expect much of the future time; we please ourselves with fond anticipations of joy, and with proud hopes of wealth, power, or renown. Thus it is that the mind is never in a state of satisfied repose, and the whole sum of human bliss is made up by the recollections we borrow from the past, and the expectations we entertain of the future. The present is never a season of happiness, which is a relative enjoyment, and can only be estimated by its absence. Neither are our ideas of this grand pursuit of our lives at all definite. Nothing can be more discordant and contradictory than the different notions which different persons or people have attached to the term happiness. One places it in wealth, another in power, a third in splendor, and a fourth in the contempt of all. Perhaps the sum of human bliss was as correctly estimated by the South Sea Indian, as it is frequently done by his more enlightened European brethren. A South Sea Indian becoming tired of life, put an end to it, by stabbing himself to the heart. The deed excited universal horror, and the grief of his family was uncontrollable. "Alas," cried a relative, "what evil spirit could have prompted him to this deed! He was blessed beyond many of his countrymen. Had he not always plenty of train-oil for his subsistence? Had he not a smooth white fish-bone, twelve inches long, run through his nose? What more could be wanting to complete his happiness?"

November 21. The bottomlands continue to improve both in quality and extent, and the growth of cane is more vigorous and green, and affords a nutritious food for our horse. The bluffs on each side of the valley continue, and are covered by the yellow pine. At the distance of six miles below our last night's encampment, the river receives its first tributary from the left in a stream of a size nearly equal to itself, which enters at the foot of a very lofty bluff, nearly at right angles, and the river below their junction is visibly increased in size. The extreme limpidity of the water of this stream gives rise to a species of deception of which we have this day had a serious proof. It is so clear, white, and transparent, that the stones and pebbles in its bottom, at a depth of eight or ten feet, are reflected through it with the most perfect accuracy as to color, size, and position, and at the same time appear as if within two or three feet of the surface of the water. Its depth cannot, therefore, be judged by the eye with any probability of that degree of exactness which can be had by looking into common clear streams. The explanation of this phenomenon is referable to the extreme degree of the purity of the water, which holds no fine particles of earth in suspension, and admits the rays of light to pass through it without being intercepted or refracted by those particles.

In attempting to ford the river where the water appeared to be two, or at most three feet deep, the horse suddenly plunged in below his depth, and was compelled to swim across, by which our baggage got completely wetted. Our tea, meal, salt, sugar, &c. was either greatly damaged, or entirely spoiled; our skins, blankets, and clothing, were also soaked with water, and such part of our powder as was not bottled shared the same fate. This proved a serious misfortune, as our situation precluded the possibility of getting new supplies. It was near night when this accident happened, and we immediately encamped, and began to dry our effects, and save what was not wholly ruined, in which we consumed a considerable part of the night. The weather continues mild and pleasant. We have passed innumerable flocks of turkey in the course of this day: also bear, deer, pigeon, duck, and squirrel. General course, south-southeast. Distance twelve miles. . . .

January 4, 1819. It began snowing a little after midnight, and continued until daybreak. Engaged in digging at the mines, and viewing the country. The prairies, which commence at the distance of a mile west of this river, are the most extensive, rich, and beautiful, of any which I have ever seen west of the Mississippi river. They are covered by a coarse wild grass, which attains so great a height that it completely hides a man on horseback in riding through it. The deer and elk abound in this quarter, and the buffalo is occasionally seen in droves upon the prairies, and in the open highland woods. Along the margin of the river, and to a width of from one to two miles each way, is found a vigorous growth of forest-trees, some of which attain an almost incredible size. The lands consist of a rich black alluvial soil, apparently deep, and calculated for corn, flax, and hemp. The riverbanks are skirted with cane, to the exclusion of all other underbrush; and the lands rise gently from the river for a mile, terminating in highlands, without bluffs, with a handsome growth of hickory and oak, and a soil which is probably adapted for wheat, rye, oats, and potatoes. Little prairies of a mile or two in extent are sometimes seen in the midst of a heavy forest, resembling some old cultivated field, which has been suffered to run into grass.

Near our present encampment are some bluffs, which serve to diversify the scene, and at the foot of which is situated a valuable lead-mine. A country thus situated, cannot fail to present a scene of great beauty in the season of verdure, and even now, in the depth of winter, wears a pleasing aspect. It is a mixture of forest and plain, of hills and long sloping valleys, where the tall oak forms a striking contrast with the rich foliage of the evergreen cane, or the waving field prairie-grass. It is an assemblage of beautiful groves, and level prairies, of river alluvion, and highland precipice, diversified by the devious course of the river, and the distant promontory, forming a scene so novel, yet so harmonious, as to strike the beholder with admiration; and the effect must be greatly heightened, when viewed under the influence of a mild clear atmosphere, and an invigorating sun, such as is said to characterize this region during the spring and summer. . . .

January 5. . . . About noon we reached and forded Findley's Fork, a stream we had encamped upon, in our journey west, on the last day of December. Two miles beyond, in ascending a valley, we discovered a bee-tree, which Mr. Pettibone and myself chopped down. It was a large white oak, (*quercus alba,*) two and a half feet across at the butt, and contained, in a hollow limb, several gallons of honey. This was the first discovery of wild honey which accident had thrown in our way, and as soon as the saccharine treasure was laid bare, by cutting open the hollow limb, we began unceremoniously to partake. And although two months' residence in the woods had left little in our personal appearance, or mode of living, to denote our acquaintance with polished society; and our appetites, by continual exercise, the want of vegetable food, and sometimes the total want of food of any kind for one, two, and even three days together, had become voracious and gross, to a degree that excited our own astonishment; yet, when we retired a few yards to view the beastly voraciousness and savage deportment of the two hunters during this sweet quaternary repast, we could not resist the most favorable conclusions concerning our own deportment, and physical decorum upon that occasion. It should here be remarked, that the white hunters in this region, (and I am informed it is the same with the Indians,) are passionately fond of wild honey, and whenever a tree containing it is found, it is the custom to assemble around it, and feast, even to a surfeit. Upon the present occasion we had no bread, which, although it prevented us from partaking so liberally as we otherwise should, did not seem in any degree to operate as a restraint upon them. On the contrary, they ate prodigiously. Each stood with a long comb of honey, elevated with both hands, in front of the mouth, and at every bite left the semi-circular dented impression of a capacious jaw, while the exterior muscles of the throat and face were swelled by their incessant exertions to force down the unmasticated lumps of honey, which rapidly followed each other into the natural repository — the stomach. When this scene of gluttony was ended, the dog also received his share, as the joint co-partner and sharer of the fatigues, dangers, and enjoyments of the chase; and in no instance have we observed this compact between the dog and the hunter to have been violated, for it is recorded in a manner less subject to obliteration or distinction than our fugitive agreements upon paper; it is recorded among the powerful habits of uncivilized man, corporeally and mentally imprinted. The honey then left was tied up in a wet deerskin, which communicates no taint; and appended to the saddle of one of the horses, thus carried along.

Timothy Dwight
(1752–1817)

Born on what was then the western frontier of Massachusetts, sixth-generation American Timothy Dwight was part of a powerful family and was the grandson of Jonathan Edwards. In 1765 Dwight entered Yale, where he was an accomplished student and tutor but was also somewhat notorious for wanting to expand the traditional college curriculum to include *belles lettres*. Indeed, Dwight wrote poetry and had literary ambitions of his own, and he is often remembered as having been a member—along with fellow Yale tutor John Trumbull and others—of the New England literary circle known as the "Connecticut Wits." After graduation Dwight was ordained and soon became a prominent minister in the region's Congregationalist clergy. In 1795 he returned to New Haven and assumed the presidency of Yale, a position he held for twenty-two years, until his death in 1817. A firm administrator and stiff moralist whose orthodox theology was outlined in *Theology Explained and Defended* (1818–19), Dwight was also a traveler of wide interests, and each year he spent the break between college terms traveling throughout New England. Beginning in the 1790s his notes from these trips are quite personal, but over the course of the next several decades his journaling evolved into a performance designed for publication. Traveling on horseback and by foot—and, in his later years, by chaise—Dwight saw most of New England and recorded his observations in what some critics have considered excruciating detail. But it is this level of detail that also makes the posthumously published, four-volume *Travels in New England and New York* (1821–22) so valuable and interesting a window onto the life, politics, and environment of the region. And while *Travels* has been recognized as American history, travel literature, and theological writing, the book, replete with superb descriptions of the New England landscape, is also an important contribution to American nature writing. In the following descriptions of the majestic forests of the White and Green Mountains, Dwight braids close observations of trees and lyrical descriptions of autumnal foliage with expressions of the sternly providential worldview that caused some readers to nickname him "the Pope of New England."

From *Travels in New England and New York* (1821–1822)

From this spot the mountains speedily began to open with increased majesty, and in several instances rose to a perpendicular height little less than a mile. The bosom of both ranges was overspread in all the inferior regions by a mixture of evergreens with trees whose leaves are deciduous. The annual foliage had been already changed by the frost. Of the effects of this change it is perhaps impossible for an inhabitant of Great Britain, as I have been assured by several foreigners, to form an adequate conception without visiting an American forest. When I was a youth, I remarked that Thomson had entirely omitted in his Seasons this fine part of autumnal imagery. Upon inquiring of an English gentleman the probable cause of the omission, he informed me that no such scenery existed in Great Britain. In this country it is often among the most splendid beauties of nature. All the leaves of trees which are not evergreens are by the first severe frost changed from their verdure toward the perfection of that color which they are capable of ultimately assuming, through yellow, orange, and red to a pretty deep brown. As the frost affects different trees and the different leaves of the same tree in very different degrees, a vast multitude of tinctures are commonly found on those of a single tree, and always on those of a grove or forest. These colors also in all their varieties are generally full, and in many instances are among the most exquisite which are found in the regions of nature. Different sorts of trees are susceptible of different degrees of this beauty. Among them the maple is preeminently distinguished by the prodigious varieties, the finished beauty, and the intense luster of its hues, varying through all the dyes between a rich green and the most perfect crimson, or more definitely, the red of the prismatic image.

There is, however, a sensible difference in the beauty of this appearance of nature in different parts of the country, even where the forest trees are the same. I have seen no tract where its splendor was so highly finished as in the region which surrounds Lancaster for a distance of thirty miles. The colors are more varied and more intense, and the numerous evergreens furnish, in their deep hues, the best groundwork of the picture.

I have remarked that the annual foliage on these mountains had been already changed by the frost. Of course, the darkness of the evergreens was finely illumined by the brilliant yellow of the birch, the beech, and the cherry, and the more brilliant orange and crimson of the maple. The effect of this universal diffusion of gay and splendid light was to render the preponderating deep green more solemn. The mind encircled by this scenery irresistibly remembered that the light was the light of decay, autumnal and melancholy. The dark was the gloom of evening, approximating to night. Over the whole, the azure of the sky cast a deep, misty blue, blending toward the summits every other hue, and predominating over all.

As the eye ascended these steeps, the light decayed and gradually ceased. On the inferior summits rose crowns of conical firs and spruces. On the superior eminences, the trees, growing less and less, yielded to the chilling atmosphere, and marked the limit of forest vegetation. Above, the surface was covered with a mass of shrubs, terminating at a still higher elevation in a shroud of dark colored moss.

As we passed onward through this singular valley, occasional torrents formed by the rains and dissolving snows at the close of winter had left behind them in many places perpetual monuments of their progress in perpendicular, narrow, and irregular paths of immense length, where they had washed the precipices naked and white from the summit of the mountain to the base.

Wide and deep chasms also at times met the eye, both on the summits and the sides, and strongly impressed the imagination with the thought that a hand of immeasurable power had rent asunder the solid rocks and tumbled them into the subjacent valley. Over all, hoary cliffs, rising with proud supremacy, frowned awfully on the world below and finished the landscape.

By our side the Saco was alternately visible and lost, and increased almost at every step by the junction of tributary streams. Its course was a perpetual cascade, and with its sprightly murmurs furnished the only contrast to the majestic scenery around us. . . .

It is impossible for a person traveling through this cleft of the Green Mountains not to experience the most interesting emotions. The unceasing gaiety of the river and the brilliancy of its fine borders create uncommon elasticity of mind, animated thoughts, and sprightly excursions of fancy; while the rude and desolate aspect of the mountains, the huge, misshapen rocks, the precipices, beyond description barren and dreary, awaken emotions verging toward melancholy, and mild and elevated conceptions. Curiosity grows naturally out of astonishment, and inquiry of course succeeds wonder. Why, the mind instinctively asks, were these huge piles of ruin thus heaped together? What end could creative wisdom propose in forming such masses of solid rock and accumulating such collections of bleak and barren mountains, unfit for habitation and apparently useless to man? Several thousands of years these piles have already existed, and have hitherto accomplished no conceivable end, but to shelter the wolf or the bear, or to furnish a passage or a den to the prowling savage, or to yield an asylum to the small and timorous tribes of mankind from the invasions of the powerful and heroic.

Wild and mountainous scenes have engrossed the attention of men in all ages. To poets, and among others to the poetical savage, they have ever been commanding objects, and have fascinated the imagination with their rude sublimity and awful grandeur. In modern days, philosophers, under the influence of a fancy little less engrossed, have explored these lofty desolate regions for purposes which escaped the research of antiquity. . . .

When we had reached the highest point of the mountain, we were struck with a novel appearance of the forest trees. In their figure they always resembled a dwarf, stunted in his stature and laterally overgrown. The stems, boughs, and branches were universally thick, short, and clumsy. As every tree on the higher part of this summit was of this peculiar figure, it must undoubtedly have been owing to the great elevation. It cannot be owing to the soil, which here, as well as further down, was very rich. On ground exactly resembling it in appearance, about one hundred feet below the point, Mr. Wilbur sowed, the preceding year, the seed of the grass called foxtail. The growth which sprang from this seed was now as high as a man's waist.

Short as the trees were on this summit, they were sufficiently thick and tall to prevent us from gaining the prospect which we had expected. There was no remedy for this disappointment but to climb to their tops. Their peculiar figure, however, made this an easy task. The view was immense and of amazing grandeur. On the northwest rose the mountains west of Lake Champlain, extending in a vast range, terminated only by the capacity of the eye. The Green Mountains, almost immediately beneath us on the east, stretched northward and southward through an astonishing extent. Beyond them on the northeast, ascended the high conical point of Monadnock at the distance of fifty miles. In the southeast, at the same distance, rose the peak of Mount Tom. Taconic lifted its head in the south at the distance of forty miles. A little northward of the other point of Saddle Mountain, the summits of the Catskill Mountains magnificently overtopped every other part of the globe within our horizon. You will easily suppose that we felt a total superiority to all the humble beings who were creeping on the footstool beneath us. The village of Williamstown shrunk to the size of a farm; and its houses, church, and colleges appeared like the habitations of martins and wrens.

On this delightful spot we spent about two hours, and about two more in accomplishing our descent. Near the base we met our companions, who had just arrived from Bennington, and were preparing to ascend the mountain. Upon being informed that it would be impossible for them to compass their object at this late hour, they postponed it till the next day.

Both this mountain and that immediately north of it, called Williamstown Mountain, exhibit an interesting specimen of the progress of vegetation in the spring. At the bottom and throughout a certain extent of the acclivity, comprising sometimes a third and sometimes a fourth of the whole ascent, the forest trees shoot out their leaves about the same time with those in the valley beneath. Above this extent, all the trees retain their bare, wintry aspect. Within a week, another division of the mountain immediately above this becomes green also, while the superior parts still retain their barren, leafless appearance. Through these parts the vegetation ascends in the same successive manner, until the whole surface is covered with verdure. Ordinarily, three weeks, and sometimes four, are required to complete this curious progress. . . .

In the progress of this journey I was forcibly struck with the wisdom of Divine Providence displayed in the growth and decay of forests. The leaves of the vast collection of trees denoted by this name constitute an immense mass of vegetable matter. Were they to be heaped together, as vegetable substances often are by the hand of man, they would, I presume, go through the usual process of fermentation and putrefaction. In this case they must become, throughout the surrounding country, not only offensive and intolerable, but productive of the various fatal diseases which owe their origin to decaying vegetables. It would be impossible, therefore, for man to fix his habitation in their neighborhood, either with comfort or safety. Nay, a country universally forested, as North America was antecedently to the colonization of it by Europeans, would be absolutely uninhabitable to the end of time. For every planter who made the attempt would have perished while he was endeavoring to clear sufficient ground to furnish himself and his family with sustenance.

The leaves of forest trees, it is well known, are universally deciduous, those of evergreens falling as usually and regularly as others. In this climate the leaves of all trees except evergreens are almost invariably bitten by frost before they fall. In consequence of this fact, the juices of the leaf are exhaled through the small ruptures occasioned by freezing. The frame of the leaf, if I may give it this appellation, is in this manner stiffened while it hangs on the tree, and does not descend till it has become perceptibly ligneous and as incapable of fermentation as the wood itself. When it reaches the ground, it lies, of course, lightly and loosely on the surface, as do all the others which follow it, constituting together a mass so little compacted as to permit a free circulation of the air throughout every part of the accumulation. Hence the mass, whenever it is wet with rain, becomes soon dried, and the decay is suffered to go on only with such a moderate degree of rapidity as to preserve the whole perfectly sweet and fragrant. By this curious process forested grounds are kept always healthy, and are not less friendly to the human constitution than those of which are under the most perfect culture. Of course, the planter sits down in them with an entire certainty that he has nothing to dread; an endemial disease is unknown until settlements have advanced far toward complete cultivation.

The mass of leaves formed and preserved in this manner is, together with the trees which bore them, converted by a slow process of decay into vegetable mold. This mold appears to be the best of all manures, being suited to more kinds and producing higher degrees of vegetation than any other. Thus in forested grounds provision is made for a continually increasing fertility. Every subsequent growth of trees becomes of course larger and finer than the preceding, until the forest arrives to its utmost height and perfection.

In the meantime, this mass of leaves covering the surface entirely prevents the springing of grass within the limits of the forest, and throughout a small breadth of the circumjacent ground. The seeds of forest trees will not germinate among grass. By preventing or destroying this kind of vegetation, therefore, an opportunity is furnished for these seeds to shoot, and thus to perpetuate, and gradually to enlarge, the growth of the forest. But to this end it is further necessary that the seed should lie on the surface, very few of them being capable of springing when sunk below it even at a very little distance. Equally do they need to be continually enveloped in moisture. The leaves, lying so loose, permit the seeds to descend to the earth through their interstices; and the lowest stratum is regularly and sufficiently moist for this purpose. Thus they furnish all the means of enabling the seeds to germinate and the stems to acquire ultimately their highest perfection. . . .

Behind this point another, much more remote, stretches out in the same direction, exhibiting a form of finished elegance, and seeming an exactly suitable limit for the sheet of water which fills the fine scoop between these arms. Still farther southward, the lake opens in boundless view, and presents in a perfect manner the blending of unlimited waters with the sky.

Over these points assembled, as if to feast our eyes at the commencement of the evening, after our arrival, one of the most beautiful collections of clouds ever seen by a votary of nature. They were of elegant forms, and of hues intense and refulgent. The richest crimson, fading into the tinges of the pink and the rose, adorned them on one side; and gold burnished into the highest brilliancy, on the other. Several strata of these splendors, extending over one tenth of the horizon, lay above each other, in the most fascinating variety of fantastical beauty; while others, single, in pairs, or in small groups, vied with the larger assemblages in contributing to the glory of the scene. Toward the southwest and northeast, two long ranges of leaden-colored clouds, with fleeces of mist hanging beneath them, reached round two thirds of the horizon. These at intervals were all along changed, sometimes gradually, and sometimes suddenly, into the gayest crimson and the most vivid purple, alternated in such a manner, as to defy the utmost efforts both of the pen and the pencil. The sky above, of that pure bright aspect which succeeds a storm when it becomes clear with a soft serenity, was varied from a glowing yellow, a brilliant straw color, and a willow green into a light, and finally into a darker, azure: the beautiful blue of autumn.

Beneath all this glory the lake, a boundless field of polished glass, glittered alternately with the variegated splendor of the clouds, and the hues of the sky, softening and improving the brilliancy of both with inimitable delicacy, and leaving on the mind the impression of enchantment rather than of reality. Not a breath was felt: not a leaf trembled; not a sound was heard: not a fluctuation disturbed the elegance of the surface. A lively imagination would easily have fancied that a paradise might be found beyond this charming expansion. . . .

Edwin James
(1797–1861)

Following their victory in the War of 1812, Americans pursued Jefferson's ambition to consolidate control of the interior wilderness of North America. In 1817 the newly elected president Monroe and his secretary of war, John C. Calhoun, organized the "Yellowstone Expedition," a large military and scientific surveying contingent intended to explore and map the Western territories while helping to sweep the Mississippi Valley clean of British settlement and trade. The scientific arm of the expedition, led by Major Stephen H. Long (1784–1864), consisted of a number of prominent naturalists including Thomas Say (1787–1843), zoologist and nephew of William Bartram, and Titian Ramsay Peale (1799–1885), natural history artist and youngest son of Charles Willson Peale. A Vermont native and protégé of naturalist John Torrey (1796–1873), Edwin James was a medical doctor and botanist who joined Long's expedition in May 1820. For an ambitious young botanist, James's timing could hardly have been better. By June 30, the Long party spotted the front range of the Rocky Mountains, where James collected hundreds of specimens and witnessed sublime mountain landscapes. As the excerpt below recounts, on July 14, 1820, James and four other adventurers became the first whites to reach summit on the 14,110-foot mountain that had defeated Zebulon Pike's efforts in 1806; and although the informal name "Pike's Peak" ultimately prevailed, Long actually named the mountain "James' Peak" in honor of the botanist whose pioneering ascent silenced Pike's claim that the mountain was so rugged that it would remain forever unclimbed. During his journey with Long, James collected more than seven hundred species of plants, at least one hundred of which were new to science. Although James's two-volume *Account of an Expedition from Pittsburgh to the Rocky Mountains* . . . (1822–23) was disparaged by some for its sharp criticism of America's virulent expansionist ideology, the book offered a detailed account of the little-known Rockies and "Great American Desert" (Great Plains), and it was so influential that it became the primary source for James Fenimore Cooper's 1826 novel, *The Prairie*. More than a dozen plants — including, for example, cliffbush (*Jamesia americana*) and James's saxifrage (*Telesonix jamesii*) are named in Edwin James's honor; the blue columbine (*Aquilegia caerulea*), which he discovered, is now the state flower of Colorado.

From *Account of an Expedition from Pittsburgh to the Rocky Mountains . . .* (1822–1823)

In ascending, we found the surface in many places, covered with this loose and crumbled granite, rolling from under our feet, and rendering the ascent extremely difficult. We began to credit the assertions of the guide, who had conducted us to the foot of the Peak; and left us with the assurance, that the whole of the mountain to its summit, was covered with loose sand and gravel, so that though many attempts had been made by the Indians and by hunters to ascend it, none had ever proved successful. We passed several of these tracks, not without some apprehension for our lives, as there was danger when the foothold was once lost of sliding down, and being thrown over precipices.

After clambering with extreme fatigue over about two miles, in which several of these dangerous places occurred, we halted at sunset in a small cluster of fir trees. We could not, however, find a piece of even ground large enough to lie down upon, and were under the necessity of securing ourselves from rolling into the brook, near which we encamped, by means of a pole placed against two trees. In this situation we passed an uneasy night, and, though the mercury fell only to 54°, felt some inconvenience from cold.

On the morning of the 14th, as soon as daylight appeared, having suspended in a tree, whatever articles of clothing could be dispensed with, our blankets and provisions, except about three pounds of bison flesh, we continued the ascent, hoping to be able to reach the summit of the Peak, and return to the same camp in the evening. After passing about half a mile of rugged and difficult traveling, like that of the preceding day, we crossed a deep chasm, opening towards the bed of the small stream we had hitherto ascended, and following the summit of the ridge between these, found the way less difficult and dangerous.

Having passed a level tract of several acres, covered with the aspen poplar, a few birches and pines, we arrived at a small stream running towards the south, nearly parallel to the base of the conic part of the mountain, which forms the summit of the Peak. From this spot, we could distinctly see almost the whole of the Peak, its lower half thinly clad with pines, junipers, and other evergreen trees; the upper a naked conic pile of yellowish rocks, surmounted here and there with broad patches of snow; but the summit appeared so distant, and the ascent so steep, that we despaired of accomplishing the ascent, and returning on the same day.

In marshy places about this part of the mountain, we saw an undescribed white flowered species of caltha, some Spediculariae, the shrubby cinquefoil, (Potentilla *fruticosa, Ph.*) and many alpine plants.

The day was agreeably bright and calm. As we ascended rapidly, a manifest change of temperature was perceptible, and before we reached the outskirts of the timber, a little wind was felt from the northeast. On this part of the mountain, the yellow flowered stonecrop, (Sedum *stenopetalum, Ph.*) is almost the only herbaceous plant which occurs. The boundary of the region of forests, is a defined line encircling the peak in a part which, when seen from the plain, appeared near the summit, but when we arrived at it, a greater part of the whole elevation of the mountain, seemed still before us. Above the timber the ascent is steeper, but less difficult than below, the surface being so highly inclined, that the large masses when loosened roll down, meeting no obstruction, until they arrive at the commencement of the timber. The red cedar, and the flexile pine, are the trees which appear at the greatest elevation. These are small, having thick and extremely rigid trunks, and near the commencement of the woodless part of the mountain, they have neither limbs nor bark on the side exposed to the descending masses of rocks. These trees have not probably grown in a situation so exposed, as to be unable to produce or retain bark or limbs on one side; the timber must formerly have extended to a greater elevation on the sides of this peak, than at present, so that those trees, which are now on the outskirts of the forest, were formerly protected by their more exposed neighbors.

A few trees were seen above the commencement of snow, but these are very small and entirely procumbent, being sheltered in the crevices and fissures of the rock. There are also the roots of trees to be seen at some distance, above the part where any are now standing.

A little above the point where the timber disappears entirely, commences a region of astonishing beauty, and of great interest on account of its productions; the intervals of soil are sometimes extensive, and are covered with a carpet of low but brilliantly flowering alpine plants. Most of these have either matted procumbent stems, or such as including the flower, rarely rise more than an inch in height. In many of them, the flower is the most conspicuous and the largest part of the plant, and in all, the coloring is astonishingly brilliant.

A deep blue is the prevailing color among these flowers, and the Pentstemon *erianthera,* the mountain Columbine, (Aquilegia *caerulea*) and other plants common to less elevated districts, were here much more intensely colored, than in ordinary situations.

It cannot be doubted, that the peculiar brilliancy of coloring, observed in alpine plants, inhabiting near the utmost limits of phaenogamous vegetation, depends in a great measure on the intensity of the light transmitted from the bright and unobscured atmosphere of those regions, and increased by reflection from the immense impending masses of snow. May the deep cerulean tint of the sky, be supposed to have an influence in producing the corresponding color, so prevalent in the flowers of these plants?

At about two o'clock we found ourselves so much exhausted, as to render a halt necessary. Mr. Wilson who had accompanied us as a volunteer, had been left behind some time since, and could not now be seen in any direction. As we felt some anxiety on his account, we halted and endeavored to apprise him of our situation; but repeated calls, and the discharging of the rifleman's piece produced no answer. We therefore determined to wait some time to rest, and to eat the provisions we had brought, hoping in the meantime he would overtake us.

Here, as we were sitting at our dinner, we observed several small animals, nearly of the size of the common gray squirrel, but shorter and more clumsily formed. They were of a dark gray color, inclining to brown, with a short thick head, and erect rounded ears. In habits and appearance, they resemble the prairie dog, and are believed to be a species of the same genus. The mouth of their burrow is usually placed under the projection of a rock, and near these we afterwards saw several of the little animals, watching our approach and uttering a shrill note, somewhat like that of the ground squirrel. Several attempts were made to procure a specimen of this animal, but always without success, as we had no guns but such as carried a heavy ball.

After sitting about half an hour, we found ourselves somewhat refreshed, but much benumbed with cold. We now found it would be impossible to reach the summit of the mountain, and return to our camp of the preceding night, during that part of the day which remained; but as we could not persuade ourselves to turn back, after having so nearly accomplished the ascent, we resolved to take our chance of spending the night, on whatever part of the mountain, it might overtake us. Wilson had not yet been seen, but as no time could be lost, we resolved to go as soon as possible to the top of the Peak, and look for him on our return. We met, as we proceeded, such numbers of unknown and interesting plants, as to occasion much delay in collecting, and were under the disagreeable necessity of passing by numbers which we saw in situations difficult of access. As we approached the summit, these became less frequent, and at length ceased entirely. Few cryptogamous plants are seen about any part of the mountain, and neither these nor any others occur frequently on the top of the Peak. There is an area of ten or fifteen acres, forming the summit, which is nearly level, and on this part scarce a lichen is to be seen. It is covered to a great depth with large splintery fragments of a rock, entirely similar to that found at the base of the Peak, except, perhaps, a little more compact in its structure.

By removing a few of these fragments, they were found to rest upon a bed of ice, which is of great thickness, and may, perhaps, be as permanent and as old as the rocks, with which it occurs.

It was about 4 o'clock P.M., when we arrived on the summit. In our way we had attempted to cross a large field of snow, which occupied a deep ravine, extending down half a mile from the top, on the southeastern side of the Peak. This was found impassable, being covered with a thin ice, not sufficiently strong to bear the weight of a man. We had not been long on the summit, when we were rejoined by the man, who had separated from us near the outskirts of the timber. He had turned aside, and lain down to rest, and afterwards pursued the ascent by a different route.

From the summit of the Peak, the view towards the north, west, and southwest, is diversified with innumerable mountains, all white with snow; and on some of the more distant, it appears to extend down to their bases. Immediately under our feet on the west, lay the narrow valley of the Arkansas, which we could trace running towards the northwest, probably more than sixty miles.

On the north side of the Peak, was an immense mass of snow and ice. The ravine, in which it lay, terminated in a woodless and apparently fertile valley, lying west of the first great ridge, and extending far towards the north. This valley must undoubtedly contain a considerable branch of the Platte. In a part of it, distant probably thirty miles, the smoke of a fire was distinctly seen, and was supposed to indicate the encampment of a party of Indians.

To the east lay the great plain, rising as it receded, until, in the distant horizon, it appeared to mingle with the sky. A little want of transparency in the atmosphere, added to the great elevation from which we saw the plain, prevented our distinguishing the small inequalities of the surface. The Arkansas with several of its tributaries, and some of the branches of the Platte, could be distinctly traced as on a map, by the line of timber along their courses.

On the south the mountain is continued, having another summit (probably that ascended by Captain Pike,) at this distance of eight or ten miles. This, however, falls much below the High Peak in point of elevation, being wooded quite to its top. Between the two lies a small lake, about a mile long and half a mile wide, discharging eastward into the Boiling-spring creek. A few miles farther towards the south, the range containing these two peaks terminates abruptly.

The weather was calm and clear, while we remained on the Peak, but we were surprised to observe the air in every direction filled with such clouds of grasshoppers, as partially to obscure the day. They had been seen in vast numbers about all the higher parts of the mountain, and many had fallen upon the snow and perished. It is perhaps difficult to assign the cause, which induces these insects to ascend to those highly elevated regions of the atmosphere. Possibly they may have undertaken migrations to some remote district, but there appears not the least uniformity in the direction of their movements. They extended upwards from the summit of the mountain, to the utmost limit of vision, and as the sun shone brightly, they could be seen by the glittering of their wings, at a very considerable distance.

About all the woodless parts of the mountain, and particularly on the summit, numerous tracks were seen resembling those of the common deer, but they most probably have been those of the bighorn. The skulls and horns of these animals we had repeatedly seen near the licks and saline springs at the foot of the mountain, but they are known to resort principally about the most elevated and inaccessible places.

The party remained on the summit only about half an hour. In this time the mercury fell to 42°, the thermometer hanging against the side of a rock, which in all the early part of the day, had been exposed to the direct rays of the sun. At the encampment of the main body in the plains, a corresponding thermometer stood, in the middle of the day, at 96°, and did not fall below 80°, until a late hour in the evening.

Great uniformity was observed in the character of the rock about all the upper part of the mountain. It is a compact, indestructible aggregate of quartz and feldspar, with a little hornblende in very small particles. Its fracture is fine granular or even, and the mass exhibits a tendency to divide when broken into long, somewhat splintery fragments. It is of a yellowish-brown color, which does not perceptibly change by long exposure to the air. It is undoubtedly owing to the close texture and the impenetrable firmness of this rock, that so few lichens are found upon it. For the same reason it is little subject to disintegration by the action of frost. It is not improbable that the splintery fragments which occur in such quantities on all the higher parts of the Peak, may owe their present form to the agency of lightning; no other cause seems adequate to the production of so great an effect.

Near the summit, some large detached crystals of feldspar, of a pea-green color, were collected; also large fragments of transparent, white and smoky quartz, and an aggregate of opaque white quartz, with crystals of hornblende.

About five in the afternoon we began to descend, and a little before sunset arrived at the commencement of the timber, but before we reached the small stream at the bottom of the first descent, we perceived we had missed our way. It was now become so dark, as to render an attempt to proceed extremely hazardous, and as the only alternative, we kindled a fire, and laid ourselves down on the first spot of level ground we could find. We had neither provisions nor blankets; and our clothing was by no means suitable for passing the night in so bleak and inhospitable a situation. We could not, however, proceed without imminent danger from precipices, and by the aid of a good fire, and no ordinary degree of fatigue, we found ourselves able to sleep during a greater part of the night.

Solomon Bayley
(n.d.)

As is often the case with the authors of fugitive slave narratives, information about the life and work of Solomon Bayley remains fragmentary. Born into slavery in Delaware, Bayley was later taken to Virginia, where—according to the laws then governing the terms of his bondage—he should rightly have become a free man. Instead, he was forcibly kept in slavery, separated from his family, and moved to the backcountry to prevent his legitimate efforts to have the courts affirm his freedom. Bayley seems to have worked first as a cooper—a trade he gave up because he disapproved of its connection with the sale of liquor—and later as a successful farmer. In addition to the trials he endured as a slave, he was apparently subjected to the additional suffering caused by the sale and subsequent death of his only son and the illness and death of both his daughters. Bayley eventually escaped and fled, and the dangerous adventures that brought him from bondage to freedom are recounted in *A Narrative of Some Remarkable Incidents, in the Life of Solomon Bayley, Formerly a Slave, in the State of Delaware, North America*, which was written sometime before 1820 and published in London by abolitionist Robert Hunard in 1825. Like many fugitive slave narratives, Bayley's *Narrative* depicts the wilderness as both a terrifying realm of exile and a nurturing refuge from pursuit. In the following excerpt, Bayley attributes his salvation in the wilderness to the thick woods in which he hides and the charmed circle of protection created by flying birds—natural elements that he interprets providentially, as sure signs of a beneficent God. A devoutly religious man, Bayley was a member of the "new connexion" Methodist sect founded during the late eighteenth century. After escaping slavery and being reunited with his wife, in 1827 he sailed to Liberia—then a fledgling west African colony that had been founded in 1821 as a settlement for freed American slaves—where he remained for five years, helping repatriated former slaves to resume the rights and privileges they had been so long denied in bondage.

From *A Narrative of Some Remarkable Incidents, in the Life of Solomon Bayley, Formerly a Slave . . .* (1825)

I was born a slave in the state of Delaware, and was one of those slaves that were carried out of Delaware into the state of Virginia; and the laws of Delaware did say, that slaves carried out of that state should be free; whereupon I moved to recover my freedom. I employed lawyers, and went to court two days, to have a suit brought to obtain my freedom. After court I went home to stay until the next court, which was about six weeks off. But two days before the court was to sit, I was taken up and put on board of a vessel out of Hunting Creek, bound to Richmond, on the western shore of Virginia, and there put into Richmond jail, and irons were put on me; and I was brought very low. In my distress I was often visited with some symptoms of distraction. At length I was taken out of jail, and put into one of the backcountry wagons, to go toward the going down of the sun. Now consider, how great my distress must have been, being carried from my wife and children, and from my natural place, and from my chance for freedom.

On the third day my distress was bitter, and I cried out in my heart, "I am past all hope:" and the moment I said I was past all hope, it pleased the father of all mercy to look on me, and he sent a strengthening thought into my heart, which was this: that he that made the heavens and the earth, was able to deliver me. I looked up to the sky, and then to the trees and ground, and I believed in a moment, that if he could make all these, he was able to deliver me. Then did that scripture come into my mind, which I had heard before, and that was, "they that trust in the Lord, shall never be confounded." I believed that was a true word, and I wanted to try that word, and got out of the wagon; but I thought I was not fit to lay hold of the promise: yet another thought came into my mind, and that was, that I did not know to what bounds his mercy would extend. I then made haste and got out of the wagon, and went into the bushes; I squatted down to see what would follow. Now there were three wagons in company, and four white people; they soon missed me, and took out one of the horses and rode back, and were gone about three-quarters of an hour, and then returned, and put the horse in the wagon again, and went on their way; and that was the last I ever saw or heard of them. I sat still where I was till night, and then walked out into the road and looked up to the sky, and I felt very desolate. Oh! the bitterness of distress which I then felt, for having sinned against God; whom if I had been careful to obey in all things, he would have spared me all my troubles. Oh! it is a dangerous thing to cast off fear, and to restrain prayer before God. If we do that which we believe will please him, with a desire to obtain his favor, it is a real prayer; but if we do, or say, that which we believe will displease him, that is to cast off fear, and to restrain prayer before him.

When night came and I walked out of the bushes, I felt very awful. I set off to walk homewards, but soon was chased by dogs, at the same house where the man told the wagoner he had taken up a runaway three days before. But it pleased the highest, to send out a dreadful wind, with thunder and lightning, and rain; which was the means by which I escaped, as I then thought, as I traveled along that night. Next day I was taken with the dysentery, which came on so bad, I thought I must die; but I obtained great favor, and kept on my feet, and so I got down to Richmond; but had liked to have been twice taken, for twice I was pursued by dogs.

But after I got to Richmond, a colored man pretended to be my friend, and then sent white people to take me up; but a little while before they came, it came expressly into my mind, that he would prove treacherous and betray me. I obeyed the impression immediately, and left the place I was in, and presently there came with clubs to take me, as it did appear, two white men and a colored man. When I saw them I was in an hollow place on the ground, not far from where the colored man left me: at sight of them I was struck with horror and fear, and the fear that came into my soul, took such impression on my animal frame, that I felt very weak: I cried to the Maker of heaven and earth to save me, and he did so. I lay there and prayed to the Lord, and broke persimmon tree bushes, and covered myself: when night came on, I felt as if the great God had heard my cry. Oh! how marvelous is his loving kindness toward men of every description and complexion. Though he is high, yet hath he respect unto the lowly, and will hear the cry of the distressed when they call upon him, and will make known his goodness and his power. I lay there till night, and then with great fear I went into the town of Richmond, and inquired the way over the river to go to Petersburg, where I stayed near three weeks, in which time, severe and painful were my exercises: I appeared to be shut up in such a straight case, I could not see which way to take. I tried to pray to the Lord for several days together, that he would be pleased to open some way for me to get along. And I do remember, that when I was brought to the very lowest, suddenly a way appeared, and I believe it was in the ordering of a good providence.

It was so; there came a poor distressed colored man to the same house where I had taken refuge: we both agreed to take a craft, and go down James River, which was attended with great difficulty, for we met with strict examination twice, and narrowly escaped; we had like to have been drowned twice, once in the river, and once in the bay. But how unable were we to offer unto God that tribute of praise due to his name, for the miracle of grace shown to us in our deliverance! Surely wisdom and might are his, and all them that walk in pride he is able to abase. Oh!

> "Let all the world fall down and know
> That none but God such power can show."

We got safe over to the eastern shore of the Chesapeake Bay, where his wife and mine were. And now, reader, I do not tell thee how glad I was, but will leave thee to judge, by supposing it had been thy own case. . . .

But I will go on to tell of my difficulties. After I came over the bay, I went to see my wife, but was still in trouble; and it was thought best to leave the state of Virginia and go to Dover, and then if my master came after me, to bring suit at Dover, and have a trial for my freedom. The distance from where I then was to Dover, was about one hundred and twenty miles: so I started and traveled at nights, and lay by in the day time. I went on northwards, with great fear and anxiety of mind. It abode on my mind that I should meet with some difficulty before I got to Dover: however I tried to study on the promises of the Almighty, and so traveled on until I came to a place called Anderson's Cross-Roads; and there I met with the greatest trial I ever met with in all my distress. But the greater the trial, the greater the benefit, if the mind be but stayed on that everlasting arm of power, whom the winds and the waves obey. It was so, that I called at the crossroads, to inquire the way to Camden, and I thought I would go to the kitchen where the black people were; but when the door was opened, it was a white man I saw, of a portly appearance, with a sulky down look. Now the day was just a breaking: he raised up out of his bed, and came towards the door and began to examine me, and I did not know what to say to him; so he soon entangled me in my own talk, and said, I doubt you are a lying: I said I scorn to lie; but I felt very weak and scared, and soon bid him farewell and started. I went some distance along the road, and then went into the woods, and leaned my back against a tree to study, and soon fell to sleep; and when I waked, the sun was up, and I said to myself, if I stand sleeping about here, and that man that examined me in the morning comes to look for me and finds me, he may tie me before I get awake; for the poor fellow that came across the bay with me told me that he traveled all night, and in the morning he met a colored man, and passed on, and went into the woods and lay down, and went to sleep; and he said there came white men and tied him, and waked him up to go before the justice; but so it was, he got away from them and found me at Petersburg. So considering on what he had told me, and that man's examining me in the morning, I did not know what to do. I concluded to look for a thick place and lay down, and then another thought came into my mind, and that was, to look for a thin place, and there lie down. So I concluded to do so; withal I thought to take a sally downwards, as I inquired of the man to go upwards, I thought by going a little downwards, would be a dodge, and so I should miss him: I thought this plan would do. I then looked for a thin place, and lay down and slept till about nine o'clock, and then waked; and when I awoke, I felt very strange: I said to myself I never felt so in all my distress: I said something was going to happen to me today. So I studied about my feelings until I fell to sleep, and when I awoke, there had come two birds near to me; and seeing the little strange looking birds, it roused up all my senses; and a thought came quick into my mind that these birds were sent to caution me to be away out of this naked place; that there was danger at hand. And as I was about to start, it came into my mind with great energy and force, "if you move out of this circle this day, you will be taken"; for I saw the birds went all round me: I asked myself what this meant, and the impression grew stronger, that I must stay in the circle which the birds made. At the same time a sight of my faults came before me, and a scanty sight of the highness and holiness of the great Creator of all things. And now, reader, I will assure thee I was brought very low, and I earnestly asked what I should do: and while I waited to be instructed, my mind was guided back to the backcountries, where I left the wagons about sixty or seventy miles from Richmond, towards the sun-setting; and a question arose in my mind, how I got along all that way, and to see if I could believe that the great God had helped me notwithstanding my vileness. I said in my heart, it must be the Lord, or I could not have got along, and the moment I believed in his help, it was confirmed in my mind, if he had begun to help me, and if he did send those birds, he would not let anything come into the circle the birds had made; I therefore tried to confirm myself in the promises of God, and concluded to stay in the circle; and so being weary, traveling all night, I soon fell to sleep; and when I awaked, it was by the noise of the same man that examined me in the morning, and another man, an old conjuror, for so I called him. And the way they waked me was by their walking in the leaves, and coming right towards me. I was then sitting on something about nine inches high from the ground, and when I opened my eyes and saw them right before me, and I in that naked place and the sun a shining down on me about eleven o'clock, I was struck with dread, but was afraid to move hand or foot: I sat there, and looked right at them; and thought I, here they come right towards me; and the first thought that struck my mind was, am I a going to sit here until they come and lay hands on me? I knew not what to do; but so it was, there stood a large tree about eleven or twelve yards from me, and another big tree had fallen with the top limbs round it: and so it was, through divine goodness, they went the other side of the tree, and the tree that had fallen, was between them and me. Then I fell down flat upon my face, on the ground; as I raised up my head to look, I saw the actions of this old craftsman; he had a stick like a surveyor's rod; he went along following his stick very diligently. The young man that examined me in the morning, had a large club, with the big end downwards, and the small end in his hand; he looked first one side, and then on the other: the old man kept on away past me about sixty yards, and then stopped; and I heard him say, "he h'ant gone this way." Then he took his stick and threw it over his shoulder, and pointed this way and that way, until he got it right towards me; and then I heard him say, "come let us go this way." Then he turned his course and came right towards me: then I trembled, and cried in my heart to the Lord, and said, what shall I do? what shall I do? and it was impressed on my mind immediately, "Stand still and see the salvation of the Lord"; the word that was spoken to the children of Israel when at the Red Sea. And I said in my heart, bless the Lord, O my soul; I will try the Lord this time. Here they come; and still that word sounded in my heart; "Stand still and see the salvation of the Lord." They came not quite so near me as the circle the birds had made, when the old man sheered off, and went by me; but the young man stopped and looked right down on me, as I thought, and I looked right up into his eyes; and then he stood and looked right into my eyes, and when he turned away, he ran after the old man, and I thought he saw me; but when he overtook the old man, he kept on, and then I knew he had not seen me. Then I said, bless the Lord, he that gave sight to man's eyes, hath kept him from seeing me this day: I looked up among the trees, and said, how dreadful is this place. I said, two great powers have met here this day; the power of darkness, and the power of God; and the power of God has overthrown the power of darkness for me a sinner.

Timothy Flint
(1780–1840)

Like Timothy Dwight, Timothy Flint was a native New Englander and a Congregationalist clergyman. But unlike Dwight, who viewed backwoodsmen as "idle," "profligate," and generally uncivilized, Flint energetically defended the "amiable" and "virtuous" men and women he met in the Western wilderness as a "hardy, adventurous, hospitable, rough, but sincere and upright race of people." Beginning in 1815, Flint spent a full decade traveling as a missionary through the valleys and prairies of the Ohio and Mississippi, the Illinois and Missouri. On the basis of his journeys in the region, he published *Recollections of the Last Ten Years Passed in Occasional Residences and Journeyings in the Valley of the Mississippi* . . . in 1826. The book was popular in part because it confirmed the dominant American ideology of the period, with its assertion that the vast geography of the interior wilderness foretold the advent of a great American political and economic empire. Although *Recollections* reflects the expansionist agenda of the age, it is also a lively and carefully crafted work of imaginative literature that owes a great deal to Flint's own literary hero and fellow traveler, Chateaubriand. In Flint's eye, the frontier landscape is one of hope, excitement, and infinite individual and national prospects—a romantic New World garden in which all things are possible. Although Flint went on to write several romantic novels and to serve as the literary editor of the *Knickerbocker* and *Western Monthly* magazines, *Recollections* remains his most influential and accomplished work. The following excerpts from it suggest Flint's compelling literary range: his first views of the Mississippi emphasize both the beauty and the prospects of the region; his account of an earthquake on the lower Mississippi shows how the challenges of wilderness life bring frontier dwellers together (in 1840, Flint himself survived being buried alive when a tornado toppled a house); and his description of alligator-infested bayous, while relatively unsympathetic to wetlands and their native creatures, clearly demonstrates his ability to bring landscapes to life through powerful literary language.

From *Recollections of the Last Ten Years Passed in Occasional Residences and Journeyings in the Valley of the Mississippi* . . . (1826)

The twenty-eighth of April, 1816, we came in sight of what had long been the subject of our conversations, our inquiries, and curiosity, the far-famed Mississippi. It is a view, which has left on my mind a most deep and durable impression, marking a period, from which commenced a new era in my existence. We had been looking forward to this place as the pillars of Hercules. The country on this side had still some unbroken associations with our native land. This magnificent river, almost dividing the continent, completely severed this chain. We were now, also, to experience the novelty of propelling a boat against the current of one of the mightiest and most rapid rivers in the world. The junction of the Ohio and Mississippi does not impress that idea of physical grandeur, which fills up your anticipations. But allow the fancy to range the boundless forests and prairies, through which it brings down the sweeping tribute, which it has collected from distant and nameless mountains, and from a hundred shores, and you will not contemplate this mighty stream without an intense interest. A sharp point, almost at right angles with either river, mingles their waters in the midst of deep and ancient forests, where the eye expatiates over vast and swampy woods, perhaps fifty miles in extent. Turn the point, and your eye catches the vast Mississippi, rolling down his mass of turbid waters, which seem, compared with the limpid and greenish-colored waters of the Ohio, to be of almost a milky whiteness. They exactly resemble waters in which white ashes have been mixed and remain suspended. A speculation was got up, to form a great city at the delta, and in fact they raised a few houses upon piles of wood. The houses were inundated, and when we were there, "they kept the town," as the boatmen phrased it, in a vast flat boat, a hundred feet in length, in which there were families, liquor shops, drunken men and women, and all the miserable appendages to such a place. To render the solitude of the pathless forest on the opposite shore more dismal, there is one gloomy-looking house there.

Having turned the point, and made our boat fast to the young willows, we reposed to give scope to our own contemplations. Our hands demanded the usual compliment, and having received it in moderation, pronounced themselves sufficiently cheered to begin their task. The margin of the stream is marked with a beautiful growth of low willows and cottonwoods, and the river, though it had overflowed the banks, and was high among the trees, was, from twenty to thirty feet from the shore, not very swift. We began to pull the boat up the stream, by a process, which, in the techniques of the boatmen, is called "bushwhacking." It consists, by commencing at the bow, to seize a handful of bushes, or a single branch, and to pull upon them and walk towards the stern, as the boat ascends. The crew follow each other in this way in succession to the stern, and walk round to the bow, on the opposite side. The banks slope so rapidly, that the "setting pole" is not long enough, in the general way, for use on the opposite side, and they commonly put two hands to the oars. Whenever we come to a point, and have to encounter the full force of the current, we cross the river, in order to get into the easier current upon the opposite shore. We shall remark, elsewhere, upon the singular but almost uniform configuration of the western rivers, by which they are scooped out into points and bends. When the river is low, there is a sandbar opposite the bend, and the current is invariably much stronger in the bend, than over the sandbar.

We mark a very obvious difference between the aspect of the Ohio and the Mississippi. The breadth of the two rivers is nearly the same; and they present at their junction nearly the same appearances of swamp and inundation. They have much the same growth on their banks; and yet they have a character very unlike each other. The Ohio is calm and placid, and except when full, its waters are limpid to a degree. The face of the Mississippi is always turbid, the current everywhere sweeping and rapid; and it is full of singular boils, where the water, for a quarter of an acre, rises with a strong circular motion, and a kind of hissing noise, forming a convex mass of waters above the common level, which roll down and are incessantly renewed. The river seems always in wrath, tearing away the banks on one hand with gigantic fury, with all their woods, to deposit the spoils in another place.

To form any adequate ideas of our impressions of this new scene which I am attempting to record, you will naturally bear in remembrance what kind of family it was, that was viewing it. We were not accustomed to traveling. We had been reared in stillness and seclusion, where we had contemplated the world rather in books than in reality. The Mississippi, too, at that time was to the great proportion of the American people, as it was to us, the "ultima Thule"—a limit almost to the range of thought. This stream, instead of being ploughed by a hundred steamboats, had seen but one. The astonishing facilities for traveling, by which it is almost changed to flying, had not been invented. The thousand travelers for mere amusement, that we now see on the roads, canals, and rivers, were then traveling only in books. The stillness of the forest had not been broken by the shouting of turnpike-makers. The Mississippi forest had seldom resounded, except with the cry of wild beasts, the echo of thunder, or the crash of undermined trees, falling into the flood. Our admiration, our unsated curiosity at that time, would be matter of surprise at the present, to the thousands of hackneyed travelers on this stream, to whom all this route, and all its circumstances, are as familiar as the path from the bed to the fire.

For myself, I shall never forget my first impressions upon beginning to ascend this river, on the banks of which I have passed so many years, and suffered so many misfortunes,—and at the period of life, too, when time is most valuable, and impressions the deepest. The scene was entirely novel, and we beheld every thing, as though the water, the plants, the trees of the Mississippi, would be different from the same things elsewhere. Our first advances on the stream were well calculated to satisfy such expectations of gratified curiosity, as we had formed. The day was beautiful, the temperature soft and genial. The vegetable kingdom on the banks, had the peculiar grandeur of its empire in that region, which must be seen, and not described, in order to be felt. Even the small willows, which we grasped in our hands, as we were drawing the boat up the stream, were full of flowers, which when crushed, yielded out that fragrance which is peculiar to them; a fragrance like the odor of burning coffee, and a few other aromatics, raising the ideas of nectar and ambrosia.

On the other side, the river had only so far overflowed its banks, as to leave the tall and verdant meadow grass, and water plants of the most tender green, above the water. Innumerable multitudes and varieties of waterfowl, of different forms, and plumage, and hues, were pattering in the water among this grass; or were raising their several cries, as we frightened them from their retreat. We easily obtained as many as we wished; and when roused to the wing by our guns, they soon settled down in another place. Flocks of that species, called wood ducks, were continually flying between the river and the woods, where, in the hollows of the trees, they were rearing their young. The huge sized cottonwoods, so regular and beautiful in their form, so bright in a verdure surpassing that of northern trees, were in themselves objects of curiosity. To us, under such circumstances, this novel and fresh scene revived those delightful images of youth, the springtime of existence, which are most fondly cherished and longest remembered.

In the excitement of this cheerful and new mode of traveling, I forgot sickness and sorrow, and the appalling prospect of carrying a young and helpless family, without friends, and but slenderly provided with resources, to a new and an untried world. Perhaps the first half day that we passed in ascending the river under every favorable omen, was the happiest period that we ever experienced, as it respects mere physical enjoyment. Let those deride our excitement then, and that which I now feel, only in the recollection of our delight, who are not capable of entering into similar feelings, and placing themselves in the position of a family constituted like mine. . . .

From all the accounts, corrected one by another, and compared with the very imperfect narratives which were published, I infer that the shock of these earthquakes in the immediate vicinity of the center of their force, must have equaled in their terrible heavings of the earth, anything of the kind that has been recorded. I do not believe that the public have ever yet had any adequate idea of the violence of the concussions. We are accustomed to measure this by the buildings overturned, and the mortality that results. Here the country was thinly settled. The houses, fortunately, were frail and of logs, the most difficult to overturn that could be constructed. Yet, as it was, whole tracts were plunged into the bed of the river. The graveyard at New Madrid, with all its sleeping tenants, was precipitated into the bend of the stream. Most of the houses were thrown down. Large lakes of twenty miles in extent were made in an hour. Other lakes were drained. The whole country, to the mouth of the Ohio in one direction, and to the St. Francis in the other, including a front of three hundred miles, was convulsed to such a degree as to create lakes and islands, the number of which is not yet known,—to cover a tract of many miles in extent, near the Little Prairie, with water three or four feet deep; and when the water disappeared, a stratum of sand of the same thickness was left in its place. The trees split in the midst, lashed one with another, and are still visible over great tracts of country, inclining in every direction and in every angle to the earth and the horizon. They described the undulation of the earth as resembling waves, increasing in elevation as they advanced, and when they had attained a certain fearful height, the earth would burst, and vast volumes of water, and sand, and pit-coal were discharged, as high as the tops of the trees. I have seen a hundred of these chasms, which remained fearfully deep, although in a very tender alluvial soil, and after a lapse of seven years. Whole districts were covered with white sand, so as to become uninhabitable. The water at first covered the whole country, particularly at the Little Prairie; and it must have been, indeed, a scene of horror, in these deep forests and in the gloom of the darkest night, and by wading in the water to the middle, to fly from these concussions, which were occurring every few hours, with a noise equally terrible to the beasts and birds, as to men. The birds themselves lost all power and disposition to fly, and retreated to the bosoms of men, their fellow sufferers in this general convulsion. A few persons sunk in these chasms, and were providentially extricated. One person died of affright. One perished miserably on an island, which retained its original level in the midst of a wide lake created by the earthquake. The hat and clothes of this man were found. A number perished, who sunk with their boats in the river. A bursting of the earth just below the village of New Madrid, arrested this mighty stream in its course, and caused a reflux of its waves, by which in a little time a great number of boats were swept by the ascending current into the mouth of the *Bayou*, carried out and left upon the dry earth, when the accumulating waters of the river had again cleared their current.

There was a great number of severe shocks, but two series of concussions were particularly terrible; far more so than the rest. And they remark that the shocks were clearly distinguishable into two classes; those in which the motion was horizontal, and those in which it was perpendicular. The latter were attended with the explosions, and the terrible mixture of noises, that preceded and accompanied the earthquakes, in a louder degree, but were by no means so desolating and destructive as the other. When they were felt, the houses crumbled, the trees waved together, the ground sunk, and all the destructive phenomena were more conspicuous. In the interval of the earthquakes there was one evening, and that a brilliant and cloudless one, in which the western sky was a continued glare of vivid flashes of lightning, and of repeated peals of subterranean thunder, seeming to proceed, as the flashes did, from below the horizon. They remark that the night, so conspicuous for subterranean thunder, was the same period in which the fatal earthquakes at Caracas occurred, and they seem to suppose these flashes and that event parts of the same scene.

One result from these terrific phenomena was very obvious. The people of this village had been noted for their profligacy and impiety. In the midst of these scenes of terror, all, Catholics and Protestants, praying and profane, became of one religion, and partook of one feeling. Two hundred people, speaking English, French, and Spanish, crowded together, their visages pale, the mothers embracing their children,—as soon as the omen that preceded the earthquakes became visible, as soon as the air became a little obscured, as though a sudden mist arose from the east,—all, in their different languages and forms, but all deeply in earnest, betook themselves to the voice of prayer. . . .

At the distance of a mile or two from the river, there are first thick cane brakes, then a series of lakes, exactly resembling the river in their points and bends, and in the color of their waters. When the river is high, it pours its redundant waters into these lakes and *Bayous,* and the water is in motion for a width of twenty miles. These lakes are covered with the large leaves, and in the proper season the flowers of the "nymphea nelumbo," the largest and most splendid flower that I have ever seen. I have seen them of the size of the crown of a hat; the external leaves of the most brilliant white, and the internal of a beautiful yellow. They are the enlarged copy of the New England pond lily, which has always struck me as the most beautiful and fragrant flower of that country. These lakes are so entirely covered with these large conical leaves, nearly of the size of a parasol, and a smaller class of aquatic plant, of the same form of leaves, but with a yellow flower, that a bird might walk from shore to shore without dipping its feet in water; and these plants rise from all depths of water up to ten feet.

Beyond these lakes, there are immense swamps of cypress, which swamps constitute a vast proportion of the inundated lands of the Mississippi and its waters. No prospect on earth can be more gloomy. The poetic Styx or Acheron had not a greater union of dismal circumstances. Well may the cypress have been esteemed a funereal and lugubrious tree. When the tree has shed its leaves, for it is a deciduous tree, a cypress swamp, with its countless interlaced branches, of a hoary gray, has an aspect of desolation and death, that often as I have been impressed with it, I cannot describe. In summer its fine, short, and deep green leaves invest these hoary branches with a drapery of crepe. The water in which they grow is a vast and dead level, two or three feet deep, still leaving the innumerable cypress "knees," as they are called, or very elliptical trunks, resembling circular beehives, throwing their points above the waters. This water is covered with a thick coat of green matter, resembling green buff velvet. The mosquitoes swarm above the water in countless millions. A very frequent adjunct to this horrible scenery is the moccasin snake with his huge scaly body lying in folds upon the side of a cypress knee; and if you approach too near, lazy and reckless as he is, he throws the upper jaw of his huge mouth almost back to his neck, giving you ample warning of his ability and will to defend himself. I traveled forty miles along this river swamp, and a considerable part of the way in the edge of it; in which the horse sunk at every step half up to his knees. I was enveloped for the whole distance with a cloud of mosquitoes. Like the ancient Avernus, I do not remember to have seen a single bird in the whole distance except the blue jay. Nothing interrupted the death-like silence, but the hum of mosquitoes.

There cannot be well imagined another feature to the gloom of these vast and dismal forests, to finish this kind of landscape, more in keeping with the rest, than the long moss, or Spanish beard, and this funereal drapery attaches itself to the cypress in preference to any other tree. There is not, that I know, an object in nature, which produces such a number of sepulchral images as the view of the cypress forests, all shagged, dark, and enveloped in the hanging festoons of moss. If you would inspire an inhabitant of New England, possessed of the customary portion of feeling, with the degree of homesickness which would strike to the heart, transfer him instantly from the hill and dale, the bracing air and varied scenery of the North, to the cypress swamps of the South, that are covered with the long moss.

Anne Newport Royall
(1769–1854)

Travel writer, journalist, and political activist Anne Newport Royall was among the most formidable, colorful, and outspoken women in antebellum America. Royall was born in colonial Maryland and later lived in Sweet Springs, Virginia, where in 1794 she married Revolutionary War veteran Major William Royall—a man nearly thirty years her senior whom her mother was then serving as housekeeper. Major

Royall died in 1812, leaving his wife a considerable estate that was eventually lost in protracted legal disputes with other family members. Widowed and without comfortable means, Anne Royall decided upon a most unlikely and arduous course to financial solvency: she would support herself as a professional travel writer. Against all odds, she succeeded admirably, covering ground from Maine to Louisiana and publishing five travel books in as many years between 1826 and 1831. When not on the road, Royall lived in Washington, D.C., where she was a well-known public figure and a journalist who interviewed every U.S. president from John Quincy Adams to Franklin Pierce. In 1831 Royall ceased regular travels and began writing, editing, and publishing *Paul Pry*, a newspaper devoted to watchdogging Washington politicians and exposing cases of indolence, ignorance, nepotism, and graft. Her fearless work with this paper (and its successor, *The Huntress*) earned Royall the respect of some, the scorn of others, and the reputation, among historians of American journalism, as the "Grandmother of the Muckrakers." Royall boasted that "no paper, perhaps, has ever had so many enemies," and she might even have agreed with the assessment of one of those enemies, P. T. Barnum, who disparaged her as "the eccentric old lady." In the first of the following two excerpts from her debut travel book, *Sketches of History, Life, and Manners, in the United States* (1826), we see how Royall combines specific notes regarding the flora, fauna, and geography of Virginia's mountains with a more general appreciation for the Appalachian highlands and the perspectives they afford. The second excerpt from *Sketches* is of considerable historical importance, for it takes us inside the halls of the nation's first public repository of natural history specimens and exhibits: Charles Willson Peale's American Museum in Philadelphia.

From *Sketches of History, Life, and Manners, in the United States* (1826)

The whole country has a romantic appearance. Sometimes you see flocks of sheep hanging upon a precipice; sometimes you behold a drove of cattle, far beneath your feet, grazing in a deep vale; anon you see a herd of deer retreating before you in graceful bounds. Again, from a deep recess, you behold with affright, a traveler, picking his way with unconcern, on a precipice over your head; and now, from a rock on high, you see the silver streams, and all the vast expanse of mountains, farms and meadows, to an immense distance.—Thus the scenery is perpetually changing. The following catalogue comprises the principal growth of the forest, viz.—White oak, black oak, swamp oak, red oak, chestnut, spruce, white pine, pitch pine, dogwood, hickory, sassafras, gum-ash, linn, walnut, cherry, sugar maple, poplar, birch, locust, cedar, mulberry, sycamore, wild cucumber-tree, pawpaw, laurel, crab apple, alder, hemlock, yellow willow, and persimmon. Shrubs of various kinds abound, both in the valleys and mountains, and in no country upon the globe are to be found a greater variety of medicinal plants; a description of them alone would fill a volume. The mountains are covered with whortleberries and ivy, and the valleys with hazel, wild gooseberry, and redwood. A shrub called pipestem grows on the savannahs. It must be observed that those savannahs are level; these, and a narrow strip of land found at intervals on the margin of the streams, is all the flat land in this country. This pipestem is a curiosity; it grows to the height of from three to five feet, straight as an arrow, of equal size from top to bottom, and perfectly free from branch or protuberance. It is without leaves, excepting small tufts, resembling grass, at the extremity of innumerable slender branches, which terminate the top. This pipestem is hollow, like a reed, and about the same size. Doct. Raglin, of the Sweet Springs, informed me, that in cutting one of these for a riding switch, he observed a small worm enclosed in the cavity of the stem, and upon examining a number of those shrubs, he found that the pith was eaten out by these worms: some had just commenced, some had eaten halfway, and some were completely eaten through: those that were without worms were without pith. The worm was very small and active, of a whitish hue. As you go from the sweet springs to the salt sulphur, at Uniontown, you have this pipestem for miles to your left: the inhabitants use them for pipestems, for which they answer equal to the reed, and from whence it took its name: it grows in the coldest soil, as these savannahs are mostly upon the tops of mountains. But little white pine is found west of Greenbriar river, or the Allegheny mountain. Peach-trees and pear-trees do not flourish, but apples, plums and cherries abound.

Animals.— The same animals have already been mentioned. The wild animals are bears, wolves, deer, panthers, wildcats, raccoons, foxes, ground hogs, and opossums, (these last are rare,) rabbits, squirrels, white and striped ground squirrels, and the skunk: all of which are numerous in the mountains, and will forever continue the proprietors of those immense wilds. The bears, wolves, panthers, and wild cats, often come down amongst the farmers, and commit great depredations, chiefly in the night, and return to their hiding places before day. Wolves have been known to attack and kill grown cattle, and even horses. There is a species of the squirrel kind in Greenbriar county which the people call the "Ferrydidle"; it is in size between the ground squirrel and gray squirrel, and nearly the color of a fox squirrel; it is very tame and active; it frequents the barns and farmyards of the inhabitants; upon the approach of the farmer it disappears with the rapidity of lightning: it will bound from the top of the barn to the ground! Capt. Williams' lady caught one of the white ground squirrels in the winter and kept it as a pet; it was white as snow when she caught it, and its eyes were red, but in summer it turned of a brownish color with bright golden stripes, its eyes changed also from red to brown. They are frequently seen by hunters both in summer and winter, but are very shy; they never come near the farms. Pied and white deer are common, west of the Alleghenies.

Natural Curiosities.— In Greenbriar county, there is a natural bridge over a creek sixty feet wide; it is said to be from 180 to 200 feet perpendicular, which nearly equals the height of the natural bridge in Rockbridge county: this bridge is about twenty miles northeast of Lewisburg. This information I received from Capt. John Williams. These counties abound with caves; the most remarkable of which, is the Singing cave, in Monroe. This cave is three miles in length; it runs under a mountain, and from it great quantities of saltpeter have been made. It is of unequal breadth. In the same county is what is called the Hanging-rock, about six miles southwest of the road that leads from Fincastle to the sweet springs, and about ten miles from the latter place. It is on the highest part of what is called Price's, or the middle mountain, and is considerably higher than it. From the top of the sweet spring mountain, from which it is nine miles distant, it looks like a huge house hanging from a precipice. I have been on this rock: it is amazingly large. It can easily be ascended by fetching a circuit as you approach it, up the mountain, which is three miles in height from the valley below, over which it projects. The main body of the rock reclines in the bosom of the mountain, while it presents a perpendicular front, which projects to a wonderful extent clear of the mountain on the north side. When you are on the top of this rock, you have one of the grandest views in the United States, you can see to the distance of an hundred miles, in every direction: you can see the peak of Oater east, North Carolina south, with the naked eye. You see eight counties at one view, to say nothing of the endless mass of mountains of which the globe seems made. Over this vast expanse, farms are here and there distinguished, which appear in small spots no larger than a lettuce bed; these, and the streams that run near the ridges of the mountains, render the whole superlatively grand. The rock itself combines enough of the awful and sublime to gratify the most enthusiastic admirer of the works of nature. Particularly that part of it which projects over the mountain. This is partly convex and partly smooth; it may be about an hundred and fifty feet from the top to the bottom, though it is hard to ascertain, from the nature of its figure and situation. It commands, however, a view of the valley beneath it. But no one has the courage to approach the edge of this precipice. The Salt-pond, on this same mountain, is not only a great natural curiosity, but amongst the greatest phenomena of nature. The mountain just mentioned keeps a southwest course from the Hanging rock, and enlarges as it proceeds until it gains Montgomery county, Va. (adjoining Giles,) in which is the Salt-pond. This pond is on the top of the highest part of the mountain, from which, it takes the name of the "Salt-pond mountain." But what is singular, no bottom has, as yet, been discovered. It has been rising for several years: the last time I heard from it, it was from three quarters to a mile in diameter: myriads of trout and other fish live in it, and the margin used to be covered with cranberries, but lately they are overflowed by the rising of the water. Some think it will form a mighty river some day, when it can be no longer confined within its present limits. Though no visible stream issues from this pond, yet, a very bold stream rushes out of the mountain about three miles distant from it, which might lead one to believe that it had some communication with this lake. It strikes me that the water has a brackish taste, from which it probably took its name. . . .

Mammoth Skeleton.— Height over the shoulders, 11 feet; do. over the hips, 9 feet; length from the rump to the chin, 15 feet; length from the tusks to the end of the tail, following the curve of the backbone, 31 feet; width of the hips, 5 feet 8 inches; length of the skeleton, in a straight line, 17 feet 6 inches; width of the head, 3 feet 2 inches; circumference of the thigh bone, 1 foot 6 inches; length of the longest rib, 4 feet 7 inches; circumference of the grinder, 1 foot 6½ inches; weight of the skeleton, 1000 pounds. The skeleton is entire, except two of the ribs, which are made of wood. The back is curved, something like what is called a roach-backed horse; the head is shaped very much like that of the elephant, wide at the top, and tapering off suddenly at the chin; the hind part is much lower than the shoulder, as may be seen.

This skeleton was found by accident, in Ulster county, N.Y. on a farm belonging to Mr. John Mastin, as he was digging for marl. It was in a morass, and the water flowed in so fast upon him that he was forced to desist from digging. In 1801, Mr. C. W. Peale, of Philadelphia, purchased the right of digging for the skeleton, and after six weeks of intense labor, his efforts were crowned with success. He obtained the skeleton perfect, except what has been mentioned. These particulars I transcribed, from a printed account kept in the museum, which was furnished me through the politeness of Mr. Peale the younger. Although I was not thrown into hysterics at the sight of the mammoth skeleton, I found enough of the marvelous in the museum to remunerate for the disappointment. Amongst these were the sea lion, the skeleton of a horse, which, when living, measured 20 hands in height, with a human figure on its back! a sheep weighing 214 lbs. (*ovis aris,*) the devil-fish—in short, ten thousand things wonderful and pleasing. What Mr. Jefferson said of the natural bridge, might with as much propriety be said of Peale's museum, viz. that it was worth a trip across the Atlantic. Here are 1100 birds of different kinds, 250 quadrupeds, 3,450 insects, fish, wax figures, and what was very pleasing to me, 200 portraits of our most distinguished men. The quadrupeds, birds, and sea animals, are stuffed, (that is, their skins,) the hair, and even the gloss on the feathers, are perfect, and all standing upon their feet, in full size. I shall notice a few of them, and of the principal curiosities, of which there are not a few.

The most remarkable is the sea lion; what surprised me is the eye, which is of glass, very large, full, fierce, and as natural as though it were living; even the eyelash was entire. The animal in size is enormous, greater than the largest ox: then there is the elephant seal, which is still larger! It lies flat on the floor, and has four feet, or rather claws, stuck on its sides, with a tail resembling that of a fish. These animals are covered with hair like that of a thrifty horse, of a bright brown; the elephant seal, much the lightest color: they are singular curiosities as to size. The devilfish is twelve feet in length and fifteen round the body, weighing upwards of 2000 pounds! And then a cow with six feet, or legs rather, two of them are on her shoulders, doubled up, as cattle do, when lying down; she was a full grown cow. The sheep is very large indeed, the sight of it alone was worth ten dollars; the wool is abundant and long; it is remarkable for great length of body, for the shortness of its legs, and a huge flat tail. Next there was a cameleopard, of which I had often read; this has a very slender body, and in appearance between a deer and a horse: its lean long forelegs contrasted with the shortness of the hind legs, gave it an unnatural and awkward appearance; it resembles a horse when in the act of rising, with his forefeet stretched out and his hinder parts on the ground. A great Missouri bear and the largest Buffalo bull, an old buck elk, with his tremendous horns on his head; and the whole family of the deer kind. All those animals and many others, are standing on their feet, facing each other, and as near as possible, presenting something like a furious combat of the most awful looking wild beasts, amongst which the tiger, and the lion, which last with his dreadful jaws extended, seems to threaten the whole affair of them with instant destruction. Besides those which are on the floor, the apartment appropriated to wild beasts is lined with large shelves from bottom to top, which are filled with the smaller species of animals; amongst these I was gratified to find the hyena, such as it is described, with fury and vengeance in its countenance, and under it a famished wolf standing over a lamb which he had just killed, and was in the act of tearing to pieces. This was the most natural representation of the whole; the bowels of the sheep looked as though they had that instant been torn out of the body, and the blood besmeared upon the wool seemed yet warm. On these shelves stand on their feet, looking you in the face, the whole tribe of small quadrupeds; amongst these is the whole generation of monkeys, a subject of much amusement to the country people, particularly two of those human-looking animals who are dressed in clothes, sitting on stools engaged at shoemaking; it is surprising how the mischief and cunning peculiar to the countenance of these animals can be so perfectly retained. One of them had his shoe, (about an inch long,) on his knee, fastened with a strap, under his foot, while he is boring with the awl, the ends in his hands ready to thrust through the hole, with all the eagerness of a person in a great hurry.

From the wild beasts I went to that part of the museum where the birds are exhibited. If I found matter of wonder and astonishment before, I now found equal matter of pleasure and delight, mingled, however, with the prodigious. The birds are classed and disposed in regular order, upon shelves, in a large room, which stretches the whole length of the building. The room is narrow, the birds on one side and large windows on the other, of no inconsiderable size. Upon these shelves the birds are placed on their feet, and close shut up with glass to preserve them from dust, and being handled by visitors; the name of each bird is written in large letters, and either laid at its feet or fastened to it. Beginning with the largest, we have first the ostrich, which may be called the mammoth of birds; the one in the museum, however, was not a full grown one, although it measures six feet from the bottom to the top of the head. They have a body in shape something like the turkey, the neck proportionably longer, and forms about one third of its height; it is of a dark (but not of a black) color; the feathers are as fine as silk, differing little in texture from those worn by the ladies. This one was much injured, having had its tail pulled out. Its wings have nothing but the pinion, or wing bones, common to other fowls, covered with a sort of down. The leg bone of a full grown ostrich was standing by the other, which came up to its neck, two-thirds of its height! It was four feet in length, and as thick as a man's wrist: what then must have been the height of the ostrich! nine feet at least. There were lying by it two of the eggs; the largest was five inches in length, and four in width; they are smooth, and of a cream color. The whooping crane seems to be a candidate for size with the ostrich. It is nearly as large, similar in shape, but of a beautiful white. The oron bird, of Africa, is also very large, and exceedingly beautiful. It is of a deep shining black, with deep red checks, viz. tufts of feathers on each side of its head. The gaber, of Africa, is likewise large, four feet in height, it has a bill eight inches in length. But the pelican and the Patagonian penguin were to me greater curiosities. The pelican has a long bill, eight or nine inches, and from the under part hangs a pouch, extending from the tip end of the bill to the throat, the size of a beef's bladder, and looks precisely like one, being thin and transparent: It is said to carry its food in it. The Patagonian penguin is in shape like the old-fashioned pudding bags, standing on its end with the pudding in it. It has neither legs or neck; its feet are stuck on one end of its misshapen body, and its head on the other. Besides these there were swans, geese, and a great variety of ducks, parrots, and a thousand others, the least remarkable of which is worthy the attention of the refined and the curious: but it was the smaller birds whose plumage astonished me most. These beauteous little creatures abound in the museum, and afford the most pleasing and rational of all entertainments. Neither language nor pencil could paint that brilliancy of tint, or that delicacy of shade, which diversify their plumage. I was completely surfeited, the eye riots in beauty. The description of those birds in books gives you scarcely any idea of them.

François-René, Vicomte de Chateaubriand (1768–1848)

A French nobleman best known as a major literary figure in the Romantic Movement that swept Europe during the first decades of the nineteenth century, François-René, Vicomte de Chateaubriand, was also a New World traveler whose imaginative representations of the American wilderness were widely read and extremely influential. Chateaubriand came to America in 1791, the year William Bartram's *Travels* was published. But where he traveled, and for how long, has for two centuries been a matter of critical debate. By his own account, Chateaubriand came to America as an adventurer seeking the elusive Northwest Passage and traveled for an extended period throughout nearly all of the country east of the Mississippi. This claim is clearly false, and it is likely that he remained in America for less than four months, and that he saw only a small part of the landscapes he later described in purported firsthand accounts. Instead, Chateaubriand depended heavily upon his imagination and upon facts gleaned from the work of other literary naturalists including William Bartram and Jonathan Carver. Despite the liberties he took in imaginatively constructing the American landscape to serve his own literary purposes, it was Chateaubriand's descriptions—rather than more factual accounts by other travelers—that most powerfully influenced popular European perceptions of the American land. For example, his best-selling novel *Atala* (1801), a classic work of Rousseauistic primitivism and exoticism, is an Indian romance set in a picturesque but fabricated American wilderness. *Travels in America* (1827), written a remarkable thirty-five years after his short trip to America, is an example of Chateaubriand's thorough literary romanticizing of American nature. Indeed, the following excerpt from *Travels* describes a wild Florida that the author almost certainly never saw; instead, he combined his own observations made along the Ohio River with descriptions of Florida that he found in the pages of William Bartram's *Travels*. But it is not sufficient to dismiss Chateaubriand as a liar or plagiarist, for if nature writing is part observation, it is also part imagination. As the following "description" shows, it was Chateaubriand's superbly graceful, lyrical, visual, and romantic prose style that captured the imagination of his readers.

From *Travels in America* (1827)

Description of a Few Sites in the Interior of the Floridas

We were driven by a cool wind. The river was going to lose itself in a lake opening before us to form a basin of about nine leagues' circumference. Three islands rose from the middle of this lake; we sailed toward the largest, where we arrived at eight o'clock in the morning.

We disembarked on the edge of a plain circular in form; we put our boat in the shelter of a group of chestnuts that grew almost in the water. We built our hut on a small rise. The easterly breeze was blowing and cooled the lake and the forests. We broke our fast with corncakes and scattered through the island, some to hunt, others to fish or to gather plants.

We noticed a kind of hibiscus. This enormous plant, which grows in low and humid parts, rises to more than ten or twelve feet and ends in a sharp pointed cone; the leaves, smooth and slightly furrowed, are enlivened by beautiful crimson flowers, which can be seen from great distances.

The *Agave vivipara* rose still higher in the salty inlets, and formed a forest of grasses 30 feet high. The ripe seed of this grass sometimes germinates on the plant itself, so that the young seedling falls to earth already formed. As the *Agave vivipara* grows at the edge of running water, its bare seed borne away by the waters would be exposed to perish: nature has prepared them while still on the old plant for those specific circumstances, so they are able to fix themselves by their little roots when they escape from the maternal bosom.

The American cypress was common on the island. The stem of this cypress resembles that of a knotty reed, and its leaves resemble a leek: the savages call it *apoya matsi*. The Indian girls of loose morals crush this plant between two stones and rub their breasts and arms with it.

We crossed a field covered with yellow-flowered jacobaea, pink-blossomed althea, and obelia, whose crown is dark red. Light winds playing on the tips of these plants broke them into waves of gold, pink, and dark red, or dug long furrows in the verdure.

The senega, which is abundant in the swampy lands, resembled in form and color shoots of red willow; some branches crawled along the ground, others rose into the air. Senega has a slightly bitter and aromatic taste. Near it grew the Carolina morning glory, whose leaf imitates an arrowhead. These two plants are to be found everywhere the rattlesnake exists: the one heals the snake's bite; the second is so powerful that the savages, after having rubbed their hands with it, handle with impunity these fearsome reptiles. The Indians tell that the Great Spirit took pity on the redskin warriors with bare legs, and he himself sowed these salutary herbs in spite of the protestations of the souls of the snakes. . . .

Continuing our way and observing the mosses, the hanging gramineous plants, the disheveled shrubs, and all the host of plants of melancholy demeanor which decorate ruins, we observed a kind of pyramidal primrose seven to eight feet high, with greenish black oblong serrated leaves; its flower is yellow. In the evening this flower begins to open; it spreads wide during the night; dawn finds it in all its splendor; toward the middle of the morning it withers; it falls at noon. It lives only a few hours, but it passes these hours beneath a serene sky. So of what importance is the brevity of its life?

A few steps from there was spread out a border of mimosa or sensitive plant; in the songs of the savages, the soul of the maiden is often compared to that plant.

Returning to our camp, we crossed a stream edged with dionaeas; a multitude of ephemera buzzed about them. There were also on this expanse three kinds of butterflies: one white as alabaster, another black as jet with wings crossed by yellow bands, the third having a forked tail and four golden wings barred with blue and spotted with dark red. Attracted by the plants, insects alighted on the dionaeas. But no sooner had they touched the leaves than they closed up and enveloped their prey.

Upon our return to our *ajouppa*, we went fishing to console ourselves for the lack of success on the hunt. We embarked in the boat with lines and nets and skirted the coast of the eastern part of the island at the edge of the covering of algae and along the shaded capes. The trout were so voracious that we caught them on unbaited hooks; the fish called goldfish were abundant. There is nothing more beautiful than this little king of the waters: he is about five inches long; his head is ultramarine; his sides and belly sparkle like fire; a longitudinal brown stripe crosses his sides; the iris of his wide eyes shines like burnished gold. This fish is carnivorous.

At some distance from the shore, in the shade of a bald cypress, we noticed little mud pyramids rising beneath the water up to the surface. A legion of gold fish patrolled the approaches of this citadel in silence. Suddenly the water boiled; the gold fish fled. Crayfish armed with pincers, coming out of the assaulted place, overcame their brilliant enemies. But soon the scattered bands returned to the charge, vanquished the besieged in turn, and the brave but slow garrison backed into the fortress to gather strength.

The crocodile, floating like the trunk of a tree, the trout, the pike, the perch, the cannelet, the bass, the bream, the drumfish, the goldfish, all mortal enemies of one another, swam pell-mell in the lake and seemed to have called a truce in order to enjoy together the beauty of the evening. The azure fluid was painted in changing colors. The waters were so pure that it seemed possible to touch with the finger the actors of this scene being played 20 feet deep in their crystal grotto.

To regain the inlet where we had our camp we had only to abandon ourselves to the current and the breezes. The sun was approaching its setting. In the foreground of the island appeared live oaks whose horizontal branches formed a parasol, and azaleas shining like coral formations.

Behind this foreground rose the most charming of all trees, the papaya. Its straight, grayish, carved trunk 20 to 25 feet high, supports a tuft of long ribbed leaves that are shaped like the gracious S of an ancient vase. The fruit, shaped like a pear, is distributed around the stem: you would take them for glass crystals; the whole tree resembles a column of chased silver surmounted by a Corinthian urn.

Finally, in the background the magnolias and the sweet gums rose gradually into the air.

The sun was setting behind the curtain of trees on the plain. As it descended, the movements of shade and light spread something magical over the scene: there a ray shone through the dome of a great tree and sparkled like a carbuncle set in the somber foliage; here, the light diverged among the trunks and branches and cast on the grass growing columns and moving trellises. In the skies were clouds of all colors, some motionless, resembling great promontories or old towers next to a torrent, others floating in pink smoke or in flakes of white silk. A moment sufficed to change the aerial scene. One could see the flaming maws of furnaces, great heaps of coals, rivers of lava, burning landscapes. The same hues were repeated without mixing; fire stood out on fire, pale yellow on pale yellow, purple on purple. Everything was brilliant, everything was enveloped, penetrated, saturated with light.

But nature laughs at the paintbrush of man. When she seems to have attained her greatest beauty, she smiles and becomes even more beautiful.

To our right were the Indian ruins; to our left, our hunting camp; the island spread before us its landscapes engraved or modeled in the waters. To the east, the moon, touching the horizon, seemed to rest motionless on the faraway hills; to the west, the vault of heaven seemed blended into a sea of diamonds and sapphires in which the sun, half-plunged, seemed to be dissolving.

The animals of creation were, as we, attentive to this great spectacle: the crocodile, turned toward the luminary of day, spewed from his open maw the lake water in a colored spray; perched on a dried branch, the pelican praised in his own manner the Master of nature, while the stork flew away to bless Him above the clouds!

We too shall sing Thee, God of the universe, who hast lavished so many marvels! The voice of a man will be lifted with the voice of the wilderness: Thou wilt make out the accents of the weak son of woman in the midst of the music of the spheres which Thy hand sets in motion, in the midst of the bellowing of the abyss whose doors Thou hast sealed.

Upon our return to the island, I had an excellent meal: fresh trout seasoned with canneberge tips was a dish worthy of a king's table. Thus was I much more than a king. If chance had placed me on the throne and a revolution had cast me from it, instead of eking out my misery in Europe as did Charles and James, I would have said to the covetous: "You want my position, well try the job; you will see it is not so desirable. Slay one another over my old mantle; in the forests of America I shall enjoy the liberty you have given back to me."

We had a neighbor at our supper. A hole similar to the burrow of a badger was the home of a tortoise; the recluse came out of her cave and started walking gravely along the water. These tortoises are little different from sea turtles; they have a longer neck. We didn't kill the peaceful queen of the island.

After supper I sat down by myself on the shore; all that could be heard was the sound of the waves lapping along the beach; fireflies shone in the darkness and were eclipsed when they crossed a moonbeam. I fell into that kind of reverie known to all travelers. No distinct remembrance of myself remained; I felt myself living as a part of the great whole and vegetating with the trees and the flowers. That is perhaps the most pleasant condition for man, for even when he is happy there is in his pleasures a certain foundation of bitterness, an indefinable something that could be called the sadness of happiness. The traveler's reverie is a sort of plenitude of the heart and emptiness of the mind which allows one to enjoy his existence in repose: it is by thought that we trouble the felicity which God gives us: the soul is peaceful; the mind is troubled.

The Indians of Florida tell that in the middle of a lake there is an island where live the most beautiful women in the world. The Muskogees several times tried the conquest of the magical island; but the Elysian retreats, fleeing before their canoes, finally disappeared: a natural image of the time we lose pursuing our chimeras. In that country there was also a Fountain of Youth. Who would want to grow younger?

The next day before sunrise we left the island, crossed the lake, and entered again on the river by which we had descended. This river was full of alligators. These animals are only dangerous in the water, especially when one is disembarking. On land, a child could easily outdistance them walking at an ordinary pace. A way of avoiding their ambushes is to set the grasses and reeds on fire. There is then the curious spectacle of great expanses of water capped with a curtain of flame.

When the crocodile of these regions has reached full growth, it measures about 20 to 24 feet from the head to the tail. Its body is as large as that of a horse. This reptile would have exactly the form of the common lizard if its tail were not compressed on the two sides as is a fish's. It is covered with bulletproof scales, except around the head and between the legs. Its head is about three feet long; the nostrils are wide; the upper jaw of the animal is the only one that moves; it opens to form a right angle with the lower jaw. Beneath the upper jaw are placed two large teeth like the tusks of a boar, which give the monster a terrible appearance.

The female of the alligator lays whitish eggs on land which she covers with grasses and mud. These eggs, sometimes as many as a hundred, form with the mud that covers them little heaps four feet high and five feet in diameter at their base. The sun and the fermentation of the clay hatch the eggs. One female does not distinguish her own eggs from the eggs of another female; she takes under her protection all the sun's broods. Is it not strange to find among the crocodiles the communal children of Plato's republic?

The heat was oppressive; we were sailing in the midst of swamps; our boats were leaking, for the sun had melted the pitch of the caulking. Often we received burning blasts from the north; our scouts predicted a storm because the savanna rat was going up and down the branches of the live oak incessantly; the mosquitoes were tormenting us frightfully. We could see swamp fire in the low spots.

We spent the night very uncomfortably without any ajouppa on a peninsula surrounded by swamps; the moon and all objects were drowned in a red fog. This morning there has been no breeze, and we reembarked to try to reach an Indian village a few miles away; but it has been impossible for us to go up the river very long, and we have had to disembark on the tip of a cape covered with trees, from where we enjoy an immense view. Clouds are rising up from beneath the horizon on the northwest and are slowly climbing into the sky. We are making a shelter for ourselves as best we can with branches.

The sun is becoming overcast, the first rolls of thunder are heard; the crocodiles answer them with a low rumble, as one thunderclap answers another. An immense column of clouds is extending to the northeast and the southeast; the rest of the sky is a dirty copper color, half-transparent and tinged with lightning. The wilderness lit by a false light and the storm suspended over our heads ready to break offer a scene full of splendor.

Here is the storm! Imagine a deluge of fire without wind or water; the smell of sulfur fills the air; nature is illuminated as if by the light of a conflagration.

Now the cataracts of the abyss open up; the raindrops are not separated from one another: a veil of water joins the clouds to the earth.

The Indians say that the noise of the thunder is caused by immense birds fighting in the air and by the efforts being made by an old man to vomit up a viper of fire. To prove this assertion they show trees where lightning has traced the image of a snake. Often the storms set fire to the forests; they continue burning until the fire is stopped by some watercourse. These burned-out forests are transformed into lakes and swamps.

The curlews, whose voices we hear in the sky in the middle of the rain and thunder, announce the end of the hurricane. The wind is tearing apart the clouds whose remnants are flying across the sky; the thunder and the lightning attached to their sides follow them; the air is becoming cold and sonorous. Of the deluge there remain only drops of water which fall like beads from the leaves of the trees.

John James Audubon
(1785–1851)

Although born in Santo Domingo (now Haiti), the illegitimate son of a French plantation owner and his Creole mistress, Jean Jacques Fougere Audubon was raised in France, where he was trained in the aristocratic arts of fencing, dancing, music, and painting. In 1803 Audubon's father Americanized the name of his eighteen-year-old son and sent him across the Atlantic to look after some family property near Philadelphia. Here young Audubon underwent a rather sudden transformation, and within months had begun styling himself "the American Woodsman"—an identity he later cultivated and marketed to win European subscribers to his books. From 1803 to 1820 Audubon, like William Bartram before him, failed at one business venture after another before finally devoting himself entirely to the study of natural history. Although Audubon's earliest bird drawings date from 1805, it was not until 1820 that he resolved upon the ambitious goal of depicting all the birds of his adopted homeland. The ultimate result was *The Birds of America* (1827–38), a monumental work consisting of 435 double-elephant-folio-sized plates (39.5 by 29.5 inches) containing life-sized representations of more than a thousand American birds. This was followed by the octavo edition of *Birds* (1840–44), the most successful natural history book ever published up to that time. Although Audubon is known foremost as a student and painter of birds—for example, he pioneered bird-banding experiments and was among the first artists to depict birds in motion—he was also a superb writer of frontier tales and natural history. His "Episodes," sixty short essays describing his travel adventures from 1808 to 1834, contribute to the tradition of frontier literature developed by the Southwest humorists and by Mark Twain, and contain romantic descriptions of American wilderness akin to those written by his own literary heroes, Washington Irving and James Fenimore Cooper. A tireless itinerant naturalist, painter, writer, promoter, and—to the dismay of some, hunter—Audubon was a devout American nationalist who saw his work as an important means of indexing the possibilities for the rising American nation. Much of Audubon's finest natural history writing, including the following essay on the life and habits of the Bald Eagle, appears in his five-volume *Ornithological Biography* (1831–39).

From *Ornithological Biography* (1831–1839)

*The White-Headed Eagle (*Falco Leucocephalus, Linn.*)*

The figure of this noble bird is well known throughout the civilized world, emblazoned as it is on our national standard, which waves in the breeze of every clime, bearing to distant lands the remembrance of a great people living in a state of peaceful freedom. May that peaceful freedom last forever!

The great strength, daring, and cool courage of the White-headed Eagle, joined to his unequalled power of flight, render him highly conspicuous among his brethren. To these qualities did he add a generous disposition towards others, he might be looked up to as a model of nobility. The ferocious, overbearing, and tyrannical temper which is ever and anon displaying itself in his actions, is, nevertheless, best adapted to his state, and was wisely given him by the Creator to enable him to perform the office assigned to him.

To give you, kind reader, some idea of the nature of this bird, permit me to place you on the Mississippi, on which you may float gently along, while approaching winter brings millions of waterfowl on whistling wings, from the countries of the north, to seek a milder climate in which to sojourn for a season. The Eagle is seen perched, in an erect attitude, on the highest summit of the tallest tree by the margin of the broad stream. His glistening but stern eye looks over the vast expanse. He listens attentively to every sound that comes to his quick ear from afar, glancing now and then on the earth beneath, lest even the light tread of the fawn may pass unheard. His mate is perched on the opposite side, and should all be tranquil and silent, warns him by a cry to continue patient. At this well-known call, the male partly opens his broad wings, inclines his body a little downwards, and answers to her voice in tones not unlike the laugh of a maniac. The next moment, he resumes his erect attitude, and again all around is silent. Ducks of many species, the Teal, the Wigeon, the Mallard and others, are seen passing with great rapidity, and following the course of the current; but the Eagle heeds them not: they are at that time beneath his attention. The next moment, however, the wild trumpet-like sound of a yet distant but approaching Swan is heard. A shriek from the female Eagle comes across the stream,—for, kind reader, she is fully as alert as her mate. The latter suddenly shakes the whole of his body, and with a few touches of his bill, aided by the action of his cuticular muscles, arranges his plumage in an instant. The snow-white bird is now in sight: her long neck is stretched forward, her eye is on the watch, vigilant as that of her enemy; her large wings seem with difficulty to support the weight of her body, although they flap incessantly. So irksome do her exertions seem, that her very legs are spread beneath her tail, to aid her in her flight. She approaches, however. The Eagle has marked her for his prey.

As the Swan is passing the dreaded pair, starts from his perch, in full preparation for the chase, the male bird, with an awful scream, that to the Swan's ear brings more terror than the report of the large duck-gun.

Now is the moment to witness the display of the Eagle's powers. He glides through the air like a falling star, and, like a flash of lightning, comes upon the timorous quarry, which now, in agony and despair, seeks, by various maneuvers, to elude the grasp of his cruel talons. It mounts, doubles, and willingly would plunge into the stream, were it not prevented by the Eagle, which, long possessed of the knowledge that by such a stratagem the Swan might escape him, forces it to remain in the air by attempting to strike it with his talons from beneath. The hope of escape is soon given up by the Swan. It has already become much weakened, and its strength fails at the sight of the courage and swiftness of its antagonist. Its last gasp is about to escape, when the ferocious Eagle strikes with his talons the under side of its wing, and with unresisted power forces the bird to fall in a slanting direction upon the nearest shore.

It is then, reader, that you may see the cruel spirit of this dreaded enemy of the feathered race, whilst, exulting over his prey, he for the first time breathes at ease. He presses down his powerful feet, and drives his sharp claws deeper than ever into the heart of the dying Swan. He shrieks with delight, as he feels the last convulsions of his prey, which has now sunk under his unceasing efforts to render death as painfully felt as it can possibly be. The female has watched every movement of her mate; and if she did not assist him in capturing the Swan, it was not from want of will, but merely that she felt full assurance that the power and courage of her lord were quite sufficient for the deed. She now sails to the spot where he eagerly awaits her, and when she has arrived, they together turn the breast of the luckless Swan upwards, and gorge themselves with gore.

At other times, when these Eagles, sailing in search of prey, discover a Goose, a Duck, or a Swan, that has alighted on the water, they accomplish its destruction in a manner that is worthy of your attention. The Eagles, well aware that waterfowl have it in their power to dive at their approach, and thereby elude their attempts upon them, ascend in the air in opposite directions over the lake or river, on which they have observed the object which they are desirous of possessing. Both Eagles reach a certain height, immediately after which one of them glides with great swiftness towards the prey; the latter, meantime, aware of the Eagle's intention, dives the moment before he reaches the spot. The pursuer then rises in the air, and is met by its mate, which glides toward the waterbird, that has just emerged to breathe, and forces it to plunge again beneath the surface, to escape the talons of this second assailant. The first Eagle is now poising itself in the place where its mate formerly was, and rushes anew to force the quarry to make another plunge. By thus alternately gliding, in rapid and often repeated rushes over the ill-fated bird, they soon fatigue it, when it stretches out its neck, swims deeply, and makes for the shore, in the hope of concealing itself among the rank weeds. But this is of no avail, for the Eagles follow it in all its motions, and the moment it approaches the margin, one of them darts upon it, and kills it in an instant, after which they divide the spoil.

During spring and summer, the White-headed Eagle, to procure sustenance, follows a different course, and one much less suited to a bird apparently so well able to supply itself without interfering with other plunderers. No sooner does the Fish Hawk make its appearance along our Atlantic shores, or ascend our numerous and large rivers, than the Eagle follows it, and, like a selfish oppressor, robs it of the hard-earned fruits of its labor. Perched on some tall summit, in view of the ocean, or of some watercourse, he watches every motion of the Osprey while on wing. When the latter rises from the water, with a fish in its grasp, forth rushes the Eagle in pursuit. He mounts above the Fish Hawk, and threatens it by actions well understood, when the latter, fearing perhaps that its life is in danger, drops its prey. In an instant, the Eagle, accurately estimating the rapid descent of the fish, closes his wings, follows it with the swiftness of thought, and the next moment grasps it. The prize is carried off in silence to the woods, and assists in feeding the ever-hungry brood of the Eagle.

This bird now and then procures fish himself, by pursuing them in the shallows of small creeks. I have witnessed several instances of this in the Perkiomen Creek in Pennsylvania, where, in this manner, I saw one of them secure a number of *Red-fins*, by wading briskly through the water, and striking at them with his bill. I have also observed a pair scrambling over the ice of a frozen pond, to get at some fish below, but without success.

It does not confine itself to these kinds of food, but greedily devours young pigs, lambs, fawns, poultry, and the putrid flesh of carcasses of every description, driving off the vultures and carrion crows, or the dogs, and keeping a whole party at defiance until it is satiated. It frequently gives chase to the vultures, and forces them to disgorge the contents of their stomachs, when it alights and devours the filthy mass. A ludicrous instance of this took place near the city of Natchez, on the Mississippi. Many Vultures were engaged in devouring the body and entrails of a dead horse, when a White-headed Eagle accidentally passing by, the vultures all took to wing, one among the rest with a portion of the entrails partly swallowed, and the remaining part, about a yard in length, dangling in the air. The Eagle instantly marked him, and gave chase. The poor vulture tried in vain to disgorge, when the Eagle, coming up, seized the loose end of the gut and dragged the bird along for twenty or thirty yards, much against its will, until both fell to the ground, when the Eagle struck the vulture, and in a few moments killed it, after which he swallowed the delicious morsel.

I have heard of several attempts made by this bird to destroy children, but have never witnessed any myself, although I have little doubt of its having sufficient daring to do so.

The flight of the White-headed Eagle is strong, generally uniform, and protracted to any distance, at pleasure. Whilst traveling, it is entirely supported by equal easy flappings, without any intermission, in as far as I have observed it, by following it with the eye or the assistance of a glass. When looking for prey, it sails with extended wings, at right angles to its body, now and then allowing its legs to hang at their full length. Whilst sailing, it has the power of ascending in circular sweeps, without a single flap of the wings, or any apparent motion either of them or of the tail; and in this manner it often rises until it disappears from the view, the white tail remaining longer visible than the rest of the body. At other times, it rises only a few hundred feet in the air, and sails off in a direct line, and with rapidity. Again, when thus elevated, it partially closes its wings, and glides downwards for a considerable space, when, as if disappointed, it suddenly checks its career, and reassumes its former steady flight. When at an immense height, and as if observing an object on the ground, it closes its wings, and glides through the air with such rapidity as to cause a loud rustling sound, not unlike that produced by a violent gust of wind passing amongst the branches of trees. Its fall towards the earth can scarcely be followed by the eye on such occasions, the more particularly that these falls or glidings through the air usually take place when they are least expected. . . .

It is supposed that Eagles live to a very great age,—some persons have ventured to say even a hundred years. On this subject, I can only observe, that I once found one of these birds, which, on being killed, proved to be a female, and which, judging by its appearance, must have been very old. Its tail and wing-feathers were so worn out, and of such a rusty color, that I imagined the bird had lost the power of molting. The legs and feet were covered with large warts, the claws and bill were much blunted, it could scarcely fly more than a hundred yards at a time, and this it did with a heaviness and unsteadiness of motion such as I never witnessed in any other bird of the species. The body was poor and very tough. The eye was the only part which appeared to have sustained no injury. It remained sparkling and full of animation, and even after death seemed to have lost little of its luster. No wounds were perceivable on its body.

The White-headed Eagle is seldom seen alone, the mutual attachment which two individuals form when they first pair seeming to continue until one of them dies or is destroyed. They hunt for the support of each other, and seldom feed apart, but usually drive off other birds of the same species. They commence their amatory intercourse at an earlier period than any other *land bird* with which I am acquainted, generally in the month of December. At this time, along the Mississippi, or by the margin of some lake not far in the interior of the forest, the male and female birds are observed making a great bustle, flying about and circling in various ways, uttering a loud cackling noise, alighting on the dead branches of the tree on which their nest is already preparing, or in the act of being repaired, and caressing each other. In the beginning of January incubation commences. I shot a female, on the 17th of that month, as she sat on her eggs, in which the chicks had made considerable progress.

The nest, which in some instances is of great size, is usually placed on a very tall tree, destitute of branches to a considerable height, but by no means always a dead one. It is never seen on the rocks. It is composed of sticks, from three to five feet in length, large pieces of turf, rank weeds, and Spanish moss in abundance, whenever that substance happens to be near. When finished, it measures from five to six feet in diameter, and so great is the accumulation of materials, that it sometimes measures the same in depth, it being occupied for a great number of years in succession, and receiving some augmentation each season. When placed in a naked tree, between the forks of the branches, it is conspicuously seen at a great distance. The eggs, which are from two to four, more commonly two or three, are of a dull white color, and equally rounded at both ends, some of them being occasionally granulated. Incubation lasts for more than three weeks, but I have not been able to ascertain its precise duration, as I have observed the female on different occasions sit for a few days in the nest, before laying the first egg. Of this I assured myself by climbing to the nest every day in succession, during her temporary absence,—a rather perilous undertaking when the bird is sitting.

I have seen the young birds when not larger than middle-sized pullets. At this time, they are covered with a soft cottony kind of down, their bill and legs appearing disproportionately large. Their first plumage is of a grayish color, mixed with brown of different depths of tint, and before the parents drive them off from the nest, they are fully fledged. As a figure of the Young White-headed Eagle will appear in the course of the publication of my Illustrations, I shall not here trouble you with a description of its appearance. I once caught three young Eagles of this species, when fully fledged, by having the tree on which their nest was, cut down. It caused great trouble to secure them, as they could fly and scramble much faster than any of our party could run. They, however, gradually became fatigued, and at length were so exhausted as to offer no resistance, when we were securing them with cords. This happened on the border of Lake Pontchartrain, in the month of April. The parents did not think fit to come within gunshot of the tree while the axe was at work.

The attachment of the parents to the young is very great, when the latter are yet of a small size; and to ascend to the nest at this time would be dangerous. But as the young advance, and, after being able to take wing and provide for themselves, are not disposed to fly off, the old birds turn them out, and beat them away from them. They return to the nest, however, to roost, or sleep on the branches immediately near it, for several weeks after. They are fed most abundantly while under the care of the parents, which procure for them ample supplies of fish, either accidentally cast ashore, or taken from the Fish Hawk, together with rabbits, squirrels, young lambs, pigs, opossums, or raccoons. Everything that comes in the way is relished by the young family, as by the old birds.

The young birds begin to breed the following spring, not always in pairs of the same age, as I have several times observed one of these birds in brown plumage mated with a full-colored bird, which had the head and tail pure white. I once shot a pair of this kind, when the brown bird (the young one) proved to be the female.

This species requires at least four years before it attains the full beauty of its plumage when kept in confinement. I have known two instances in which the white of the head did not make its appearance until the sixth spring. It is impossible for me to say how much sooner this state of perfection is attained, when the bird is at full liberty, although I should suppose it to be at least one year, as the bird is capable of breeding the first spring after birth.

The weight of Eagles of this species varies considerably. In the males, it is from six to eight pounds, and in the females from eight to twelve. These birds are so attached to particular districts, where they have first made their nest, that they seldom spend a night at any distance from the latter, and often resort to its immediate neighborhood. Whilst asleep, they emit a loud hissing sort of snore, which is heard at the distance of a hundred yards, when the weather is perfectly calm. Yet, so light is their sleep, that the cracking of a stick under the foot of a person immediately wakens them. When it is attempted to smoke them while thus roosted and asleep, they start up and sail off without uttering any sound, but return next evening to the same spot.

Before steam-navigation commenced on our western rivers, these Eagles were extremely abundant there, particularly in the lower parts of the Ohio, the Mississippi, and the adjoining streams. I have seen hundreds going down from the mouth of the Ohio to New Orleans, when it was not at all difficult to shoot them. Now, however, their number is considerably diminished, the game on which they were in the habit of feeding, having been forced to seek refuge from the persecution of man farther in the wilderness. Many, however, are still observed on these rivers, particularly along the shores of the Mississippi.

In concluding this account of the White-headed Eagle, suffer me, kind reader, to say how much I grieve that it should have been selected as the Emblem of my Country. The opinion of our great Franklin on this subject, as it perfectly coincides with my own, I shall here present to you. "For my part," says he, in one of his letters, "I wish the Bald Eagle had not been chosen as the representative of our country. He is a bird of bad moral character; he does not get his living honestly;

you may have seen him perched on some dead tree, where, too lazy to fish for himself, he watches the labor of the Fishing-Hawk; and when that diligent bird has at length taken a fish, and is bearing it to his nest for the support of his mate and young ones, the Bald Eagle pursues him, and takes it from him. With all this injustice, he is never in good case, but, like those among men who live by sharping and robbing, he is generally poor, and often very lousy. Besides, he is a rank coward: the little King Bird, not bigger than a Sparrow, attacks him boldly, and drives him out of the district. He is, therefore, by no means a proper emblem for the brave and honest Cincinnati of America, who have driven all the *King Birds* from our country; though exactly fit for that order of knights which the French call *Chevaliers d'Industrie*."

It is only necessary for me to add, that the name by which this bird is universally known in America is that of *Bald Eagle*, an erroneous denomination, as its head is as densely feathered as that of any other species, although its whiteness may have suggested the idea of its being bare.

Ralph Waldo Emerson
(1803–1882)

Best known as a prominent Transcendentalist, a major literary figure of the American Romantic period, an influential mentor of Henry Thoreau, and as the author of *Nature* (1836) and such famous essays as "Self-Reliance" (1841) and "Experience" (1844), Ralph Waldo Emerson was perhaps the greatest nineteenth-century American natural philosopher. A native Bostonian who graduated from Harvard and Harvard Divinity School, Emerson was in 1829 ordained as Unitarian minister of the Second Church of Boston — the church of Increase and Cotton Mather. But despite his success as a preacher, Emerson soon came to question and to doubt the mediating role of the institutional church in individual spiritual life. In 1832 he resigned the ministry, instead devoting himself to the natural history he had already begun to read and to incorporate into his sermons. Indeed, the first four lectures of his new, secular career as public intellectual were on the subject of natural history. Delivered in 1833–34, well before the stunning debut of *Nature*, Emerson used these foundational lectures to explore seminal ideas that would resonate throughout his life's work: that there is a mysterious, powerful relationship between human and nonhuman nature; that particular aspects of the natural world serve as analogies to human spiritual and intellectual faculties; that the order, flow, and dynamism inherent in natural systems indicates potential for human growth and development; that science might prove an effective means to the end of human enlightenment and self-knowledge; and that the study of natural history was a technique by which the "individual soul" could be radically expanded and ennobled. But Emerson was clearly more a natural philosopher than a natural scientist. Whereas Henry Thoreau was deeply engaged in specific observations of particular natural phenomena, Emerson's tendency was to generalize and abstract from natural facts in order to address matters of the soul. Already present in "The Uses of Natural History" (1833), the first of Emerson's hundreds of public lectures, is the classic Emersonian inclination to apply natural history as a means by which the individual might access aesthetic, intellectual, and spiritual truths.

From "The Uses of Natural History" (1833)

[L]et us inquire what are the advantages which may be expected to accrue from the greater cultivation of Natural Science.

They are in my judgment great and manifold, and probably more than can be now enumerated. I do not think we are yet masters of all the reasons that make this knowledge valuable to us. They will only disclose themselves by a more advanced state of science. I say this because we have all a presentiment of relations to external nature, which outruns the limits of actual science. I lately had an opportunity of visiting that celebrated repository of natural curiosities the Garden of Plants in Paris; and except perhaps to naturalists only I ought not to speak of the feelings it excited in me. There is the richest collection in the world of natural curiosities arranged for the most imposing effect. The mountain and morass and prairie and jungle, the ocean, and rivers, the mines and the atmosphere have been ransacked to furnish whatever was rich and rare; the types of each class of beings — Nature's proof impressions;—to render account of her three kingdoms to the keen insatiable eye of French science.

In spacious grounds skillfully laid out, and shaded with fine groves and shrubberies, you walk among the animals of every country, each in his own paddock with his mates, having his appropriate food before him,—his habits consulted in his accommodation. There towers the camelopard nearly twenty feet high, whose promenade and breakfast attract as much attention as the king's; the lions from Algiers and Asia; the elephants from Siam — whose bath is occasionally performed with great applause from the boys;—our own countrymen, the buffalo and the bear from New Hampshire and Labrador. All sizes and all stripes of tigers, hyenas, leopards, and jackals; a herd of monkeys; not to mention the great numbers of sheep, goats, llamas, and zebras, that sleep, browse, or ruminate in their several country fashions, (as much at ease as in their own wilds,) for the amusement of the whole world in the heart of the capital of France.

Moving along these pleasant walks, you come to the botanical cabinet, an enclosed garden plot, where grows a grammar of botany—where the plants rise, each in its class, its order, and its genus, (as nearly as their habits in reference to soils will permit,) arranged by the hand of Jussieu himself. If you have read Decandolle with engravings, or with a *hortus siccus,* conceive how much more exciting and intelligible is this natural alphabet, this green and yellow and crimson dictionary, on which the sun shines, and the winds blow.

The Cabinet of Natural History is contained in a large stone edifice in the center of the grounds.

It is a prodigality to visit in one walk all the various halls in this great gallery of Nature. The ornithological chambers require an entire day: For who would mix and confound so fine and delicate sensations? This house of stuffed birds is a finer picture gallery than the Louvre. The whole air is flushed with the rich plumage and beautiful forms of the birds. The fancy colored vests of those elegant beings make me as pensive as the hues and forms of a cabinet of shells have done before. They fill the mind with calm and genial thought. Some of the birds have a fabulous beauty that seems more appropriate to some sultan's garden in the Arabian Nights Entertainments than to a real tangible scientific collection. You see the favorites of nature,—creatures in whose form and coat seems to have been a design to charm the eye of cultivated taste. Observe that parrot of the parrot tribe called *Psittacus Erythropterus.* You need not write down his name for he is the beau of all birds and you will find him as you will find a Raphael in a gallery. Then the hummingbirds so little and so gay—from the least of all, the *Trochilus Niger* not so big as a beetle—to the *Trochilus Pella* with his irresistible neck of gold and silver and fire; and the *Trochilus Delalandi* from Brazil whom the French call the magnificent fly (*La mouche magnifique*) or glory in miniature. The birds of Paradise are singularly delicate and picturesque in their plumage. The manucode or royal Paradisaea from New Guinea, the red Paradisaea, and the Paradisaea Apoda, seem each more beautiful than the last and each, if seen alone, would be pronounced a peerless creature. I watched the different groups of people who came in to the gallery, and noticed that they picked out the same birds to point to the admiration of their companions. They all noticed the Veuve à épaulettes—the widow with epaulettes—a grotesque black fowl called Emberiza Longicauda with fine shoulder ornaments and a long mourning tail, and the Ampelis Cotinga. All admired the *Phasianus Argus,* a pheasant that appeared to have made its toilette after the pattern of the peacock, and the *Trogon pavoninus,* called also the Couroucon. But it were vain to enumerate even the conspicuous individuals in the parti-colored assembly. There were black swans and white peacocks, the famous venerable ibis come hither to Paris out of Egypt, both the sacred and the rosy; the flamingo with a neck like a snake; the toucan, rightly denominated the rhinoceros; and a vulture whom to meet in a wilderness would make the flesh creep, so truculent and executioner-like he stood.

The cabinet of birds was a single and even small part of that noble magazine of natural wonders. Not less complete, scarcely less attractive is the collection of stuffed beasts, prepared with the greatest skill to represent the forms and native attitudes of the quadrupeds. Then follow the insects, the reptiles, the fishes, the minerals. In neighboring apartments is contained the collection of comparative anatomy, a perfect series from the skeleton of the *balaena* which reminds every one of the frame of a schooner, to the upright form and highly developed skull of the Caucasian race of man.

The eye is satisfied with seeing and strange thoughts are stirred as you see more surprising objects than were known to exist; transparent lumps of amber with gnats and flies within; radiant spars and marbles; huge blocks of quartz; native gold in all its forms of crystallization and combination, gold in threads, in plates, in crystals, in dust; and silver taken from the earth molten as from fire. You are impressed with the inexhaustible gigantic riches of nature. The limits of the possible are enlarged, and the real is stranger than the imaginary. The universe is a more amazing puzzle than ever, as you look along this bewildering series of animated forms, the hazy butterflies, the carved shells, the birds, beasts, insects, snakes, fish, and the upheaving principle of life everywhere incipient, in the very rock aping organized forms. Whilst I stand there I am impressed with a singular conviction that not a form so grotesque, so savage, or so beautiful, but is an expression of something in man the observer. We feel that there is an occult relation between the very worm, the crawling scorpions, and man. I am moved by strange sympathies. I say I will listen to this invitation. I will be a naturalist.

Under the influence of such thoughts, I say that I suppose many inducements to the study of Natural History will disclose themselves as its secrets are penetrated. Besides that the general progress of the science has given it a higher and higher place in the public estimation is there not every now and then some inexplicable fact or new class of relations suggested which for the time seems not so much to invite as to defy scientific solution? For example, what known laws are to classify some of the astounding facts embodied in the Report of the Committee of the French Institute in 1830 upon the subject of Animal Magnetism — a committee too, considering the persons and the circumstances, who might be regarded as a picked jury of the most competent scientific persons on earth? But not to venture upon this dangerous ground, the debatable land of the sublime and the ridiculous, let me confine my attention to the enumeration of certain specific advantages easily marked and understood which may serve as the commendation of the objects of this society.

1. It is the lowest and yet not a bad recommendation of the occupations of the Naturalist that they are serviceable to the health. The ancient Greeks had a fable of the giant Antaeus, that when he wrestled with Hercules, he was suffocated in the grip of the hero, but every time he touched his mother earth, his strength was renewed. The fable explains itself of the body and the mind. Man is the broken giant, and in all his weakness he is invigorated by touching his mother earth, that is, by habits of conversation with nature. It is good for the body exhausted by the bad air, and artificial life of cities, to be sent out into the fresh and fragrant fields, and there employed in exploring the laws of the creation. The study of Botany deserves the attention of those interested in Education, for this, if for no other cause. The wild rose will reflect its hues upon the cheek of the lover of nature. It is well known that the celebrated Wilson was led to the study of Ornithology for the benefit of his enfeebled health, and in his enthusiastic rambles in the wilderness his constitution was established whilst he enlarged the domain of science.

The mountain minerals will pay their searcher with active limbs and refreshed spirits. And he who wanders along the margin of the sounding sea for shellfish or marine plants, will find strength of limb and sharpness of sight and bounding blood in the same places. Dig your garden, cross your cattle, graft your trees, feed your silkworms, set your hives — in the field is the perfection of the senses to be found, and quiet restoring Sleep, —

His poppy grows among the Corn.

2. In the second place, the main advantage to be proposed from the study of natural history is that which may seem to make all further argument needless; to be itself the manifest ground on which the study stands in the favor of mankind, I mean the direct service which it renders to the cultivator and the world, the amount of useful economical information which it communicates. The proof of this assertion is the history of all discoveries, almost the history of civilization itself. It is the earth itself and its natural bodies that make the raw material out of which we construct our food, clothing, fuel, furniture, and arms. And it is the Naturalist who discovers the virtues of these bodies and the mode of converting them to use. . . .

3. But it is high time to enumerate a third reason for the cultivation of natural history which is the *delight which springs from the contemplation of this truth*, independent of all other considerations. I should be ashamed to neglect this good, in too particular a showing what profit was to accrue from the knowledge of nature. The knowledge itself, is the highest benefit. He must be very young or very sordid who wishes to know what good it will do him to understand the sublime

mechanism on which the stability of the solar system and the faithful return of the seasons depend. What good will it do him? Why, the good of knowing that fact. Is not that good enough?—Moreover is it not disgraceful to be served by all the arts and sciences at our tables, and in our chambers and never know who feeds us, nor understand the cunning they employ? I cannot but think it becoming that every gentleman should know why he puts on a white hat in summer, and a woolen coat in winter; and why his shoes cannot be made until the leather is tanned. Better sit still than be borne by steam, and not know how; or guided by the needle and the quadrant through thousands of miles of sea, without a mark in the horizon, and brought to a little dent in the shore on the other half the globe, as truly as if following a clew in the hand—and never ask how that feat is accomplished.

Bias was asked what good, education would do for a boy;—"When he goes there," pointing to the marble seats of the theater, he replied, "that he might not be a stone sitting upon a stone." Every fact that is disclosed to us in natural history removes one scale more from the eye; makes the face of nature around us so much more significant. . . .

Thus knowledge will make the face of the earth significant to us: it will make the stones speak and clothe with grace the meanest weed. Indeed it is worth considering in all animated nature what different aspect the same object presents to the ignorant and the instructed eye. It only needs to have the eye informed, to make everything we see, every plant, every spider, every moss, every patch of mold upon the bark of a tree, give us the idea of fitness, as much as the order and accommodation of the most ingeniously packed dressing box. For, every form is a history of the thing. The comparative anatomist can tell at sight whether a skeleton belonged to a carnivorous or herbivorous animal—to a climber, a jumper, a runner, a digger, a builder. The conchologist can tell at sight whether his shell were a river or a sea shell, whether it dwelt in still or in running waters, whether it were an annual or a perennial covering, and many the like particulars. And this takes away the sense of deformity from all objects; for, everything is a monster till we know what it is for. A ship, a telescope, a surgical instrument, a box of strange tools are puzzles and painful to the eye, until we have been shown successively the use of every part, and then the thing tells its story at sight, and is beautiful. A lobster is monstrous to the eye the first time it is seen, but when we have been shown the use of the case, the color, the tentacula, and the proportion of the claws, and have seen that he has not a scale nor a bristle, nor any part, but fits exactly to some habit and condition of the creature; he then seems as perfect and suitable to his sea-house, as a glove to a hand. A *man* in the rocks under the sea, would indeed be a monster; but a lobster is a most handy and happy fellow there. So there is not an object in nature so mean or loathsome, not a weed, not a toad, not an earwig, but a knowledge of its habits would lessen our disgust, and convert it into an object of some worth; perhaps of admiration. Nothing is indifferent to the wise. If a man should study the economy of a spire of grass — how it sucks up sap, how it imbibes light, how it resists cold, how it repels excess of moisture, it would show him a design in the form, in the color, in the smell, in the very posture of the blade as it bends before the wind. . . .

4. There is a fourth good purpose answered by the study of Natural History which deserves a distinct enumeration. I refer to its salutary effect upon the mind and character of those who cultivate it. It makes the intellect exact, quick to discriminate between the similar and the same, and greedy of truth.

Moreover I hope it will not be thought undue refinement to suppose that long habits of intimate acquaintance with nature's workmanship, which is always neat, simple, masterly, accustoms her scholars to think and work in her style. All our ideas of sublimity and beauty are got from that source. Our contrivances are good but will not bear comparison with hers. . . .

5. I have spoken of some of the advantages which may flow from the culture of natural science: health; useful knowledge; delight; and the improvement of the mind and character. I should not do the subject the imperfect justice in my power if I did not add a fifth. It is in my judgment the greatest office of natural science (and one which as yet is only begun to be discharged) to explain man to himself. The knowledge of the laws of nature,—how many wild errors—political, philosophical, theological, has it not already corrected! The knowledge of all the facts of all the laws of nature will give man his true place in the system of being. But more than the correction of specific errors by the disclosure of particular facts, there yet remain questions of the highest interest which are unsolved and on which a far more profound knowledge of Nature will throw light. . . .

And this, because the whole of Nature is a metaphor or image of the human Mind. The laws of moral nature answer to those of matter as face to face in a glass. "The visible world," it has been well said, "and the relations of its parts is the dial plate of the invisible one." In the language of the poet,

> For all that meets the bodily sense I deem
> Symbolical, one mighty alphabet
> For infant minds.

It is a most curious fact that the axioms of geometry and of mechanics only translate the laws of ethics. Thus, A straight line is the shortest distance between two points; The whole is greater than its part; The smallest weight may be made to lift the greatest, the difference of force being compensated by time; Reaction is equal to action; and a thousand the like propositions which have an ethical as well as a material sense. They are true not only in geometry but in life; they have a much more extensive and universal signification as applied to human nature than when confined to technical use. And every common proverb is only one of these facts in nature used as a picture or parable of a more extensive truth; as when we say, "A bird in the hand is worth two in the bush." "A rolling stone gathers no moss." " 'Tis hard to carry a full cup even." "Whilst the grass grows the steed starves."—In themselves these are insignificant facts but we repeat them because they are symbolical of moral truths. These are only trivial instances designed to show the principle. But it will probably be found to hold of all the facts revealed by chemistry or astronomy that they have the same harmony with the human mind.

And this undersong, this perfect harmony does not become less with more intimate knowledge of nature's laws but the analogy is felt to be deeper and more universal for every law that Davy or Cuvier or Laplace has revealed. It almost seems as if according to the idea of Fontenelle, "We seem to recognize a truth the first time we hear it."

I look then to the progress of Natural Scicncc as to that which is to develop new and great lessons of which good men shall understand the moral. Nature is a language and every new fact we learn is a new word; but it is not a language taken to pieces and dead in the dictionary, but the language put together into a most significant and universal sense. I wish to learn this language—not that I may know a new grammar but that I may read the great book which is written in that tongue. A man should feel that the time is not lost and the efforts not misspent that are devoted to the elucidation of these laws; for herein is writ by the Creator his own history. . . .

John D. Godman
(1794–1830)

By the end of his short life, editor, naturalist, and medical doctor John Godman was among the most accomplished physical anatomists in America. But Godman's early life was unusually troubled: both his parents died by the time he was five years old, and the aunt who subsequently cared for him died shortly thereafter. The orphan lived with his sister until 1811 when, like Benjamin Franklin, he was apprenticed to a printer. In 1814 he joined the navy and participated in the defense of Baltimore Harbor's Fort McHenry against bombardment by the British during the War of 1812 (this battle inspired Francis Scott Key to pen the "Star-Spangled Banner") and afterward studied medicine in Baltimore and at the University of Maryland. In 1821 he married Angelica Kauffman Peale, the granddaughter of Charles Willson Peale. Godman later held faculty appointments at the Medical College of Ohio and at Rutgers Medical College, and served as an editor of several important medical journals (including the publication later known as the *American Journal of Medical Sciences*). Godman translated and wrote a number of books, among which the most important is his three-volume *American Natural History* (1825–28), an erudite work that is the first descriptive study of mammals by an American naturalist. But in his last years Godman shifted away from scientific anatomy and instead wrote a series of wonderfully gentle, insightful, and philosophical nature essays that appeared as occasional pieces in the Philadelphia journal *The Friend;* these essays were later collected in the posthumously published *Rambles of a Naturalist.* Like Henry Thoreau, Godman loved to saunter, observe, and study the minute details of the natural world. Also like Thoreau, he suffered terribly from the tuberculosis that eventually took his life. As Godman neared death, he continued to take modest walks on the outskirts of Germantown and Philadelphia. He especially loved the semi-urban wildlands of Turner's Lane and Frankford and Wissahickon Creeks, where, following his own curiosity about nature, he made the observations recorded in the essays excerpted below. Although written by a dying man, these remarkable essays have a freshness and immediacy that remind us that nearby nature can be as fascinating and engaging as a remote wilderness.

From *Rambles of a Naturalist* (1833)

Ramble Number One

From early youth devoted to the study of nature, it has always been my habit to embrace every opportunity of increasing my knowledge and pleasures by actual observation, and I have found ample means of gratifying this disposition, wherever my place has been allotted by Providence. When an inhabitant of the country, it was sufficient to go a few steps from the door to be in the midst of numerous interesting objects; when a resident of the crowded city, a healthful walk of half an hour placed me where my favorite enjoyment was offered in abundance; and now, when no longer able to seek in fields and woods and running streams for that knowledge which cannot readily be elsewhere obtained, the recollection of my former rambles is productive of a satisfaction, which past pleasures but seldom bestow. Perhaps a statement of the manner in which my studies were pursued, may prove interesting to those who love the works of nature, and may not be aware how great a field for original observation is within their reach, or how vast a variety of instructive objects are easily accessible, even to the occupants of a bustling metropolis. To me it will be a source of great delight to spread these resources before the reader, and enable him so cheaply to participate in the pleasures I have enjoyed, as well as place him in the way of enlarging the general stock of knowledge by communicating the results of his original observations.

One of my favorite walks was through Turner's lane, near Philadelphia, which is about a quarter of a mile long, and not much wider than an ordinary street, being closely fenced in on both sides; yet my reader may feel surprised when informed that I found ample employment for all my leisure, during six weeks, within and about its precincts. On entering the lane from the Ridge road, I observed a gentle elevation of the turf beneath the lower rails of the fence, which appeared to be uninterruptedly continuous; and when I had cut through the verdant roof with my knife, it proved to be a regularly arched gallery or subterranean road, along which the inhabitants could securely travel at all hours without fear of discovery. The sides and bottom of this arched way were smooth and clean, as if much used; and the raised superior portion had long been firmly consolidated by the grass roots, intermixed with tenacious clay. At irregular and frequently distant intervals, a side path diverged into the neighboring fields, and by its superficial situation, irregularity, and frequent openings, showed that its purpose was temporary, or had been only opened for the sake of procuring food. Occasionally I found a little gallery diverging from the main route beneath the fence, towards the road, and finally opening on the grass, as if the inmate had come out in the morning to breathe the early air, or to drink of the crystal dew which daily gemmed the close cropped verdure. How I longed to detect the animal which tenanted these galleries, in the performance of his labors! Farther on, upon the top of a high bank, which prevented the pathway from continuing near the fence, appeared another evidence of the industry of my yet unknown miner. Half a dozen hillocks of loose, almost pulverized earth were thrown up, at irregular distances, communicating with the main gallery by side passages. Opening one of these carefully, it appeared to differ little from the common gallery in size, but it was very difficult to ascertain where the loose earth came from, nor have I ever been able to tell, since I never witnessed the formation of these hillocks, and conjectures are forbidden, where nothing but observation is requisite to the decision. My farther progress was now interrupted by a delightful brook which sparkled across the road over a clear sandy bed; and here my little galleries turned into the field, coursing along at a moderate distance from the stream. I crept through the fence into the meadow on the west side, intending to discover, if possible, the animal whose works had first fixed my attention, but as I approached the bank of the rivulet something suddenly retreated towards the grass, seeming to vanish almost unaccountably from sight. Very carefully examining the point at which it disappeared, I found the entrance of another gallery or burrow, but of very different construction from that first observed. This new one was formed in the grass, near and among whose roots and lower stems a small but regular covered way was practiced. Endless, however, would have been the attempt to follow this, as it opened in various directions, and ran irregularly into the field, and towards the brook, by a great variety of passages. It evidently belonged to an animal totally different from the owner of the subterranean passage, as I subsequently discovered, and may hereafter relate. Tired of my unavailing pursuit, I now returned to the little brook, and seating myself on a stone, remained for some time unconsciously gazing on the fluid which gushed along in unsullied brightness over its pebbly bed. Opposite to my seat, was an irregular hole in the bed of the stream, into which, in an idle mood, I pushed a small pebble with the end of my stick. What was my surprise, in a few seconds afterwards, to observe the water in this hole in motion, and the pebble I had pushed into it gently approaching the surface. Such was the fact; the hole was the dwelling of a stout little crayfish or fresh water lobster, who did not choose to be incommoded by the pebble, though doubtless he attributed its sudden arrival to the usual accidents of the stream, and not to my thoughtless movements. He had thrust his broad lobster-like claws under the stone, and then drawn them near to his mouth; thus making a kind of shelf; and as he reached the edge of the hole, he suddenly extended his claws, and rejected the encumbrance from the lower side, or downstream. Delighted to have found a living object with whose habits I was unacquainted, I should have repeated my experiment, but the crayfish presently returned with what might be called an armful of rubbish, and threw it over the side of his cell, and down the stream as before. Having watched him for some time while thus engaged, my attention was caught by the considerable number of similar holes along the margin and in the bed of the stream. One of these I explored with a small rod, and found it to be eight or ten inches deep, and widened below into a considerable chamber, in which the little lobster found a comfortable abode. Like all of his tribe, the crayfish makes considerable opposition to being removed from his dwelling, and bit smartly at the stick with his claws: as my present object was only to gain acquaintance with his dwelling, he was speedily permitted to return to it in peace.

Under the end of a stone lying in the bed of the stream, something was floating in the pure current, which at first seemed like the tail of a fish, and being desirous to obtain a better view, I gently raised the stone on its edge, and was rewarded by a very beautiful sight. The object first observed was the tail of a beautiful salamander, whose sides were of a pale straw color, flecked with circlets of the richest crimson. Its long lizard like body seemed to be semitransparent, and its slender limbs appeared like mere productions of the skin. Not far distant, and near where the upper end of the stone had been, lay crouched, as if asleep, one of the most beautifully colored frogs I had ever beheld. Its body was slender compared with most frogs, and its skin covered with stripes of bright reddish brown and grayish green, in such a manner as to recall the beautiful markings of the tiger's hide; and since the time alluded to, it has received the name of *Tigrina* from Leconte, its first scientific describer. How long I should have been content to gaze at these beautiful animals, as they lay basking in the living water, I know not, had not the intense heat made me feel the necessity of seeking a shade. It was now past 12 o'clock, I began to retrace my steps towards the city; and without any particular object moved along by the little galleries examined in the morning. I had advanced but a short distance, when I found the last place where I had broken open the gallery was *repaired.* The earth was perfectly fresh, and I had lost the chance of discovering the miner, while watching my new acquaintances in the stream. Hurrying onward, the same circumstance uniformly presented; the injuries were all efficiently repaired, and had evidently been very recently completed. Here was one point gained; it was ascertained that these galleries were still inhabited, and I hoped soon to become acquainted with the inmates. But at this time, it appeared fruitless to delay longer, and I returned home, filled with anticipations of pleasure from the success of my future researches. These I shall relate on another occasion, if such narrations as the present be thought of sufficient interest to justify their presentation to the reader. . . .

Ramble Number Four

My next visit to my old hunting ground, the lane and brook, happened on a day in the first hay harvest, when the verdant sward of the meadows was rapidly sinking before the keen edged scythes swung by vigorous mowers. This unexpected circumstance afforded me considerable pleasure, for it promised me a freer scope to my wanderings, and might also enable me to ascertain various particulars, concerning which my curiosity had long been awakened. Nor was this promise unattended by fruition of my wishes. The reader may recollect, that, in my first walk, a neat burrow in the grass, above ground, was observed, without my knowing its author. The advance of the mowers explained this satisfactorily, for in cutting the long grass, they exposed several nests of field mice, which, by means of these grass-covered alleys, passed to the stream in search of food or drink, unseen by their enemies, the hawks and owls. The numbers of these little creatures were truly surprising; their fecundity is so great, and their food so abundant, that were they not preyed upon by many other animals, and destroyed in great numbers by man, they would become exceedingly troublesome. There are various species of them, all bearing a very considerable resemblance to each other, and having to an incidental observer much of the appearance of the domestic mouse. Slight attention, however, is requisite to perceive very striking differences, and the discrimination of these will prove a source of considerable gratification to the enquirer. The nests are very nicely made, and look much like a bird's nest, being lined with soft materials, and usually placed in some snug little hollow, or at the root of a strong tuft of grass. Upon the grass roots and seeds these nibblers principally feed; and where very abundant, the effects of their hunger may be seen in the brown and withered aspect of the grass they have injured at the root. But under ordinary circumstances, the hawks, owls, domestic cat, weasels, crows, &c. keep them in such limits, as prevent them from doing essential damage.

I had just observed another and a smaller grassy covered way, where the mowers had passed along, when my attention was called towards a wagon at a short distance, which was receiving its load. Shouts and laughter, accompanied by a general running and scrambling of the people, indicated that some rare sport was going forward. When I approached, I found that the object of chase was a jumping mouse, whose actions it was truly delightful to witness. When not closely pressed by its pursuers, it ran with some rapidity in the usual manner, as if seeking concealment. But in a moment it would vault into the air, and skim along for ten or twelve feet, looking more like a bird than a little quadruped. After continuing this for some time, and nearly exhausting its pursuers with running and falling over each other, the frightened creature was accidentally struck down by one of the workmen, during one of its beautiful leaps, and killed. As the hunters saw nothing worthy of attention in the dead body of the animal, they very willingly resigned it to me; and with great satisfaction I retreated to a willow shade, to read what nature had written in its form for my instruction. The general appearance was mouse-like; but the length and slenderness of the body, the shortness of its fore limbs, and the disproportionate length of its hind limbs, together with the peculiarity of its tail, all indicated its adaptation to the peculiar kind of action I had just witnessed. A sight of this little creature vaulting or bounding through the air, strongly reminded me of what I had read of the great kangaroo of New Holland; and I could not help regarding our little jumper as in some respects a sort of miniature resemblance of that curious animal. It was not evident, however, that the jumping mouse derived the aid from its tail, which so powerfully assists the kangaroo. Though long and sufficiently stout in proportion, it had none of the robust muscularity which, in the New Holland animal, impels the lower part of the body immediately upward. In this mouse, the leap is principally, if not entirely effected by a sudden and violent extension of the long hind limbs, the muscles of which are strong, and admirably suited to their object. We have heard that these little animals feed on the roots, &c. of the green herbage, and that they are every season to be found in the meadows. It may perhaps puzzle some to imagine how they subsist through the severities of winter, when vegetation is at rest, and the earth generally frozen. Here we find another occasion to admire the all-perfect designs of the awful Author of nature, who has endowed a great number of animals with the faculty of retiring into the earth, and passing whole months in a state of repose so complete, as to allow all the functions of the body to be suspended, until the returning warmth of the spring calls them forth to renewed activity and enjoyment. The jumping mouse, when the chill weather begins to draw nigh, digs down about six or eight inches into the soil, and there forms a little globular cell, as much larger than his own body as will allow a sufficient covering of fine grass to be introduced. This being obtained, he contrives to coil up his body and limbs in the center of the soft dry grass, so as to form a complete ball; and so compact is this, that, when taken out, with the torpid animal, it may be rolled across a floor without injury. In this snug cell, which is soon filled up and closed externally, the jumping mouse securely abides through all the frosts and storms of winter, needing neither food nor fuel, being utterly quiescent, and apparently dead, though susceptible at any time of reanimation, by being very gradually stimulated by light and heat.

The little burrow under examination, when called to observe the jumping mouse, proved to be made by the merry musicians of the meadows, the field crickets, *acheta campestris*. These lively black crickets are very numerous, and contribute very largely to that general song which is so delightful to the ear of the true lover of nature, as it rises on the air from myriads of happy creatures rejoicing amid the bounties conferred on them by Providence. It is not *a voice* that the crickets utter, but a regular vibration of musical chords, produced by nibbing the nervures of the elytra against a sort of network intended to produce the vibrations. The reader will find an excellent description of the apparatus in Kirby and Spence's book, but he may enjoy a much more satisfactory comprehension of the whole, by visiting the field cricket in his summer residence, see him tuning his viol, and awakening the echoes with his music. By such an examination as may be there obtained, he may derive more knowledge than by frequent perusal of the most eloquent writings, and perhaps observe circumstances which the learned authors are utterly ignorant of.

Washington Irving
(1783–1859)

Author of the tales "Rip Van Winkle" and "The Legend of Sleepy Hollow," New Yorker Washington Irving was among the best-loved, most prolific, and best-selling American writers of the early nineteenth century, and he was the first American fiction writer to win international acclaim. In his own day, Irving was an American celebrity—an urbane gentleman lawyer, historian, satirist, and diplomat widely admired for his sharp wit and graceful literary style. Although Irving's most memorable fiction is noteworthy for its pioneering use of American rural and wilderness settings, Irving himself was neither explorer nor naturalist; instead, this highly polished literary luminary spent much of his life living and traveling in the civilized society and pastoral countryside of Europe. It was upon his return, in 1832, from a seventeen-year residence abroad that Irving immediately resolved upon going west to spend the fall amid the oceanic plains landscapes then being celebrated in such works as James Fenimore Cooper's novel *The Prairie* (1826). Irving and several companions went first to Cincinnati, then traveled down the Ohio and up the Mississippi to St. Louis, and from there rode horseback across the present state of Missouri before launching in earnest onto the Great Plains. Traveling with a government commission deep into Indian Territory, Irving made it as far west as present-day western Oklahoma on his journey, which he recorded in a series of field notebooks. Material from the "Western Notebooks" was later crafted into the painterly prose and dynamic adventure narrative *A Tour on the Prairies* (1835), a book so successful that Irving quickly followed it with several other Western works: *Astoria* . . . (1836) and *The Adventures of Captain Bonneville* . . . (1837). Before leaving on his Western journey, Irving had written that his goal was to "see those fine countries of the 'far west,' while still in a state of pristine wildness, and behold herds of buffaloes scouring their native prairies, before they are driven beyond the reach of a civilized tourist." As the following account of his first successful buffalo hunt shows, Irving the "civilized tourist" did accomplish his goal — but not without contributing to the destruction of the "pristine wildness" whose disappearance he professed to lament.

From *A Tour on the Prairies* (1835)

The Grand Prairie — A Buffalo Hunt

After proceeding about two hours in a southerly direction, we emerged toward midday from the dreary belt of the Cross Timber, and to our infinite delight beheld "the great Prairie" stretching to the right and left before us. We could distinctly trace the meandering course of the main Canadian, and various smaller streams, by the strips of green forest that bordered them. The landscape was vast and beautiful. There is always an expansion of feeling in looking upon these boundless and fertile wastes; but I was doubly conscious of it after emerging from our "close dungeon of innumerous boughs."

From a rising ground Beatte pointed out the place where he and his comrades had killed the buffaloes; and we beheld several black objects moving in the distance, which he said were part of the herd. The Captain determined to shape his course to a woody bottom about a mile distant, and to encamp there for a day or two, by way of having a regular buffalo hunt, and getting a supply of provisions. As the troop defiled along the slope of the hill toward the camping ground, Beatte proposed to my messmates and myself, that we should put ourselves under his guidance, promising to take us where we should have plenty of sport. Leaving the line of march, therefore, we diverged toward the prairie; traversing a small valley, and ascending a gentle swell of land. As we reached the summit, we beheld a gang of wild horses about a mile off. Beatte was immediately on the alert, and no longer thought of buffalo hunting. He was mounted on his powerful half-wild horse, with a lariat coiled at the saddlebow, and set off in pursuit; while we remained on a rising ground watching his maneuvers with great solicitude. Taking advantage of a strip of woodland, he stole quietly along, so as to get close to them before he was perceived. The moment they caught sight of him a grand scamper took place. We watched him skirting along the horizon like a privateer in full chase of a merchantman; at length he passed over the brow of a ridge, and down into a shallow valley; in a few moments he was on the opposite hill, and close upon one of the horses. He was soon head and head, and appeared to be trying to noose his prey; but they both disappeared again below the hill, and we saw no more of them. It turned out afterward that he had noosed a powerful horse, but could not hold him, and had lost his lariat in the attempt.

While we were waiting for his return, we perceived two buffalo bulls descending a slope, toward a stream, which wound through a ravine fringed with trees. The young Count and myself endeavored to get near them under covert of the trees. They discovered us while we were yet three or four hundred yards off, and turning about, retreated up the rising ground. We urged our horses across the ravine, and gave chase. The immense weight of head and shoulders, causes the buffalo to labor heavily uphill; but it accelerates his descent. We had the advantage, therefore, and gained rapidly upon the fugitives, though it was difficult to get our horses to approach them, their very scent inspiring them with terror. The Count, who had a double-barreled gun loaded with ball, fired, but it missed. The bulls now altered their course, and galloped downhill with headlong rapidity. As they ran in different directions, we each singled one and separated. I was provided with a brace of veteran brass-barreled pistols, which I had borrowed at Fort Gibson, and which had evidently seen some service. Pistols are very effective in buffalo hunting, as the hunter can ride up close to the animal, and fire at it while at full speed; whereas the long heavy rifles used on the frontier, cannot be easily managed, nor discharged with accurate aim from horseback. My object, therefore, was to get within pistol shot of the buffalo. This was no very easy matter. I was well mounted on a horse of excellent speed and bottom, that seemed eager for the chase, and soon overtook the game; but the moment he came nearly parallel, he would keep sheering off, with ears forked and pricked forward, and every symptom of aversion and alarm. It was no wonder. Of all animals, a buffalo, when close pressed by the hunter, has an aspect the most diabolical. His two short black horns, curve out of a huge frontlet of shaggy hair; his eyes glow like coals; his mouth is open, his tongue parched and drawn up into a half crescent; his tail is erect, and tufted and whisking about in the air, he is a perfect picture of mingled rage and terror.

It was with difficulty I urged my horse sufficiently near, when, taking aim, to my chagrin, both pistols missed fire. Unfortunately the locks of these veteran weapons were so much worn, that in the gallop, the priming had been shaken out of the pans. At the snapping of the last pistol I was close upon the buffalo, when, in his despair, he turned round with a sudden snort and rushed upon me. My horse wheeled about as if on a pivot, made a convulsive spring, and, as I had been leaning on one side with pistol extended, I came near being thrown at the feet of the buffalo.

Three or four bounds of the horse carried us out of the reach of the enemy; who, having merely turned in desperate self-defense, quickly resumed his flight. As soon as I could gather in my panic-stricken horse, and prime the pistols afresh, I again spurred in pursuit of the buffalo, who had slackened his speed to take breath. On my approach he again set off full tilt, heaving himself forward with a heavy rolling gallop, dashing with headlong precipitation through brakes and ravines, while several deer and wolves, startled from their coverts by his thundering career, ran helter-skelter to right and left across the waste.

A gallop across the prairies in pursuit of game is by no means so smooth a career as those may imagine, who have only the idea of an open level plain. It is true, the prairies of the hunting ground are not so much entangled with flowering plants and long herbage as the lower prairies, and are principally covered with short buffalo grass; but they are diversified by hill and dale, and where most level, are apt to be cut up by deep rifts and ravines, made by torrents after rains; and which, yawning from an even surface, are almost like pitfalls in the way of the hunter, checking him suddenly, when in full career, or subjecting him to the risk of limb and life. The plains, too, are beset by burrowing holes of small animals, in which the horse is apt to sink to the fetlock, and throw both himself and his rider. The late rain had covered some parts of the prairie, where the ground was hard, with a thin sheet of water, through which the horse had to splash his way. In other parts there were innumerable shallow hollows, eight or ten feet in diameter, made by the buffaloes, who wallow in sand and mud like swine. These being filled with water, shone like mirrors, so that the horse was continually leaping over them or springing on one side. We had reached, too, a rough part of the prairie, very much broken and cut up; the buffalo, who was running for his life, took no heed of his course, plunging down breakneck ravines, where it was necessary to skirt the borders in search of a safer descent. At length we came to where a winter stream had torn a deep chasm across the whole prairie, leaving open jagged rocks, and forming a long glen bordered by steep crumbling cliffs of mingled stone and clay. Down one of these the buffalo flung himself, half tumbling, half leaping, and then scuttled along the bottom; while I, seeing all further pursuit useless, pulled up, and gazed quietly after him from the border of the cliff, until he disappeared amidst the windings of the ravine.

Nothing now remained but to turn my steed and rejoin my companions. Here at first was some little difficulty. The ardor of the chase had betrayed me into a long, heedless gallop. I now found myself in the midst of a lonely waste, in which the prospect was bounded by undulating swells of land, naked and uniform, where, from the deficiency of landmarks and distinct features, an inexperienced man may become bewildered, and lose his way as readily as in the wastes of the ocean. The day, too, was overcast, so that I could not guide myself by the sun; my only mode was to retrace the track my horse had made in coming, though this I would often lose sight of, where the ground was covered with parched herbage.

To one unaccustomed to it, there is something inexpressibly lonely in the solitude of a prairie. The loneliness of a forest seems nothing to it. There the view is shut in by trees, and the imagination is left free to picture some livelier scene beyond. But here we have an immense extent of landscape without a sign of human existence. We have the consciousness of being far, far beyond the bounds of human habitation; we feel as if moving in the midst of a desert world. As my horse lagged slowly back over the scenes of our late scamper, and the delirium of the chase had passed away, I was peculiarly sensible to these circumstances. The silence of the waste was now and then broken by the cry of a distant flock of pelicans, stalking like specters about a shallow pool; sometimes by the sinister croaking of a raven in the air, while occasionally a scoundrel wolf would scour off from before me; and, having attained a safe distance, would sit down and howl and whine with tones that gave a dreariness to the surrounding solitude.

After pursuing my way for some time, I descried a horseman on the edge of a distant hill, and soon recognized him to be the Count. He had been equally unsuccessful with myself; we were shortly after rejoined by our worthy comrade, the Virtuoso, who, with spectacles on nose, had made two or three ineffectual shots from horseback.

We determined not to seek the camp until we had made one more effort. Casting our eyes about the surrounding waste, we descried a herd of buffalo about two miles distant, scattered apart, and quietly grazing near a small strip of trees and bushes. It required but little stretch of fancy to picture them so many cattle grazing on the edge of a common, and that the grove might shelter some lowly farmhouse.

We now formed our plan to circumvent the herd, and by getting on the other side of them, to hunt them in the direction where we knew our camp to be situated: otherwise, the pursuit might take us to such a distance as to render it impossible to find our way back before nightfall. Taking a wide circuit, therefore, we moved slowly and cautiously, pausing occasionally, when we saw any of the herd desist from grazing. The wind fortunately set from them, otherwise they might have scented us and have taken the alarm. In this way, we succeeded in getting round the herd without disturbing it. It consisted of about forty head, bulls, cows, and calves. Separating to some distance from each other, we now approached slowly in a parallel line, hoping by degrees to steal near without exciting attention. They began, however, to move off quietly, stopping at every step or two to graze, when suddenly a bull that, unobserved by us, had been taking his siesta under a clump of trees to our left, roused himself from his lair, and hastened to join his companions. We were still at a considerable distance, but the game had taken the alarm. We quickened our pace, they broke into a gallop, and now commenced a full chase.

As the ground was level, they shouldered along with great speed, following each other in a line; two or three bulls bringing up the rear, the last of whom, from his enormous size and venerable frontlet, and beard of sunburnt hair, looked like the patriarch of the herd; and as if he might long have reigned the monarch of the prairie.

There is a mixture of the awful and the comic in the look of these huge animals, as they bear their great bulk forward, with an up and down motion of the unwieldy head and shoulders; their tail cocked up like the queue of Pantaloon in a pantomime, the end whisking about in a fierce yet whimsical style, and their eyes glaring venomously with an expression of fright and fury.

For some time I kept parallel with the line, without being able to force my horse within pistol shot, so much had he been alarmed by the assault of the buffalo in the preceding chase. At length I succeeded, but was again balked by my pistols missing fire. My companions, whose horses were less fleet, and more wayworn, could not overtake the herd; at length Mr. L., who was in the rear of the line, and losing ground, leveled his double-barreled gun, and fired a long raking shot. It struck a buffalo just above the loins, broke its backbone, and brought it to the ground. He stopped and alighted to dispatch his prey, when borrowing his gun, which had yet a charge remaining in it, I put my horse to his speed, again overtook the herd which was thundering along, pursued by the Count. With my present weapon there was no need of urging my horse to such close quarters; galloping along parallel, therefore, I singled out a buffalo, and by a fortunate shot brought it down on the spot. The ball had struck a vital part; it could not move from the place where it fell, but lay there struggling in mortal agony, while the rest of the herd kept on their headlong career across the prairie.

Dismounting, I now fettered my horse to prevent his straying, and advanced to contemplate my victim. I am nothing of a sportsman; I had been prompted to this unwonted exploit by the magnitude of the game, and the excitement of an adventurous chase. Now that the excitement was over, I could not but look with commiseration upon the poor animal that lay struggling and bleeding at my feet. His very size and importance, which had before inspired me with eagerness, now increased my compunction. It seemed as if I had inflicted pain in proportion to the bulk of my victim, and as if there were a hundred-fold greater waste of life than there would have been in the destruction of an animal of inferior size.

To add to these after-qualms of conscience, the poor animal lingered in his agony. He had evidently received a mortal wound, but death might be long in coming. It would not do to leave him here to be torn piecemeal, while yet alive, by the wolves that had already snuffed his blood, and were skulking and howling at a distance, and waiting for my departure; and by the ravens that were flapping about, croaking dismally in the air. It became now an act of mercy to give him his quietus, and put him out of his misery. I primed one of the pistols, therefore, and advanced close up to the buffalo. To inflict a wound thus in cool blood, I found a totally different thing from firing in the heat of the chase. Taking aim, however, just behind the fore-shoulder, my pistol for once proved true; the ball must have passed through the heart, for the animal gave one convulsive throe and expired.

While I stood meditating and moralizing over the wreck I had so wantonly produced, with my horse grazing near me, I was rejoined by my fellow sportsman, the Virtuoso; who, being a man of universal adroitness, and withal, more experienced and hardened in the gentle art of "venery," soon managed to carve out the tongue of the buffalo, and delivered it to me to bear back to the camp as a trophy.

Thomas Cole
(1801–1848)

Like John James Audubon before him, Thomas Cole was better known as a painter than as a writer. Widely recognized as the founder of the influential style of American Romantic landscape painting associated with the Hudson River School — which also included Asher Durand, J. F. Kensett, Jasper Cropsey, and Cole's protégé, Frederic Church — Cole helped turn the creative resources of American artists from imitation of European models toward the sublime beauty of their own land. In a series of paintings depicting the wilderness of the Hudson River Valley, the Catskills, and the White Mountains, he represented American nature as a lovely, dynamic, and dramatic green world in which the human presence was radically deemphasized and the sense of divinity in wilderness was the implied subject. Although he was a painter, Cole was closely connected with the literary figures of his place and time, especially fellow New Yorkers Washington Irving, James Fenimore Cooper, and

William Cullen Bryant. Cole actually based several paintings solely upon descriptions of the Catskill Mountains that appeared in Cooper's novels, and his friendship with Bryant was so close that Asher Durand celebrated it in *Kindred Spirits* (1849), a now famous painting depicting Cole and Bryant standing together in the timeless American wilderness. But *Kindred Spirits* depicts more than simply friendship, for it also symbolizes the kinship between nature writing and landscape painting during the early and mid–nineteenth century. Cole's artistic project was akin to that of such wilderness romanticizers as Cooper and Bryant, but it was also closely related to the Transcendentalists' approach: like Emerson and Thoreau, Cole placed before Americans the grandeur of their own national landscape, compelling them to see their native land as an aesthetic, cultural, and spiritual resource. In his influential "Essay on American Scenery," which first appeared in *American Monthly Magazine* in 1836 (the same year Emerson's *Nature* was published), Cole's energetic nationalist agenda is to redeem the maligned American landscape from unexamined assumptions regarding the superiority of European landscapes. He insists not only that American lands are lovely "scenes of solitude," but that they are "undefiled works" through which we see the infinite creativity of God the landscape artist.

From "Essay on American Scenery" (1836)

The Essay, which is here offered, is a mere sketch of an almost illimitable subject—American Scenery; and in selecting the theme the writer placed more confidence in its overflowing richness, than in his own capacity for treating it in a manner worthy of its vastness and importance.

It is a subject that to every American ought to be of surpassing interest; for, whether he beholds the Hudson mingling waters with the Atlantic—explores the central wilds of this vast continent, or stands on the margin of the distant Oregon, he is still in the midst of American scenery—it is his own land; its beauty, its magnificence, its sublimity—all are his; and how undeserving of such a birthright, if he can turn towards it an unobserving eye, an unaffected heart!

Before entering into the proposed subject, in which I shall treat more particularly of the scenery of the Northern and Eastern States, I shall be excused for saying a few words on the advantages of cultivating a taste for scenery, and for exclaiming against the apathy with which the beauties of external nature are regarded by the great mass, even of our refined community.

It is generally admitted that the liberal arts tend to soften our manners; but they do more—they carry with them the power to mend our hearts.

Poetry and Painting sublime and purify thought, by grasping the past, the present, and the future—they give the mind a foretaste of its immortality, and thus prepare it for performing an exalted part amid the realities of life. And *rural nature* is full of the same quickening spirit — it is, in fact, the exhaustless mine from which the poet and the painter have brought such wondrous treasures — an unfailing fountain of intellectual enjoyment, where all may drink, and be awakened to a deeper feeling of the works of genius, and a keener perception of the beauty of our existence. For those whose days are all consumed in the low pursuits of avarice, or the gaudy frivolities of fashion, unobservant of nature's loveliness, are unconscious of the harmony of creation —

> Heaven's roof to them
> Is but a painted ceiling hung with lamps;
> No more — that lights them to their purposes —
> They wander 'loose about'; they nothing see,
> Themselves except, and creatures like themselves,
> Short lived, short sighted.

What to them is the page of the poet where he describes or personifies the skies, the mountains, or the streams, if those objects themselves have never awakened observation or excited pleasure? What to them is the wild Salvator Rosa, or the aerial Claude Lorrain?

There is in the human mind an almost inseparable connection between the beautiful and the good, so that if we contemplate the one the other seems present; and an excellent author has said, "it is difficult to look at any objects with pleasure — unless where it arises from brutal and tumultuous emotions — without feeling that disposition of mind which tends towards kindness and benevolence; and surely, whatever creates such a disposition, by increasing our pleasures and enjoyments, cannot be too much cultivated."

It would seem unnecessary to those who can see and feel, for me to expatiate on the loveliness of verdant fields, the sublimity of lofty mountains, or the varied magnificence of the sky; but that the number of those who *seek* enjoyment in such sources is comparatively small. From the indifference with which the multitude regard the beauties of nature, it might be inferred that she had been unnecessarily lavish in adorning this world for beings who take no pleasure in its adornment. Who in groveling pursuits forget their glorious heritage. Why was the earth made so beautiful, or the sun so clad in glory at his rising and setting, when *all* might be unrobed of beauty without affecting the insensate multitude, so they can be "lighted to their purposes?"

It *has not* been in vain — the good, the enlightened of all ages and nations, have found pleasure and consolation in the beauty of the rural earth. Prophets of old retired into the solitudes of nature to wait the inspiration of heaven. It was on Mount

Horeb that Elijah witnessed the mightly wind, the earthquake, and the fire; and heard the "still small voice"—that voice is YET heard among the mountains! St. John preached in the desert;—the wilderness is YET a fitting place to speak of God. The solitary Anchorites of Syria and Egypt, though ignorant that the busy world is man's noblest sphere of usefulness, well knew how congenial to religious musings are the pathless solitudes.

He who looks on nature with a "loving eye," cannot move from his dwelling without the salutation of beauty; even in the city the deep blue sky and the drifting clouds appeal to him. And if to escape its turmoil — if only to obtain a free horizon, land and water in the play of light and shadow yields delight—let him be transported to those favored regions, where the features of the earth are more varied, or yet add the sunset, that wreath of glory daily bound around the world, and he, indeed, drinks from pleasure's purest cup. The delight such a man experiences is not merely sensual, or selfish, that passes with the occasion leaving no trace behind; but in gazing on the pure creations of the Almighty, he feels a calm religious tone steal through his mind, and when he has turned to mingle with his fellow men, the chords which have been struck in that sweet communion cease not to vibrate.

In what has been said I have alluded to wild and uncultivated scenery; but the cultivated must not be forgotten, for it is still more important to man in his social capacity — necessarily bringing him in contact with the cultured; it encompasses our homes, and, though devoid of the stern sublimity of the wild, its quieter spirit steals tenderly into our bosoms mingled with a thousand domestic affections and heart-touching associations — human hands have wrought, and human deeds hallowed all around.

And it is here that taste, which is the perception of the beautiful, and the knowledge of the principles on which nature works, can be applied, and our dwelling-places made fitting for refined and intellectual beings.

If, then, it is indeed true that the contemplation of scenery can be so abundant a source of delight and improvement, a taste for it is certainly worthy of particular cultivation; for the capacity for enjoyment increases with the knowledge of the true means of obtaining it.

In this age, when a meager utilitarianism seems ready to absorb every feeling and sentiment, and what is sometimes called improvement in its march makes us fear that the bright and tender flowers of the imagination shall all be crushed beneath its iron tramp, it would be well to cultivate the oasis that yet remains to us, and thus preserve the germs of a future and a purer system. And now, when the sway of fashion is extending widely over society — poisoning the healthful streams of true refinement, and turning men from the love of simplicity and beauty, to a senseless idolatry of their own follies — to lead them gently into the pleasant paths of Taste would be an object worthy of the highest efforts of genius and benevolence. The spirit of our society is to contrive but not to enjoy—toiling to produce more toil—accumulating in order to aggrandize. The pleasures of the imagination, among which the love of scenery holds a conspicuous place, will alone temper the harshness of such a state; and, like the atmosphere that softens the most rugged forms of the landscape, cast a veil of tender beauty over the asperities of life.

Did our limits permit I would endeavor more fully to show how necessary to the complete appreciation of the Fine Arts is the study of scenery, and how conducive to our happiness and well-being is that study and those arts; but I must now proceed to the proposed subject of this essay—American Scenery!

There are those who through ignorance or prejudice strive to maintain that American scenery possesses little that is interesting or truly beautiful—that it is rude without picturesqueness, and monotonous without sublimity—that being destitute of those vestiges of antiquity whose associations so strongly affect the mind, it may not be compared with European scenery. But from whom do these opinions come? From those who have read of European scenery, of Grecian mountains, and Italian skies, and never troubled themselves to look at their own; and from those traveled ones whose eyes were never opened to the beauties of nature until they beheld foreign lands, and when those lands faded from the sight were again closed and forever; disdaining to destroy their transatlantic impressions by the observation of the less fashionable and unfamed American scenery. Let such persons shut themselves up in their narrow shell of prejudice—I hope they are few,—and the community increasing in intelligence, will know better how to appreciate the treasures of their own country.

I am by no means desirous of lessening in your estimation the glorious scenes of the old world—that ground which has been the great theater of human events—those mountains, woods, and streams, made sacred in our minds by heroic deeds and immortal song—over which time and genius have suspended an imperishable halo. No! But I would have it remembered that nature has shed over *this* land beauty and magnificence, and although the character of its scenery may differ from the old world's, yet inferiority must not therefore be inferred; for though American scenery is destitute of many of those circumstances that give value to the European, still it has features, and glorious ones, unknown to Europe.

A very few generations have passed away since this vast tract of the American continent, now the United States, rested in the shadow of primeval forests, whose gloom was peopled by savage beasts, and scarcely less savage men; or lay in those wide grassy plains called prairies—

> The Gardens of the Desert, these
> The unshorn fields, boundless and beautiful.

And, although an enlightened and increasing people have broken in upon the solitude, and with activity and power wrought changes that seem magical, yet the most distinctive, and perhaps the most impressive, characteristic of American scenery is its wildness.

It is the most distinctive, because in civilized Europe the primitive features of scenery have long since been destroyed or modified—the extensive forests that once overshadowed a great part of it have been felled—rugged mountains have been smoothed, and impetuous rivers turned from their courses to accommodate the tastes and necessities of a dense population—the once tangled wood is now a grassy lawn; the turbulent brook a navigable stream—crags that could not be removed have been crowned with towers, and the rudest valleys tamed by the plow.

And to this cultivated state our western world is fast approaching; but nature is still predominant, and there are those who regret that with the improvements of cultivation the sublimity of the wilderness should pass away: for those scenes of solitude from which the hand of nature has never been lifted, affect the mind with a more deep toned emotion than aught which the hand of man has touched. Amid them the consequent associations are of God the creator—they are his undefiled works, and the mind is cast into the contemplation of eternal things. . . .

Yet I cannot but express my sorrow that the beauty of such landscapes are quickly passing away—the ravages of the axe are daily increasing—the most noble scenes are made desolate, and oftentimes with a wantonness and barbarism scarcely credible in a civilized nation. The wayside is becoming shadeless, and another generation will behold spots, now rife with beauty, desecrated by what is called improvement; which, as yet, generally destroys Nature's beauty without substituting that of Art. This is a regret rather than a complaint; such is the road society has to travel; it may lead to refinement in the end, but the traveler who sees the place of rest close at hand, dislikes the road that has so many unnecessary windings.

I will now conclude, in the hope that, though feebly urged, the importance of cultivating a taste for scenery will not be forgotten. Nature has spread for us a rich and delightful banquet. Shall we turn from it? We are still in Eden; the wall that shuts us out of the garden is our own ignorance and folly.

Harriet Martineau
(1802–1876)

The author of more than fifty books and fifteen hundred articles on a wide range of subjects including politics, economics, and public policy, Harriet Martineau was among the most prolific women writers of the nineteenth century. Born in Norwich, England, to a Unitarian family with French Huguenot roots, she was unusually well educated for a woman of the period (she claimed, for example, that she could "think in Latin"), and she began publishing articles while still a teenager. Although she was ill and deaf for much of her life—and, indeed, was a complete invalid for a number of years until, by her own account, she was cured by mesmerism—Martineau was a tenacious woman and an energetic social reformer who remained productive throughout her life. The first of her many books, *Illustrations of Political Economy* (1832–34), was so successful that it enabled her to make a two-year journey to America in 1834–36. During her travels Martineau was a courageously outspoken critic of the oppression of African Americans and women—arguing, for example, that American women deserved better access to education, so that "marriage need not be their only object in life." Of the two books Martineau wrote about her experiences in America, *Society in America* (1837) includes a strong abolitionist critique of American political economy, while *Retrospect of Western Travel* (1838) is a more personal and more lyrical account of the landscapes she visited. In the following excerpts from *Retrospect*, we see the unique perspective of a British woman traveler on the Mississippi River during the mid–nineteenth century. And although Martineau's feminist critique of American society is implicit in certain of her comments about fellow passengers on the voyage, the heart of her travel writing is her keen appreciation for the beauty of the land. After her American tour Martineau returned to Europe and settled in the English Lake District near Windermere, where she spent the rest of her life writing and socializing with visitors including William and Dorothy Wordsworth, Thomas Carlyle, Charlotte Brontë, and George Eliot.

From *Retrospect of Western Travel* (1838)

This morning we seemed to be lost among islands in a waste of waters. The vastness of the river now began to bear upon our imaginations. The flatboats we met looked as if they were at the mercy of the floods, their long oars bending like straws in the current. They are so picturesque, however, and there is something so fanciful in the canopy of green boughs under which the floating voyagers repose during the heat of the day, that some of us proposed building a flatboat on the Ohio, and floating down to New Orleans at our leisure.

Adams Fort, in the state of Mississippi, afforded the most beautiful view we had yet seen on the river. The swelling hills, dropped with wood, closed in a reach of the waters, and gave them the appearance of a lake. White houses nestled in the clumps; goats, black and white, browsed on the points of the many hills; and a perfect harmony of coloring dissolved the whole into something like a dream. This last charm is as striking to us as any in the vast wilderness through which the "Father of Waters" takes his way. Even the turbid floods, varying their hues with the changes of light and shadow, are a fit element of the picture, and no one wishes them other than they are.

In the afternoon we ran over a log; the vessel trembled to her center; the ladies raised their heads from their work; the gentlemen looked overboard; and I saw our yawl snagged as she was careering at the stern. The sharp end of the log pricked through her bottom as if she had been made of brown paper. She was dragged after us, full of water, till we stopped at the evening wooding-place, when I ran to the hurricane deck to see her pulled up on shore and mended. There I found the wind so high that it appeared to me equally impossible to keep my seat and to get down; my feather-fan blew away, and I expected to follow it myself—so strangling was the gust—one of the puffs which take the voyager by surprise amid the windings of this forest-banked river. The yawl was patched up in a surprisingly short time. The deck passengers clustered round to lend a hand, and the blows of the mallet resounded fitfully along the shore as the gust came and passed over. . . .

In the evening only one firefly was visible; the moon was misty, and faint lightning flashed incessantly. Before morning the weather was so cold that we shut our windows, and the next day there was a fire in the ladies' cabin. Such are the changes of temperature in this region.

The quantity of driftwood that we encountered above Natchez was amazing. Some of it was whirling slowly down with the current, but much more was entangled in the bays of the islands, and detained in incessant accumulation. It can scarcely be any longer necessary to explain that it is a mistake to suppose this driftwood to be the foundation of the islands of the Mississippi. Having itself no foundation, it could not serve any such purpose. The islands are formed by deposits of soil brought down from above by the strong force of the waters. The accumulation proceeds till it reaches the surface, when the seeds contained in the soil, or borne to it by the winds, sprout, and bind the soft earth by a network of roots, thus providing a basis for a stronger vegetation every year. It is no wonder that superficial observers have fallen into this error respecting the origin of the new lands of the

Mississippi, the rafts of driftwood look so like incipient islands; and when one is fixed in a picturesque situation, the gazer longs to heap earth upon it, and clothe it with shrubbery. . . .

I believe it was about three hours after midnight when I was awakened by a tremendous and unaccountable noise overhead. It was most like plowing through a forest, and crashing all the trees down. The lady who shared my stateroom was up, pale and frightened, and lights were moving in the ladies' cabin. I did not choose to cause alarm by inquiry; but the motion of the boat was so strange, that I thought it must waken everyone on board. The commotion lasted, I should think, about twenty minutes, when I suppose it subsided, for I fell asleep. In the morning I was shown the remains of hailstones, which must have been of an enormous size, to judge by what was left of them at the end of three hours. Mr. E. told me that we had been in the utmost danger for above a quarter of an hour, from one of the irresistible squalls to which this navigation is liable. Both the pilots had been blown away from the helm, and were obliged to leave the vessel to its fate. It was impossible to preserve a footing for an instant on the top; and the poor passengers who lay there had attempted to come down, bruised with the tremendous hail (which caused the noise we could not account for), and seeing, with the pilot, no other probability than that the hurricane deck would be blown completely away; but there was actually no standing room for these men, and they had to remain above and take their chance. The vessel drove madly from side to side of the dangerous channel, and the pilots expected every moment that she would founder. I find that we usually made much more way by night than by day, the balance of the boat being kept even while the passengers are equally dispersed and quiet, instead of running from side to side, or crowding the one gallery and deserting the other.

I was on the lookout for alligators all the way up the river, but could never see one. A deck passenger declared that a small specimen slipped off a log into the water one day when nobody else was looking; but his companions supposed he might be mistaken, as alligators are now rarely seen in this region. Terrapins were very numerous, sometimes sunning themselves on floating logs, and sometimes swimming, with only their pert little heads visible above water. Wood pigeons might be seen flitting in the forest when we were so close under the banks as to pry into the shades, and the beautiful blue jay often gleamed before our eyes. No object was more striking than the canoes which we frequently saw, looking fearfully light and frail amid the strong current. The rower used a spoon-shaped paddle, and advanced with amazing swiftness; sometimes crossing before our bows, sometimes darting along under the bank, sometimes shooting across a track of moonlight. Very often there was only one person in the canoe, as in the instance I have elsewhere mentioned of a woman who was supposed to be going on a visit twenty or thirty miles up the stream. I could hardly have conceived of a solitude so intense as this appeared to me, the being alone on that rushing sea of waters, shut in by untrodden forests; the slow fish hawk wheeling overhead, and perilous masses of driftwood whirling down the current; trunks obviously uprooted by the forces of nature, and not laid low by the hand of man. What a spectacle must our boat, with its gay crowds, have appeared to such a solitary! what a revelation that there was a busy world still stirring somewhere; a fact which, I think, I should soon discredit if I lived in the depths of this wilderness, for life would become tolerable there only by the spirit growing into harmony with the scene, wild and solemn as the objects around it.

The morning after the storm the landscape looked its wildest. The clouds were drifting away, and a sungleam came out as I was peeping into the forest at the wooding-place. The vines look beautiful on the black trunks of the trees after rain. Scarcely a habitation was to be seen, and it was like being set back to the days of creation, we passed so many islands in every stage of growth. I spent part of the morning with the L.'s, and we were more than once alarmed by a fearful scream, followed by a trampling and scuffling in the neighboring gallery. It was only some young ladies, with their work and guitar, who were in a state of terror because some green boughs *would* sweep over when we were close under the bank. They could not be reassured by the gentlemen who waited upon them, nor would they change their seats; so that we were treated with a long series of screams, till the winding of the channel carried us across to the opposite bank.

In the afternoon we came in sight of New Madrid, in the State of Missouri; a scattered small place, on a green tableland. We sighed to think how soon our wonderful voyage would be over, and at every settlement we reached repined at being there so soon. While others went on shore, I remained on board to see how they looked, dispersed in the woods, grouped round the woodpiles, and seated on logs. The clergyman urged my going, saying, "It's quite a retreat to go on shore." This gentleman is vice-president of an educational establishment for young ladies, where there are public exhibitions of their proficiency, and the poor ignorant little girls take degrees. Their heads must be so stuffed with vainglory that there can be little room for anything else.

There were threatenings of another night of storm. The vessel seemed to labor much, and the weather was gusty, with incessant lightnings. The pilots said that they were never in such danger on the river as for twenty minutes of the preceding night. The captain was, however, very thankful for a few hours of cold weather; for his boat was so overcrowded as to make him dread, above all things, the appearance of disease on board. Some of us went to bed early this night, expecting to be called up to see the junction of the Ohio with the Mississippi by such light as there might be two hours after midnight. Mr. E. promised to have me called, and on the faith of this I went to sleep at the usual time. I had impressed him with my earnest desire not to miss this sight, as I had seen no junction of large rivers, except that of the Tombigbee with the Alabama. Mrs. B. would not trust to being called, but sat up, telling her husband that it was now his turn to gratify her, and he must come for her in good time to see the spectacle. Both she and I were disappointed, however. When I awoke it was five o'clock, and we were some miles into the Ohio. Mr. E. had fallen asleep, and awaked just a minute too late to make it of any use to rouse me. Mr. B. had put his head into his wife's room to tell her that the cabin floor was so completely covered with sleepers that she could not possibly make her way to the deck, and he shut the door before she could open her lips to reply. Her lamentations were sad. "The three great rivers meeting and all; and the little place on the point called Trinity and all; and I having sat up for it and all! It is a bad thing on some accounts to be married. If I had been a single woman, I could have managed it all for myself, I know."

However, junctions became frequent now, and we saw two small ones in the morning, to make up for having missed the large one in the night. When I went up on deck I found the sun shining on the full Ohio, which was now as turbid as the Mississippi, from the recent storms. The stream stood in among the trees on either bank to a great depth and extent, it was so swollen. The most enormous willows I ever saw overhung our deck, and the beechen shades beyond, where the turf and unencumbered stems were dressed in translucent green, seemed like a palace of the Dryads. How some of us fixed our eyes on the shores of free Illinois! After nearly five months of sojourn in slaveland, we were now in sight of a free state once more. I saw a settler in a wild spot, looking very lonely among the tall trees; but I felt that I would rather be that man than the wealthiest citizen of the opposite state, who was satisfied to dwell there among his slaves.

At eleven o'clock on this the ninth and last day of our voyage we passed Paducah, in Kentucky, a small neat settlement on the point of junction of the Tennessee and Ohio. Preparations were going on before our eyes for our leaving the boat; our luggage and that of the L.'s, who joined company with us, was brought out; cold beef and negus were provided for us in the ladies' cabin, the final sayings were being said, and we paid our fare, fifty dollars each, for our voyage of twelve hundred miles. Smithland, at the mouth of the Cumberland river, soon appeared; and, as we wished to ascend to Nashville without delay, we were glad to see a small steamboat in waiting. We stepped on shore, and stood there, in spite of a shower, for some time, watching the "Henry Clay" plowing up the river, and waving our handkerchiefs in answer to signals of farewell from several of the multitude who were clustered in every part of the noble vessel.

If there be excess of mental luxury in this life, it is surely in a voyage up the Mississippi, in the bright and leafy month of May.

Jane Johnston Schoolcraft (Bame-wa-was-ge-zhik-a-quay) (Ojibwa) (1800–1841) and Henry Rowe Schoolcraft (1793–1864)

Henry R. Schoolcraft was an explorer and geologist (see his *Journal of a Tour into the Interior of Missouri and Arkansaw* . . . [1821], included earlier in this volume) who became an Indian agent on the northwestern frontier when, in 1822, he was appointed to the post at Sault Sainte Marie. Schoolcraft was among the most active anthropologists and folklorists working in the first half of the nineteenth century, and he was a devoted student of Native American cultures, languages, and narratives. His popular 1839 book, *Algic Researches, Comprising Inquiries Respecting the Mental Characteristics of the North American Indians,* introduced many Anglo-Americans to the imaginative richness of Native American oral traditions, while also serving as the source of Henry Wadsworth Longfellow's romanticized version of Indian life in *Hiawatha* (1855). However, Henry Schoolcraft has received too much of the credit due his wife, Jane Johnston Schoolcraft, whom he married in 1823. Jane Johnston (Bame-wa-was-ge-zhik-a-quay) was an Ojibwa Indian, the daughter of Susan Johnston (Ozha-guscoday-way-quay) and granddaughter of Chippewa Chief Waub Ojeeg. It was through Jane Johnston and her family that Henry Schoolcraft accessed the traditional lore and legends of the Ojibwa people, and it was Jane who not only collected but also translated most of the tales that appeared in *Algic Researches.* Henry Schoolcraft credited his wife's contribution only in a perfunctory note, but it is fair to say that the cultural and linguistic access and acumen necessary to render these tales are more her skills than his own. Indeed, the unusual value of the oral narratives recorded in the book derives from the accuracy of their translations and the richness of the tribal cultural context in which they are situated. In the following Ojibwa tale, "Ojeeg Annung," we see a number of thematic and stylistic elements characteristic of Native American narratives: an animistic worldview in which animals and other natural elements possess language and moral agency; a quest motif in which a human hero must collaborate with natural forces in order to succeed; a recursive narrative structure in which ritual acts or their incantation are repeated;

and a conclusion in which aspects of the natural world — in this case the summer season and a particular celestial constellation — are explained by the events of the tale.

From *Algic Researches, Comprising Inquiries Respecting the Mental Characteristics of the North American Indians* (1839)

Ojeeg Annung; or, The Summer-Maker; An Ojibwa Tale

There lived a celebrated hunter on the southern shores of Lake Superior, who was considered a Manitou by some, for there was nothing but what he could accomplish. He lived off the path, in a wild, lonesome place, with a wife whom he loved, and they were blessed with a son, who had attained his thirteenth year. The hunter's name was Ojeeg, or the Fisher, which is the name of an expert, sprightly little animal common to the region. He was so successful in the chase, that he seldom returned without bringing his wife and son a plentiful supply of venison, or other dainties of the woods. As hunting formed his constant occupation, his son began early to emulate his father in the same employment, and would take his bow and arrows, and exert his skill in trying to kill birds and squirrels. The greatest impediment he met with, was the coldness and severity of the climate. He often returned home, his little fingers benumbed with cold, and crying with vexation at his disappointment. Days, and months, and years passed away, but still the same perpetual depth of snow was seen, covering all the country as with a white cloak.

One day, after a fruitless trial of his forest skill, the little boy was returning homeward with a heavy heart, when he saw a small red squirrel gnawing the top of a pine burr. He had approached within a proper distance to shoot, when the squirrel sat up on its hind legs and thus addressed him:

"My grandchild, put up your arrows, and listen to what I have to tell you." The boy complied rather reluctantly, when the squirrel continued: "My son, I see you pass frequently, with your fingers benumbed with cold, and crying with vexation for not having killed any birds. Now, if you will follow my advice, we will see if you cannot accomplish your wishes. If you will strictly pursue my advice, we will have perpetual summer, and you will then have the pleasure of killing as many birds as you please; and I will also have something to eat, as I am now myself on the point of starvation.

"Listen to me. As soon as you get home you must commence crying. You must throw away your bow and arrows in discontent. If your mother asks you what is the matter, you must not answer her, but continue crying and sobbing. If she offers you anything to eat, you must push it away with apparent discontent, and continue crying. In the evening, when your father returns from hunting, he will inquire of your mother what is the matter with you. She will answer that you came home crying, and would not so much as mention the cause to her. All this while you must not leave off sobbing. At last your father will say, 'My son, why is this unnecessary grief? Tell me the cause. You know I am a spirit, and that nothing is impossible for me to perform.' You must then answer him, and say that you are sorry to see the snow continually on the ground, and ask him if he could not cause it to melt, so that we might have perpetual summer. Say it in a supplicating way, and tell him this is the cause of your grief. Your father will reply, 'It is very hard to accomplish your request, but for your sake, and for my love for you, I will use my utmost endeavors.' He will tell you to be still, and cease crying. He will try to bring summer with all its loveliness. You must then be quiet, and eat that which is set before you."

The squirrel ceased. The boy promised obedience to his advice, and departed. When he reached home, he did as he had been instructed, and all was exactly fulfilled, as it had been predicted by the squirrel.

Ojeeg told him that it was a great undertaking. He must first make a feast, and invite some of his friends to accompany him on a journey. Next day he had a bear roasted whole. All who had been invited to the feast came punctually to the appointment. There were the Otter, Beaver, Lynx, Badger, and Wolverine. After the feast, they arranged it among themselves to set out on the contemplated journey in three days. When the time arrived, the Fisher took leave of his wife and son, as he foresaw that it was for the last time. He and his companions traveled in company day after day, meeting with nothing but the ordinary incidents. On the twentieth day they arrived at the foot of a high mountain, where they saw the tracks of some person who had recently killed an animal, which they knew by the blood that marked the way. The Fisher told his friends that they ought to follow the track, and see if they could not procure something to eat. They followed it for some time; at last they arrived at a lodge, which had been hidden from their view by a hollow in the mountain. Ojeeg told his friends to be very sedate, and not to laugh on any account. The first object that they saw was a man standing at the door of the lodge, but of so deformed a shape that they could not possibly make out who or what sort of a man it could be. His head was enormously large; he had such a queer set of teeth, and no arms. They wondered how he could kill animals. But the secret was soon revealed. He was a great Manitou. He invited them to pass the night, to which they consented.

He boiled his meat in a hollow vessel made of wood, and took it out of this singular kettle in some way unknown to his guests. He carefully gave each their portion to eat, but made so many odd movements that the Otter could not refrain from laughing, for he is the only one who is spoken of as a jester. The Manitou looked at him with a terrible look, and then made a spring at him, and got on him to smother him, for that was his mode of killing animals. But the Otter, when he felt him on his neck, slipped his head back and made for the door, which he passed in safety; but went out with the curse of the Manitou. The others passed the night, and they conversed on different subjects. The Manitou told the Fisher that he would accomplish his object, but that it would probably cost him his life. He gave them his advice, directed them how to act, and described a certain road which they must follow, and they would thereby be led to the place of action.

They set off in the morning, and met their friend, the Otter, shivering with cold; but Ojeeg had taken care to bring along some of the meat that had been given him, which he presented to his friend. They pursued their way, and traveled twenty days more before they got to the place which the Manitou had told them of. It was a most lofty mountain. They rested on its highest peak to fill their pipes and refresh themselves. Before smoking, they made the customary ceremony, pointing to the heavens, the four winds, the earth, and the zenith; in the meantime, speaking in a loud voice, addressed the Great Spirit, hoping that their object would be accomplished. They then commenced smoking.

They gazed on the sky in silent admiration and astonishment, for they were on so elevated a point, that it appeared to be only a short distance above their heads. After they had finished smoking, they prepared themselves. Ojeeg told the Otter to make the first attempt to try and make a hole in the sky. He consented with a grin. He made a leap, but fell down the hill stunned by the force of his fall; and the snow being moist, and falling on his back, he slid with velocity down the side of the mountain. When he found himself at the bottom, he thought to himself, it is the last time I make such another jump, so I will make the best of my way home. Then it was the turn of the Beaver, who made the attempt, but fell down senseless; then of the Lynx and Badger, who had no better success.

"Now," says the Fisher to the Wolverine, "try your skill; your ancestors were celebrated for their activity, hardihood, and perseverance, and I depend on you for success. Now make the attempt." He did so, but also without success. He leaped the second time, but now they could see that the sky was giving way to their repeated attempts. Mustering strength, he made the third leap, and went in. The Fisher nimbly followed him.

They found themselves in a beautiful plain, extending as far as the eye could reach, covered with flowers of a thousand different hues and fragrance. Here and there were clusters of tall, shady trees, separated by innumerable streams of the purest water, which wound around their courses under the cooling shades, and filled the plain with countless beautiful lakes, whose banks and bosom were covered with waterfowl, basking and sporting in the sun. The trees were alive with birds of different plumage, warbling their sweet notes, and delighted with perpetual spring.

The Fisher and his friend beheld very long lodges, and the celestial inhabitants amusing themselves at a distance. Words cannot express the beauty and charms of the place. The lodges were empty of inhabitants, but they saw them lined with mocuks of different sizes, filled with birds and fowls of different plumage. Ojeeg thought of his son, and immediately commenced cutting open the mocuks and letting out the birds, who descended in whole flocks through the opening which they had made. The warm air of those regions also rushed down through the opening, and spread its genial influence over the north.

When the celestial inhabitants saw the birds let loose, and the warm gales descending, they raised a shout like thunder, and ran for their lodges. But it was too late. Spring, summer, and autumn had gone; even perpetual summer had almost all gone; but they separated it with a blow, and only a part descended; but the ends were so mangled, that, wherever it prevails among the lower inhabitants, it is always sickly.

When the Wolverine heard the noise, he made for the opening and safely descended. Not so the Fisher. Anxious to fulfill his son's wishes, he continued to break open the mocuks. He was, at last, obliged to run also, but the opening was now closed by the inhabitants. He ran with all his might over the plains of heaven, and, it would appear, took a northerly direction. He saw his pursuers so close that he had to climb the first large tree he came to. They commenced shooting at him with their arrows, but without effect, for all his body was invulnerable except the space of about an inch near the tip of his tail. At last one of the arrows hit the spot, for he had in this chase assumed the shape of the Fisher after whom he was named.

He looked down from the tree, and saw some among his assailants with the totems of his ancestors. He claimed relationship, and told them to desist, which they only did at the approach of night. He then came down to try and find an opening in the celestial plain, by which he might descend to the earth. But he could find none. At last, becoming faint from the loss of blood from the wound on his tail, he laid himself down towards the north of the plain, and, stretching out his limbs, said, "I have fulfilled my promise to my son, though it has cost me my life; but I die satisfied in the idea that I have done so much good, not only for him, but for my fellow-beings. Hereafter I will be a sign to the inhabitants below for ages to come, who will venerate my name for having succeeded in procuring the varying seasons. They will now have from eight to ten moons without snow." He was found dead next morning, but they left him as they found him, with the arrow sticking in his tail, as it can be plainly seen, at this time, in the heavens.

John Kirk Townsend
(1809–1851)

Philadelphian and Quaker John Kirk Townsend was a gifted amateur ornithologist whose great opportunity came in 1834, when botanist Thomas Nuttall invited Townsend to join him on Nathaniel Wyeth's transcontinental expedition along the route later known as the Oregon Trail. Nuttall (the "Mr. N." in the following selection) had resigned his position at Harvard in order to study Far Western plants, and he considered Townsend a good choice to study the little-known birds of the Western territories. Having traveled from Philadelphia all the way to Independence before heading farther west with Wyeth's party of seventy men, Nuttall and Townsend soon found themselves in scientific terra incognita, where they collected hundreds of plant and bird specimens that were new to science. After five months crossing the continent the party arrived at Fort Vancouver, where Townsend remained for several years studying the birds of the coastal Northwest. Townsend finally proceeded to additional bird studies in the Sandwich Islands (Hawaii) before rounding Cape Horn and returning to Philadelphia in November 1837—nearly four years after he had left there. So significant was Townsend's collection of Western birds that John James Audubon, then at work on *The Birds of America* (1827–38), obtained as many of Townsend's specimens as he could; ultimately, 74 of the 508 bird species Audubon included in the octavo edition of *Birds* (1840–44) came from Townsend. But Townsend also left a rich literary legacy, for the account of his great adventure, *Narrative of a Journey across the Rocky Mountains, to the Columbia River* . . . (1839) is a classic of nineteenth-century Western exploration and nature writing. In the following selections we see that Townsend is not just a "bird chief" (as the Northwest Indians called him) in whose honor many species are named, but also an honest reporter whose developing ethical sensibility — and his unfortunate lapses from it — prefigure the environmental epiphanies so important to contemporary nature writing. In one particularly powerful example, Townsend's sincere lament, as he looks into the "large, soft, black eyes" of an innocent antelope he has just mortally wounded, is remarkably similar to the famous passage, in *A Sand County Almanac* (1949), in which Aldo Leopold deeply regrets killing a wolf as he watches the "green fire" dying in its eyes. Townsend himself died young, a victim of cumulative poisoning caused by the arsenic powder he used to preserve bird specimens.

From
Narrative of a Journey across the Rocky Mountains, to the Columbia River . . . (1839)

May 23, 1834. . . . I had determined to kill a buffalo, and as I had seen it several times done with so much apparent ease, I considered it a mere moonshine matter, and thought I could compass it without difficulty; but now I had attempted it, and was grievously mistaken in my estimate of the required skill. I had several times heard the guns of the hunters, and felt satisfied that we should not go to camp without meat, and was on the point of altering my course to join them, when, as I wound around the base of a little hill, I saw about twenty buffalo lying quietly on the ground within thirty yards of me. Now was my time. I took my picket from my saddle, and fastened my horse to the ground as quietly as possible, but with hands that almost failed to do their office, from my excessive eagerness and trembling anxiety. When this was completed, I crawled around the hill again, almost suspending my breath from fear of alarming my intended victims, until I came again in full view of the unsuspecting herd. There were so many fine animals that I was at a loss which to select; those nearest me appeared small and poor, and I therefore settled my aim upon a huge bull on the outside. Just then I was attacked with the "*bull fever*" so dreadfully, that for several minutes I could not shoot.

At length, however, I became firm and steady, and pulled my trigger at exactly the right instant. Up sprang the herd like lightning, and away they scoured, and my bull with them. I was vexed, angry, and discontented; I concluded that I could never kill a buffalo, and was about to mount my horse and ride off in despair, when I observed that one of the animals had stopped in the midst of his career. I rode towards him, and sure enough, there was my great bull trembling and swaying from side to side, and the clotted gore hanging like icicles from his nostrils. In a few minutes after, he fell heavily upon his side, and I dismounted and surveyed the unwieldy brute, as he panted and struggled in the death agony.

When the first ebullition of my triumph had subsided I perceived that my prize was so excessively lean as to be worth nothing, and while I was exerting my whole strength in a vain endeavor to raise the head from the ground for the purpose of removing the tongue, the two hunters joined me, and laughed heartily at my achievement. Like all inexperienced hunters, I had been particular to select the largest bull in the gang, supposing it to be the best, (and it proved, as usual, the poorest,) while more than a dozen fat cows were nearer me, either of which I might have killed with as little trouble.

As I had supposed, my companions had killed several animals, but they had taken the meat of only one, and we had, therefore, to be diligent, or the camp might suffer for provisions. It was now past midday; the weather was very warm, and the atmosphere was charged with minute particles of sand, which produced a dryness and stiffness of the mouth and tongue, that was exceedingly painful and distressing. Water was now the desideratum, but where was it to be found? The arid country in which we then were, produced none, and the Platte was twelve or fourteen miles from us, and no buffalo in that direction, so that we could not afford time for so trifling a matter. I found that Mr. Lee was suffering as much as myself, although he had not spoken of it, and I perceived that Richardson was masticating a leaden bullet, to excite the salivary glands. Soon afterwards, a bull was killed, and we all assembled around the carcass to assist in the manipulations. The animal was first raised from his side where he had lain, and supported upon his knees, with his hoofs turned under him; a longitudinal incision was then made from the nape, or anterior base of the hump, and continued backward to the loins, and a large portion of the skin from each side removed; these pieces of skin were placed upon the ground, with the under surface uppermost, and the *fleeces*, or masses of meat, taken from along the back, were laid upon them. These fleeces, from a large animal, will weigh, perhaps, a hundred pounds each, and comprise the whole of the hump on each side of the vertical processes, (commonly called the *hump ribs*,) which are attached to the vertebra. The fleeces are considered the choice parts of the buffalo, and here, where the game is so abundant, nothing else is taken, if we except the tongue, and an occasional marrowbone.

This, it must be confessed, appears like a useless and unwarrantable waste of the goods of Providence; but when are men economical, unless compelled to be so by necessity? Here are more than a thousand pounds of delicious and savory flesh, which would delight the eyes and gladden the heart of any epicure in Christendom, left neglected where it fell, to feed the ravenous maw of the wild prairie wolf, and minister to the excesses of the unclean birds of the wilderness. But I have seen worse waste and havoc than this, and I feel my indignation rise at the recollection. I have seen dozens of buffalo slaughtered merely for the tongues, or for practice with the rifle; and I have also lived to see the very perpetrators of these deeds, lean and lank with famine, when the meanest and most worthless parts of the poor animals they had so inhumanly slaughtered, would have been received and eaten with humble thankfulness.

But to return to ourselves. We were all suffering from excessive thirst, and so intolerable had it at length become, that Mr. Lee and myself proposed a gallop over to the Platte river, in order to appease it; but Richardson advised us not to go, as he had just thought of a means of relieving us, which he immediately proceeded to put in practice. He tumbled our mangled buffalo over upon his side and with his knife opened the body, so as to expose to view the great stomach, and still crawling and twisting entrails. The good missionary and myself stood gaping with astonishment, and no little loathing, as we saw our hunter plunge his knife into the distended paunch, from which gushed the green and gelatinous juices, and then insinuate his tin pan into the opening, and by depressing its edge, strain off the water which was mingled with its contents.

Richardson always valued himself upon his politeness, and the cup was therefore first offered to Mr. Lee and myself, but it is almost needless to say that we declined the proffer, and our features probably expressed the strong disgust which we felt, for our companion laughed heartily before he applied the cup to his own mouth. He then drank it to the dregs, smacking his lips, and drawing a long breath after it, with the satisfaction of a man taking his wine after dinner. Sansbury, the other hunter, was not slow in following the example set before him, and we, the audience, turned our backs upon the actors.

Before we left the spot, however, Richardson induced me to taste the blood which was still fluid in the heart, and immediately as it touched my lips, my burning thirst, aggravated by hunger, (for I had eaten nothing that day,) got the better of my abhorrence; I plunged my head into the reeking ventricles, and drank until forced to stop for breath. I felt somewhat ashamed of assimilating myself so nearly to the brutes, and turned my ensanguined countenance towards the missionary who stood by, but I saw no approval there: the good man was evidently attempting to control his risibility, and so I smiled to put him in countenance; the roar could no longer be restrained, and the missionary laughed until the tears rolled down his cheeks. I did not think, until afterwards, of the horrible ghastliness which must have characterized my smile at that particular moment.

When we arrived at the camp in the evening, and I enjoyed the luxury of a hearty draft of water, the effect upon my stomach was that of a powerful emetic: the blood was violently ejected without nausea, and I felt heartily glad to be rid of the disgusting encumbrance. I never drank blood from that day. . . .

May 28. We fell in with a new species of game today;—a large band of wild horses. They were very shy, scarcely permitting us to approach within rifle distance, and yet they kept within sight of us for some hours. Several of us gave them chase, in the hope of at least being able to approach sufficiently near to examine them closely, but we might as well have pursued the wind; they scoured away from us with astonishing velocity, their long manes and tails standing out almost horizontally, as they sprang along before us. Occasionally they would pause in their career, turn and look at us as we approached them, and then, with a neigh that rang loud and high above the clattering of the hoofs, dart their light heels into the air and fly from us as before. We soon abandoned this wild chase, and contented ourselves with admiring their sleek beauty at a distance.

In the afternoon, I committed an act of cruelty and wantonness, which distressed and troubled me beyond measure, and which I have ever since recollected with sorrow and compunction. A beautiful doe antelope came running and bleating after us, as though she wished to overtake the party; she continued following us for nearly an hour, at times approaching within thirty of forty yards, and standing to gaze at us as we moved slowly on our way. I several times raised my gun to fire at her,—but my better nature as often gained the ascendancy, and I at last rode into the midst of the party to escape the temptation. Still the doe followed us, and I finally fell into the rear, but without intending it, and again looked at her as she trotted behind us. At that moment, my evil genius and love of sport triumphed; I slid down from my horse, aimed at the poor antelope, and shot a ball through her side. Under other circumstances, there would have been no cruelty in this; but here where better meat was so abundant, and the camp was so plentifully supplied, it was unfeeling, heartless murder. It was under the influence of this too late impression, that I approached my poor victim She was writhing in agony upon the ground, and exerting herself in vain efforts to draw her mangled body farther from her destroyer; and as I stood over her, and saw her cast her large, soft, black eyes upon me with an expression of the most touching sadness, while the great tears rolled over her face, I felt myself the meanest and most abhorrent thing in creation. But now a finishing blow would be mercy to her, and I threw my arm around her neck, averted my face, and drove my long knife through her bosom to the heart. I did not trust myself to look upon her afterwards, but mounted my horse, and galloped off to the party, with feelings such as I hope never to experience again. For several days the poor antelope haunted me, and I shall never forget its last look of pain and upbraiding.

The bluffs on the southern shore of the Platte, are, at this point, exceedingly rugged, and often quite picturesque; the formation appears to be simple clay, intermixed, occasionally, with a stratum of limestone, and one part of the bluff bears a striking and almost startling resemblance to a dilapidated feudal castle. There is also a kind of obelisk, standing at a considerable distance from the bluffs, on a wide plain, towering to the height of about two hundred feet, and tapering to a small point at the top. This pillar is known to the hunters and trappers who traverse these regions, by the name of the "*chimney*." Here we diverged from the usual course, leaving the bank of the river, and entered a large and deep ravine between the enormous bluffs.

The road was very uneven and difficult, winding from amongst innumerable mounds six to eight feet in height, the space between them frequently so narrow as scarcely to admit our horses, and some of the men rode for upwards of a mile kneeling upon their saddles. These mounds were of hard yellow clay, without a particle of rock of any kind, and along their bases, and in the narrow passages, flowers of every hue were growing. It was a most enchanting sight; even the men noticed it, and more than one of our matter-of-fact people exclaimed, *beautiful*,

beautiful! Mr. N. was here in his glory. He rode on ahead of the company, and cleared the passages with a trembling and eager hand, looking anxiously back at the approaching party, as though he feared it would come ere he had finished, and tread his lovely prizes underfoot.

The distance through the ravine is about three miles. We then crossed several beautiful grassy knolls, and descending to the plain, struck the Platte again, and traveled along its bank. Here one of our men caught a young antelope, which he brought to the camp upon his saddle. It was a beautiful and most delicate little creature, and in a few days became so tame as to remain with the camp without being tied, and to drink, from a tin cup, the milk which our good missionaries spared from their own scanty meals. The men christened it "*Zip Coon*" and it soon became familiar with its name, running to them when called, and exhibiting many evidences of affection and attachment. It became a great favorite with every one. A little pannier of willows was made for it, which was packed on the back of a mule, and when the camp moved in the mornings, little *Zip* ran to his station beside his long-eared hack, bleating with impatience until someone came to assist him in mounting.

On the afternoon of the 31st, we came to green trees and bushes again, and the sight of them was more cheering than can be conceived, except by persons who have traveled for weeks without beholding a green thing, save the grass under their feet. We encamped in the evening in a beautiful grove of cottonwood trees, along the edge of which ran the Platte, dotted as usual with numerous islands.

In the morning, Mr. N. and myself were up before the dawn, strolling through the umbrageous forest, inhaling the fresh, bracing air, and making the echoes ring with the report of our gun, as the lovely tenants of the grove flew by dozens before us. I think I never before saw so great a variety of birds within the same space. All were beautiful, and many of them quite new to me; and after we had spent an hour amongst them, and my game bag was teeming with its precious freight, I was still loath to leave the place, lest I should not have procured specimens of the whole.

None but a naturalist can appreciate a naturalist's feelings — his delight amounting to ecstasy — when a specimen such as he has never before seen, meets his eye, and the sorrow and grief which he feels when he is compelled to tear himself from a spot abounding with all that he has anxiously and unremittingly sought for.

This was peculiarly my case upon this occasion. We had been long traveling over a sterile and barren tract, where the lovely denizens of the forest could not exist, and I had been daily scanning the great extent of the desert, for some little oasis such as I had now found; here was my wish at length gratified, and yet the caravan would not halt for me; I must turn my back upon the *El Dorado* of my fond anticipations, and hurry forward over the dreary wilderness which lay beyond.

What valuable and highly interesting accessions to science might not be made by a party, composed exclusively of naturalists, on a journey through this rich and unexplored region! The botanist, the geologist, the mammalogist, the ornithologist, and the entomologist, would find a rich and almost inexhaustible field for the prosecution of their inquiries, and the result of such an expedition would be to add most materially to our knowledge of the wealth and resources of our country, to furnish us with new and important facts relative to its structure, organization, and natural productions, and to complete the fine native collections in our already extensive museums.

Nicolas Point
(1799–1868)

Born at Rocroi, France, on the Belgian border, Nicolas Point began to study for the priesthood after the defeat of Napoleon in 1815; he was accepted into the Society of Jesus in 1819 and ordained a Jesuit priest in 1831. Because Jesuits were persecuted throughout Europe during this period, however, he was forced to move from France to Switzerland to Spain before being sent to America in 1835. Point went first to Kentucky and then Louisiana, where he founded the Jesuit St. Charles College at Grand Cocteau. In 1840 Father Point was reassigned to St. Louis, where he began the greatest adventure of his life: he had been selected to join Father Pierre Jean De Smet on his missionary voyage into the little-known Flathead, Coeur d'Alene, and Blackfoot Indian territory of the Rocky Mountains. Leaving for the Western wilderness with his fellow priests in late April of 1841, Point, who had been appointed official diarist for the expedition, began keeping meticulous notes; he also began making the sketches and paintings of frontier and Indian life for which he would later be justly celebrated. By mid-September the Catholics had established a mission among the Flathead Indians, on the Bitterroot River, near present-day Missoula, Montana. And when the Flatheads departed for their annual winter buffalo hunt, Father Point went with them, enduring four months of winter travel in order to continue the religious instruction he had begun in the fall. The following year Point was sent even farther into the wilderness, this time to establish a mission among the Coeur d'Alene people and to evangelize among the Blackfoot Indians. During the mid-1840s Point's health began to fail, and he left the wilderness for less strenuous work in the Canadian missions. In Montreal Point used the field notes he kept while living in the wilderness from 1840 to 1847 to compose his *Recollections of the Rocky Mountains* (*Souvenirs des Montagnes Rocheuses*), a detailed account of wilderness and Indian life that remained in manuscript until 1967. The following selections from *Recollections* suggest that Father Point's zeal as a priest was matched by his appreciation for the Far Western landscapes, animals, and wildflowers that his work as a wilderness missionary allowed him to witness.

From *Recollections of the Rocky Mountains* (1840–1847/1967)

Next to the Missouri, which is for the West what the Mississippi is for the North and South, the most beautiful rivers of this area are the Kansas, the Platte, the Sweetwater, and the Green. The first, which empties directly into the Missouri, is quite remarkable for the large number of its great tributaries. Between the Kansas and the Platte we counted eighteen tributaries, which presupposed a large number of springs and, consequently, a very compact soil. The contrary is true in the vicinity of the Platte. Even on the buttes, which run parallel to the low shore for some distance, there are neither springs nor woods, since the soil, practically all sand, is so porous that water runs to the lower level of the valleys almost as soon as it falls. Hence the neighboring plains are very fertile and especially beautiful in the spring because of the great variety of flowers which grow there. By picking fifteen of each variety, I was able, on the eve of the Feast of the Sacred Heart, to fill an entire basket to honor this great day. The most common of the flowers is the *epinette des prairies*, a small five-petal flower of yellow color. The plains on which they bloom, when seen from a distance, seem to have no green at all; all is a yellow-gold, similar to the color of the narcissus in northern France. Beside *la Cheminee*, the *pricleper* together with the *turnsol*, is dominant.

The prettiest of them is the *Cactus Americana*, which had already been domesticated in European flower beds. I never saw anything as pure and vivid as the bloom of this charming flower. All shades of rose and green decorate the exterior of the blossom, which, like that of the lily, widens at the top. The flower, surrounded by a great many thorns, is only two inches from the earth and grows naturally only in the desert. Thus it, more than the rose, could be the symbol of the pleasures of this world. The most elegant flower is something like the European campanula, but surpasses it by the gracefulness of its form and the delicacy of its colors, which vary from pure white to dark blue. The noblest of them, found only on the mountains, is the "Needle of Adam." Its stem is about three feet high. Halfway up the stem begins a pyramid of blossoms matted closely together, shaded lightly with red, and narrowing to a point at the top. Its base is protected by a kind of tough, long and sharp leaf. From the roots can be made soap, often called Mexican soap, and, in times of emergency, this root might also serve as food.

We saw three other remarkable flower varieties, so rare that, even in America, their names were not generally known. The first one, whose bronze leaves are arranged something like the capital of a Corinthian column, we named the *Corinthienne*. The second, something of a straw color, which, because of the arrangement of its stem and branches reminded one of the dream which caused Joseph to be hated by his brothers, we named the *Josephine*. The third, which had around a yellow disk, shaded in black and red, seven or eight stems of blossoms, each one of which might have been a beautiful flower in itself, was named *la dominicale*, not only because it appeared to us to be the mistress of all the flowers found in the area, but also because it was first found on a Sunday. . . .

Everyone has heard of the rattlesnakes and mosquitoes which have been mentioned so frequently in accounts by the first missionaries in America. I will, therefore, mention them only to thank God publicly for the protection he gave us from the former and for the patience he gave us to endure the latter. On the feast of St. Francis Regis, the wagoners, without once leaving the trail, killed a dozen rattlesnakes with their whips. The menacing heads of these reptiles, and their rattling tails always warn one of their hostile intentions. Next to the more destructive winged insects, the small, inoffensive ant is very common. At almost every step, one found anthills of several feet in diameter constructed, not of grain, as in our European fields and gardens, but out of small pebbles. This observation would seem to necessitate a modification of that opinion which holds that ants exercise foresight in storing food and in constructing their dwellings. The grain, which ants collect in Europe, could well serve to feed them during the winter. But does it really serve that purpose as directly as the other? This seems to me scarcely probable, especially since provisions of another nature can be found in their individual cells. At any rate, the wonderful instinct with which God has endowed them for the continual preservation of their species is admirable. Why are these hills composed of tiny globules, and why are the globules arranged in little mounds? Why are the mounds given a specific inclination, and why is the entry always made on the side opposite to the prevailing wind? All of these things point to some kind of wisdom in these tiny heads.

In his account of the missions in Paraguay, Muratori remarks that the hummingbird sings like a nightingale. He professed to be amazed to find that such a tiny body could emit such a surprisingly loud sound. Unless the hummingbirds in South America differ from those I saw, one must hold that only by a kind of analogy did that noted author add pleasing song to the undoubted beauty of the hummingbirds' plumage. This minute *chef-d'oeuvre* of elegance nourishes itself only with the honey it finds in the blossoms of flowers. It draws the honey out by means of its tongue, which it can extend after the manner of bees. While partaking of the honey, the bird stops in flight and appears to be humming as a bee does among flowers. But if one listens intently and looks closely, one discovers that the humming sound comes from the extraordinarily rapid beat of the tiny wings.

I do not know how the prairie dog got its name. In shape, size, color, agility, and timidity, it resembles a squirrel more than a dog. Some think it to be a kind of marmot. Each single family of prairie dogs has its own burrow. On the prairies, families are so very numerous that they form villages. These villages differ from those of the beaver in that, instead of being on a stream's bank, they are located as far from water as possible. It is said that the prairie dog feeds only on grass roots and drinks dew. A tradition of travelers in the West, which borders somewhat on the fantastic, has it that the prairie dogs sometimes leave their burrows en masse to form a general assembly. When a prairie dog hears or sees something hostile, it scampers into its burrow and from there gives forth a piercing cry which is repeated from burrow to burrow, putting the entire colony on the alert. Since it is naturally very curious, however, in a few minutes it pokes its nose out of its hole. The hunter chooses that moment to shoot it. This requires a great deal of skill, for the small animal, endowed with great agility and piercing sight, ordinarily does not expose more than the top of its head.

What is said about the strength of the beaver's four small teeth is very true. I have seen trees, more than two feet in diameter, cut in two by these apparently feeble instruments. I do not know if what is said in addition to this is true. Some hold that before felling the trees which are to serve in the construction of their dams they examine, among the trees suitable to this purpose, those which lean toward the spot on which they are to be used. If none of the trees offers this advantage, they wait until a good wind comes to their assistance and, while the wind is bending the tree, set to work and soon have the tree toppling.

There is a kind of frog which differs essentially from those we see in Europe, in that it has a tail and lives in arid places which are stony and hot. I have heard it called a salamander. . . .

Two long months had passed since our entry into the wilderness, but at last we were arriving, if not at the end of our journey and of the greatest perils, at least at the Rocky Mountains to which our most ardent prayers had so long transported us. A celebration was held in camp in honor of these mountains. Why are they called rocky? Because they are composed of granite and flint. Some travelers have given them the more pompous name of "Backbone of the World" because they are the principal chain which divides the North American continent lengthwise. This great chain is buttressed on the west by the Cordilleras and on the east by the Wind River Range. It was toward mid-July that we crossed the highest ridge of the latter. Behind us we had the tributaries of the Missouri; before us lay the rivers that empty into the Pacific. What a magnificent view! But who could describe the majesty of the wilderness as we then saw it? At this sight, a single need filled our souls, that of exclaiming like the King Prophet, "From the rising of the sun until its setting the name of the Lord is admirable." And we carved into the bark of a cedar which overlooked all this majesty the ever-adorable Name at which every knee in Heaven, on earth, and in Hell bends. May this blessed name be for those who pass after us a sign of hope and salvation! . . .

On this plain, called Peter's Cave, there was an abundance of camass. The flower of this plant is a beautiful blue in color and makes the plain on which it abounds look like a lake. The flower of the bitterroot, has shades of rose. The roots differ greatly in shape. The bitterroot's is long and odd-looking. That of the camass is like that of an onion, which it also resembles in the disposition of its layers inside.

The bitterroot is indeed so bitter to the taste that a civilized mouth can scarcely bear it. The root of the camass tastes something like a prune and a chestnut. It is eaten with pleasure, but its digestion is accompanied by very disagreeable effects for those who do not like strong odors or the sound that accompanies them. The root is gathered by means of a stick with a claw on one end, giving it the appearance of a shoemaker's hammer. While the left hand grasps the stick, which is like the handle of the hammer, the right hand thrusts the claw into the earth and extracts the root with as much rapidity as skill. This work is relegated to the women, being carried on from sunrise to four o'clock in the afternoon. To preserve the bitterroot it has only to be dried in the sun. But to preserve the camass, and above all to make it palatable, it must be cooked. To do this you dig in the earth a circular hole a few inches in depth and with a diameter about equal to that of an ordinary wagon wheel. This done, you fill the hole with wood, which you burn until you have a bed of glowing embers. On this bed of embers you spread stones and over the stones a layer of earth. On the layer of earth you spread the roots and over the roots a second layer of earth. On this you place a sufficiently large quantity of wood to maintain a fire for thirty or forty hours. When all this has been done, you have a food which can be preserved for years. But, to succeed, a great deal of care, skill, and experience is required. Hence, success at this undertaking is a mark of distinction for the women.

The cooking of moss, called in some countries Spanish bread, proceeds in the same manner. But the Flathead never has recourse to such mean fare. He prefers, in case of a famine, to eat the pellicle found between the bark and the wood of certain trees.

There was in the area in which we found ourselves a variety of edible roots. There was a small white carrot of excellent flavor and a potato which would, perhaps, differ little from ours if it were cultivated. But since it never reaches a size exceeding two or three centimeters in diameter and is fairly scarce, it is for the Indian a treasure that remains buried. The other species, introduced by our brothers, replaces it abundantly.

The large animals still showed themselves only on the edge of a forest, too thick to be easily penetrated. While waiting for better game, the hunters amused themselves pursuing antelope, which appeared here and there on the way. This pretty animal, called *cabri* (kid or goat) by the French *voyageurs,* resembles the roe deer in shape and size. But the antler of the male, which has only two prongs, is smaller, and its coat, like that of the stag, is white on the rump and belly. When it goes through the woods, its ordinary gait is an elegant little trot. From time to time, it stops in its tracks, turns toward the hunter and examines him curiously. This is the moment to fire. If the hunter misses his shot, the animal darts away like an arrow. But in a moment he stops again to get a better look at the hunter. The hunter, who knows its weakness, attracts it by waving a brilliantly colored object. The poor animal, drawn on by this bait, comes closer. But its curiosity causes its death.

Occasionally there can be seen a kind of sheep, called bighorn because of its relatively large horns which curve downward so that the tips are near its mouth. In quality, the flesh of the bighorn is next to that of the buffalo. Then come the hind, the roe deer, and antelope, and finally the white ram. I must add, too, the elk which, in the quality of its meat, is almost the equal of the buffalo. The snout of those noble animals, like the hump of the buffalo, is one of the choicest of morsels. . . .

Tomorrow is the Feast of the Maternity of the Most Blessed Virgin Mary. On the day after the missionary is to leave the Flatheads to go among the Coeur d'Alenes. Yesterday confessions began, for many would like to communicate before the missionary leaves. Today confessions should be finished, but already the day is declining and we are still marching along the crest of the mountains. Only after a forced march of ten hours do we descend onto the plain. There we find warm weather again. There also flows majestically the Great Fork of the Missouri, whose waters, separating and then joining, form an island. In addition to good pasturage, there are large trees that will protect us from the sun tomorrow and wood with which we can warm ourselves this evening.

A huge fire is lighted before the lodge, which serves also as a chapel, so that during the night the penitents may wait for confession without too much discomfort. The next day, ninety persons approach the Communion rail. In the evening, mothers bring their children to be blessed by the priest, and the final ceremony is the planting of a cross.

It would be difficult to imagine a more beautiful spectacle. On the horizon there is a chain of summits already covered with snow. Below them is a mass of rocks shaded in red, yellow, blue, and everything that autumn has to offer of the richest in color and form. Immediately before us is brush, mixed with the huge trees and a waterfall foaming as it descends into a basin. The leaves rustle in the evening breeze and the sun lights this magnificent panorama with its final rays. This is what you might have admired had you been with us on this day.

George Catlin
(1796–1872)

Like John James Audubon, Thomas Cole, and Nicolas Point, George Catlin is better known as a painter than a writer, though he did extremely important work in both media. Born in Wilkes-Barre, Pennsylvania, the fifth of fourteen children, Catlin was raised with "books reluctantly held in one hand, a rifle or fishing pole grasped firmly in the other." Though he was trained to the law, Catlin preferred drawing and being outdoors, and so in 1823 moved to Philadelphia, where he soon became a successful portrait painter—and where he may have received instruction at Charles Willson Peale's American Museum. By 1826 Catlin had moved to New York but was resolved upon going west to draw and paint among the Native American peoples already being displaced, removed, and destroyed by liquor, disease, and U.S. policy. Catlin's epic travels through Indian country began in 1831, when General William Clark—who had crossed the continent with Meriwether Lewis a quarter century earlier—invited him to St. Louis and helped direct his initial journey west. That year and the next he visited and sketched Plains Indians including the Sioux, Iowa, Sauk, Fox, Kansa, Oto, Omaha, and Missouri. In 1832 he traveled two thousand miles up the Missouri River and on to the mouth of the Yellowstone—a long voyage that introduced him to the Lakota, Blackfoot, Assiniboin, Ojibwa, Crow, Cree, and Mandan peoples. Two years later he explored up the Arkansas River and visited the Osage, Pawneee, and Kiowa, and in 1837 he went south to paint among the Yuchi, Muskogee, and Miccosukee. Throughout these amazing journeys into the remote wilderness of Indian country, Catlin made hundreds of field sketches and took voluminous notes that he later developed into the mature paintings and books that are now among the richest extant representations of nineteenth-century Native American people and land. His most important work, *Letters and Notes on the Manners, Customs, and Conditions of the North American Indians* (1841) effectively combined textual and pictorial art to argue for the nobility and fragility of Indian cultures (the book also established him as the chief rival of Indian ethnologist Henry R. Schoolcraft). And although the racial bias common to the period is clear in Catlin's suggestion of a "nation's Park" in which buffalo and Indian would coexist as "thrilling specimen[s]," his condemnation of the wanton slaughter of bison and his sensitivity to the dependence of Indian peoples upon the great herds was well ahead of its time.

From
Letters and Notes on the Manners, Customs, and Conditions of the North American Indians (1841)

Letter No. 31

Mouth of Teton River, Upper Missouri. There are several varieties of the wolf species in this country, the most formidable and most numerous of which are white, often sneaking about in gangs or families of fifty or sixty in numbers, appearing in distance, on the green prairies like nothing but a flock of sheep. Many of these animals grow to a very great size, being I should think, quite a match for the largest Newfoundland dog. At present, whilst the buffaloes are so abundant, and these ferocious animals are glutted with the buffalo's flesh, they are harmless, and everywhere sneak away from man's presence; which I scarcely think will be the case after the buffaloes are all gone, and they are left, as they must be, with scarcely anything to eat. They always are seen following about in the vicinity of herds of buffaloes and stand ready to pick the bones of those that the hunters leave on the ground, or to overtake and devour those that are wounded, which fall an easy prey to them. While the herd of buffaloes are together, they seem to have little dread of the wolf, and allow them to come in close company with them. The Indian then has taken advantage of this fact, and often places himself under the skin of this animal, and crawls for half a mile or more on his hands and knees, until he approaches within a few rods of the unsuspecting group, and easily shoots down the fattest of the throng.

The buffalo is a very timid animal, and shuns the vicinity of man with the keenest sagacity; yet, when overtaken, and harassed or wounded, turns upon its assailants with the utmost fury, who have only to seek safety in flight. In their desperate resistance the finest horses are often destroyed; but the Indian, with his superior sagacity and dexterity, generally finds some effective mode of escape.

During the season of the year whilst the calves are young, the male seems to stroll about by the side of the dam, as if for the purpose of protecting the young, at which time it is exceedingly hazardous to attack them, as they are sure to turn upon their pursuers, who have often to fly to each other's assistance. The buffalo calf, during the first six months is red, and has so much the appearance of a red calf in cultivated fields, that it could easily be mingled and mistaken amongst them. In the fall, when it changes its hair it takes a brown coat for the winter, which it always retains. In pursuing a large herd of buffaloes at the season when their calves are but a few weeks old, I have often been exceedingly amused with the curious maneuvers of these shy little things. Amidst the thundering confusion of a throng of several hundreds or several thousands of these animals, there will be many of the calves that lose sight of their dams; and being left behind by the throng, and the swift passing hunters, they endeavor to secrete themselves, when they are exceedingly put to it on a level prairie, where naught can be seen but the short grass of six or eight inches in height, save an occasional bunch of wild sage, a few inches higher, to which the poor affrighted things will run, and dropping on their knees, will push their noses under it, and into the grass, where they will stand for hours, with their eyes shut, imagining themselves securely hid, whilst they are standing up quite straight upon their hind feet and can easily be seen at several miles distance. It is a familiar amusement for us accustomed to these scenes, to retreat back over the ground where we have just escorted the herd, and approach these little trembling things, which stubbornly maintain their positions, with their noses pushed under the grass, and their eyes strained upon us, as we dismount from our horses and are passing around them. From this fixed position they are sure not to move, until hands are laid upon them, and then for the shins of a novice, we can extend our sympathy; or if he can preserve the skin on his bones for the furious buttings of its head, we know how to congratulate him on his signal success and good luck. In these desperate struggles, for a moment, the little thing is conquered, and makes no further resistance. And I have often, in concurrence with a known custom of the country, held my hands over the eyes of the calf, and breathed a few strong breaths into its nostrils; after which I have, with my hunting companions, rode several miles into our encampment, with the little prisoner busily following the heels of my horse the whole way, as closely and as affectionately as its instinct would attach it to the company of its dam! . . .

It is truly a melancholy contemplation for the traveler in this country, to anticipate the period which is not far distant, when the last of these noble animals, at the hands of white and red men, will fall victims to their cruel and improvident rapacity; leaving these beautiful green fields, a vast and idle waste, unstocked and unpeopled for ages to come, until the bones of the one and the traditions of the other will have vanished, and left scarce an intelligible trace behind.

That the reader should not think me visionary in these contemplations, or romancing in making such assertions, I will hand him the following item of the extravagancies which are practiced in these regions, and rapidly leading to the results which I have just named.

When I first arrived at this place, on my way up the river, which was in the month of May, in 1832, and had taken up my lodgings in the Fur Company's fort, Mr. Laidlaw, of whom I have before spoken, and also his chief clerk, Mr. Halsey, and many of their men, as well as the chiefs of the Sioux, told me, that only a few days before I arrived, (when an immense herd of buffaloes had showed themselves on the opposite side of the river, almost blackening the plains for a great distance,) a party of five or six hundred Sioux Indians on horseback, forded the river about midday, and spending a few hours amongst them, recrossed the river at sundown and came into the Fort with *fourteen hundred fresh buffalo tongues,* which were thrown down in a mass, and for which they required but a few gallons of whiskey, which was soon demolished, indulging them in a little, and harmless carouse.

This profligate waste of the lives of these noble and useful animals, when, from all that I could learn, not a skin or a pound of the meat (except the tongues), was brought in, fully supports me in the seemingly extravagant predictions that I have made as to their extinction, which I am certain is near at hand. In the above extravagant instance, at a season when their skins were without fur and not worth taking off, and their camp was so well stocked with fresh and dried meat, that they had no occasion for using the flesh, there is a fair exhibition of the improvident character of the savage, and also of his recklessness in catering for his appetite, so long as the present inducements are held out to him in his country, for its gratification. . . .

Whilst the herd is together, the wolves never attack them, as they instantly gather for combined resistance, which they effectually make. But when the herds are traveling, it often happens that an aged or wounded one, lingers at a distance behind, and when fairly out of sight of the herd, is set upon by these voracious hunters, which often gather to the number of fifty or more, and are sure at last to torture him to death, and use him up at a meal. The buffalo, however, is a huge and furious animal, and when his retreat is cut off, makes desperate and deadly resistance, contending to the last moment for the right of life — and oftentimes deals death by wholesale, to his canine assailants, which he is tossing into the air or stamping to death under his feet.

During my travels in these regions, I have several times come across such a gang of these animals surrounding an old or a wounded bull, where it would seem, from appearances, that they had been for several days in attendance, and at intervals desperately engaged in the effort to take his life. But a short time since, as one of my hunting companions and myself were returning to our encampment with our horses loaded with meat, we discovered at a distance, a huge bull, encircled with a gang of white wolves; we rode up as near as we could without driving them away, and being within pistol shot, we had a remarkably good view, where I sat for a few moments and made a sketch in my note-book; after which, we rode up and gave the signal for them to disperse, which they instantly did, withdrawing themselves to the distance of fifty or sixty rods, when we found to our great surprise, that the animal had made desperate resistance, until his eyes were entirely eaten out of his head — the grizzle of his nose was mostly gone — his tongue was half eaten off, and the skin and flesh of his legs torn almost literally into strings. In this tattered and torn condition, the poor old veteran stood bracing up in the midst of his devourers, who had ceased hostilities for a few minutes, to enjoy a sort of parley, recovering strength and preparing to resume the attack in a few moments again. In this group, some were reclining, to gain breath, whilst others were sneaking about and licking their chaps in anxiety for a renewal of the attack; and others, less lucky, had been crushed to death by the feet or the horns of the bull. I rode nearer to the pitiable object as he stood bleeding and trembling before me, and said to him, "Now is your time, old fellow, and you had better be off." Though blind and nearly destroyed, there seemed evidently to be a recognition of a friend in me, as he straightened up, and, trembling with excitement, dashed off at full speed upon the prairie, in a straight line. We turned our horses and resumed our march, and when we had advanced a mile or more, we looked back, and on our left, where we saw again the ill-fated animal surrounded by his tormentors, to whose insatiable voracity he unquestionably soon fell a victim . . .

It is not enough in this polished and extravagant age, that we get from the Indian his lands, and the very clothes from his back, but the food from their mouths must be stopped, to add a new and useless article to the fashionable world's luxuries. The ranks must be thinned, and the race exterminated, of this noble animal, and the Indians of the Great Plains left without the means of supporting life, that white men may figure a few years longer, enveloped in buffalo robes — that they may spread them, for their pleasure and elegance, over the backs of their sleighs, and trail them ostentatiously amidst the busy throng, as things of beauty and elegance that had been made for them!

Reader! listen to the following calculations, and forget them not. The buffaloes (the quadrupeds from whose backs your beautiful robes were taken, and whose myriads were once spread over the whole country, from the Rocky Mountains to the Atlantic Ocean) have recently fled before the appalling appearance of civilized man, and taken up their abode and pasturage amid the almost boundless prairies of the West. An instinctive dread of their deadly foes, who made an easy prey of them whilst grazing in the forest, has led them to seek the midst of the vast and treeless plains of grass, as the spot where they would be least exposed to the assaults of their enemies; and it is exclusively in those desolate fields of silence (yet of beauty) that they are to be found — and over these vast steppes, or prairies, have they fled, like the Indian, towards the "setting sun"; until their bands have been crowded together, and their limits confined to a narrow strip of country on this side of the Rocky Mountains.

This strip of country, which extends from the province of Mexico to Lake Winnipeg on the North, is almost one entire plain of grass, which is, and ever must be, useless to cultivating man. It is here, and here chiefly, that the buffaloes dwell; and with, and hovering about them, live and flourish the tribes of Indians, whom God made for the enjoyment of that fair land and its luxuries.

It is a melancholy contemplation for one who has traveled as I have, through these realms, and seen this noble animal in all its pride and glory, to contemplate it so rapidly wasting from the world, drawing the irresistible conclusion too, which one must do, that its species is soon to be extinguished, and with it the peace and happiness (if not the actual existence) of the tribes of Indians who are joint tenants with them, in the occupancy of these vast and idle plains.

And what a splendid contemplation too, when one (who has traveled these realms, and can duly appreciate them) imagines them as they *might* in future be seen, (by some great protecting policy of government) preserved in their pristine beauty and wildness, in a *magnificent park*, where the world could see for ages to come, the native Indian in his classic attire, galloping his wild horse, with sinewy bow, and shield and lance, amid the fleeting herds of elks and buffaloes. What a beautiful and thrilling specimen for America to preserve and hold up to the view of her refined citizens and the world, in future ages! A *nation's Park*, containing man and beast, in all the wild and freshness of their nature's beauty!

I would ask no other monument to my memory, nor any other enrollment of my name amongst the famous dead, than the reputation of having been the founder of such an institution.

Lucy Hooper
(1816–1841)

The "language of flowers" book, an immensely popular nineteenth-century literary form, might justly be considered a lost subgenre of American nature writing. Flower books, which evolved from the popular genres of the almanac and the illustrated gift book, were usually written and edited by women and sought to explore and celebrate the symbolic, allegorical, and mythic significance of specific plants, trees, and flowers. Although language of flowers literature has a long history in both Eastern and European cultures, American flower books were in vogue from the 1830s through the 1860s, a period that produced scores of these works, including Sarah Josepha Hale's *Flora's Interpreter* (1832), Catharine H. Waterman's *Flora's Lexicon* (1839), Frances Sargent Osgood's *The Poetry of Flowers and Flowers of Poetry* (1841), Sarah Carter Edgarton Mayo's *Fables of Flora* (1844), and C. M. Kirtland's *Poetry of Flowers* (1848). The language of flowers book excerpted below is *The Lady's Book of Flowers and Poetry . . .* (1842), edited (and partially written) by American poet Lucy Hooper. Hooper, who lived most of her life in Brooklyn, was a well-educated woman whose dual passion for botany and poetry are clearly reflected in her work. Although she died of tuberculosis at age twenty-five, Hooper was able to complete what is among the most interesting and accomplished of the American flower books. *The Lady's Book* is organized by species of flower, each of which is celebrated in a poem (or poems) by various writers—including, notably, Longfellow and Bryant. But beneath the conventional sentimentality of this beautifully illustrated "friendship offering" we see an accomplished botanist and purveyor of popular science, for Hooper includes various educational apparatus including a "Botanical Introduction" (in which she argues for the adoption of Linnaean taxonomy), a "Complete Floral Dictionary," and a practical guide to the "Management of Plants in Rooms." In her prose headnotes to each flower entry, a number of which appear below, Hooper combines scientific information, mythic and literary allusions, and lyrical appreciation of each species. Indeed, language of flower books such as Hooper's might be seen as a popular corollary to the Transcendentalists' more intellectualized assertion that, as Emerson wrote in *Nature* (1836), the natural world is a "perpetual allegory" within which "[e]very natural fact is a symbol of some spiritual fact."

From *The Lady's Book of Flowers and Poetry* . . . (1842)

The Rose

The different kinds of Roses are quite numerous; and botanists find it very difficult to determine with accuracy which are species and which are varieties. On this account, Linnaeus, and some other eminent authors, are inclined to think that there is only one real species of Rose, which is the Rosa Canina, or Dog rose of the hedges, &c., and that all the other sorts are accidental varieties of it. However, according to the Linnaean arrangement, they stand divided into fourteen species, each comprehending varieties, which in some sorts are but few, in others numerous.

Poetry is lavish of Roses: it heaps them into beds, weaves them into crowns, twines them into arbors, forges them into chains, and plants them in the bosom of beauty. It not only delights to bring in the Rose itself upon every occasion, but seizes each particular beauty it possesses as an object of comparison with the loveliest works of Nature;—as soft as a Rose leaf; as sweet as a Rose; Rosy Clouds; &c. &c. The eastern poets have united the Rose with the nightingale—the Venus of Flowers with the Apollo of birds.—The Rose is supposed to burst forth from its bud at the song of the nightingale. . . .

The Gentian

This genus of plant has received its name in honor of Gentius, a King of Illyria, who is said to have discovered one of the species of it. He is also supposed to have experienced its virtues on his army, as a cure for the plague.

The Gentians are very numerous, and many of them eminently beautiful. They are generally very difficult to preserve in a garden; and, being long-rooted, very few are adapted for planting in pots. The smaller kinds, however, may be so cultivated: as the Swallow-wort-leaved, which does not exceed a foot in height, and has large light-blue bell-shaped flowers, blowing in July and August. The roots only are perennial; the stalks decay annually: and of most of the species the flowers appear but once in two or three years. The March Gentian has also fine blue flowers, though few in number, and blows in August and September. This species grows naturally in England and many other parts of Europe. . . .

Sunflower, Marigold, and Heliotrope

The Sunflower does not derive its name, as some have supposed, from turning to the sun, but from the resemblance of the full-blown flower to the sun itself: Gerard remarks, that he has seen four of these flowers on the same stem, pointing to the four cardinal points. This flower is a native of Mexico and Peru, and looks as if it grew from their own gold. It flowers from June to October.

The principal species of Sunflower are — the Dwarf Annual, the Perennial, the Dark Red, and the narrow-leaved.

Several of the Sunflowers are natives of Canada, where they are much admired and cultivated by the inhabitants, in gardens, for their beauty; in the United States we sow whole acres of land with them, for the purpose of preparing oil from their seeds, of which they produce an immense number.

The Sunflower was formerly called Marigold also, as the Marigold was termed Sunflower. Gerard styles it the Sun marigold.

In old authors, the name for the plant, which is now more strictly and properly designated the Marigold, is Golds, or Rudds. Golds, or Gouldes, is a name given by the country-people to a variety of yellow flowers; and the name of the Virgin Mary has been added to many plants which were anciently, for their beauty, named after Venus, of which the Marigold is one: Costmary, the Virgin Mary's Costus, is another.

The Field Marigold is a native of most parts of Europe, and differs but little from the garden Marigold, except in being altogether smaller.

There are many varieties of the Garden Marigold; one of which, the Proliferous, called by Gerard the fruitful Marigold, is, as he says, "called by the vulgar sort of women, Jack-an-apes on horseback." Although this species of Marigold is generally yellow, there is a variety with purple flowers.

Linnaeus has observed, that the Marigold is usually open from nine in the morning to three in the afternoon. This circumstance attracted early notice, and on this account the plant has been termed *Solsequia* (Sun-follower), and *Solis sponsa* (Spouse of the Sun).

The Heliotrope is the same with the Turnsole, both names being derived from words which signify to turn with the sun.

The Sunflower is of the class *Syngenesia*, and order *Polygamia Frustanea*; the Marigold of the same class, but of the order *Polygamia Necessaria*; and the Heliotrope of the class *Pentandria*, and order *Monogynia*. . . .

The Acanthus

The Acanthus is found in hot countries, along the shores of great rivers.

It grows freely in our climate; and Pliny assures us that it is a garden herb, and is admirably adapted for ornament and embellishment. The ancients tastefully adorned their furniture, vases, and most costly attire, with its elegant leaves. And Virgil says, that the robe of Helen was bordered with a wreath of acanthus in relief.

This beautiful model of the arts has become their emblem; and he will be talented indeed, who shall produce anything to excel its richness. If any obstacle resists the growth of the acanthus, it seems to struggle to overcome it, and to vegetate with renewed vigor. So genius, when acted upon by resistance or opposition, redoubles its attempts to overthrow every impediment.

It is said that the architect, Callimach, passing near the tomb of a young maiden who had died a few days before the time appointed for her nuptials, moved by tenderness and pity, approached to scatter some flowers on her tomb. Another tribute to her memory had preceded his. Her nurse had collected the flowers which should have decked her on her wedding-day; and, putting them with the marriage veil, in a little basket, had placed it near the grave upon a plant of acanthus, and then covered it with a tile. In the succeeding spring the leaves of the acanthus grew round the basket; but, being stayed in their growth by the projecting tile, they recoiled and surmounted its extremities. Callimach, surprised by this rural decoration, which seemed the work of the Graces in tears, conceived the capital of the Corinthian column, a magnificent ornament, still used and admired by the whole civilized world. . . .

The Vervain

It were well if botanists would attach a moral idea to every plant they describe; we might then have an universal dictionary of the Sentiment of Flowers — generally understood,—which would be handed down from age to age, and might be renewed, without changing their characters, every succeeding spring.

The altars of Jupiter are overthrown; those ancient forests, that witnessed the mysteries of Druidism, exist no longer; and the pyramids of Egypt shall one day disappear, buried, like the sphinx, in the sands of the desert; but the lotus and the acanthus shall ever flower upon the banks of the Nile, the mistletoe will always flourish upon the oak, and the vervain upon the barren knolls.

Vervain was used by the ancients for divers kinds of divinations; they attributed to it a thousand properties; among others, that of reconciling enemies; and when the Roman heralds at arms were dispatched with a message of peace or war to other nations, they wore a wreath of vervain.

The Druids held this plant in great veneration, and, before gathering it, they made a sacrifice to the earth. Probably they used it for food.

We are told that the worshippers of the sun, in performing their services, held branches of vervain in their hands. Venus Victorious wore a crown of myrtle interwoven with vervain, and the Germans to this day give a hat of vervain to the new married bride, as putting her under the protection of that goddess. Pliny also tells us that it was made use of by the Druids in casting lots, in drawing omens, and in other magical arts. . . .

The Lilac

The lilac is consecrated to the first emotion of love, because nothing is more delightful than the sensations it produces by its first appearance on the return of spring. The freshness of its verdure, the pliancy of its tender branches, the abundance of its flowers,—their beauty, though brief and transient,—their delicate and varied colors;—all their qualities summon up those sweet emotions which enrich beauty, and impart to youth a grace divine.

Albano was unable to blend, upon the palette which love had confided to him, colors sufficiently soft and delicate to convey the peculiarly beautiful tints which adorn the human face in early youth;

The velvet down that spreads the cheek;

Van Spaendock himself laid down his pencil in despair before a bunch of lilac. Nature seems to have aimed to produce massy bunches of these flowers, every part of which should astonish by its delicacy and its variety. The gradation of color, from the purple bud to the almost colorless flowers, is the least charm of these beautiful groups, around which the light plays and produces a thousand shades, which all blending together in the same tint, forms that matchless harmony which the painter despairs to imitate, and the most indifferent observer delights to behold. What labor has Nature bestowed to create this fragile shrub, which seems only given for the gratification of the senses! What an union of perfume, of freshness, of grace, and of delicacy! What variety in detail! What beauty as a whole! . . .

The Laurel

The Greeks and Romans consecrated crowns of laurel to glory of every kind. With them they adorned the brows of warriors and of poets, of orators and philosophers, of the vestal virgin and the emperor.

This beautiful shrub is found in abundance in the island of Delphos, where it grows naturally on the banks of the river Peneus. There, its aromatic and evergreen foliage is borne up by its aspiring branches to the height of the loftiest trees; and it is alleged that by a secret and peculiar power they avert the thunderbolt from the shores they beautify. The beautiful Daphne was the daughter of the river Peneus. She was beloved by Apollo; but, preferring virtue to the love of the most eloquent of gods, she fled, fearing that the eloquence of his speech should lead her from the paths of virtue. Apollo pursued her; and as he caught her, the nymph invoked the aid of her father, and was changed into the laurel.

In our free land, where letters are so extensively cultivated, they who succeed in exciting popular favor meet with more remuneration than in ancient days; but how few have been honored so highly as their merits demand, until the last debt of nature has been paid, and then the marble bust, wreathed with bay, is raised to immortalize his fame, when his ears are become deaf to praise. He seldom receives his honors due while he enjoys the beauties of this terrestrial globe. . . .

Nathaniel Hawthorne
(1804–1864)

Among the most celebrated and studied American fiction writers, Nathaniel Hawthorne is best known as the author of novels such as *The Scarlet Letter* (1850) and *The House of the Seven Gables* (1851) and short stories such as those contained in the collections *Twice-Told Tales* (1837) and *Mosses from an Old Manse* (1846). Born in Salem, Massachusetts, Hawthorne resolved upon a literary career early in life, and after graduating from Bowdoin College in 1825 he spent twelve years in literary seclusion while writing his first novel and early tales. Hawthorne's first substantial literary success came in 1837 with the publication of *Twice-Told Tales,* a book of short stories that included "The Minister's Black Veil." During the following years Hawthorne continued writing, spent six months living at the experimental Brook Farm commune, and married Sophia Peabody. In 1842 the Hawthornes moved to the Transcendentalist hub of Concord, Massachusetts, where they rented and occupied the "Old Manse"—the home that had been built in 1770 by Ralph Waldo Emerson's grandfather, William, and where Emerson himself completed the first draft of *Nature* (1836). Here Hawthorne spent what he later described as his three happiest years, and here he wrote some of his finest tales, including "The Birthmark," "Rappaccini's Daughter," and "The Artist of the Beautiful." When those now-famous stories appeared in the superb collection *Mosses from an Old Manse,* they were among a number of other pieces including "Buds and Bird-Voices," which had been previously published in the *United States Magazine and Democratic Review* in June 1843. This wonderful but often overlooked nature essay—an eloquent literary appreciation of the spring season that was clearly composed under the influence of his Transcendentalist neighbors—suggests how pleased Hawthorne was to witness the arrival of the New England spring through the open windows of the Old Manse. His observations of birds and plants are accompanied by a poignant sense of renewal that finds graceful expression in his lyrical prose. Little wonder that, writing in an 1850 review of *Mosses*, Hawthorne's friend Herman Melville (who dedicated *Moby-Dick* [1851] to Hawthorne) declared this seasonal nature essay "a delicious thing."

From "Buds and Bird-Voices" (1843)

Balmy Spring—weeks later than we expected, and months later than we longed for her—comes at last, to revive the moss on the roof and walls of our old mansion. She peeps brightly into my study-window, inviting me to throw it open, and create a summer atmosphere by the intermixture of her genial breath with the black and cheerless comfort of the stove. As the casement ascends, forth into infinite space fly the innumerable forms of thought or fancy, that have kept me company in the retirement of this little chamber, during the sluggish lapse of wintry weather;—visions, gay, grotesque, and sad; pictures of real life, tinted with nature's homely gray and russet; scenes in dreamland, bedizened with rainbow-hues, which faded before they were well laid on;—all these may vanish now, and leave me to mold a fresh existence out of sunshine. Brooding meditation may flap her dusky wings, and take her owl-like flight, blinking amid the cheerfulness of noontide. Such companions befit the season of frosted windowpanes and crackling fires, when the blast howls through the black ash-trees of our avenue, and the drifting snowstorm chokes up the wood-paths, and fills the highway from stone wall to stone wall. In the spring and summer time, all somber thoughts should follow the winter northward, with the somber and thoughtful crows. The old, paradisiacal economy of life is again in force; we live, not to think, nor to labor, but for the simple end of being happy; nothing, for the present hour, is worthy of man's infinite capacity, save to imbibe the warm smile of heaven, and sympathize with the reviving earth.

The present Spring comes onward with fleeter footsteps, because winter lingered so unconscionably long, that, with her best diligence, she can hardly retrieve half the allotted period of her reign. It is but a fortnight, since I stood on the brink of our swollen river, and beheld the accumulated ice of four frozen months go down the stream. Except in streaks here and there upon the hillsides, the whole visible universe was then covered with deep snow, the nethermost layer of which had been deposited by an early December storm. It was a sight to make the beholder torpid, in the impossibility of imagining how this vast white napkin was to be removed from the face of the corpselike world, in less time than had been required to spread it there. But who can estimate the power of gentle influences, whether amid material desolation, or the moral winter of man's heart! There have been no tempestuous rains,—even, no sultry days,—but a constant breath of southern winds, with now a day of kindly sunshine, and now a no less kindly mist, or a soft descent of showers, in which a smile and a blessing seemed to have been steeped. The snow has vanished as if by magic; whatever heaps may be hidden in the woods and deep gorges of the hills, only two solitary specks remain in the landscape; and those I shall almost regret to miss, when, tomorrow, I look for them in vain. Never before, methinks, has spring pressed so closely on the footsteps of retreating winter. Along the roadside, the green blades of grass have sprouted on the very edge of the snowdrifts. The pastures and mowing fields have not yet assumed a general aspect of verdure; but neither have they the cheerless brown tint which they wear in latter autumn, when vegetation has entirely ceased; there is now a faint shadow of life, gradually brightening into the warm reality. Some tracts, in a happy exposure—as, for instance, yonder southwestern slope of an orchard, in front of that old red farmhouse, beyond the river—such patches of land already wear a beautiful and tender green, to which no future luxuriance can add a charm. It looks unreal—a prophecy—a hope—a transitory effect of some peculiar light, which will vanish with the slightest motion of the eye. But beauty is never a delusion; not these verdant tracts, but the dark and barren landscape, all around them, is a shadow and a dream. Each moment wins some portion of the earth from death to life; a sudden gleam of verdure brightens along the sunny slope of a bank, which, an instant ago, was brown and bare. You look again, and behold an apparition of green grass!

The trees, in our orchard and elsewhere, are as yet naked, but already appear full of life and vegetable blood. It seems as if, by one magic touch, they might instantaneously burst into full foliage, and that the wind, which now sighs through their naked branches, might make sudden music amid innumerable leaves. The moss-grown willow-tree, which, for forty years past, has overshadowed these western windows, will be among the first to put on its green attire. There are some objections to the willow; it is not a dry and cleanly tree, and impresses the beholder with an association of sliminess. No trees, I think, are perfectly agreeable as companions, unless they have glossy leaves, dry bark, and a firm and hard texture of trunk and branches. But the willow is almost the earliest to gladden us with the promise and reality of beauty, in its graceful and delicate foliage, and the last to scatter its yellow, yet scarcely withered leaves, upon the ground. All through the winter, too, its yellow twigs give it a sunny aspect, which is not without a cheering influence, even in the grayest and gloomiest day. Beneath a clouded sky, it faithfully remembers the sunshine. Our old house would lose a charm, were the willow to be cut down, with its golden crown over the snow-covered roof, and its heap of summer verdure.

The lilac-shrubs, under my study-window, are likewise almost in leaf; in two or three days more, I may put forth my hand, and pluck the topmost bough in its freshest green. These lilacs are very aged, and have lost the luxuriant foliage of their prime. The heart, or the judgment, or the moral sense, or the taste, is dissatisfied with their present aspect. Old age is not venerable, when it embodies itself in lilacs, rosebushes, or any other ornamental shrubs; it seems as if such plants, as they grow only for beauty, ought to flourish in immortal youth, or, at least, to die before their sad decrepitude. Trees of beauty are trees of Paradise, and therefore not subject to decay, by their original nature, though they have lost that precious birthright by being transplanted to an earthly soil. There is a kind of ludicrous unfitness in the idea of a time-stricken and grandfatherly lilac-bush. The analogy holds good in human life. Persons who can only be graceful and ornamental—who can give the world nothing but flowers—should die young, and never be seen with gray hair and wrinkles, any more than the flower-shrubs with mossy bark and blighted foliage, like the lilacs under my window. Not that beauty is worthy of less than immortality—no; the beautiful should live forever—and thence, perhaps, the sense of impropriety, when we see it triumphed over by time. Apple-trees, on the other hand, grow old without reproach. Let them live as long as they may, and contort themselves into whatever perversity of shape they please, and deck their withered limbs with a springtime gaudiness of pink-blossoms, still they are respectable, even if they afford us only an apple or two in a season. Those few apples—or, at all events, the remembrance of apples in bygone years—are the atonement which utilitarianism inexorably demands, for the privilege of lengthened life. Human flower-shrubs, if they will grow old on earth, should, beside their lovely blossoms, bear some kind of fruit that will satisfy earthly appetites; else neither man, nor the decorum of nature, will deem it fit that the moss should gather on them.

One of the first things that strike the attention, when the white sheet of winter is withdrawn, is the neglect and disarray that lay hidden beneath it. Nature is not cleanly, according to our prejudices. The beauty of preceding years, now transformed to brown and blighted deformity, obstructs the brightening loveliness of the present hour. Our avenue is strewn with the whole crop of Autumn's withered leaves. There are quantities of decayed branches, which one tempest after another has flung down, black and rotten; and one or two with the ruin of a bird's nest clinging to them. In the garden are the dried bean-vines, the brown stalks of the asparagus-bed, and melancholy old cabbages, which were frozen into the soil before their unthrifty cultivator could find time to gather them. How invariably, throughout all the forms of life, do we find these intermingled memorials of death! On the soil of thought, and in the garden of the heart, as well as in the sensual world, lie withered leaves; the ideas and feelings that we have done with. There is no wind strong enough to sweep them away; infinite space will not garner them from our sight. What mean they? Why may we not be permitted to live and enjoy, as if this were the first life, and our own the primal enjoyment, instead of treading always on these dry bones and moldering relics, from the aged accumulation of which springs all that now appears so young and new? Sweet must have been the springtime of Eden, when no earlier year had strewn its decay upon the virgin turf, and no former experience had ripened into summer, and faded into autumn, in the hearts of its inhabitants! That was a world worth living in! Oh, thou murmurer, it is out of the very wantonness of such a life, that thou feignest these idle lamentations! There is no decay. Each human soul is the first created inhabitant of its own Eden. We dwell in an old moss-covered mansion, and tread in the worn footprints of the past, and have a gray clergyman's ghost for our daily and nightly inmate; yet all these outward circumstances are made less than visionary, by the renewing power of the spirit. Should the spirit ever lose this power — should the withered leaves, and the rotten branches, and the moss-covered house, and the ghost of the gray past, ever become its realities, and the verdure and the freshness merely its faint dream — then let it pray to be released from earth. It will need the air of heaven, to revive its pristine energies!

What an unlooked-for flight was this, from our shadowy avenue of black ash and Balm of Gilead trees, into the infinite! Now we have our feet again upon the turf. Nowhere does the grass spring up so industriously as in this homely yard, along the base of the stone wall, and in the sheltered nooks of the buildings, and especially around the southern doorstep; a locality which seems particularly favorable to its growth; for it is already tall enough to bend over, and wave in the wind. I observe that several weeds — and, most frequently, a plant that stains the fingers with its yellow juice — have survived, and retained their freshness and sap throughout the winter. One knows not how they have deserved such an exception from the common lot of their race. They are now the patriarchs of the departed year, and may preach mortality to the present generation of flowers and weeds.

Among the delights of spring, how is it possible to forget the birds! Even the crows were welcome, as the sable harbingers of a brighter and livelier race. They visited us before the snow was off, but seem mostly to have departed now, or else to have betaken themselves to remote depths of the woods, which they haunt all summer long. Many a time shall I disturb them there, and feel as if I had intruded among a company of silent worshippers, as they sit in sabbath-stillness among the treetops. Their voices, when they speak, are in admirable accordance with the tranquil solitude of a summer afternoon; and, resounding so far above the head, their loud clamor increases the religious quiet of the scene, instead of breaking it. A crow, however, has no real pretensions to religion, in spite of his gravity of mien and black attire; he is certainly a thief, and probably an infidel. The gulls are far more respectable, in a moral point of view. These denizens of sea-beaten rocks, and haunters of the lonely beach, come up our inland river, at this season, and soar high overhead, flapping their broad wings in the upper sunshine. They are among the most picturesque of birds, because they so float and rest upon the air as to become almost stationary parts of the landscape. The imagination has time to grow acquainted with them; they have not flitted away in a moment. You go up among the clouds, and greet these lofty-flighted gulls, and repose confidently with them upon the sustaining atmosphere. Ducks have their haunts along the solitary places of the river, and alight in flocks upon the broad bosom of the overflowed meadows. Their flight is too rapid and determined for the eye to catch enjoyment from it, although it never fails to stir up the heart with the sportsman's ineradicable instinct. They have now gone farther northward, but will visit us again in autumn.

The smaller birds — the little songsters of the woods, and those that haunt man's dwellings, and claim human friendship by building their nests under the sheltering eaves, or among the orchard-trees — these require a touch more delicate and a gentler heart than mine, to do them justice. Their outburst of melody is like a brook let loose from wintry chains. We need not deem it a too high and solemn word, to call it a hymn of praise to the Creator; since Nature, who pictures the reviving year in so many sights of beauty, has expressed the sentiment of renewed life in no other sound, save the notes of these blessed birds. Their music, however, just now, seems to be incidental, and not the result of a set purpose. They are discussing the economy of life and love, and the site and architecture of their summer residences, and have no time to sit on a twig, and pour forth solemn hymns, or overtures, operas, symphonies, and waltzes. Anxious questions are asked; grave subjects are settled in quick and animated debate; and only by occasional accident, as from pure ecstasy, does a rich warble roll its tiny waves of golden sound through the atmosphere. Their little bodies are as busy as their voices; they are in a constant flutter and restlessness. Even when two or three retreat to a treetop, to hold council, they wag their tails and heads all the time, with the irrepressible activity of their nature, which perhaps renders their brief span of life in reality as long as the patriarchal age of sluggish man. The blackbirds, three species of which consort together, are the noisiest of all our feathered citizens. Great companies of them — more than the famous "four-and-twenty," whom Mother Goose has immortalized — congregate in contiguous treetops, and vociferate with all the clamor and confusion of a turbulent political meeting. Politics, certainly, must be the occasion of such tumultuous debates; but still — unlike all other politicians — they instill melody into their individual utterances, and produce harmony as a general effect. Of all bird-voices, none are more sweet and cheerful to my ear than those of swallows, in the dim, sun-streaked interior of a lofty barn; they address the heart with even a closer sympathy than Robin Redbreast. But, indeed, all these winged people, that dwell in the vicinity of homesteads, seem to partake of human nature, and possess the germ, if not the development, of immortal souls. . . .

Thank Providence for Spring! The earth — and man himself, by sympathy with his birthplace — would be far other than we find them, if life toiled wearily onward, without this periodical infusion of the primal spirit. Will the world ever be so decayed, that spring may not renew its greenness? Can man be so dismally age-stricken, that no faintest sunshine of his youth may revisit him once a year? It is impossible. The moss on our timeworn mansion brightens into beauty; the good old pastor, who once dwelt here, renewed his prime, regained his boyhood, in the genial breezes of his ninetieth spring. Alas for the worn and heavy soul, if, whether in youth or age, it have outlived its privilege of springtime sprightliness! From such a soul, the world must hope no reformation of its evil — no sympathy with the lofty faith and gallant struggles of those who contend in its behalf. Summer works in the present, and thinks not of the future; Autumn is a rich conservative; Winter has utterly lost its faith, and clings tremulously to the remembrance of what has been; but Spring, with its outgushing life, is the true type of the Movement!

William Cullen Bryant
(1794–1878)

The author of celebrated nature poems including "To a Waterfowl" and "A Forest Hymn," William Cullen Bryant was among the most revered landscape poets of the nineteenth century. Washington Irving praised Bryant's ability to describe natural objects with "a pensive grace that blends them all into harmony"; Ralph Waldo Emerson wrote that "if Bryant is in the world we have more tolerance & more love for the changing sky, the mist, the rain, the bleak overcast day, the indescribable sunrise & the immortal stars"; and Asher Durand, in his painting *Kindred Spirits* (1849), made Bryant the representative figure standing beside Thomas Cole in the sublime American wilderness. But Bryant was also an environmental journalist and travel writer of tremendous influence. As editor of the *New York Evening Post* newspaper, Bryant used editorials to alert his readers to the value of protecting natural areas from development. "A New Public Park," included here, was part of his campaign for the establishment of an urban park in New York City. It was Bryant who first suggested the idea, and he supported the appointment of pioneer conservationist Frederick Law Olmsted as the first superintendent of what later became Central Park. Bryant also made extensive travels, from which he dispatched letters describing his observations for publication in the *Post.* Through these letters Bryant showed readers the beauty of the American land and lamented the development of the pristine wilderness he encountered in his journeys. So popular were Bryant's missives from the field that they were thrice collected into independent volumes: *Letters of a Traveller . . .* (1850), *Letters of a Traveller — Second Series* (1859), and *Letters From the East* (1869). It was in Bryant's travel letters that many Americans caught their first glimpse of Midwestern prairies, Vermont mountains, Georgia river marshes, and Florida coral reefs; as they walked to their jobs at warehouses, offices, and docks, New Yorkers read Bryant's descriptions of the prairie-wolf, alligator, sturgeon, and copperhead. By expanding Americans' sense of their land through his travel letters, and by arguing for the protection of local and urban nature through his editorials, Bryant used the medium of the newspaper — as well as the lyric poem — to celebrate the role of landscape in American culture.

"A New Public Park" (*New York Evening Post,* July 3, 1844)

The heats of summer are upon us, and while some are leaving the town for shady retreats in the country, others refresh themselves with short excursions to Hoboken or New Brighton, or other places among the beautiful environs of our city. If the public authorities who expend so much of our money in laying out the city, would do what is in their power, they might give our vast population an extensive pleasure ground for shade and recreation in these sultry afternoons which we might reach without going out of town.

On the road to Harlem, between Sixty-eighth street on the south, and Seventy-seventh street on the north, and extending from Third avenue to the East River, is a tract of beautiful woodland, comprising sixty or seventy acres, thickly covered with old trees, intermingled with a variety of shrubs. The surface is varied in a very striking and picturesque manner, with craggy eminences, and hollows, and a little stream runs through the midst. The swift tides of the East river sweep its rocky shores, and the fresh breeze of the bay comes in, on every warm summer afternoon, over the restless waters. The trees are of almost every species that grows in our woods: — the different varieties of oak, the birch, the beech, the linden, the mulberry, the tulip tree, and others: the azalea, the kalmia, and other flowering shrubs are in bloom here at their season, and the ground in spring is gay with flowers. There never was a finer situation for the public garden of a great city. Nothing is wanted but to cut winding paths through it, leaving the woods as they now are, and introducing here and there a jet from the Croton aqueduct, the streams from which would make their own waterfalls over the rocks, and keep the brook running through the place always fresh and full. In the English Garden at Munich, a pleasure ground of immense extent, laid out by our countryman Count Rumford, into which half the population pours itself on summer evenings, the designer of the ground was obliged to content himself with artificial rocks, brought from a distance and cemented together, and eminences painfully heaped up from the sand of the plain. In the tract of which we speak, nature has done almost everything to our hands, excepting the construction of paths.

As we are now going on, we are making a belt of muddy docks all around the island. We should be glad to see one small part of the shore without them, one place at least where the tides may be allowed to flow pure, and the ancient brim of rocks which borders the waters left in its original picturesqueness and beauty. Commerce is devouring inch by inch the coast of the island, and if we would rescue any part of it for health and recreation it must be done now.

All large cities have their extensive public grounds and gardens, Madrid and Mexico their Alamedas, London its Regent's Park, Paris its Champs Elysées, and Vienna its Prater. There are none of them, we believe, which have the same natural advantages of the picturesque and beautiful which belong to this spot. It would be of easy access to the citizens, and the public carriages which now rattle in almost every street in this city, would take them to its gates. The only objection which we can see to the place would be the difficulty of persuading the owners of the soil to part with it.

If any of our brethren of the public press should see fit to support this project, we are ready to resign in their favor any claim to the credit of originally suggesting it.

From *Letters of a Traveller* . . . (1850)

We were soon upon the broad waters of Lake Huron, and when the evening closed upon us we were already out of sight of land. The next morning I was awakened by the sound of rain on the hurricane deck. A cool east wind was blowing. I opened the outer door of my stateroom, and snuffed the air which was strongly impregnated with the odor of burnt leaves or grass, proceeding, doubtless, from the burning of woods or prairies somewhere on the shores of the lake. For mile after mile, for hour after hour, as we flew through the mist, the same odor was perceptible: the atmosphere of the lake was full of it.

"Will it rain all day?" I asked of a fellow-passenger, a Salem man, in a white cravat.

"The clouds are thin," he answered; "the sun will soon burn them off."

In fact, the sun soon melted away the clouds, and before ten o'clock I was shown, to the north of us, the dim shore of the Great Manitoulin Island, with the faintly descried opening called the West Strait, through which a throng of speculators in copper mines are this summer constantly passing to the Sault de Ste. Marie. On the other side was the sandy isle of Bois Blanc, the name of which is commonly corrupted into Bob Low Island, thickly covered with pines, and showing a tall lighthouse on the point nearest us. Beyond another point lay like a cloud the island of Mackinaw. I had seen it once before, but now the hazy atmosphere magnified it into a lofty mountain; its limestone cliffs impending over the water seemed larger; the white fort—white as snow—built from the quarries of the island, looked more commanding, and the rocky crest above it seemed almost to rise to the clouds. There was a good deal of illusion in all this, as we were convinced as we came nearer, but Mackinaw with its rocks rising from the most transparent waters that the earth pours out from her springs, is a stately object in any condition of the atmosphere. The captain of our steamer allowed us but a moment at Mackinaw; a moment to gaze into the clear waters, and count the fish as they played about without fear twenty or thirty feet below our steamer, as plainly seen as if they lay in the air; a moment to look at the fort on the heights, dazzling the eyes with its new whiteness; a moment to observe the habitations of this ancient village, some of which show you roofs and walls of red-cedar bark confined by horizontal strips of wood, a kind of architecture between the wigwam and the settler's cabin. A few baskets of fish were lifted on board, in which I saw trout of enormous size, trout a yard in length, and whitefish smaller, but held perhaps in higher esteem, and we turned our course to the straits which lead into Lake Michigan.

I remember hearing a lady say that she was tired of improvements, and only wanted to find a place that was finished, where she might live in peace. I think I shall recommend Mackinaw to her. I saw no change in the place since my visit to it five years ago. It is so lucky as to have no backcountry, it offers no advantages to speculation of any sort; it produces, it is true, the finest potatoes in the world, but none for exportation. It may, however, on account of its very cool summer climate, become a fashionable watering place, in which case it must yield to the common fate of American villages and improve, as the phrase is. . . .

Yesterday evening we left the beautiful island of Mackinaw, after a visit of two days delightfully passed. We had climbed its cliffs, rambled on its shores, threaded the walks among its thickets, driven out in the roads that wind through its woods—roads paved by nature with limestone pebbles, a sort of natural macadamization, and the time of our departure seemed to arrive several days too soon. . . .

But I should mention that before leaving Mackinaw, we did not fail to visit the principal curiosities of the place, the Sugar Loaf Rock, a remarkable rock in the middle of the island, of a sharp conical form, rising above the trees by which it is surrounded, and lifting the stunted birches on its shoulders higher than they, like a tall fellow holding up a little boy to overlook a crowd of men—and the Arched Rock on the shore. The atmosphere was thick with smoke, and through the opening spanned by the arch of the rock I saw the long waves, rolled up by a fresh wind, come one after another out of the obscurity, and break with roaring on the beach.

The path along the brow of the precipice and among the evergreens, by which this rock is reached, is singularly wild, but another which leads to it along the shore is no less picturesque—passing under impending cliffs and overshadowing cedars, and between huge blocks and pinnacles of rock.

I spoke in one of my former letters of the manifest fate of Mackinaw, which is to be a watering place. I cannot see how it is to escape this destiny. People already begin to repair to it for health and refreshment from the southern borders of Lake Michigan. Its climate during the summer months is delightful; there is no air more pure and elastic, and the winds of the south and southwest, which are so hot on the prairies, arrive here tempered to a grateful coolness by the waters over which they have swept. The nights are always, in the hottest season, agreeably cool, and the health of the place is proverbial. The world has not many islands so beautiful as Mackinaw, as you may judge from the description I have already given of parts of it. The surface is singularly irregular, with summits of rock and pleasant hollows, open glades of pasturage and shady nooks. To some, the savage visitors, who occasionally set up their lodges on its beach, as well as on that of the surrounding islands, and paddle their canoes in its waters, will be an additional attraction. I cannot but think with a kind of regret on the time which, I suppose is near at hand, when its wild and lonely woods will be intersected with highways, and filled with cottages and boardinghouses. . . .

I had not space in my last letter, which was written from Keene in New Hampshire, to speak of a visit I had just made to the White Mountains. Do not think I am going to bore you with a set description of my journey and ascent of Mount Washington; a few notes of the excursion may possibly amuse you.

From Conway, where the stagecoach sets you down for the night, in sight of the summits of the mountains, the road to the Old Notch is a very picturesque one. You follow the path of the Saco along a wide valley, sometimes in the woods that overhang its bank, and sometimes on the edge of rich grassy meadows, till at length, as you leave behind you one summit after another, you find yourself in a little plain, apparently enclosed on every side by mountains.

Further on you enter the deep gorge which leads gradually upward to the Notch. In the midst of it is situated the Willey House, near which the Willey family were overtaken by an avalanche and perished as they were making their escape.

It is now enlarged into a house of accommodation for visitors to the mountains. Nothing can exceed the aspect of desolation presented by the lofty mountain-ridges which rise on each side. They are streaked with the paths of landslides, occurring at different periods, which have left the rocky ribs of the mountains bare from their bald tops to the forests at their feet, and have filled the sides of the valley with heaps of earth, gravel, stones, and trunks of trees.

From the Willey house you ascend, for about two miles, a declivity, by no means steep, with these dark ridges frowning over you, your path here and there crossed by streams which have made for themselves passages in the granite sides of the mountains like narrow staircases, down which they come tumbling from one vast block to another. I afterward made acquaintance with two of these, and followed them upward from one clear pool and one white cascade to another till I was tired. The road at length passes through what may be compared to a natural gateway, a narrow chasm between tall cliffs, and through which the Saco, now a mere brook, finds its way. You find yourself in a green opening, looking like the bottom of a drained lake with mountain summits around you. Here is one of the houses of accommodation from which you ascend Mount Washington.

If you should ever think of ascending Mount Washington, do not allow any of the hotel-keepers to cheat you in regard to the distance. It is about ten miles from either the hotels to the summit, and very little less from any of them. They keep a set of worn-out horses, which they hire for the season, and which are trained to climb the mountain, in a walk, by the worst bridle paths in the world. The poor hacks are generally tolerably surefooted, but there are exceptions to this. Guides are sent with the visitors, who generally go on foot, strong-legged men, carrying long staves, and watching the ladies lest any accident should occur; some of these, especially those from the house in the Notch, commonly called Tom Crawford's, are unmannerly fellows enough.

The scenery of these mountains has not been sufficiently praised. But for the glaciers, but for the peaks white with perpetual snow, it would be scarcely worthwhile to see Switzerland after seeing the White Mountains. The depth of the valleys, the steepness of the mountainsides, the variety of aspect shown by their summits, the deep gulfs of forest below, seamed with the open courses of rivers, the vast extent of the mountain region seen north and south of us, gleaming with many lakes, took me with surprise and astonishment. Imagine the forests to be shorn from half the broad declivities — imagine scattered habitations on the thick green turf and footpaths leading from one to the other, and herds and flocks browsing, and you have Switzerland before you. I admit, however, that these accessories add to the variety and interest of the landscape, and perhaps heighten the idea of its vastness.

I have been told, however, that the White Mountains in autumn present an aspect more glorious than even the splendors of the perpetual ice of the Alps. All this mighty multitude of mountains, rising from valleys filled with dense forests, have then put on their hues of gold and scarlet, and, seen more distinctly on account of their brightness of color, seem to tower higher in the clear blue of the sky. At that season of the year they are little visited, and only awaken the wonder of the occasional traveler.

It is not necessary to ascend Mount Washington, to enjoy the finest views. Some of the lower peaks offer grander though not so extensive ones; the height of the main summit seems to diminish the size of the objects beheld from it. The sense of solitude and immensity is however most strongly felt on that great cone, overlooking all the rest, and formed of loose rocks, which seem as if broken info fragments by the power which upheaved these ridges from the depths of the earth below. At some distance on the northern side of one of the summits, I saw a large snowdrift lying in the August sunshine.

The Franconia Notch, which we afterwards visited, is almost as remarkable for the two beautiful little lakes within it, as for the savage grandeur of the mountain-walls between which it passes.

Margaret Fuller
(1810–1850)

One of the leading intellectuals of nineteenth-century New England, Margaret Fuller was a writer, teacher, editor, feminist, journalist, and Transcendentalist of exceptional talent and education. As a young woman Fuller taught at several schools including Bronson Alcott's Temple School in Boston, contributed reviews and poems to journals and newspapers, and published translations of German literature. In 1840 she followed the promptings of her friend Ralph Waldo Emerson and became editor of the Transcendentalist journal *The Dial.* During this period Fuller also conducted her famous "Conversations" in Boston (1839–44)—meetings of women intellectuals (men were admitted only later) who engaged in informed discussions of serious subjects including literature, art, philosophy, and politics. In May 1843 she left Boston on a four-month tour of the upper Midwest, then the nation's western frontier. Traveling with her friend James Freeman Clarke and his sister Sarah Ann, Fuller began her western tour at Niagara, making a wide swing through the Great Lakes region before ending at Buffalo. Traveling by train, ship, carriage, and on foot, Fuller kept detailed field notebooks describing the landscapes and people of the recently settled prairie states. Returning to Boston in mid-September, she began a program of research to augment her firsthand observations of Western land and life—research she pursued as the first woman reader ever admitted to the Harvard library. The product of her travels and reading, published with Emerson's help in 1844, was the eclectic, multigeneric *Summer on the Lakes, in 1843*. Part travelogue, part social critique, and part nature writing, *Summer on the Lakes* is a rich, digressive book that has much in common with Henry Thoreau's *A Week on the Concord and Merrimack Rivers* (1849). The following selection from *Summer,* written from nineteenth-century America's leading tourist attraction—Niagara Falls—shows Fuller's intellectual tendency to shun easy sentimentalizing in favor of a more considered aesthetic response to nature. Fuller later moved to Europe, married the Italian Count Giovanni Ossoli, and gave birth to a son, Angelo. On their return to America in July 1850, the Ossolis were shipwrecked just off shore at Fire Island, New York, where they perished in a storm. Although Emerson sent Henry Thoreau to Fire Island to search for remains, neither Fuller's body nor her manuscripts were ever recovered.

From *Summer on the Lakes, in 1843* (1844)

Niagara, June 10, 1843

Since you are to share with me such footnotes as may be made on the pages of my life during this summer's wanderings, I should not be quite silent as to this magnificent prologue to the, as yet, unknown drama. Yet I, like others, have little to say where the spectacle is, for once, great enough to fill the whole life, and supersede thought, giving us only its own presence. "It is good to be here," is the best as the simplest expression that occurs to the mind.

We have been here eight days, and I am quite willing to go away. So great a sight soon satisfies, making us content with itself, and with what is less than itself. Our desires, once realized, haunt us again less readily. Having "lived one day" we would depart, and become worthy to live another.

We have not been fortunate in weather, for there cannot be too much, or too warm sunlight for this scene, and the skies have been lowering, with cold, unkind winds. My nerves, too much braced up by such an atmosphere, do not well bear the continual stress of sight and sound. For here there is no escape from the weight of a perpetual creation; all other forms and motions come and go, the tide rises and recedes, the wind, at its mightiest, moves in gales and gusts, but here is really an incessant, an indefatigable motion. Awake or asleep, there is no escape, still this rushing round you and through you. It is in this way I have most felt the grandeur—somewhat eternal, if not infinite.

At times a secondary music rises; the cataract seems to seize its own rhythm and sing it over again, so that the ear and soul are roused by a double vibration. This is some effect of the wind, causing echoes to the thundering anthem. It is very sublime, giving the effect of a spiritual repetition through all the spheres.

When I first came I felt nothing but a quiet satisfaction. I found that drawings, the panorama, &c. had given me a clear notion of the position and proportions of all objects here; I knew where to look for everything, and everything looked as I thought it would.

Long ago, I was looking from a hillside with a friend at one of the finest sunsets that ever enriched this world. A little cowboy, trudging along, wondered what we could be gazing at. After spying about some time, he found it could only be the sunset, and looking, too, a moment, he said approvingly "that sun looks well enough"; a speech worthy of Shakespeare's Cloten, or the infant Mercury, up to everything from the cradle, as you please to take it.

Even such a familiarity, worthy of Jonathan, our national hero, in a prince's palace, or "stumping" as he boasts to have done, "up the Vatican stairs, into the Pope's presence, in my old boots," I felt here; it looks really *well enough*, I felt, and was inclined, as you suggested, to give my approbation as to the one object in the world that would not disappoint.

But all great expressions which, on a superficial survey, seems so easy as well as so simple, furnishes, after a while, to the faithful observer its own standard by which to appreciate it. Daily these proportions widened and towered more and more upon my sight, and I got, at last, a proper foreground for these sublime distances. Before coming away, I think I really saw the full wonder of the scene. After awhile it so drew me into itself as to inspire an undefined dread, such as I never knew before, such as may be felt when death is about to usher us into a new existence. The perpetual trampling of the waters seized my senses. I felt that no other sound, however near, could be heard, and would start and look behind me for a foe. I realized the identity of that mood of nature in which these waters were poured down with such absorbing force, with that in which the Indian was shaped on the same soil. For continually upon my mind came, unsought and unwelcome, images, such as never haunted it before, of naked savages stealing behind me with uplifted tomahawks; again and again this illusion recurred, and even after I had thought it over, and tried to shake it off, I could not help starting and looking behind me.

As picture, the Falls can only be seen from the British side. There they are seen in their veils, and at sufficient distance to appreciate the magical effects of these, and the light and shade. From the boat, as you cross, the effects and contrasts are more melodramatic. On the road back from the whirlpool, we saw them as a reduced picture with delight. But what I liked best was to sit on Table Rock, close to the great fall. There all power of observing details, all separate consciousness, was quite lost.

Once, just as I had seated myself there, a man came to take his first look. He walked close up to the fall, and, after looking at it a moment, with an air as if thinking how he could best appropriate it to his own use, he spat into it.

This trait seemed wholly worthy of an age whose love of *utility* is such that the Prince Puckler-Muskau suggests the probability of men coming to put the bodies of their dead parents in the fields to fertilize them and of a country such as Dickens has described; but these will not, I hope, be seen on the historic page to be truly the age or truly the America. A little leaven is leavening the whole mass for other bread.

The whirlpool I like very much. It is seen to advantage after the great falls; it is so sternly solemn. The river cannot look more imperturbable, almost sullen in its marble green, than it does just below the great fall; but the slight circles that mark the hidden vortex, seem to whisper mysteries the thundering voice above could not proclaim,—a meaning as untold as ever.

It is fearful, too, to know, as you look, that whatever has been swallowed by the cataract, is like to rise suddenly to light here, whether uprooted tree, or body of man or bird.

The rapids enchanted me far beyond what I expected; they are so swift that they cease to seem so; you can think only of their beauty. The fountain beyond the Moss Islands, I discovered for myself, and thought it for some time an accidental beauty which it would not do to leave, lest I might never see it again. After I found it permanent, I returned many times to watch the play of its crest. In the little waterfall beyond, nature seems, as she often does, to have made a study for some larger design. She delights in this,—a sketch within a sketch, a dream within a dream. Wherever we see it, the lines of the great buttress in the fragment of stone, the hues of the waterfall, copied in the flowers that star its bordering mosses, we are delighted; for all the lineaments become fluent, and we mold the scene in congenial thought with its genius.

People complain of the buildings at Niagara, and fear to see it further deformed. I cannot sympathize with such an apprehension: the spectacle is capable to swallow up all such objects; they are not seen in the great whole, more than an earthworm in a wide field.

The beautiful wood on Goat Island is full of flowers; many of the fairest love to do homage here. The Wake Robin and May Apple are in bloom now; the former, white, pink, green, purple, copying the rainbow of the fall, and fit to make a garland for its presiding deity when he walks the land, for they are of imperial size, and shaped like stones for a diadem. Of the May Apple, I did not raise one green tent without finding a flower beneath. . . .

As I rode up to the neighborhood of the falls, a solemn awe imperceptibly stole over me, and the deep sound of the ever-hurrying rapids prepared my mind for the lofty emotions to be experienced. When I reached the hotel, I felt a strange indifference about seeing the aspiration of my life's hopes. I lounged about the rooms, read the stage bills upon the walls, looked over the register, and, finding the name of an acquaintance, sent to see if he was still there. What this hesitation arose from, I know not; perhaps it was a feeling of my unworthiness to enter this temple which nature has erected to its God.

At last, slowly and thoughtfully I walked down to the bridge leading to Goat Island, and when I stood upon this frail support, and saw a quarter of a mile of tumbling, rushing rapids, and heard their everlasting roar, my emotions overpowered me, a choking sensation rose to my throat, a thrill rushed through my veins, "my blood ran rippling to my finger's ends." This was the climax of the effect which the falls produced upon me—neither the American nor the British fall moved me as did these rapids. For the magnificence, the sublimity of the latter I was prepared by descriptions and by paintings. When I arrived in sight of them I merely felt, "ah, yes, here is the fall, just as I have seen it in picture." When I arrived at the terrapin bridge, I expected to be overwhelmed, to retire trembling from this giddy eminence, and gaze with unlimited wonder and awe upon the immense mass rolling on and on, but, somehow or other, I thought only of comparing the effect on my mind with what I had read and heard. I looked for a short time, and then with almost a feeling of disappointment, turned to go to the other points of view to see if I was not mistaken in not feeling any surpassing emotion at this sight. But from the foot of Biddle's stairs, and the middle of the river, and from below the table rock, it was still "barren, barren all." And, provoked with my stupidity in feeling most moved in the wrong place, I turned away to the hotel, determined to set off for Buffalo that afternoon. But the stage did not go, and, after nightfall, as there was a splendid moon, I went down to the bridge, and leaned over the parapet, where the boiling rapids came down in their might. It was grand, and it was also gorgeous; the yellow rays of the moon made the broken waves appear like auburn tresses twining around the black rocks. But they did not inspire me as before. I felt a foreboding of a mightier emotion to rise up and swallow all others, and I passed on to the terrapin bridge. Everything was changed, the misty apparition had taken off its many-colored crown which it had worn by day, and a bow of silvery white spanned its summit. The moonlight gave a poetical indefiniteness to the distant parts of the waters, and while the rapids were glancing in her beams, the river below the falls was black as night, save where the reflection of the sky gave it the appearance of a shield of blued steel. No gaping tourists loitered, eyeing with their glasses, or sketching on cards the hoary locks of the ancient river god. All tended to harmonize with the natural grandeur of the scene. I gazed long. I saw how here mutability and unchangeableness were united. I surveyed the conspiring waters rushing against the rocky ledge to overthrow it at one mad plunge, till, like topping ambition, o'erleaping themselves, they fall on t'other side, expanding into foam ere they reach the deep channel where they creep submissively away.

Then arose in my breast a genuine admiration, and a humble adoration of the Being who was the architect of this and of all. Happy were the first discoverers of Niagara, those who could come unawares upon this view and upon that, whose feelings were entirely their own.

John C. Frémont (1813–1890) and Jessie Benton Frémont (1834–1902)

John Charles Frémont, the explorer, soldier, and politician who was nicknamed "The Pathfinder," was among the best-known and most controversial public figures of mid-nineteenth-century America. At the heart of Frémont's long and troubled career are his five major Western expeditions (1842, 1843–44, 1845–46, 1848–49, 1853–54), and the books these journeys inspired. Frémont began his career as an apprentice surveyor, topical engineer, and cartographer on various government expeditions before serving as the controversial leader of the Western expeditions—surveying missions that filled in many blank spaces on the map of the West, but sometimes resulted in disaster for the men in Frémont's charge. Frémont's ambitions for fame and fortune were shared fully by his wife, Jessie Benton Frémont, the daughter of influential Missouri senator Thomas Hart Benton. From the time of their marriage in 1841 until her own death in 1902, Jessie served as the tireless guardian of the family reputation and legacy and as the unnamed collaborator and amanuensis to whom much of the credit for her husband's books is due. Indeed, the couple effectively cowrote the most popular Frémont works: John made the journeys and provided the maps, scientific data, and field notebooks; Jessie recrafted the field notes with a stylistic, narrative, and literary flair that made these books, though initially issued as government reports, among the best-selling works of the period. Perhaps the most exciting of Frémont's journeys was his second expedition, on which he surveyed and mapped the continent from St. Louis all the way to the Pacific. After successfully reaching Vancouver, Frémont decided to return east by an unknown route, planning to track south along the eastern Sierra and then east across the Great Basin (which he named). In the first of the following excerpts from his 1845 *Report,* the Frémonts relate John's rather romantic discovery and naming of western Nevada's Pyramid Lake, which he finds "set like a gem in the mountains." The second excerpt recounts Frémont's unprecedented crossing of the Sierra Nevada in the dead of winter—a crossing on which his bedraggled men (including Kit Carson) barely survived the five-week snowshoe trek up the eastern slope peaks, past Lake Tahoe, and down into the Sacramento Valley. Although Frémont's subsequent efforts as a politician, Civil War general, and gold baron were mostly failures, his several books of Western topography, travel, and adventure had a tremendous influence upon Americans' sense of the Western landscape as the destined arena of vast national prospects.

From *Report of the Exploring Expedition to the Rocky Mountains in the Year 1842, and to Oregon and North California in 1843–1844* (1845)

November 18, 1843. The camp was now occupied in making the necessary preparations for our homeward journey, which, though homeward, contemplated a new route, and a great circuit to the south and southeast, and the exploration of the Great Basin between the Rocky Mountains and the Sierra Nevada. Three principal objects were indicated, by report or by maps, as being on this route, the character or existence of which I wished to ascertain, and which I assumed as landmarks, or leading points, on the projected line of return. The first of these points was the Klamath lake, on the tableland between the head of Fall River, which comes to the Columbia, and the Sacramento, which goes to the Bay of San Francisco; and from which lake a river of the same name makes its way westwardly direct to the ocean. This lake and river are often called Klamath. . . . From this lake our course was intended to be about southeast, to a reported lake called Mary's, at some days' journey in the Great Basin; and thence, still on southeast, to the reputed Buenaventura River, which has had a place in so many maps, and countenanced the belief of the existence of a great river flowing from the Rocky Mountains to the Bay of San Francisco. From the Buenaventura the next point was intended to be in that section of the Rocky Mountains which includes the heads of Arkansas River, and of the opposite waters of the California Gulf; and thence down the Arkansas to Bent's Fort, and home.

This was our projected line of return—a great part of it absolutely new to geographical, botanical, and geological science—and the subject of reports in relation to lakes, rivers, deserts, and savages hardly above the condition of mere wild animals, which inflamed desire to know what this terra incognita really contained. It was a serious enterprise, at the commencement of winter, to undertake the traverse of such a region, and with a party consisting only of twenty-five persons, and they of many nations—American, French, German, Canadian, Indian, and colored—and most of them young, several being under twenty-one years of age. . . .

January 10, 1844. We continued our reconnaissance ahead, pursuing a south direction in the basin along the ridge, the camp following slowly after. On a large trail there is never any doubt of finding suitable places for encampments. We reached the end of the basin, where we found, in a hollow of the mountain which enclosed it, an abundance of good bunch grass. Leaving a signal for the party to encamp, we continued our way up the hollow, intending to see what lay beyond the mountain. The hollow was several miles long, forming a good pass, the snow deepening to about a foot as we neared the summit. Beyond, a defile between the mountains descended rapidly about two thousand feet; and filling up all the lower space was a sheet of green water, some twenty miles broad. It broke upon our eyes like the ocean.

The neighboring peaks rose high above us, and we ascended one of them to obtain a better view. The waves were curling in the breeze, and their dark-green color showed it to be a body of deep water. For a long time we sat enjoying the view, for we had become fatigued with mountains, and the free expanse of moving waves was very grateful. It was set like a gem in the mountains, which, from our position, seemed to enclose it almost entirely. At the western end it communicated with the line of basins we had left a few days since; and on the opposite side it swept a ridge of snowy mountains, the foot of the great Sierra. Its position at first inclined us to believe it Mary's Lake, but the rugged mountains were so entirely discordant with descriptions of its low rushy shores and open country, that we concluded it some unknown body of water, which it afterward proved to be.

On our road down, the next day, we saw herds of mountain sheep, and encamped on a little stream at the mouth of the defile, about a mile from the margin of the water, to which we hurried down immediately. The water is so slightly salt that, at first, we thought it fresh, and would be pleasant to drink when no other could be had. The shore was rocky—a handsome beach, which reminded us of the sea. On some large granite boulders that were scattered about the shore, I remarked a coating of a calcareous substance, in some places a few inches, and in others a foot in thickness. Near our camp, the hills, which were of primitive rock, were also covered with this substance, which was in too great quantity on the mountains along the shore of the lake to have been deposited by water, and has the appearance of having been spread over the rocks in mass. . . .

January 13. We followed again a broad Indian trail along the shore of the lake to the southward. For a short space we had room enough in the bottom; but after traveling a short distance, the water swept the foot of precipitous mountains, the peaks of which are about three thousand feet above the lake. The trail wound along the base of these precipices, against which the water dashed below, by a way nearly impracticable for the howitzer. During a greater part of the morning the lake was nearly hid by a snowstorm, and the waves broke on the narrow beach in a long line of foaming surf, five or six feet high.

The day was unpleasantly cold, the wind driving the snow sharp against our faces; and, having advanced only about twelve miles, we encamped in a bottom formed by a ravine, covered with good grass, which was fresh and green. We did not get the howitzer into camp, but were obliged to leave it on the rocks until morning. We saw several flocks of sheep, but did not succeed in killing any. Ducks were riding on the waves, and several large fish were seen. The mountainsides were crusted with the calcareous cement previously mentioned.

There were chenopodiaceous and other shrubs along the beach; and, at the foot of the rocks, an abundance of *Ephedra occidentalis*, whose dark-green color makes them evergreens among the shrubby growth of the lake. Toward evening the snow began to fall heavily, and the country had a wintry appearance.

The next morning the snow was rapidly melting under a warm sun. Part of the morning was occupied in bringing up the gun; and, making only nine miles, we encamped on the shore, opposite a very remarkable rock in the lake, which had attracted our attention for many miles. It rose, according to our estimate, six hundred feet above the water; and, from the point we viewed it, presented a pretty exact outline of the great pyramid of Cheops. . . . Like other rocks along the shore, it seemed to be encrusted with calcareous cement. This striking feature suggested a name for the lake, and I called it Pyramid Lake; and though it may be deemed by some a fanciful resemblance, I can undertake to say that the future traveler will find a much more striking resemblance between this rock and the pyramids of Egypt than there is between them and the object from which they take their name.

The elevation of this lake above the sea is four thousand eight hundred and ninety feet, being nearly seven hundred feet higher than the Great Salt Lake, from which it lies nearly west, and distant about eight degrees of longitude. The position and elevation of this lake make it an object of geographical interest. It is the nearest lake to the western rim, as the Great Salt Lake is to the eastern rim, of the Great Basin which lies between the base of the Rocky Mountains and the Sierra Nevada, and the extent and character of which, its whole circumference and contents, it is so desirable to know. . . .

February 3. Tonight we had no shelter, but we made a large fire around the trunk of one of the huge pines; and covering the snow with small boughs, on which we spread our blankets, soon made ourselves comfortable. The night was very bright and clear, and though the thermometer was only down to 10°, a strong wind which sprang up at sundown made it intensely cold, and this was one of the bitterest nights during the journey.

Two Indians joined our party here; and one of them, an old man, immediately began to harangue us, saying that ourselves and animals would perish in the snow, and that if we would go back, he would show us another and a better way across the mountain. He spoke in a very loud voice, and there was a singular repetition of phrases and arrangement of words which rendered his speech striking and not unmusical.

We had now begun to understand some words, and, with the aid of signs, easily comprehended the old man's simple ideas. "Rock upon rock—rock upon rock—snow upon snow—snow upon snow," said he; "even if you get over the snow, you will not be able to get down from the mountains." He made us the sign of precipices, and showed us how the feet of the horses would slip, and throw them off from the narrow trails which led along their sides.

Our Chinook, who comprehended even more readily than ourselves, and believed our situation hopeless, covered his head with his blanket and began to weep and lament. "I wanted to see the whites," said he; "I came away from my own people to see the whites, and I wouldn't care to die among them; but here"—and he looked around into the cold night and gloomy forest, and, drawing his blanket over his head, began again to lament. . . .

February 10. . . . The wind kept the air filled with snow during the day; the sky was very dark in the southwest, though elsewhere very clear. The forest here has a noble appearance: the tall cedar is abundant; its greatest height being one hundred and thirty feet, and circumference twenty, three or four feet above the ground; and here I see for the first time the white pine, of which there are some magnificent trees. Hemlock spruce is among the timber, occasionally as large as eight feet in diameter four feet above the ground; but, in ascending, it tapers rapidly to less than one foot at the height of eighty feet. I have not seen any higher than one hundred and thirty feet, and the slight upper part is frequently broken off by the wind. The white spruce is frequent; and the red pine (*Pinus colorado* of the Mexicans), which constitutes the beautiful forest along the flanks of the Sierra Nevada to the northward, is here the principal tree, not attaining a greater height than one hundred and forty feet, though with sometimes a diameter of ten. Most of these trees appeared to differ slightly from those of the same kind on the other side of the continent.

The elevation of the camp, by the boiling point, is eight thousand and fifty feet. We are now one thousand feet above the level of the South Pass in the Rocky Mountains; and still we are not done ascending. The top of a flat ridge near was bare of snow, and very well sprinkled with bunch grass, sufficient to pasture the animals two or three days, and this was to be their main point of support. This ridge is composed of a compact trap, or basalt, of a columnar structure; over the surface are scattered large boulders of porous trap. The hills are in many places entirely covered with small fragments of volcanic rock.

Putting on our snowshoes, we spent the afternoon in exploring a road ahead.

The glare of the snow, combined with great fatigue, had rendered many of the people nearly blind; but we were fortunate in having some black silk handkerchiefs, which, worn as veils, very much relieved the eyes. . . .

February 13. We continued to labor on the road, and in the course of the day had the satisfaction to see the people working down the face of the opposite hill, about three miles distant. During the morning we had the pleasure of a visit from Mr. Fitzpatrick, with the information that all was going on well. A party of Indians had passed on snowshoes, who said they were going to the western side of the mountain after fish. This was an indication that the salmon were coming up the streams; and we could hardly restrain our impatience as we thought of them, and worked with increased vigor.

The meat train did not arrive this evening, and I gave Godey leave to kill our little dog (Klamath), which he prepared in Indian fashion—scorching off the hair, and washing the skin with soap and snow, and then cutting it up into pieces, which were laid on the snow. Shortly afterward the sleigh arrived with a supply of horse meat; and we had tonight an extraordinary dinner—pea soup, mule, and dog.

February 14. With Mr. Preuss, I ascended today the highest peak near us, from which we had a beautiful view of a mountain lake at our feet, about fifteen miles in length, and so entirely surrounded by mountains that we could not discover an outlet. We had taken with us a glass; but though we enjoyed an extended view, the valley was half hidden in mist, as when we had seen it before. Snow could be distinguished on the higher parts of the coast mountains; eastward, as far as the eye could extend, it ranged over a terrible mass of broken snowy mountains, fading off blue in the distance. . . .

February 24. . . . The character of the forest continued the same, and among the trees, the pine with short leaves and very large cones was abundant, some of them being noble trees. We measured one that had ten feet diameter, though the height was not more than one hundred and thirty feet. All along the river was a roaring torrent, its fall very great; and descending with a rapidity to which we had long been strangers, to our great pleasure oak trees appeared on the ridge, and soon became very frequent; on these I remarked unusually great quantities of mistletoe. Rushes began to make their appearance; and at a small creek where they were abundant, one of the messes was left with the weakest horses, while we continued on.

The opposite mountainside was very steep and continuous—unbroken by ravines, and covered with pines and snow; while on the side we were traveling, innumerable rivulets poured down from the ridge. Continuing on, we halted a moment at one of these rivulets, to admire some beautiful evergreen trees, resembling live oak, which shaded the little stream. They were forty to fifty feet high, and two in diameter, with a uniform tufted top; and the summer green of their beautiful foliage, with the singing birds, and the sweet summer wind which was whirling about the dry oak leaves, nearly intoxicated us with delight; and we hurried on, filled with excitement, to escape entirely from the horrid region of inhospitable snow to the perpetual spring of the Sacramento.

George Copway (Kah-ge-ga-gah-bowh) (Ojibwa) (1818–1869)

Like Samson Occom (Mohegan) (1723–92) and William Apess (Pequot) (1798–?), George Copway (Kah-ge-ga-gah-bowh) was a Native American historian and autobiographer who wrote primarily as a means of introducing a white audience to Indian culture. And like Jane Johnston Schoolcraft (Bame-wa-was-ge-zhik-a-quay), Copway was an Ojibwa who chose a white spouse while remaining deeply concerned about the welfare and autonomy of Native peoples. Born in Upper Canada to a traditional Ojibwa family, Copway was Christianized at an early age and was educated in Illinois before becoming a missionary to Indian peoples in Wisconsin and Minnesota. In 1847 he published *The Life, History and Travels of Kah-ge-ga-gah-bowh, a Young Indian Chief of the Ojebwa Nation. . .* , a popular book that was widely reprinted under various titles. Using his new popularity as leverage, Copway energetically wrote and lectured against the U.S. government's 1850 plan to remove the Ojibwa from lands promised them in an 1842 treaty. In support of his cause he attempted to recruit influential new friends including Henry Wadsworth Longfellow, Washington Irving, and James Fenimore Cooper — white writers whose success often depended upon romanticizing the Indian for the benefit of white audiences. The first full-length autobiography written by a Native American raised within traditional Indian culture, Copway's *Life, History and Travels* deftly adopts, adapts, and co-opts Indian stereotypes in order to reeducate his white audience about Native American culture. Although Copway's prose displayed many of the romantic and sentimental tropes common to Longfellow, Irving, and Cooper, it successfully challenged the common iconography of Indian as bloodthirsty savage. In particular, Copway's explanation of the Ojibwa reverence for the places and creatures of "nature's wide domain" offered a powerful means to connect animistic Native American beliefs with nature-loving American Romantic authors and their audience.

From *The Life, History and Travels of Kah-ge-ga-gah-bowh, a Young Indian Chief of the Ojebwa Nation . . .* (1847)

Early as I can recollect, I was taught that it was the gift of the many spirits to be a good hunter and warrior; and much of my time I devoted in search of their favors. On the mountaintop, or along the valley, or the water brook, I searched for some kind intimation from the spirits who made their residence in the noise of the waterfalls.

I dreaded to hear the voice of the angry spirit in the gathering clouds. I looked with anxiety to catch a glimpse of the wings of the Great Spirit, who shrouded himself in rolling white and dark clouds — who, with his wings, fanned the earth, and laid low the tall pines and hemlock in his course — who rode in whirlwinds and tornadoes, and plucked the trees from their woven roots — who chased other gods from his course — who drive the Bad Spirit from the surface of the earth, down to the dark caverns of the deep. Yet he was a kind spirit. My father taught me to call that spirit Ke-sha-mon-e-doo — *Benevolent spirit* — for his ancestors taught him no other name to give to that spirit who made the earth, with all its variety and smiling beauty. His benevolence I saw in the running of the streams, for the animals to quench their thirst and the fishes to live; the fruit of the earth teemed wherever I looked. Every thing I saw smilingly said Ke-sha-mon-e-doo nin-ge-oo-she-ig — *the Benevolent spirit made me*. . . .

I was born in *nature's wide domain!* The trees were all that sheltered my infant limbs — the blue heavens all that covered me. I am one of Nature's children; I have always admired her; she shall be my glory; her features — her robes, and the wreath about her brow — the seasons — her stately oaks, and the evergreen — her hair — ringlets over the earth, all contribute to my enduring love of her; and wherever I see her, emotions of pleasure roll in my breast, and swell and burst like waves on the shores of the ocean, in prayer and praise to Him who has placed me in her hand. It is thought great to be born in palaces, surrounded with wealth — but to be born in nature's wide domain is greater still!

I was born sometime in the fall of 1818, near the mouth of the river Trent, called in our language, Sah-ge-dah-we-ge-wah-noong, while my father and mother were attending the annual distribution of the presents from the government to the Indians. I was the third of our family; a brother and sister being older, both of whom died. My brother died without the knowledge of the Savior, but my sister experienced the power of the loving grace of God. One brother, and two stepbrothers, are still alive.

I remember the tall trees, and the dark woods — the swamp just by, where the little wren sang so melodiously after the going down of the sun in the west — the current of the broad river Trent—the skipping of the fish, and the noise of the rapids a little above. It was here I first saw the light; a little fallen down shelter, made of evergreens, and a few dead embers, the remains of the last fire that shed its genial warmth around, were all that marked the spot. When I last visited it, nothing but fir poles stuck in the ground, and they were leaning on account of decay. Is this dear spot, made green by the tears of memory, any less enticing and hallowed than the palaces where princes are born? I would much more glory in this birthplace, with the broad canopy of heaven above me, and the giant arms of the forest trees for my shelter, than to be born in palaces of marble, studded with pillars of gold! Nature will be nature still, while palaces shall decay and fall in ruins. Yes, Niagara will be Niagara a thousand years hence! the rainbow, a wreath over her brow, shall continue as long as the sun, and the flowing of the river! While the work of art, however impregnable, shall in atoms fall. . . .

I was taught early to hunt the deer. It was a part of our father's duty to teach us how to handle the gun as well as the bow and arrow. I was early reminded to hunt for myself; and thirst to excel in hunting began to increase; no pains were spared, no fatigue was too great, and at all seasons I found something to stimulate me to exertion, that I might become a good hunter. For years I followed my father, observed how he approached the deer, the manner of getting it upon his shoulders to carry it home. The appearance of the sky, the sound of the distant waterfalls in the morning, the appearance of the clouds and the winds, were to be noticed. The step, and the gesture, in traveling in search of the deer, were to be observed.

Many a lecture I received when the deer lay bleeding at the feet of my father; he would give me an account of the nobleness of the hunter's deeds, and said that I should never be in want whenever there was any game, and that many a poor aged man could be assisted by me. "*If you reverence the aged, many will be glad to hear of your name*," were the words of my father. "The poor man will say to his children, 'my children, let us go to him, for he is a great hunter, and is kind to the poor, he will not turn us away empty.' The Great Spirit, who has given the aged a long life, will bless you. You must never laugh at any suffering object, for you know not how soon you may be in the same condition: never kill any game needlessly." Such was his language when we were alone in the woods. Ah! they were lessons directed from heaven.

In the spring but few deer were killed, because they were not in good order, the venison being poor, and the skin so thin, that it was no object to kill them. To hunt deer in the summer was my great delight, which I did in the following manner:—During the day I looked for their tracks, as they came on the shore of the lake or river during the night; they came there to feed. If they came on the bank of the river, I lighted pitch pine, and the current of the river took the canoe along the shore. My lantern was so constructed that the light could not fall on one spot, but sweep along the shore. The deer could see the light, but were not alarmed by it, and continued feeding on the weeds. In this way, I have approached so close that I could have reached them with my paddle. In this manner our forefathers shot them, not with a gun, as I did, but with the bow and arrow. Bows were made strong enough, so that the arrows might pierce through them.

Another mode of hunting on the lakes, preferred by some, is shooting without a light. Many were so expert, and possessed such an accuracy in hearing, that they could shoot successfully in the dark, with no other guide than the noise of the deer in the water; the position of the deer being well known, in this way, the darkest night. . . .

I loved to hunt the bear, the beaver, and the deer but now, the occupation has no charms for me. I will now take the goose quill, for my *bow,* and its point for my *arrow.* If perchance I may yet speak; when my poor aching head lies low in the grave; when the hand that wrote these recollections shall have crumbled into dust; then these pages will not have been written in vain.

"O! Land of rest for thee I sigh—
When will the season come,
When I shall lay my armor by,
And dwell in peace at home."

The beaver was hunted in the spring and fall. They were either trapped or shot. Among all the animals that live in the water, the beaver is of the kindest disposition, when tamed; it is a very cleanly animal; sits on its broad tail on the ground while feeding; feeds all night, and sleeps most of the day. The beaver skin was once worth from eight to ten dollars apiece, or four dollars per pound.

The otter, too, is much valued. The whites buy the skins, and make caps of them. They are mostly caught in traps. In the fall and spring they are always on the move.

The otter is a greedy animal; it can be tamed, but when hungry becomes cross, and often bites. If it be a half mile off, it will scent any food preparing in the wigwam.

When about five years old, I commenced shooting birds, with a small bow and arrow. I have shot many a bird, but am no more a marksman. I used to feel proud when I used to carry home my own game. The first thing that any of the hunters shot, was cooked by the grandfather and grandmother, and there was great rejoicing, to inspire the youthful hunter with fresh ardor. Day after day I searched for the gray squirrel, the woodpecker, the snipe, and the snowbird, for this was all my employment.

The gun was another instrument put into my hands, which I was taught to use both carefully and skillfully. Seldom do accidents occur from the use of firearms among our people. I delighted in running after the deer, in order to head and shoot them. It was a well-known fact that I ranked high among the hunters. I remember the first deer I ever shot, it was about one mile north of the village of Keene. The Indians, as has just been said, once had a custom, which is now done away, of making a great feast of the first deer that a younger hunter caught: the young hunter, however, was not to partake of any of it, but wait upon the others. All the satisfaction he could realize, was to thump his heels on the ground, while he and others were singing the following hunter's song:

> "Ah yah ba wah, ne gah me koo nah vah!
> Ah yah wa seeh, ne gah me koo nah nah."
> The fattest of the bucks I'll take,
> The choicest of all animals I'll take. . . .

It was in visiting the interior that we always suffered most. I will here narrate a single circumstance which will convey a correct idea of the sufferings to which the Indians were often exposed. To collect furs of different kinds for the traders, we had to travel far into the woods and remain there the whole winter. Once we left Rice Lake in the fall, and ascended the river in canoes, above Bellmont Lake. There were five families about to hunt with my father, on his grounds. The winter began to set in, and the river having frozen over, we left the canoes, the dried venison, the beaver, and some flour and pork; and when we had gone farther north, say about sixty miles from the whites, for the purpose of hunting, the snow fell for five days in succession to such a depth that it was impossible to shoot or trap anything. Our provisions were exhausted, and we had no means to procure any more. Here we were. The snow about five feet deep; our wigwam buried; the branches of the trees falling around us, and cracking from the weight of the snow.

Our mother boiled birch bark for my sister and myself, that we might not starve. On the seventh day some of them were so weak that they could not raise themselves, and others could not stand alone. They could only crawl in and out of the wigwam. We parched beaver skins and old moccasins for food. On the ninth day none of the men were able to go abroad, except my father and uncle. On the tenth day, still being without food, those only who were able to walk about the wigwam were my father, my grandmother, my sister, and myself. O how distressing to see the starving Indians lying about the wigwam with hungry and eager looks; the children would cry for something to eat. My poor mother would heave *bitter sighs of despair,* the tears falling from her cheeks profusely as she kissed us. Wood, though plenty, could not be obtained, on account of the feebleness of our limbs.

My father, at times, would draw near the fire, and rehearse some prayer to the gods. It appeared to him that there was no way of escape; the men, women and children dying; some of them were speechless. The wigwam was cold and dark, and covered with snow. On the eleventh day just before daylight, my father fell into a sleep; he soon awoke and said to me, "My son, the Great Spirit is about to bless us; this night in my dream I saw a person coming from the east, walking on the tops of the trees. He told me that we should obtain two beavers this morning about nine o'clock. Put on your moccasins and go along with me to the river, and we will hunt the beaver, perhaps for the last time." I saw that his countenance beamed with delight; he was full of confidence. I put on my moccasins and carried my snowshoes, staggering along behind him, about half a mile. Having made a fire near the river, where there was an air hole, through which the beaver had come up during the night, my father tied a gun to a stump, with the muzzle towards the air hole; he also tied a string to the trigger, and said "should you see the beaver rise, pull the string and you will kill it." I stood by the fire with the string in my hand. I soon heard a noise occasioned by the blow of his tomahawk; he had killed a beaver, and he brought it to me. As he laid it down, he said, "then the Great Spirit will not let us die here"; adding, as before, "if you see the beaver rise, pull the string." He left me, I soon saw the nose of one; but I did not shoot. Presently another came up; I pulled the trigger, and off the gun went. I could not see for some time for the smoke. My father ran towards me, took the two beavers and laid them side by side; then pointing to the sun, said, "Do you see the sun? The Great Spirit informed me that we should kill these two about this time this morning. We will yet see our relatives at Rice Lake; now let us go home and see if they are still alive." We hastened home, and arrived just in time to save them from death.

Henry David Thoreau
(1817–1862)

While often associated with the metaphysical insights and anti-materialist social critique that have helped make *Walden* (1854) a monument of American nature writing, Henry Thoreau was also a passionate student and practitioner of natural history. No stranger to the roots of nature writing, Thoreau was an enthusiastic reader of earlier American naturalists including William Wood, John Josselyn, Cotton Mather, and William Bartram, as well as nineteenth-century environmental writers including John James Audubon, Susan Cooper, and many others included in this volume. Thoreau was born and raised in Concord, Massachusetts, where, after graduating from Harvard, he lived among fellow Transcendentalists including his close friend Ralph Waldo Emerson. In 1845 he built a small cabin on Emerson's land near the shores of Walden Pond, where he lived for just over two years studying nature while exploring the ennobling virtues of a deliberately pursued "life in the woods." But Thoreau also went to the pond to write a book about the two-week river trip he had taken in 1839 with his beloved brother John, who in 1842 contracted tetanus and died in Henry's arms. Published in 1849 as *A Week on the Concord and Merrimack Rivers*, Thoreau's first book—and the only book besides *Walden* he published in his lifetime—was a commercial failure. When the publisher shipped the unsold copies of the work to Thoreau, he wrote in his journal, with characteristic courage and wit: "I have now a library of nearly nine hundred volumes, over seven hundred of which I wrote myself." But if *A Week* was a financial failure, it succeeded in other ways; although a digressive and uneven work, it stands as one of the most innovative mid-nineteenth-century literary attempts to synthesize natural history knowledge and field observations with personal insights and philosophical exploration of the aesthetic, ethical, and spiritual relationship between human and nonhuman nature. In the following excerpt from the "Saturday" chapter of *A Week*, the insights of the amateur ichthyologist are combined with the lyricism of the nature writer and the ethical stance of the environmentalist—a man who energetically takes up the "just cause" of the migratory shad against "the Corporation with its dam."

From *A Week on the Concord and Merrimack Rivers* (1849)

Whether we live by the seaside, or by the lakes and rivers, or on the prairie, it concerns us to attend to the nature of fishes, since they are not phenomena confined to certain localities only, but forms and phases of the life in nature universally dispersed. The countless shoals which annually coast the shores of Europe and America, are not so interesting to the student of nature, as the more fertile law itself, which deposits their spawn on the tops of mountains, and on the interior plains; the fish principle in nature, from which it results that they may be found in water in so many places, in greater or less numbers. The natural historian is not a fisherman, who prays for cloudy days and good luck merely, but as fishing has been styled, "a contemplative man's recreation," introducing him profitably to woods and water, so the fruit of the naturalist's observations is not in new genera or species, but in new contemplations still, and science is only a more contemplative man's recreation. The seeds of the life of fishes are everywhere disseminated, whether the winds waft them, or the waters float them, or the deep earth holds them; wherever a pond is dug, straightway it is stocked with this vivacious race. They have a lease of nature, and it is not yet out. The Chinese are bribed to carry their ova from province to province in jars or in hollow reeds, or the waterbirds to transport them to the mountain tarns and interior lakes. There are fishes wherever there is a fluid medium, and even in clouds and in melted metals we detect their semblance.

Think how in winter you can sink a line down straight in a pasture through snow and through ice, and pull up a bright, slippery, dumb, subterranean silver or golden fish! It is curious, also, to reflect how they make one family, from the largest to the smallest. The least minnow, that lies on the ice as bait for pickerel, looks like a huge sea-fish cast up on the shore. In the waters of this town there are about a dozen distinct species, though the inexperienced would expect many more.

It enhances our sense of the grand security and serenity of nature, to observe the still undisturbed economy and content of the fishes of this century, their happiness a regular fruit of the summer. The Freshwater Sunfish, Bream, or Ruff, *Pomotis vulgaris*, as it were, without ancestry, without posterity, still represents the Freshwater Sunfish in nature. It is the most common of all, and seen on every urchin's string; a simple and inoffensive fish, whose nests are visible all along the shore, hollowed in the sand, over which it is steadily poised through the summer hours on waving fin. Sometimes there are twenty or thirty nests in the space of a few rods, two feet wide by half a foot in depth, and made with no little labor, the weeds being removed, and the sand shoved up on the sides, like a bowl. Here it may be seen early in summer assiduously brooding, and driving away minnows and larger fishes, even its own species, which would disturb its ova, pursuing them a few feet, and circling round swiftly to its nest again: the minnows, like young sharks, instantly entering the empty nests, meanwhile, and swallowing the spawn, which is attached to the weeds and to the bottom, on the sunny side. The spawn is exposed to so many dangers, that a very small proportion can ever become fishes, for beside being the constant prey of birds and fishes, a great many nests are made so near the shore, in shallow water, that they are left dry in a few days, as the river goes down. These and the lamprey's are the only fishes' nests that I have observed, though the ova of some species may be seen floating on the surface. The breams are so careful of their charge that you may stand close by in the water and examine them at your leisure. I have thus stood over them half an hour at a time, and stroked them familiarly without frightening them, suffering them to nibble my fingers harmlessly, and seen them erect their dorsal fins in anger when my hand approached their ova, and have even taken them gently out of the water with my hand; though this cannot be accomplished by a sudden movement, however dexterous, for instant warning is conveyed to them through their denser element, but only by letting the fingers gradually close about them as they are poised over the palm, and with the utmost gentleness raising them slowly to the surface. Though stationary, they keep up a constant sculling or waving motion with their fins, which is exceedingly graceful, and expressive of their humble happiness; for unlike ours, the element in which they live is a stream which must be constantly resisted. From time to time they nibble the weeds at the bottom or overhanging their nests, or dart after a fly or a worm. The dorsal fin, besides answering the purpose of a keel, with the anal, serves to keep the fish upright, for in shallow water, where this is not covered, they fall on their sides. As you stand thus stooping over the bream in its nest, the edges of the dorsal and caudal fins have a singular dusty golden reflection, and its eyes, which stand out from the head, are transparent and colorless. Seen in its native element, it is a very beautiful and compact fish, perfect in all its parts, and looks like a brilliant coin fresh from the mint. It is a perfect jewel of the river, the green, red, coppery, and golden reflections of its mottled sides being the concentration of such rays as struggle through the floating pads and flowers to the sandy bottom, and in harmony with the sunlit brown and yellow pebbles. Behind its watery shield it dwells far from many accidents inevitable to human life.

There is also another species of bream found in our river, without the red spot on the operculum, which, according to M. Agassiz, is undescribed.

The Common Perch, *Perca flavescens,* which name describes well the gleaming, golden reflections of its scales as it is drawn out of the water, its red gills standing out in vain in the thin element, is one of the handsomest and most regularly formed of our fishes, and at such a moment as this reminds us of the fish in the picture, which wished to be restored to its native element until it had grown larger; and indeed most of this species that are caught are not half grown. In the ponds there is a light-colored and slender kind, which swim in shoals of many hundreds in the sunny water, in company with the shiner, averaging not more than six or seven inches in length, while only a few larger specimens are found in the deepest water, which prey upon their weaker brethren. I have often attracted these small perch to the shore at evening, by rippling the water with my fingers, and they may sometimes be caught while attempting to pass inside your hands. It is a tough and heedless fish, biting from impulse, without nibbling, and from impulse refraining to bite, and sculling indifferently past. It rather prefers the clear water and sandy bottoms, though here it has not much choice. It is a true fish, such as the angler loves to put into his basket or hang at the top of his willow twig, in shady afternoons along the banks of the stream. So many unquestionable fishes he counts, and so many shiners, which he counts and then throws away. Old Josselyn in his "New England's Rarities," published in 1672, mentions the Perch or River Partridge.

The Chivin, Dace, Roach, Cousin Trout, or whatever else it is called, *Leuciscus pulchellus,* white and red, always an unexpected prize, which, however, any angler is glad to hook for its rarity. A name that reminds us of many an unsuccessful ramble by swift streams, when the wind rose to disappoint the fisher. It is commonly a silvery soft-scaled fish, of graceful, scholarlike and classical look, like many a picture in an English book. It loves a swift current and a sandy bottom, and bites inadvertently, yet not without appetite for the bait. The minnows are used as bait for pickerel in the winter. The red chivin, according to some, is still the same fish, only older, or with its tints deepened as they think by the darker water it inhabits, as the red clouds swim in the twilight atmosphere. He who has not hooked the red chivin is not yet a complete angler. Other fishes, methinks, are slightly amphibious, but this is a denizen of the water wholly. The cork goes dancing down the swift rushing stream, amid the weeds and sands, when suddenly, by a coincidence never to be remembered, emerges this fabulous inhabitant of another element, a thing heard of but not seen, as if it were the instant creation of an eddy, a true product of the running stream. And this bright cupreous dolphin was spawned and has passed its life beneath the level of your feet in your native fields. . . .

The Pickerel, *Esox reticulatus*, the swiftest, wariest, and most ravenous of fishes, which Josselyn calls the Freshwater or River Wolf, is very common in the shallow and weedy lagoons along the sides of the stream. It is a solemn, stately, ruminant fish, lurking under the shadow of a pad at noon, with still, circumspect, voracious eye, motionless as a jewel set in water, or moving slowly along to take up its position, darting from time to time at such unlucky fish or frog or insect as comes within its range, and swallowing it at a gulp. I have caught one which had swallowed a brother pickerel half as large as itself, with the tail still visible in its mouth, while the head was already digested in its stomach. Sometimes a striped snake, bound to greener meadows across the stream, ends its undulatory progress in the same receptacle. They are so greedy and impetuous that they are frequently caught by being entangled in the line the moment it is cast. Fishermen also distinguish the brook pickerel, a shorter and thicker fish than the former.

The Horned Pout, *Pimelodus nebulosus*, sometimes called Minister, from the peculiar squeaking noise it makes when drawn out of the water, is a dull and blundering fellow, and like the eel vespertinal in his habits, and fond of the mud. It bites deliberately as if about its business. They are taken at night with a mass of worms strung on a thread, which catches in their teeth, sometimes three or four, with an eel, at one pull. They are extremely tenacious of life, opening and shutting their mouths for half an hour after their heads have been cut off. A bloodthirsty and bullying race of rangers, inhabiting the fertile river bottoms, with ever a lance in rest, and ready to do battle with their nearest neighbor. I have observed them in summer, when every other one had a long and bloody scar upon his back, where the skin was gone, the mark, perhaps, of some fierce encounter. Sometimes the fry, not an inch long, are seen darkening the shore with their myriads.

The Suckers, *Catostomi Bostonienses* and *tuberculati*, Common and Horned, perhaps on an average the largest of our fishes, may be seen in shoals of a hundred or more, stemming the current in the sun, on their mysterious migrations, and sometimes sucking in the bait which the fisherman suffers to float toward them.

The former, which sometimes grow to a large size, are frequently caught by the hand in the brooks, or like the red chivin, are jerked out by a hook fastened firmly to the end of a stick, and placed under their jaws. They are hardly known to the mere angler, however, not often biting at his baits, though the spearer carries home many a mess in the spring. To our village eyes, these shoals have a foreign and imposing aspect, realizing the fertility of the seas.

The Common Eel, too, *Muraena Bostoniensis*, the only species of eel known in the State, a slimy, squirming creature, informed of mud, still squirming in the pan, is speared and hooked up with various success. Methinks it too occurs in picture, left after the deluge, in many a meadow high and dry.

In the shallow parts of the river, where the current is rapid, and the bottom pebbly, you may sometimes see the curious circular nests of the Lamprey Eel, *Petromyzon Americanus*, the American Stone-Sucker, as large as a cart wheel, a foot or two in height, and sometimes rising half a foot above the surface of the water. They collect these stones, of the size of a hen's egg, with their mouths, as their name implies, and are said to fashion them into circles with their tails. They ascend falls by clinging to the stones, which may sometimes be raised, by lifting the fish by the tail. As they are not seen on their way down the streams, it is thought by fishermen that they never return, but waste away and die, clinging to rocks and stumps of trees for an indefinite period; a tragic feature in the scenery of the river bottoms, worthy to be remembered with Shakespeare's description of the seafloor. They are rarely seen in our waters at present, on account of the dams, though they are taken in great quantities at the mouth of the river in Lowell. Their nests, which are very conspicuous, look more like art than any thing in the river.

If we had leisure this afternoon, we might turn our prow up the brooks in quest of the classical trout and the minnows. Of the last alone, according to M. Agassiz, several of the species found in this town, are yet undescribed. These would, perhaps, complete the list of our finny contemporaries in the Concord waters.

Salmon, Shad, and Alewives, were formerly abundant here, and taken in weirs by the Indians, who taught this method to the whites, by whom they were used as food and as manure, until the dam, and afterward the canal at Billerica, and the factories at Lowell, put an end to their migrations hitherward; though it is thought that a few more enterprising shad may still occasionally be seen in this part of the river. It is said, to account for the destruction of the fishery, that those who at that time represented the interests of the fishermen and the fishes, remembering between what dates they were accustomed to take the grown shad, stipulated, that the dams should be left open for that season only, and the fry, which go down a month later, were consequently stopped and destroyed by myriads. Others say that the fishways were not properly constructed. Perchance, after a few thousands of years, if the fishes will be patient, and pass their summers elsewhere, meanwhile, nature will have leveled the Billerica dam, and the Lowell factories, and the Grass-ground River run clear again, to be explored by new migratory shoals, even as far as the Hopkinton pond and Westborough swamp. . . .

Shad are still taken in the basin of Concord River at Lowell, where they are said to be a month earlier than the Merrimack shad, on account of the warmth of the water. Still patiently, almost pathetically, with instinct not to be discouraged, not to be *reasoned* with, revisiting their old haunts, as if their stern fates would relent, and still met by the Corporation with its dam. Poor shad! where is thy redress? When Nature gave thee instinct, gave she thee the heart to bear thy fate? Still wandering the sea in thy scaly armor to inquire humbly at the mouths of rivers if man has perchance left them free for thee to enter. By countless shoals loitering uncertain meanwhile, merely stemming the tide there, in danger from sea foes in spite of thy bright armor, awaiting new instructions, until the sands, until the water itself, tell thee if it be so or not. Thus by whole migrating nations, full of instinct, which is thy faith, in this backward spring, turned adrift, and perchance knowest not where men do *not* dwell, where there are *not* factories, in these days. Armed with no sword, no electric shock, but mere Shad, armed only with innocence and a just cause, with tender dumb mouth only forward, and scales easy to be detached. I for one am with thee, and who knows what may avail a crowbar against that Billerica dam?—Not despairing when whole myriads have gone to feed those sea monsters during thy suspense, but still brave, indifferent, on easy fin there, like shad reserved for higher destinies. Willing to be decimated for man's behoof after the spawning season. Away with the superficial and selfish phil-*anthropy* of men,—who knows what admirable virtue of fishes may be below low-water mark, bearing up against a hard destiny, not admired by that fellow creature who alone can appreciate it! Who hears the fishes when they cry? It will not be forgotten by some memory that we were contemporaries. Thou shalt ere long have thy way up the rivers, up all the rivers of the globe, if I am not mistaken. Yea, even thy dull watery dream shall be more than realized. If it were not so, but thou wert to be overlooked at first and at last, then would not I take their heaven. Yes, I say so, who think I know better than thou canst. Keep a stiff fin then, and stem all the tides thou mayest meet.

Susan Fenimore Cooper
(1813–1894)

Daughter of popular novelist James Fenimore Cooper, whose descriptions of frontier life helped make wilderness a fit subject for American literature, Susan Fenimore Cooper was a writer, editor, and naturalist of considerable skill. Susan Cooper grew up in Cooperstown, New York—which had been established by her grandfather, William Cooper—spending much of her time rambling the neighboring fields and forests to study plants and birds. Although early-nineteenth-century Cooperstown was a rural, agricultural village, Cooper was unusually well educated for a woman of her day: she had been schooled in Paris and had traveled in Europe, and she was an avid reader of major American naturalists including Thomas Jefferson, Alexander Wilson, Thomas Nuttall, and John James Audubon. Although Cooper's first book was the pseudonymously published novel *Elinor Wyllys* (1846)—and although much of her later work was devoted to promoting her father's literary reputation—her greatest gift was as a nature writer and editor of nature writing. Cooper edited British naturalist John Leonard Knapp's *Country Rambles* . . . (1853) and was also editor of one of the first anthologies of nature poetry to include American work, *The Rhyme and Reason of Country Life* (1854). Her great work, *Rural Hours* (1850), is the first fully developed book of nonfiction nature writing by an American woman. Published four years before Henry Thoreau's *Walden* (1854)—and Thoreau himself read the book—*Rural Hours* is an eloquent regional literary natural history in which Cooper brings what we would now call a bioregional perspective to her study of the natural world; like Thoreau, she is devoted to cultivating a rich sense of place on her home ground. Cooper's book also anticipates the nature writing of our own day in its elegiac quality—its desire to measure, lament, and discourage exploitative land use practices that result in the extermination of species. And *Rural Hours* is, as the following excerpt shows, one of the first American books to explicitly advocate forest preservation. Cooper is well ahead of her time in celebrating the aesthetic, cultural, and spiritual value of the forests: "[I]ndependently of their market values in dollars and cents, the trees have other values," she asserts; "they have their importance in an intellectual and in a moral sense."

From *Rural Hours* (1850)

July 28, 1849. Passed the afternoon in the woods.

What a noble gift to man are the forests! What a debt of gratitude and admiration we owe for their utility and their beauty!

How pleasantly the shadows of the wood fall upon our heads, when we turn from the glitter and turmoil of the world of man! The winds of heaven seem to linger amid these balmy branches, and the sunshine falls like a blessing upon the green leaves; the wild breath of the forest, fragrant with bark and berry, fans the brow with grateful freshness; and the beautiful woodlight, neither garish nor gloomy, full of calm and peaceful influences, sheds repose over the spirit. The view is limited, and the objects about us are uniform in character; yet within the bosom of the woods the mind readily lays aside its daily littleness, and opens to higher thoughts, in silent consciousness that it stands alone with the works of God. The humble moss beneath our feet, the sweet flowers, the varied shrubs, the great trees, and the sky gleaming above in sacred blue, are each the handiwork of God. They were all called into being by the will of the Creator, as we now behold them, full of wisdom and goodness. Every object here has a deeper merit than our wonder can fathom; each has a beauty beyond our full perception; the dullest insect crawling about these roots lives by the power of the Almighty; and the discolored shreds of last year's leaves wither away upon the lowly herbs in a blessing of fertility. But it is the great trees, stretching their arms above us in a thousand forms of grace and strength, it is more especially the trees which fill the mind with wonder and praise.

Of the infinite variety of fruits which spring from the bosom of the earth, the trees of the wood are the greatest in dignity. Of all the works of the creation which know the changes of life and death, the trees of the forest have the longest existence. Of all the objects which crown the gray earth, the woods preserve unchanged, throughout the greatest reach of time, their native character: the works of man are ever varying their aspect; his towns and his fields alike reflect the unstable opinions, the fickle wills and fancies of each passing generation; but the forests on his borders remain today the same they were ages of years since. Old as the everlasting hills, during thousands of seasons they have put forth, and laid down their verdure in calm obedience to the decree which first bade them cover the ruins of the Deluge.

But, although the forests are great and old, yet the ancient trees within their bounds must each bend individually beneath the doom of every earthly existence; they have their allotted period when the mosses of Time gather upon their branches; when, touched by decay, they break and crumble to dust. Like man, they are decked in living beauty; like man, they fall a prey to death; and while we admire their duration, so far beyond our own brief years, we also acknowledge that especial interest which can only belong to the graces of life and to the desolation of death. We raise our eyes and we see collected in one company vigorous trunks, the oak, the ash, the pine, firm in the strength of maturity; by their side stand a young group, elm, and birch, and maple, their supple branches playing in the breezes, gay and fresh as youth itself; and yonder, rising in unheeded gloom, we behold a skeleton trunk, an old spruce, every branch broken, every leaf fallen,—dull, still, sad, like the finger of Death.

It is the peculiar nature of the forest, that life and death may ever be found within its bounds, in immediate presence of each other; both with ceaseless, noiseless, advances, aiming at the mastery; and if the influences of the first be the most general, those of the last are the most striking. Spring, with all her wealth of life and joy, finds within the forest many a tree unconscious of her approach; a thousand young plants springing up about the fallen trunk, the shaggy roots, seek to soften the gloomy wreck with a semblance of the verdure it bore of old; but ere they have thrown their fresh and graceful wreaths over the moldering wood, half their own tribe wither and die with the year. We owe to this perpetual presence of death an impression calm, solemn, almost religious in character, a chastening influence, beyond what we find in the open fields. But this subdued spirit is far from gloomy or oppressive, since it never fails to be relieved by the cheerful animation of living beauty. Sweet flowers grow beside the fallen trees, among the shattered branches, the season through; and the freedom of the woods, the unchecked growth, the careless position of every tree, are favorable to a thousand wild beauties, and fantastic forms, opening to the mind a play of fancy which is in itself cheering and enlivening, like the bright sunbeams which checker with golden light the shadowy groves. That character of rich variety also, stamped on all the works of the creation, is developed in the forest in clear and noble forms; we are told that in the field we shall not find two blades of grass exactly alike, that in the garden we shall not gather two flowers precisely similar, but in those cases the lines are minute, and we do not seize the truth at once; in the woods, however, the same fact stands recorded in bolder lines; we cannot fail to mark this great variety of detail among the trees; we see it in their trunks, their branches, their foliage; in the rude knots, the gnarled roots; in the mosses and lichens which feed upon their bark; in their forms, their coloring, their shadows. And within all this luxuriance of varied beauty, there dwells a sweet quiet, a noble harmony, a calm repose, which we seek in vain elsewhere, in so full a measure.

These hills, and the valleys at their feet, lay for untold centuries one vast forest; unnumbered seasons, ages of unrecorded time passed away while they made part of the boundless wilderness of woods. The trees waved over the valleys, they rose upon the swelling knolls, they filled the hollows, they crowded the narrow glens, they shaded the brooks and springs, they washed their roots in the lakes and rivers, they stood upon the islands, they swept over the broad hills, they crowned the heads of all the mountains. The whole land lay slumbering in the twilight of the forest. Wild dreams made up its half-conscious existence. . . .

It is to be feared that few among the younger generation now springing up will ever attain to the dignity of the old forest trees. Very large portions of these woods are already of a second growth, and trees of the greatest size are becoming every year more rare. It quite often happens that you come upon old stumps of much larger dimensions than any living trees about them; some of these are four, and a few five feet or more in diameter. Occasionally, we still find a pine erect of this size; one was felled the other day, which measured five feet in diameter. There is an elm about a mile from the village seventeen feet in girth, and not long since we heard of a basswood or linden twenty-eight feet in circumference. But among the trees now standing, even those which are sixty or eighty feet in height, many are not more than four, or five, or six feet in girth. The pines, especially, reach a surprising elevation for their bulk.

As regards the ages of the larger trees, one frequently finds stumps about two hundred years old; those of three hundred are not rare, and occasionally we have seen one which we believed to claim upward of four hundred rings. But as a rule, the largest trees are singled out very early in the history of a settlement, and many of these older stumps of the largest size have now become so worn and ragged, that it is seldom one can count the circles accurately. They are often much injured by fire immediately after the tree has been felled, and in many other instances decay has been at work at the heart, and one cannot, perhaps, count more than half the rings; measuring will help, in such cases, to give some idea; by taking fifty rings of the sound part, and allowing the same distance of the decayed portion for another fifty. But this is by no means a sure way, since the rings vary very much in the same tree, some being so broad that they must have sensibly increased the circumference of the trunk in one year, to the extent, perhaps, of an inch, while in other parts of the same shaft you will find a dozen circles crowded into that space. In short, it is seldom one has the satisfaction of meeting with a stump in which one may count every ring with perfect accuracy. It is said that some of the pines on the Pacific coast, those of Oregon and California, have numbered nine hundred rings; these were the noble Lambert pines of that region. Probably very few of our own white pines can show more than half that number of circles.

It is often said, as an excuse for leaving none standing, that these old trees of forest growth will not live after their companions have been felled; they miss the protection which one gives to another, and, exposed to the winds, soon fall to the ground. As a general rule, this may be true; but one is inclined to believe that if the experiment of leaving a few were more frequently tried, it would often prove successful. There is an elm of great size now standing entirely alone in a pretty field of the valley, its girth, its age, and whole appearance declaring it a chieftain of the ancient race — the "Sagamore elm," as it is called — and in spite of complete exposure to the winds from all quarters of the heavens, it maintains its place firmly. The trunk measures seventeen feet in circumference, and it is thought to be a hundred feet in height; but this is only from the eye, never having been accurately ascertained. The shaft rises perhaps fifty feet without a branch, before it divides, according to the usual growth of old forest trees. Unfortunately, gray branches are beginning to show among its summer foliage, and it is to be feared that it will not outlast many winters more; but if it die tomorrow, we shall have owed a debt of many thanks to the owner of the field for having left the tree standing so long.

In these times, the hewers of wood are an unsparing race. The first colonists looked upon a tree as an enemy, and to judge from appearances, one would think that something of the same spirit prevails among their descendants at the present hour. It is not surprising, perhaps, that a man whose chief object in life is to make money, should turn his timber into banknotes with all possible speed; but it is remarkable that any one at all aware of the value of wood, should act so wastefully as most men do in this part of the world. Mature trees, young saplings, and last year's seedlings, are all destroyed at one blow by the axe or by fire; the spot where they have stood is left, perhaps, for a lifetime without any attempt at cultivation, or any endeavor to foster new wood. One would think that by this time, when the forest has fallen in all the valleys — when the hills are becoming more bare every day — when timber and fuel are rising in prices, and new uses are found for even indifferent woods — some forethought and care in this respect would be natural in people laying claim to common sense. The rapid consumption of the large pine timber among us should be enough to teach a lesson of prudence and economy on this subject. It has been calculated that 60,000 acres of pine woods are cut every year in our own State alone; and at this rate, it is said that in twenty years, or about 1870, these trees will have disappeared from our part of the country! But unaccountable as it may appear, few American farmers are aware of the full value and importance of wood. . . .

But independently of their market price in dollars and cents, the trees have other values: they are connected in many ways with the civilization of a country; they have their importance in an intellectual and in a moral sense. After the first rude stage of progress is past in a new country — when shelter and food have been provided — people begin to collect the conveniences and pleasures of a permanent home about their dwellings, and then the farmer generally sets out a few trees before his door. This is very desirable, but it is only the first step in the track; something more is needed; the preservation of fine trees, already standing, marks a farther progress, and this point we have not yet reached. It frequently happens that the same man who yesterday planted some half dozen branchless saplings before his door, will today cut down a noble elm, or oak, only a few rods from his house, an object which was in itself a hundred-fold more beautiful than any other in his possession. In very truth, a fine tree near a house is a much greater embellishment than the thickest coat of paint that could be put on its walls, or a whole row of wooden columns to adorn its front; nay, a large shady tree in a dooryard is much more desirable than the most expensive mahogany and velvet sofa in the parlor. Unhappily, our people generally do not yet see things in this light. But time is a very essential element, absolutely indispensable, indeed, in true civilization; and in the course of years we shall, it is to be hoped, learn farther lessons of this kind. Closer observation will reveal to us the beauty and excellence of simplicity, a quality as yet too little valued or understood in this country. And when we have made this farther progress, then we shall take better care of our trees. We shall not be satisfied with setting out a dozen naked saplings before our door, because our neighbor on the left did so last year, nor cut down a whole wood, within a stone's throw of our dwelling, to pay for a Brussels carpet from the same piece as our neighbor's on the right; no, we shall not care a stiver for mere show and parade, in any shape whatever, but we shall look to the general proprieties and fitness of things, whether our neighbors to the right or the left do so or not.

How easy it would be to improve most of the farms in the country by a little attention to the woods and trees, improving their appearance, and adding to their market value at the same time! Thinning woods and not blasting them; clearing only such ground as is marked for immediate tillage; preserving the wood on the hilltops and rough sidehills; encouraging a coppice on this or that knoll; permitting bushes and young trees to grow at will along the brooks and watercourses; sowing, if need be, a grove on the bank of the pool, such as are found on many of our farms; sparing an elm or two about the spring, with a willow also to overhang the well; planting one or two chestnuts, or oaks, or beeches, near the gates or bars; leaving a few others scattered about every field to shade the cattle in summer, as is frequently done, and setting out others in groups, or singly, to shade the house—how little would be the labor or expense required to accomplish this, and how desirable would be the result! Assuredly, the pleasing character thus given to a farm and a neighborhood is far from being beneath the consideration of a sensible man.

But there is also another view of the subject. A careless indifference to any good gift of our gracious Maker, shows a want of thankfulness, as any abuse or waste, betrays a reckless spirit of evil. It is, indeed, strange that one claiming to be a rational creature should not be thoroughly ashamed of the spirit of destructiveness, since the principle itself is clearly an evil one. Let us remember that it is the Supreme Being who is the Creator, and in how many ways do we see his gracious providence, his Almighty economy, deigning to work progressive renovation in the humblest objects when their old forms have become exhausted by Time! There is also something in the care of trees which rises above the common labors of husbandry, and speaks of a generous mind. We expect to wear the fleece from our flocks, to drink the milk of our herds, to feed upon the fruits of our fields; but in planting a young wood, in preserving a fine grove, a noble tree, we look beyond ourselves to the band of household friends, to our neighbors — ay, to the passing wayfarer and stranger who will share with us the pleasure they give, and it becomes a grateful reflection that long after we are gone, those trees will continue a good to our fellow-creatures for more years, perhaps, than we can tell.

Howard Stansbury
(1806–1863)

Born in New York City, Howard Stansbury was a civil engineer before being appointed to the newly formed Army Corps of Topographical Engineers in 1838. After working on projects around the Great Lakes and New England, and serving at the Dry Tortugas during the Mexican War, Stansbury received the major assignment of his career: to survey and map the entire Salt Lake and its valley. In 1849 — the year of the great gold rush — Stansbury's eighteen-man reconnaissance party traveled as far west as Fort Bridger, in present-day southwestern Wyoming, and from there pioneered a new route to Salt Lake. Stansbury then led his men on an unprecedented circumambulation of the lake, and in November 1849 they became the first whites to complete an entire land circuit of Salt Lake. Stansbury's explorations of the great lake were preceded by those of Captain Benjamin Bonneville, who visited the area in 1831 and John C. Frémont, who came through on his 1843–44 expedition; indeed, Stansbury did not realize that the mysterious cross he discovered carved in a tree on what is now called Frémont Island had been made by Frémont's guide, Kit Carson. Stansbury demonstrated resourcefulness and good judgment in facing the challenges of mud, heat, lack of water, scant forage, and harsh weather, and his written account — replete with engaging descriptions of the fantastic landscapes, creatures, and fossils of the eastern Great Basin — is far more lyrical than most exploration narratives of the period. Published in 1852 as a U.S. government document titled *Exploration and Survey of the Valley of the Great Salt Lake of Utah . . .*, Stansbury's report was republished commercially and was widely read by Americans then hungry for firsthand views of Western landscapes. Stansbury was honored in the naming of the cliff rose species *Purshia stansburiana,* and the common side-blotched lizard, *Uta stansburiana.*

From
Exploration and Survey of the Valley of the Great Salt Lake of Utah . . . (1852)

October 22, 1849. . . . The evening was mild and bland, and the scene around us one of exciting interest. At our feet and on each side lay the waters of the Great Salt Lake, which we had so long and so ardently desired to see. They were clear and calm, and stretched far to the south and west. Directly before us, and distant only a few miles, an island rose from eight hundred to one thousand feet in height, while in the distance other and larger ones shot up from the bosom of the waters, their summits appearing to reach the clouds. On the west appeared several dark spots, resembling other islands, but the dreamy haze hovering over this still and solitary sea threw its dim, uncertain veil over the more distant features of the landscape, preventing the eye from discerning any one object with distinctness, while it half revealed the whole, leaving ample scope for the imagination of the beholder. The stillness of the grave seemed to pervade both air and water; and, excepting here and there a solitary wild-duck floating motionless on the bosom of the lake, not a living thing was to be seen. The night proved perfectly serene, and a young moon shed its tremulous light upon a sea of profound, unbroken silence. . . .

October 25. . . . In passing over this mud-plain, the glare from the oozy substance of which it is composed was extremely painful to the eyes. Leaving it behind us, we ascended a ridge to the west of it, two or three miles broad, passing over some remains of shales and altered limestone with conglomerate, the crest being composed of porous trap, underlying the sedimentary rocks, and cropping out to the west. It may be remarked here, that the general direction of all the ridges noticed in this region is north and south, and they terminate most frequently in sharp, bold promontories, to the south. A herd of antelope was seen on this ridge, numbering about a hundred, but too wild to be approached.

Descending its western slope, we came into another plain, somewhat similar to the last in form, but much more extensive in all directions, and densely covered with artemisia. Over this desolate, barren waste, we traveled until nearly dark, when we reached a rocky promontory, constituting the southern point of a low ridge of hills jutting into the plain from the north. The rock was porous trap, in which no stratification could be made out. The mules having been without water or grass the whole day, and our stock of the former being insufficient to give them even their stinted allowance of one poor pint, we halted for a couple of hours, and drove them upon the side of the mountain to pick what they could get from the scanty supply of dry bunchgrass that grew in tufts upon its side. The prospect of water now began to be rather gloomy; and I was obliged to put the party upon allowance, lest we should be left entirely destitute. At eight o'clock we replaced the packs upon our mules, all of which began to show the effects of their unusual abstinence, and rode on till near midnight by the light of the moon, in a southwesterly direction, over a country similar to that we had traversed during the day; when, finding the indications of water growing less and less promising, and that our animals were nearly worn out, we halted, and, covered with our blankets, we lay down on the ground till morning, regardless of a heavy shower that fell during the night.

October 26. The poor animals presented this morning a forlorn appearance, having been now without a drop of water for more than twenty-four hours, during eighteen of which they had been under the saddle, with scarcely anything to eat. I now began to feel somewhat anxious. Should our mules give out before we could reach the mountains west of us, to which I had determined to direct our course as speedily as possible, we must all perish in the wilderness. Sweeping the horizon with a telescope, I thought I discovered something that looked like willows to the northwest, distant about four or five miles. Reanimated by this gleam of hope, we saddled up quickly and turned our steps in that direction. We soon had the lively satisfaction of finding our expectations confirmed; for, arriving at the spot, we found, after some search, a small spring welling out from the bottom of a little ravine, which having with some labor been cleaned out, we soon enjoyed a plentiful, most needed, and most welcome supply of excellent water for all. . . .

November 7. Ther. at sunrise, 47°. Starting early in the morning, we crossed to the eastern side of the valley, followed the base of the mountain to its northern extremity, and reached the shores of the Great Salt Lake near Black Rock, whence we crossed the valley of the Jordan, over sterile artemisia plains, and reached the city in the afternoon—being the first party of white men that ever succeeded in making the entire circuit of the lake by land. Attempts had, in early times, been made to circumnavigate it in canoes, by some trappers in search of beaver; but they all proved unsuccessful, from want of fresh water.

The examination just completed proves that the whole western shore of the lake is bounded by an immense level plain, consisting of soft mud, frequently traversed by small, meandering rills of salt and sulfurous water, with occasional springs of fresh, all of which sink before reaching the lake. These streams seem to imbue and saturate the whole soil, so as to render it throughout miry and treacherous. For a few months, in midsummer, the sun has sufficient influence to render some portions of the plain, for a short time, dry and hard: in these intervals the traveling over it is excellent; but one heavy shower is sufficient to reconvert the hardened clay into soft, tenacious mud, rendering the passage of teams over it toilsome, and frequently quite hazardous.

These plains are but little elevated above the present level of the lake, and have, beyond question, at one time formed a part of it. It is manifest to every observer, that an elevation of but a few feet above the present level of the lake would flood this entire flat to a great distance north and south, and wash the base of the Pilot Peak range of mountains, which constitute its western boundary; thus converting what is now a comparatively small and insignificant lake into a vast inland sea. This extensive area is, for the most part, entirely denuded of vegetation, excepting occasional patches of artemisia and greasewood. The minute crystals of salt which cover the surface of the moist, oozy mud, glisten brilliantly in the sunlight, and present the appearance of a large sheet of water so perfectly, that it is difficult, at times, for one to persuade himself that he is not standing on the shore of the lake itself. High rocky ridges protrude above the level plain, and resemble great islands rising above the bosom of this desert sea.

The mirage, which frequently occurs, is greater here than I ever witnessed elsewhere, distorting objects in the most grotesque manner, defying all calculation as to their size, shape, or distances, and giving rise to optical illusions almost beyond belief. With the exception of the two valleys lying at the south end of the lake, the country is, as a place of human habitation, entirely worthless. There is, however, one valuable use to which it may and perhaps will be applied: its extent, and perfectly level surface, would furnish a desirable space on which to measure a degree of the meridian. . . .

May 7. After moving camp some few miles above, started for an island in the lake, apparently fifteen or twenty miles to the southward, to place a triangulation station upon it. The wind had been southerly during the night, and had raised such a sea that I found it impossible to force the boat through the water, whose ponderous waves struck upon our bows with a power that was irresistible. After rowing some eight miles, we gave it up and returned to camp.

One of the party, in attempting to cut across the country today, got lost, and as he did not return by dark, signal-fires were lighted upon one or two of the neighboring eminences to guide him to camp. He returned by bedtime, very much exhausted by his wanderings, having been without food or water since sunrise.

May 8. The day being calm and the water smooth, renewed the attempt made yesterday to reach the island to the southward, taking with us blankets, provisions, and water, prepared to encamp upon it, if necessary. We reached the island after a row of four hours. The water was bold and deep nearly the whole distance — fifteen, seventeen, and twenty feet; and ten feet, within a hundred and fifty feet of the shore.

There are two islands here, one of them quite small, and lying within one hundred yards to the northward of the larger one, of which it has at one time formed a part. We landed at the head of a beautiful little sandy bay, on the eastern side, which has its counterpart on the western, the two being separated by a low, narrow neck of land, forming a delightful little nook, and separating the lofty pile of rock forming the northern part of the island from the rocky cliffs which extend to its southern extremity.

The whole neck and the shores on both of the little bays were occupied by immense flocks of pelicans and gulls, disturbed now for the first time, probably, by the intrusion of man. They literally darkened the air as they rose upon the wing, and, hovering over our heads, caused the surrounding rocks to re-echo with their discordant screams. The ground was thickly strewn with their nests, of which there must have been some thousands. Numerous young, unfledged pelicans, were found in the nests on the ground, and hundreds half-grown, huddled together in groups near the water, while the old ones retired to a long line of sand-beach on the southern side of the bay, where they stood drawn up, like Prussian soldiers, in ranks three or four deep, for hours together, apparently without motion.

Fredrika Bremer
(1801–1865)

Swedish writer, traveler, pacifist, social critic, and feminist Fredrika Bremer was born in 1801 in Åbo (Turku), Finland, where naturalist Peter Kalm had studied seventy years earlier. A best-selling novelist whose many books include *Scenes from Everyday Life* (1828), *The President's Daughter* (1834), and the important feminist novel *Hertha* (1856), Bremer often focused her work on the problems of women and the working classes in gaining access to education, vocational opportunities, and social equality. Bremer's contribution to American nature writing was inspired by her 1849–51 American tour—a trip during which she traveled through the South, Northeast, and upper Midwest. On her journey she visited literary luminaries including Washington Irving, Nathaniel Hawthorne, James Fenimore Cooper, and Ralph Waldo Emerson and met with prominent women activists and abolitionists including Lucretia Mott, Harriet Beecher Stowe, and Lydia Maria Child. While traveling in the United States Bremer wrote a series of letters to her sister, Agathe, who meanwhile died before Bremer returned to Sweden in 1851. Although she had not intended to document her North American tour for publication, after returning home she revised the letters and collected them as the 1853 book *Hemmen I den Nya verlden*, a popular travelogue republished the same year in an English translation entitled *The Homes of the New World. . . . Homes* is a fascinating work of travel literature that, like Harriet Martineau's *Retrospect of Western Travel* (1838), includes an outspoken feminist critique of slavery and other American social injustices, often contrasting such injustices with the impressive beauty and grandeur of the American land. In the following excerpts from *Homes,* Bremer travels two American rivers—the Mississippi and the St. Johns—commenting on the sublimity and the mythic potential of the New World landscape, which she predicts will become "an empire for all the nations of the earth."

From *The Homes of the New World: Impressions of America* (1853)

Letter XXI: Cape May, New Jersey

August 27, 1850. I now, my beloved child, am preparing to set off to the great West, which stands before me in a kind of mythological nebulosity, half mist, half splendor, and about which I know nothing rightly, excepting that it is great, great, great! How? Why? In what way? Whether it is peopled by gods or giants, giants of frost and hobgoblins, or by all those old mythological gentry together—I have yet to discover. That Thor and Loki yet wrestle vigorously in that fairy-tale-like Utgard, is however, what I quite anticipate, and that the goblins are at home there also, that I know, because of certain "spiritual rappings or knockings," as they are called, of which I have heard and read some very queer things since I have been in this country. These are a standing subject in the newspapers at this time, and are treated partly in jest and partly in earnest. But I shall certainly find Iduna with the apple of the Hesperides in that Eden of the setting sun. Do not the Allegheny Mountains and Niagara stand as giant watchers at its entrance, to open the portals of that new garden of Paradise, the latest home of the human race? Those glorious cherubim forbid not the entrance; they invite it, because they are great and beautiful.

The people of Europe pour in through the cities of the eastern coast. Those are the portals of the outer court; but the West is the garden where the rivers carry along with them gold, and where stands the tree of Life and of Death. There the tongue of the serpent and the voice of God are again heard by a new humanity.

That great enigmatical land of the West, with its giant rivers, and giant falls, and giant lakes; with its valley of the Mississippi and its Rocky Mountains, and its land of gold and the Pacific Ocean; with its buffaloes and its golden hummingbirds; the land which nourishes states as the children of men, and where cities grow great in a human life; where the watchword of existence is growth, progress! this enigmatic, promised land, this land of the future, I shall now behold! . . .

Letter XXVI: On the Mississippi

October 15. Was this, then, indeed, the Mississippi, that wild giant of nature, which I had imagined would be so powerful, so divine, so terrible? Here its waters were clear, of a fresh, light-green color, and within their beautiful frame of distant violet-blue mountains, they lay like a heavenly mirror, bearing on their bosom verdant, vine-covered islands, like islands of the blessed. The Mississippi was here in its youth, in its state of innocence as yet. It has not as yet advanced very far from its fountains; no crowd of steamboats muddy its waters. The Menomonie and one other, a still smaller boat, are the only ones which ascend the river above Galena; no cities cast into it their pollution; pure rivers only flow into its waters, and aborigines and primeval forests still surround it. Afterward, far below and toward the world's sea, where the Mississippi comes into the life of the states, and becomes a statesman, he has his twelve hundred steamers, and I know not how many thousand sailing-boats, gives himself up to cities and the population of cities, and is married to the Missouri: then it is quite different; then is it all over with the beauty and innocence of the Mississippi.

But now, now it was beautiful, and the whole of that evening on the Mississippi was to me like an enchantment. . . .

October 16. A glorious morning, as warm as summer! It rained in the night, but cleared up in the morning; those dense, dark masses of cloud were penetrated, rent asunder by the flashing sunbeams; and bold, abrupt shadows, and heavenly lights played among the yet bolder, more craggy and more picturesque hills. What an animated scene it was! and I was once more alone with America, with my beloved, my great and beautiful sister, with the sibyl at whose knee I sat listening and glancing up to her with looks full of love. Oh what did she not communicate to me that day, that morning full of inspiration, as amid her tears she drank in the heavenly light, and flung those dark shadows, like a veil, back from her countenance, that it might be only the more fully illumined by the Divine light! Never shall I forget that morning!

They came again and again, during the morning, those dark clouds, spreading night over those deep abysses; but again they yielded, again they gave place to the sun, which finally prevailed, alone, triumphant, and shone over the Mississippi and its world in the most beautiful summer splendor; and the inner light in my soul conversed with the outward light. It was glorious!

The further we advanced, the more strangely and fantastically were the cliffs on the shore splintered and riven, representing the most astonishing imagery. Halfway up, probably four or five hundred feet above the river, these hills were covered with wood now golden with the hue of autumn, and above that, rising, as if directly out of it, naked, ruin-like crags, of rich red brown, representing fortifications, towers, half-demolished walls, as of ancient, magnificent strongholds and castles. The castle ruins of the Rhine are small things in comparison with these gigantic remains of primeval ages; when men were not, but the Titans of primeval nature, Megatheriums, Mastodons, and Ichthyosaurians rose up from the waters, and wandered alone over the earth.

It was difficult to persuade oneself that many of these bold pyramids and broken temple-facades had not really been the work of human hands, so symmetrical, so architectural were these colossal erections. I saw in two places human dwellings, built upon a height; they looked like birds'-nests upon a lofty roof; but I was glad to see them, because they predicted that this magnificent region will soon have inhabitants, and this temple of nature worshipers in thankful and intelligent human hearts. The country on the other side of these precipitous crags is highland, glorious country, bordering the prairie-land — land for many millions of human beings! Americans will build upon these hills beautiful, hospitable homes, and will here labor, pray, love, and enjoy. An ennobled humanity will live upon these heights.

Below, in the river, at the feet of the hill-giants, the little green islands become more and more numerous. All were of the same character; all were lovely islands, all one tangle of wild vine. The wild grapes are small and sour, but are said to become sweet after they have been frosted. It is extraordinary that the wild vine is everywhere indigenous to America. America is of a truth Vineland. . . .

Letter XXXVIII, Savannah, Georgia

May 13, 1851. St. Johns River — in the Indian language, Welaka, or the Lake-River — is like a chain of larger and smaller lakes, linked together by narrow but deep straits, which wind in innumerable sinuosities between shores, the wonderful scenery of which is scarcely to be imagined, if none similar to it have been seen before. Here is again primeval forest such as I saw on the Savannah River, but still richer in its productions, because Welaka flows, for the greater part, under a tropical sky, and below the boundary which frost approaches. We see here thick groves and belts of palmettos; here are wild orange-groves laden with brilliant fruit which there are no hands to gather; masses of climbing plants, vanilla, wild vines, convolvuluses, and many others, cover the shores in indescribable luxuriance, forming themselves into clumps and bushes as they grow over the trees, and cypresses, which present dark green pyramids, altars, perfect temples with columns, arches, porticoes, shadowy aisles, and, on all hands, the most beautiful, the most ornamental festoons flung along and over the clear river. From amid the masses of foliage towers upward the fan-palm, with its beautiful crown, free and fantastic; the magnolia stands full of snow white flowers, and, preeminent amid that republic of plants, flowers, and multitudes of trees, stand the lofty cypresses like protecting, shadowy patriarchs, stretching out horizontally their light green heads, with long, waving mosses hanging down from their strong branches.

Here is the life of Nature in its luxuriance, but it is the realm and reign of the old pagan god of Nature, old Pan, which embraces both the good and the evil, life and death, with the same love, and which recognizes no law and no ordination but that of production and decay. Beneath these verdant, leafy arches which overshadow the water lie the peaceful tortoise, and the cruel alligator also, waiting for its prey. Elks inhabit these natural temples; also panthers, tigers, and black bears. Around these columns of leaves and flowers wind the rattlesnake and the poisonous moccasin, and that beautiful, romantic forest is full of small, poisonous, noxious creatures. But more dangerous than all is the pleasant air which comes laden, during the summer, with the miasmas of the primeval forests and the river, bringing to the colonist fever and slowly consuming diseases, and causing these wondrously beautiful shores still to lack human inhabitants. Small settlements have been commenced here and there on the river, but have, after a few years, been deserted and left to decay.

It is, however, precisely this primeval life in the wilderness, this wild, luxuriant beauty defying the power of man, and vigorous in its own affluence, which is so unspeakably interesting to me, and which supplies me with an incessant festival. And the air is so pleasant, and the magnolias so full of flower, the river so full of life, alligators and fishes splashing about, large and beautiful waterfowl on all hands—everything is so luxuriant, so wonderfully rich, wild, and lovely, it is a never-ending fairy scene, especially in the evenings, when the moon rises and throws her mystic half light and half shadow into the arches and pillared aisles of these marvelous natural temples. . . .

Our journey was enchanting the whole day; we emerged from the narrow, winding river-passes into a large, clear lake, surrounded by luxuriant verdant banks. The affluence of vegetation and animal life seemed to increase with every hour; the Flora of the tropics and the atmosphere of the tropics seemed to approach; we advanced into the home of eternal summer. The wild sugarcane, the maiden-cane grew along the banks, and showed that the soil was favorable for sugar cultivation. The temple of Nature became still richer. Beautiful, gorgeous flowers, red and blue, upon long stalks, white lilies, and gigantic water-plants, among which was the tall *Alisma plantago,* shone like stems of light beneath the dark green arches; flocks of little green parrots flew twittering over the wild sugarcane and into the palm-groves; wild turkeys, larger than our tame ones, were seen on the shores; lovely, slender waterfowl fluttered fearlessly around us, and equally fearless, but much less lovely, thousands of alligators swam in front of and on each side of our vessel, and fish leaped and splashed about as if they were out of their senses, but whether from terror or from joy I know not. It was a grand spectacle the whole way. . . .

The only annoyance I experienced the whole way was the lust of shooting which possessed one of the passengers in particular, and who was not contented with shooting alligators right and left, but who even shot the lovely waterfowl, which, however, he could not make any use of, and it was distressing to me to see them fall down wounded, here and there, among the weeds. I took the liberty of speaking my mind to him about this needless shooting. He smiled, agreed with what I said, and continued to shoot. I wished him, *in petto,* bad digestion!

As regards the alligators, I could not have very much compassion on them. They are so hideous to behold, and are so terrible; for, though they do not attack grown people unless in self-defense, still they carry off the little negro children without ceremony. They swim, with the upper part of the body above the water, so that it is not difficult to hit them with a bullet in the body and the forelegs. On this they dive down, or, if severely wounded, turn on one side; they are often seen like masses of living mud, rolling themselves on the shore to hide themselves among the water-reeds that grow there. Their number and their fearlessness here are amazing. It is said that even two years ago they were so numerous that it was difficult for boats to get along. They make a sort of grunting or bellowing sound, and it is said that early in the spring, at pairing-time, they make a horrible noise.

I spent the whole day on the piazza, dividing my attention between natural scenes and the perusal of Columbus's journal, which he kept during his first voyage of discovery among the enchanting islands of the New World. . . .

What an empire, what a world is North America, embracing all climates, natural scenery, and productions. It is indeed an empire for all the nations of the earth.

FURTHER READING

The following selected bibliography is intended to be neither authoritative nor exhaustive; indeed, a comprehensive bibliography of early American nature writing (considered broadly) would itself be book length (for example, see the entries for Bell, Meisel, and Tucher, below). Instead, offered here is a selective list of several hundred books that I have found particularly valuable and interesting, and that I believe will be especially useful to students and scholars of the place-based literatures of early America.

In the section on primary works (arranged chronologically), I have listed nonfiction books and monographs by authors whose work I would very likely have excerpted in this volume, had space permitted. Because most of these materials are available on microfilm, in special collections, or as scholar's reprints (rather than in particular, authoritative scholarly editions), I have omitted specific edition publication information. It is my hope that this list will offer fruitful directions for future scholarship, and that it may encourage scholarly studies, editions, and reprints of some of these superb but nearly forgotten works of early American nature writing.

The section on secondary works (arranged alphabetically) omits articles, single-author studies, works solely on British and continental natural history, and narrowly disciplinary scholarship but does include critical and reference volumes that provide useful insights into the general field of early American nature writing. Although readers who approach this field with a specific generic, thematic, regional, historical, or ideological interest (e.g., environmental memoir, ornithological literature, southern nature writing, exploration narrative, preservationist writing) are likely to find these secondary sources rather general, they may nevertheless find many helpful starting points among the works listed here.

PRIMARY WORKS

Giovanni da Verrazzano, "To his Most Serene Majesty the King of France . . ." (1524)

Jacques Cartier, *Voyages* (1534–1541)

A Gentleman of Elvas, *The Discovery and Conquest of Terra Florida* (1557)

M. John Hawkins, *The Voyage Made by M. John Hawkins, Esq.* (1565)

David Ingram, "The Relation of David Ingram" (1568/1589)

Rene Goulaine de Laudonniere, *A Notable Historie Containing Foure Voyages Made by Certaine French Captaines unto Florida* (1587)

José de Acosta, *Natural and Moral History of the Indies* (1590)

Gabriel Archer, *The Relation of Captaine Gosnol's Voyage to the North Part of Virginia . . .* (1602)

John Brereton, *A Brief and True Relation of the Discoverie of the North Part of Virginia . . .* (1602)

Samuel de Champlain, *The Voyages and Explorations of Samuel de Champlain* (1603–1616)

James Rosier, *A True Relation of the Most Prosperous Voyage . . .* (1605)

Henry Hudson, *A Second Voyage or Employment of Master Henry Hudson, for Finding a Passage to the East Indies by the North-East, Written by Himselfe* (1608/1625)
Marke Lescarbot, *The Voyage of Monsieur de Monts into New France* (1609)
Abacuk Pricket, *A Larger Discourse of the Same Voyage [Henry Hudson's Fourth Voyage], and the Successe Thereof* (1610)
William Bradford and Edward Winslow ("G. Mourt"), *Mourt's Relation, or, Journall of the beginning and proceedings of the English Plantation setled at Plimoth in New England . . .* (1622)
Christopher Levett, "Discovery of Diverse Rivers and Harbors . . ." (1624)
Edward Winslow, *Good Newes from New England* (1624)
Francis Higginson, *New England's Plantation* (1630)
William Bradford, *Of Plymouth Plantation* (1630–1650/1856)
Richard Mather, *Journal [of a Voyage to New England]* (1635/1846)
John Underhill, *Newes from America; or, A New and Experimentall Discoverie of New England* (1638)
Edward Taylor, *Diary* (1660–1670s/1880–1881)
John Lederer, *The Discoveries of John Lederer* (1672)
Father Marquette, *A Discovery of Some New Countries and Nations in Northern America* (1673/1698)
John Banister, *The Natural History of Virginia* (1678–1692/ 1970)
Nicolas De La Salle, *Relation of the Discovery of the Mississippi River* (1682)
Mary Rowlandson, *A True History of the Captivity and Restoration of Mrs. Mary Rowlandson* (1682)
Increase Mather, "ΚΟΜΗΤΟΓΡΑΦΙΑ [Kometographia], or, Discourse Concerning Comets; wherein the Nature of BLAZING STARS is Enquired into" (1683); *Remarkable Providences, Illustrative of the Earlier Days of American Colonisation* (1684)
Samuel Sewall, *Phaenomena quaedam Apocalyptica ad Aspectum Novi Orbis configurata* (1697)
William Byrd II, *The History of the Dividing Line betwixt Virginia and North Carolina* (1728–29/1841); *A Journey to the Land of Eden* (1733/1841)
Cadwallader Colden, *Observations on the Situation, Soil, Climate, Water Communications, Boundaries &c of the Province of New York* (1738); *An Explication of the First Causes of Action in Matter, and of the Cause of Gravitation* (1745)
John Clayton, *Flora Virginica . . .* (1739–1743)
Jane Colden, *Flora of New York* (c. 1750/1963)
John Bartram, *Travels in Pensilvania and Canada* (1751)
Martha Daniell Logan, "The Gardener's Kalender" (1752)
Jonathan Carver, *Travels Through the Interior Parts of North America* (1766/1778)
William Stork, *An Account of East-Florida . . .* (1767)
Samson Occom (Mohegan), *A Short Narrative of My Life* (1768)
John Woolman, *Journal* (1774)
James Adair, *The History of the American Indians* (1775)

Alexander Garden, "An Account of the *Gymnotus Electricus*, or Electrical Eel . . ." (1775)
Bernard Romans, *A Concise Natural History of East and West Florida* (1775)
Fray Franscisco Silvestre Velez de Escalante, *The Dominguez-Escalante Journal* (1776)
Thomas Hutchins, *A Topographical Description of Virginia, Pennsylvania, Maryland, and North Carolina . . .* (1778); *An Historical Narrative and Topographical Description of Louisiana and West-Florida . . .* (1784)
Johann David Schoepf, *Travels in the Confederation* (1783–1784)
Daniel Boone, *The Adventures of Colonel Daniel Boone* (1784)
John Marrant, *A Narrative of the Lord's Wonderful Dealings with John Marrant* (1785)
Marquis de Chastellux, *Travels in North-America* (1786)
Manasseh Cutler, *An Explanation of the Map which Delineates that Part of the Federal Lands Comprehended between Pennsylvania West Line, the Rivers Ohio and Sioto, and Lake Erie . . .* (1787)
Johann Reinhold Forster, *Observations Made During a Voyage Round the World* (1787)
Mary Coburn Dewees, *Journal of a Trip from Philadelphia to Lexington in Kentucky* (1787–1788/1936)
Andre Michaux, *Journal* (1787–1796)
Jedidiah Morse, *The American Geography* (1789)
Gilbert Imlay, *A Topographical Description of the Western Territory of North America . . .* (1793)
Hendrick Aupaumut (Mahican), *A Short Narration of My Last Journey to the Western Contry* (1794/1827)
Samuel Williams, *The Natural and Civil History of Vermont* (1794)
Benjamin Smith Barton, *A Memoir Concerning the Fascinating Faculty which has been Ascribed to the Rattle-Snake . . .* (1799); *A Discourse on Some of the Principal Desiderata in Natural History, and on the Best Means of Promoting the Study of This Science, in the United-States* (1807)
Thaddeus Mason Harris, *The Journal of a Tour into the Northwest Territory of the Alleghany Mountains* (1803)
Francois Andre Michaux, *Travels to the Westward of the Alleghany Mountains* (1804); *The North American Sylva* (1818–1819)
Peter Custis and Thomas Freeman, *An Account of the Red River in Louisiana . . .* (1806)
Isaac Weld Jr., *Travels Through the States of North America . . .* (1807)
Anthony Glass, *Journal of a Voyage from Nackitosh into the Interior of Louisiana . . .* (1808–1809/1975)
John Edwards Caldwell, *A Tour through a Part of Virginia . . .* (1809)
William Cooper, *A Guide in the Wilderness; or, The History of the First Settlements in the Western Counties of New York with Useful Instructions to Future Settlers* (1810)
Zebulon Montgomery Pike, *An Account of Expeditions to the Sources of the Mississippi and through the Western Parts of Louisiana* (1810)
Benjamin Silliman, "An Account of the Meteor, Which Burst Over Weston in Connecticut, in December, 1807, and of the Falling of Stones on that Occasion" (1810); "Consis-

tency of the Discoveries of Modern Geology with the Sacred History of the Creation and the Deluge" (1833); "Address Delivered before the Association of American Geologists and Naturalists . . ." (1842)

Henry Marie Brackenridge, *Views of Louisiana* (1814)

Stephen Harriman Long, "Voyage in a Six-Oared Skiff to the Falls of St. Anthony" (1817)

William Maclure, *Observations on the Geology of the United States of America* . . . (1817)

James Kirke Paulding, *Letters from the South* (1817)

Amos Eaton, *A Manual of Botany* . . . (1817); "Geology and Meteorology West of the Rocky Mountains" (1834)

Juan Bautista Alvarado, *The Reminiscences of Juan Bautista Alvarado* (1819)

Thomas Nuttall, *A Journal of Travels into the Arkansa Territory* (1821)

Jacob Fowler, *The Journal of Jacob Fowler* (1821–1822/1898)

Paul Wilhelm, *Travels in North America* (1822–1824/1835)

David Douglas, *Journal* . . . (1823–1827/1914)

John Torrey, *A Flora of the Middle and Northern Sections of the United States* . . . (1823)

Zakahar Tchitchinoff, *The Reminiscences of Zakahar Tchitchinoff* (1824)

Thomas Say, *American Entomology* (1824–1828)

Daniel Drake, *Geological Account of the Valley of the Ohio* (1825)

James Ellsworth Dekay, *Anniversary Address on the Progress of the Natural Sciences in the United States* . . . (1826)

August Cilly, *Voyage* (1826–1829)

Duke Berhard of Saxe-Weimar-Eisenach, *Travels of Duke Berhard of Saxe-Weimar-Eisenach Through North America* . . . (1828)

Almira Hart Lincoln Phelps, *Familiar Lectures on Botany* . . . (1829)

Sandor Boloni Farkas, *Journey in North America* (1831)

Sarah Hale, *Flora's Interpreter: or, The American Book of Flowers and Sentiments* (1832)

Alexander Philip Maximilian, *Travels in the Interior of North America* . . . (1832–1834/1906)

Thomas Hamilton, *Men and Manners in America* (1833)

Davy Crockett, *Narrative of the Life of David Crockett* (1834)

Augustus Gould, *A System of Natural History; Containing Scientific and Popular Descriptions of Man, Quadrupeds, Birds, Fishes, Reptiles, and Insects* (1834)

Charles Fenno Hoffman, *A Winter in the West* (1835); *Wild Scenes in the Forest and Prairie* (1839)

Alexis de Tocqueville, *Democracy in America* (1835–1840)

Constantine Samuel Rafinesque, *A Life of Travels* (1836)

F[rederick] A[dolph] Wislizenus, *A Journey to the Rocky Mountains* . . . (1839/1912)

Richard Henry Dana, *Two Years Before the Mast* (1840)

John Bachman, *The Viviparous Quadrupeds of North America* (1840–1852)

William Darlington, "A Plea for a National Museum and Botanic Garden . . ." (1841); "Book of Wonders! or, Marvellous Chronicle Containing an Authentic Account of Extraordinary Events and Occurrences in Nature . . ." (1846)

Thaddeus William Harris, *A Treatise on Some of the Insects of New England* . . . (1842)

George William Featherstonhaugh, *Excursions through the Slave States* (1844)

Mary Townsend, *Life in the Insect World . . .* (1844)
Charles Lyell, *Travels in North America* (1845)
James William Abert, *Diary [of an Expedition to the Southwest . . .]* (1846–1847/1966)
William Emory, *Notes of a Military Reconnoissance from Fort Leavenworth, in Missouri, to San Diego, in California . . .* (1848); *Notes of Travel in California, Comprising the Prominent Geographical, Agricultural, Geological, and Mineralogical Features of the Country . . .* (1849); *Notes on the Survey of the Boundary Line between Mexico and the United States* (1851)
Henry William Herbert, *Frank Forester's Field Sports of the United States . . .* (1848); *Frank Forester's Fish and Fishing of the United States . . .* (1849)
Katherine Haun, *Diary [A Woman's Trip Across the Plains]* (1849)
Francis Parkman, *The California and Oregon Trail* (1849)
James Fenimore Cooper, "American and European Scenery Compared" (1852)
George William Curtis, *Lotus-Eating: A Summer Book* (1852)
Charles Olliffe, *American Scenes: Eighteen Months in the New World* (1852)
George P. Putnam, ed. *The Home Book of the Picturesque: American Scenery, Art, and Literature* (1852)
Lydia Allen Rudd, *Journal [Notes by the Wayside En Route to Oregon]* (1852)
Elisha Kane, *The U.S. Grinnell Expedition in Search of Sir John Franklin . . .* (1853)
Philip Pendleton Kennedy, *The Blackwater Chronicle, a Narrative of an Expedition into the Land of Canaan . . .* (1853)
John Palliser, *Solitary Rambles and Adventures of a Hunter in the Prairies* (1853)
S[amuel] W[ashington] Woodhouse, *Report on the Natural History of the Country Passed Over by the [Zuni-Colorado] Exploring Expedition . . .* (1853)
Friedrich Gerstacker, *Wild Sports in the Far West* (1854)

SECONDARY WORKS

Abir-Am, Pnina G., and Dorinda Outram, eds. *Uneasy Careers and Intimate Lives: Women in Science, 1789–1979*. New Brunswick, N.J.: Rutgers UP, 1987.
Adams, Alexander B. *Eternal Quest: The Story of the Great Naturalists*. New York: Putnam, 1969.
Bakeless, John. *The Eyes of Discovery: The Pageant of North America as Seen by the First Explorers*. Philadelphia: Lippincott, 1950.
Barber, Lynn. *The Heyday of Natural History, 1820–1870*. New York: Doubleday, 1980.
Barclay, Donald A., James H. Maguire, and Peter Wild, eds. *Into the Wilderness Dream: Exploration Narratives of the American West, 1500–1805*. Salt Lake City: U of Utah P, 1994.
Bates, Marston. *The Nature of Natural History*. New York: Scribner's, 1950.
Bell, Whitfield J., Jr. *Early American Science: Needs and Opportunities for Study*. Williamsburg, Va.: Institute of Early American History and Culture, 1955.
Bonta, Marcia Meyers. *Women in the Field: America's Pioneering Women Naturalists*. College Station: Texas A&M UP, 1991.

Brebner, J. Bartlett, *The Explorers of North America, 1492–1806*. New York: World Publishing, 1933.

Bryson, Michael A. *Visions of the Land: Science, Literature, and the American Environment from the Era of Exploration to the Age of Ecology*. Charlottesville: UP of Virginia, 2002.

Buell, Lawrence. *The Environmental Imagination: Thoreau, Nature Writing, and the Formation of American Culture*. Cambridge: Harvard UP, 1995.

Carroll, Peter N. *Puritanism and the Wilderness: The Intellectual Significance of the New England Frontier, 1629–1700*. New York: Columbia UP, 1969.

Cronon, William. *Changes in the Land: Indians, Colonists, and the Ecology of Colonial New England*. New York: Hill & Wang, 1983.

Daniels, George H. *Science in the Age of Jackson*. New York: Columbia UP, 1968.

Dear, Peter, ed. *The Literary Structure of Scientific Argument: Historical Studies*. Philadelphia: U of Pennsylvania P, 1991.

DeVoto, Bernard. *The Course of Empire*. Boston: Houghton Mifflin, 1952.

Egerton, Frank N., ed. *History of American Ecology*. New York: Arno P, 1977.

Ekirch, Arthur A., Jr. *Man and Nature in America*. New York: Columbia UP, 1963.

Elman, Robert. *First in the Field: America's Pioneering Naturalists*. New York: Mason/Charter, 1977.

Evans, Howard Ensign. *Pioneer Naturalists: The Discovery and Naming of North American Plants and Animals*. New York: Henry Holt, 1993.

Ewan, Joseph. *Rocky Mountain Naturalists*. Denver: Denver UP, 1950.

Farber, Paul Lawrence. *Finding Order in Nature: The Naturalist Tradition from Linnaeus to E. O. Wilson*. Baltimore: Johns Hopkins UP, 2000.

Fishman, Gail. *Journeys through Paradise: Pioneering Naturalists in the Southeast*. Gainesville: UP of Florida, 2000.

Foucalt, Michel. *The Order of Things: An Archeology of the Human Sciences*. New York: Pantheon, 1970.

Franklin, Wayne. *Discoverers, Explorers, Settlers: The Diligent Writers of Early America*. Chicago: U of Chicago P, 1979.

Friedenberg, Daniel M. *Life, Liberty, and the Pursuit of Land: The Plunder of Early America*. Buffalo: Prometheus, 1992.

Gates, Barbara, and Ann Shteir, eds. *Natural Eloquence: Women Reinscribe Science*. Madison: U of Wisconsin P, 1997.

Geiser, Samuel W. *Naturalists of the Frontier*. Dallas: Southern Methodist UP, 1948.

Goetzmann, William H. *Exploration and Empire: The Explorer and the Scientist in the Winning of the American West*. Austin: Texas State Historical Association, 1993.

Greene, John C. *American Science in the Age of Jefferson*. Ames: Iowa State UP, 1984.

Gross, Alan G. *The Rhetoric of Science*. Cambridge: Harvard UP, 1990.

Hallock, Thomas. *From the Fallen Tree: Frontier Narratives, Environmental Politics, and the Roots of a National Pastoral, 1743–1826*. Chapel Hill: U of North Carolina P, 2003.

Hanley, Wayne. *Natural History in America: From Mark Catesby to Rachel Carson*. New York: Quadrangle, 1977.

Harshberger, J. W. *The Botanists of Philadelphia and Their Work.* Philadelphia: T. C. Davis, 1899.

Hicks, Philip M. "Development of the Natural History Essay in American Literature." Diss. U of Pennsylvania, 1924.

Hindle, Brooke, ed. *Early American Science.* New York: Science History Publications, 1976.

———. *The Pursuit of Science in Revolutionary America, 1735–1789.* Chapel Hill: U of North Carolina P, 1956.

Hollingsworth, Buckner. *Her Garden Was Her Delight.* New York: Macmillan, 1962.

Horwitz, Howard. *By the Law of Nature: Form and Value in Nineteenth-Century America.* New York: Oxford UP, 1991.

Huth, Hans. *Nature and the American: Three Centuries of Changing Attitudes.* Berkeley: U of California P, 1957.

Irmscher, Christoph. *The Poetics of Natural History: From John Bartram to William James.* New Brunswick, N.J.: Rutgers UP, 1999.

Jardine, N., J. A. Secord, and E. C. Spary, *Cultures of Natural History.* Cambridge: Cambridge UP, 1996.

Jehlen, Myra, and Michael Warner. *The English Literatures of America, 1500–1800.* New York: Routledge, 1997.

Jenkins, Alan. C. *The Naturalists: Pioneers of Natural History.* New York: Mayflower, 1978.

Jones, Howard Mumford. *O Strange New World: American Culture: The Formative Years.* New York: Viking P, 1964.

Jordan, Terry G., and Matti Kaups. *The American Backwoods Frontier: An Ethnic and Ecological Interpretation.* Baltimore: Johns Hopkins UP, 1992.

Kass-Simon, G., and Patricia Farnes. *Women of Science: Righting the Record.* Bloomington: Indiana UP, 1990.

Kastner, Joseph. *A Species of Eternity.* New York: Knopf, 1977.

Keeney, Elizabeth B. *The Botanizers: American Scientists in Nineteenth-Century America.* Chapel Hill: U of North Carolina P, 1992.

Kolodny, Annette. *The Land before Her: Fantasy and Experience of the American Frontiers, 1630–1860.* Chapel Hill: U of North Carolina P, 1984.

———. *The Lay of the Land: Metaphor as Experience and History in American Life and Letters.* Chapel Hill: U of North Carolina P, 1975.

Krutch, Joseph Wood, ed. *Great American Nature Writing.* New York: William Sloane, 1950.

Larson, James. *Interpreting Nature: The Science of Living Form from Linnaeus to Kant.* Baltimore: Johns Hopkins UP, 1994.

Lawson-Peebles, Robert. *Landscape and Written Expression in Revolutionary America: The World Turned Upside Down.* Cambridge: Cambridge UP, 1988.

Lloyd, Clare. *The Travelling Naturalists.* London: Croom Helm, 1985.

Locke, David. *Science as Writing.* New Haven: Yale UP, 1992.

Lyon, Thomas J. *This Incomperable Lande: A Guide to American Nature Writing.* Rev. ed. Minneapolis: Milkweed, 2001.

McKelvey, Susan D. *Botanical Exploration of the Trans-Mississippi West, 1790–1850*. Jamaica Plain, Mass.: Arnold Arboretum of Harvard U, 1955.
Meisel, Max. *A Bibliography of American Natural History: The Pioneer Century, 1769–1865*. 3 vols. Brooklyn, N.Y.: Premier, 1924–29.
Merchant, Carolyn. *Ecological Revolutions: Nature, Gender, and Science in New England*. Chapel Hill: U of North Carolina P, 1989.
Merrill, Lynn L. *The Romance of Victorian Natural History*. New York: Oxford UP, 1989.
Meyers, Amy R. *Art and Science in America: Issues of Representation*. San Marino, Calif.: Huntington Library Press, 1998.
Miall, Louis Compton. *The Early Naturalists: Their Lives and Work (1530–1789)*. London: Macmillan, 1912.
Mitchell, Lee Clark. *Witnesses to a Vanishing America: The Nineteenth-Century Response*. Princeton: Princeton UP, 1981.
Moring, John. *Early American Naturalists: Exploring the American West, 1804–1900*. New York: Cooper Square P, 2002.
Nash, Roderick. *Wilderness and the American Mind*. 4th ed. New Haven: Yale UP, 2001.
Nicolson, Marjorie Hope. *Mountain Gloom and Mountain Glory: The Development of the Aesthetics of the Infinite*. Ithaca: Cornell UP, 1959.
Norwood, Vera, ed. *Made from This Earth: American Women and Nature*. Chapel Hill: U of North Carolina P, 1993.
Pachter, Marc, and Frances Wein, eds. *Abroad in America: Visitors to the New Nation, 1776–1914*. Reading, Mass.: Addison-Wesley, 1976.
Peattie, Donald Culross. *Green Laurels: The Lives and Achievements of the Great Naturalists*. New York: Simon & Schuster, 1936.
Porter, Charlotte. *The Eagle's Nest: Natural History and American Ideas, 1812–1842*. Tuscaloosa: U of Alabama P, 1986.
Raby, Peter. *Bright Paradise: Victorian Scientific Travellers*. Princeton: Princeton UP, 1996.
Rae, Noel. *Witnessing America: The Library of Congress Book of Firsthand Accounts of Life in America, 1600–1900*. New York: Stonesong P, 1996.
Regis, Pamela. *Describing Early America: Bartram, Jefferson, Crèvecoeur, and the Rhetoric of Natural History*. DeKalb: Northern Illinois UP, 1992.
Reingold, Nathan, ed. *Science in Nineteenth-Century America: A Documentary History*. New York: Hill & Wang, 1964.
Rogers, Robert Emmons. *The Voice of Science in Nineteenth-Century Literature*. Boston: Atlantic Monthly P, 1921.
Savage, Henry, Jr. *Discovering America, 1700–1875*. New York: Harper & Row, 1979.
———. *Lost Heritage: Wilderness America through the Eyes of Seven Pre-Audubon Naturalists*. New York: William Morrow, 1970.
Schatzberg, Walter, Ronald A. Waite, and Jonathan K. Johnson, eds. *The Relations of Literature and Science: An Annotated Bibliography of Scholarship, 1880–1980*. New York: Modern Language Association, 1987.
Scholnick, Robert J., ed. *American Literature and Science*. Lexington: U of Kentucky P, 1992.

Shepard, Paul. *Man in the Landscape: A Historic View of the Esthetics of Nature.* College Station: Texas A&M UP, 1991.

Slotkin, Richard. *Regeneration through Violence: The Mythology of the American Frontier, 1600–1860.* Middletown, Conn.: Wesleyan UP, 1973.

Smallwood, William Martin, and Mabel Sarah Coon Smallwood. *Natural History and the American Mind.* New York: Columbia UP, 1941.

Stearns, Raymond Phineas. *Science in the British Colonies of America.* Urbana: U of Illinois P, 1970.

Stephens, Lester D. *Science, Race, and Religion in the American South: John Bachman and the Charleston Circle of Naturalists, 1815–1895.* Chapel Hill: U of North Carolina P, 2000.

Struik, Dirk J. *Yankee Science in the Making.* Boston: Little, Brown, 1948.

Stuckey, Ronald L. *Development of Botany in Selected Regions of North America before 1900.* New York: Arno P, 1978.

Sweet, Timothy. *American Georgics: Economy and Environment in Early American Literature.* Philadelphia: U of Pennsylvania P, 2002.

Thomas, Keith. *Man and the Natural World: A History of the Modern Sensibility.* New York: Pantheon, 1983.

Tinling, Marion, ed. *With Women's Eyes: Visitors to the New World, 1775–1918.* Norman: U of Oklahoma P, 1993.

Tucher, Andrea J. *Natural History in America, 1609–1860; Printed Works in the Collections of the American Philosophical Society, the Historical Society of Pennsylvania, the Library Company of Philadelphia.* New York: Garland, 1985.

Welch, Margaret. *The Book of Nature: Natural History in the United States, 1825–1875.* Boston: Northeastern UP, 1998.

Wilson, David Scofield. *In the Presence of Nature.* Amherst: U of Massachusetts P, 1978.

Worster, Donald. *Nature's Economy: A History of Ecological Ideas.* 2nd ed. Cambridge: Cambridge UP, 1994.

SOURCES AND CREDITS

Following are the sources for the texts excerpted in this book—either as section epigraphs or as selections—arranged in order of their appearance. Credited selections indicate the publisher by whose permission the text is reprinted, while uncredited selections are within the public domain. In a very few cases, items remain uncredited because repeated attempts to locate or contact their publishers were unsuccessful.

BOOK EPIGRAPH

Christopher Columbus, *The Four Voyages of Christopher Columbus*, ed. and trans. J. M. Cohen (New York: Penguin Books, 1969). Reprinted by permission of Penguin Books Ltd.

PART ONE: THE FIFTEENTH, SIXTEENTH, AND SEVENTEENTH CENTURIES

[epigraph] Samuel Sewall, *Phaenomena Quadedam Apocalyptica* (Boston: Bartholomew Green and John Allen, 1697).

Christopher Columbus, *The Four Voyages of Christopher Columbus*, ed. and trans. J. M. Cohen (New York: Penguin Books, 1969). Reprinted by permission of Penguin Books Ltd.

Amerigo Vespucci, *Letters from a New World: Amerigo Vespucci's Discovery of America*, trans. David Jacobson (New York: Marsilio, 1992). Reprinted by permission of Marsilio Publishers.

Pietro Martire d'Anghiera, *De Orbe Novo: The Eight Decades of Peter Martyr D'Anghera*, trans. Francis Augustus MacNutt (New York: G. P. Putnam's Sons, 1912).

Gonzalo Fernández de Oviedo y Valdés, *Natural History of the West Indies*, trans. Sterling A. Stoudemire. North Carolina Studies in the Romance Languages and Literatures, no. 32 (Chapel Hill: U of North Carolina P, 1959). Copyright © 1959 by the University of North Carolina Press, renewed 1987 by Sterling A. Stoudemire. Used by permission of the publisher.

Alvar Núñez Cabeza de Vaca, *Adventures in the Unknown Interior of America*, trans. Cyclone Covey (1961; reprint: Albuquerque: U of New Mexico P, 1983).

Pedro de Castañeda de Nájera, *The Journey of Coronado, 1540–1542*, trans. and ed. George Parker Winship (New York: Allerton Books, 1922).

Jean Ribaut, *The Whole & True Discouerye of Terra Florida*, ed. H. M. Biggar (Deland: Florida State Historical Society, 1927).

Thomas Hariot, *A Brief and True Report of the New-found Land of Virginia*, in *The Principal Nauigations . . . of the English Nation* (Glasgow: Glasgow UP, 1903–5).

John Smith, *The Complete Works of Captain John Smith, 1580–1631*, ed. Philip L. Barbour (Chapel Hill: U of North Carolina P, 1986). Reprinted by permission of University of North Carolina Press.

William Wood, *New England's Prospect*, ed. Alden T. Vaughan (Amherst: U of Massachusetts P, 1977). Reprinted by permission of University of Massachusetts Press.

Thomas Morton, *New English Canaan*, ed. Charles Francis Adams Jr. (Boston: Prince Society, 1883).

Anne Bradstreet, *The Complete Works of Anne Bradstreet*, ed. Joseph R. McElrath Jr. and Allan P. Robb (Boston: Twayne, 1981). Copyright © 1981 Macmillan Reference USA. Reprinted by permission of The Gale Group.

John Josselyn, *John Josselyn: Colonial Traveler*, ed. Paul J. Lindholdt (Hanover: UP of New England, 1988). Reprinted by permission of University Press of New England.

Jasper Danckaerts, *Journal of Jasper Danckaerts*, ed. Bartlett Burleigh James (New York: Charles Scribner's Sons, 1913).

Louis Hennepin, *A New Discovery of a Vast Country in America*, ed. Reuben Gold Thwaites (Chicago: A. C. McClurg, 1903).

PART TWO: THE EIGHTEENTH CENTURY

[epigraph] Daniel Boone, *The Adventures of Colonel Daniel Boon, Formerly a Hunter: Containing a Narrative of the Wars of Kentucky* (1784). In *A Topographical Description of the Western Territory of North America*, 3d ed., by Gilbert Imlay (London: J. Debrett, 1797).

Sarah Kemble Knight, *The Journal of Madam Knight*, ed. George Parker Winship (Boston: Small, Maynard, 1920).

Robert Beverley, *The History and Present State of Virginia*, ed. Louis B. Wright (Chapel Hill: U of North Carolina P, 1947). Reprinted by permission of University of North Carolina Press.

John Lawson, *A New Voyage to Carolina*, ed. Hugh Talmage Lefler (Chapel Hill: U of North Carolina P, 1967). Reprinted by permission of University of North Carolina Press.

Cotton Mather, *The Christian Philosopher*, ed. Winton U. Solberg (Urbana: U of Illinois P, 1994).

Jonathan Edwards, *The Works of Jonathan Edwards*, vol. 6, ed. Wallace E. Anderson (New Haven: Yale UP, 1980). Reprinted by permission of Yale University Press.

Paul Dudley, "An Essay upon the Natural History of Whales." In *Philosophical Transactions of the Royal Society*, vol. 39 (London: Royal Society, 1735–36).

Mark Catesby, *Catesby's Birds of Colonial America*, ed. Alan Feduccia (Chapel Hill: U of North Carolina P, 1985). Reprinted by permission of University of North Carolina Press.

Eliza Lucas Pinckney, *The Letterbook of Eliza Lucas Pinckney, 1739–1762*, ed. Elise Pinckney (Chapel Hill: U of North Carolina P, 1972). Reprinted by permission of University of North Carolina Press.

Peter Kalm, *Travels into North America*, trans. John Reinhold Forster (Barre, Mass.: Imprint Society, 1972).

Benjamin Franklin, *The Ingenious Dr. Franklin: Selected Scientific Letters of Benjamin Franklin*, ed. Nathan G. Goodman (Philadelphia: U of Pennsylvania P, 1931). Reprinted by permission of University of Pennsylvania Press.

John Winthrop, *A Lecture on Earthquakes* (Boston: Edes & Gill, 1755).

Pedro Font, *Font's Complete Diary: A Chronicle of the Founding of San Francisco,* trans. Herbert Eugene Bolton (Berkeley: U of California P, 1933). Copyright © 1933 The Regents of University of California. Reprinted by permission of the publisher.

J. Hector St. John de Crèvecoeur, *Letters from an American Farmer* (London: J. M. Dent & Sons, 1912).

John Ferdinand Dalziel Smyth, *A Tour in the United States of America* (London: G. Robinson, J. Robson, & J. Sewell, 1784).

Thomas Jefferson, *Notes on the State of Virginia,* ed. William Peden (Chapel Hill: U of North Carolina P, 1954). Reprinted by permission of University of North Carolina Press.

William Bartram, *Travels Through North and South Carolina, Georgia, East and West Florida . . .* (Philadelphia: James & Johnson, 1791).

James Smith, *An Account of the Remarkable Occurrences in the Life and Travels of Col. James Smith.* In *American Captivity Narratives,* ed. Gordon M. Sayre (Boston: Houghton Mifflin, 2000). Copyright © 2000 by Houghton Mifflin Company. Reprinted by permission of the publisher.

Charles Willson Peale, *The Selected Papers of Charles Willson Peale and His Family,* vol. 2, ed. Lillian B. Miller (New Haven: Yale UP, 1988). Reprinted by permission of Yale University Press.

PART THREE: THE NINETEENTH CENTURY THROUGH *WALDEN*

[epigraph] John Palliser, *Solitary Rambles and Adventures of a Hunter in the Prairies* (London: John Murray, 1853).

Meriwether Lewis and William Clark, *Original Journals of the Lewis and Clark Expedition,* ed. Reuben Gold Thwaites (New York: Dodd, Mead, 1904–5).

Alexander Wilson, *American Ornithology; or, The Natural History of the Birds of the United States* (New York: J. W. Bouton, 1877).

John Bradbury, *Travels in the Interior of America, in the Years 1809, 1810, and 1811 . . .* (London: Sherwood, Neely, and Jones, 1817).

Henry Rowe Schoolcraft, *Rude Pursuits and Rugged Peaks: Schoolcraft's Ozark Journal, 1818–1819,* ed. Milton D. Rafferty (Fayetteville: U of Arkansas P, 1996). Copyright © 1996 by Milton D. Rafferty. Reprinted by permission of University of Arkansas Press.

Timothy Dwight, *Travels in New England and New York,* ed. Barbara Miller Solomon (Cambridge: Belknap Press of Harvard UP, 1969). Copyright © 1969 by the President and Fellows of Harvard College. Reprinted by permission of the publisher.

Edwin James, *Account of an Expedition from Pittsburgh to the Rocky Mountains, Performed in the Years 1819 and '20 . . .* (Philadelphia: Carey & Lea, 1823).

Solomon Bayley, *A Narrative of Some Remarkable Incidents, in the Life of Solomon Bayley, Formerly a Slave, in the State of Delaware, North America . . .* (London: Harvey & Darton, 1825).

Timothy Flint, *Recollections of the Last Ten Years Passed in Occasional Residences and Journeyings in the Valley of the Mississippi . . .* (Boston: Cummings, Hilliard, 1826).

Anne Newport Royall, *Sketches of History, Life, and Manners, in the United States* (New Haven: n.p., 1826).

François-René, Vicomte de Chateaubriand, *Chateaubriand's Travels in America*, trans. Richard Switzer (Lexington: U of Kentucky P, 1969). Used by permission of University of Kentucky Press.

John James Audubon, *Ornithological Biography; or, An Account of the Habits of the Birds of the United States of America . . .*, 5 vols. (Edinburgh: A. Black, 1831–39).

Ralph Waldo Emerson, *The Early Lectures of Ralph Waldo Emerson*, vol. 1, ed. Stephen E. Whicher and Robert E. Spiller (Cambridge: Harvard UP, 1959). Copyright © 1959 by the President and Fellows of Harvard College. Reprinted by permission of the publisher.

John D. Godman, *Rambles of a Naturalist* (Philadelphia: J. J. Ash, 1833).

Washington Irving, *A Tour on the Prairies*, ed. John Francis McDermott (Norman: U of Oklahoma P, 1956). Copyright © 1956 by the University of Oklahoma Press, Norman. Reprinted by permission of the publisher.

Thomas Cole, "Essay on American Scenery." In *American Monthly Magazine* 1 (January 1836). Reprinted in *American Art, 1700–1960: Sources and Documents*, ed. John W. McCoubrey (Englewood Cliffs: Prentice Hall, 1965).

Harriet Martineau, *Retrospect of Western Travel* (London: Saunders & Otley, 1838).

Henry Rowe Schoolcraft, *Algic Researches, Comprising Inquiries Respecting the Mental Characteristics of the North American Indians* (New York: Harper & Brothers, 1839).

John Kirk Townsend, *Narrative of a Journey across the Rocky Mountains, to the Columbia River*, ed. George A. Jobanek (Corvallis: Oregon State UP, 1999). Reprinted by permission of Oregon State University Press.

Nicolas Point, *Wilderness Kingdom: Indian Life in the Rocky Mountains, 1840–1847*, trans. Joseph P. Donnelly (New York: Holt, Rinehart & Winston, 1967).

George Catlin, *Letters and Notes on the Manners, Customs, and Conditions of the North American Indians . . .* (London: Tosswill & Myers, 1841). Reprinted as *North American Indians*, ed. Peter Matthiessen (New York: Viking Penguin, 1989).

Lucy Hooper, *The Lady's Book of Flowers and Poetry . . .* (New York: J. C. Riker, 1842).

Nathaniel Hawthorne, "Buds and Bird-Voices." In *United States Magazine and Democratic Review*, 13 (June 1843). Reprinted in *Mosses from an Old Manse*, vol. 10 in *The Centenary Edition of the Works of Nathaniel Hawthorne*, ed. J. Donald Crowley (Columbus: Ohio State UP, 1974).

William Cullen Bryant, *Letters of a Traveller; or, Notes of Things Seen in Europe and America* (New York: George P. Putnam, 1850).

Margaret Fuller, *Summer on the Lakes, in 1843*, ed. Susan Belasco Smith (Urbana: U of Illinois P, 1991).

John C. Frémont, *Report of the Exploring Expedition to the Rocky Mountains in the Year 1842, and to Oregon and North California in 1843–1844* (28th Cong., 2nd sess., 1845, S. Doc. 174). Reprinted in *Narratives of Exploration and Adventure*, ed. Allan Nevins (New York: Longmans, Green, 1956).

George Copway (Kah-ge-ga-gah-bowh), *Life, Letters and Speeches*, ed. A. LaVonne Brown